Aging and Society

Fifth Edition

Aging and Society

A Canadian Perspective

Mark Novak
San Jose State University

Lori Campbell
McMaster University

THOMSON

NELSON

Australia   Canada   Mexico   Singapore   Spain   United Kingdom   United States

THOMSON
★
NELSON

Aging and Society, Fifth Edition
by Mark Novak and Lori Campbell

Associate Vice President and Editorial Director:
Evelyn Veitch

Publisher, Social Sciences and Humanities:
Joanna Cotton

Acquisitions Editor:
Cara Yarzab

Marketing Manager:
Lenore Taylor

Developmental Editor:
Sandra de Ruiter

Photo Researcher:
Kristiina Bowering

Permissions Coordinator:
Kristiina Bowering

Senior Production Editor:
Bob Kohlmeier

Copy-Editor:
Madeline Koch

Proofreader:
Sarah Robertson

Indexer:
Dennis A. Mills

Production Coordinator:
Hedy Sellers

Creative Director:
Angela Cluer

Interior-Design Modifications:
Sarah Battersby

Cover Design:
Anne Bradley

Cover Image:
Sean Murphy/Stone/Getty Images

Compositor:
Alicja Jamorski

Printer:
Transcontinental

Library and Archives Canada Cataloguing in Publication

Novak, Mark W.
Aging & society : a Canadian perspective / Mark Novak, Lori Campbell. — 5th ed.

Includes bibliographical references and index.
ISBN 0-17-641663-3

1. Aging—Canada. 2. Older people—Canada. 3. Older people—Canada—Social conditions. 4. Gerontology—Canada. I. Campbell, Lori D. (Lori Debra), 1953– II. Title. III. Title: Aging and society.

HQ1064.C2N68 2005   305.26'0971
C2004-904478-8

Contents

Preface

Many changes have taken place in Canadian gerontology since the fourth edition of this text was published. New researchers have entered the field of aging. The government has released many reports that summarize studies of health, housing, and pension reform. And the results of studies by consortia of researchers and research centres have begun to appear. These studies will shape social policy in this new century.

As the twenty-first century unfolds, the study of aging will increase in importance. Canada's population will have more older people than ever before. These people will make new demands on Canada's health care, retirement income, and housing resources. They will also bring new interests, new skills, and a new perspective on aging. People young and old will need to understand the realities of aging in this new age.

The fifth edition of this book has the same goals as the first four editions. To begin with, we want a readable book—one that students can read without stumbling over social science jargon and dense academic prose. We have defined most technical terms within the text so that students will not have to flip to a glossary or interrupt their reading by looking at footnotes. We also present examples, charts, or graphs to illustrate difficult points. This edition includes key terms and study questions that students can use to review and test their knowledge. These study aids will free students to think about the ideas contained in the text.

Second, we want a text that presents aging in the context of Canada's history and social life. In the past, gerontology instructors had to use U.S. texts in our aging courses, and each year we had to delete large sections of the text from the assigned readings. Canadian students don't need to know how many older people live in Arizona, the workings of the U.S. Social Security system, or the differences between aging black, white, and Hispanic Americans. These are interesting topics, but Canada has its own geographic regions, social policies, and mix of cultures and ethnic groups. Canadian students should first learn about aging in their own country.

Third, we want a text that describes Canada's social institutions—its health care, income, and housing systems, as well as its family and community life. Canadian students should know, for example, that their health care system provides free health care benefits to all older

people and that the retirement income system provides a basic income to older Canadians. These systems create a social safety net for older people and provide the basis for a decent old age today.

Canadian students should also know that older adults face problems in their society. Many Canadians hold negative stereotypes about older people (look at the number of lotions designed to hide wrinkled skin); the fast pace of modern society often pushes older people to the sidelines (imagine trying to cross a six-lane street if you have arthritis in your legs); and some groups of older people (many of them very old women) still live in poverty. Canadian society needs improvement. Students need to know what parts of the social system work for older people and what parts work against them. *Aging and Society: A Canadian Perspective* gives students the facts about aging and helps them sort through and understand the issues surrounding aging today.

This new edition has a fourth goal: to improve on the fourth edition. Many instructors and students across the country have used the fourth edition. We too have used it in our classes with hundreds of students. Our students and our colleagues have commented on what they liked and did not like about the text. We have used their comments to create this new edition.

As in earlier editions, this one refers to classic Canadian studies and the most up-to-date facts and figures on aging in Canada. It contains exhibits that present case studies of older people today or discuss current issues in the field. This edition also has some new sections that reflect new research in the field of aging. Where appropriate, the new edition makes reference to the impact of technology on seniors' lives. This includes the use of computers to maintain contact with family members and to join new communities.

Chapter 1 now contains information on intergenerational equity and societal ageism. We have brought this material forward so that students can learn, early in their reading, about the socio-political context of aging. Chapter 2 includes a discussion of current research activity in Canada, and a section on ethical issues in research.

Chapter 3 contains up-to-date demographic facts and new material on aging around the world. Chapter 4 contains thoroughly updated information and statistics based on the latest Canadian data. Chapter 5 has more information on disability and activity limitation. It looks at how physical activity, health promotion, and self-care can improve health and well-being in later life. Chapter 6 contains a new and more detailed discussion of mental disorders, including Alzheimer's disease and depression. Chapter 8 discusses health care reform. It documents the continuing increase in home care and the growing interest in long-term care. The chapter also includes a discussion of the Romanow report, the federal government report on health care reform. The chapter discusses the implications of this report for older people.

Chapter 9 contains the latest information on pensions in Canada. It continues to show that financial inequality exists between single women (many of them widows) and men in later life. Chapter 10 contains material on new retirement options such as "disrupted careers." Chapter 11 contains new information on homeless seniors, new housing options such as "flexhousing," life leases, and shared equity. The chapter also looks at issues related to driving a car in later life. Chapter 13 now has two major sub-sections. The first sub-section deals with family life and contains new information on partner status, including common-law unions. The chapter also looks at new types of relationships such as "living apart together." The second sub-section looks closely at informal supports. This includes both support provided by older adults (such as grandparenting) as well as support provided to older people (such as help with shopping). Researchers have carried out extensive work in both of these fields.

This edition, like those before it, documents the aging of Canadian society. It shows the issues that occupy our thinking. And it shows the ways that society and individuals have adapted to aging. The first edition of this book, nearly 20 years ago, laid down many of the issues discussed here. That edition looked to the future and saw a growing number of older people. It saw that Canada would have to reshape its policies and programs to meet their needs. Later editions tracked the changes that took place as Canadian society aged.

This edition continues that tradition. But the issues of the past exist as real challenges today. Canada has become an older society. Income inequality, early retirement, community-based health care, the importance of active living, and family caregiver burden all affect more people than ever before. Soon the baby boom generation will enter old age. This generation will make new demands on society and will call for new responses. This fifth edition of *Aging and Society: A Canadian Perspective* points to some of the emerging issues in aging and to the challenges that lie ahead.

Organization

This book begins by describing large-scale (macroscopic) changes in society. It then shows how these changes affect people and social institutions. It concludes by showing how individuals respond to these changes and how individuals' actions give new direction to society. The structure of the book reflects a dialectical model of social change.

Part 1, Gerontology Today (Chapters 1 and 2), introduces students to the field of aging. It shatters many of the myths people have about aging and shows the range of topics gerontologists study. It also describes the theories and methods gerontologists use when they study aging.

Part 2, Historical Change (Chapters 3 and 4), looks at the changes in Canada's history and demographic structure that led to population aging (the increased proportion of older people in the population). It also places aging in Canada in a world context.

Part 3, Maturational Change (Chapters 5, 6, and 7), looks at individual aging—the physical, psychological, and developmental changes that come with age.

Part 4, Institutional Change (Chapters 8 through 14), examines Canada's institutions—the health care, social security, and housing systems as well as the family, the community, and the institutions responsible for death and dying.

Special Features

A number of features make this both a useful and an easy-to-use book.

First, the chapters are organized into topics that most instructors cover in their courses. Each chapter represents a unit of study and presents the facts and issues related to one topic (e.g., housing or health care). This division allows instructors to use this text in either a one- or a two-term course. Instructors of a two-term course are able to use the entire book, while those teaching one-term courses can assign specific chapters and know that a topic will be covered in depth. A one-term course, for example, might include those chapters that deal specifically with population aging and Canada's social institutions (i.e., Chapters 1, 3, 4, 8, 9, 10, and 11).

Second, each chapter starts with an outline of the chapter's contents and an introduction to its main themes.

Third, in each chapter the text is supplemented by exhibits, including graphs, charts, and excerpts from other publications. Some of the exhibits present controversies in the literature; others contain case studies that show the human side of aging. Most graphs and charts have accompanying explanations that describe them and show their relation to the text.

Fourth, each chapter concludes with a series of main points that summarize the text, a list of study questions, and an annotated list of important sources students can consult for further reading.

Fifth, the book concludes with a reference list of all the sources referred to in the text, in alphabetical order by author surname. Each listing has beside it a number (or series of numbers) that corresponds to the chapter(s) that contain the reference. A student will find this list helpful when doing a research paper. All the references in Chapter 11 (Housing and Transportation), for example, have an "11" beside them. A student who decides to do a research paper on housing can quickly pick out all the references for housing and transportation.

General Acknowledgments

Joanna Cotton, Social Sciences and Humanities Publisher in Higher Education at Nelson, and Cara Yarzab, Acquisitions Editor, guided us through the early stages of this project. Glen Herbert and Sandra de Ruiter, Developmental Editors at Nelson, contacted instructors throughout the country for comments on the fourth edition and worked diligently to get this edition out on time. Like all good editors, Joanna, Cara, Glen, and Sandra cleared away technical and editorial problems so that we could focus on the research and writing. Bob Kohlmeier served as Production Editor, and Madeline Koch and Sarah Robertson capably handled copy-editing and proofreading, respectively. We thank them for their support.

Zeni Espinosa and Sharon Cancilla coordinated administrative assistance on our behalf. We thank them and the other staff members for their hard work and attention to detail.

Canadian colleagues in the field of gerontology sent us their papers and research reports. We cannot thank them all here, but we want to acknowledge that they helped make this a better text. We also thank the reviewers who took time from their busy schedules to read the text carefully and make helpful comments: Jody Bain of the University of Victoria, Pearl Crichton of Concordia University, Ti King of Lakehead University, Robert Lewis of Memorial University of Newfoundland, Bev Matthews of Mount Royal College, Herb Northcott

of the University of Alberta, and Edward Thompson of Conestoga College. We alone take responsibility for the text's shortcomings.

Author's Acknowledgments

Lori Campbell

I wish to thank Mark Novak for his support, patience, and kindness on this project. I feel privileged to have had the opportunity to work with, and learn from, such a fine person and academic. Mark demonstrated an unwavering commitment to the project, a genuine concern for the academic needs of students, and an amazing generosity and sharing in the collaborative process.

My appreciation to my family: my siblings Jane, Lynn, and Joe, and their partners and children. To my "2Ps," Payton and Paris, who continue to sparkle and shine as they grow. Thank you for bringing such joy and delight into my life.

To my partner, Michael Carroll, thank you for your unconditional love, support, and encouragement in all I do—academically and in life. I feel truly fortunate to share my life—and our dogs Barkey and Bronney—with such a loving and remarkable person. No heart could have a warmer or happier haven than mine has with you.

I dedicate this book in most loving memory of my parents, Leon and Dorothy Campbell, who are in my thoughts and my heart in all I do. My parents demonstrated to me what it truly means to care about family and others, and how to live and age with great strenth, integrity, compassion, and humour. I owe them much more than I could ever express.

Mark Novak

My wife, Mona, helped me by reading the chapters and preparing the summary points, key terms, and study questions at the end of each chapter. She has made the book more useful to students. My son Daniel helped with the preparation of the bibliography. I thank both of them for their time and their careful work.

It has been a pleasure working with Lori Campbell, my co-author, and sharing ideas with her as we went along. She has been a friendly critic, a careful scholar, and a hard worker. She has brought many new insights and resources to the text. Students will benefit from her knowledge and her sensitivity as a teacher.

I owe special thanks to my mentor and close friend, Hans Mohr. His intellectual integrity inspires all my work. I can never repay him, only thank him for his support and friendship.

I dedicate this book to my family—my wife, Mona, and my sons, Christopher, Jonathan, Sean, and Daniel. We have some new family members as this edition goes to press—Shona, Megan, and our new grandson, Tobin. All of them deserve credit for lightening my spirits with their good humour and love.

Part One

1

Gerontology Today

Chapter One
Aging Today

Photo © PHOTICK/Index Stock Imagery

INTRODUCTION

Everyone needs to know about aging. First, all of us are getting older. While some of us are over 65 already, most adults not yet 65 will become part of the older population between now and the year 2040.[1] We will want to make old age as good a time of life as it can be.

Second, when those of you who are younger students reach middle age, your parents, aunts, uncles, neighbours, and older friends will have grown old. You will want to know about aging so that you can help them live the best old age possible.

Third, more people work with the elderly than ever before, and more will find themselves working with the elderly in the future. In 2000, Canada had 3.8 million people aged 65 and over. Older Canadians make up more than 13 percent of the population today, and experts predict that this proportion will grow to 9 million people or 25 percent of the population by 2041 (Health Canada 2001a). Nurses, social workers, teachers, family counsellors, and even travel agents will have more and more older people as clients.

An older population will also put new demands on Canada's **social structures**. Sociologists define a social structure as a relatively stable pattern of social interactions. The family, the education system, and the health care system all fit this definition, and they will change in the following ways as Canadian society ages:

- More Canadians will live in three- and four-generation families. And many people will become grandparents while they are still active in their careers.

- Schools and universities will attract more older students than ever before. These students will want flexible schedules. They will also need different kinds of teaching methods and different grading schemes than younger students.

- The health care system will also change. The current system favours the treatment of acute (short-term) illness, but older people tend to have chronic ailments such as arthritis, hearing problems, and diabetes. An aging society needs to prevent illness before it occurs.

Gerontology is the discipline that studies aging systematically. It looks at the subject from two points of view: how aging affects the individual and how an aging population will change society. This chapter describes

(1) myths and realities of aging, (2) stereotyping and attitudes toward aging, and (3) ageism and social policy.

MYTHS AND REALITIES OF AGING

Gerontology has two goals. First, scholars and researchers work to produce accurate knowledge about aging. Second, professionals who work with older people apply this knowledge to create a better life for their clients. Academic gerontologists try to decrease prejudice and stereotyping in society by writing about the facts of aging today. Consider the following myths and the facts that gerontologists have found to replace them.

Myth: People feel lonely and lost in retirement. They often get sick and die shortly after they retire.

Reality: Few people face sickness or loneliness due to retirement (McDonald and Wanner 1990). Given the chance to retire with a decent income, most people do so as soon as they can. McDonald and Wanner report that retirement has little, if any, effect on health, social activity, or life satisfaction or happiness. The health of some workers improves when they retire. Many start new careers, take up volunteer work, or go back to school.

Myth: People in older age groups face a higher risk of criminal victimization than people in younger age groups.

Reality: Older people report more fear of crime than younger people. The Canadian General Social Survey (cited in Lindsay 1999) studied people's feelings of safety. The study found that older people showed the greatest fear of walking in their neighbourhood. For example, 57 percent of women aged 65 and over compared with 41 percent of women aged 45 to 64 felt very or somewhat unsafe walking in their neighbourhood after dark. Men aged 65 and over, compared with younger men, also showed a greater fear of walking in their neighbourhood. Nineteen percent of older men, compared with 11 percent of men aged 45 to 64, felt very or somewhat unsafe walking alone in their neighbourhood after dark. More than a quarter of older women and 17 percent of older men said they felt very or somewhat worried when home alone at night. Saco and Nathalie (2001) found that, compared to younger people, older people tended to stay home because they feared crime.

Loss of social networks due to retirement, death of a spouse, and staying home may lead to increased fear of crime. But this fear of crime does not fit the facts about

---

1. The terms "old," "elderly," "aged," and "senior" in this text refer to people aged 65 and over unless another age is given.

Exhibit 1.1

FACTS ON AGING QUIZ

Try the following quiz to see how much you know about aging in Canada. The quiz is based on Palmore's "Facts on Aging: A Short Quiz" (1977), but it incorporates suggestions made by Canadian researchers who have revised Palmore's work (Matthews, Tindale, and Norris 1985). The answers are on page 16. You will find the facts to support these answers throughout this book.

True or False?

1. At least 15 percent of the aged in Canada are living in long-stay institutions (e.g., nursing homes, mental hospitals, homes for the aged).

2. British Columbia has a higher proportion of older people in its population than any other province.

3. Older people today have less contact with their families than older people had in the past.

4. Older people stand a higher risk of criminal victimization than people in other age groups.

5. Memory declines with age.

6. A decline in sexual vigour in older men is usually due to hormone deficiencies.

7. Retirees more often feel depressed, bored, and ill than those who keep working.

8. Most older people in rural areas depend on public transportation to get around.

9. The body's systems go into a steady decline from age 40 on.

10. The majority of older people have incomes below the poverty level (as defined by the federal government).

Source: Reprinted with permission from the *Canadian Journal on Aging*.

crime against the elderly. Ponies and her colleagues (1989), for instance, found that only 6 percent of their sample had property or money stolen from them by a stranger since turning age 65. Studies in Britain, the United States, and Canada show that older people run less risk of victimization than any other age group. A Canadian survey found that older people made up only 3 percent of victims of violent crimes (Statistics Canada 1994). And older people had the lowest homicide rate and the lowest rate of attack on their person or property compared to all other age groups (Lindsay 1999).

Brillion (1987, 10) says that "elderly people are largely under-victimized, proportionately, for all types of crime." The Canadian Urban Victimization Survey (Solicitor General of Canada 1983, 3) sums up these findings. It states that "contrary to popular belief ... elderly people are relatively unlikely to be victimized by crime.... In fact, the actual sample counts of sexual assault and robbery incidents for those over 60 were so low that estimated numbers and rates are unreliable."

Older people do face relatively high rates of certain kinds of crimes. For example, compared with younger people, they run a higher risk of being victims of fraud. Crime surveys in Canada report that people aged 65 and

over make up over half the victims of fraud. People aged 60 and over make up three-quarters of the people defrauded of more than $5000. And a large majority of this group gets cheated more than once (National Advisory Council on Aging 2001a).

The National Advisory Council on Aging (NACA) (Plouffe 1991) consulted 125 older people on consumer fraud. About a fifth of these people claimed that a salesperson or company had tried to cheat them. Fourteen percent said that advertising had misled them. Ten percent said they knew a senior who had lost money through fraud. The Internet provides a new channel for crooks to use in cheating older people. This may increase fraud against older people as the computer becomes more of a part of their daily lives.

NACA reported a number of conditions that create a higher risk of fraud among older people. These included lack of information, social isolation, and lack of wariness in business relations. Donahue (2001, 36) reports that ethnic seniors face further risk due to the language barrier, trust in Canadians, trust in their ethnic community, and fear of reprisal. One respondent said, "Even if we know it is fraud, what can we do? We do not know the channels to fight. We do not know the language."

Some fraud prevention programs have begun for older people. Project Phone Busters in Canada handles complaints of telemarketing fraud. The project receives between 100 and 120 calls per day. More than half the complaints come from people aged 60 and over (Ontario Provincial Police 1997). A group called Senior Busters works with Phone Busters to advise and support senior victims of fraud.

Myth: Most old people live in institutions.

Reality: Only a small percentage of older people live in **special-care homes** for the aged—nursing homes, hospitals, or other long-term-care settings—at any given time. Lindsay (1999) reports that, in 1996, 3.9 percent of older men and 7.8 percent of older women lived in special-care homes. The likelihood of institutionalization increases with age. Only 1.3 percent of men and 1.6 percent of women aged 65 to 74 years lived in special-care homes. But this figure jumps to 22 percent of men and 34.4 percent of women aged 85 and over.

Institutionalization rates have slowed over the past several decades. In 1971, for example, 10.2 percent of older people lived in an institution. By 1996 that figure had dropped to 7.3 percent (Lindsay 1999). Today, most institutions house the very old, sick, and frail elderly—people with few social supports, who cannot live on their own. Current moves in Canada toward increased community care may lead to less institutionalization in the future.

ATTITUDES TOWARD OLD AGE

People hold many **stereotypes** about old age. Sociologists define a stereotype as an exaggerated and often prejudiced view of a type of person or group of people. People who hold a stereotype do not check it to see if it is true. If they meet someone who does not fit the stereotype, they think he or she is an exception. Stereotypes often have some basis in truth, but they exaggerate and distort the truth. Often they lead to discrimination (Page 1997).

When it comes to old age, we hold both positive and negative stereotypes: the wise old farmer and the kindly grandmother, the dirty old man and the sex-starved spinster. Grant and his colleagues (2001) asked 240 men and women aged 18 to 86 in Newfoundland about how they thought an older person would respond to a set of attitude questions. Younger people in the study thought that older people would give socially and politically conservative answers. People in the study thought that liberal views would decrease with age. The researchers conclude that both young and old people hold traditional age stereotypes.

Ryan and Heaven (1988) studied the attitudes of 120 adults toward older people in 40 situations. The people in this study assigned older people less often to situations that required competence and more often to those that called for benevolence. These adults thought of older people as kinder but less able than younger people.

● **Exhibit 1.2**

A New Myth about Aging

A student passed the following story along to us. She said she heard it from someone who heard it from a Nova Scotia fisherman. Maybe it will become a part of our Canadian mythology about aging.

The ferry between Cape Breton and St. John's was having a rough passage. The seas were so rough that the captain decided that it was too dangerous to take the boat right to the dock. Instead, he anchored in the harbour. He manoeuvred the boat so that passengers could get off, but he kept the boat far enough from the quay walls to keep the boat safe. The crew set up a makeshift gangway made of wood planks and a rope handrail on either side. The heaving of the boat and the springiness of the planks made the passengers reluctant to cross to the shore. The crew and shore personnel persuaded and encouraged the passengers to get them to cross. At last, a small, frail-looking old lady came from below. She hesitated to cross the gangway, but finally she worked up her courage and inched across. Many people watched her make her way and the people on shore almost carried her the last few feet. People began to cheer as she set herself on the shore. Then she turned to face the boat; she cupped her hands and called, "It's all right, Mother. You can come down now."

In another study, Ryan and her colleagues (1998) found that, compared to younger telephone users (mean age 22 years), older telephone users (mean age 73 years) reported fewer problems using the telephone. Still, younger people in this study believed that a 75-year-old would have more trouble using the telephone than a 25-year-old. A study of undergraduate students' attitudes toward eyewitness testimony also found ambivalence toward older people (Brimacombe et al. 1997). The study found that undergraduates rated older adults as honest, but as less credible witnesses than younger adults.

Many of our stereotypes consist of negative views of older people and old age. Knox and Gekoski (1989) asked undergraduate students in an experimental study to compare young, middle-aged, and older people. The study found that students gave older people lower ratings than those who were middle-aged on such qualities as autonomy, effectiveness, and personal acceptability. Page (1997) had an elderly woman call to rent an apartment. He then had a young woman and a young man each make a similar call. In a fourth case a young man called on behalf of an older woman. Page found that the elderly woman and the young man calling on behalf of an elderly woman got three to four times more negative responses than the two younger people. He concludes that "persons identified as elderly still face the prospect of rejection" (Page 1997, 59).

Stereotyping even influences retail sales staff. One woman, in a NACA study of attitudes toward older people, said that "salespersons can be impatient if you are choosing something and are not swift enough." Another woman said that "salespeople will talk to me rather than to my mother who is 85" (NACA 1993e, 20).

Even older people sometimes hold negative views about old age. A study of age bias found that older and younger people in the study saw memory success as more typical of younger people (Bieman and Bouchard 1998). They saw memory failure as more typical of older people, and they linked this failure to lack of ability and worry.

Gerontologists call prejudice against older people **ageism**. Robert Butler (1969) coined the term ageism. He says that ageism comes about because the young and the middle-aged feel distaste for aging. They see old age as a time of weakness, sickness, and dying. Ageism also comes about because people know little about old age, and because what they know is based on myth and fear. Palmore (1994) considers it one of the three great "isms" of our day (along with racism and sexism).

In Canadian society today, people learn to be prejudiced against the old. These negative views come from many sources. Cruikshank (2003, 138) found negative

attitudes toward older women in fairy and folk tales. These tales often portray the older women as witches. According to one folk saying, "if the devil can't come himself, he sends an old woman." Cruikshank discusses how, in *Gulliver's Travels*, Jonathan Swift created the Struldbruggs, a people who grow old but never die. Gulliver's interpreter calls them "peevish, covetous, morose, vain, talkative." He describes them as selfish and impotent, and Gulliver says they are "the most mortifying sight I ever beheld; and the women are more horrible than the men."

Berman and Sobkowska-Ashcroft (1986, 1987) reviewed the treatment of older people in great books from the Bible to those of the twentieth century. They found that comedies almost always make fun of older people. Wortley (1998) found negative attitudes toward women in some ancient Greek poems. These poems especially criticized courtesans who relied on their beauty in their youth. Overall, in philosophy, literature, and the theatre, Berman and Sobkowska-Ashcroft found that "negative traits outnumber positive traits by about two to one" (1986, 141).

Jokes give a negative view of old age and older people as well. Palmore (1971) conducted a classic study of attitudes to older people in humour. He looked at 264 jokes taken from 10 popular joke books. He found that one-quarter of the jokes took a positive view of aging and about one-fifth took a neutral view, but more than half of them showed a negative attitude to aging or the aged. He also found a double standard in jokes about age. Jokes about women, more often than those about men, portrayed older people negatively. A more recent study by Bowd (2003) also found stereotypes of older people in jokes. He chose more than 4000 jokes from three published joke books. He found that 102 of these jokes presented a stereotype of the older person. The jokes included stereotypes of impotent men, unattractive women, and childishness in old age.

These jokes project our own fears about aging onto older people. But do these fears have a basis in fact? Studies generally find high life satisfaction among older people. A study by the Commonwealth Fund (1993), for example, looked at aging in five developed nations (Canada, the United States, the United Kingdom, western Germany, and Japan). The study found that 58 percent of older Canadians said they felt "generally very content." This surpassed the other countries in the study (except the United States with 61 percent). The Canadian Community Health Survey sampled 25 000 community-dwelling Canadians aged 15 and over in 2002 (Statistics Canada 2003v). The survey found that

● Exhibit 1.3

WHAT IS IT LIKE TO BE OLD?

We cannot know the answer to this question until we reach old age ourselves. But Professor Paul Baker of the University of Victoria set out, at age 33, to learn about aging firsthand. In the story that follows he describes his experiment with old age.

"You're too young to be a gerontologist. How can somebody who's only 33 know what it's like to be 83?" This reaction from one of the few older students in my course on the sociology of aging bothered me. My first instinct was to haul out my academic/scientific defences and claim that you don't have to be an X to study X's (be they old, female, black, or handicapped).

But I was left with the uncomfortable feeling that maybe she was right, maybe I was missing some of the more subjective and emotional aspects of aging by working only with "hard," "objective" data. Then I ran across John Griffin's classic book, *Black Like Me*, written in 1961. Griffin dyed his skin and passed as a black man in the southern United States for a month. His book showed how different the world was for a black man, and made a lot of white people realize what racism meant at the human level.

So, how could I become old? The answer was obvious: the same kind of makeup that turned Dustin Hoffman old in *Little Big Man* might work for me, and, with the help of a makeup artist in Vancouver, plus some old clothes, a cane, and a grey wig, I made the transformation. The makeup took several hours to apply, and hurt like hell going on and coming off, but it worked.

My main interest was in experiencing society's reactions to an old man. I walked around in Victoria and Vancouver about a dozen times, in different places, at night and during the day. And what I found was pretty much what I expected; a few people go out of their way to help the old, a few turn their backs, and most people simply ignore them.

One "young" woman (my own age) waited patiently for me as I struggled up the stairs at the Victoria Institute of Gerontology, held the door open, and said, "Have a nice day." I felt very uncomfortable: I was really a young, healthy male but was masquerading as a decrepit old man; I actually felt like I was a "burden" and almost told her I could open doors for myself, even if I was old.

On the other hand, I was shoved off the sidewalk in front of the Empress Hotel by a large, noisy bunch of tourists. It may have been accidental, but I felt angry and frustrated. On crowded streets I could no longer stride along and know that other people would move aside. I had to be on the defensive, anticipating others' moves. Crossing busy streets became a totally different experience. I hung back so that the crowds could bolt across as soon as the light changed, and then I shuffled along, keeping my eye on the cars, which seemed like racehorses just itching for the gates to open. The lights always started flashing "DON'T WALK" before I was across. What was I supposed to do, the bunny hop?

I experimented with getting in and out of cars and using buses. The basic lesson I learned was that the world gets bigger and faster for an old man, and I became acutely aware of this dramatic change because I was really young, and hadn't gradually accepted the inevitable changes of aging.

I discovered a sense of comradeship of the old, who had the time to sit and talk. I also found a subtle difference between old Victoria and big Vancouver: it seemed easier to be old here, partly because of the size and pace, but maybe also because in Victoria we have so many old people. I think we have learned to be a little more patient.

Would I do it again? Probably not ... pretending to be old hurt my back, my legs, my feet. It was hard to explain to friends and neighbours what I was doing. I think I'll wait for old age to creep up on me slowly, and, in the meantime, I think I have gained a better understanding for my old friends.

Source: Paul Baker, 1983, *Old Before My Time* [videotape], distributed by the Centre on Aging, University of Victoria, Victoria, BC V8W 2Y2. Reprinted by permission of Paul Morgan Baker.

older people showed the highest proportion of people very satisfied with life. They also showed the lowest proportion of people who felt dissatisfied or very dissatisfied with life.

Married seniors, those in good health, those with more education and better income all report high life satisfaction (Clarke et al. 2000). In a study of 195 Canadian adults, Webster (1998) found that older adults scored higher than younger adults on the University of Newfoundland Scale of Happiness. Michalos and his colleagues (2001) compared the life satisfaction of the general population in British Columbia with the life satisfaction of older people (aged 55 to 97). They found that, compared to the general population, on almost all dimensions older people reported higher levels of life satisfaction. The older people in the study did not feel stereotyped and they said they felt that someone really cared about them. Northcott (1982, 77) says that "old age looks far more attractive than stereotypes suggest."

"One antidote to ageism," Butler (1993, 77) says, "is knowledge, the primary intervention." Research shows that stereotypes about old age decrease with increased education. Ragan and Bowen (2001), for example, conducted a controlled study of 64 female college students. They found that correct information improved students' attitudes toward older people. Palmore (1977) devised a "Facts on Aging Quiz (FAQ)." Researchers and educators have used this quiz with people from a variety of backgrounds. Studies report that scores improve with education. People with a high-school education or less, for example, average 57 percent correct. Undergraduates do somewhat better, averaging 64 percent. Gerontology students and faculty on average score 83 percent (Palmore 1988). A study in Canada by Greenslade (cited in Palmore 1988) found that nurses with no gerontology training scored 61 percent correct, but a group with training in geriatrics scored 83 percent.

Matthews, Tindale, and Norris (1985) gave a modified version of Palmore's quiz to public health nurses and also to students and faculty at the University of Guelph (see Exhibit 1.1). They found that the people with the most knowledge about aging scored best on the quiz. Undergraduate students just completing a gerontology course scored highest. Students in an introductory human development course scored lowest. Their results suggest that when people learn about aging, their concept of old age improves. Hooyman and Kiyak (1993) report that stereotyping decreases when older and younger people see each other as individuals with good and bad traits.

Dooley and Frankel (1990) studied a friendly visiting program where adolescents visited a specific senior each week. They found that adolescents who had a positive perception of the person they visited made a favourable attitude change toward seniors in general. This evidence supports the idea that knowledge about aging and satisfying contact with older people can relieve fears and replace negative stereotypes with a more positive view of old age. Kenyon (1992, 4) says that "all people in an aging society need to be sensitive to their own assumptions ... of aging."

The study of aging shows that old age has its compensations. Older people in Canada have guaranteed incomes, subsidized housing, and free medical care. They also get reduced rates on buses, hotels, and car rentals. Other bonuses include tax breaks, free tuition at many universities, and financial support for recreation programs.

Marshall and McPherson (1993) say that Canadian society has an ambivalent view of aging. Ageism exists alongside care and concern for older people. They say that Canada has "been called an ageist society, yet no societies in world history have provided a larger proportion of societal wealth to provide income security, health care, and shelter for the aged" (7).

The study of aging shows that the attitudes of others cause some of the worst problems older people face. McMullin and Marshall (2001) studied garment workers in Montreal. The workers said they felt that the owners' ageist attitudes and actions put pressure on them and in some cases forced them to retire. They felt that the owners and managers gave them less credit for their experience than they deserved, and that the owners focused on decreases in their speed and strength.

The owners and managers denied any ageist attitudes. They said they focused only on productivity and outcomes. But the researchers found that the owners gave the older workers the hardest jobs and did not adapt the speed of the work to accommodate older workers' abilities. The researchers say that the owners and managers used the decline in speed and precision of older workers as an excuse to force them out of work. A more flexible attitude and an appreciation of the older workers' contribution to the workplace would have allowed older workers to stay at work.

Other studies of attitudes toward older workers show that ageism in the workplace exists. Underhill, Marshall, and Deliencourt (1997) asked counsellors at Human Resources Centres of Canada about employers' attitudes toward older workers. Sixty-two percent of the counsellors agreed that "employers believe that older workers should step aside" and 50 percent agreed that "employers believe that older workers have low productivity"; 84 percent agreed that "employers discriminate against older workers in hiring practices" (cited in Marshall 2001, 7). Marshall (2001, 7) concludes that ageist beliefs "are so widespread as to affect the working opportunities of middle-aged and older individuals."

Canada's National Advisory Council on Aging studied how older people feel about society's view of aging. One person told the NACA that "some people confound aging with illness." Another said: "People confuse the 90% of older people who are able with the 10% that are not" (NACA 1993e, 10–11).

Kalish (1979) described a **new ageism**. This refers to the belief that older people need special treatment due to poor health, poverty, and lack of social support. This form of ageism tries to do good, but it often does the opposite. Binstock (1983) calls this a **compassionate stereotype**. This stereotype attempts to create sympathy for older people, but it doesn't give a true picture of later life. A NACA study (1993e, 10–11) found that older people themselves don't support compassionate stereotyping. One older person in this study said, "I get tired of the 'good for you' attitude, as if it were surprising that someone 65-plus can be involved in a number of physical, intellectual, and volunteer programs."

Older people today face many of the traditional stereotypes about old age. But as the population has aged, a new form of prejudice has emerged. This type of ageism focuses on the cost of having an older population.

AGEISM AND SOCIAL POLICY

Stereotypes and ageism most often focus on the individual. They exaggerate the physical and mental changes that come with age. But ageism can also focus on population aging. This type of ageism reflects a fear of an aging society. Some commentators have begun to express this new form of ageism. They see the new generation of older people as a burden on Canadian society. They fear that an increased number and proportion of older people will lead to higher costs for pensions and health care. And they fear that this will lead to economic and social collapse.

Gee and Gutman (2000, 6) cite some examples of this attack on the older population at the start of their book *The Overselling of Population Aging: Apocalyptic Demography, Intergenerational Challenges, and Social Policy.*

• Barbara Beck, writing for *The Globe and Mail* on December 29, 1995, writes, "the deal between the generations is under severe threat, as the costs of state pensions rise. Many countries are running out of people to pay those contributions.... But the argument between the generations is not just about pensions. Medical expenses, too, will burgeon as people get older."

• Shawn McCarthy and Rob Carrick, writing for *The Globe and Mail* on April 11, 1998, say, "faced with the daunting demographic challenges of an aging baby-boom ... Canadians—younger ones in particular—are skeptical ... the CPP [Canadian Pension Plan] will be around for their retirement. And they have every reason to worry."

• Edward Greenspon, writing for *The Globe and Mail* on October 3, 1996, writes, "Canadians have rarely received so few benefits for their tax dollars, and the difficult times are just beginning. The consequences of this will be profound: tense interregional conflict, *clashes between young and old people*, and if things get really bad, class warfare [emphasis added by Gee and Gutman]."

These writers play on the public fear of an aging society. They stereotype the older population as dependent, unproductive, and costly. And they speak in apocalyptic terms as if population aging will lead to the collapse of society as we know it.

Discussions of aging within this worldview often come down to the issue of the fair distribution of resources to the older and younger generations (Jacobs 1990). Rosenzweig (1991), for example, dealt with this topic in an address given at the annual meeting of the Gerontological Society of America. He said that unless older people willingly give up some of their current benefits in a time of scarcity, they will create a "disastrous" effect on society. "Of every nondefense, noninterest dollar in the federal budget [in the United States]," he said, "47 cents is spent on programs for people age 65 and over." He added that this "will grow to more than 50 cents by 1995 and 57 cents by 2000." He projected that these costs will lead to a conflict between retirees and the rest of society, including future retirees. And he said that leaders of interest groups ought to help their members "shape a conception of their interests that fits their own immediate needs into the needs of the larger community on whose overall well-being their own ultimately depends."

Other U.S. authors, such as Peter G. Peterson, speak of a "demographic iceberg" that will sink Western society (Cruikshank 2003, 27). These writers propose limits on old age benefits and point to older people as an unfair economic burden on the young. The issue of **intergenerational equity** has sparked debate and controversy. In the U.S., it led to the creation of a group called **Americans for Generational Equity (AGE)**. This group grew from fewer than a hundred members in 1985 to more than a thousand members in 1990 (Wisensale 1993). AGE believes that young and middle-aged people cannot pay the high costs for services to older and younger people. AGE proposes cuts to programs for older people to free up money for the young. For example, it proposes to replace Social Security in the U.S. with a system of welfare for the poorest older people (Quadagno 1991). One member of AGE proposed that health care providers should deny some treatments to older people (quoted in Binstock 1992).

Other U.S. groups like the **Concord Coalition** propose a means test for Social Security and Medicare. The coalition says that only people who earn under $40 000 per year should get Social Security and Medicare. Cruikshank (2003, 27) reports that in 1999 the Concord Coalition "took out a full-page ad in the *New York Times* to attack a proposal to use part of the budget surplus to

strengthen Social Security and Medicare." These groups gather support by pitting the interests of older people against those of the young. They argue that programs for older people take money from programs for poor children. Townson (1994, 14) says that in the United States the media have taken up the cause of "kids versus canes."

Some gerontologists feel that Canada can avoid the U.S. tendency to blame older people for society's economic problems. Clark (1993) believes that broad-based social programs in Canada create a sense of common interest. For example, Canada's national health care system serves people of all ages. For this reason, it tends to unify national concerns around good health regardless

---

● **Exhibit 1.4**

SETTING LIMITS ON HEALTH CARE

Ageism shows up in discussions of health care policy. Daniel Callahan, in his 1987 book *Setting Limits: Medical Goals in an Aging Society*, suggests one way to deal with the rising costs of health care: ration health care for the elderly. He cites three reasons for this proposal. First, compared with children, older people as a group use a large amount of health care. Second, a large and growing portion of research and technology goes to reverse the health conditions of the elderly. Third, more than a fair share of money for health care to the elderly goes to care for dying people.

Callahan wants to make rationing by age an accepted part of medical practice. He argues against the use of medical need as a criterion for treating older people. Instead, he proposes that we base the decision to treat an illness on age or on the concept of the "natural life span," which Callahan defines as 70 to 80 years (137). He argues that society should commit itself to high-quality care for people throughout this span. But, beyond this point, medicine and government support of health care should focus on the relief of suffering, not the extension of life. This policy, he says, would remove the burden of high health care costs for the very old. He presents the following three principles for the use of age as a way to decide on treatment:

1. Medical care should not resist death after patients have lived their natural life span.

2. Medical care should relieve suffering only for those who have lived their natural life span.

3. Medical technologies that can extend life beyond the natural life span should not be used for this purpose.

These policies, Callahan argues, would remove the uncertainty older people and their children face about the high cost of treatment; it would lead to a high quality of life until late old age; and it would remove the social threat posed by the rising cost of health care for the elderly.

Callahan's proposal rests on the stereotype of older people as sick and costly members of society. His approach blames older people for the high cost of health care. He scapegoats older people and then proposes to sacrifice them to solve the problem of rising costs.

But Glass (1993) says that age serves as a weak basis for making decisions about life and death issues. For example, studies show that older people of the same age vary in their health and need for health care. Even some very old people report good health. Also, Callahan assumes that an older frail person has less social worth than a younger healthy person. "The criterion of social worth values the individual only as an instrument of society and not as a person deserving of respect simply because he or she is a human being" (Glass 1993, 75). Kathleen Glass (1993, 80) argues that each person (whatever his or her age) deserves treatments that "best serve their interest or their wishes *as they have defined them*."

What do you think of Callahan's proposal? Is health care rationing based on age a good way to contain health care costs? What are the dangers of taking this approach?

of age. Clark says that "what is interpreted in the U.S. as a crisis is simply seen in Canada as a challenge to good government" (498).

A study by Stone, Rosenthal, and Connidis (1998) shows that influential Canadian researchers take a broad view of intergenerational equity. They look beyond public exchanges of funds (such as Canada's Old Age Security program) to include parent–child exchanges of informal supports. They also look at the mutual exchanges (of money and services) between adult children and their aging parents. And they look at support levels and types of support given and received by many age groups. Some studies conclude that "*over the life course, private exchange of supports between parents and children is not balanced. It heavily favours the children*" (66; italics in the original). Up to age 70, older people give more support to their children than they receive. And they continue to give to their children throughout their lives.

These findings question the "investment concept" (Stone, Rosenthal, and Connidis 1998, 96) of intergenerational equity common in the U.S. debate. In the U.S. view, each generation looks at what it has put into the system and judges whether it will get back more or less than it put in. Stone and his colleagues support a long view of exchange. They propose that giving and receiving over the life course strengthens social bonds between the generations. They see children's dependence on parents over most of a lifetime as a normal part of social and familial life. And they see giving to parents in later life as a way for the young to pay back their parents for this support. They propose that we view this as "a foundation of social cohesion."

Myles and Teichroew say that the intergenerational equity controversy has "had little impact in Canada. The prospect of the fiscal burden expected as a result of a long-term process of population aging has been received with relative equanimity by public, corporate, and policy elites" (1991, 85; see also Myles 2000). Ng found that Canadians have generally talked about "continued sharing and cooperation among generations" (1992, 15). Northcott's 1994 research supports this view. He studied the attitudes of the public toward the idea of an aging crisis. He found that "age was not significantly related to attitudes towards policies designed to respond to the aging crisis. He concluded that population aging will not necessarily lead to intergenerational conflict" (Maurier and Northcott 2000).

Still, rumblings in the Canadian press and in public debate suggest that Canadian society shows some concern about generational equity. Loveland (1994), for example, in a submission to the House of Commons,

says that "it is abundantly clear that this huge government debt 'belongs' to older Canadians, as opposed to younger Canadians." He goes on to ask for greater equity between young and old and for reduced benefits for older people.

Connidis (2001, 253) points to "deficit reduction, downsizing, and cost cutting in public and private spheres" as evidence that Canada, like the U.S., sees older people as the source of increased costs.

This debate over the cost of an older population will go on in the years ahead. And the growing size of the older population will draw attention to the costs of public pensions, health care, and other services. Blaming older people for this shift in resource allocation will not lead to a better life for older or younger people. The public needs good information about the costs and the benefits of social policies. We all have parents and grandparents. We'll all be old someday. We want to live in a society that cares for people at every age.

A NEW VIEW OF OLD AGE

Stereotypes and ageism give a simplistic picture of individual and societal aging. Research shows that older people live rich and complex lives that contradict the stereotypes. For example, most people aged 50 to 70 have good incomes, little or no mortgage, and no children to support. These people have money to spend and active lifestyles. Recreation programs, education, and travel services appeal to this group (Fletcher 1990). The increased affluence, better education, and more active lifestyles of older people have led the corporate world to see the potential in later life.

Foot and Stoffman (1998) say that retail companies have begun to target the older consumer. Foot and Stoffman report that baby boomers will pay for quality and service when they buy a product. For example, Ikea, the furniture company, has begun to offer delivery and assembly in order to attract older customers. Some companies now market services and products to the needs and desires of seniors.

Companies have developed drugs to improve male sexual potency, chemical treatments to hide wrinkles, and new hair colours to enhance an older woman's looks. Foot and Stoffman (1998) report that beer makers have created new premium brands for older consumers. They also say that clothing makers have redefined the sizes of clothing in order to salve the egos of older customers. "Even men's waist sizes have been relaxed by some manufacturers who are putting 32-inch labels on pants that fit comfortably around spongy 34-inch waists" (132). All of these products support a new model of later life. They meet the needs of older people who see themselves as active, energetic, and engaged. This view of later life rejects the image of aging as a decline.

Advertisements have also begun to take a more positive view of older people. Kaufert and Lock (1997) looked at the visual image of menopausal women portrayed in pharmaceutical ads. They found a shift from a negative image in the 1970s to a positive image in the 1990s. The new ads portray women with healthy teeth, hair, and skin. The ads show them playing with grandchildren and socializing with friends. The researchers say that the ads portray a fit and sexually active woman. Nemeth (1994, 27) says that "advertisers now poke fun at the aged only at their peril." For example, a TV ad for Doritos tortilla chips showed a steamroller squashing a confused older woman into wet cement. The company faced public outrage after it aired the commercial. "The contrite manufacturer," Nemeth says, "delivered cases of free chips to a food bank" to soothe public anger.

Today, many newspapers cover the senior beat. Kleyman (2002) reports that, in the U.S. in 2002, 15 daily news reporters spent full- or nearly full-time covering seniors' issues (compared to 10 in 1997). Another 35 news organizations assign staff to seniors' issues. Also, compared with the past, the mass media present an image of healthier, more active older people (Robinson 1998). David Poltrack, an executive vice president at CBS, says that when the baby boom generation reaches its 50s these people will want to watch shows that meet their needs (S.C. Taylor 1995). Television shows now sometimes feature single, independent, older women. The Rolling Stones, in their 60s, tour and produce albums. Jane Fonda and Cher, both over 50, promote fitness through aerobic exercise videos. One TV commercial has an elderly 90-pound saleswoman carry a 200-pound man out of a store to try her pizza because he "only goes out for pizza." Robinson (1998) reports that many TV advertisements place older people outdoors, and 93 percent of the ads he studied promoted a positive view of older people.

The July/August 2003 issue of the American Association of Retired Persons (AARP) magazine contained articles on the Korean War, the cost of drugs, and an age-bias settlement. You might expect to see these articles in a magazine for seniors. It contained articles on travel, gourmet cooking, and sexual satisfaction. These articles reflect the new interests and lifestyles of older people today.

Some critics believe that this new positive view of later life creates a new stereotype. Katz and Marshall (2003), for example, note that our consumer society pressures older people to use drugs and products to remain sexually and physically youthful. They say that this promotes an impossible ideal that ignores other ways to age. According to them, many of the new images of aging marginalize the very old, older people with disabilities, and older people with a different view of aging.

A number of authors say that claims of agelessness or youthfulness in spirit deny the uniqueness of later life. For instance, Gibson (2000) found that even organizations designed for self-development in later life deny some of the realities of aging. England's U3A (University of the Third Age), an educational organization, says that education keeps people young. Gibson objects to this view of a youthful mind inside an aging body. She says that older people should feel proud of their experience, wisdom, and freedom from their youthful mistakes. Andrews (2000) also challenges the idea of a youthful self within an aging body. This mind–body split, she says, rejects the aging body. She says that older people and society should embrace aging in all its forms. Cruikshank (2003, 168) proposes "frankness about decline and loss of capacity." She argues against the "false cheerfulness" of the more upbeat view of aging.

This debate shows a healthy interest in redefining old age. It captures the diversity of later life as older people work out new ways of aging. In one study, Clarke (2002) looked at older women's views on beauty in later life. These women felt the pressure toward thinness exerted by the modern fashion ideal, but they rejected the current ideal of extreme thinness. They preferred a more rounded body shape for themselves. These women also emphasized the importance of inner beauty. They found beauty in an individual's personality, relations to others, and inner happiness. Clarke concludes that social ideals shape an older woman's view of herself: "ageist norms ... denigrate older women and older women's bodies" (440). But, she says, older women can and do challenge these norms. "Many of the women in my study," she points out, "provide an important example of how oppressive social values can be resisted and how individuals may ... offer alternatives to ageist interpretations of later life" (440).

More change needs to take place in society and in our attitudes in order to have a more balanced view of later life. We need to allow for many ways to grow old. Some people want to engage in energetic activities that we associate with youth. Other older people define later life as a time to use their wisdom, share their memories, and offer community leadership. Some people will live vibrant healthy lives into late old age. Others will live with chronic illness. Some will seem youthful to us, others will look old. No single right way to grow old exists. And none of these ways should meet with social rejection.

Some changes in Canadian society suggest that ageism will lessen over time. First, Canada will have more older people in the future. Many of them will live in good health until late old age. They will serve as role models for a healthy, productive old age. Second, compared with earlier generations, people will enter old age with more education and technical knowledge. This will allow older people to remain a valuable part of their communities and of the workforce (if they choose). The generation gap in part reflected an education gap between the generations, which will lessen in the future. Third, the small size of younger age groups may open up opportunities for older people to work into later ages if they choose. This would provide some older people with better incomes in later life. And it would decrease the stereotype of the older person as dependent, obsolete, and irrelevant.

● Exhibit 1.5

EVENTS TODAY'S CENTENARIANS HAVE WITNESSED IN THEIR LIFETIME

Year	Age in that year	Event
1901	0–10	Marconi sends first transatlantic message between England and Newfoundland
1905		Alberta and Saskatchewan become provinces
1910	10–20	First electric street lamps lit in Toronto
1914		World War I begins
1918		World War I ends
1920	20–30	Canadian women win right to vote
1927		Lindbergh makes first transatlantic flights
1929		Stock market collapses and Great Depression begins
1931	30–40	Penicillin discovered
1939	40–50	World War II begins
1945		World War II ends
1946		Baby boom begins
1948		30 percent of Canadian homes have refrigerators
1949		Newfoundland becomes a province
1950	50–60	First "automatic" washing machines arrive
1952		CBC broadcasts first television show
1960	60–70	Contraceptive pills available in Canada
1972	70–80	State-funded universal medicare introduced across Canada
1980	80–90	Era of the personal computer begins
1990	90–100	Dot-com stock market bubble
2001	100+	World Trade Center bombing and terrorism threat worldwide

This chart shows the tremendous amount of change that the oldest Canadians have witnessed in their lifetimes. Centenarians today played an active role in many of these events, including World War I and World War II. These changes and many others have shaped and reshaped their world. World events have also shaped the older person's character and personality. This view of the past century challenges the belief that older people resist change and can't adapt to a changing world.

What changes have occurred in your parents' lifetimes? In your own? Create a chart that lists the changes you've witnessed in history, technology, and society. How have you responded to these changes? Can you guess what changes you will witness in the future?

Source: Adapted from Statistics Canada, 2002, "Time Line: The Events Today's Centenarians Have Witnessed in Their Lifetime," http://www12.statcan.ca/english/census01/Products/Analytic/companion/age/timelinet.cfm, accessed on September 15, 2004. Reprinted with permission.

CONCLUSION

Gerontology can help us to understand the facts and the issues about aging. It can move discussion from stereotype, prejudice, and discrimination to understanding. Gerontology shows that old age forms a normal part of the life cycle. Nearly all of us will enter old age some day. And we'll bring with us the attitudes and experiences of a lifetime. Gerontology can help overcome ageism by presenting a more balanced and accurate view of aging and older people. It can change people's attitudes toward aging and give them more knowledge about their families, their friends, and themselves.

Summary

1. The growth of the older population in Canada has made aging a major social issue—one that will affect all of us.

2. Gerontology has two goals: first, to increase our knowledge about old age and, second, to improve the quality of life in old age. In Canada today, these goals take the form of scholarly research and the practical application of research findings.

3. Canadians have both positive and negative images of aging and older people. Many of these stereotypes have little basis in fact. Negative attitudes can lead to prejudice and discrimination against older people.

4. Population aging has led to a new form of ageism. Some writers scapegoat the older population and blame older people for rising pension and health care costs. These writers predict economic collapse and intergenerational conflict. They propose a reduction in support for older people. Gerontologists refute these claims and present a more balanced view of Canadian society in the future.

5. New images of aging have begun to emerge. These include the image of the ever-youthful person; the active, engaged senior; and the older person who accepts aging and the physical changes it brings.

6. A growing population of healthy and active older people will lead Canadians to rethink their views of aging. Gerontology tries to replace stereotypes with facts, information, and a clearer understanding of later life.

Study Questions

1. Why should students know about aging? How will an aging population affect social structures like education, health care, and the family?

2. What is ageism? Where do negative attitudes toward aging come from? How can people develop a more positive attitude toward aging?

3. Define the term "gerontology." What are the two main goals of this discipline?

4. State three common myths about aging. Explain why these myths are false.

5. Why do some writers predict intergenerational conflict? Do you think this will take place in Canada? Why or why not?

6. Explain why older consumers have become a force in the marketplace. What types of products do older consumers prefer? How has the image of the older consumer changed in the past few years?

7. What troubles some older people about the image of later life as an extension of youth? What response have some seniors made to the image of the older person as ever-youthful?

Key Terms

ageism prejudice against older people. (7)

Americans for Generational Equity (AGE) a group that believes that young and middle-aged people cannot pay the high costs for services to older and younger people, and proposes cuts to programs for older people to free up money for the young. (10)

compassionate stereotype a stereotype that attempts to create sympathy for older people, but does not give a true picture of later life. (10)

Concord Coalition a U.S. group that proposes a means test for Social Security and Medicare. (11)

gerontology the discipline that studies aging systematically. (4)

intergenerational equity the call for a smaller proportion of public support for older people; based on the belief that older people use a disproportionate share of public resources. (10)

new ageism the belief that older people need special treatment due to poor health, poverty, and lack of social support. (10)

social structures a relatively stable pattern of social interactions. (4)

special-care homes nursing homes, hospitals, or other long-term care settings. (6)

stereotypes an exaggerated and often prejudiced view of a type of person or group of people. (6)

Selected Readings

Gee, E.M.T., and G. Gutman, eds. *The Overselling of Population Aging: Apocalyptic Demography, Intergenerational Challenges, and Social Policy.* Don Mills, ON: Oxford University Press, 2000.

This book presents articles by Canadian gerontologists. Topics include pension reform, health care, caregiving, and family life. The articles challenge the myth that population aging will lead to social conflict and economic collapse. The writers show that through social planning Canadian society can respond to the challenges of population aging.

Maurier, W.L., and H.C. Northcott. *Aging in Ontario: Diversity in the New Millennium.* Calgary: Detselig Enterprises, 2000.

A close look at aging in one Canadian province. The study focuses on the diversity of the older population and presents a factual analysis of aging today. It also shows how gerontologists look at aging and how their work can give a clear understanding of later life.

Novak, M.W., ed. *Aging and Society: A Canadian Reader.* Toronto: Nelson Canada, 1995.

A collection of topical articles by Canadian gerontologists, bringing together articles published in professional journals, government reports, and chapters from books. Topics include myths and realities of aging, cultural diversity, health care, housing, income, and retirement. The readings reflect Canadian concerns about aging, such as living in winter cities and Aboriginal health care.

Answers to Quiz in Exhibit 1.1

All 10 statements are false.

Chapter Two
Theories and Methods

INTRODUCTION

In 1980, the Gerontological Society of America (GSA) and the Association for Gerontology in Higher Education (AGHE) set out to define the discipline of gerontology (Foundations Project 1980). They asked 111 scholars, researchers, and professionals in the field to describe a basic education program in gerontology. These experts came from such different disciplines as biomedicine and economics, and their descriptions of the exact content and boundaries of gerontology varied. But they did agree that three broad areas of study should make up the core of a gerontology curriculum: biomedicine, psychosocial studies, and socioeconomic-environmental studies.

The first area, biomedicine, looks at the changes in physiology and health that come with age. This area includes studies of the biochemical causes of aging, studies of reaction time and stress, and studies of dementia. Experts disagreed least about the curriculum content for this area; this may be due to the long tradition of biomedical research on aging.

The second area, psychosocial studies, examines the changes that take place within individuals and between individuals and groups. This includes studies of memory, learning, and personality, as well as research on family and friendship ties, recreation, and leisure activities of older adults.

The third area, socioeconomic-environmental studies, concentrates on the effects of aging on social structures such as health care and education. It also looks at the effects of social structures on the aging individual and includes the study of income policies, health care systems, and formal social supports.

Social gerontology includes psychosocial, socioeconomic-environmental, and practice-related research. It looks at aging from the points of view of both the individual and the social system. Social gerontologists

---

● **Exhibit 2.1**

THEORIES IN THE STUDY OF AGING

Levels of Theory

Micro
individual social interaction

Macro
social structures, social processes

Theoretical Perspectives

Interpretive
how individuals define
and create social world

Functionalist
social order based on
cooperation and consensus

Conflict
society based on conflict
between social groups

Theories

social constructionism
symbolic interactionism
social phenomenology
ethnomethodology
social exchange

structural functionalism
modernization
disengagement
continuity
activity
age stratification
life course

political economy
moral economy
feminist theories

This chart presents the most influential theories in the study of aging. It summarizes the discussion in the text.

often take an interest in physical and health care changes that come with age. But the focus of the social gerontologist differs from that of the physiologist or biochemist. When social gerontologists look at biological or physical change in old age, they ask how these changes affect the individual's social life or society as a whole. They want to know how diseases in old age affect hospital costs or how changes in lung capacity affect a person's ability to work. They also want to know how a social norm such as retirement affects an older person's health, how changes in family life in Canada affect the psychological well-being of older adults, or what counselling methods work best with new retirees. Researchers use a variety of methods to examine these and other questions. And they have begun to give added attention to gerontological theory (Bengtson, Burgess, and Parrott 1997; Bengtson, Rice, and Johnson 1999; Marshall 1999; McMullin 2000). This chapter will look at (1) the theories that gerontologists use to guide their research and to interpret their findings, (2) the methods researchers use to gather data, and (3) current and future developments in Canadian research on aging.

THEORY IN THE STUDY OF AGING

Social gerontologists use theory to guide research and to interpret the results of their studies. A good theory helps a researcher choose research methods, questions, and samples. Bengtson and his colleagues (1999, 5) see the primary value of theory as providing "a set of lenses through which we can view and make sense of what we observe in research."

Theories create a structure that explains why things happen the way they do. For instance, research shows that women get more of their retirement income from public pension sources than men. Why does this difference exist? And is this an important finding or a trivial fact? Theory offers a framework for explaining research findings and for building knowledge and understanding. Feminist theory, for example, would trace this difference to gender inequalities in the workplace. Women have less opportunity to pay into private pension plans during their middle years. This forces them to rely on public pension sources in old age, and it forces some women to live in poverty.

Theory gives an interpretation to the facts. But no one theory in gerontology can explain all the facts about aging (Bengtson, Burgess, and Parrott 1997). And sometimes a researcher will use several theories to explain the results of a study. Authors often select theories to fit their

sense of how the world works. If you know the assumptions that underlie a theory, you know the strengths and limitations of using that theory, and you know the biases that each theory brings to the explanation of results. The theory used will guide the collection of data as well as how that data is interpreted.

Social gerontologists have generally used sociological or social-psychological theories in their work. Sometimes they have adapted these theories to fit the study of aging. Theory helps to disentangle the effects of history, biology, and social life on the aging person.

Two Levels of Theory

Theories describe all sorts of human activity and relationships, from individual attitudes to societal structures. The following discussion categorizes theories by placing them into a framework, and also gives examples of how gerontologists apply these theories in their work.

Gerontologists often classify theories into two categories: (1) micro level and (2) macro level. But be aware that sometimes these levels overlap and some theories fit into both categories (Bengtson, Burgess, and Parrott 1997).

Micro-level theories focus on individuals and their interactions. They are used to explain phenomena such as the relationship between adult children and their parents, changes in memory with age, and the effect of negative attitudes on an older person's self-image. **Macro-level theories** "examine social structures or structural elements as they influence experiences and behaviors" (Bengtson, Burgess, and Parrott 1997, S76). Such theories explain phenomena such as the effect of industrialization on older people's status, the history and impact of public pensions, and how gender and income affect older people's well-being. Critics of micro-level theories say they focus too much on people's actions. They ignore or take little account of economic conditions and social policies. Critics of macro-level theories say that this approach tends to minimize people's ability to act and overcome the limits of social structures.

Three Theoretical Perspectives

Both micro- and macro-level theories can take one of three perspectives: (1) the interpretive perspective, (2) the functionalist perspective, or (3) the conflict perspective.

The Interpretive Perspective

The **interpretive perspective** focuses almost exclusively on the micro level of social life. It looks at how people define situations, how they create social order, and how they relate to one another in daily life. Social gerontologists, historically, have made the least use of this perspective, although interest in this approach has increased significantly in the last few years. Theories within this perspective include social constructionism (Bengtson, Burgess, and Parrott 1997), social exchange theory (Homans 1961), the symbolic interactionist perspective, social phenomenology, and ethnomethodology (Garfinkel 1967), as well as an even earlier tradition pioneered by Max Weber (1905/1955). Mead (1934), for example, said that objects and events have no meaning in themselves. People give them meaning through everyday interaction. Grey hair can be a sign of wisdom in one society but a sign of decline in another. People give meanings to objects and then base their actions on these meanings. Some people will refuse to wear a hearing aid because to them it symbolizes decrepitude and weakness. The interpretive perspective views the individual as a creator of social order and organization. This perspective asks the question, "How does a recognizable, predictable social order come about?" (Berger and Luckman 1967; Garfinkel 1967; Schutz 1967). The interpretive perspective can give a good understanding of how people interpret their social world, how they interact with one another, and why they do what they do. Canadian gerontologists have used this approach to study how caregivers for people with Alzheimer's disease maintain their identity in the face of caregiving stress (MacRae 2002). They have studied the self-concept of women who have osteoporosis (Wilkins 2001). And they have looked at the social construction of elder abuse and neglect (Harbison and Morrow 1998). These studies demonstrate some of the strengths of an interpretive perspective.

For example, MacRae (2002) used a symbolic interactionist framework to study caregivers for people with Alzheimer's disease (AD). She looked at how family members help a parent or spouse cope with the loss of self that the disease causes. MacRae found that family members employ a number of strategies to help their relative preserve some of his or her former identity. One strategy involves concealing the diagnosis from others to avoid the label of dementia. A second strategy involves interpreting inappropriate behaviour as caused by the disease and not by the "real person." A third strategy involves assisting their relative with dressing and grooming so he or she will present an unchanged image of self to others. These strategies help family members preserve the identity of their relative. MacRae shows that this process takes place through daily interactions between the caregivers and their care receivers.

A symbolic interactionist perspective helps us recognize that objects and behaviours can have more than one meaning. MacRae's research, for example, shows

that family members can help a care receiver look normal when that individual enters the social world. Also, MacRae's work shows that members of the same family often have different interpretations of how much the person with AD has changed and how much of the person's former self remains. MacRae (2003, 414) concludes that "while selves are at risk because of the effects of AD, whether identity is lost or retained is very much dependent upon 'the eye of the beholder.'" MacRae's work demonstrates the value of using an interpretive perspective to study identity maintenance in the case of people with Alzheimer's disease.

The interpretive perspective has weaknesses as well as strengths. For example, it gives only the subjective or individual point of view on social life. It tends to ignore the connections that exist between micro-level social interactions and the larger social forces or structures in society, such as the health care system. This means that it cannot answer many of the questions that gerontologists ask. The interpretive perspective, for example, cannot tell us how health care policies will have to change to serve an aging society. It also says little about power and conflict between social groups. For example, it cannot explain income inequality between men and women in old age or the effects of ethnicity on social status in later life. Fortunately, the functionalist and conflict perspectives do look at these questions.

The Functionalist Perspective

The **functionalist perspective** fits within a **positivist worldview**. It holds that social order is based on consensus, cooperation, and shared norms and values. Within this perspective, all parts of society serve a role or function to keep society in a state of balance or equilibrium. While the interpretive perspective asks "How do people create their social world through interaction with one another?," the functionalist perspective asks, "What is the structure of the society that people live in and how do the parts of this structure function?"

The structural functionalist theories that grew out of Emile Durkheim's work in nineteenth-century France best express the functionalist perspective (Parsons 1937, 1951). Durkheim's studies, *The Division of Labor* and *Suicide,* serve as models for this approach. Structural functionalist theories treat society as a system that consists of social institutions such as the family, the military, and educational institutions. These systems keep society in a dynamic equilibrium. They adjust to one another as the system responds to internal and external pressures. For example, a structural functionalist would say that the increased number of women in the labour force has led to a decrease in the number of full-time family caregivers for frail older people. This, in turn, has led to more community care programs sponsored by government health services. The health care system has changed to meet new family demands, and this change serves the useful function of restoring society's balance.

Structural functionalism sometimes draws the analogy between society and a living organism. Just as our bodies will adjust to an increase in our blood sugar, so will society adjust to changes in its internal condition. An increase in the number of older people, for example, may lead society to increase funding to health promotion programs. Structural functionalism predicts that society will attempt to create an orderly transition to a new, stable state.

Structural functionalism also assumes that shared norms and values shape individual behaviour. People conform to these norms through social pressure, but also through belief in society's underlying value system. The values expressed in the commandment "Honour thy father and mother" show up in everyday behaviour and in social policies. Failure to honour a parent may lead to informal sanctions, such as criticism from a sister or brother. Extreme neglect may lead to the charge of abuse and legal sanctions. Functionalism draws connections between large-scale (macro) social structures and individuals' social roles and actions.

Finally, structural functionalism assumes that society changes or evolves in a positive direction. It explains social problems as dysfunctions, and it proposes to correct these dysfunctions through the use of experts in planning and the helping professions.

Historically, gerontologists used the functionalist perspective more than any other perspective in their study of aging. Gerontology's most influential early theories—disengagement theory (Cumming and Henry 1961), activity theory (Neugarten, Havighurst, and Tobin 1968) (both discussed in Chapter 7), and modernization theory (Cowgill and Holmes 1972)—all rely on structural functionalist assumptions. Riley (1971, 1987; Riley, Foner, and Waring 1988; Riley, Johnson, and Foner 1972) also produced a dominant theory based on structural functionalist principles: age stratification theory.

Age stratification theory, or its more recent identification as the "aging and society paradigm" (Riley 1994; Riley, Foner, and Riley, Jr. 1999), "focuses on the role of social structures in the process of individual aging and the stratification by age in the society" (Bengtson, Burgess, and Parrott 1997, S81). Age stratification theory focuses on the movement of age cohorts over the life cycle. It identifies similarities and differences between and among different age cohorts. Gerontologists define an age cohort as a group of people born in the same

period of time. All the people born between 1945 and 1950, for example, form an age cohort. According to age stratification theory, people in each cohort move or flow through society's predetermined age grades as they age. (An age grade is a period of life defined by society. Childhood, adolescence, and young adulthood are all age grades in Canada.)

People born in the same period experience the transitions from one stage to another at roughly the same time. They also experience the same historical events at the same time in their life cycle. People who are in their 50s today, for example, experienced the cultural changes of the 1960s in their teens and early 20s. These people still have an interest in the music of that period, and classic rock radio programs cater to this large group. People in their 40s today lived through the 1960s as children. They may recall the events of that decade, but the cultural, social, and political turmoil of those years had less effect on them.

Age stratification theorists say that society also changes as people age, so the norms and roles learned by each new cohort change as society changes. The norms of adult behaviour that people learn in their childhood, for example, may no longer fit when these same people reach adulthood. Many older people today were taught in their childhood that sex outside of marriage was immoral. Now, due to the death of a spouse or the influence of changing values and lifestyles of their children and grandchildren, many older people have changed their point of view. Similarly, many younger people will rethink their own values as they age and as society changes.

Age cohorts constantly move along as if on an escalator. As one group leaves an age grade, a new group takes its place. Each age grade (youth, young adulthood, and so on) places expectations on its members and offers people new roles. Also, each cohort brings new norms and values to its age grade.

This leads to a dialectic between individuals and societal structures. Changes in norms and values bring changes in social organizations. These changes, in turn, shape the process of aging. For example, new cohorts of older people, with interests in travel and education, will affect the traditional programs offered in senior centres. Some senior centres may close because they cannot meet the demands of these new seniors. Others may remain open by adapting their programs to serve newer cohorts of older people. These changes in programs will also change the way younger and middle-aged people think about later life.

Age stratification theory relies on many of the assumptions of the structural functionalist approach to aging. First, it assumes that norms and values influence individual aging. Second, it describes the relationship between the individual and society as a feedback loop. Change begins with the individual cohort or with large-scale historical or social change. These changes then lead to change in other parts of the social system. Third, the theory tends to see society as a homogeneous set of structures and functions that all people experience in the same way.

Age stratification theory has a number of strengths. First, it has helped to separate age differences (between cohorts) from age changes over the life course (aging). Second, it highlights the impact of historical and social changes on individuals and cohorts (Bengtson, Burgess and Parrott 1997). Third, it highlights the relationship between aging and social structures (Marshall 1996). Bengtson and his colleagues (1997, S82) say that age stratification theory "provides new ways to explore differences related to time, period, and cohort."

This perspective also has its limits. For example, people of the same age do not all experience the world in the same way. An elderly Chinese woman who has just arrived in Canada will see the world differently from a French-Canadian man born in Montreal. The age stratification theory overlooks each person's interpretation of the world. It makes little reference to individual control or action. The theory also makes little reference to the tensions and conflicts between social groups in society or to issues of power (Marshall 1995a).

There is also little focus in age stratification theory on how characteristics such as gender, social class, race, and ethnicity can create inequalities within age cohorts. For example, it says little about the differences between growing old as a poor woman compared with growing old as an upper-middle-class man. Such variations within cohorts may have a greater influence on people's lives and their experiences in aging than the norms and values related to their age grade. A person's race or gender will lead to different behaviours and to different responses to sociohistorical events. A person's race or gender will also determine the choices he or she has available (Stoller and Gibson 1997). For example, a policy change such as a decrease in government pension payments will have different effects on poor older women and wealthy older men.

Age stratification theory has its limits, but it has made a major contribution to our understanding of aging. It orders many complex phenomena and helps us to see the relationship between the individual and society. The **life course approach**, a functionalist approach, bridges both the micro- and macro-levels of analysis by incorporating social interaction and social structure within its framework (Bengtson, Burgess, and Parrott 1997). Researchers use this approach to explain (1) the

changes that take place over time, (2) age-related and socially recognized life transitions, and (3) the interaction of social life, history, culture, and personal biography (Bengtson, Burgess, and Parrott 1997; George 1996). At the micro or individual level, the life course approach looks at how events and conditions early in life can affect later life. At the macro or societal level, the life course approach shows how social change and historical events can create differences between cohorts (Elder 2000; Uhlenberg and Miner 1996).

Some researchers (e.g., George 1996) say that no unified, systematic approach to the life course exists. Rather, the life course approach merges theoretical approaches from many disciplines, including sociology and psychology. The life course approach recognizes variety in life course patterns and differences between age cohorts. It also recognizes differences within age cohorts due to differences in race, ethnicity, social class, and gender (Stoller and Gibson 1997). This approach takes into account the diversity of roles and role changes across the life course. The life course approach recognizes aging as a lifelong, dynamic, interactive, and multidirectional process. For example, an older person may show some loss of memory over time but may stay physically active, and may even take up new activities in later life. Aging involves stability in some areas of life, decline in others, and improvement in others.

The life course approach looks at **transitions** and **trajectories**. Transitions refer to changes in social status or social roles (when those changes occur, how long they last, etc.). Transitions include marriage, divorce, remarriage, widowhood, and parenthood. Work-related transitions also occur, for example, getting a first job or retiring. Trajectories refer to long-term patterns of stability and change. They often include many transitions. One marital status trajectory may involve the transition to marriage, a subsequent divorce, then a remarriage, and finally a transition to widowhood. Another marital status trajectory may involve only one marriage for life. This involves only the transition to a first marriage and, for one of the couple, the transition to widowhood.

The life course approach has made a number of contributions to the study of aging. First, it bridges the macro level and the micro level of analysis by recognizing the importance of social structures and historical context, as well as individual experiences and meanings. It helps us to understand the diversity within and between cohorts. Second, the approach brings together sociological, psychological, anthropological, and historical approaches to the study of aging. Third, the life course approach understands aging as a dynamic process that takes place throughout life.

This approach has some limitations. Its broad focus on society, culture, and the individual makes it hard to define as a single theory. Furthermore, as Bengtson and his colleagues (1997, S80) say, "it is very difficult to incorporate into a single analysis the many contextual variables ... that this approach identifies." Still, the life course approach encourages us to think about the many individual and social forces that affect aging.

The Conflict Perspective

Historically, few gerontologists have used the **conflict perspective** in their work. But a new interest has developed in social conflict and aging. Researchers understand that social and structural inequalities experienced earlier in life can lead to poverty and other disadvantages in later life. For example, women are more likely than men to earn less income, work part-time, or have disrupted work histories due to child care or care for other family members. Public and private pension programs tend to reward those with higher incomes and stable work histories. This means that many women will be financially disadvantaged in their later years. Researchers have begun to study the causes of poverty in later life, women and gender discrimination, the ideology of aging as a social problem, and pensions and policies. The conflict perspective holds that society consists of conflicts between dominant and subordinate social groups.

The **political economy theory** that grew out of the work of Karl Marx exemplifies the conflict perspective. This theory focuses on conflict and change in social life. It traces this conflict to the struggle between social classes and to the resulting dominance of some groups and the subordination of others in society.

Marxist theory says that, for example, if managers view older workers as slower and weaker, they will also see these workers as less useful to industry as they age. Therefore, companies will tend to fire or retire older workers and replace them with younger workers who will work faster and for lower wages (McMullin and Marshall 2001).

Studies on political economy and aging look at aging in the modern state. They also examine the structural conditions in society that create inequality in old age. Gerontologists have looked at the impact of retirement and pensions on aging (Phillipson 1999), the structural situation of women and retirement (Zimmerman et al. 2000), and social policy in an aging society (Estes 1999; Hudson 1999).

The political economy approach traces the origins of older people's problems to the political and economic structure of capitalist society (Minkler 1999b). It also looks at how social programs and policies for older people serve the interests of middle-aged, middle-class professionals, and can reinforce class, gender, and racial inequalities in later life.

Early work by Myles (1984) used the political economy approach to study pensions in Canada and other liberal democracies. He traces the development of modern, state-run pension plans to the struggle between labour and the owners of the means of production. Workers today expect pensions to form part of their wage package, but many employers resist paying this money. For this reason, employers support government pension programs. This allows them to pay less into workers' pension programs.

It was also for this reason that Canada's *Old Age Security Act* of 1951 gained the support of industrialists. More recently, labour unions have played an important role in deciding pension entitlements. Myles (1984) found that increased labour union organization leads to better public pensions, as do the increased political power of working-class parties and the right to strike. He also found that the electoral process itself leads to better pensions. Political parties pay attention to have-not voters when an active electoral process exists.

Myles's (1984) early work shows the strengths of the political economy approach to aging. First, it places the study of aging in the context of large political, historical, economic, and social forces. Second, it views public pensions as the outcome of a struggle between competing groups. Third, it predicts that economic and political forces will shape future changes in public pensions.

The political economy approach looks beyond the individual to understand the forces that shape individual aging today. It broadens gerontologists' understanding of aging and offers another way to interpret the origins and effects of social policies. Recent work by Myles (2000), for example, examines the distribution of income among older Canadians. It looks at income in the context of recent improvements in Canada's public and private retirement income system. He finds that since the early 1980s, the average income of older Canadians has increased significantly, particularly among lower-income seniors. And this has decreased income inequality among older Canadian.

The political economy approach emphasizes the impact of history and economics on individuals. It shows how the state and social policies can increase or decrease social inequalities (Quadagno and Reid 1999). Sometimes, though, the political economy approach overemphasizes the poverty and problems older people face. It also tends to view the individual as the product of political and economic forces, and pays little attention to individuals' interpretations of social life. It says little about the ways in which individuals shape their world through their interactions with others. As Bengtson and his colleagues (1997, S83) say, this perspective too often "paints a picture of all elders as powerless, forced to exist under oppressive structural arrangements with no control over their own lives."

Feminist theories, within the conflict perspective, bridge both the micro and macro levels of analysis. They recognize the importance of social interaction and social structure in the study of aging (Bengtson, Burgess, and Parrott 1997). Feminist theories hold that society is gendered by nature. Feminist social gerontologists believe that gender defines social interaction and life experiences, including the experience of aging. Furthermore, within a patriarchal system (such as North American society), gender-based inequalities are created and perpetuated. This results in social advantages for men (for instance, higher wages and better pensions) and disadvantages for women (higher rates of poverty in old age).

Feminist theorists criticize other theories of aging and aging research for not focusing enough on gender relations or on women's experiences. Neysmith (1995a), for example, says that gerontologists need to explore women's experiences without constant reference to the experiences of men. Hooyman and her colleagues (2002) state that researchers and practitioners need to find new approaches to address gender, race, and class inequalities that exist across the life course.

Feminist research in aging has focused on many issues: mother–daughter conflict (Ray 2003), the impact of domestic violence on older women (Vinton 1999), women and retirement (Richardson 1999), and the social invisibility of older lesbians (Fullmer, Shenk, and Eastland 1999).

Feminist theories have made several contributions to the study of aging. First, feminist theories, like the life course approach, recognize the importance of social structure, social interaction, and individual characteristics (primarily gender, but also race, ethnicity, and social class) (Bengtson, Burgess, and Parrott 1997). Second, they present a more inclusive picture of aging and older adults, by focusing on the majority of the older population—women—and on issues that are relevant to women's lives. Third, feminist theories of aging challenge the traditional focus on men in research (Calasanti 1996) and the ageist biases in "mainstream" feminist theories that ignore issues of age (Calasanti and Slevin 2001; McMullin 1995).

Feminist theories have some limitations. They are too diffuse to form one unified "theory." Also, some gerontologists say that feminist theories are biased or value-laden. They see gender as too narrow a focus for the study of aging. Furthermore, feminist theories have been criticized for the so-called feminization of aging. Critics say that feminist theories deny the gendered nature of aging for men (Bengtson, Burgess, and Parrott 1997; Bengtson, Rosenthal, and Burton 1996) and overlook experiences important to older men. Feminist theories have also been criticized for their preoccupation with the problems and disadvantages older women face. Critics say that feminist theory overlooks the positive experience of aging for many women and overlooks their contributions to society (Gibson 1996). Still, feminist theories of aging have made gender an explicit theme in the study of aging and later life.

Further Developments in Gerontological Theory

Theories try to make sense of the complex, multidimensional facts of aging. The theories discussed here show that no single explanation of aging can account for everything we know. But we must have theories in order to understand the mass of detailed information that researchers gather (Bengtson, Rice, and Johnson 1999; George 1995; Marshall 1995a). As Bengtson and his colleagues (1997, S84) say, "theory is not a marginal, meaningless 'tacked-on' exercise to presenting results in an empirical paper. Rather, cumulative theory-building represents the core of the foundation of scientific inquiry and knowledge."

What theoretical ideas will emerge in social gerontology in the years ahead? Marshall (1995a) and others support the wider use of interpretive theories in gerontology. **Dialectical theory** (one type of interpretive theory), for example, says that aging has many dimensions (physical, psychological, social, and historical). Dialectical theory focuses on the asynchronies that exist among these dimensions. For example, a sudden illness (a physical change) or the death of a spouse (a social loss) can lead to a psychological crisis. Dialectical gerontology highlights the crises and tensions in individual and social life. It argues that these moments of crisis force a person to reflect critically on his or her own life and on the social environment. This reflection on life crises and our responses to them lead to growth and development. Dialectical theory and other interpretive theories (hermeneutic and critical theories) work to foster self-understanding and personal development.

Moral economy theory, a complement to political economy theory, grew out of the work of E.P. Thompson in England. Political economy theorists and researchers have begun to use this perspective to explore issues like retirement, senior power, and long-term care (Minkler and Estes 1999). This approach to the study of aging looks at the shared moral assumptions held by members of a society. Studies that use this approach look at values such as justice and fairness in society and how they affect social policies. The moral economy theory is concerned with the social consensus that underlies issues such as justice between the generations, pension entitlements, and access to health care.

Marshall (1995a) predicts an increased focus on a political economy perspective, interpretive approaches such as phenomenology and symbolic interactionism, critical and feminist theories, and life course perspectives. Bengtson and his colleagues (1999) say that "theory is the compass with which to navigate through vast seas of data. It is the means by which data are transformed into meaningful explanations, or stories, about the processes and consequences of aging." Gerontological theories offer many explanations of aging. Their variety reflects the many dimensions of gerontological research. Each of these perspectives gives us a different insight into what it means to age.

RESEARCH ISSUES AND METHODS

Research Issues

Gerontologists use a variety of theories to direct their research and explain their findings. They also use a number of methods that help them study the process of aging. The proper use of these methods ensures that researchers come up with reliable and valid findings. Improper use can lead to biased and confusing results. The following discussion will give a glimpse of the methodological issues that gerontologists face in trying to study continuity and change in later life.

Gerontologists generally place changes in old age into one of three categories:

1. **Age effects** due to physical decline. These changes appear with the passage of time. They include an increase in the body's fat-to-muscle ratio, a decline in lung elasticity, and decreases in bone density. They also include environmentally caused changes such as wrinkled skin and cataracts caused by the sun.

2. **Cohort effects** related to the time of a person's birth. A cohort refers to a group of people born around the same time (usually within a five- or ten-year period). People born in a certain cohort often share a common background and experience of the world. People born just after World War II, for example, are in the cohort that was the first to be exposed to large doses of television. This new technology shaped their entertainment habits and lifestyles.

3. **Period or environmental effects** due to the time of measurement. This category includes social or historical effects on measurement, such as an ongoing war, changes in health habits (for example, increased exercise), or changes in health care policies. These effects have different influences on different age cohorts.

Gerontologists try to disentangle these effects in order to understand the causes of aging. They use a number of research designs to look at these three effects in their attempts to understand change in later life.

Studies on aging done in the 1960s supported many of the negative stereotypes of aging. Much of the early research on aging used a **cross-sectional research design**. This type of method studies people from many age groups at one point in time. Early studies done in psychology, for example, found that older age groups, compared with younger age groups, scored lower on intelligence tests. This finding supported the view that people get "simple-minded" as they get older. But these early studies tended to confuse differences *between age groups* (cohort effects) with *changes due to aging* (age effects). In the 1980s, research by Baltes and Schaie (1982) found that younger people had more education than older people. This, they said, might account for a large part of the differences in younger and older people's test scores.

Most researchers who study aging still use a cross-sectional design. This method allows researchers to gather data in a short time at a low cost. It also allows policymakers to assess and meet the needs of different age groups fairly quickly. Researchers in a single study can ask a broad range of questions that give a detailed snapshot of a group of people at one point in time (Charness 1995).

Still, this method causes problems. As the early intelligence studies show, cross-sectional studies confound cohort effects (such as lower education levels in older cohorts) with age changes (e.g., changes in intelligence due to increasing age). The findings from cross-sectional studies cannot tell us whether aging (maturation) leads to changes in intelligence, health, or any other condition or behaviour that changes over time.

Longitudinal research designs attempt to overcome this problem. A longitudinal study looks at a single group of people at two or more points in time. For example, a longitudinal study of how aging affects intelligence might test the same group of people at 10-year intervals. These results give a truer picture of the effects of age on intelligence, because this kind of study avoids the problem of trying to compare different cohorts (e.g., people with different educational backgrounds due to the historical conditions in their childhood).

Gerontologists use longitudinal studies when they want to learn about age changes, but this method also creates problems. Environmental changes (period effects)—historical events, changes in the economy, or changes in political values—can confound changes due to aging. Havens (1995b) says that longitudinal studies of older people face special problems. These include loss of people in the study due to death, illness, and moving; inability to respond due to chronic illness or cognitive decline; and a shift in the sex ratio due to the deaths of more men than women in later life (see also Chipperfield, Havens, and Doig 1997). These examples show the kinds of problems gerontologists can face when they search for the causes of change in later life.

A third method, **time-lag comparison design**, tries to overcome the problems raised by simple cross-sectional and simple longitudinal designs. Time-lag studies look at different groups of people of the same age at different points in time (e.g., 70-year-olds in 1985, 1995, and 2005). This type of study tries to measure differences between cohorts. Like cross-sectional and longitudinal methods, the time-lag method also presents problems. It confounds cohort effects with environmental ones. If a research study finds that 70-year-olds in 2005 visited doctors less often than 70-year-olds did in 1985, this difference may be because of the better health of 70-year-olds in 2005 (a cohort effect) or it may be because of a change in the health care system, perhaps higher costs to users (an environmental effect).

Each type of study creates problems when it comes to interpreting results. In addition, longitudinal and time-lag studies pose practical problems. First, they often take many years to complete—years during which researchers must wait before they can show results to granting agencies or to the public. Second, they are expensive to maintain. The cost can force the researcher to apply for new grants for each wave of the research. The researcher must compete with all other applicants, but cannot tailor sample size or limit the research to fit new funding conditions (Havens 1995a). Third, subjects in longitudinal studies drop out (or die), biasing results in later rounds of the study. Fourth, longitudinal studies require institutional support. The time needed to complete a longitudinal study can be so long that researchers themselves may die or move before the study ends. For this reason, some longitudinal studies take place through a research centre or university. The

institution can see the study through and provide a home for the data (Havens 1995a).

Gerontologists have solved some of these problems by turning simple cross-sectional and simple longitudinal designs into **sequential designs**. Researchers create sequential designs by looking at a series of cross-sectional studies during a longer longitudinal study. The cross-sectional studies allow for quick data collection. The longitudinal study provides a check on cross-sectional findings. These two methods together also provide time-lag data on the sampled members of same-aged groups at different times.

The Aging in Manitoba Longitudinal Study offers this kind of option to researchers by providing comparable data on health and health care needs for a random sample of older people in Manitoba at different times (Chipperfield, Havens, and Doig 1997). In this project, which began in 1971, three independent cross-sectional studies were conducted (in 1971, 1976, and 1983). The groups were then followed over time (1983–84 and 1990). This method produced both cross-sectional and longitudinal data (within a sequential design). With a third follow-up survey providing data over 25 years, the Aging in Manitoba Longitudinal Study is the longest continuous population-based study of aging in Canada.

This type of study allows researchers to compare the needs of different age groups in a given year (e.g., 66- to 75-year-olds and 76- to 85-year-olds in 1990). It also allows researchers to study the changes in these groups' needs over time (e.g., whether the needs of the sample of 66- to 75-year-olds have changed between 1976 and 1990). The researchers can also see whether social changes have affected all age groups (e.g., whether all groups of older people used hospitals more in 1971 than in 1990). They can then separate period effects—effects due to social conditions at the times of measurement (e.g., new medical care policies)—from effects due to aging (such as the need for more medical care as a person ages).

These complex designs still do not untangle time of measurement, age, and cohort effects, although they do give researchers more information about the group under study. Attempting to neutralize variables takes a great deal of time and effort. Without the effort, the researchers could make a fundamental error in understanding. But, even with it, the researcher still has to explain, for example, the specific historical events that led to changes in health care use or how these events translated themselves into different behaviours. Whatever method the researcher chooses, logical reasoning and judgment must be used to make sense of research findings.

Types of Research Methods

Gerontologists use psychological tests and surveys to study aging, but they also use other research methods. Researchers in each dimension of aging (biomedical, psychosocial, socioeconomic-environmental) have their preferred methods.

Pharmacologists, chemists, and neurophysiologists use laboratory techniques and controlled experiments to study aging; historians use libraries, archives, diaries, and even paintings; literary scholars use plays, novels, and poetry. Kuehne (1998–99) proposes the use of community-based action-research to help build intergenerational communities. Some studies require more than one method—a questionnaire survey of a large population, for example, may include a psychological test, and an anthropological field study may include the study of a society's literature and history as well as a measurement of the people's physical condition.

Researchers have recently expanded their interest in certain research issues. Many Statistics Canada publications, for example, now routinely include separate information on age groups over 65 (e.g., groups aged 65 to 74, 75 to 84, and 85 and over) (Lindsay 1999). This approach recognizes that we need more information about the growing population of very old people. It also recognizes that age cohorts among the 65 and over group often differ from one another. Smaller age groupings give more information about differences among older people. Researchers also focus more now on the differences between men and women as they age. Studies of retirement, widowhood, caregiving, and social life, among other topics, all show the importance of gender differences in later life. Gerontologists' interests continue to grow and expand. As this happens, researchers will develop and use the methods that best answer their questions.

Quantitative and Qualitative Methodologies

Social gerontologists use both quantitative and qualitative methods in research on aging. But **quantitative methods** remain the dominant approach in much of the gerontological research. Quantitative methods emphasize relationships between and among factors (variables) through numerical measurement (quantity, amount, frequency) (Neuman 2003). "Quantitative research refers to counts and measures of things" (Berg 1998, 3). While there are many different methods used in quantitative research, very often data are gathered through surveys or other questionnaires. Researchers then summarize

responses into numerical values for statistical analysis. Examples of Canadian studies that use quantitative methods include research on the links between informal and formal care of the elderly (Denton 1997), attachment style and well-being in elderly adults (Webster 1997), older adults' perceptions of health care and health care delivery (Shapiro, Tate, Wright, and Plohman 2000), and the prediction of adult sons' level of involvement in caregiving for parents (Campbell and Martin-Matthews 2003).

The use of **qualitative methods** in research on aging has grown significantly in recent years. Qualitative researchers "look at social life from multiple points of view and explain how people construct identities" (Neuman 2003, 146). They seek to understand the social world and social experience of individuals from the subjects' own perspective. Qualitative research does not use statistical procedures or quantification of the data to obtain findings. Qualitative research uses many methods, including interviews, life histories, field observation, case studies, and content analysis. It uses an interpretive theoretical approach to understand these data (Berg 1998).

Neuman (2003, 146) says that "instead of trying to convert social life into variables or numbers, qualitative researchers borrow ideas from the people they study and place them within the context of a natural setting." Researchers try to understand the meanings people bring to social interactions. Examples of Canadian qualitative studies include research on caregivers' experiences of living with a memory-impaired spouse (O'Connor 1999), the process that allows caregivers to combine employment and care to older relatives (Guberman and Maheu 1999), friendship ties of older women (MacRae 1996), and women's perspectives on informal care of the elderly (Aronson 1998).

Quantitative and qualitative methods each have their strengths and limitations. Quantitative methods, for example, allow researchers to gather a great deal of information on a wide range of issues. Moreover, they can analyze a large sample and generalize their results to a larger population. But quantitative researchers structure their research questions and give respondents limited choices. This kind of research offers little opportunity to capture the "rich description" of individuals' subjective experiences or perceptions of their social world (Lincoln and Guba 2000; Neuman 2003).

Qualitative methods allow researchers to appreciate the complexity of social interactions and behaviours. These methods study how individuals understand and give meaning to their lives (Del Balso and Lewis 1997). Qualitative research also has its limits. Researchers often use small sample sizes, a practice that limits generalization to a larger population. Some researchers combine both quantitative and qualitative methods in one study (Neuman 2003).

Ethical Issues in Research

Research studies on human subjects face ethical challenges. And studies of certain frail or vulnerable groups pose unique problems. Researchers need to consider the ethical implications of studying institutionalized older people, those living in poverty (Kayser-Jones and Koenig 1994), the socially isolated (Russell 1999), and people with Alzheimer's disease or another cognitive impairment (Karlawish 2004).

Researchers need to consider at least three ethical issues: (1) the need for informed consent, (2) the need to guard subjects against harm or injury, and (3) the need to protect individuals' privacy (Neuman 2003).

Informed consent means that the researcher tells the subject the facts about the research and gets written permission from the subjects before they take part in a study. Individuals must freely give their consent without any coercion. They need to understand that they can decide not to answer any questions without explanation. And they need to know that they can withdraw from the study at any time. Older people who live in long-term care facilities and socially isolated people may feel some pressure to take part in a study (Kayser-Jones and Koenig 1994; Russell 1999).

Researchers must also guard against doing harm or injury to study participants. This includes physical harm and psychological harm. A person might feel embarrassed or upset at some questions they feel they have to answer. Researchers need to minimize risk to participants throughout the research process (Neuman 2003).

Researchers also seek to protect participants from potential harm by protecting their identity. Researchers can do this by making sure that data analysis cannot reveal an individual's identity. The researcher should also promise to keep personal information private.

Older people with Alzheimer's disease or other types of dementia present special challenges in research. For example, they may not be able to give true voluntary informed consent (Neuman 2003). If the mental competency of an individual is in question, the researchers must get written permission from someone who has the legal authority to make such decisions. A family member or staff member in a nursing home may have this authority. Permission from a substitute decision maker allows for research at all stages of the disease (Dukoff and Sunderland 1997; Karlawish 2004).

Universities and other funding agencies have ethics review boards to evaluate potential risks that participants might face. The ethics review board must approve each study, weigh the potential risks and benefits, and then give permission for research to proceed. This process protects participants from potential harm and ensures that researchers act ethically and responsibly in their research.

THE FUTURE OF GERONTOLOGICAL THEORY AND METHODS

What theories and methods will gerontologists use in the future? First, gerontologists will create new and more sophisticated quantitative methods, including structural equation models, longitudinal factor analysis, and multivariate effects models. As computer power increases and as gerontologists apply methods used in other social sciences, gerontologists will be able to test new and more complex theories. Hendricks (1997) proposes the use of recent models from natural science—chaos theory and catastrophe theory—to explain aging. These theories and models question the assumptions of linear, probabilistic analyses that gerontologists use today. Hendricks challenges gerontology "to develop mind-sets and measures that address the possibility of non-linear processes" (205). This approach would include the study of unpredictable and dramatic changes in individuals' lives and in their families, work, and neighbourhoods. It would also include a study of how people modify their life course through their own interpretations of their lives.

Second, gerontologists will continue to link the micro and macro levels of theory. Age stratification theory, life course approaches, and feminist theories come closest to doing this now, although they have their limitations. They try to explain a great deal, but they remain too broad or abstract. Researchers support the further development of political economy and phenomenological theories, as well as feminist theories, life course approaches, and exchange theory (Bengtson, Burgess, and Parrott 1997; Marshall 1995a). These theories allow gerontologists to stand back and analyze social processes. These approaches reveal hidden sides of aging and explore ways to create a good old age.

Third, qualitative methods will continue to grow in importance in gerontological research. Qualitative methods can explore the experience of aging at a time when more and more people will want to know about that experience. Gubrium and Holstein (1997, 6) say that qualitative methods attempt "to understand social reality on its own terms 'as it really is.'" Qualitative research prizes the richness and diversity of everyday social life. This type of research takes us into the world of older people and their communities. It reveals their experiences of later life. Still, the positivist paradigm that dominates gerontology continues to give less value to qualitative study and makes it riskier for researchers to build a career on this kind of work.

Fourth, technology will expand research opportunities. Connell (1998) points out that laptop computers allow researchers to enter interview data in the field. She also describes the use of video-based technology to study behaviour problems in long-term care settings. Video recording technology allows researchers to observe behaviour without a researcher present. This method allows researchers to gather data throughout the day, and a number of researchers can observe and analyze the same data. Researchers have used this technology to study wandering behaviour and the causes of falls in nursing homes.

Fifth, studies in the humanities will add new methods to gerontological research such as linguistic analysis, the study of paintings and photos, autobiographical analysis, and narrative gerontology. New topics of interest in the future will lead to new approaches to the study of aging.

In turn, researchers will develop new methods as they work to answer new questions about aging.

Chappell (1995, 26) says that "the research question ... should drive our methodological approach and not vice versa." Researchers should choose the method that best suits their needs. A bias for or against one research method or another only stifles the search for knowledge. A more open approach to varied methods will lead to a better understanding of aging.

CONCLUSION

Research in gerontology now goes on in many disciplines, including biology, economics, social work, health sciences, psychology, and sociology. Researchers also have access to the latest gerontology research through the use of online databases. Still, more research on aging in Canada needs to be done. For instance, a review of the abstracts for the 2002 annual meeting of the Canadian Association on Gerontology (CAG) (2002) shows that researchers presented more papers on health-related issues than on any other subject. A review of the Ageline database in 2003 found a strong focus on income, caregiving, and health issues. Government funding for research on these policy-related issues, in part, explains the concentration on these topics. But we also need to know about healthy older people because most older people live healthy, active lives.

● Exhibit 2.2

ANGLOPHONE AND QUEBEC GERONTOLOGY: TWO SOLITUDES?

Anglophone Canadians have often overlooked francophone research, as have other North American scholars. As Béland (1988) pointed out a number of years ago, and what remains true today, francophone researchers often publish their work in French and tend to publish in research reports rather than in refereed journals. For these reasons, their work has not reached the wider North American academic community. Lesemann (2001, 58) says that English-Canadian and Quebec gerontology today exist as "two solitudes." He remarks on the "comparative lack of knowledge of one another that seems to exist ... despite the efforts at collaboration that have been made over the years" (58). He traces this lack of knowledge to the impact of politics and culture on research and scholarship. McPherson (2001) says

that language also forms a barrier to collaboration. Relatively few English-speaking scholars today can work in French and so they know little about Quebec gerontology.

But, as Béland's review shows, francophone researchers have conducted community studies that could interest a wider audience. They have also conducted social and social-psychological studies that speak to important issues like the loneliness and isolation of the elderly (Béland 1997), family caregivers' assessment of the quality of geriatric services (Roberge et al. 2002), and women's perceptions of physical activity and aging (Beausoleil and Martin 2002). Anglophone gerontologists could benefit from wider exposure to this research.

● Exhibit 2.3

LARGE-SCALE GERONTOLOGY RESEARCH IN CANADA

Canadian gerontologists use many methods and theories to study aging. They have conducted interactionist studies of dying patients as well as large-scale surveys of health care system use. The past 20 years have seen an increase in national studies conducted by interdisciplinary teams. The federal government funded most of these studies and they have an application to social policy and program development (Chappell 1995).

In December 1987, for example, Health and Welfare Canada funded the Collaborative Study Centre to study Alzheimer's disease and other dementias. The centre linked the University of Ottawa's Department of Epidemiology, the federal Laboratory Centre for Disease Control, and experts from various disciplines at universities across the country. This study produced the first national picture of the incidence and impact of dementia in Canada. It also produced the first nationwide data of this kind in the world (Eastwood et al. 1992).

In May 1988, the federal government's Canadian Strategy for Science and Technology (Innov-Action) spent $240 million to establish a project called Networks of Centres of Excellence (NCE) across Canada. The program set up 15 national networks with more than 500 scientists to "promote fundamental and long term applied research and to provide an opportunity for the nation's best researchers to work together in support of Canada's long term industrial competitiveness" (Inter-Council 1988, 1).

The NCE sponsored the Canadian Aging Research Network (CARNET), which began in 1990. CARNET had four research programs based at the universities of Toronto, Guelph, and Manitoba. Research in this program included studies of formal supports, new products to enhance independent living, work and eldercare, and cognitive function. CARNET also developed relationships with corporate partners to develop useful products and technology. Numerous reports and academic papers on this work have appeared in the literature and researchers continue to publish research based on CARNET data (for example, Campbell and Martin-Matthews 2003).

In 2003, a major interdisciplinary project entitled "Workforce Aging in the New Economy: A Comparative Study of Information Technology Employment" received funding from Social Sciences and Humanities Research Council in the amount of $2.9 million. This multidisciplinary, cross-national study examines the growth in information technology, employment, and workforce aging in Canada, the United States, the European Union, and Australia. Julie McMullin, a sociologist at the University of Western Ontario, heads an international consortium of 16 researchers from all the participating regions. This research, focusing on the workplace in the new economy, will help countries respond to an aging workforce and diversity in the workplace.

These studies all show a trend toward large-scale, interdisciplinary research among Canadian researchers. Collaborative studies save money by pooling researchers' skills and resources. They also create interdisciplinary teams that can carry out sophisticated analyses of large data sets. This research and the many other studies conducted by researchers throughout Canada expand our knowledge and understanding of aging. They also help governments, social service agencies, and professionals to plan better programs for older people.

Social gerontologists now see the need to focus on the social conditions that lead to good aging. Lesemann (2001, 65) reports that, compared to the past, Canadian researchers now look at "the strengths and resources available to the older person ... [in order to] make them more autonomous." He notes the improvement in older peoples' lives due to better social supports, better income, and greater understanding of later life. This will lead to more questions for researchers. For example, what do people of different ethnic backgrounds need as they age? Do the needs of people in rural areas differ from those of people in cities? Do older people have unique educational needs? How do they learn best? How will early retirees use their time? Researchers have begun to ask these and other questions about aging.

Summary

1. Three broad areas make up the field of gerontology: biomedicine, psychosocial studies, and socioeconomic-environmental studies. Social gerontology includes psychosocial and socioeconomic-environmental studies, as well as practice-related research.

2. Gerontologists use theory to guide their research and to interpret their results. Micro- and macro-level theories exist. They include interpretive, functionalist, and conflict theories. Each theoretical approach gives a different and valuable insight into aging.

3. Gerontologists have developed methods to distinguish age effects (changes due to age) from changes in groups due to differences in cohorts, historical events, and the effects of repeated testing.

4. Gerontologists also borrow methods from traditional disciplines such as biology, chemistry, history, philosophy, and anthropology. Researchers have begun to shift their interests as their knowledge grows. New statistical reports now present separate statistics for the oldest age groups. New critical methods of analysis have also emerged as gerontology has grown.

5. Gerontologists use both qualitative and quantitative methods for studying aging and older adults. They use methods that suit their research questions and their discipline. Methods include literary analysis, archival research, and econometric analysis, among others.

6. Gerontology today is one of the fastest-growing fields of study. It can make old age a better time of life by increasing knowledge about aging. It can help modify and create social structures that meet the needs of older people.

Study Questions

1. List and describe the three main areas that make up the field of gerontology. What areas does social gerontology include? Compare the major focus of the social gerontologist with the focus of the medical gerontologist.

2. Explain the function of a sociological theory. Gerontologists classify theories into two categories. Define these two levels of theory and the three perspectives that these levels of theory can take. Critique each of these perspectives.

3. State the major characteristics of gerontological theories. What theoretical ideas may emerge in social gerontology in the future? Where will future theorists look for new theoretical insights?

4. What is the most significant problem with using a cross-sectional method to gather gerontological data? How can researchers overcome this problem?

5. What are the benefits of using a longitudinal research design? What are the weaknesses?

6. Discuss the strengths and limitations of qualitative and quantitative methods.

7. List at least six methods that gerontologists use to study aging.

8. How does gerontological research benefit society?

Key Terms

age effects an effect on a person's life related to physical decline or change due to the aging process. (27)

age stratification theory a theory that focuses on the movement of age cohorts over the life course, and on "the role of social structures in the process of individual aging and the stratification by age in the society" (Bengtson, Burgess, and Parrott 1997, S81). (23)

cohort effects an effect on a person's life related to the time of the person's birth. (27)

conflict perspective a perspective that holds that society consists of conflicts between dominant and subordinate social groups. (25)

cross-sectional research design a research method that studies people from many age groups at one point in time. (27)

dialectical theory a type of interpretive theory that says aging has many dimensions (physical, psychological, social, and historical) and focuses on the differences among them. (26)

feminist approach an approach that views gender as a defining characteristic in social interaction and life experiences, as well as in the process and experience of aging; gender is seen as socially constructed, with men being more advantaged than women in society. (26)

functionalist perspective a perspective that holds that social order is based on consensus, cooperation, and shared norms and values, that all parts of society serve a role or function to keep society in a state of balance or equilibrium. (22)

interpretive perspective a perspective that focuses almost exclusively on the micro level of social life. It looks at how people define situations, how they create social order, and how they relate to one another in daily life. (21)

life course approach a functionalist approach that bridges both the micro- and macro-levels of analysis by incorporating social interaction and social structure within its framework. (24)

longitudinal research design a research method that looks at a single group of people at two or more points in time. (27)

macro-level theories theories that "examine social structures or structural elements as they influence experiences and behaviors" (Bengtson, Burgess, and Parrott 1997, S76). (21)

micro-level theories theories that focus on individuals and their interactions, and that are used to explain phenomena such as the relationship between adult children and their parents, changes in memory with age, and the effect of negative attitudes on older people's self-esteem. (21)

moral economy theory a theory that focuses on shared values and social norms that shape popular beliefs in the legitimacy of certain practices and policies; this theory complements political economy theory. (26)

period or environmental effects an effect on a person's life due to the time of measurement. This would include historical, social, or environmental effects, such as an ongoing war, changes in health habits (e.g., increased exercise), or changes in health care policies that have different influences on different age cohorts. (27)

political economy theory a theory that focuses on conflict and change in social life. It traces this conflict to the struggle between social classes and to the resulting dominance of some groups and the subordination of others in society. (25)

positivist worldview theoretical perspective based on the belief that knowledge is built by studying observable facts and their relationship to one another. (22)

qualitative methods research methods that include in-depth interviews, analysis of the content of documents or artifacts, and observation. Researchers use these methods to understand individuals' social world and experience from the subjects' own perspective. (29)

quantitative methods research methods that use statistical methods and mathematical models to analyze data that include census data, national social surveys, and epidemiological studies. (29)

sequential design a research method that looks at a series of cross-sectional studies during a longitudinal study. (28)

time-lag comparison design a research method that examines different groups of people of the same age at different points in time (e.g., 70-year-olds in 1985, 1995, and 2005). (28)

transitions changes in social status or social roles such as marriage, divorce, remarriage, widowhood, and parenthood. (24)

trajectories long-term patterns of stability and change that often include many transitions. (24)

Selected Readings

Bengtson, V.L., and K.W. Schaie, eds. *Handbook of Theories of Aging.* New York: Springer, 1999.

Well-known researchers in the fields of biology, biomedical science, psychology, and social science discuss the latest theories and concepts in their fields. This volume contains chapters on the history of theory development, theories of everyday competence, and political economy theory. It also contains a section on the application of theory to practice and public policy. A challenging book for students new to the field, but a good resource for research and more advanced writing.

Gubrium, J.F., and J.A. Holstein. *The New Language of Qualitative Methods.* New York: Oxford University Press, 1997.

A detailed and sympathetic look at qualitative methods. Gubrium has used this method in most of his research and writing. He has thought deeply about the uses of this method, its benefits, and its challenges. The book reviews four major approaches to qualitative research and explores new ways to think about and use qualitative methods. The authors use examples of qualitative gerontological research throughout the book. A good resource for anyone thinking of doing qualitative research.

Matthews, A.M., ed. "Methodological Diversity." *Canadian Journal on Aging* 14(1), 1995. Special issue.

This issue contains articles by English- and French-Canadian gerontologists that discuss both quantitative and qualitative research issues. These issues include an analysis of feminist methodologies, longitudinal research, and action research. A good look at the diverse methods used by Canadian gerontologists.

Neuman, W.L. *Social Research Methods: Qualitative and Quantitative Approaches,* 5th ed. Boston: Allyn and Bacon, 2003.

This text presents a clear introduction to qualitative and quantitative research methods, and the benefits of combining different approaches in social research.

Part Two

Historical Change

Chapter Three

Aging Then and Now

Photo courtesy of Lori Campbell

INTRODUCTION

In Laurel Creek, West Virginia, old men retire to the porch. They watch the traffic go by, they talk to friends and neighbours, and they arrange for part-time work. Life on the porch in the early years of retirement allows a man to keep in contact with the community. When a man gets older and his health fails, life on the porch allows him to draw on his social credit. People stop to check on him, and they make trips to the store to get his groceries. If bad health keeps him indoors, his absence from the porch alerts people that he may need extra help. When a man nears death, he may come out to the porch to receive last visits from friends and neighbours. Life on the porch keeps a man part of the community until he dies (*Human Behavior Magazine* 1977).

Life on the porch matches an ideal we have of late old age. It reminds us of another time, a time when people grew up and died in the same town, when neighbours knew one another well, and when the young respected the old. Today, many people feel that old age has become devalued. We push old people aside in retirement, advertisers tell everyone to "think young," and even birthday cards make fun of aging. One card reads, "Roses are red, violets are blue, thank goodness I'm not older than you." It seems that in the past people enjoyed old age, but that in modern society this is less so because older people get little respect or attention.

Has old age become worse over time? Did simpler societies offer a golden age to the old? Or do we just like to believe things were better in the past?

Social gerontologists try to answer these questions. They take two approaches: some gerontologists study past societies to see how they viewed and treated older people; others study modern societies to see how different social structures lead to different experiences of old age. This chapter will examine both points of view. It will look at (1) how aging differs in different types of societies, (2) how social structures affect aging, and (3) how aging today differs from aging in the past.

FOUR TYPES OF SOCIETIES

Sociologists Gerhard and Jean Lenski (1974) describe four stages of sociocultural evolution. These stages correspond to four types of societies: hunting and gathering, horticultural, agricultural (agrarian), and industrial. They also list specialized types of societies, including herding and fishing societies. Recently, sociologists have described a new sociocultural stage: the post-industrial society. This chapter will look at four major societal types: (1) hunting and gathering, (2) agricultural, (3) industrial, and (4) post-industrial societies. Each type has a unique social organization. And each exists today. They all also represent a historical evolution from the simplest to the most complex forms of social life. A look at these societies will show the impact of social organization on the status and treatment of older people. This review will also give a picture of how aging has changed over time.

Hunting and Gathering Societies

Humans lived in hunting and gathering bands for a million years or more and settled into agriculture between only 10 000 and 20 000 years ago. People in hunting and gathering societies survive by gathering wild plants and by stalking or trapping wild game. These groups (sometimes as few as 20 people) move constantly from place to place in search of food. They resemble an extended family. Their technology is simple, consisting mainly of bows, spears, and fire, and they have no permanent settlement.

Most simple societies have undergone rapid change in the past few years. Industry has destroyed many of their habitats, and some groups find themselves confined to reserves. Other groups have adapted to new technologies and new opportunities and now work for the large companies and government projects that use their land. These contacts have led to changes in traditional nomadic life. The discussion below refers to traditional hunting and gathering life as it existed in the past and where it exists in the present. Where possible, the discussion compares traditional life with life for these people today.

Archaeologists estimate that people in hunting and gathering societies had a short life expectancy by modern standards. For example, Native peoples in Canada, before the Europeans arrived, may have had an average life expectancy of 30 or 40 years (Northcott and Wilson 2001). Cowgill and Holmes (1972) report that these societies defined a person as old by age 45 or 50; and Simmons (1960, 1970), in a study of 71 contemporary simple societies, says that people in these societies were considered old at 50 or 60 years of age. He estimates, on the basis of scarce data, that these societies rarely had more than 3 percent of their people over age 65. Therefore, when the terms "old" and "elderly" are used here in connection with simple societies, they refer to people 50 to 60 years old.

Early work by Cowgill (1972) and Press and McKool (1972) present four conditions that lead to support for an older person in simple societies. First, the person needs an important role to play in social life; second, the older person must live near and fit into his or her extended family; third, he or she must control some important material or informational resource; and fourth, the group must value collective rather than individual development (Sokolovsky 1990). Few simple societies fulfill all these conditions, so treatment of older people varies among them.

Amoss and Harrell (1981) say that one condition more than the others leads to a good old age in primitive societies: The old have high status when their contribution to subsistence outweighs their cost to the group. Older people do well when they still have a valued role to play in the culture. Their ability to give to the group depends on two things. First, the culture must offer alternative roles for older people to play as they lose their strength, and, second, the older person must have good health.

Canada's Inuit serve as a good example of a present-day hunting and gathering society. They live in a climate that demands physical strength to survive, but they love and respect their elders and allow their older members to take part in social life as long as they can (Holmes and Holmes 1995). Men, for example, "retire" slowly from work. As a man loses his strength, younger male members of the community or household do more of the winter hunting. The older man may then take shorter hunting trips or teach the young how to hunt. Older Inuit women have an easier time moving into old age than do men (this is true of women in most nomadic societies). They pass the heavy work on to younger women and spend more time taking care of the children. "Because women's work is less demanding ... the decreasing physical capability of a woman does not appear so obviously or so dramatically[11] (Guemple 1974, cited in Holmes and Holmes 1995).

Collings (2000, 2001) found that the ability to manage decreased health and a good attitude defined successful aging among the Inuit. Successfully aging older men and women find their own ways to adapt to decreases in their strength. Older men will start to hunt early in the spring in order to stockpile food for the winter. They may also strike a bargain with young hunters—for example, the older man may fix the gear while the younger man hunts. Older women sometimes adopt children. The Inuit allow their elders to play new roles in society as their health and strength decline. They value their old as much for their knowledge and wisdom as for their work. A person gives something to the group when he or she recalls and passes on the knowledge of Inuit lore. This social role makes the old person useful to the group and improves his or her status and treatment in the community (Holmes and Holmes 1995).

Not all groups make these accommodations for older members. The Chipewyan, for instance, who live in Canada's northern prairies, have no roles for older men to play. The Chipewyan do not place a high value on knowledge of tribal lore or craftwork. A man has status when he succeeds at hunting, but when he stops hunting, he loses respect and power in the group, and people label him "elderly." Men will do anything to avoid this label. Some continue to hunt even when their health fails. Sharp (1981) reports the case of a man who had just recovered from a heart attack and had emphysema but still went into the bush alone. His wife worried that he would kill himself through over-exertion, but he would rather risk his life than be called old. The Chipewyan offer fewer options to older men than do the Inuit.

Most of these simple societies have changed in the recent past due to contacts with the modern world. Elders on Holman Island in the Northwest Territories "now watch color televisions in the comfort of heated homes equipped with running water and electricity" (Condon 1987, cited in Holmes and Holmes 1995). They no longer rely on their contribution to group survival but get government pensions. Graburn (1969, cited in Holmes and Holmes 1995) found that pensions freed elders from economic dependence on their families. This payment gave elders new status as well as a source of income for their children. But, at the same time, the cash economy led to less respect for older people. Modernization has decreased the role of elders as educators and caregivers to their grandchildren. In some cases, children (who learn English in school) cannot understand their grandparents' language.

Researchers report that hunting and gathering societies distinguish between two different stages of old age. In the first, a person retires from the heavy work of middle age, but he or she still has good health. In the second stage, the older person gets sick or becomes demented or frail. Simmons (1960) calls people in this second group the "overaged."

In Inuit society, older people keep their status as long as they do some useful work for the group. Their status drops if illness makes them dependent. People make fun of the frail elderly, say nasty things to them, or ignore them. The overaged get the worst cuts of meat, have little money, and have to do without trade goods. A stranger may take in an Inuit who outlives his or her spouse, children, and close relatives, but this person will get little respect and will have to do the worst work (Guemple 1977).

The Inuit also abandon their aged when they become liabilities to the group. They do this as a last resort and encourage the older person to make the

● Exhibit 3.1

Do Nomadic People Abandon Their Elders?

In any nomadic society, if people live too long and become decrepit or demented, the group may abandon or kill them.

Jacob Bronowski (1976) shows this in his film series and book *The Ascent of Man.* In Iran, he follows a nomadic group called the Bakhtiari on their yearly journey to their summer pastures. The tribe climbs over six mountain ranges, through high passes and snow, until it reaches the Bazuft River.

Bronowski says the test for the group comes at the river. The Bazuft, a trickle in summer, swells each year with melting snow and spring rain. The group— men, women, and animals—must swim across. For the young, crossing the Bazuft stands as a test of adulthood. For them, life begins, but for the old, Bronowski says, life ends. The camera records in detail the struggle to cross the river. The current batters horses, donkeys, sheep, goats, and people. The young men swim for their lives and help the animals get across. But then the camera pulls back to focus on two figures among the rocks—a dog and an old man. The dog races back and forth looking from the man to the group below. The man sits silently with his back against the rocks watching the tribe cross the river. No emotion shows on his face. He no longer has

the strength to cross the river, and the tribe will go on without him. "Only the dog is puzzled to see a man abandoned," Bronowski says. "The man accepts the nomad custom; he has come to the end of his journey" (1976, 64).

Life in many nomadic cultures demands this kind of choice. The tribe must move on to survive, and the old, who cannot keep up, get left behind. This man accepts his fate. He may have left his own parents to die in the same way. This dramatic case shows the dark side of life in primitive society. "In a vigorous community," Colin Turnbull (1961, 35–36) says, "where mobility is essential, cripples and infirm people can be a handicap and may even endanger the safety of the group."

A study by Robert Maxwell and J. Philip Silverman (1977, 37) found that 80 percent of the societies that did not value the elderly lived as nomads for at least part of the year. The harsher the environment, the greater the chance a group will kill or abandon its aged. Killing the aged shows up most often in societies that have irregular food supplies, move often, and live in severe climates (Simmons 1970, 240).

decision (Guemple 1980). But sometimes the group will withdraw its support rapidly, thus hastening death (Holmes and Holmes 1995).

Glascock and Feinman (1981) found this same ambivalence to old age in 57 simple societies they studied. They found that in 35 percent of the societies, younger people treated older members well, and in 80 percent young people showed respect for the aged. Many of these same societies abandoned and killed their elderly (Maxwell and Silverman 1977). Glascock and Feinman (1981) found non-supportive treatment (abandoning and killing the aged) in some form in 84 percent of the simple societies they studied. This, they say, contradicts the idea that all simpler societies support the aged. Research shows that simple societies vary in how they treat the aged and that treatment of the aged often depends on how much an older person contributes to or takes from the group.

Agricultural Societies

People in agricultural societies live on food produced from farming the land. These societies have more complex technologies than hunting and gathering societies. They also have more complex social structures, including social classes and bureaucracies.

Humans settled into villages and cities for the first time in the Middle East, China, and India about 10 000 years ago at the end of the last Ice Age. For the first time in human history, societies gathered a surplus of food. In these societies, older people often owned property, and they used property rights to get support from the young. "Property rights," Simmons (1970, 36) says, "have been lifesavers for the aged.... The person who controlled property was able to get more out of life and to get it much longer. Indeed, the importance of property for old age security can hardly be overrated."

As a general rule, in agricultural societies, those with land command the most respect, those without land the least. All over the world, property rights create a legal dependence of the young on the old (Amoss and Harrell 1981). Old people among the Gwembe Tonga of Zambia get power by owning livestock and land (Colson and Scudder 1981). Older people among the Etal Islanders of Micronesia gain respect when they own property. The Etal look down on old people who hold on to all their land, but they think of a person as foolish if he or she gives it all away. The land serves as an inheritance bribe (Nason 1981).

Americans in the past also used property to hold power in old age. Fischer (1978) studied aging in the United States from 1607 to the 1970s. He found that young men had to wait to inherit their fathers' land before they could start families. In the seventeenth and eighteenth centuries, that meant a son might reach age 40 before he owned the farm. Fischer (1978, 52) calls the land "an instrument for generational politics"; parents used it to ensure good treatment in their old age.

Fischer (1978) also found that this kind of coercion bred hostility. The diaries of Colonel Landon Carter, for example, report signs of growing anger between the younger and older generations. One night in 1776, Colonel Carter reports, his son, Robert Wormeley Carter, invited friends over for gambling with cards. When the enraged Colonel ordered the game to stop, his son exploded and called his father a tyrant. The two men almost came to blows. After that the Colonel carried a pistol with him in the house. He wrote in his diary, "Surely it is happy our laws prevent parricide.... Good God! That such a monster is descended from my loins!" (Greene 1965, cited in Fischer 1978, 75).

Other agricultural societies in the past also expressed their dislike for the aged, some more openly than Americans. The Greek playwright Aristophanes mocked the old in his plays; Aristotle derided the way most people grew old (although he thought a philosopher could live a good life even in old age). Greek poems mock older people who want to hold on to youth (Wortley 1998). And in the Renaissance, Machiavelli portrayed the old man as a lecherous fool in his play *La Clizia*. These writings show a special dislike for older people who deny aging.

Tension between the generations sometimes surfaced in song. An Austrian folksong (Berkner 1972, cited in Fischer 1978, 69) says:

> Papa, when will you give me the farm?
> Papa, when will you give me the house?
> When will you finally move to your little room
> And tend your potato patch?

Studies of English Canadians in the late nineteenth century show the same tensions between the young and the old. Historical accounts indicate that parents gave a great deal of thought to how they would pass their land down to their children (Gagan 1983b; Mays 1983), and the children, who worked to improve the family farm, sometimes into their 30s, expected to get it as a reward for their work. In 1853, Susannah Moodie wrote that "death is looked upon by many Canadians more as a matter of ... change of property into other hands, than as a real domestic calamity" (Moodie 1853, cited in Gagan 1983b, 185).

Ontario farmers kept intergenerational tension low by passing the land down before they died (a method still used today) (Keating 1996). Synge (1980) says that the older people stayed on the land with the inheriting child and his family. The young or the old couple built a new house nearby. According to one woman, the parents-in-law "stayed on in the house till they built a place out back for them" (Synge 1980, 138). Getting the land early in life must have reduced some tensions between the generations, but it created others. Selling the land to the young risked the older generation's old-age security. Parents, when they did sell the land to their children, often kept a few acres for themselves to maintain their independence in old age (Mays 1983).

In Canada in the early twentieth century, the family provided the most support to older people. Snell (1996) says that older people with little income or poor health often went to live with a child or grandchild. Snell reports that in some cases children moved into their parents' house to care for them. In other cases, the older and younger generations moved to live near each other in order to ensure support for the elderly parents. Sometimes the elderly parent moved from one child's house to another's in order to spread the costs and benefits of parent care. Scattered historical reports show that older people who lived with their children often helped with gardening, household repairs, or child rearing. Snell says that this exchange of support characterized family life in rural Canada (see also Montigny 1997).

Prentice and her colleagues (1996) report that, in New France in the eighteenth century, an older woman who gave up her farm to a younger family member often received a pension. For example, a woman who lived in the Richelieu valley in 1760 got a pension for "heat, light, clothing, and houseroom." She also got "16 minots (bushels) of flour, 1/4 minot of salt, and 120 pounds of salt pork." Another pension allowed a woman "two pairs of French shoes every year" (44). These pensions provided older women with some support.

Prentice and her colleagues (1996, 124) say that in the 1850s in Canada women had few rights to ownership of the land. Widows did have a right of dower to one-third of her husband's land. But a husband's will could ignore this right, so land often passed down to a son when the woman's husband died (Benoit 2000). This left a widow with only a small pension. And this pension sometimes depended on her willingness to stay widowed. "Control 'from the grave' continued in many farming regions well into the 20th century."

The content of farmers' wills in Ontario, like those in New France, suggests some worry about future security. Wills stated exactly what the inheriting son was to do for his parents. One will describes in detail the kind of food ("flour, pork and butter and milk, potatoes and other vegetables"), the kind of firewood ("plenty of good wood ready for use"), the transportation ("a horse and buggy"), and the cash ("$100 a year") that a son had to give his mother for the rest of her life (Gagan 1983b, 186). Snell (1996, 75, 101) says that parents used "maintenance agreements to gain support from children, based on the fear that such support would not otherwise be forthcoming."

Inequality in Old Age in Agricultural Societies

Treatment of the aged in agricultural societies differed by social class. The elderly who owned land in these societies had power until they died. For this reason, older people who owned land commanded the greatest respect in societies from Canada to traditional China (Ikels 1981). The poor and landless lived less well and got little respect.

"To be old and poor and outcast in early America," Fischer (1978, 60) says, "was certainly not to be venerated but rather to be despised.... Old age seems actually to have intensified the contempt visited upon a poor man. A rich old man was the more highly respected because he was old, but the aged poor were often scorned." A New Jersey law in 1720 ordered police to search ships for old people and to send them away. In one case the crew of a ship placed a poor, sick old man on a barren island and left him there to die (Fischer 1978).

Fischer also describes drunk, crippled old men who hid in cellars and roamed the wharves at night looking for food. Poor old widows had low status too, but their womanhood made old age and poverty worse (as it did in most countries). Without money a woman was degraded and left to depend on others for support. Neighbours sometimes forced old widows to move away to keep poor rates down. Even their own children sometimes turned them away. "If the aged poor were only a small minority [in early America]," Fischer (1978, 61) says, "their misery was great."

Laslett (1976) reports that in Elizabethan England, the Poor Law of 1601 made children responsible for their aged parents, but only their parents. This excluded other relatives from aid by law. The existence of a law that spells out the relations between the generations suggests that custom bound children to their parents less than we may have thought. Laslett says that in some cases a parent who lived with his or her children got listed in official records as a "lodger, receiving parish relief" (95). In other cases, the children moved into the family cottage and left their widowed mothers and sisters in poorhouses. The rise of the nuclear family in the West, according to Laslett (1995), imposed a hardship on older people.

Stearns (1977, 119), in a study of customs in France, says that "older women were treated horribly in the popular culture of traditional society." Villages expected widows over age 45 to stay single, and literature made fun of older women. Even the grandmother role got little prestige. Other historians have also documented the suffering of the aged poor in the past and in less industrialized societies (Hufton 1975).

These reports about aging in agricultural society give the impression that many older people lived in poverty. But relatively few older people lived in poverty in pre-industrial Canada. Canadian historians report that most older people "lived independently and were capable of maintaining themselves" (Montigny 1997, 52). Those who needed help got support from their families and neighbours. Indeed, "intense poverty in old age was still the exception" (Haber and Gratton 1994, cited in Myles 2002, 327). Most people in poverty had no working adult children to help support them.

Snell (1996) found that in Canada community support softened the effects of poverty or isolation in old age. He reports on many cases where neighbours and friends support an older person in need. They provide a room and food or at least try to get the older person formal help. But most families had little extra to give to older family members. So a poor older person in a household might push the limits of family and community support. For instance, a farmer in eastern Ontario took in a 73-year-old widower, and provided the man with room and board in return for some light chores. But, the farmer says, the man "cannot do much ... [and] we would like to be free of him" (Snell 1996, 62).

Prentice and her colleagues (Rubio and Waterson 1986, cited in Prentice et al. 1996, 124) report on another case in Ontario from the 1905 diary of Lucy Maud Montgomery. She writes:

Uncle John and Prescott have been suing grandmother shamefully all summer. In short, they have been trying to turn her out ... Grandmother's absurd will put her completely in their power—the power of selfish, domineering men eaten up with greed. Grandmother told them she would *not* leave the home she had lived and worked for sixty years and since then Uncle John has never spoken to her or visited her.

The current picture of life in pre-industrial society shows that most older people maintained a decent standard of living. But some people faced hard times in old age. The existence of poor older people and their marginal condition argue against the idea of a golden age in pre-industrial society.

Agricultural society, in its treatment of older people, looks like a mirror image of primitive society. In the simplest societies the old had no wealth, but they received respect as long as they gave to the group. The !Kung San roam the Kalahari desert throughout their lives and have little property. The young revere their elders as storytellers, spiritual leaders, and healers (Biesele and Howell 1981). In agricultural societies, the elderly get the most respect if they own property and keep it from their children until late in life or until they die. In such a society, "a firm hold on the strings of a fat purse was one effective compensation for declining physical powers" (Simmons 1970, 46; see also Cowgill 1986, 108). The old may be respected in this kind of society, but they are not often loved by the young (Fischer 1978).

Modern Industrial Society

The agricultural revolution created a new form of society. Agriculture produced a surplus of food and gave rise to the first cities. It created social classes and based status on ownership of property. This kind of society dominated until the middle of the eighteenth century, when three interrelated changes began to reshape social life: (1) industrialization, (2) urbanization, and (3) the demographic transition.

These changes took place over 200 years, and they still affect society today. They began at various times in different places, and sometimes one type of change—economic change, demographic change, or a change in values—had more influence on a society than another. Scholars still argue over which change came first in which society, but taken together these three changes revolutionized social life and led to a new age of older people.

Industrialization

By the nineteenth century, most of Europe had begun to industrialize. Industry began to use steam and water

power to increase productivity; the factory system gathered workers and raw materials in cities; and transportation systems spread the production of factories to all classes and countries. Some countries industrialized before others, and some more quickly, but by 1850 industrialization had changed the shape of European society (Stearns 1967).

Industrialization both caused and resulted from the breakup of rural life. Cottage industries, in which small groups of workers in villages produce mostly for local needs, failed as the factories produced more and cheaper goods. At the same time, parents could no longer keep their sons on the farm with the promise of future inheritance. As death rates declined, families had too many sons who wanted the land. The younger sons had to move to the city to find work, and the city welcomed them as a cheap source of labour. The new pace of work and life in the city freed young people from traditional ties and beliefs (Stearns 1967), and led to a decrease in the status of older people.

Industrialization decreased the status of older people in another way. Companies looked for ways to get the older, supposedly less effective worker out of the workplace. In the United States in the 1920s, for example, some companies used physical exams to screen out older workers (Holmes and Holmes 1995). Also, retirement rules, supported by both labour and management, forced older workers out of work. Management liked retirement because it allowed them to release workers who were costly because they had seniority. Unions supported retirement because in return they won seniority rights (rules about being first hired, last fired) from management (Haber 1978). In short, unions traded older workers' right to work for younger workers' job security. Retirement expressed in a formal rule the decline of the older person's status in industrial society.

Snell (1996) points out that these changes came about gradually in Canada. Workers with little in the way of savings continued to work. And those who worked had an income similar to the incomes of younger workers. Only in the 1930s and 1940s did modern patterns of retirement emerge in Canada. Still, over time, older workers found that work became harder to find. They often had to take work in low-paying and marginal jobs as janitors or household labourers. Some people complained about discrimination due to their age.

Urbanization

Canadian society changed from a rural to an urban one between 1851 and 1950 (Biggs and Bollman 1991). During the nineteenth century, both men and women migrated to the cities. Cross (1983) found that Montreal attracted large numbers of young women from the crowded countryside. Bradbury (1983) describes Montreal in 1871 as a city in transition from pre-industrial to industrial life. Accounts of this time say little about the elderly.

Katz (1975) gives one of the few reports on what life was like for older people in a Canadian town. He studied Hamilton, Ontario, between 1851 and 1861. In a report on 597 land-owning men in 1851, he counted only 26 men out of 597 aged 60 or over, or about 4 percent of the population. (Men among the poorer classes died younger and probably made up a smaller portion of the population than the landowners.) Men who owned land had the most security in old age, and men aged 60 and over were the largest group of landowners. However, after age 60, Katz shows, a man's power began to decrease, and men over 60 had a greater chance of having less land from one year to the next than any other group. Men 60 and over were also the least likely to have a servant (a sign of wealth). After age 60, Katz says, men often "decline[d] into difficult circumstances" (63).

Synge (1980) says that in small businesses and on farms older people could adjust their work to suit their health and strength, but in industrial cities older people had to meet the demands of the workplace or quit. No public pensions existed in the nineteenth century, and many older people in the cities had no private savings. In addition, they often had to take the lowest forms of work, move into public homes for the aged, or live in poverty, especially if they were without children (Haber 1983, 1993).

In North America, urban life undermined traditional society in another way. The cities supported a market system in which individuals could accumulate wealth outside the family structure. Inequality in society began to grow as some individuals gathered wealth for themselves through trade. Those who were successful turned from public affairs to private concerns. This focus on the self broke the individual's communal bonds, including those that linked the older to the younger generation (Fischer 1978).

Synge (1980), who studied working-class families in Ontario in the early twentieth century, found that city life made old age an uncertain time. Young people earned their own wages and gave money to their parents while they lived at home. But when these children grew up and moved out, parents lost this income. Few social services existed for older people, and an unmarried daughter often looked after her parents as they aged. Families sometimes passed the job of care from one child to the next. Synge reports the case of one old woman who lived for periods of time with each of her children for her last 25 years.

Katz (1975) found that few older people in Hamilton lived with their married children, and the poorest households were least likely to house an older relative. Only 8 percent of households in 1851 and 10 percent in 1861 had adults of two or more generations. "Only when old age and loneliness were combined would a parent move in with her children" (254).

Katz (1975) also found that, from 1851 to 1861, 58.8 percent of women aged 60 to 69 were widowed, almost double the rate of men. Women of the poorest social class (Irish Catholic women) faced an eight-times greater chance of widowhood than women of the highest class (Canadian-born Protestant women). Poor widows had little or no savings and no pensions from their husbands. The poorest women, especially those without children, would finally be recipients of charity (a special charity, the Ladies' Benevolent Society, was created to help them) or live in a "house of refuge and industry."

Snell (1996) found that in the late 1800s Ontario built a network of poorhouses or houses of refuge that served poor older people. Similar houses existed in Nova Scotia, New Brunswick, and Newfoundland. These institutions began by serving all poor people—orphans, unwed mothers, and older people—but over time, more and more of these homes focused on care for older people. Poorhouses gradually became homes for the elderly and were an important public response to the needs of older people.

On the surface, the new freedom and equality in urban industrial Canada made all people more alike, but for the old they meant a decrease in status. "A really democratic ethic," Cowgill (1986, 51) says, "is incompatible with any system of stratification based on ascribed statuses.... You cannot have gerontocracy [rule of the eldest] and democracy at the same time."

The Demographic Transition

The demographic transition refers to the changes in population that led to a high proportion of older people among the developed nations (of Western Europe and North America). This transition, which took place in North America at the end of the nineteenth century along with industrialization and urbanization, was a three-stage process. The stages outline how European and North American societies shifted from a youthful to an older population structure.

Stage 1: 1300–1750   Before the eighteenth century, population had been relatively stable. High birth rates were balanced by high death rates. French studies of the seventeenth century estimate that there were about eight children to a normal marriage and that about 70 percent

Exhibit 3.2

DEMOGRAPHIC TRANSITION THEORY

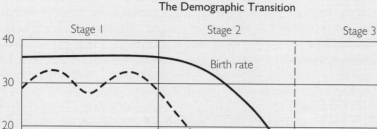

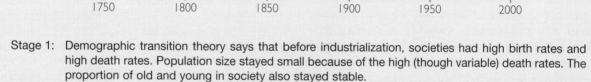

The Demographic Transition

Stage 1: Demographic transition theory says that before industrialization, societies had high birth rates and high death rates. Population size stayed small because of the high (though variable) death rates. The proportion of old and young in society also stayed stable.

Stage 2: Industrialization led to a decrease in death rates. Birth rates stayed high, and the population grew in size. These societies had a growing proportion of young people.

Stage 3: Further into industrialization the birth rate dropped. Death rates remained low, and population size stayed stable. The birth rate sometimes fluctuated (as with the baby boom of 1944–1965). Society had a growing proportion of older people.

Source: Chart based on personal communication with W.W. McVey, 1987. Courtesy of Wayne McVey.

of the households had children. Children made up 45 percent of the French population at that time (compared with half that rate in industrial societies today).

Only a small number of people lived to old age in pre-industrial society. Figures exist only for scattered populations before 1800, but they give some idea of the proportions of people 65 and over. A national census in Iceland in 1703 reported 4.6 percent of the population was 65 and over; Belgrade in 1733 reported 2.1 percent; and Nishinomiya, Japan, in 1713 reported 6.6 percent. A listing of counties in England from 1599 to 1796 showed people aged 65 or over made up between 1.4 percent and 6.4 percent of the population. Rarely did the 65-and-over population top 10 percent in any place in Europe, and Laslett (1976) cautions that past the age of 60 people tended to exaggerate their age.

Stage 2: 1750–1850 Three phenomena caused rapid population growth in Europe from 1750 on, and also changed the proportion of young and old people in society. First, the death rate decreased, because war fatalities decreased, the cycle of epidemics ended, improved hygiene in cities led to better health, border controls stopped the spread of disease, and food supplies increased due to better climate and more open land (Braudel 1981).

Second, the birth rate stayed high and in some cases increased. New lands opened and allowed earlier marriage in the countryside. Young people in the cities, who did not have to wait for their parents' land, married young. Better nutrition and more opportunity led people to have more children.

Third, the number and proportion of young people in the population began to grow and the total population increased.

Stage 3: 1850–Present   Both the birth rate and death rate in Western Europe had declined by 1900, completing the transition to an aging population. The biggest change in death rates came from improvements in the general standard of living. Diet and hygiene in the cities improved. Clean underwear, soap, coal for heat, and glass in the windows all helped people stay healthier. Improved housing and more efficient treatment of water and sewage decreased disease. As the standard of living rose, the virulence of disease, and so the death rate, declined.

These changes led all social classes to decrease the number of children per family (Stearns 1967). Middle-class families led the way. They had smaller families to ensure that their children would have the money needed to remain in the middle class. Rural families followed the trend later in order to ensure that each of their children would get a good portion of land. Children had a different meaning in agricultural and industrial societies. In an agricultural society, children are an economic asset: they help produce food, care for the farm, and increase a family's wealth. In an urban society, children are an economic liability. They cost money to raise, and the family gets little economic benefit from them. These facts led to a decreased birth rate.

From 1850 onward, the proportion of older people in the developed nations grew. Longer life expectancy meant that more people lived into old age. But more than anything else, it was the decrease in the birth rate after industrialization that led to a higher proportion of older people in society.

The three trends mentioned previously—industrialization, urbanization, and the demographic transition—put an end to almost all of the following conditions, each of which had supported the high status of older people:

1. ownership and control of property

2. a monopoly on special knowledge

3. ancestor worship and a high value placed on tradition (where the old provide a link to the gods)

4. society organized around kinship and family

5. small, stable communities

6. high mutual dependence of group members

7. small numbers of older people

8. special roles for the aged (Eisdorfer 1981; Rosow 1965)

In the past two centuries, the economy, the structure of family life, and the relations of the old to the young changed. Old age became more common, but it also lost its privileged status (Fischer 1978).

Modernization Theory

Some researchers believe that a sharp break took place as societies moved from an agricultural to an industrial way of life. This break, where it occurred, affected all social institutions and social relations. **Modernization theory** holds that this shift to an urban life, with high technology and complex institutions, leads to a decrease in the status of older people.

Cowgill and Holmes (1972) refer to the shift from agricultural to urban society as a process of modernization. Modernization is "the transformation of a total society from a relatively rural way of life based on animate power, limited technology, relatively undifferentiated institutions, parochial and traditional outlook and values, toward a predominantly urban way of life based on inanimate sources of power, highly developed scientific technology, highly differentiated institutions matched by segmented individual roles, and a cosmopolitan outlook which emphasized efficiency and progress" (Cowgill 1974, 127).

Cowgill and Holmes (1972) theorized that the status of older people decreases with increases in modernization. They reviewed studies of 14 contemporary societies from around the world. These ranged from a study of the Sidamo of southwestern Ethiopia, to two studies of Israeli society (one of a kibbutz), to a study of the aged in the U.S.S.R. They found that small numbers of older people, ancestor worship, low social change, extended families, a value system that emphasized the importance of the group, stable residence, and low literacy (where the group values the old for their knowledge) all lead to high status in old age. In modern societies, where such conditions are reversed, older people have low status. The authors concluded that these trends support modernization theory.

Other research supports this theory. Palmore and Whittington (1971) studied the change in status of the elderly in the United States between 1940 and 1969. They used a "similarity index" to compare the status of the aged (65 and over) and the non-aged (14 to 64 years old), and found a decrease for the aged in the number of weeks and hours worked as well as a decrease in income and education level compared with younger people. They found improvements only in the health status of the elderly. They conclude that even with improvements in health and health care, the elderly lost status relative to the young over the 30 years they studied.

A later study by Palmore and Manton (1974) also supports the idea that status drops in old age in modern society. The authors compared people 65 and over with people 25 to 64 in 31 countries. They used an "equality index" (EI) to compare these groups. The EI measured employment status (employed or not employed), occupation for those employed, and years of education completed for each group. The researchers then computed the similarity of the young and the old in each country. (A score of 100 means perfect equality.) EI scores ranged from the 90s for developing countries such as Iran to the 50s for developed nations such as the United States or Canada. "This indicates," the researchers write, "that the socioeconomic status of the aged is almost equal that of younger adults in some underdeveloped countries, but has apparently declined to about one-half of equality in some of the modernized countries" (207). Bengtson and his colleagues (1975) studied more than 5000 men in six developing countries and found that negative views of aging increased with increased modernization.

Other writers, many of them historians, have criticized modernization theory. Laslett (1976) says that the theory compares the present, with its problems, to an idealized past. He shows, to the contrary, that the treatment and status of the aged varied from time to time and from place to place before modernization (as it varies today among simpler societies). O'Rand (1990) says that modernization theory cannot account for the complexities of social change. It misses the differences within the older population based on age cohort differences, socioeconomic differences, and historical conditions. Within a single society, researchers often find ambivalent feelings toward the aged (Trexler 1982; Vatuk 1982).

Most people think of Japan as a country that reveres its elderly. Traditional tenets urge respect and honour for the elderly, and the Japanese try to follow this rule (Plath 1972). But Plath found a second view of aging in Japanese culture, referred to as *obasute* or "discarding granny." This theme of abandoning the old, he says, runs through Japanese literature from the sixth to the twentieth centuries. Even within industrial societies, the treatment and status of the aged have differed from class to class and between women and men (Achenbaum and Stearns 1978; Quadagno 1980).

A study by Cherry and Magnuson-Martinson (1981) also questions the simple application of modernization theory to all developing nations. They propose that researchers look at the country's political economy to understand the status of the aged. These writers studied the status of older people in modern China. They learned that China had a tradition of great respect for the elderly based on authority, power, and prestige,

but that this system of age stratification had declined in recent years. They did not find, however, that industrialization, urbanization, education, or demographic change accounted for the decreased status of the old. Instead, their research showed that the decline in older people's status came about as a result of government social and economic policies.

Communist laws, for example, ended arranged marriages, which was one way the old had maintained power over the young, and gave married couples more autonomy. Land reform also led to less control of property by the old and less leverage of fathers over sons. The Chinese government emphasized equality between the generations. Older people would now get recognition for helping their families with child care, housework, or industrial work.

Cherry and Magnuson-Martinson (1981) suggest some modifications to modernization theory be made based on their work. First, the theory needs to take into account social policies that affect age-group relationships. Second, a society can alter the status of the aged directly (through political action) rather than through processes of modernization. Third, some groups in a society will experience a greater change in status than others (e.g., men compared with women).

Some research describes a middle ground between the pro- and anti-modernization camps. Cohn (1982) found that the status of the old does drop at the start of modernization. Changes in education, leading to more professional and technical jobs, cause this drop. But, as modernization increases, the educational and occupational gap between the old and the young decreases. The modern welfare state has "tended to treat older adults rather generously" (Maddox 1988, 3). Improved retirement benefits, more adult education, and job retraining will raise the status of the aged in the future.

Post-Industrial Society

Countries such as Canada have gone through the industrial revolution and have developed service-based **post-industrial societies**. Today, some people in these societies still live badly in old age—they have poor housing, poor nutrition, bad health, and little money. Also, studies show that some people still hold negative attitudes toward the aged. Baker (1983a) studied Canadian university students' attitudes toward various ages. He found that the youngest and oldest ages received the lowest ratings. Middle-aged people received the highest ratings. He found the same pattern in attitudes regardless of the social class, gender, or age of the people making the judgment. He describes the findings as an inverted U with status low early in life, rising to mid-life, and falling in old age.

Graham and Baker (1989) replicated this study with a sample of older people (mean age 67). Their results showed that the older people gave less negative ratings to all age groups, and they rated the young and old less negatively compared with the middle-aged. Still, the researchers discovered the same inverted-U curve in the older sample's ratings as was found in the earlier university student sample. The researchers say that these similar findings from two diverse samples support the idea that Canadians see old age as a time of low status.

Knox and Gekoski (1989) studied 1400 undergraduates' judgments and attitudes toward age. They studied two different approaches to making judgments. The researchers found that, regardless of the rating method, students gave older people the lowest rating on two of three scales—effectiveness and personal acceptability.

A study of selected Canadian literature for children (de Vries 1987) found some loving portrayals of older people. "Older characters always have their annoying side but attempts are made to appreciate their point of view" (43). A study of novels over four decades found both positive and negative views of old age. Matthews and Thompson (1985) studied 40 novels, half of them winners of the Governor General's Award for Fiction. They found that most older characters had high self-esteem and high life satisfaction, but they also concluded that more recent novels treated the aged as comic figures and saw this as a possible sign of growing negative attitudes to the old.

These studies show that in Western society people feel ambivalent toward old age. Kastenbaum and Ross (1975, 5) call this an "approach-avoidance dilemma."

● Exhibit 3.3

THE DEGA AND THE NACIREMA: THEN AND NOW

More than 45 years ago, an anthropologist named Horace Miner described some of the peculiar body rituals among a tribe called the Nacirema. Most of his writing concerned the repressive sexual attitudes and primitive medical practices of that culture. Very little was said about the position of older people among the Nacirema. However, an unpublished manuscript was recently discovered which describes the relationship between the Nacirema and another tribe called the Dega. This manuscript was written in 1958 by Dr. L.N. Rekab of Adanac University, and portions of it are presented below.

I believe this material is vitally important because it gives us an eyewitness account of the abuses inflicted upon the Dega by the Nacirema culture, and because it offers a historical baseline by which we can judge the progress which has been made since that time.

For some time now, members of the Dega tribe have been migrating into the village occupied by the Nacirema. Relations between the two cultures are far from cordial. Perhaps the best way to describe the situation is that the Nacirema treat the Dega like visiting relatives who have overstayed their welcome. The Nacirema prohibit the Dega from taking any active part in the economy, except for some childcare work, or tending the sick and the lame among their own group. This work is called *gnireet-nulov* and

is never rewarded with pay or goods. The Nacirema explain that the Dega refuse to accept compensation because that would take away the honour of *gnireet-nulov* and turn it into mere labour. The Dega told me they had never been offered any pay.

The Dega appear to be slaves to the Nacirema, although neither group seems aware of the relationship. The Dega are not subjected to long days of hard labour, but are kept in a state of enforced idleness. They are given a meagre allowance for food and clothing, called a *noisnep*, which gives them a standard of living not much better than the poorest Nacirema. Some of them are permitted to live in their own individual huts, but many of the Dega are forced to live in group quarters called *gnisrun* homes. They are confined to small rooms, usually shared with another Dega, all their personal possessions are taken away from them, and they are tended by apprentices of the village witch doctor.

The daily life of the Dega is occupied mainly by sedentary activities. The Nacirema encourage them to play children's games and to do some weaving, but the articles they produce are given away, not sold in the market. A favorite pastime of the Dega is a sport called *flog*. Small white rocks are hit with a stick, over a large area of long grass, sand pits, and ponds. The aim of the game is to find the rock after you hit it. Each player has to buy a dozen special rocks from the Nacirema who makes them, who is called the *orp*. The player who returns at the end of the day with the

● Exhibit 3.3 (cont.)

THE DEGA AND THE NACIREMA: THEN AND NOW

most rocks is given free drinks by the other players. Sometimes the wealthy Nacirema also play *flog*, but never on the same day as the Dega. The Nacirema complain that the Dega take too long to finish the game. One of the Dega told me that the reason they played so slowly was that they had nothing else to do anyway, so enjoyed the company and the fresh air....

The temple is the major gathering place for the Dega. They attend the religious ceremonies regularly, but conversations with the priest and the Dega revealed a curious discrepancy. While the priest was sure that they believed fervently in the religious teaching, most of the Dega said that they did not really believe, but like to see their friends and listen to the music.

The temple is also used for activities which are a major source of excitement for the Dega. The most popular activity is a game of chance called *ognib* which consists of chanting by the priest and the creation of magic geometric shapes by the Dega. At the end of each chant, one of the players shouts the name of the game and jumps up and down with great excitement. The priest inspects the magic shape to see if it has been done correctly, and if it was, presents a clay pot to the winner....

The sexual practices of the Dega are either nonexistent, or are very well hidden. No births have ever been observed among the Dega, so it may be inferred that they are beyond their reproductive years. However, there seems to be no sexual activity at all. I asked one Nacirema warrior if he had ever heard of such activity among the Dega, but he just laughed loudly, saying that would be like two rocks trying to lay an egg! When I asked if any Nacirema had sexual relations with the Dega, he turned pale, spat on the ground, and told me he would rather sleep with a wild pig. Even though some of the Dega are very good-looking, the Nacirema consider them all as sterile, sexless individuals.

What will become of the Dega? Their future looks bleak, but I observed that new members arrive almost daily from the forest outside the village. Because of this immigration, there seems to be an increase in their numbers each month. When food was scarce, there was some talk among the young Nacirema warriors of attacking the Dega, but this was discouraged by the older warriors, who seemed more sympathetic to them.

The total population in the village seems to be kept in check by the disappearance of the Nacirema warriors after the ceremony of the gold sundial. This ceremony occurs only among the oldest of the Nacirema, who are given a small sundial and sent off into the forest to rest before they battle with the great spirits. Only one warrior ever returned while I was in the village, and he had gone crazy. He came back and began embracing the Dega, crying out "Brother! Sister!" ... He was put out of his deluded misery by a young warrior.

What has happened in the quarter century since Dr. Rekab wrote this account? Well, the Dega have not died out. In fact, their numbers have increased dramatically since then, and most of the abuses put upon them by the Nacirema have disappeared. The gnisrun homes have been improved, the noisnep plans are providing a better standard of living for the Dega, and the Dega themselves are taking on a more active role in Nacirema society. To be sure, there are still some problems that need solving. However, it is a sure bet that the Dega will never again be second-class citizens.

Source: B. Hess and E. Markson, © 1987, "The Dega and the Nacirema," *Growing Old in America*, 3rd ed., New Brunswick, NJ: Transaction Publishers. Reprinted by permission of Transaction Publishers.

They say that limited resources and the physical decline that come with old age make it unattractive in all societies. On the other hand, most people know and like older individuals, and at all times in history younger people have cared for and loved their aged relatives and friends.

In spite of some negative attitudes toward old age, older people as a group in North America live materially better lives than older people at any time in history.

Schulz (1980) reports "major breakthroughs" in private and public programs that deal with economic problems in old age. He cites as proof the increase of private pensions, property tax relief, and a rise of almost 100 percent in U.S. Social Security benefits from 1970 to 1980. He could also have included in his list improvements in Canada's Old Age Security benefits, the Canada Pension Plan, and free nationwide health care coverage for the elderly. All these programs increase older people's independence and freedom.

Some writers predict an age-irrelevant society in the future (Neugarten 1980). This kind of society will treat individuals on the basis of what they can do, rather than on the basis of sex, race, or age. This fits with the trend in North America today to eliminate racism and sexism. Fischer (1978) points to the end of mandatory retirement as a sign of this trend, and Atchley (1980) cites better treatment of old age on television as a sign of improved attitudes toward and treatment of the elderly in post-industrial nations.

AGING IN THE WORLD TODAY

The United Nations (UN) recognizes the demographic challenges faced by developed and developing nations. It declared 1999 the International Year of the Older Person (IYOP). Canada's motto for that year was "Canada, a society for all ages" (Canada Coordinating Committee 1999). The UN focused on four themes: raising awareness of aging, looking beyond 1999, reaching out to younger people, and networking between nations on policy and research. This last theme—networking between nations—will grow in importance as nations struggle with common issues. Countries can learn from one another, though the diversity of governments, cultures, and economic systems in the world will force nations to look for unique solutions. Chappell (1999a, 1) says that the IYOP reflected a new paradigm in the study of aging. "The new paradigm," she says, "promotes the life course perspective, age integration, and the interrelatedness of aging and development." This perspective puts the life of the individual in the social, historical, and economic context of society. It looks at aging as the product of social as well as individual (biological and physiological) forces.

The U.S. Bureau of the Census calls the global increase in the number of older people "a social phenomenon without historical precedent" (American Association of Retired Persons [AARP] 1998, 7). In 2000, about 16 percent of the population of the developed nations such as the United States, Australia, the United Kingdom, and Canada were over age 60 (United Nations 2002). Australia, Western Europe countries, the Russian Federation, Japan, and Canada had 12 percent or more of their populations over age 65. Europe had a greater proportion of older people than any other continent. One projection estimates that the United Kingdom, for example, will have nearly one-third of its population (29.4 percent) aged 60 or over in the year 2025.

This increase in the older population will be caused mostly by a decrease in birth rates and, to a lesser extent, by increased longevity. Italy reports the lowest birth rates in human history. It now has more people over age 60 than under age 20 (United Nations 2002). The United Nations (2002) reports that by 2050 Italy may have as many people aged 60+ as working. The developed nations will see increases in health care and pension costs. These nations have a number of options. For example, they can change pension policies and encourage people to work longer, or they can raise taxes or increase the national debt (Anderson and Hussey 2000). But they will all have to reduce costs and yet provide services to their aging populations (Henripin 1994; Secretariat of the European Commission 1992).

The developing nations (such as the Latin American, African, and Middle Eastern countries) make up three-quarters of the world's population, and they too will see changes in their population structures. These countries have relatively young populations, with large numbers of children and proportionately few older people, some with as few as 3 percent of the population aged 65 and over (e.g., Bangladesh and Afghanistan) (United Nations 2002). But the death rates in these countries have begun to fall and many more people now live into old age.

The low proportion of people aged 65 and over in the developing nations, compared with that in the developed nations, tells only part of the story of aging in these countries. First, the United Nations (2002) projects that between 2000 and 2025 the world population of older people (65 and over) will nearly double to more than 800 million people. About two-thirds of the world's older people will live in the developing nations (AARP 1998). Today, "Hong Kong, Singapore and China are all witnessing the fastest population aging the world has ever seen" (Chi 2001, 119). In 2025, the UN predicts that about 86 percent of the older people in the developing world will live in Asia. Second, the less-developed countries will show the greatest percentage increase of older people. The UN says that between 2000 and 2050, the 60-and-over population in the developed countries will increase by 70 percent. That population in the developing countries will more than quadruple in this same time. Nearly 80 percent of the world's older population will live in the less-developed countries in 2050 (UN 2003). These nations will also see increases in their oldest old populations (people aged 80 and over). Third, the developing countries have few public services to meet the needs of their aging populations.

The developing countries face other problems as well. When nations develop, the young often move to the cities (AARP 1998; Apt 2002; Holmes and Holmes

● Exhibit 3.4

PERCENTAGES OF POPULATION AGED 60 YEARS AND OVER, SELECTED REGIONS AND NATIONS, 2000, 2025, AND 2050

Regions	2000	2025	2050
World	10.0	15.0	21.1
Africa	5.1	6.3	10.2
Latin America/Caribbean	8.0	14.0	22.5
North America	16.2	25.1	27.2
Asia	8.8	14.7	22.6
Europe	20.3	28.8	36.6
Oceania	13.4	19.7	23.3
Canada	16.7	27.9	30.5
China	10.1	19.5	29.9
Egypt	6.3	11.5	20.8
France	20.5	28.7	32.7
Israel	13.2	18.5	24.8
Jamaica	9.6	14.5	24.0
Japan	23.2	35.1	42.3
Kenya	4.2	5.9	13.0
Mexico	6.9	13.5	24.4
Russian Federation	18.5	26.0	37.2
Sweden	22.4	32.4	37.7

European countries that first went through demographic transitions have the largest proportions of older people. More than a century ago, in 1900, more than 7 percent of the populations of France and Sweden were aged 65 and over. (France had 8.2 percent in 1900; Sweden had 8.4 percent in 1900). England and Wales, along with Germany, became older societies around 1930; both had 7.4 percent of their population aged 65 and over in that year (Laslett 1976). The high death rates for young men and the low birth rates during World War II speeded up societal aging in these countries. By 2000, 20.5 percent of France's population was over age 60; that of England and Wales was 20.6 percent and Sweden had a 22.4 percent rate. In 2000, Japan topped the list with more than 23 percent of its population over age 60 (United Nations 2002).

The figures in this chart show that the world population will age in the years ahead. Decreased birth and death rates will lead to population aging in all parts of the world. Each region and each selected country above shows the trend toward population aging. The developed nations will have the largest proportions of older people. But the developing nations will also have high proportions of people aged 60 and over.

Note: The above chart uses age 60 and over to define an aged population and presents proportions of older people for a sample of countries.

Source: United Nations Secretariat, Population Division of the Department of Economics and Social Affairs, 2002, *World Population Prospects: The 1994 Review* (United Nations Publication, Sales No. E.95.XIII.16), *World Population Ageing: 1950–2050*, http://www.un.org/esa/population/publications/worldageing19502050, accessed July 8, 2003. Reprinted with permission.

1995). The young feel less tied to the land and feel less obligation to care for their elders. This leaves the aged in rural villages with little family or social support (Chi 2001). Also, changing gender roles lead women to work outside the home, so older people are left without the family supports that former generations could rely on. Villages lack communications, transportation, supplies, and services that the elderly need. Modernization in India, for example, leaves elders without the support of tradition or the presence of modern social services (Bhat and Dhruvarajan 2001).

Older workers sometimes return to their home countries after years of working in another country. They have no work, no skills, and no pensions, and will grow old in poverty (DeLehr 1988). In rural settings, old people must work as long as they have the strength. In larger centres a growing number of older people survive by "scratching out a living from rubbish dumps or peddling goods on the streets" (7). She predicts things will get worse unless these countries develop basic services to help older people.

New problems have grown up that further place the older person at risk. AIDS now plagues many developing countries. Canada's National Advisory Council on Aging (2002a) reports that in Thailand two-thirds of the adults with HIV-related illnesses receive care at home from their 60- and 70-year-old parents. African elders face unique challenges. The AIDS epidemic in Africa has hit the working-age population, leading to the loss of middle-aged caregivers for African elders. Also, AIDS has left many older Africans as the sole caregiver for their orphaned grandchildren. "In some parts of Africa," the AARP says, "AIDS is actually called the 'grand mothers' disease'" (AARP 1998, 19).

Developing countries need more information about their older populations, and they need to plan for an aging society (Sennott-Miller 1994). Countries with social programs and pension plans in place will need to adapt these programs to serve more older people (Chee 2000; Oh and Warnes 2001). Gerontologists need new theories of aging to explain the changes taking place in these countries (see Exhibit 3.5) and new plans for social change that fit the needs of an aging world.

Solutions that fit Western developed countries do not necessarily fit the developing nations (Apt 2002).

● Exhibit 3.5

CONTROVERSY: MODERNIZATION VS. DEPENDENCY THEORY

Modernization theory views developed industrial societies as the model for less-developed countries and proposes that less-developed countries set up policies for older people such as those used in developed countries (Neysmith and Edwardh 1983). But developed countries' solutions often do not fit the needs of developing societies. Some theorists propose an alternative theory of aging—dependency theory.

Dependency theory uses a critical Marxist approach to the study of aging. It says that the social and economic structures in a society create the status of the old and that to understand the developing world gerontologists have to understand aging with regard to the economic relations between nations. Dependency theory looks at the societal and worldwide forces that decide the fate of older people (Hendricks 1982).

Dependency theory begins with the fact that structured inequality exists between developed and less-developed societies. Less-developed or peripheral countries now depend on the developed or core countries for their economic well-being. The peripheral countries of Latin America, Africa, and Asia pro-

duce raw materials, crops, and manufactured goods for the core countries. The core countries decide what a peripheral country should grow or make for its markets. This keeps the peripheral country dependent and poor, and disrupts its economic, familial, and political life.

Younger people in developing countries move off the land to work in the cities. Also, the gap between rich and poor people in these nations grows. Families, for example, grow less food for their own use. They begin to grow cash crops for export. This makes it harder for them to support large families that include older members (Gillin 1986). Older people also lose status in these societies because their knowledge does not serve the core nation's needs. "Old people do not simply become out of date, they are made obsolete. If one goal of gerontology is to upgrade the quality of life for older people in any given society, then it must first understand the structural imperatives that have shaped their control over potential resources" (Hendricks 1982). Dependency theory adds this understanding to the study of aging and society.

Katz (1996) says that even the Western view of aging does not fit many nations' needs. He says that the Western, problem-centred approach to aging makes traditional views of old age look "ineffectual and disorganized" (3). Western gerontology "is premised on moral and social understandings of the individual vastly different from those of India [and other developing nations] and is designated for different political, economic, and cultural realities" (3). Western societies evolved away from family-centred supports for older people (Kertzner 1995). The developed countries created pensions and other welfare programs for their older citizens. But this approach requires an economy and political system that supports these programs.

The developing countries have neither the social services nor the economic resources to help the elderly poor. Nor can these countries afford the housing, health, or welfare services for the old that Western countries have set up. The AARP reports that 155 countries had social security programs in 1993. These programs covered about a third of the people aged 60 and over in the world. But these programs remain unstable and in some cases they have failed (AARP 1998). Also, only about one-third of the working population gets benefits. Often these benefits add up to only small amounts. Many older people in these countries will face economic and social hardship.

CONCLUSION

Did older people live better lives in the past than they do today? Can we learn something about aging from past societies? Will aging in the future differ from aging today?

Older people's status in the past differed from time to time, from place to place, and from class to class.

Some societies treated their aged badly, some treated them well, but all of these societies had fewer older people than societies today. We cannot look to the past for ways to create a good old age today. The large number of older people in the world today is a new phenomenon. And Laslett (1976, 96) says, "It calls for invention rather than imitation."

In the future, as in the past, aging will differ from society to society. The wealthier nations will have the best chance of creating a materially satisfying old age for their people. The poorer societies will struggle under the burden of more people, old and young. Shrestra (2000) notes that care for the old has a low priority among public policy concerns in many developing countries.

One thing, however, seems certain: Aging populations will challenge all countries in the world. In 2002, the UN published its "International Strategy for Action on Ageing." This strategy calls for improved attitudes toward older people, more effective policies, and more supportive communities. The UN looks to governments worldwide to achieve these goals. But the economy, the political system, the culture, the level of development, and the age structure of a society will all affect how governments respond to this challenge.

Canada, like other countries, cannot copy past societies in its treatment of older people, but it can learn something from the past and from simpler societies. The !Kung San elders heal the sick through dance and music. In traditional Chinese culture, the older woman works as a matchmaker. Among the Coast Salish tribe of British Columbia the old serve as ritual leaders. Wherever older people have had valued roles to play in their societies, they have lived respected and purposeful lives. Canada can make this a goal of its policies for older people.

Summary

1. Culture, custom, and the economic life of the group all influence how a society treats its older members. A study of four types of societies—hunting and gathering, agricultural, industrial, and post-industrial—shows that treatment of the aged differed in the past from time to time and from place to place. None of these societies created a golden age for older people.

2. Like most societies, past and present, modern Western societies show an ambivalence toward the aged. Negative stereotypes exist, and some discrimination against the aged takes place. Modern societies also offer older people independence, a high standard of living, and many opportunities for life satisfaction.

3. The developed nations have a high percentage of older people. They will have to shift resources to serve the changing needs of their populations. Post-industrial societies show an ambivalence toward older people. They provide pensions and services, but they also show prejudice toward older people.

4. Modernization theory predicts a decline in the status and treatment of the aged in modern society compared with societies in the past. Some studies that compare developed and developing countries today support modernization theory, but critics of the theory argue that it oversimplifies life in the past, ignores differences in treatment of the elderly within societies, and undervalues the opportunities for a good old age today.

5. The developing countries have large numbers of older people, even though older people make up a relatively small percentage of their populations. This increase in the numbers of older people presents developing countries with problems of service delivery and health care support. Population aging has become a worldwide challenge. The response a nation makes to the challenge will depend on its traditions, culture, level of development, and economic strength.

Study Questions

1. Identify and describe the four major types of societies. How are older people treated in each of these societies?

2. What are the four conditions that lead to support for an older person in simple societies? How do these conditions determine the way these societies treat older people? How has modernization affected the status of elders?

3. How did older people command status and respect in agricultural societies? What kind of tension did this create?

4. Define the process of modernization. What three changes created the modern industrial society? How did these three things influence the status and treatment of older people? Why do some researchers criticize modernization theory?

5. Explain why older people in the developed countries live better materially now than at any time in the past.

6. What problems will the developing countries face as their older populations grow in size?

Key Terms

modernization theory this theory holds that a shift to urban life, with high technology and complex institutions, leads to a decrease in the status of older people. (48)

post-industrial society a society such as Canada's that has gone through the industrial revolution and become a service-based, complex society. (49)

Selected Readings

Albert, S.M., and M.G. Cattell. *Old Age in Global Perspective: Cross-Cultural and Cross-National Views.* New York: G.K. Hall, 1994.

The authors use field research and national surveys to describe aging around the world. The book discusses older people's living arrangements, social relationships, and the life course. The book also looks at the effects of modernization on old age.

Cole, Thomas R. *The Journey of Life.* New York: Cambridge University Press, 1992.

The author, a historian, traces the meaning of aging from the Middle Ages to the present. He focuses his more recent analyses on the United States. Cole shows different views of aging, as a personal problem, as something to manage and control, and as something to deny. He suggests that today we need a full picture of life that includes aging and death, and suggests that our view of aging today needs to include notions of spiritual growth, a legacy, and wisdom. Cole shows how one society, the United States, has grappled with the meaning of aging over time.

Sokolovsky, J., ed. *The Cultural Context of Aging: Worldwide Perspectives.* New York: Bergin and Garvey, 1990.

This book focuses on aging in a variety of cultures. Articles include research on supports for older members of the !Kung San of Botswana, grandparenting among Native Americans, and the elderly in modern Japan. A picture of the diversity of aging worldwide.

Chapter Four
Aging in Canada

Photo © Walter Hodges/CORBIS/MAGMA

INTRODUCTION

When people think about aging, they think about their family, their friends, or themselves getting older. But societies age too. From 1901 to 2001, Canada's population grew almost six times in size (Statistics Canada 2003o). During this same period, the older population grew by more than 13 times, more than twice the rate of the general population. The proportion of people aged 65 and over rose from 5 percent of the total population in 1901 to 13 percent of Canada's population in 2001 (Health Canada 2001a; Statistics Canada 2002b).[1] This makes Canada's population one of the oldest in the world. And demographers expect Canadian society to age even more in the next 50 years.

This chapter will look at (1) why Canadian society has aged, (2) the population structure of Canada today, and (3) the impact of population aging on health care and pension programs.

CANADA COMES OF AGE

Canada is a relatively young nation compared to the European countries. Until 1900, less than 5 percent of its population was aged 65 and over, and the country aged gradually through the first part of this century. In 1951, Canada had 7.8 percent of its population over age 65 (Lindsay 1999). By 2000, Canada had 3.8 million people, or 13 percent of its population, aged 65 and over (Health Canada 2001a). By 2041, the portion of Canada's population aged 65 and over could be one-quarter of the total population, five times the proportion of older people in 1901 (Health Canada 2001a; Lindsay 1999).

What caused Canada to age in the twentieth century? What will keep it aging in the years ahead? And what effect will population aging have on Canadian society? A look at Canada's population, past and present, will answer these questions.

Demographers study three conditions that affect a population's size and structure: immigration, death rates, and birth rates. Each of these demographic forces caused the Canadian population to age from the mid-1800s to the present.

Immigration

Of the three demographic forces—immigration, birth rates, and death rates—immigration played the smallest part in the aging of Canada's population (Moore, Rosenberg, and McGuinness 1997). It also affected different parts of Canada in different ways. Waves of immigration in the early twentieth century brought new groups of young adults to Canada. Between 1901 and 1911, 1.5 million people arrived in Canada, as many as in the previous 40 years combined. Immigration in the first decade of the twentieth century accounted for 44 percent of Canada's total population increase in those years (Statistics Canada 1981). Most of these immigrants came to Canada as children or young adults (20 to 34 years old) (Northcott 1988). These young people (and the families they raised) helped keep Canada's population young at the start of this century (see Exhibit 4.1).

Immigration continued to add to Canada's population until the start of the Great Depression. Between 1901 and 1931, successive waves of immigration brought from 3.5 to 4.5 million people to Canada. These immigrants did more than simply increase the number of people in Canada; they also changed the face of Canadian society. Immigrants before 1900 came mostly from the British Isles, but Leacy (1983) reports that Canadians of "other European" origin rose from 37 percent of the European-born population in 1881 to 43 percent of the same population in 1911. Germans, Norwegians, Mennonites, Doukhobors, Chinese, and southern and eastern Europeans arrived in large numbers. Most of these immigrants were young males.

Many of the eastern Europeans, along with Icelanders and Mennonites, settled on the Prairies. Manitoba in the 1880s and Saskatchewan around 1911 had high birth rates due to the large number of young immigrants in their populations (Henripin 1972). This large wave of immigration partly explains the drop in the proportion of people over age 65 in Canada from 5 percent in 1901 to 4.7 percent in 1911 and 4.8 percent in 1921. This same group added to Canada's older population as they aged. Lindsay (1999) estimates that, in 1996, 61 percent of all immigrants aged 65 and over arrived in Canada before 1961. Many older immigrants came to Canada during World War II and the first years after the war.

Foreign-born older people made up 27 percent of Canada's older population in 1996 (Lindsay 1999). This proportion dropped steadily, due to decreased immigration, from a high of 38.8 percent in 1961 (Norland 1994). The proportion of foreign-born people in the older population may increase somewhat in the next few years. A

---

1. Most studies use the population aged 65 and over to measure population aging. We will use this figure (unless otherwise noted) to allow for a comparison of different societies, past and present.

Exhibit 4.1

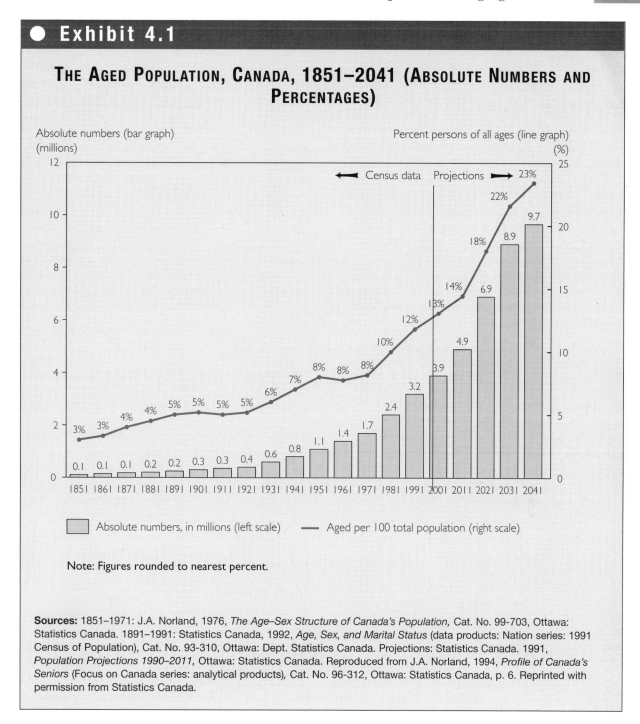

THE AGED POPULATION, CANADA, 1851–2041 (ABSOLUTE NUMBERS AND PERCENTAGES)

Absolute numbers (bar graph) (millions)

Percent persons of all ages (line graph) (%)

◄— Census data   Projections —►

Absolute numbers, in millions (left scale)

Aged per 100 total population (right scale)

Note: Figures rounded to nearest percent.

Sources: 1851–1971: J.A. Norland, 1976, *The Age–Sex Structure of Canada's Population,* Cat. No. 99-703, Ottawa: Statistics Canada. 1891–1991: Statistics Canada, 1992, *Age, Sex, and Marital Status* (data products: Nation series: 1991 Census of Population), Cat. No. 93-310, Ottawa: Dept. Statistics Canada. Projections: Statistics Canada. 1991, *Population Projections 1990–2011,* Ottawa: Statistics Canada. Reproduced from J.A. Norland, 1994, *Profile of Canada's Seniors* (Focus on Canada series: analytical products), Cat. No. 96-312, Ottawa: Statistics Canada, p. 6. Reprinted with permission from Statistics Canada.

major wave of immigration in the early 1950s accounts for about 6 percent of Canada's growth from 1946 to 1978. These immigrants have begun to increase the size of the foreign-born older population (McDaniel 1986).

More recent immigration patterns will change the character of the older population in the future. In the period before 1961, most of Canada's immigrants—almost 90 percent—came from the United Kingdom or Europe (Chard, Badets, and Leo 2000, cited in Lindsay 2000b). By the early 1990s, the largest portion of immigrants came from the developing countries of Asia, the Caribbean, South America, and Central America—57.4

percent from Asia, and 13.2 percent from the Caribbean, South and Central America. In the 1990s, more than half of immigrants came from East and South Asian countries—India and China, particularly Hong Kong (Statistics Canada 2001a). Nearly all (91 percent) of immigrants aged 65 and over today come as family members of Canadian residents (Lindsay 1999).

Compared with other demographic forces, immigration has little effect on the aging of Canada's population (Moore, Rosenberg, and McGuinness 1997). For example, in 1995 people aged 65 and over made up only 4 percent of all immigrants. Fertility, not immigration, causes population aging or rejuvenation (Denton, Feaver, and Spencer 1998). But immigration does increase the diversity of Canadian society, and it creates new challenges for families, communities, and groups that serve older people (Gee, Kobayashi, and Prus 2003).

Death Rates

The **death rate** is the number of deaths per 1000 people in a population. By the late nineteenth and early twentieth centuries, death rates began to drop across the country. The most reliable figures for this period come from Quebec. Henripin and Peron (1972, cited in Beaujot and McQuillan 1982) say that the crude death rate in Quebec dropped by half from 24 per 1000 in 1871–75 to 12.9 by 1921–25. These figures probably overestimate the drop in death rates for Canada as a whole. Historians say that Canada's large cities still suffered from high death rates (Artibise 1977; Cross 1983; Gagan 1983a; Torrance 1981), but a steady, if not dramatic, decline did take place. Life expectancy at birth rose from 41.9 years for men and 44.2 years for women born in 1851 to 60.0 years for men and 62.1 years for women born in 1931. Life expectancy at age 65 had increased to 78 years for men and 78.7 years for women by 1931. This meant that more people lived longer and that more lived into late old age (Lavoie and Oderkirk 1993; Nagnur 1986).

Life expectancy increased steadily for men and women at all ages between 1941 and 1981, but infants gained the most years (see Exhibit 4.2). **Infant mortality rates** (the death rates of children less than one year old) decreased dramatically over this century. By 2001, the infant mortality rate had fallen to about one-half of 1 percent of live births (compared with about 10 percent in 1921) (Parliament 1987; Statistics Canada 2003d).

Control of childhood disease, better prenatal care, and improved nutrition account for most of this change. Lavoie and Oderkirk (1993; see also Lavoie 1992) say that in the mid-nineteenth century epidemics of cholera

(in 1832), typhus (in 1846–49), and smallpox (in 1885–86) led to high infant and child mortality. Nagnur and Nagrodski (1988, 26) report that "infectious and parasitic diseases, including tuberculosis, accounted for almost 15% of deaths in 1921; in 1986, however, only about half of one percent of all deaths were the result of these diseases." From 1931 to 2001 in Canada, life expectancy at birth increased from 60 years to 77.1 years for men and from 62 years to 82.2 years for women (Statistics Canada 2003d).

Since 1951, Canada has also seen a drop in the most common cause of death in adulthood—cardiovascular disease (which includes ischemic heart disease, strokes, arterial disease, hypertension, and rheumatic heart disease) (Parliament 1989). People in the oldest cohorts show some of the greatest improvements in life expectancy. Dumas (1990, 64), for example, says that "the most spectacular progress [in the extension of life expectancy has been] realized at very advanced ages: the probability of living 10 years beyond one's 80th birthday rose from 28% in 1966 to 41% in 1986, or nearly 50 per cent." As a result of this trend, between 1986 and 1998 the proportion of Canadians aged 75 to 84 increased by more than 25 percent and the proportion aged 85 and over increased by more than 33 percent (Lindsay 1999). Statistics Canada projects that the group aged 85 and over will make up 4 percent of the total population in 2041 (four times the proportion in 1998) (Lindsay 1999).

Today, Canada, along with Japan, Sweden, Denmark, Norway, and the United States, has some of the highest life expectancies in the world (in Canada 77.1 years for males at birth and 81.2 years at birth for women in 2001) (Statistics Canada 2003d). And this means that more Canadians than ever before will enter old age.

Birth Rates

The **birth rate** is the number of births per 1000 women in a population. A change in fertility causes population aging (Denton, Feaver, and Spencer 1998). A population ages when its proportion of younger people declines. Quebec in the 1700s, for example, had a young population and one of the highest birth rates ever recorded. From 1700 to 1730, women averaged births of one child every two years until they reached age 30. Women who reached the age of 50 averaged eight or nine children. In the middle of the eighteenth century, the average was 13 children apiece (Henripin 1972). During this time the birth rate ran two to six times higher than the death rate. Quebec's population grew 20 times from 1608 to 1765, and by one and a half times again by 1851 (Kalbach and McVey 1979). Death rates in Quebec began to decline

Exhibit 4.2

EVOLUTION OF LIFE EXPECTANCY BY AGE AND SEX, CANADA, 1921–1996

	At Birth		At Age 65		At Age 85	
Year	Males	Females	Males	Females	Males	Females
1921*	58.8	60.6	13.0	13.6	4.1	4.3
1931*	60.0	62.1	13.0	13.7	4.1	4.4
1941*	63.0	66.3	12.8	14.1	4.1	4.4
1951	66.4	70.9	13.3	15.0	4.3	4.7
1961	68.4	74.3	13.6	16.1	4.6	5.0
1971	69.4	76.5	13.8	17.6	5.0	5.9
1981	71.9	79.1	14.6	18.9	5.2	6.6
1991	74.6	81.0	15.8	20.0	5.5	7.0
1996	75.7	81.4	16.3	20.2	5.7	7.0

* The 1921 figures exclude Quebec and the 1921–41 figures exclude Newfoundland.

This table shows a steady increase in life expectancy at birth, at age 65, and at age 85 from 1941 to 1996 for both sexes, with one exception: life expectancy at age 85 for women levelled off for 1996. Note that until 1996, women gained more in life expectancy than men at birth and at age 65 in each time period. This may be due to differences in lifestyles, habits, or environmental conditions (e.g., working conditions). Recent figures show a change in this trend. Men at birth and at age 65 gained more years in life expectancy than women between 1981 and 1996. Changes in work patterns and lifestyles for men and women may account for this reversal.

Source: Adapted from Colin Lindsay, *A Portrait of Seniors in Canada,* 3rd ed., October 1999, Cat. No. 89-519, Tables 4.1 and 4.2, pp. 67–68; and Josée Normand, "The Health of Women," in *Women in Canada 2000: A Gender-Based Statistical Report,* Cat. No. 89-503-XPE, Table 3.13, p. 75. Reprinted with permission from Statistics Canada.

after 1780, but despite this the province's birth rate was still high and the population stayed young (Henripin 1972; Kalbach and McVey 1979).

Frontier regions in Ontario also had high birth rates. McInnis (1977) and Henripin (1972) report rates similar to Quebec's in rural Ontario in the mid-nineteenth century. A writer of the time reported that children "in Canada [are a man's] greatest blessing, and happy is that man who has a quiver full of them" (Philpot 1871, cited in Gagan 1983b). McInnis says that Upper Canada at the time "had one of the highest birth rates in the world" (1977, 202). Gagan (1983b) estimates that settled Ontario families in Peel County had eight to nine children. New immigrants to Canada before 1830 often had more.

Canada began its demographic transition around 1850 as the birth rate decreased. Henripin (1972) shows that the birth rate in Canada as a whole dropped by about 30 percent from 1851 to 1951 (with a sharp drop

during the 1930s). Though the provinces all showed the same declining trend, their individual rates varied: The Quebec birth rate dropped least, by about 20 percent from 1851 to 1921; Ontario showed a sharp drop of about 50 percent during this same time; Manitoba between 1881 and 1921 showed a drop of more than 60 percent; and Saskatchewan showed a similar drop between 1901 and 1921 (Henripin 1972). This drop in the birth rate, more than any other demographic change, led to the aging of Canadian society.

Baby Boom and Baby Bust

Two phenomena affecting the birth rate, the **baby boom** and the **baby bust**, account for the greatest changes in Canadian population from 1951 to the present.

From 1947 to the early 1960s, Canada went through a baby boom (Foot and Stoffman 1998). Beaujot and McQuillan (1982, 220–21) define the **fertility rate** as

● **Exhibit 4.3**

MEDIAN AGE* OF THE POPULATION, CANADA, 1881–2006 (EXCLUDING NEWFOUNDLAND)

Year	Median Age	Year	Median Age
1881	20.1	1966	25.6
1891	21.4	1971	26.2
1901	22.7	1976	27.8
1911	23.8	1981	29.6
1921	23.9	1986	31.6
1931	24.7	1991	33.5
1941	27.0	1996	35.3
1951	27.7	2001	37.6
1961	26.3	2006	39.5 (projected)
		2011	41.0 (projected)

* Half the population is older and half is younger than the median age.

Canada's median age rose 17.5 years from 1881 to 2001. The table shows a jump of 2.3 years in the median age between 1931 and 1941. This reflects the sharp drop in the birth rate during the Depression years. The table also shows a rise in the median age until 1951, followed by a drop from 1952 to 1966. During these years, the rise in the birth rate (the baby boom) led to a decrease in the median age by 2.1 years to 25.6 years. In 1976, the median age rose again to above its 1951 high of 27.7. By 1986, more than half the population was over the age of 30. The aging of the baby boom cohorts will increase the median age in the years ahead. Statistics Canada projects a continued increase in the median age into the middle of the twenty-first century.

Sources: Dominion Bureau of Statistics, 1964, *Census of Canada (1961 Census), Bulletin* 7: 1–4, Ottawa: Queen's Printer; Statistics Canada, 1968, *1966 Census of Canada*, Vol. 1 (1–11), Ottawa: Queen's Printer; Statistics Canada, 1973, *Census of Canada (1971 Census), Bulletin* 1: 2–3, Ottawa: Information Canada; Statistics Canada, 1978, cited in W.E. Kalbach and W.W. McVey, 1979, *The Demographic Bases of Canadian Society*, 2nd ed., Toronto: McGraw-Hill Ryerson, 161, Table 6:3; M.S. Devereaux, 1987, "Aging of the Canadian Population," *Canadian Social Trends*, Winter, 37–38; C. McKie, 1993, "Population Aging: Baby Boomers into the 21st Century," *Canadian Social Trends*, Summer, 2–6; and M.V. George et al., 1994, *Population Projections for Canada, Provinces and Territories 1993–2016*, Ottawa: Ministry of Industry, Science and Technology. Adapted from *Annual Demographic Statistics*, Cat. No. 91-213, and from Statistics Canada (2002a),[11] Median Age, Canada, 1901–2011,[11] http://www12.statcan.ca/english/census01/Products/Analytic/companion/age/cdamedaget.cfm, accessed September 27, 2003. Reprinted with permission from Statistics Canada.

"the average number of children that would be born alive to a woman during her lifetime if she were to pass through all her childbearing years conforming to the age-specific fertility rates of a given year." Between 1941 and 1961, the total fertility rate rose from 2.83 to 3.84. The **age-specific birth rate** (the number of births in a given age group per 1000 women in that age group) nearly doubled for 15- to 19-year-olds, going from 30.7 to 58.2 (Statistics Canada 1978, cited in Beaujot and McQuillan 1982). Women averaged four children each at the height of the baby boom (Foot and Stoffman 1998).

Total births soared from 264 000 in 1941 to almost 476 000 in 1961 (Statistics Canada 1978, cited in Beaujot and McQuillan 1982).

Foot and Stoffman (1998, 25) say that "Canada's was the loudest baby boom in the industrialized world." Owram (1996, 5) says that after World War II "society seemed to revolve around babies … sometimes it seemed like everybody was pregnant or had a new baby." Foot and Stoffman (1998) trace the baby boom to two conditions: a good economy (people felt confident about the future) and a large number of immigrants (many of

● Exhibit 4.4

CANADA'S OLDEST SENIORS

Canada has more very old people (aged 80 and over) in its population than ever before. And demographers predict a growing number of very old people in the future. Few studies have looked at this age group. The National Advisory Council on Aging (NACA) talked with Canada's oldest seniors to learn something about their lives and how they see the world. The excerpts below show the varied perspectives very old people have on aging and on living in late old age.

> "It is very peculiar being over 100 ... and fun. I'm a rare breed, a museum piece. They bring people in to look at me. I would say that I have had a very good life. There have been bad times but I am happy now, although my health is slowly deteriorating. Last night, I went to hear my grand-daughter and her husband in a Gilbert and Sullivan musical. I was an actress and singer when I was young. They must get it from me." (101-year-old widow living in a long-term care facility)

"You shouldn't be congratulated for living too long. It's a question of endurance.... Nothing works properly in my body, from teeth to toes.... Old age is a form of punishment. The more you go on, the more you endure. I hate every minute of it." (87-year-old single woman living in a long-term care facility)

"I really mourn the loss of my friends. I miss most of all having someone to share news or encounters, reports of the day when I return from shopping or an outing. I sometimes find myself saying 'I must tell Mary about that,' and then I remember that she is no longer around. We used to be a close group of six and now I am the only one left." (87-year-old widow living in a seniors' housing complex).

"I was born blind and have been living here for 40 years. Last year, I married a fellow resident who has cerebral palsy. I am happier than I have ever been in my life because I am so much in love. Life is good to me now." (80-year-old woman living in a long-term facility)

Source: National Advisory Council on Aging, 1992, *The NACA Position on Canada's Oldest Seniors: Maintaining the Quality of Their Lives.* Ottawa: National Advisory Council on Aging. Courtesy of the National Advisory Council on Aging, Health Canada, 2000.

childbearing age). The baby boom reversed a general trend of decreased fertility rates that had begun in the nineteenth century. It also reversed a century-long trend in population aging (excluding the years 1911 to 1931) that began in the late nineteenth century.

After 1961, Canada went into a baby bust cycle. Foot and Stoffman (1998) trace the baby bust to two trends: the use of the birth control pill and the increased participation of women in the labour force. During the baby bust, the total fertility rate dropped from 3.84 (children per woman) in 1961 to 2.81 in 1966, a rate below that of 1941. It dropped further to 1.49 in 2000 (Beaujot and McQuillan 1982; 1994; Denton and Spencer 2003; Dumas and Bélanger). Lavoie and Oderkirk (1993) say that Canada's low fertility rate today falls below the level (2.1) needed to replace the population.

Low fertility led to a sharp drop in the number of young people in Canada. Between 1976 and 2002, for example, the population of people 0 to 14 years old decreased from 5.9 million to 5.8 million, which was a decrease, from 26 percent of the population (in 1976) to 18 percent of the population (in 2002) (McKie 1993;

Statistics Canada 1989a; Statistics Canada 2003p). Statistics Canada projects a continuing decline in the proportion of the population made up of younger people in the years ahead. A medium growth projection by Statistics Canada estimates that the younger population (under age 18) will fall to 19 percent of the population in 2041, while the older population will grow to 25 percent of the population (George et al. 1994; Health Canada 2001a; Lindsay 1999; McKie 1993).

This decrease in the birth rate, especially the sharp drop since the 1960s, speeded up the rate of population aging in Canada. Between 1961 and 2002, the population aged 65 and over rose by more than five percentage points, moving from 7.6 to 12.7 percent of Canada's population. The older population will increase sharply again in the early decades of the twenty-first century when the baby boom generation moves into old age. Demographers project an increase of the older population of two and a half times (to over 9 million people) from 1998 to 2041 (Health Canada 2001a; Lindsay 1999). They project that the group aged 85 and over will multiply four times during this same period.

● Exhibit 4.5

HOW TO READ A POPULATION PYRAMID

Population pyramids graphically portray a society's population structure at a certain point in time and allow researchers to compare societies at a glance.

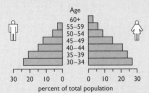

Most pyramids have the same design:

The title: The title contains the name of the country and the year this "snapshot" was taken. The title answers the questions what? where? when?

The centre line: The centre line divides the pyramid by sex—males on the left, females on the right.

The base: The horizontal axis can represent absolute numbers or percentages. The pyramids for Canada (see Exhibit 4.6) use percentages. The centre line marks 0, and each main point on the baseline marks 1 percent of the pop-

ulation (males to the left of the centre, females to the right).

The tiers: Each tier or level of the pyramid stands for an age cohort (conventionally a five-year group). The lowest tier stands for the youngest age cohort (0 to 4 years old), and as one moves up the pyramid the cohorts get older. The top cohort (90+ in the Canadian pyramids) contains everyone over a certain age. (Note that this large top tier takes in a larger age span than the other tiers. It includes people from age 90 to over 100.)

Pyramids allow a viewer to compare age cohorts within a country (e.g., the size of young cohorts can be compared with the size of older cohorts), to compare sex differences within cohorts (by comparing the size of a tier to the right and left of the centre line), and to see unusually large or small cohorts at a glance. Gerontologists also use population pyramids to study population change over time and to compare one country with another.

Summary of Population Aging in Canada

Canada's demographic transition took place from before 1850 to the present in three stages. In the first stage, before 1850, Canada had both high death and high birth rates, and, in Ontario and the Maritimes, a high rate of immigration. These forces kept the average age of Canadians low. In Ontario in the mid-nineteenth century, half the population over the age of 15 was made up of men under the age of 30 (Gagan 1983a). Statistics Canada data puts the **median age** of Canadians in 1901 at 22.7 (compared with a median age of 37.6 in 2001 (Statistics Canada 2002a).

The second stage of the transition began after 1850 as major declines in birth and death rates took place (Kalbach and McVey 1979). This stage differed from the second stage in Europe's demographic transition, where death rates declined and birth rates stayed high for some time before they dropped to complete the transition. In Canada, both birth and death rates dropped (with some important fluctuations in birth rates) until the present.

These changes transformed Canada from a young nation (under 4 percent aged 65 and over) in the late 1800s to an older nation (with about 7 percent of the population aged 65 and over) by 1950.

Today, in the third stage of the transition, Canada has low death rates, low birth rates, and an aging population. As this century progresses, Canada's population pyramid will change from that of a wide-based, triangular shape to a more rectangular one (see Exhibit 4.6).

AGING IN CANADA TODAY

Older people differ by age, sex, marital status, and health. They come from different ethnic backgrounds, have lived through varying historical events, and live in diverse parts of the country. These differences make older people one of the most heterogeneous age groups in Canada.

The Aging of the Older Population

The older population itself has aged in the past century. In 1901, people aged 85 and over made up 5.1 percent of the

● Exhibit 4.6

POPULATION PYRAMIDS BY AGE GROUP AND SEX, CANADA, 1991, 2011, 2031

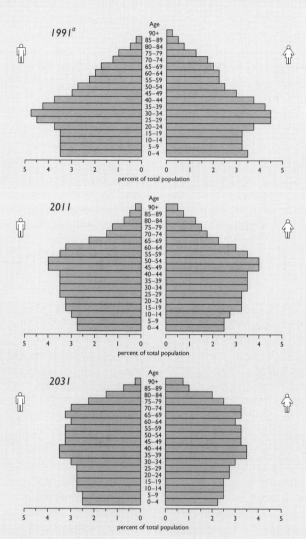

[a] Estimates based on 1991 census; standard projection as of January 17, 2000.

These pyramids show at least three important trends: the dramatic growth in size of the older age cohorts (aged 40+); a continued higher proportion of women compared with men in the oldest cohorts; and the movement of the baby boom cohorts into old age. The 2031 pyramid is top-heavy, with small younger age groups below a large older population.

Sources: Adapted in part from M.V. George et al., 1994, *Population Projections for Canada, Provinces and Territories, 1993–2016,* Cat. No. 91-520, Ottawa: Ministry of Industry Trade and Commerce; and F.T. Denton, C.H. Feaver, and B.G. Spencer, 2000, *Projections of the Population and Labour Force to 2046*, SEDAP Research Paper No. 15, Hamilton: McMaster University. Reprinted with permission from Statistics Canada.

older population; by 2000, they made up 10.7 percent of the older population (Statistics Canada 2002a; United Nations 2002). The age 85-and-over group will more than double in size between 1998 and 2016 and will grow almost fourfold by 2041, when it will constitute 17.6 percent of the older population (Health Canada 2001b; Lindsay 1999). Women in 2000 made up 70 percent of the population over age 85 (United Nations 2002). Longer life expectancy and larger numbers of people entering this age group account for this growth. Stone and Frenken (1988, 35) say that this trend will lead to "a veritable population explosion among seniors of advanced age."

An Ontario White Paper says that "the increase in the number of elderly citizens, and particularly the older elderly, is creating a new generation of issues" (cited in Stone and Frenken 1988, 35). These issues will influence social policy and the use of resources in the future. For example, the group aged 85 and over, compared with people aged 65 to 74, shows higher rates for institutionalization, disability, and poor health. Health Canada's Division of Aging and Seniors says that "in 1996, for example, seniors aged 85 and over made up almost half (46%) of all seniors in health-related institutions, whereas they represented only about 10% of the total senior population" (Health Canada 2001b). They also show a greater need for daily support. This group will need more institutional support, medical care, household maintenance, and community health care support in the future (Conference of Deputy Ministers of Health 1999).

At the same time that the oldest cohorts grow in size, the younger cohorts aged 65 and over will also get larger. Projections show more than a doubling in the population aged 65 to 74 between 1998 and 2041 (Lindsay 1999). This large number of older Canadians will make new demands on society. The younger elderly will change retirement patterns by retiring early or by staying at work past age 65. This group will want more recreational and educational opportunities. Services such as job bureaus, schools, and counselling programs will also be needed to serve these people.

Programs for all types of older people will cost taxpayers more money. In 2002–02, for example, Canada spent $26.6 billion on its income security system (compared with $11 billion in 1984) (Human Resources Development Canada 2003a). More of this money went to older people than to any other age group. The single largest amount of this money went to the **Old Age Security** program (including the **Guaranteed Income Supplement** and the **Allowance**). If the proportion of older people more than doubles in the next 50 years as expected, will the public be willing to pay out even more

of the country's income for older people? Or will the costs lead to resentment and a crisis in Canadian society? We will discuss these issues in more detail later in this chapter under the topic of dependency ratios.

Ethnicity

In 1996, immigrants made up 27 percent of the older population. But immigrants made up only 17 percent of the overall Canadian population in that year. Immigrants made up a larger percentage of the older population than of any other age group. Three-quarters of these immigrant seniors moved to Canada before 1970. Most moved to Canada to join their families. This trend of family reunification continues today.

Most older immigrants (71 percent) have come from Europe. Another large group (16 percent) of older immigrants have come from Asia. About 6 percent of older immigrants have come from the United States. Smaller groups (around 2 percent of the older immigrant population) have come from Africa, Central and South America, and the Caribbean. By contrast, younger immigrants tend to come from Asia, Africa, the Caribbean, and Central and South America (Lindsay 1999). As these younger people age, they will create greater diversity among the older population (Canadian Council on Social Development 1999).

About 1.3 million people in Canada in 2001 identified themselves as Aboriginal. This group has a relatively young population (Statistics Canada 2003a). They have a median age of 24.7 compared to a non-Aboriginal median age of 37.7. The Aboriginal group has about 40 000 seniors. The Aboriginal senior population grew by 40 percent between 1996 and 2001 (about four times the rate of growth of the non-Aboriginal older population). Still, due to high fertility rates and the large number of younger Aboriginal people, seniors make up only about 4.1 percent of the Aboriginal population. This group faces unique challenges due to high rates of chronic illness, such as diabetes and high blood pressure, in later life.

Many older immigrants today, who learned a language other than English in their native countries, continue to use this language at home. For example, about 4 percent of older people know neither English nor French. And about 11 percent of older people speak only a non-official language at home (Lindsay 1999). Having now reached old age, these immigrants make the older population today an ethnically diverse group.

Gerber (1983) reports that both the size of an ethnic group and the proportion of older people in the group determine the institutional supports that older people can expect from their group. A large group with a mod-

Exhibit 4.7

CANADIAN SNOWBIRDS: ARE THEY A GREY PERIL?

Some older Canadians stay in place, others move within Canada. But some choose a third option. They migrate south for the winter. These "snowbirds" settle in Florida, Arizona, Texas, and other southern states. Most of them stay in the United States for less than six months of the year because the Canadian health system requires at least six months' residence in Canada. These seniors move to their winter homes when the snow falls and return to Canada again in the spring.

Longino (1988b) found that Florida attracts more older Canadians (60+) than any other non-border state. He also reports that many Floridians along with other Sunbelt natives have a "gray peril mentality" (Longino 1988a). They fear that older seasonal migrants will place a burden on local social and health care services.

To test this idea, Longino and a group of Canadian and U.S. researchers conducted a survey of Canadian seasonal migrants in Florida. They asked about Canadians' background, health, social life, and migration patterns. This survey included the responses of 2731 (mostly English-speaking) Canadians who lived in Florida in 1986 (Tucker and Marshall 1988; Tucker et al. 1988). The people who answered the survey had a median age of 69.2 years, more than half (57 percent) were between 65 and 74 years old, and about a fifth (21 percent) were aged 75 or older. Nearly all of them (89.6 percent) were married. More than half had graduated from high school, and most reported former middle- to upper-middle-class occupations (Tucker and Marshall 1988). Most of them had children, siblings, or friends who lived in Florida (Longino et al. 1991). And most of them (80 percent) still owned homes in Canada (Tucker et al. 1992).

Tucker et al. (1988) reviewed the health status of these people. More than 80 percent of them reported excellent or good health (see also Martin et al. 1992). Only about 10 percent of any age and gender group reported any sick days. Less than 10 percent of the sample had recently consulted a family doctor or other health professional. And few of these people used any health or social services in Florida.

Most of the snowbirds in this study reported good physical and psychological health, good social supports, and high life satisfaction (Mullins et al. 1989). A third of them said that they had better health when they visited Florida. One respondent said, "My wife finds that her bronchitis is ... considerably better in Florida, as a result of the sun and warmth" (Tucker et al. 1988, 227).

This study shows that Canadian seasonal migrants make few demands on Florida's health care or social service system. The large majority of these people live healthy, active lives. Marshall and Tucker (1990) reported that Canadian snowbirds at that time spent about $1200 per month (in U.S. dollars) during their typical five-month stay. They also create demands for housing, goods, and services. Most of them (89 percent) moved to Florida for the climate or for the lifestyle (67 percent). A later study of French Canadian snowbirds in Florida suggests that they too use few local health care services. French Canadians tended to be younger as a group and to have a larger family network to rely on (Tucker et al. 1992). Longino (1988a, 451) says that "the search for [an] ... impact on specialized services for the aging by seasonal migrants has turned up disappointingly little evidence for the gray peril."

erate proportion of its population aged 65 and over can provide a more complete community life for its elderly. A small group with a high proportion of older people may be able to offer little support. Also, the concentration of the group (how close to one another members live), their location (urban or rural), the proportion of old-old to young-old, family size, and cultural values all affect the number of supports older people can draw on. People of Chinese, Greek, and Italian backgrounds, for example, tend to have large families, live in cities, and live with their children (Brotman 1998). Older members

of these groups, compared to members of smaller groups, have more access to community resources and family support in old age.

This brief look at ethnicity and aging shows that ethnic groups vary in their size, their location, their proportion of older people, and their institutional completeness, a term that refers to the amount of community support they offer their older members. For this reason, Driedger and Chappell (1987, 75) say that "ethnicity can have significant implications for care and supportiveness in old age," and so policies for older people from different types of groups (large, small; rural, urban) will have to vary. Driedger and Chappell advise planners and policy-makers to take ethnicity into account, along with socio-economic status and physical mobility, when designing programs for older people. (See Chapter 7 for a more detailed discussion of ethnicity and aging.)

Geographic Mobility

Older people follow internal migration patterns similar to those of younger people, but they are less mobile than the non-aged (Lindsay 1999). In 1996, for example, 5 percent of older people made a residential move. But 20 percent of people aged 25 to 44 moved in that year. The

---

● **Exhibit 4.8**

ENJOYING THE GOOD LIFE

Older Canadians who move after retirement often choose to live on the West Coast. The warm weather and the large number of older people with similar interests make this a good retirement spot. The cases described below fit the type of migration that Litwak and Longino (1987) call "amenity migration." This often begins with a couple vacationing in a spot for a number of years. The couple then decides to settle there after retirement. In this excerpt from a 1992 Maclean's *magazine article, reporter James Deacon describes the amenities and social life that attracted the Perrigos and their neighbours to Qualicum Beach, British Columbia.*

A brilliantly sunny morning in late July greeted Ladies' Day at the Qualicum Beach Memorial Golf Club. As the first groups finished their rounds, they gathered in the clubhouse to add up their scores. Nearly all of the women were in their 60s, and most had moved to the Vancouver Island community from somewhere else in Canada. One of the golfers, Beth Perrigo, 64, said that she first visited Qualicum Beach 13 years ago, while vacationing from Ottawa with her husband Howard and their two children. Perrigo said that she was strongly attracted by the town, which overlooks the Strait of Georgia 40 km north of Nanaimo. "We bought a lot and just sat on it," she says. In 1989, Howard Perrigo retired from his job with the federal government. The couple had already decided that they did not want to stay in Ottawa ("My husband got tired of shovelling snow.") The Perrigos considered wintering in Florida, but in the end chose Qualicum Beach, attracted by the mild climate and relaxed lifestyle that has made the province the most popular retirement region in the country.

According to federal census figures, during the 12-month period to June, 1991, almost 4,600 new arrivals from elsewhere in Canada were over 65. The temperate West Coast climate has traditionally attracted older Canadians to such cities as Vancouver and Victoria. Now, provincial officials say that migrating senior citizens have made smaller communities on the east coast of Vancouver Island, including Nanaimo, Qualicum Beach, Parksville and Comox, into some of the province's most popular retirement areas. Other pensioners, including many Albertans, favor communities in the mainland's south-central Okanagan Valley....

As in many retirement communities, Qualicum Beach's municipally owned golf course is a busy social centre. Sitting with Perrigo at a table overlooking the golf course and the strait beyond, Wilma Bleakley, 66, and Gladys Morton, 70, discussed the area's mild climate as being one of the main attractions for senior citizens. "There may be two weeks when we can't play golf," said Morton, who moved to Qualicum Beach from the central B.C. mining town of Hendrix Lake. "But that's about it."

Patricia and Conrad Nadeau lived in an ocean-view home in Lions Bay, 30 minutes northwest of Vancouver, but were lured to the Island by its weather and the abundance of recreational opportunities. Conrad Nadeau, a semi-retired insurance executive, and Patricia, a keen gardener, bought a two-bedroom condominium alongside Morningstar Golf Course, six km east of Qualicum Beach, and moved in eight months ago. Surveying her flourishing garden, which backs onto the golf course, Patricia Nadeau said: "I don't think we could do any better than this." Clearly, that judgment is shared by the thousands of retirement-aged Canadians who have responded to the attractions of British Columbia.

Source: J. Deacon, "Enjoying the Good Life," Maclean's, August 24, 1992, 50. Reprinted with permission of Maclean's magazine.

● Exhibit 4.9

MAP OF CANADA

Population Aged 65 and Over, by Province, 1998

Province	000s	% of total provincial population
Newfoundland	62.0	11.4
Prince Edward Island	17.7	13.0
Nova Scotia	123.3	13.2
New Brunswick	97.1	12.9
Quebec	912.3	12.4
Ontario	1417.9	12.4
Manitoba	154.8	13.6
Saskatchewan	149.2	14.6
Alberta	288.4	9.9
British Columbia	509.2	12.7

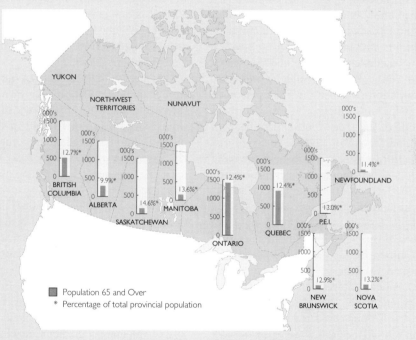

■ Population 65 and Over
* Percentage of total provincial population

This map shows the distribution of older people throughout Canada. It shows the number and proportion of older people in each province. Note that Ontario and Quebec have the largest number of older people, but a relatively small proportion of older people. Saskatchewan and Manitoba have the largest proportions of older people in their populations. The large proportion of older people in some provinces points to smaller numbers of young people in those provinces. British Columbia, with the third highest number of older people, is a prime migration spot for retirees. But the large number of young people (and young in-migrants) in that province keeps the proportion of older people relatively low.

Source: Adapted from Colin Lindsay, 1999, *A Portrait of Seniors in Canada*, Table 1.3, p. 23. Cat. No. 89-519-XPE. Ottawa: Minister of Industry.

majority of older movers move within their communities. The 1995 General Social Survey found that three-quarters of Canadians aged 60 and over who moved in the previous five years moved no further than 50 kilometres. Many moved no more than 10 kilometres. Only 10 percent of older movers moved more than 200 kilometres. Many older movers simply moved from a larger home to an apartment in their community (Che-Alford and Stevenson 1998). Only a small percentage of older people move between provinces, so interprovincial moves have only a small impact on provincial older populations. British Columbia, for example, received 23 percent of all interprovincial older movers in 2001, but older in-migrants represent only a small percentage of older people in the province (Statistics Canada 2001e).

Litwak and Longino (1987) describe three stages of later life when people may choose to move. The first is the retirement stage, when freedom from the need to live near work allows people to move to a more pleasant climate and to have a more relaxed lifestyle. Some of these people move out of the country to the U.S. sunbelt (see Exhibit 4.7). Others move to Canadian retirement sites like Niagara-on-the-Lake and Victoria (see Exhibit 4.8). People in good health, with grown children, and with a good income in later life tend to make lifestyle-related moves (Hayward 2001). In the second, or disability stage, physical limitation may lead the older person to move closer to children or others who can give them help. The likelihood of this type of move increases with age (Che-Alford and Stevenson 1998). The severe disability stage is the third phase, and it requires the older person to move to a nursing home or other institution.

Northcott (1988) reports a peak in migration among older age groups around retirement age (60 to 69 years). This corresponds to Litwak and Longino's retirement stage. Many of these people moved within their communities. But some moved out of their locality, and they most often relocated to improve their quality of life (Northcott 1988). Alberta showed the greatest rates of gain in older migrants in 1997–98, followed by Ontario and New Brunswick. During this same period, Quebec and Saskatchewan showed the greatest net losses of older people due to migration (Health Canada 1999d; Lindsay 1999). British Columbia, the Northwest Territories, the Yukon, Saskatchewan, Manitoba, Nova Scotia, P.E.I., and Newfoundland also showed losses during this period (Health Canada 1999d; Lindsay 1999). New Brunswick showed a small net gain in older migrants. Older people, who moved away in their middle years to find work, may migrate back in their retirement (Moore and Pacey 2003).

Migration patterns show a multidirectional flow. But some trends do appear. Litwak and Longino's (1987)

second and third stages of migration help explain these trends. Older people most often say that they moved to buy a new home, to change the size of their home, or to move to a less expensive home, or to move to a home with special features (Che-Alford and Stevenson 1998; Lindsay 1997). Older people also say that they move to be near family or to care for a family member. People move to get more support as they age (Moore, Rosenberg, and McGuinness 1997). Older people tend to move from farms to towns or cities, and most older movers relocate within their local area. Provinces, towns, and neighbourhoods with increased numbers of older people will face new challenges in the future.

Increased Numbers and Proportions of Older Women

The death rates for older women have decreased faster than they have for older men through most of this century. In 1931, the life expectancy for a 65-year-old woman was 13.7 years; in 1961, it was 16.1 years; and for 2005, it is estimated to be 20.3 years (for a 65-year-old man it was only 13.0 years in 1931, 13.6 years in 1961, and estimated at 16.5 years in 2005) (Lindsay 1999; United Nations 2003).

As a result of these changes, the proportion of older women in the population has grown. At the beginning of the twentieth century, there were 105 men for every 100 women aged 65 and over, and in the mid-1950s older men still outnumbered older women. But by the 1960s the pattern reversed itself. By 2000, there were 74.9 men for every 100 women aged 65 and over. Projections show that men will begin to catch up to women in the future. Projections for 2050 show that the ratio of men to women aged 65 and over will increase to 78.6 men per 100 women. In that year, women will make up 56 percent of all people aged 65 and over (United Nations 2002). For the age group 85 and over, the ratio of men to women will decrease until 2011 (from 44 in 1991 to 39 in 2011). It will then rise to 42 in 2031 (Norland 1994).

This means that policies and programs for older people will have a greater impact on women than on men. Women will live longer and so will be affected by programs for older people for more years. This is especially true of health care, housing, and income support programs. We will study these programs in detail in the chapters ahead. For now, we will look at the overall impact of population aging on Canada's economy.

THE IMPACT OF POPULATION AGING

The Dependency Ratio and the Cost of an Aging Population

Concern about the increasing numbers of older people typically pits the old against the young. An editorial in the *Calgary Herald*, for example, told its readers to prepare for "an astonishing increase in the tax burden" due to an aging society (cited in Denton and Spencer 1999, 3). Siegel (1994, cited in Denton and Spencer 1999, 3) refers to the "colossal challenges of our rapidly aging society." An editorial in *The Globe and Mail* (1993) calls the baby boom generation "a massive unfunded liability." "It's probable," the editorial goes on to say, "that those in the baby boom's wake will rebel at paying ... to subsidize the retirement of a generation that may well be better off than they are."

These sources assume a high dependence of older people on the young, and they suggest that the young will rebel against or resent the burden of a large older population. Gee and Gutman (2000) say that this fear has little basis in the demographic fact. They call this extreme view "**apocalyptic demography**." And they say that it distorts the likely effects of population aging.

Gerontologists use a figure called the **overall dependency ratio** to gauge the burden that the old and the young place on people in middle age. Experts arrive at this ratio by adding the number of people under age 20 to the number of people aged 65 and over. They then compare this figure to the population aged 20 to 64:

$$\frac{\text{(Population aged 0 to 19)} + \text{(Population aged 65+)}}{\text{Population aged 20 to 64}}$$

(Some writers use ages 0 to 14 or 0 to 17 as the age span for the younger group.)

Denton, Feaver, and Spencer (1998) used the dependency ratio to look at dependency in Canada. They found that while the ratio of people aged 65 and over to those aged 20 to 64 will more than double from 1996 to 2041, the proportion of young people will decline. When they combined these projected changes in the young and old populations, they found that this led to "a somewhat lower overall dependency ratio for the first two decades of the new century compared to 1996. Then the overall dependency ratio will increase." In spite of this increase, in 2041 (when the baby boom will have created large increases in the over-65 population) the overall dependency ratio may not be much higher than in 1971 (Denton, Feaver, and Spencer 1998; Denton and Spencer 1999). Denton, Feaver, and Spencer (1998,

103–104) conclude that "the overall dependency ratio (which declined rapidly between 1961 and 1991) will rise, but will still be low by historical standards."

Exhibit 4.10 shows dependency projections based on moderate demographic change. This box introduces the concept of the elderly and youth dependency ratios. The **elderly dependency ratio** refers to the number of people aged 65 and over divided by the population aged 20 to 64. The **youth dependency ratio** refers to the number of people aged 0 to 19 divided by the population aged 20 to 64. These ratios show how these two subgroups contribute to the total dependency ratio.

Denton, Feaver, and Spencer (1986, 86) say that figures such as these should reassure "those who are concerned about the possible inability of the economy to support its dependent population, young and old, in the decades ahead." But not everyone agrees with this conclusion. The Ontario Ministry of Treasury and Economics says that the **crude dependency rates**, which are based solely on the number of people in each group, presented here tell only part of the story. These rates tell us little about the economic burden of an older population (Stone and Fletcher 1980).

Scarth (2003), for example, says that it costs more to serve an older population because health care for the old costs more than education for the young. Some studies (Robson, cited in Scarth 2003) say that Canada may need a 3 percent increase in its gross domestic product (GDP) to finance social service programs in the future.

Denton and Spencer (1995; 1997; 1999), in a series of studies, also project large increases in government expenditures in the future as Canada ages. They predict a steady increase in the total cost of health care, education, and social security between 1986 and 2041. Population aging accounts for most of this increase. They report, for example, that by 2011 social security costs (for the old) will surpass education costs (for the young) as a percent of the GDP. Social security costs will triple between 1986 and 2041, while education costs will increase by about 10 percent. Likewise, health care costs will more than double between 1986 and 2041.

A report by the Canadian Council on Social Development (CSSD) (1999) says that 7 percent of total public health costs went to care for children under age 15 in the early 1990s. But 48 percent of total public health costs went to care for people aged 65 and over. The largest share of health spending went to older people, and only their share grew between 1980–81 and 1994–95. Likewise, the amount spent on the Old Age Security and other income security programs increased nearly 50 percent during this period. And Canada Pension Plan payments increased nearly 300 percent during this time. The CCSD

● **Exhibit 4.10**

DEPENDENCY RATES FOR CANADA, SELECTED YEARS FROM 1921 TO 2036

Year	Elderly Dependency (65+/20–64)	Youth Dependency (0–19/20–64)	Overall Dependency
1921	.09	.84	.94
1941	.12	.67	.79
1961	.15	.83	.98
1981	.16	.54	.71
2001	.21	.41	.62
2011	.23	.37	.60
2031	.43	.37	.80
2041	.46	.36	.82

These figures show a fairly steady increase in the elderly dependency ratio over the years shown here. They also show a fairly steady decrease in the youth dependency ratio (except for the sudden jump during the baby boom years around 1961). The overall dependency decreases through the early years of the twenty-first century. It then increases only to the 1941 level in the years after 2031. These figures suggest that an older population will not create an undue burden on Canadian society.

Note: Projections for the years from 1921 to 1961 assume modest increases in life expectancy of 0.8 years per five-year period, a total fertility rate of 1.8, and immigration of 250 000 gradually decreasing to 200 000 by 2011. Projections from 1981 onward assume a life expectancy increase of 6.5 years for men and 5.1 years for women, a fertility rate of 1.66, and an immigration rate of 200 000 per year.

Source: B. Desjardins, 1993, *Population Ageing and the Elderly,* Cat. No. 91-533E, Ottawa: Minister of Industry, Science and Technology. Reprinted with permission from Statistics Canada. Recent data adapted from F.T. Denton, C.H. Feaver, and B.G. Spencer, 1998, "The Future Population of Canada, Its Age Distribution, and Dependency Relations," *Canadian Journal on Aging* 17(1): 83–109. Reprinted with permission.

reports that spending on older people between 1980–81 and 1994–95 increased more rapidly than did their proportion in the population.

Burke (1991) says that in the years between 1980 and 2040, pension costs will rise more than any other expense, and he projects a 204 percent increase over this time. If this comes to pass, pensions will "account for 38% of social spending, up from just 24% in 1980" (7). At the same time, health care costs will increase by 118 percent and account for 33 percent of social spending (compared with 29 percent in 1980). These trends would lead to an increase in social spending of 87 percent in Canada, which is high compared with predictions of 65 percent for the United States and 40 percent for Japan. It seems as if the apocalyptic demographers have a point when they warn about the crisis due to population aging.

Evans and his colleagues (2001, 162), in an article entitled "Apocalypse No," challenge the prediction of economic crisis. They agree that "'apocalypse' cannot be definitively ruled out." But they say that the data so far do not support the link between population aging and runaway health care costs.

Evans and his colleagues (2001) reviewed economic data from the British Columbia health care system. They studied acute hospital use, physicians' services, and drug use. They looked at the impact of population aging on the costs of these services. They found that, in spite of rising numbers of older people in British Columbia, the per capita use rate of hospitals declined from 1969 to the late 1990s. They found that in-patient days per capita decreased because of changes in health care practices over the 30-year period. Hospitals tended to send people home sooner and they increased same-day surgical care. Evans and his colleagues go on to show that projections for the age 65 population in 1969 should have led to "truly hair-raising" costs—triple the 1969 cost by the end of the twentieth century and another doubling for the next 25 years (169). In reality, the researchers show, acute care hospital use rates have decreased by half for the 65-and-over population since 1969. This study shows the danger of projecting costs based on population growth figures alone.

A similar study of physician services and pharmaceutical use did reveal an increase in per capita costs. But the researchers show that increases in the number of physicians as well as the rising cost of drugs accounts for most of this change. For example, the total expenditure on drugs in British Columbia increased more than threefold between 1985 and 1999—an annual increase of 9 percent. Forces other than population aging, like the increased cost of new and expensive drugs, account for most of the rise in drug expenditures.

Evans and his colleagues (2001, 181) conclude that population aging plays only a small role in the increase in overall health care costs and an "almost undetectable" role in the rising cost of drugs. Other forces, such as rising drug prices, more expensive drugs, and the number of doctors, play a larger role in explaining increased costs. The researchers say that "the evidence from British Columbia is quite clear.... Changes in the age structure of the overall population have not in the past been major contributors to trends in the per capita utilization of these three categories of health care services, and they will not be in the future" (176).

Researchers may disagree about the specific impact of an aging population on health and income resources. But nearly all of them agree that more health care and retirement income resources will go to serve older people and that this will cost more money. This shift in resources to the older population will force Canadians to make some hard choices. Burke (1991, 8), for example, says that "Canadians will most likely have to choose between increasing tax rates and social security contributions or lower levels of social benefits." The next 50 years will see increased debate over the allocation of health and income resources.

These reports on the future look gloomy. But dependency ratios tell only part of the story (Denton, Feaver, and Spencer 1998). Myles and Boyd (1982, 259) say that "alarmist exercises in futurology ... have pro-

duced more oversight than insight" when it comes to the issue of dependency in the future. Even small changes in Canada's economy and social norms, for example, could lead to large decreases in the effective dependency rate (Chen 1987). The **effective dependency rate** is based on the real differences in the costs for older and younger age groups. Denton, Feaver, and Spencer (1986, 90) say that "non-demographic forces [e.g., changes in the demand for services, increases in per capita worker output, or changes in the federal government's commitment to fund programs] could easily be more important quantitatively than demographic ones in their effects on government expenditures."

Most projections, for example, assume a traditional retirement age of 65 (when people become entitled to Old Age Security payments). But government policy could change and this age could be raised. Denton and Spencer (2002, 354) say that this would "both reduce pension costs and increase the ability of the economy to meet those costs." Northcott (1992, 15) says that society could deal with "the social 'problem' of population aging" by defining it away.

Also, dependency ratios ignore the fact that people save in one part of their lives and use these savings later on (Denton and Spencer 2000). Today, many middle-aged workers have private pension plans and savings. In the future, compared to pensioners today, they may rely less on government pension supplements when they reach old age. More flexible retirement plans will allow some people to work full- or part-time after age 65. The Canada Pension Plan has changed its rules to make both early and late retirement more attractive. All these trends will change current dependency patterns and alter future projections (Chen 1987).

A stronger economy would also ease the dependency burden. Even a small improvement in the income of middle-aged people, compared with costs for services to the old, would significantly decrease the effective dependency rate. The Ontario Ministry of Treasury and Economics (1979) found that if income for working people increased even 1 percent faster than dependency costs, the effective dependency rates would be less than in 1976. In a strong economy, higher costs for services to the elderly may not create a burden for the middle-aged.

Weller and Bouvier (1981) point to one of the greatest weaknesses of using dependency rates to project into the future. They say that dependency rates focus too narrowly on the costs of having more older people in society. They remind us that an older population will also bring benefits, such as a lower crime rate and increased concern for fitness, diet, and disease prevention. These trends have already begun. Larger numbers of older people may also improve the economy. They will likely spend their savings to consume the services of travel agencies, restaurants, and professionals (McDaniel 1986). These trends may reduce some waste of social resources and create a higher quality of life for people of all ages.

McDaniel (1986) says that dependency ratios lead to **demographic determinism**. Demographic determinism assumes that population dynamics determine the future of social relations and social institutions. McDaniel believes that social policies have the greatest effect on the dependence of older people (see also Denton and Spencer 2000). Cheal (2000) agrees and proposes ongoing changes in social policies to meet the needs of an aging society. Retirement policies today, for example, encourage retirement at age 65. Ironically, countries with the highest elderly dependency ratios encourage older people to leave the workforce early. They appear to encourage and may even demand economic dependency by the older population. Likewise, patients rarely choose the treatment for their illness. The cost of health care treatment depends on choices doctors make about treatment, on the cost of drugs, and on policies that support home care options.

Demographers need to study the connections between demographic facts, political realities, and social change. How much choice do countries have in how they will respond to demographic change? What determines the choices a country makes? Are there models of preferred adaptation to an aging population? Countries such as Sweden and Norway could serve as models for Canadian policy. Already, more than 15 percent of the populations of these countries are over age 65, and they

have not faced crises as a result. Progressive programs have been put in place to serve older people, and citizens pay more in taxes to support them. These countries show that the transition to an older society can come about without social conflict and distress (Myles 1982).

CONCLUSION

Canadian society has its own history, its own mix of ethnicity, age/sex ratios, economic institutions, and values. Canada also faces its own demographic issues. The baby boom generation, for example, has got used to society's meeting its needs (for housing, child care, etc.). Canadians now expect to receive a public pension and they expect free health care in old age. Canadian discussions of societal aging often revolve around the costs of these two systems (Venne 2001). Will this generation demand an unreasonable level of social support as it ages? Or will the baby boomers develop a broader view of their relationship to society and moderate their expectations?

Canada will face unknown political, economic, and social challenges in the years ahead and will have to discover its own responses to population aging (Denton and Spencer 2003). Friedland and Summer (1999, 5) say that "society can and will adjust [to an aging population] as it has done before. But adjustment will be easier if the challenges are addressed in a rational manner today." Preparation for the future will take planning, thought, and creative social action, and all of us will play a part in this societal transformation.

Summary

1. Canada has a younger population than most of the other developed nations. It had 13 percent of the population aged 65 and over in 2001. Demographers project that this population will more than double by 2041 and will equal almost 23 percent of the total population.

2. Canada went through a demographic transition between 1850 and 1950. During this time, immigration increased, the death rate decreased, and, most important, the birth rate decreased. Between 1850 and 1950, the older population grew from about 4 percent of the population to almost 8 percent.

3. Canada today has a diverse older population. Older people differ by ethnicity, sex, income, education, and marital status. They also differ by age. Longer life expectancy in old age has given rise to a wide range of age groups within the older population. Large increases in the very old population will place new demands on health care and social service resources.

4. Ethnic groups vary in their size, location, proportion of older people, and the amount of community support they offer older people. Researchers and policymakers will have to take ethnicity, socioeconomic status, and physical mobility into account when designing programs for older people.

5. The growth of the older population (and the decrease in the younger population) has led some people to predict an economic crisis due to the large numbers of dependent older people. Gerontologists measure the dependence of young and old people on middle-aged people and call this measure the overall dependency ratio (or rate).

6. Experts look at dependency rates to project the future costs of an aging society. But the effect of future dependency rates will depend on a number of social conditions. A weak economy, low birth rates, low immigration rates, and a rise in costs of services for the old (compared with per capita income for the middle-aged) will increase the burden on middle-aged people. A strong economy, higher birth rates, more immigration, and a rise in per capita income for middle-aged people (compared with costs in services for the old) will mean less burden on middle-aged workers. Changes in social values and retirement ages, as well as better preparation for old age by middle-aged people today, could also decrease the dependence of older people on the young.

7. Dependency rates focus on the costs of an aging society. But an aging society may have a lower crime rate, a lower accident rate, and more concern for lifelong health and fitness. These changes would decrease the waste of social and economic resources and improve the quality of life in Canada.

8. Canada can grow old without upheaval and conflict; most of the developed nations have done so. But the transition to an aging society will take planning, thought, and creative social action.

Study Questions

1. List the three demographic forces that caused Canada's population to age from the 1850s to the present. How did each force affect societal aging?

2. What developments helped increase the life expectancy of men and women in Canada during the past century?

3. What two factors account for the greatest changes in Canada's population from 1951 to the present? How did these factors affect Canada's population?

4. State three ways that an increase in the number of older people affects public policy.

5. How does ethnicity affect the care and support of older people?

6. Where in Canada do older people tend to live? Why?

7. Describe the changes that brought about the growth of the large older female population today. What implications does this increase have for older women? For social policy?

8. What do gerontologists mean by the "overall dependency ratio"? How do gerontologists calculate this ratio? How might a higher percentage of older people affect the economy in the future?

9. What steps can we take to help reduce the potential economic costs of an older population in the future?

Key Terms

age-specific birth rate the number of births in a given age group per 1000 women in that age group. (64)

Allowance an income security program for spouses of pensioners who receive only Old Age Security income. (68)

apocalyptic demography the use of demographic facts (such as the aging of the population) to project the high cost of an aging population to predict that population aging will lead to economic and social crisis. (73)

baby boom the sharp rise in the fertility rate in Canada from about 1946 to the early 1960s (precise dates vary). (63)

baby bust the sharp drop in the fertility rate from the mid-1960s on. (63)

birth rate the number of births per 1000 women in a population. (62)

crude dependency rates rates based solely on the numbers of people in each age group. (73)

death rate the number of deaths per 1000 people in a population. (62)

demographic determinism the assumption that population dynamics determine the future of social relations and social institutions (e.g., the amount of dependency of the old on the young). (76)

effective dependency rate the rate based on differences between the costs for older and for younger age groups. (75)

elderly dependency ratio the number of people aged 65 and over divided by the population aged 20 to 64. (73)

fertility rate "the average number of children that would be born alive to a woman during her lifetime if she were to pass through all her childbearing years conforming to the age-specific fertility rates of a given year" (Beaujot and McQuillan 1982, 220–21). (63)

Guaranteed Income Supplement an income security program for the poorest older people. (68)

infant mortality rate the death rate of children less than a year old. (62)

median age half the population is older and half is younger than the median age. (66)

Old Age Security Canada's basic retirement income program, which supplements the income of nearly all of the country's older people. (68)

overall dependency ratio (or rate) the combined total number of people under age 19 and people aged 65 and over to the number of people aged 20 to 64. (73)

youth dependency ratio the number of people aged 0 to 19 divided by the population aged 20 to 64. (73)

Selected Readings

Foot, David K., and Daniel Stoffman. *Boom, Bust, and Echo 2000: Profiting from the Demographic Shift in the New Millennium*. Toronto: Macfarlane Walter & Ross, 1998.

An entertaining, informative, and readable study of how demography affects Canadian society. The authors begin with an overview of demographic changes in the later years of the twentieth century. They then look at how these changes affect housing, health, the economy, recreation, and leisure, and use demographic facts to predict future social change.

Gee, E.M., and G.M. Gutman, eds. *The Overselling of Population Aging: Apocalyptic Demography, Intergenerational Challenges, and Social Policy*. Don Mills, ON: Oxford University Press, 2000.

This collection of articles by Canadian researchers challenges the "alarmist" view of population aging. Chapters focus on topics such as aging families, hospital usage by older Canadians, intergenerational care-giving, retirement income, social policy, adult children returning home, and economics and women's pensions. This book demonstrates that in many ways older Canadians give more to the younger generations than they receive. It also argues that contrary to "much of the thinking on the subject that has gotten into the public consciousness ... population aging should never be perceived as a 'crisis.'"

Owram, Doug. *Born at the Right Time: A History of the Baby-Boom Generation.* Toronto: University of Toronto Press, 1996.

A richly documented history of the baby boom generation. The author shows how this generation has shaped Canadian society from the early 1940s to the present. He reports on the growth of suburbs, the protests of the 1960s, and the rise of the youth culture. This book will give insight into how the baby boomers may behave as seniors. It will also help younger people to understand the life experiences of this massive soon-to-be-senior generation.

Statistics Canada. *Canadian Social Trends.* Cat. No. 11-008E. Ottawa: Minister of Supply and Services, Annual.

Statistics Canada publishes this journal four times a year. Articles report on data from recent government studies in a readable magazine format and are accompanied by charts and graphs that help to interpret the statistics. Each issue contains useful and up-to-date information on topics such as demography, living arrangements, and aging in Canada. A good resource for professionals and students of aging.

Part Three

Maturational Change

Chapter Five

Personal Health and Illness

Photo © Paul Barton/CORBIS/MAGMA

INTRODUCTION

Jeanne Calment of Provence, France, died in 1997 at age 122 and 5 months. Before her death she was the oldest person in the world and the longest-lived person ever. To celebrate her 121st birthday, Mme. Calment released a four-song CD. The songs mixed rap and techno music with stories from her life (for example, she met Vincent Van Gogh in her childhood). Money she earned from the CD went to pay for a minibus for her nursing home (Mitchell 1996). When Mme. Calment died, Marie-Louise Meilleur, a French Canadian, became the oldest person in the world. Mme. Meilleur died in 1998, in a nursing home in Corbeil, Ontario. She was 117 years and 7 months old. At the time of her death, her 85-year-old son lived in the same nursing home.

How did these women live so long? For one thing, Mme. Calment stayed active throughout her life. She lived on her own in a second-floor apartment until age 110 and she rode a bicycle until age 100 (Glass 1995). Other centenarians also attribute their long life to an active lifestyle. Some say they enjoy regular sex, never worry, or drink a shot of whisky before bed. Mme. Meilleur was reported to be a vegetarian. One 100-year-old man claimed that he lived so long because he ate a pound of peanuts a day.

Scientific research supports some of these methods for longer life. Moderate drinkers live longer than teetotallers (although it is unclear why); a simple diet low in fat, salt, and sugar can decrease disease; and exercise leads to good health and possibly a longer life (Chernoff 2002). But even with good habits, a good diet, and a good environment, physiological aging takes place. These changes take place as part of normal aging. Older people on the covers of health and nutrition magazines beam good health, but they often have white hair, brown spots on their skin, and wrinkles, like older people all over the world.

Gerontologists distinguish between the **maximum life span** (the maximum number of years a member of a species can live) and **life expectancy** (the number of years at birth an average member of a population can expect to live). Scientists think that the maximum human life span of somewhere between 110 and 125 years has stayed the same for the past 100 000 years. Human life expectancy at birth, on the other hand, has increased in the past 2000 years from an average of 22 years in ancient Rome to around 75 or 80 years today (Clarfield 2002). Women have gained more in life expectancy than men. A girl born today can expect to outlive her male peers by five to six years. Technology and biomedical science continue to extend life expectancy, and if this trend continues, more and more people will live close to the maximum human life span. This means that more people will live to old age and more will live longer in old age than ever before (Stipp 1999).

The study of personal health and illness has two goals: to understand changes in the body that come with age and to apply this knowledge to extend and improve human life. This chapter will look at (1) what effects aging has on health, behaviour, and everyday life, (2) how older people cope with physical change, and (3) future changes in health and illness.

Researchers have asked two questions about the effects of physiological aging on the older person's well-being. First, do health problems increase with age? Second, does physiological aging limit the older person's activities?

SENIORS' HEALTH STATUS

Older Canadians live relatively healthy lives. More than 70 percent of older Canadians view their own health as good, very good, or excellent. Even among people aged 75 and over, 63.3 percent report good to excellent health (Health Canada 2002a; Statistics Canada 2003w). Shields and Shooshtari (2001, 39) report that "the self-perceived health of people aged 75 or older did not differ significantly from that of 35- to 44-year olds."

The National Advisory Council on Aging ([NACA] 2001c, 2003) publishes an annual report card on Canadian seniors. The 2001 and 2003 reports describe improvements in seniors' health. Compared to the past, older Canadians enjoy longer life expectancy and they expect to live more years in good health. They also report improvements in some lifestyle behaviour (such as increased physical activity in the 65 to 74 age group). Chen and Millar (2000) report an increase in some chronic illnesses between the late 1970s and the late 1990s (for example, older men show increased rates of diabetes). But they also report decreases in heart disease, high blood pressure, and arthritis. Activity limitation among seniors also decreased during this time and so did disability days.

Still, the frequency of chronic diseases remains high. Wister (1998, 10) says that an older society will go through an "epidemiological transition." This means that the society shows a decrease in acute and infectious diseases and an increase in chronic and degenerative disease. Canadian society has gone through this transition. In

● Exhibit 5.1

LIVING A GOOD AND LONG OLD AGE

The 2001 Canadian census reported there were 3795 centenarians living in Canada, a 21 percent increase from the earlier census. Women centenarians outnumber men by about four to one. But what does living this long mean for quality of life in advanced old age? Florence Himes is one example of what it is like to live past the 100-year mark.

Florence Himes may be 108 but she has yet to slow down. She is so fast on her walker she is almost a blur as she negotiates the halls of New Horizons Tower, the not-for-profit Toronto seniors' residence she has called home for 20 years. She lives in the assisted-living area on the second floor, but is up and down the elevator several times daily. Who better, then, to take on a bunch of young whipper-snappers in the residence's 200-storey stair challenge in June 2003 to raise money for low-income seniors who want to live at New Horizons.

"I told them I thought I would win," she confides. "I wanted to win. [The home's administrator] Mr. [Ian] Logan was counting on me for the money."

As six runners ran a route up and down the building's stairs, Himes rode the elevator on a gold brocade chair. At every other floor, she was up, on her walker, out in the hallway and back inside the elevator again.

"I kept asking her if she wanted to stop. I'd say 'Had enough, Nanny?' and she would say no," says Cliff Himes, her 74-year-old stepson who rode along with her. "She never gives up."

An active lifestyle is not new to Himes. She's participated in a fundraising walk within the residence—and walked the farthest and raised the most money. For years she has made doilies to sell at the Christmas sale. At 105, she was off to see Niagara Falls, and she's never missed the residence's annual outing to see the fall colours.

"If there's something going on, she wants to be a part of it, she's always been like that," her stepson says.

Widowed three times, she's lived throughout Southern Ontario, in Montreal and in Manitoba, where her family emigrated from England when she was 14. She's worked on a farm, as a dressmaker and in a munitions factory during the Second World War. She also used to mix cement, hang wallpaper, lay tiles and do her own wiring around the house. Her son Ross, a doctor, died three years ago.

Only her hearing aids indicate she has lived in three centuries.

How has she managed to live so long? "I don't worry," she says with a wide grin. "I do what I can about things and let the rest take care of itself."

What year will it be when you're 108 years old? What will you be doing? What do you think aging will be like in that year and how will it feel to be an older person then?

Source: Catherine Dunphy, 2003, "Going Strong," *Toronto Star, Comfort Life*, Our Kids Publications, http://www.ourkids.net/comfortlife/ uf2003_amazing_himes.shtml, accessed on July 28, 2004. Reprinted with permission of the author.

1996–97, 82 percent of seniors living at home reported they had at least one chronic health condition, and 28 percent said their activity was somewhat restricted by their condition (Lindsay 1999). A longitudinal study conducted in Manitoba examined health status trends over a 14-year period (Menec, Lix, and MacWilliam 2003). While this research found improvements in health over time related to heart attack, stroke, cancer, and hip fractures, the prevalence of chronic illnesses such as diabetes and dementia increased significantly over that period.

Statistics Canada found that specific groups among the older population report high rates of chronic conditions (Lindsay 1999). For example, women live longer than men, but they also experience poorer health in later life (Bélanger et al. 2002; Statistics Canada 2000a). Women report higher rates of hypertension, arthritis, and rheumatism than men. Women, compared to men, also report more falls (Fletcher and Hirdes 2002). And the oldest women (80 and older) face the highest risk of falling. Cousins and Goodwin (2002) say that a "hard fall" can prove fatal. Half of all women aged 80 and over who break a hip due to a fall die within a year. Fear of falling can lead to less activity and an even higher risk of falling. Older women, compared to men, also use more health care services, including more physician visits (Statistics Canada 2001c). Health service use may reflect

Exhibit 5.2

PERCENTAGES OF SENIORS IN PRIVATE HOUSEHOLDS WHO REPORT SELECTED CHRONIC CONDITIONS DIAGNOSED BY A HEALTH PROFESSIONAL, 1996–1997

| | Age | | | | | |
| | 65–74 | | 75–84 | | 85+ | |
Health Problem	Men	Women	Men	Women	Men	Women
Arthritis/Rheumatism	32.2	45.6	36.0	51.9	43.1	59.3
Hypertension	28.2	34.0	26.0	41.9	27.4	33.6
Heart Trouble	15.7	11.3	22.4	18.4	20.1	22.8
Chronic Bronchitis/Emphysema	6.3	4.9	8.2	7.0	—	3.0
Diabetes	11.2	8.8	13.6	9.7	—	7.4

The proportion of people who report health problems varies by age and gender. Women in every older age group have higher rates of arthritis/rheumatism and hypertension. They show an especially high risk of hypertension. Men have higher rates of heart trouble, bronchitis/emphysema, and diabetes until late old age. Many men with these diseases do not live to late old age. This may account for the drop in the rate of these diseases among very old men. Bélanger and his colleagues (2002) say that compared to men, a higher proportion of women aged 45 and over report more disabling chronic diseases. Diabetes, arthritis, and physical inactivity decreased women's disability-free life expectancy. Diabetes, smoking, arthritis, and cancer led to the greatest decreases in men's disability-free life expectancy.

Sources: Adapted from Colin Lindsay, 1999, *A Portrait of Seniors in Canada*, 3rd ed., Cat. No. 89-519, Table 4.9, p. 74. Reprinted with permission from Statistics Canada.

the continuation of a pattern of health care use by women during their middle years. These figures may also reflect a denial of health problems by men.

People with low education, low income, the unemployed, and unskilled workers are more likely to report poor health (Cairney 2000; Roberge, Berthelot, and Wolfson 1995). People with low incomes report higher rates of chronic illnesses and activity limitations than do other seniors. Poor seniors, compared to other seniors, say they engage in less physical activity (Melzer et al. 2000; NACA 2001c). Health differences between people with low and high incomes show up at all ages in later life. Poor nutrition, poor-quality housing, and lack of information all lead to poor health among low-income people. Poorer seniors risk a shorter life expectancy due to their poor health. Menec, Chipperfield, and Perry (1999) found that, compared to those who rated their health as excellent, those who rated their health as fair or poor were more than twice as likely to die within the following three to four years.

Lifestyles as well as poverty lead to poorer health. For example, financial stress and behaviour such as smoking, tranquillizer use, excessive alcohol consumption, and lack of physical activity among poorer people help explain their high rates of poor health (Cairney 2000). Low-income smokers reported the least intent to quit. This places their health at risk as they age.

LIMITS ON ACTIVITY DUE TO PHYSICAL DECLINE

More than 80 percent of older Canadians say they have one or more **chronic health problems** (Lindsay 1999). Chronic illness, which is any long-term illness such as arthritis, rheumatism, hypertension, diabetes, or heart disease, can lead to functional decline. **Functional disability** refers to a limitation on a person's ability to perform normal daily activities due to illness or injury. This measure focuses on the effects of illness on a person's

Exhibit 5.3

HIV/AIDS IN AN AGING SOCIETY

Few people think of the elderly when they hear the word AIDS. The media have linked AIDS (Acquired Immune Deficiency Syndrome) to gay men, intravenous drug users, and sexually active young people. And the data support this view. People aged 30 to 44 had a higher number of deaths from AIDS (723 deaths) than any other age group in 1992. The group aged 60 and over had only 42 deaths from AIDS in Canada in that year (Dumas and Bélanger 1994). Still, older people can and do get AIDS. And the number of older people with AIDS has begun to climb.

Celia Gibbs, a researcher at the Lakehead University Northern Education Centre for Aging, reports that one in ten Canadians with AIDS (926 people) is over age 50. Heterosexuals make up only a small percentage of older people (aged 50 and over) with AIDS. But this number may increase as AIDS spreads among younger heterosexuals. Older people can get AIDS the same way younger people do: through sexual relations, intravenous drug use, and blood transfusions. Gibbs says that "many older people do not know they have the disease, they do not expect to get it, but unknown to them, they are spreading it" (quoted in Paul 1994).

What explains this projected increase in AIDS among older people?

First, a person can have HIV (Human Immunodeficiency Virus, the cause of AIDS) 10 years or more before the body's immune system breaks down and AIDS appears. Intravenous drug users, for example, can get infected with HIV in their younger years, but might not show signs of the disease until old age. More people in the future will come into old age with the AIDS virus.

Second, some people have contracted AIDS from contaminated blood.

Third, any sexually active adult can get HIV. HIV spreads when bodily fluids such as semen or blood pass from one person (who has the disease) to someone else. Because older women have thinner uterine linings than younger women, they are more susceptible to HIV if they have sexual contact with an HIV carrier. About one older person in ten with AIDS got the disease through heterosexual activity. The person with AIDS will spread the disease to other partners. Older people may stand a greater chance of getting HIV through sexual contact because they have weaker immune systems. AIDS also progresses faster in an older person for this reason.

Fourth, older people tend to know less about safe sex practices or to think about using a condom to prevent AIDS.

Fifth, medical professionals may misdiagnose AIDS because older people have a low risk of getting AIDS.

Gibbs says that as many as 4000 older people have HIV, but have not yet got AIDS (quoted in Paul 1994). These people may need long-term health care in the future. A larger older population will include more older people with AIDS. The spread of AIDS among older people could lead to heavy use of health services.

everyday life. Health Canada (2002a) reports that more than one-quarter of older adults face activity restrictions due to health conditions (compared to only 11 percent of those aged 25 to 54). Functional limitations tend to increase with age. Half of all people aged 85 and over report a limitation on some activities due to chronic illness (Lindsay 1999; see also Hum and Simpson 2002). These chronic problems decrease the number of years people live without a disability (Bélanger et al. 2002). And this can decrease an older person's quality of life and subjective well-being (Clarke et al. 2000).

A study that compared disability levels in two groups of older Canadians found that almost twice as many people in the older group (aged 85 and older) had a functional impairment compared to those in the younger group (aged 65 to 84) (Hogan, Ebly, and Fung 1999; see also Hum and Simpson 2002). Statistics Canada (2003i) reports that 18.5 percent of people aged 65 to 74 say that pain or discomfort limits some or most of their activities. This figure jumps to 23.8 percent of people aged 75 and over. A higher proportion of women in each age group report limitations due to pain or discomfort. Compared to men, women also tend to face activity limitations earlier in life and to live for more years with these limitations. Also, poor older people have the highest rates of disability regardless of gender (NACA 1996b).

Disabilities impair some functions more than others. Disabled older adults most often say they have trouble with mobility (e.g., walking from room to room or standing for a long time). They also have trouble with agility (e.g., bending, dressing, or grasping things) and hearing. Community services can help, but many disabled seniors report that they could use more help (Dunn 1990). Older people at all ages report the need for help with heavy housework and shopping (Health and Activity Limitation Survey, cited in Chappell 1993a). But the proportion who needs this type of help increases with advanced age.

Gerontologists study the effects of functional disability on **activities of daily living (ADLs)** and **instrumental activities of daily living (IADLs)**. ADLs include bathing, moving from a bed or chair, dressing, getting to and using the toilet, eating, and walking. IADLs refer to home management activities such as using the phone, preparing meals, managing finances, shopping, and doing light housework. Limitations may range from a mild problem such as trouble dialling the phone to more serious problems such as the inability to eat unassisted or use the toilet. A drop in the ability to care for oneself signals a drop in quality of life and in the number of active years a person will live (Elgar, Worrall, and Knight 2002).

Penning and Strain (1994) studied 1406 people between the ages of 65 and 104. They found that 55 percent of these people reported problems with at least one ADL or IADL. And women reported more disability than men. But they also reported getting more help from other people (National Health and Welfare 1993). Most older people cope with declines in their health. They accept the health changes that come with age, adjust their expectations about their activities, and gradually make changes in their lives to cope with physical decline. The Canadian National Survey of Ageing and Independence (NSAI) asked older people with disabilities about their ability to cope. Eighty-five percent said that they cope "very well" or "fairly well" (National Health and Welfare 1993). Even among the most disabled seniors, those in institutions, 21 percent report that they go shopping and 18 percent manage their own finances (Statistics Canada 1993, cited in Norland 1994).

The focus on health problems and disability in later life can give the impression that nearly all older people suffer from a decline in the quality of life. Stone (2003, 64) says "it is not the case that all old people or even most old people reported having disabilities ... *more than half* do not report any disabilities." She points out that young people as well as older people can face a disability. The Health and Activity Limitation Survey (HALS), for example, found that people under age 65 made up two-thirds of all disabled people in Canada (Stone 2003). Stone calls disability "a likely product of experience with life" (66).

Also, for some seniors disability comes and goes in later life. Statistics Canada (2000a) reports that about 20 percent of older people developed a long-term activity limitation between 1994–95 and 1998–99. But about one-third of older people with long-term activity limitations (31 percent of men and 37 percent of women) overcame their limitation during this time. "Activity limitations and dependency are not necessarily long-lasting....This may reflect the natural resolution of some conditions (back problems, for example) and effective treatment of others (such as arthritis), resulting in improvements in functional ability" (29).

Disability in later life deserves researchers' attention. First, older people with disabilities need informal and sometimes formal support to maintain a high quality of life. These seniors may rely on the health care system for service. An increase in the number of disabled seniors will increase costs and will affect types of resources that the health care system needs to provide. Second, some older people cope well with their disability and some get their functioning back again. This group can help us understand how to encourage and rehabilitate disabled seniors. Third, exercise and self-care can prevent, ease, or reverse disabilities. Studies show that even people with chronic illness can improve their functioning.

COPING WITH PHYSICAL CHANGE

Moore, Rosenberg, and Fitzgibbon (1999) found that chronic conditions do not always turn into functional disability or the need for assistance with daily activities. Although over three-quarters of elderly persons have at least one chronic condition, only about half experience some functional disability. Even fewer, about one-fifth, require assistance with basic activities. Research shows that a large majority of old people live without functional handicaps on certain activities (such as toileting and bathing) (Penning and Chappell 1990; Stone 2003).

Evans and his colleagues (2001) say that healthy aging can slow the process of physical decline. For example, older people can compensate for declines in the senses, muscles, and organs as they age. More than one-third of seniors with a hearing disability, for example, use a hearing aid. Eighty-two percent of seniors with a vision disability wear glasses. And 31 percent of seniors with a mobility disability use a mobility aid (most often a cane, wheelchair, or walker) (Statistics Canada 1990b). The more mobility problems a person has, the more likely that he or she will use a mobility aid (Zimmer and Chappell 1994).

● Exhibit 5.4

A LOVE OF DANCE

Elizabeth Patterson, "on the doorstep of 70," shares her love of dance with audiences of all ages. Sharon Aschaiek describes Patterson's renewed life as a dancer and performer.

On the doorstep of 70, Patterson taught ballet for 38 years at her own school, the Oakville School of Dancing, and also worked as an examiner—a role that took her globetrotting to places such as Brazil, New Zealand, Malta, England and across Canada and the United States.

She retired 10 years ago and eventually moved to Village by the Arboretum, a Guelph, Ontario retirement community. But her first love has never been far off the radar screen.

A new interest in tap dancing led to lessons at the Oakville Senior Citizens' Recreation Centre, and before long she joined the Happy Tappers, a 19-member group that performed twice at the [RBC Seniors'] Jubilee [Concert] (an annual event sponsored by the Royal Bank of Canada).

She also began teaching tap at the Evergreen Seniors Centre in Guelph, and formed Evergreen Footlights, a dance troupe that performed its own colourful routine at the show.

But Patterson's biggest thrill came from her newest act—Two's Company, a contemporary dance piece she developed with a partner.

"It's light rock with a classical feel to it," says Patterson, who marked five years with the Jubilee this year. "You definitely know you've danced when you're done!"

Participating in the Jubilee year after year allows Patterson a chance to reconnect with old friends and to sustain her long-time love affair with dance. "I feel better when I dance. If I have a day where I'm not dancing, I can't say that I feel as good," she says. "It keep you in a good frame of mind and it keeps you healthy."

Source: Sharon Aschaiek, 2003, "Senior Idols: Annual Jubilee Put Talent Front and Centre," *Toronto Star, Comfort Life*, p. 22. Toronto-based Sharon Aschaiek (sharon@summitmediagroup.com) writes and edits for newspapers, magazines, and websites.

Sutton, Gignac, and Cott (2002) found that 92 percent of older adults with disabilities used a wide range of non-medical assistive devices and about two-thirds of them used a medical device. Most people used assistive devices for personal care and in-home mobility. Most often people used simple products to make life easier. One woman, for example, bought a cordless phone so that she could carry it with her around the house. An older person may use the microwave oven as an assistive device. She can boil water by the cupful in the microwave. This avoids the need to lift a heavy kettle. A simple device such as a bathroom grab bar can prevent falls and injury. Edwards and her colleagues (2003) estimate that grab bars could save an estimated $210 million per year in health care costs.

Zimmer, Hickey, and Searle (1997) found that people with arthritic pain tended to cut back on activity. The greater the pain, the greater the tendency to quit activities. But a group of people, called "replacers," added more passive activities to replace activities they had quit. These people often were younger than "quitters." They also tended to have a spouse, a social network, and fewer mobility problems. These researchers say that professionals should encourage arthritis patients to take up new activities. People who replace their activities will live a higher quality of life.

Cott and Gignac (1999) found that people with activity limitations used many methods to cope with their illness. These included keeping a positive attitude toward life, cutting down on household chores, and relying on others for help. Although Litwin (2000) reports that disability negatively affects a person's sense of well-being, he also found that a supportive social network improves well-being. Support from family and friends—the quality of their relationships and the frequency of help—brought disabled older people the most satisfaction. Cott and Gignac (1999) found that married people relied on a spouse for help. People without a spouse sometimes hired a homemaker to help with housework or cooking. Community meal programs can help the most dependent older people eat well (Keller et al. 1999).

Three responses to aging can decrease the effects of physiological decline: changes in the environment, improvements in technology, and changes in lifestyle.

Changes in the Environment

Sense thresholds, the points at which a person can begin to perceive a stimulus, begin to increase as early as age 30, and by age 60 most people notice changes in their senses. Lindsay (1999) reports that 4 percent of older people in private households have a hearing problem even with a hearing aid and 4 percent have a vision problem even with corrective lenses. Hearing aids may not help a person follow a conversation. They amplify all sounds, even background noises. In one case, an elderly man with a hearing aid in a university class showed up to take the course a second time. Surprised, the professor asked him why. The man said that students talking behind him, a bus depot across the street, and a noisy heating system all made his hearing aid useless. Some days he left it at home or shut it off and tried to read the professor's lips. "I only got half of what you said last time," he told the professor. "So I've come back to get the rest." This man needed a quieter classroom setting. Fozard (1990) says that "the elderly appear to benefit as much as or more than younger adults from good context" (165).

Changes in the environment—including changes in the way other people speak to or treat an older person—can help that person cope with physical decline. Also, older adults can compensate for a disability by changing their environment. For example, older people who cannot walk stairs may choose to live in a one-floor, ground-level home. Nearly all older people say they would prefer to live in their own home and never move. But few people have a home that can easily adapt to their changing physical needs as they age. Many older people face a dilemma: live in unsuitable housing (e.g., a home with an inaccessible upstairs bedroom) or move and adjust to new housing.

A demonstration project in Vancouver called "The User Friendly Demonstration Home" shows that a home can adapt to an older person's needs. The demonstration home includes "a flexible floor plan (main-floor office/bedroom, second-floor closet placed right over main-floor closet to permit later installation of a lift), lower light switches and thermostat controls, lever-action handles, reinforced bathroom walls to accommodate grab bars, wider hallways, and heated outdoor walkways. The extra construction cost—about $1000 in a three-bedroom house—is much less than the cost of retrofitting a non-senior-friendly residence" (*Ottawa Citizen*, August 14, 1999; reprinted in NACA 1999b, 4).

New designs in household products can offer a higher quality of life to older residents. New products include a bathroom sink that stops scalding water from reaching the faucet, rubber flooring in the bathroom to prevent slips and falls, window shades with pinholes that let in light with less glare, and lamps that turn on and off with a touch at the base or a voice command. As the market grows, companies will respond by designing and producing more products for older people. New technology will increase a person's ability to live in his or her own home for life.

Some architects and landscape designers have designed special gardens for nursing homes and day centres. Garden designs often include benches for residents and staff to sit with family or clients. A fountain may serve as a destination for short walks. An enclosed loop and coloured walkway can guide people who have cognitive impairment. These gardens can also allow clients or residents to care for some plants of their own. An enclosed garden offers a safe setting for outdoor activity. Designers create an environment that matches and enhances the decreased cognitive and physical abilities of the older clients or residents. For example, in one study, at a day centre that served clients with Alzheimer's, staff used the garden for calming activities. A walk in the garden soothed agitated clients (Lovering et al. 2002). Staff also used the garden for mild physical activity such as bocce or shuffleboard, and to hold group discussions. One staff member commented about the garden's effect on clients: "It's good for them, it's healthy for them. They enjoy it. I know that people benefit and are healthier from having just 20 minutes of sunlight a day" (423). The designers say that "specially designed outdoor spaces" (SDOS) can improve the quality of life of frail and confused older people (417). Specially designed spaces can help older people cope with mental and physical decline.

Improvements in Technology

In the eighteenth century, Benjamin Franklin invented bifocals. He cut his glasses in half when he found he needed to watch the speakers' expressions at the French court. Today, technology helps older people cope with aging in dozens of ways. Some people wear electronic pacemakers to regulate their hearts; people with severe arthritis can have joint replacement surgery; and in some cases a person can have a childhood problem corrected in old age.

● Exhibit 5.5

A SMALL CHANGE CAN MAKE A BIG DIFFERENCE

Health Canada (1999a) produced Canada's Physical Activity Guide to Healthy Active Living for Older Adults. *It encourages active living, makes suggestions on how to get active, and gives tips on activities that will lead to better health. The guide also provides a series of case studies to show what older people have done to live a more active life. Below we present one of these cases. It shows how a simple environmental change can open a person to a new and healthier lifestyle.*

Li is 65. She is a small woman and has never been very strong, but she has always loved gardening. She has become very depressed and bored after she retired from her job. She began to sleep a lot and rarely did any activity. She missed her yard since she moved to an apartment and did not know what to do with her time....

Li's friends began to worry about her and found her a garden plot very close to the seniors' apartments where she was living. Li was thrilled and determined to make it the best garden on the block. Every day she is out there digging, weeding, planting, and trimming ... and her energy level has improved. But what was she going to do in the winter?

One of the other gardeners told her about a mall-walking program and asked her to join it with her. Through her new friends she found out about a T'ai Chi class as well, and she loves it so much she now does it summer and winter.

Getting physically active changed Li's life. She has a whole group of new friends. Her spirits have lifted and she feels stronger and more secure.

Source: Adapted from Health Canada, 1999, *Canada's Physical Activity Guide to Healthy Active Living for Older Adults: Handbook*, Ottawa: Canada's Communications Group, p. 18.

One woman lived her first 60 years with her hip bones outside their sockets. Her muscles and ligaments allowed her to walk, but she limped and tired quickly. As she aged her muscles weakened, and her doctor said she would have to spend the rest of her life in a wheelchair. She searched for and found a doctor who agreed to operate on both her hips. He warned her that the operation would endanger her life, but she decided to go ahead with the surgery. She now has both hips in place in their sockets and she stands two inches taller than in her youth.

Technological aids to older people range from the simple (e.g., a thick piece of rubber tubing that fits over a wooden spoon handle to help a person with arthritis or a weak grip) to the complex (e.g., a battery-powered tub seat that lowers a person into the tub, reclines at the push of a button, and uses an optional turntable to help the person into and out of the tub; the portable device fits into an apartment-size bathroom). Some aids are common (e.g., rubber strips applied to the bottom of the bathtub to prevent slipping) and some are unusual (e.g., a living room chair with a seat that lifts a person to a standing position when a button is pressed). People with visual impairment, for example, use simple technologies

such as talking books and complex technologies such as computerized reading aids (Ryan et al. 2003).

McWilliam and her colleagues (2000) report that many people who need an assistive device do not use one. Gitlin (1995) says that little is known about why people adopt or reject assistive devices. But the fear of embarrassment or perception of dependence may lead some to reject an assistive device (Gignac, Cott, and Badley 2000). Aminzadeh and Edwards (2000), for example, found that about one-third of cane users and almost two-thirds of nonusers feel that a cane signifies the loss of independence and being "old." Those who used a cane tended to hold a more positive attitude about this aid. Over 85 percent of people in this study who used a cane said that it improved their functioning, made them feel safer, and prevented falls.

People can overcome negative views of assistive devices. If they do, a mobility aid can increase their autonomy and improve their quality of life (Sutton, Gignac, and Cott 2002). An assistive device can help reduce the need for medical care and can help older people stay in the community (Allen, Foster, and Berg 2001; Hoenig, Taylor, and Sloan 2003; Sutton, Gignac and Cott 2002). One U.S. study found that 80 percent of people who used assistive devices and services said they depended less on others, while 50 percent avoided entry into a nursing home (National Council on Disability, cited in McWilliam et al. 2000). Shapiro and Havens (2000) propose that government programs provide financial aid and professional advice to people who need assistive devices. They also propose a loan program for people who need devices for only a short time. Studies need to look at how people use devices and the benefits they feel they gain from them.

In the future, older people may have access to more exotic aids. For example, computerized robots may help older people with daily chores. They might help bathe and feed people in nursing homes. Voice-activated robots will pick things up or move them around. Robots may also help patients do passive exercises, help them walk, or bring them something they need. Robots could free nursing home staff from unpleasant work and allow them more enjoyable time with residents. Voice-activated robots would give aware older people who are immobilized a feeling of control over their environment, thereby increasing their life satisfaction. Research will have to see whether robots further dehumanize institutional settings, whether older people (or institutions) can afford complex machines, and whether people will use high-tech equipment if they have the chance.

Computers already allow housebound older people to order groceries, get their mail, or play Scrabble with a grandchild across the country (Kaplan 1997). Brink (1997, 1998) says that new technologies may make some disabilities less of a problem. Telebanking allows older people with a mobility problem to manage their finances from homes, and home shopping allows people to order groceries by TV or computer. People with disabilities use computers to communicate with one another and with family members. Computer websites allow people to get medical and health promotion information. All these services and resources will increase in the future. People with arthritis or visual disabilities can adjust the keyboard and screen to suit their needs.

Jessome, Parks, and MacLellan (2001) say that technology will continue to shape seniors' lives in the years ahead. But few studies have looked at the way older people use technology or respond to it. Some of the writing on seniors' use of technology points to a "digital divide" between those who have and use technology and those who don't. Age, education, income, and attitude all influence the older person's acceptance or rejection of technology. Older people who reject the use of technology may cut themselves off from life-enhancing services and supports. However, some older people reject technology because they feel that it dehumanizes former relationships (e.g., by substituting a bank machine for a bank teller).

Jessome, Parks, and MacLellan (2001) conducted focus groups with older people to hear their views of technology. Some older people in these groups expressed mistrust of technology. One focus group member said "you know the banks don't necessarily change technology to convenience [people]. It's to make more profit" (16; see also Ryan 2001). The researchers found that older adults weighed the benefits of technology against the loss of social contact and increased isolation (see Gutman 1999a). These researchers say that older people will accept technology more easily if it fits with their values and their preferred way of relating to others.

In general, compared to younger people, older people make less use of computer technology. Brink (2001) reports that, compared to younger Canadians, fewer older Canadians use the Internet (although they may spend more time online). Of all adult groups, they showed the least use of online shopping. Barriers to use include the cost of a computer, lack of access to a computer, and lack of time and skills.

Computer manufacturers may need to adjust their products to serve an older market. For example, some older adults find it difficult to use the mouse (Hendrix and Sakauye 2001). Needham (1997) says that makers of new information technology should keep systems simple, know and respond to the needs of older users, and offer help and training. For example, middle-aged and older adults show the best performance on computers that have black-on-white screens. Older people can learn a computer software package as well as younger adults if they have more time and more assistance to complete the task. Older people also tend to learn better in pairs.

People with past exposure to technology will feel the most comfortable using new technology. Still, many older people today miss the benefits of computer technology such as e-banking and comparative shopping online. Homebound older people or those who can't drive "could benefit from tele-health and distance learning" opportunities (Brink 2001, 29). Computers can help older people cope with decreases in physical ability. Support and training may help some older people cross the digital divide.

Lustbader (1997) reports that older people benefit from special methods of teaching computer skills. For example, she uses computers in personal and mental health counselling sessions with older clients. Because she has found that older people sometimes feel alienated from new technology, she teaches computer skills to overcome these feelings. She says that when clients learn computer skills they improve their self-image, increase their confidence, and discover new abilities. One 80-year-old computer-hating client began an autobiography with Lustbader's support. That project turned into a book of 24 chapters. He says: "My only regret is that I wasted all those years with pencil and paper when I could have been happily writing the Great American Novel. But I think the greatest and most significant discovery I made was that the act of pressing the on switch on that computer is the start of an unbelievable voyage of discovery" (Lester 1997, 32).

Residents in long-term care facilities can also benefit from computer technology. Namazi and McClintic (2003) trained residents to use computers. Some of the residents found the physical and mental challenges too great. But others enjoyed using the computer to search the Web and write letters to friends and family using e-mail. Malcolm and colleagues (2001) studied computer use by frail older women who lived in the community. They found that the women used computers to learn about health issues from websites and to connect with family and friends through e-mail. New generations of older people will have more experience using computers. They will feel comfortable with computerized solutions to everyday needs. Brink (2001) predicts that the current digital divide may fade away as the baby boom generation enters later life.

Technology may also alter life course transitions by allowing people to work longer (e.g., by telecommuting). One university professor retired to Mexico. He later developed a terminal illness that kept him in bed. But through the Internet he was able to teach a graduate course in detective fiction. Students got the benefit of this man's experience and wisdom, and online teaching renewed his purpose in life. A number of projects funded by the Canadian government focus on the use of computers to improve health care. One program uses the Internet to deliver cardiac rehabilitation to homebound older patients (Gutman 1999b).

Current transportation technology helps solve many disabled seniors' problems. But sometimes the technology does not meet seniors' needs. The HALS found that 92 percent of disabled seniors engage in leisure activities outside their homes (Dunn 1990). But these seniors report problems with boarding and leaving planes, long-distance buses, and trains. They also have problems with local transportation, finding it difficult to get to and wait at bus stops. Kline (1994) reports that older drivers often have trouble seeing signs in time to react to them. He proposes larger, better-lit signs in higher-contrast colours.

The HALS also found that 8 percent of people who need mobility aids do not have them; 31 percent who need a hearing aid do not have one; and 10 percent of people who need a visual aid do not have one. Seniors often report that they cannot afford the aids they need. Government programs cover only some aids and government support differs from province to province. For example, Chappell (1993a) says that government programs often provide medical equipment, but they do not always provide devices that help a person stay active and live safely. The NACA (1995c) reports that some government programs do not cover batteries for wheelchairs and lifting devices.

Assistive devices can help people stay active and live safely. But for technological aids to be useful, three things are necessary: (1) people have to know about them, (2) people have to understand their usefulness, and (3) products have to be affordable and accessible. Manufacturers need to set up norms and standards of safety and suitability for new products. Cott and Gignac (1999) show that older people will tend not to use devices that make them look different or dependent. For example, a person may use a motorized scooter to get around, but they would not use a wheelchair. Product design has to overcome an older person's resistance to appearing dependent.

Zimmer and Myers (1997) studied older people's openness to wearing protective clothing. For example, would an older person wear padded underwear to protect against hip injuries? About a third of the sample said they would. Those at highest risk showed the greatest willingness to try such an aid. This type of study shows the value of market research with an older audience. Zimmer and Chappell (1999) found that people differed in their willingness to accept new technology. They found that people who report the most concern about managing at home show the most receptivity to new technology. People with health problems most often show this concern.

Gutman (1998) predicts that future seniors' familiarity with technology will lead to greater use of aids in the future. Compared to seniors today, middle-aged people and the young-old tend to own more technological devices (including computers, VCRs, microwave ovens). New generations of older people will have more education and will feel more comfortable using computer equipment. They will feel more comfortable using the Internet to find the technology they need.

Wylde (1998, 50) says that "marketing technology to older people requires doing one's homework." Technology developers must understand what customers want, what features they prefer, and what they expect from the product. Wylde also says that age alone cannot predict use of a device. She says that developers need to know the life stage, personality, health, and attitudes of potential customers.

It is also important to know the effects of aids on a person's social life. A simple self-administered blood sugar test, for example, can cut down on the cost of a nurse's visit. But this cost-saving initiative may remove an important social contact for the older person, who may prefer to see a nurse. Finn (1997, 6) asks: "What are we losing in terms of high-touch delivery of services, or relationships with the older adults we serve, our sense of community, and our sense of privacy?" Little is known about whether technology can have side effects such as social isolation (Gutman 1999a). As well, technology can create dependence. Does an electric wheelchair help a woman who has trouble using a walker or does it put an end to her ability to walk? Researchers have begun to address these and other questions as they look at the impact of technology on older people's lives.

Changes in Lifestyle

People can also change their habits to cope with biological aging. Heavy smoking and drinking put wear and tear on the body. Smoking is one of the leading causes of serious disease and death for older Canadians (Health Canada 2002c; Little 2002). One-half of long-term smokers die from diseases related to their smoking. Smoking leads to decreased psychological well-being, poorer subjective health, and reduced levels of physical functioning (Gillis and Hirdes 1996; Health Canada 2002c). Overeating can increase a person's risk of heart disease and diabetes, and long exposure to the sun increases the risk of skin cancer. People can cut back on activities and habits that lead to decreased well-being.

Some recent figures show that people have already begun to change their habits. Smoking rates have declined in Canada since 1990. In 1996–97, for example, 36 percent of all older Canadians were former smokers (52 percent of men and 24 percent of women) (Health

● Exhibit 5.6

THE EFFECTS OF SMOKING ON THE QUALITY OF LIFE

Statistics Canada conducted the National Population Health Survey to look at health and health-related habits among people aged 45 and over. The report's conclusions show the effects of smoking on health in later life.

- Smokers spend a larger proportion of their lives coping with functional disabilities than do non-smokers, and they are far more likely to die prematurely, according to a study on the relationship between smoking and disability-free life expectancy.
- Of every 100 non-smoking men aged 45 in 1995, about 90 will survive to the age of 65, and 55 will still be living at the age of 80. Of every 100 male smokers aged 45, 80 will survive to the age of 65, and fewer than 30 will still be living at the age of 80.
- Among women, the percentage of survivors is

higher for both smokers and non-smokers. However, the consequences of tobacco use are just as evident. Among women who were aged 45 in 1995, about 70 percent of non-smokers will survive to the age of 80, compared with only about 40 percent of those who smoked.

- Non-smokers are expected to live a higher proportion of their life without any disability. Among both men and women, two-thirds of non-smokers will survive without any disability to the age of 65, compared with less than half of smokers.
- In addition, 25 percent of male non-smokers and 30 percent of female non-smokers who live to the age of 80 will have no disability, compared with less than 10 percent for both men and women who smoke.

Source: Adapted from "Impact of Smoking on Life Expectancy and Disability," excerpts from the Statistics Canada publication *The Daily*, Cat. No. 11-001, June 22, 2001, http://www.statcan.ca/english/edu/feature/smk.htm, accessed on November 24, 2003; see also http://www.statcan.ca/Daily /English/010622/d010622a.htm. Reprinted with permission.

● Exhibit 5.7

DEATH RATES AMONG PEOPLE AGED 65 AND OVER FROM SELECTED CAUSES, 1980 AND 1996

Deaths per 100 000 Population

Cause	Men 1980	Men 1996	Women 1980	Women 1996
Cancer	1414.8	1544.2	794.9	888.1
Heart Disease	2520.1	1,720.4	1,654.9	1,080.1
Strokes	612.3	413.5	550.6	357.5
Respiratory Diseases	624.0	676.6	251.2	347.9
Chronic Liver Disease and Cirrhosis	56.5	48.9	21.8	19.3

Deaths rates from heart disease, stroke, and liver diseases have declined for both men and women during this period. But the death rates from cancer and respiratory diseases have increased. Decreases in smoking among older people may account for some of the decline in heart disease and stroke death rates. The death rates from cancer and respiratory diseases, to the extent that the environment or heredity cause these deaths, may prove harder to decrease.

Note that men have higher death rates than women for all of these diseases. They have nearly double the death rate from cancer and a much higher rate of heart disease. These rates account for the shorter life expectancy of older men in Canada. Note also that women have higher rates of the leading chronic illnesses arthritis/rheumatism and hypertension (see Exhibit 5.2). Compared to men, women live more years with these chronic illnesses.

Source: Adapted from Colin Lindsay, 1999, *A Portrait of Seniors in Canada*, 3rd ed., Cat. No. 89-519, Table 4.3, p. 68. Reprinted with permission from Statistics Canada.

Canada 2002c). Compared to younger Canadians, older Canadians have a lower proportion of smokers. Lindsay (1999) reports that 31 percent of men and 26 percent of women aged 25 to 54 smoked daily in 1996–97. But only 15 percent of older men and 10 percent of older women reported smoking daily in that same year.

Often what people see as unavoidable consequences of aging falls into the category of **hypokinesia**, or physical problems due to lack of movement. For example, in Canada in 1999 older people showed the lowest rate of participation in vigorous leisure activity (such as jogging for 20 minutes). Only 19 percent of older men and 11 percent of older women said they engaged in this type of exercise. Older people also showed high rates of overweight and obesity. Two-fifths of men and one-third of women fall into the overweight category; 14 percent of men and 15 percent of women fall into the obese category (using the body mass index) (Statistics Canada

2000b). Lack of exercise causes overweight, decline in muscle and bone mass, and a loss of function. *Canada's Physical Activity Guide to Healthy Active Living for Older Adults* reports that 60 percent of seniors are not active enough to get full health benefits from activity (Health Canada 1999a). Inactivity levels could reach as high as 79 percent (based on standards of the Canadian Fitness and Lifestyle Research Institute) (Health Canada 2002b). Bélanger and his colleagues (2002) report that physical inactivity in women can decrease disability-free life expectancy by six years.

Studies show that exercise can slow the aging process, improve health, and improve physical function (Chernoff 2002; Lalive d'Epinay and Bickel 2003). Researchers list dozens of benefits from exercise in later life. They include reduced body fat, greater muscle mass, greater strength, improved cardiac output, improved endocrine-metabolic function, lower blood pressure, decreased hypertension, decreased heart disease, and decreased osteoporosis (Adams 2003; Chernoff 2002). Gillis and Hirdes (1996) looked at findings from Canada's General Social Survey. They found that greater activity led to a lower risk of psychological problems and better subjective health. McWilliam and her colleagues (2000) support this conclusion. They reviewed five rigorous studies of exercise programs and found that "regular low intensity exercise" improves mental as well as physical function and exercise leads to more functional independence (105). Gillis and Hirdes say that "there appear to be considerable gains in quality of life associated with moderate levels of physical activity compared with a sedentary lifestyle" (312). The Conference Board of Canada reports that a 1 percent increase in physical activity would result in a $10.2-million savings on health care related to ischemic heart disease. It would reduce the cost of care for adult-onset diabetes by $877 000 and for colon cancer by $407 000 (Health Canada 2002b).

Health promotion programs encourage a more active lifestyle. Programs for women should include education and counselling on exercise and other physical activities (Chernoff 2002). O'Brien and Vertinsky (1991) say that physically active women, for example, have a physical condition 10 to 20 years younger than women who do not exercise. Older athletes who take part in special national and international competitions into their 70s can match the ability of sedentary people in their 20s. Even sedentary people can gain benefits from exercise. Studies report that three months of training can bring a sedentary person's condition up to that of active people (NACA 1994d). Some medical experts believe that the body "rusts out" rather than "wears out." That is, over time organs lose their reserve capacity, and the amount of work they can do under conditions of great demand decreases. Exercising an organ can help to prevent loss of reserve function and delay the aging process.

These studies point the way to a new view of aging. Science cannot stop the aging process. But individuals can improve their environment and can delay chronic problems through lifestyle changes and exercise. Even institutionalized older people with many chronic conditions can benefit from an exercise program. Lazowski and his colleagues (1999) conducted a study of institutionalized seniors. They found that a program designed to improve strength, balance, and mobility led to significant improvements in mobility, balance, flexibility, and knee and hip strength. The researchers conclude that frail and incontinent seniors as well those with mild dementia can benefit from a challenging exercise program. Chernoff (2002) says that improvements in dietary habits and physical activity can contribute to better health and greater longevity.

Research on self-care (activities that maintain good health and help a person cope with illness) shows that individual habits can influence the aging process. Morrongiello and Gottlieb (2000, 35) say that "old age disabilities are not universal, necessarily irreversible, or determined by biological process independent of social and psychological process." Self-care can put off illness and promote productive and successful aging.

The North Shore Self-Care Study in British Columbia studied 900 older people who had one to four chronic illnesses (Wister, Gutman, and Mitchell, cited in Morrongiello and Gottlieb 2000). The study found that most of these people engaged in some self-care activity. Exercise topped the list, with 70 percent of people in the study reporting they used this method. Other self-care practices included dieting (50 percent), stress reduction methods (50 percent), and weight control (30 percent). These findings show that most older people try to maintain good health and well-being as they age. Researchers see self-care as an important way for older people to maintain independence and a high quality of life.

Evans and his colleagues (2001; see also Martel and Bélanger 2000) sum up the trends in individual health among older Canadians. First, they say, chronic disease rates have remained stable from the late 1970s to the 1990s. Even though older people remain in the community longer, rates of chronic illness and activity limitation among seniors in the community have not gone up. Second, life expectancy has increased faster than disability years have increased. This looks like a compression of illness into the later years of life. Third, "it seems safe to say that the health status of the average senior is improving. There is at least no evidence that it is declining" (Evans et al. 2001, 185). A Statistics Canada report supports this view. "All indications," the researchers say, "are that not only have Canadians added several years to their lives, but also life to their years" (Martel and Bélanger 2000, 29).

THE COMPRESSION OF MORBIDITY HYPOTHESIS

What will a longer life for Canadians mean? Will it mean more years of health and activity with a short period of illness at the end? Or will it mean a slow decline in health with more years of disability? Will we wear out quickly like Oliver Wendell Holmes's "one hoss shay" that fell apart all at once? Or will we rust out over many years like an old Chevrolet? How many people will want to live 120 years, if they know that they will spend their last 30 years in a nursing home with dementia or paralysis due to a stroke?

Researchers have developed two concepts to measure the quality of life in old age. **Disability-free life expectancy** refers to the years of remaining life free of any disability. Researchers compare this to the number of years of life expectancy. It gives an indication of the quality of life of a person's remaining years. A man at age 65 in 1996, for example, could expect to live another 16.3 years, a woman 20.2 years. They could expect to live about half of those years (8.3 years for a man and 9.2 years for a woman) free of disability (Statistics Canada 1999b).

A similar concept, **dependence-free life expectancy,** measures the number of years of remaining life that a person will live in a state free of dependence on others for daily tasks. Statistics Canada reports that men aged 65 to 69 years old in 1996 could expect on average to live 16.3 more years and 12.7 of those years would be dependence-free (Martel and Bélanger 2000). They would spend 1.5 years in a state of moderate dependence (needing help with tasks such as shopping), 1.1 years in severe dependence (they would need an assistant to help with personal care), and 0.8 years in an institution. Women in that same age group in 1996 could expect on average to live another 20.2 years. They would live 13.5 years dependence-free, 2.7 years in moderate dependence, 1.6 years in severe dependence, and 2.1 years in an institution. A man can expect to live about a fifth of his remaining years with some dependence. A woman can expect to live about a third of her later life in dependence.

These figures show that women live longer than men but spend more of those years dependent on others for their well-being. Martel, Bélanger, and Berthelot (2002, 42) report that gender creates a "double-jeopardy" for women. "Elderly men," they say, "had lower odds than did elderly women of losing their independence. And if they experienced an episode of dependence, men had significantly higher odds of recovering." Health behaviour such as smoking and lack of exercise leads to chronic illness and dependence. Smokers, compared to non-smokers, show the least likelihood of recovering from a state of dependence.

Both of these concepts (disability-free and dependence-free life expectancy) measure the quality of life in old age. As old age lengthens, researchers want to know whether people will live these added years in good health and independent or disabled and dependent on others. An active and independent older person will have a higher quality of life. This type of older population will also make less demand on the health care and social service systems.

Twenty-five years ago, Fries (1980; see also Fries and Crapo 1981) gave an optimistic answer to the question of what a longer life would mean. He predicted three things: first, that more people would live a life that approached the hypothetically fixed life span of 110 to 120 years; second, that longer life would come about primarily through the reduction of chronic illnesses such as heart disease, cancer, and stroke; and third, that severe chronic illness would occur for a short time near the end of life (the **compression of morbidity hypothesis**). Researchers have challenged all three of these predictions. A closer look at Canadian figures will show the reasons for researchers' doubts but also some support for these predictions.

Challenge 1: Canadians' life expectancy has increased over the past half-century. This trend gives the impression of rectangularization of the survival curve. Exhibit 5.8 illustrates this trend, using the example of Canadian women at three time periods.

Note that according to Exhibit 5.8, cohorts born more recently die off at a slower rate than those born earlier. Also, note the decline in numbers at later ages for the most recent cohorts. This trend almost forms a right angle on the chart and produces a **rectangularization** or **squaring to the survival curve**. Researchers conclude from these curves that a finite life span exists and that modern populations have begun to approach this limit (Clarfield 2002; Martel and Bélanger 2000).

Note something else in Exhibit 5.8. The tail of the most recent cohort does not come as close to the zero point as the tail for earlier cohorts. This means that the oldest older women show a decreasing mortality rate. And this suggests that the life span may have a flexible rather than a finite limit. It also "derectangularizes" the curve as the tail moves further to the right. This evidence suggests that we still don't know the potential human life span.

Researchers report similar findings in the United States (Schneider and Brody 1983) and in England and Wales (Grundy 1984). A model developed by Manton (1982) in the United States shows that a lower rate of chronic illness leads to lower mortality, but also to longer life expectancy. This finding goes against Fries's notion of a fixed life span. Canadian research by Kraus (1987, 59) reports a two-year increase in the "usual life span" ("the age to which only 1 percent of a birth cohort lives")— more than 100 times Fries's prediction. "Age-sex specific mortality rates in Canada in the 65–69, 70–74 ... 85+ age groups," he says, "declined from 18 percent to 11 percent in males and from 21 percent to 11 percent in females between 1974 to 1984" (Kraus 1988, 62). This trend runs counter to the rectangularization prediction.

● **Exhibit 5.8**

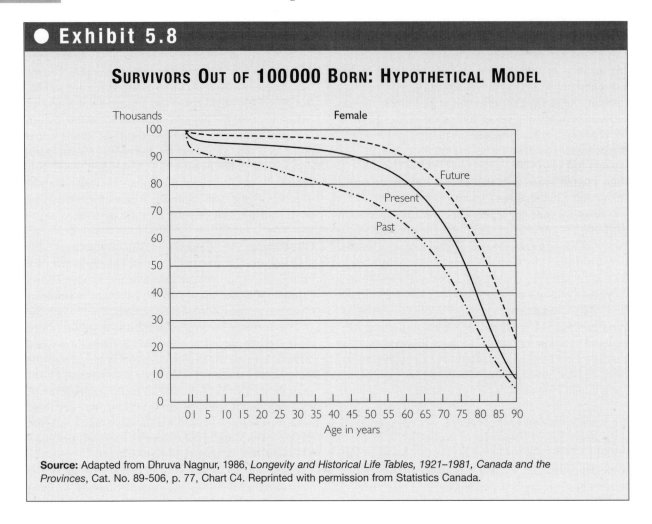

SURVIVORS OUT OF 100000 BORN: HYPOTHETICAL MODEL

Source: Adapted from Dhruva Nagnur, 1986, *Longevity and Historical Life Tables, 1921–1981, Canada and the Provinces*, Cat. No. 89-506, p. 77, Chart C4. Reprinted with permission from Statistics Canada.

Challenge 2: Fries (1986, 1990) says that longer life expectancy has come about through the decrease in acute illnesses such as smallpox, whooping cough, and diphtheria. He predicted that, in the future, decreased rates of chronic illness in old age—lung cancer, stroke, and heart disease—would lead to even longer life. This argues for the possibility of postponing illness until late old age ("the compression of morbidity") and implies a longer and healthier life.

But some writers have challenged this optimistic view of the future. They say that the major causes of illness and disease are not necessarily the major causes of death. For example, arthritis is a major cause of disability in the older population but has little impact on mortality (Bélanger et al. 2002). Also, chronic conditions that cause death (such as heart disease) produce only small amounts of disability. Many researchers now agree that chronic degenerative (but not necessarily fatal) conditions cause the most disability. These conditions include the most common illnesses reported by older

people—diabetes, respiratory problems, and arthritis and rheumatism. People live with these diseases for many years. Manton (1986, 680) concludes that "the numbers of disabled elderly adults can be expected to increase as the number of survivors to later ages increases due to mortality reduction."

Canadian data show a trend similar to other research, but also some changes in this pattern over time. For example, in Canada from 1951 to 1978, life expectancy increased 4.5 years for men and 7.5 years for women. For this same period, disabled years increased by 3.2 years for men and 6.1 years for women. This means that as life expectancy increased, so did the years of disability. This would suggest that Canadians made only small gains in disability-free years during that period (Roberge, Berthelot, and Wolfson 1995).

Barer, Evans, and Hertzman (1995) reviewed a number of studies in the United States and Canada. They conclude that "the proportion of life spent in a state of disability is increasing" (Barer, Evans, and

Hertzman 1995, 219). These studies run contrary to Fries's predictions. But other studies (Robine, Mormiche, and Sermet 1998) support the compression of morbidity hypothesis. They found that disability-free life expectancy increased faster than overall life expectancy for men and women. Also, in Canada from 1986 to 1996, life expectancy for a 65-year-old Canadian man improved by 1.1 years. And most of this time (0.7 years) was time spent in good health. Likewise for women, life expectancy increased (by 0.6 years), and they gained an additional 0.8 years of disability-free living (Martel and Bélanger 2000). These more recent findings provide some support for Fries's hypothesis.

Challenge 3:   Some trends show an increase in survivorship after the onset of chronic disease. New treatments for chronic illness explain part of this increase. But other studies found a decrease in disability despite an increase in the number of people with potentially disabling illnesses (Robine, Mormiche, and Sermet 1998). Hum and Simpson (2002) sum up recent research findings. They find that studies both support and contradict Fries's hypothesis. They say that "with so much conflicting evidence, it is difficult to draw general conclusions" (121). However, they discuss a possible middle ground. It may be that recent increases in life expectancy will mean more years lived with moderate rather than severe chronic conditions. Older people will perform many daily tasks and remain independent longer. They will also spend less of their final years with severe disability or in an institution.

Has this debate settled the issue of morbidity compression? Fries (1990) believed that healthier habits, training, and health policies could compress morbidity. Recent research finds that higher socioeconomic status (Melzer et al. 2000), smoking reduction (Bronnum-Hansen and Juel 2001), and regular physical activity (Ferrucci et al. 1999) all lead to a relative compression of morbidity. Fries also said that the variation in ability among seniors shows room for further compression of morbidity. In other words, if some people live morbidity-free lives into late old age, other people can follow this pattern. The potential for further improvement in well-being among older people has led some authors to study the phenomenon of successful aging.

SUCCESSFUL AGING

The focus by biologists on intrinsic processes has led to a more precise description of normal aging. But this research does not explain (nor does it try to explain) the differences in function among older people. It does not deal with the influence of the environment, lifestyles, and habits on physical functioning.

Rowe and Kahn (1995) understood the importance of these lifestyle and environmental influences. They developed a model to study **successful aging**. They describe three signs of successful aging: (1) low chance of disease and disability; (2) high mental and physical functioning; and (3) active engagement in social relations and productive activity. They propose that scientists look at people with these traits. The people to be studied "demonstrate little or no loss in a constellation of physiologic functions ... [and] would be regarded as more broadly successful in physiologic terms" (Rowe and Kahn 1991, 22). The research would focus on understanding the reasons for these people's success.

The concept of successful aging may be of little use to the biologist (because if people can avoid decline through lifestyle or environmental change, decline may not be part of true biological aging). But for the physiologist, the clinician, and others who work at improving life in old age, the focus on successful aging has some value. Rowe and Kahn (1991) showed that in a variety of studies, including research on metabolism, osteoporosis, cognitive functioning, mortality, and well-being, extrinsic influences such as diet, exercise, and social relations can inhibit and sometimes reverse functional decline. Reker (2001–02) examined predictors of successful aging in a longitudinal study of community-dwelling and institutionalized older adults in Canada. This research looked at dimensions of Rowe and Kahn's model (physical health, cognitive competence, and social resources) as well as other more existential measures that included purpose in life, death acceptance, and religiousness. The research found that those who scored high on measures of successful aging when the study began showed similar signs of successful aging one year later. Social resources and having a purpose in life also predicted successful aging over time for both community-dwelling and institutionalized older adults. These results provide some support for Rowe and Kahn's model.

Roos and Havens (1991) used the concept of successful aging in a longitudinal study of elderly Manitobans. Their definition of successful aging included the following criteria: the person had survived from 1971 to 1983; the person lived in the community in 1983; and the person received fewer than 59 days of home care services in 1983. The definition also included signs of well-being in measures of health, mobility, and mental ability. Roos and Havens found that 20 percent of the sample aged 65 to 84 fit the criteria for successful aging in 1983. They also found that people with the following characteristics tended to age successfully: spouse maintained his or her well-being;

good self-reported health in 1971; they did not retire due to poor health; they had no cancer or diabetes; and they had good mental status. Successful agers also reported more life satisfaction. These findings show that successful aging depends on good self-reported health, mobility, and the absence of disease (see also Fox and Gooding 1998). But it also depends on psychosocial influences such as a spouse's well-being and good mental status. Some researchers suggest that we add positive spirituality as a separate dimension to Rowe and Kahn's model of successful aging (Crowther et al. 2002).

These findings show that researchers should use an interdisciplinary approach to the study of aging. Studies should include psychosocial as well as physiological measures of functioning, and researchers should look for links between the psychosocial and the physiological findings. Also, attention needs to be paid to the people who function best in each age group, because these people may hold the key to a longer life and a better old age for everyone in the future.

CONCLUSION

People have tried to reverse or stop the process of aging at least since Ponce de Leon set out to find the fountain of youth. Drug companies have looked into the effects of animal glands, sex hormones, and chemical therapy on aging. One company that sells skin cream includes in its formula "proteins from the placentas of black sheep (because they are so resistant to disease)" (Toufexis 1986, 5l). Boutiques now offer Botox injections to erase facial wrinkles and create smoother-looking skin. These methods can make the skin softer or add water below the skin to temporarily smooth out wrinkles, but they do nothing to increase life expectancy or reverse aging.

Still, the search goes on. Scientists have explored many methods for increasing life span and extending youth. They have found that certain drugs, calorie-restricted diets, and lowered body temperatures (during hibernation) extend the lives of some animals in the laboratory.

Will any of these methods lead to a longer, healthier life for humans in the near future? Most biological researchers predict a slow increase in life expectancy in the next few years due to better health care, healthier lifestyles, and new medical technology. An end to cancer in Canada, for instance, could add a total of 12.9 years to the life expectancy of women who now have cancer. The estimated gain for men would be 11 years (Bélanger et al. 2002). The elimination of the most common causes of death would raise life expectancy at birth in 1981 to about

90 years for men and about 101 years for women (Statistics Canada 1989a). These figures still do not approach the currently estimated human life span of 110 to 120 years.

Some scientists propose an even more optimistic scenario. Crews (1993, 288), for example, says that "the possibility of human life span extension is real and interventions that postpone human aging are a likely prospect." Rose (1993, 72) says:

> Given enough time and resource, there is no reason to doubt that eventually we will be able to postpone human aging, at least to some extent.... [T]here is the further possibility that increases in the human "health span" could likewise be open-ended.... [E]volutionarily postponed aging involves an enhancement in performance at later ages, not an extended period of debility. The long-term prospect, then, is more of an extension of youth than an increase in longevity, though the latter does occur.

Any of the following changes could increase the length of life and well-being in old age: the discovery and use of gene therapy, the use of human growth hormones, or genetic postponement of aging through natural selection. These changes would both extend the human life span and increase the number of healthy years people live. This prospect would support the morbidity compression hypothesis and challenge the findings of its critics.

But the technical ability to extend life may arrive before we have worked out the social effects of this change. For example, how would personal and social life differ if people lived on average for 120 years? How would this change our ideas about youth, middle age, and old age? Would retirement at age 65 make any sense? Would people and society adjust their life cycles and careers to meet this new schedule?

Studies of people aged 100 years or older throughout the world give some clue about what a long-lived society will look like. These studies report that long-lived people have good genes, a purpose in life, physical activity, independence, close family ties, friends, good hygiene, a simple balanced diet, low stress, good self-esteem, and religious faith. In other words, centenarians live balanced lives in supportive social settings.

These findings suggest that we expand the quest for a long life beyond the realm of science fiction. We should place the search for a full life where it belongs: within the power of each of us and the society we live in. We can and will extend life through scientific research and positive changes in our lifestyle and environments. But life extension will only put off the deeper question: Can we give meaning and purpose to those added years?

Summary

1. Chronic health problems increase with age. People with a low income have more health problems than those with a higher income.

2. Although women live longer than men, they also suffer from more chronic conditions and higher rates of disability. These conditions include hypertension, arthritis, and rheumatism.

3. Changes in health in turn lead to changes in a person's ability to function on their own. Declines in ability can lead to the need for help with activities of daily living.

4. Social and health care supports as well as a more supportive environment can help older people maintain their independence.

5. Technology can help people cope with declines in health. Simple objects such as spoons can be adapted for people with arthritis, computers can increase a person's contact with others, and in the future robots and computers may help people bathe, exercise, and do daily tasks. Eyeglasses, hearing aids, and a supportive environment can make up for some losses in the senses.

6. Research shows that changes in smoking, diet, and exercise can slow the aging process. People can even improve their lung capacity and bone density through exercise. This can lead to a longer and healthier life.

7. The compression of morbidity hypothesis says that people will live longer and have more disability-free years in the future. Some research supports this hypothesis while other research suggests that a longer life may lead to more years of disability.

8. Many older people stay healthy and active as they age. They live without physical handicap and without special help. Studies of successful aging show that people can extend the number of years they live in good health. In the future, science may find a way for people to live past the current limits of the human life span.

Study Questions

1. Describe the changes in health that often occur in later life. How does income affect health in old age? Do health changes differ for men and women?

2. What effects does physical decline have on activity in later life? What do older people need in order to maintain their independence? How can older people cope with physical change?

3. Describe three broad responses to physical aging that can improve or maintain physical well-being in later life. Discuss some of the problems that can limit useful responses to physical change. How could these problems be overcome?

4. State the compression of morbidity hypothesis. Briefly discuss research that supports and challenges this hypothesis.

5. Discuss Rowe and Kahn's model of successful aging. How can this research on successful aging expand our thinking about the potential for aging well in later life?

6. What scientific developments might extend the human life span in the future? What developments might expand the span of good health?

Key Terms

activities of daily living (ADLs) activities performed daily, such as bathing, moving from a bed or chair, dressing, getting to and using the toilet, eating, and walking. (88)

chronic health problems long-term illnesses such as arthritis, rheumatism, hypertension, diabetes, and heart disease. (86)

compression of morbidity hypothesis the idea that severe chronic illness would occur for a short time near the end of life. (97)

dependence-free life expectancy the number of years of remaining life that a person will live in a state free of dependence on others for daily tasks. (97)

disability-free life expectancy the years of life remaining that are free of any disability. (97)

functional disability a limitation in the performance of normal daily activities due to illness or injury. (86)

hypokinesia physical problems due to lack of movement. (95)

instrumental activities of daily living (IADLs) home management activities such as using the phone, cooking, shopping, managing finances, and doing light housework. (88)

life expectancy the number of years at birth an average member of a population can expect to live. (84)

maximum life span the maximum number of years a member of a species can live. (84)

rectangularization or **squaring to the survival curve** the change over time in survival curves resulting in a right angle or square shape, leading researchers to conclude that a finite life span exists. (97)

successful aging aging characterized by a low chance of disease and disability, high mental and physical functioning, and active engagement in social relations and productive activity. (99)

Selected Readings

Cousins, S.O. *Exercise, Aging, and Health: Overcoming Barriers to an Active Old Age.* Philadelphia: Taylor and Francis, 1998.

> This book shows how physical activity can add to seniors' well-being. The author reviews the link between earlier life habits and activity patterns in old age. She also looks at risks and benefits of an active lifestyle. The book reports on seniors' attitudes toward physical activity and it discusses how to get older people involved in exercise and fitness programs. The book offers empirical, theoretical, and practical information on exercise in later life.

National Advisory Council on Aging, ed. *Seniors and Technology.* Cat. No. 0-662-30932-4. Ottawa: Minister of Public Works and Government Services Canada, 2001.

> A collection of well-written articles by gerontologists on topics related to seniors' use of technology. Articles range from a report on seniors' views of everyday technologies such as bank machines to a discussion of Internet and e-mail use. The essays show the attitudes of seniors toward new technologies (often ambivalent) and the benefits (such as reading assistance) that technology can bring to people as they age.

Schneider, Edward L., and John W. Rowe, eds. *Handbook of the Biology of Aging,* 4th ed. San Diego: Academic Press, 1996.

> A review of the latest findings in the field of biology and aging. Topics range from studies of cells to studies of physiological change in later life. Readers with little scientific background may find the chapters difficult to understand, but this is an excellent resource for recent findings in the biology of aging.

Chapter Six
The Psychology of Aging

6

INTRODUCTION

A few years ago, one of Canada's leading geriatric specialists gave a talk on memory to a group of seniors. He told the group that, in the absence of disease, in everyday life memory stays about the same in old age as in youth. Young people and old people both forget things, he said, but older people notice it more because they expect memory loss to come with age. A man stood up at the end of the talk and said, "I respect your views, doctor. But I know my memory has gotten worse with age. What I want to know is what I can do about it." This response fits with two things research has found out about older people and memory: first, a large proportion of older people believe they have memory problems (Lindsay 1999) and, second, memory failure upsets them, even if they forget something unimportant (Cavanaugh, Grady, and Perlmutter 1983).

Many people, older people included, accept the stereotype that cognitive decline is a normal part of aging. But recent research on memory, intelligence, and creativity questions this belief. Studies show that people can learn and grow intellectually in old age as well as in youth. On some measures, mental ability may decrease with age, but on other measures mental ability can improve. Dramatic declines in mental functioning are due to physiological disorders or distress, not to normal aging.

This chapter will look at (1) memory and intelligence in later life, (2) creativity, and (3) the psychological problems some older people face.

PSYCHOLOGICAL STUDIES OF AGING

Birren and Schroots (1996; see also Schroots 1995) describe three approaches psychologists take to the study of aging: the psychology of the aged; the psychology of age; and the psychology of aging. The **psychology of the aged**, they say, describes life in old age, with an emphasis on the biomedical view of aging as decline or disease. It supports ageism and the view of older people as a social problem. The **psychology of age** focuses on differences between age groups. It uses cross-sectional methods to study differences between age groups. For example, researchers compare the mental abilities of young and old people on measures of memory or intelligence. The **psychology of aging** studies changes in individuals over time. It uses longitudinal methods to study both gains and losses through the life cycle. The sections that follow discuss the psychology of age and the psychology of aging approaches to the study of memory and intelligence.

NORMAL CHANGES IN PSYCHOLOGICAL FUNCTIONING

The brain changes with age. The changes vary from person to person, but, in general, the brain shrinks in size, loses weight, and parts of the brain lose neurons (Albert and Killiany 2001; Vintners 2001). The brain also develops more abnormalities such as **neurofibrillary tangles**, which are neuronal fibres that wrap around one another. These tangles show up in healthy older brains and in greater numbers in cases of Alzheimer's disease (AD). Tangles appear to increase rapidly after age 70 (Vintners 2001). Albert and Killiany say that "changes in the brain are, at least in part, responsible for age-related declines in cognition" (163).

Still, research on the older brain shows that (1) changes in the brain take place gradually throughout life, (2) people lose more neurons in childhood than in healthy adulthood, (3) the nervous system has a remarkable ability to adapt to change, and (4) most neurons live through the entire life of the person (Scheibel 1996). The stability and adaptability of the adult brain allow for continuity and growth throughout life. Recent studies of learning, memory, and intelligence show the variety of changes that take place in mental functioning as people age.

LEARNING AND MEMORY

Psychologists define **memory** as the recall of information after learning has taken place. Most formal measurement of memory takes place in psychology laboratories. Psychologists in the field of aging have spent more time on the study of memory than on any other topic. Smith (1996, 236) reports that studies of memory and aging made up "34% of all the published papers in the two journals, *Psychology and Aging* and *Journal of Gerontology: Psychological Sciences.*"

Psychologists show a strong interest in memory and aging for a number of reasons. First, popular stereotypes about aging and early psychological research on memory predict a decline in memory with age. If this is true, studies of memory can trace the causes of this decline. Second, psychologists can study memory in the laboratory under controlled conditions, making research on memory relatively easy. Third, studies of memory have produced testable models of how the mind works. These models attempt to explain complex processes such as learning, forgetting, and the storage and retrieval of information. For all of these reasons, the study of memory has dominated the study of psychological aging.

Researchers break the process of remembering into a series of steps. Most researchers today use an information-processing model to guide their work (France 1990). The model includes the following steps: (1) a person perceives information, which psychologists call **sensory memory**; (2) the person acts on this information and transforms it in some way while the information sits in **short-term memory**; and (3) the person stores the information in **long-term memory**, the storehouse of knowledge that also includes the rules for applying knowledge.

Take the example of looking up and remembering a phone number. You open the phone book and see the number (sensory memory). You repeat it to yourself a few times as your eye moves from the phone book to the dial (short-term memory). You make a rhyme of the number so you can remember it later (long-term memory). The greatest mental work goes on when a person stores information in long-term memory.

Much of the research on memory and aging points to some decline in memory with age. Bäckman, Small, and Wahlin (2001) say that decline in memory occurs in both **non-episodic memory** (information oriented toward the present or the future with no reference to the time at which it was acquired, such as general knowledge of the world) and **episodic memory** (memory acquired at specific time and place, such as the recall of words memorized from a list). The decline in episodic memory begins earlier in adulthood than most people think and continues steadily with age (Bäckman et al. 2000). Episodic memory shows a greater decline with age than other types of memory. Much of the laboratory research on memory looks at episodic memory.

Many studies show that older people take longer to learn new information, longer to search for it in memory, and longer to use it when they need it. Cerella (1990) says that **latency** (the length of time a person takes to process information or make a response to a question) increases with age. Hultsch and his colleagues (1992) studied two groups of older people (one aged 65 on average, the other aged 75 on average). They found that, over three years, decrements in processing time occurred. They also found that the older group showed more decrement than the younger group. Foisy (1995) reviewed 22 studies of word memory. He found that older people showed the greatest decline in memory on free-recall tests when they had the fewest cues from the environment. Older people showed the least decline in memory on recognition tests. Foisy says that free recall probably demands more processing resources. A decline in these resources with age would account for the findings.

Cerella (1990) agrees. He says that processing time increases regardless of the content of the task. He calls this process "generalized slowing" and considers the finding to be classical and well accepted in the field of cognitive psychology. Madden (2001, 289) says that "slowing is a fundamental dimension of age-related change in cognitive function." Birren and Schroots (1996) say that such findings show the link between decreased brain integrity and mental ability.

Park (2000) uses an analogy to explain changes in mental function in later life. Think of the older mind as a computer, he says, with a large store of memory in the hard drive, but with limited random access memory. This computer will have limited memory function and will process information slowly. The processing capacity cannot make efficient use of the large store of memory. "The computer works, but perhaps a little less efficiently than one would like" (5).

Hundreds of studies have tried to sort out the effects of age on memory. In particular, the research has focused on differences in learning (acquisition and recall) between younger and older subjects. Psychologists believe that acquisition and retrieval are closely related. How someone retrieves information (how they search for and find information in memory) depends on how they acquired it (the methods they used to organize and store the information).

Laboratory Studies

Some studies have found deficits in memory in older people due to the way they learn and store information. Perfect and Dasgupta (1997) studied recall in younger and older subjects. They found that older adults recalled less than younger adults on psychological tests. They traced this difference to **encoding** (the process whereby a person puts new bits of information together with already stored information). The older adults said they could not think of encoding strategies or they used less elaborate encoding. Perfect and Dasgupta believe that encoding, rather than retrieval, accounts for the lower recall rate in older adults.

Speeded trials appear to increase the learning deficit. More than the young, older subjects miss verbal and pictorial items presented at a rapid rate. They miss late items in a list more than earlier ones, and they encode some items at the expense of others. Waugh and Barr (1982, 190) found that "the older the subject, the less efficiently and the more selectively he encodes—perhaps because ... he simply lacks the time to encode efficiently and comprehensively."

Other studies (Kausler 1982) report that older people do not automatically use **mediators**, such as picturing a word or finding a rhyme for a word, to help with remembering. Sanders et al. (1980) found that older learners take a less active and non-strategic approach to memorizing their lists, while younger ones actively organized and categorized their lists as they memorized them.

This research suggests that memory decline in older adults may be due in part to the use of inefficient processing techniques. Light (1990), for example, traces memory differences between older and younger people to deficits in older people's **working memory**. Working memory stores recent information and also manipulates this information. In addition, it processes new information while temporarily storing other information (Smith 1996).

A number of studies point to a decrease in working memory as a source of memory deficits in older people. First, older adults remember less well when irrelevant information comes between two things to be remembered (Light and Capps 1986). Second, older adults have more difficulty remembering when the material they have to remember comes in a scrambled order (Light et al. 1982). If sentences are presented in a scrambled order, the older person will have more trouble holding all the information in working memory and making sense of the information. Third, changes in topics place a greater load on working memory and lead to poorer memory in older people. When a topic changes, older people appear to forget relevant information. Salthouse and Babcock (1991) say that decreased processing efficiency leads to poorer working memory in older people. Bäckman and his colleagues (2000) report that this decline in working memory increases in late old age. Craik (2000, 82) says "it is clear that older adults have particular problems in situations where they must hold, manipulate, and integrate moderate amounts of information over short time spans."

Physical Change as the Source of Mental Decline

Cerella (1990, 201) proposes that deficits in mental functioning (such as memory) may be "distributed throughout the information-processing system rather than being localized in particular stages." He proposes that breakdowns in the older person's neural network lead to slower processing of information. Each breakdown in the network requires the input to travel a greater distance. The older the person, the greater the neural decay and the slower the processing time. This

not only explains the general slowing phenomenon, but also indicates why older people do less well on tests that emphasize speed. It also accounts for why older people may do as well as younger people on skilled tasks. These tasks use well-established neural networks.

This model, Cerella (1990) says, offers a simple explanation that replaces the many explanations related to specific tasks (such as storage and retrieval). Through this new theoretical development, "cognitive aging reemerges as a subfield of neurophysiology rather than cognitive psychology" (217). This work challenges current models of cognitive psychology.

Raz (2000) reviewed the research on the relationships between mental performance and neural activity in the brain. A number of studies asked older and younger adults to take a variety of memory tests (including encoding). The researchers then compared the brain activity of older and younger subjects. They found that, compared to younger people, older people showed less activation or no activation in certain parts of the brain during these tests. Younger and older subjects' brain function also differed when they worked on harder verbal recall tasks. More work on brain function will attempt to describe the neural sources of memory changes that come with age (Prull, Gabrieli, and Bunge 2000).

Recent work reported from the Berlin Aging Study also points to physical change as a source of cognitive decline. Lindenberger and Baltes (1997, cited in Park 2000) propose that sensory decline serves as a measure of brain integrity and has a strong impact on all cognitive abilities. They found that visual and auditory ability explained nearly all age-related decline on a series of psychological tests. Further research by this team controlled for education, social class, and income. They still found declines in cognition based on sensory decline. They say that this points to "a common factor or ensemble of factors," the decrease in the brain's structural and functional integrity.

Researchers admit that current knowledge has just begun to trace the link between the brain's function and mental performance. The second edition of the *Handbook of Aging and Cognition* (Craik and Salthouse 2000) contains reviews of the literature on brain function and mental performance. Psychologists have also studied genetics, cellular function, and brain physiology to understand mental performance (see Birren and Schaie 2001). These studies show the growing interest among psychologists in the effects of biology and physiology on mental functioning.

The Limits of Laboratory Research on Memory

Other causes besides physical aging account for the differences in memory between older and younger people found in laboratory studies. Differences in educational background and verbal ability, for example, influence results in memory studies. Cavanaugh (1983) studied the recall of TV show content and found that when subjects had low verbal ability, older people recalled less than younger people. But when younger subjects and older subjects both had high verbal ability, the study showed no difference between the scores of the two age groups. Taub (1979) found that the better a person's vocabulary, the greater the ability to retain pieces of prose in memory. Bowles and Poon (1982) found significant age differences in memory between young and old samples with a low vocabulary, but no age differences in high-vocabulary samples.

Test conditions can also influence older subjects' performance on memory tests. Researchers report that a supportive context improved older subjects' ability to learn paired words. Supports can include guidance on how to encode information, prior knowledge of a topic, or external cues to help learning (Zacks, Hasher, and Li 2000). Poon (1985) found that when older people could control the pace of their learning, they showed less decrement in memory. The design of memory tests, their content, and the use of cross-sectional designs (that compare older and younger people at one point in time) may all lead to exaggerated findings of memory decline in older people

Finally, most studies show that older people learn familiar and relevant material better than new and irrelevant material. Barrett and Wright (1981), for example, found that older people did less well than younger people on a list of words unfamiliar to them. But they showed a better rate of recall than younger people on a list of familiar words. These studies show that laboratory tests and experiments put the older learner at a disadvantage.

Laboratory studies raise an important question: How well do the results of memory research predict an older person's ability to remember details in everyday life? The answer: not very well. Memory studies done under laboratory conditions have poor ecological validity (the transferability of knowledge from lab to life) (Park and Gutchess 2000). Older people rarely learn or recall well under pressure, and research shows that they remember best when they learn information relevant and useful to them.

The Contextual Approach

The **contextual view of memory** begins with the insight that many conditions influence memory, including "the physical, psychological, and social context in which the event was experienced, the knowledge, abilities, and characteristics the individual brings to the context, [and] the situation in which we ask for evidence of remembering" (Hultsch and Deutsch 1981, 153).

Charness (1981, 1985), in his early work, reported on a study of younger and older chess players' problem-solving abilities. He found that older players had more difficulty than younger players at the same skill level in recalling positions accurately. He attributes this difficulty to older players' poorer retrieval ability. But when Charness (1981) evaluated game-playing performance, he found that skill level, not age, determined a player's ability. Older players did as well as younger players of the same skill level. "Given the retrieval deficits associated with aging," Charness asks, "why is there no deficit in molar [overall] problem-solving performance?" (1981, 34–35). Mireles and Charness (2002) in a later study used a neural network model to measure chess performance in the laboratory. They found that in a chess recall task people with a larger knowledge base achieved more accuracy on the recall task. The researchers say that preexisting knowledge can overcome the effects of systemic slowing due to neural noise.

In a study of the effects of age and skill on bridge players, Charness (1985, 1987) also found that past knowledge compensated for decreases in information processing speed. He found that older subjects reacted more slowly than younger subjects on a novel task (unrelated to bridge). But accuracy in bidding depended only on skill level, not age. Charness (1987, 241) concluded that older players may use "preassembled (and highly efficient) programs to maintain effective performance." Dixon and Bäckman (1993) propose that older people who maintain their cognitive abilities may compensate for losses. They may put more effort into a task, they may call on a past skill, or they may develop a new skill. Willis (1996) says that experts at a task use strategies that decrease their need to search for information. They more carefully select information that they need. Dixon and Bäckman say that people who have a high level of skill at a task show the greatest likelihood of using these methods.

These studies and the previous review of the literature support the idea that causes other than biological decline can influence mental performance in older people. Research shows that different types of older people (with more or less education or skill), under a variety of conditions (supportive or non-supportive) and exposed to varying types of materials to learn (relevant or irrelevant), differ in their ability to perform mental tasks or to remember specific information (Bosman 1993). Dixon and Cohen (2001) say that **competence** (a person's skill at real-world tasks) can improve with age. They go on to say that older people often show more competence in real-world tasks than psychological tests measure.

Some studies have looked directly at what older people remember about the world around them. These studies have found less of the memory deficit reported in laboratory research. Craik (2000) reports that **semantic memory**, the store of factual information,

shows little decline with age. For example, older and younger people show little difference in general knowledge questions on IQ tests. The more repeated and familiar the knowledge, the better the older person's memory. Older people have a good memory for past personal events (Zacks, Hasher, and Li 2000). The more automatic the recall (for example, driving a car in a person's own neighbourhood), the better the older person will perform (Park and Gutchess 2000).

McIntyre and Craik (1987) tested older and younger subjects on their knowledge of Canadian facts. They found that older people had less ability than younger people to recall the source of their facts. But the two groups had about the same ability to recall facts after a week, and the older group had a greater knowledge of facts about Canada at the start of the experiment. The researchers note that this study of knowledge

● Exhibit 6.1

TEACHING METHODS FOR USE WITH SENIOR STUDENTS

Hultsch and Deutsch (1981) suggest the following methods to help older people learn better in the classroom. Some of these methods should be used no matter what the student's age (taking breaks, giving immediate feedback on tests), while others apply more to seniors than to other age groups (giving visual and aural cues to help memory, speaking slowly and distinctly).

Technique	Description of the Technique
1. Pacing	Remove time pressures. Let people set their own pace.
2. Anxiety Arousal	Decrease anxiety. Decrease competition and testing. Let people get used to new ideas or techniques.
3. Fatigue	Give older students rest breaks or cut down the length of time for each lesson.
4. Difficulty	Build people up by starting with simple and moving on to more complex work. Break the work into segments.
5. Practice	Give people a chance to use what they know in different ways.
6. Feedback	Let people know how they did as soon as possible so they can fix mistakes.
7. Cues	Give older people visual and aural cues to help them with their work. Use clear diagrams, speak clearly, and repeat questions from the class so that everyone follows the discussion.
8. Organization	Group information for students. Use memory aids like pictures, mental images, or verbal cues.
9. Relevance/Experience	Find out what the older students want to know. Build on students' past experiences. Show them how to apply what they learn.

Source: Adapted from David F. Hultsch and Francine Deutsch, 1981, *Adult Development and Aging: A Life-Span Perspective,* New York: McGraw-Hill, p. 152. Copyright © 1981. Reprinted with permission of McGraw-Hill Companies.

about the world, compared with typical laboratory studies, led to smaller differences in recall between older and younger subjects.

Hultsch and Dixon (1990) reviewed the literature on memory for meaningful events and materials. They found that in some studies younger adults outperformed older people. But in others older adults performed as well as younger people. One study (Hultsch and Dixon 1983) looked at the ability of older and younger people to remember biographical sketches. The study found that younger adults remembered better when the sketch referred to a person known best to the younger adults. The researchers found equivalent recall rates for entertainment figures known to both the younger and older adults. Another study found that older people remember as well as younger people when they perform an activity related to the item they have to remember (Bäckman 1985). Poon (1985, 435) concludes a review of the research on memory by saying that "in general, evidence to date shows minimal differences in memory for familiar discourse materials that may be found in the everyday environment."

The research reported to date should end the stereotyping of older people as forgetful. Cerella and his colleagues (1993) reviewed the literature and found studies of improvements in cognitive ability with age. These studies report compensation for decline, positive effects of physical exercise on memory, and benefits from training (see Baltes and Baltes 1990). Research also shows that the use of memory aids (such as the use of a notebook) can significantly improve memory performance (Sharps and Price Sharps 1996). Park (2000, 11) says that "environmental supports" lead to improved recall. For example, an older person will do better on a multiple-choice test (with all the possible answers displayed) than on a free-recall test with no cues. Supports reduce the amount of mental processing or resource use. And this leads to better recall.

Bäckman and his colleagues (2000) summarize the literature on memory and aging. They say that "no form of memory appears to be fully resistant to the negative influence of human aging. Thus, age-related deficits may be observed in tasks assessing implicit memory ... semantic memory ... primary memory ... working memory ... and episodic memory.... However it is important to note that the size of age-related deficits and the consistency with which such deficits are observed varies systematically across different forms of memory. Specifically, age deficits tend to be *large and robust for measures of episodic memory and working memory, smaller and more contingent on demand characteristics in tasks assessing implicit and semantic memory, and even smaller in primary memory tasks*" (501, italics added).

The researchers go on to say that memory in old age varies by individual (education and gender), lifestyle (social activity), and health. Some people show greater decreases in memory than do others. Also, research shows that older people have a reserve mental capacity. Studies show that people can improve memory performance by using memory cues and by training. Salthouse and Craik (2000) say that researchers should look at ways that older people can put off the declines that come with age. They say that research should look at how older people can "optimize [their] mental capacities" (701).

INTELLIGENCE

The research on intelligence in old age parallels the research on memory. Early studies assumed that intelligence decreases in old age as the body declines. More recent research questions this simple connection between senescence and intelligence.

Psychologists use at least two definitions of **intelligence**. First, taking a global view, they refer to it as the "ability to negotiate environmental demands successfully" (Labouvie-Vief 1985, 506). Second, they take a pragmatic view, referring to it as "that which intelligence tests measure" (506) or what a person taking a test can do now. Psychologists most often use this second (more limited) definition when they conduct research on intelligence and aging.

Early research done in the 1930s reported a decline in intellectual ability after age 20 (Jones and Conrad 1933; Miles and Miles 1932; Wechsler 1939). These findings supported the idea that mental ability declines along with the body, and all IQ tests build this expectation of decline into their design. They assume that older people will score less well than younger people, and they correct for supposed age declines in their formulas for calculating IQ. The Wechsler Adult Intelligence Scale (WAIS-R) manual uses this approach. It puts the peak of intelligence at between 20 and 34 years (Wechsler 1981) and assumes that each later age group will show a decline in scores.

The actual scores on WAIS-R scales support this assumption of decline with age, but they also show that decline does not take place uniformly. Scores on the WAIS-R Verbal Scale, for example, decrease steadily from a mean score of 61.42 at ages 25 to 34 to a mean of 51.50 at ages 70 to 74 (84 percent of the younger group's score). Scores on the Performance Scale drop earlier and more sharply from 51.14 at ages 20 to 24 to a mean score of 30.62 at ages 70 to 74 (60 percent of the younger group's score) (Wechsler 1981, 26).

Other cross-sectional studies of intelligence show a similar pattern of decline in some abilities and less decline in others (Schaie and Labouvie-Vief 1974). Researchers generally agree that a significant decline in intelligence scores takes place past age 60 (Schaie 1990a). But they argue over the meaning of these findings, disagreeing on at least three issues: (1) the concept of intelligence as a single structure, (2) the methods used to produce these findings, and (3) the potential of cognitive functioning in later life.

Intelligence as Multidimensional

Current research on intelligence supports a multidimensional view of intelligence. The WAIS-R scales point to this multidimensionality. They show what Botwinick (1984) calls the "classic aging pattern." The Performance Scale scores show a much greater decrease with age than the Verbal Scale scores (40 percent versus 16 percent). "This classic aging pattern, relative maintenance of function in verbal skills as compared to performance skills, has been seen many times with a variety of different populations" (254). These findings support the idea that "both decrement and stability—or even growth—over the adult period [are] the rule" (Labouvie-Vief 1985, 502; see also Schaie 1996).

Horn and Cattell (1966, 1967; see also Cattell 1963) have developed a model of intelligence that explains these results. They describe two types of intelligence— fluid intelligence and crystallized intelligence. **Fluid intelligence** refers to reasoning, abstracting, concept formation, and problem solving. It makes little use of knowledge gained through reading, schooling, or work. Fluid intelligence relies on how well the physical and nervous systems function. Performance tests that demand the use of fluid intelligence ask subjects to manipulate unfamiliar material in new ways mentally, and they sometimes require skill at manipulating objects physically. **Crystallized intelligence** refers to the use of stored information, acculturation, and learning (Horn 1978). Verbal tests, such as a test of vocabulary or historical events, demand the use of crystallized intelligence.

This two-part model helps explain the empirical results on intelligence. Numerical and verbal skill problems measure crystallized intelligence; spatial and reasoning questions measure fluid intelligence. Fluid intelligence may follow the decline of the biological system from the teen years on, while studies of crystallized intelligence show stable intelligence scores and even increases in scores with age (Park 2000).

Schwartzman et al. (1987) conducted a longitudinal study of male Canadian army veterans of World War II.

The study found declines in spatial problem solving, or fluid intelligence, but scores on crystallized intelligence, measured by vocabulary and mechanical knowledge, increased over time. Overall, the study found that on both spatial problems and vocabulary problems individual scores changed only slightly (a 16.1 percent loss in spatial problem solving and a 10.5 percent gain in vocabulary) over 40 years.

Longitudinal versus Cross-Sectional Methods

Like studies of memory, most studies of intelligence use a cross-sectional method to draw conclusions about age changes. These studies ignore the fact that older and younger cohorts differ on more variables than just age. Few studies of intelligence have looked at the variability among individuals (differences such as educational level, social class, personal experience) in their samples. Age cohorts differ in education, test-taking ability, and vocabulary. These characteristics depend on when people were born and what they have done in their lifetimes (Schaie 1990a, 1996). When intelligence tests are used to compare different age groups at one point in time, they can lead us to mistake cohort differences for differences due to aging.

Longitudinal and sequential studies of intelligence try to overcome this problem by measuring the same groups of people at more than one point in time (Hertzog 1996). Most longitudinal studies find less decline in intelligence with age than do cross-sectional studies. Schaie (1990b, 114) studied one group over time and found that "virtually none of the individuals ... showed universal decline on all abilities monitored, even by the eighties." By age 60, he reports, three-quarters of the people in the study maintained their ability over a seven-year period on four of five measures. Even at age 81, more than half the sample maintained its ability over a seven-year period (Schaie 1990b). These findings support the idea that each person shows unique changes in mental ability with age (Birren and Schroots 1996).

Botwinick (1984) takes a less optimistic view of intellectual functioning in old age. He reports that decline sets in at about age 53. Earlier cross-sectional research showed declines around age 55. "Thus, the longitudinal sequences and the cross-sectional data are not very different" (262). Declines in intelligence occur regardless of the method used.

Botwinick (1984, 262) also says that longitudinal studies play down the effects of age on intelligence because people with low intelligence scores drop out of the studies, leaving more intelligent people at older ages. The longer the study and the greater the number of tests on the subjects who remain, the more the dropout factor affects the results. The debate over the effects of age on intelligence continues in the literature. Future research will focus on the causes of differences in intelligence within different age groups and between different cohorts.

Improvements in Cognitive Functioning in Later Life

Some research on intelligence explores ways to improve older people's intellectual functioning. Charness and Campbell (1988) tested young, middle-aged, and older people's mental calculation skills. They found that older adults gained skill in calculation in the same way that younger adults did. The older group showed "marked improvement" in their ability with practice (Charness and Campbell 1988, 127). And they equalled the starting level of the youngest group before the end of the study. The researchers conclude that the older group's improvement "is testimony to the malleability of the human information processing system, even in old age" (1988, 128). This research shows that older people can improve their performance on intelligence tests. Instruction in test-taking methods and in problem-solving strategies can improve the cognitive performance of older subjects (Schaie 1990a).

Some of these studies show long-term effects. Schaie (1996) reports that, over seven years, trained subjects compared with control subjects showed less decline in intelligence. Refresher courses can maintain the benefits of training as people age. These studies show that "the old, like the young, have more potential than is typically measured by the tests" (Botwinick 1984, 271).

Studies show that people who have good health and who live in a challenging environment score better on intelligence tests than those who do not (Gold et al. 1995; Schooler 1990). People who read books and newspapers and who travel and talk with friends keep their minds fresh. Researchers now think of the individual as modifiable. Baltes has developed a model of "selective optimization and compensation" (1997, cited in Norris 1998). For example, he says that people who age well select tasks that will likely lead to success. They maintain skills they already have, and they compensate for losses by developing new skills or knowledge. This model recognizes that aging can bring loss. But it also shows that people can adapt to change and improve their ability.

Baltes and Willis (1982, 120–21) conclude that "people can learn to make better use of their minds at any age. The logical approach [to observed decrements in mental functioning in later life] might be the devel-opment of compensatory education programs at about the time of retirement." The section in Chapter 12 on education discusses some of these programs in detail.

New Models of Mental Ability in Later Life

Schroots (1995) says that the psychology of aging describes typical changes in psychological function over time. Focusing on the mature organism, this model of aging tends to view life as a hill. Ability increases, plateaus, then declines. But, Schroots says, this view has begun to change. The study of wisdom offers a different view of psychological change in later life.

Baltes, who has conducted some of the most respected research on intelligence, says that two research findings led to changes in his thinking about mental ability in later life (Baltes and Baltes 1990). First, research shows variability between individuals. In general, younger people outperform older people on memory and intelligence tests. But, on a given measure, some older people perform better than younger people. Second, research shows **plasticity** (the ability to change and adapt) for each individual. Each person has a reserve mental capacity. Researchers have found plasticity in brain function, personality change, and skill development. Training, practice, and education can enhance this ability to grow in later life (Dixon and Cohen 2001).

Willis (1990) found this potential up to late old age. Dixon and Cohen (2001, 138) say that these findings offer a "cautiously optimistic perspective, with emphases on resilience and adaptation in late life." Baltes (1992, 1993) concludes that past research has taken too narrow a view of mental ability in later life. He says that certain types of cognitive processes, what he calls **cognitive mechanics** (the information-processing mechanisms that implement fluid intelligence), decline with age. Other types of cognitive processes, what he calls **cognitive pragmatics** (the culture- and knowledge-related applications of intelligence, similar to crystallized intelligence), improve with age (Li et al. 2004). Baltes says that knowledge and culture can enrich cognitive pragmatics throughout life.

Baltes set out to explore the "new domain" of cognitive pragmatics in old age. To do this he set up the Berlin Aging Study. This project defines **wisdom** as "expert knowledge about the important and fundamental matters of life, their interpretation and management" (Featherman, Smith, and Peterson, 1990; see also Baltes et al. 1990). The project studies wisdom by asking older people to solve real-life problems. One problem, for

● **Exhibit 6.2**

THE FIVE CRITERIA FOR WISDOM

Psychologist Paul Baltes compiled a list of five criteria for wisdom based on cognitive psychology and life-span theory. A person who had this knowledge would have "exceptional insight into life matters and good judgment and advice about difficult life problems."

1. Rich factual knowledge about life matters.
2. Rich procedural knowledge about life problems.

3. Life-span contextualism: Knowledge about the contexts of life and their temporal (developmental) relationships.
4. Relativism: Knowledge about differences in values and priorities.
5. Uncertainty: Knowledge about the relative indeterminacy and unpredictability of life and ways to manage.

Source: P.B. Baltes, J. Smith, U.M. Staudinger, and D. Sowarka, 1990, "Wisdom: One Facet of Successful Aging?" in M. Perlmutter, ed., *Late Life Potential,* pp. 63–81, Washington, DC: Gerontological Society of America. Reprinted with permission of the Gerontological Society of America, 2000.

example, asked people to respond to a suicidal call from a friend. Another one asked people to give advice to a 15-year-old girl who wants to get married (White 1993).

A person who displays wisdom has insight into life's conditions and shows good judgment. This person gives good advice. Rybash, Hoyer, and Roodin (1986) say that younger people may do better than older people in problem solving in a lab or classroom. They can answer clearly structured problems faster than older people. But older people may do better at "problem finding." That is, older people have a greater ability to shape and solve a problem in a less defined situation. Baltes (1992) reports that older people get higher scores than younger people on problems related to real-life dilemmas. More than half of the top responses, he says, come from people over age 60.

Wisdom makes older people more skilled at working in everyday life. Skills include "life planning, life management, and life review" (Dixon 2000, 32). This ability could allow older people to play a meaningful role in modern society. Baltes and his colleagues suggest that a society with more older people will have a greater storehouse of wisdom. Society could use that wisdom to redefine problems that escape rational and technical solutions (Featherman, Smith, and Peterson 1990). More older people thinking and advising about practical problems could enhance the quality of life for everyone. But, for this to occur, society first has to recognize wisdom in its older people (Baltes 1993). Then it has to have the good sense to make use of it. Baltes's work takes the first step by expanding our view of mental potential in later life.

CREATIVITY

The bulk of research on psychology and aging has focused on changes in memory and intelligence with age. Comparatively few studies have looked at creativity in later life. At least three different measures of creativity exist in the literature. First, some studies measure creative achievement by evaluating the greatness of a work or by counting the number of creative works by an individual. Second, some studies use psychological tests to measure creativity. These tests take place in the laboratory and allow for comparisons of old and young people in a number of dimensions. Third, some studies use a more global definition of creativity: fulfillment to the individual and possibly even to others (though it might not reach worldwide or historical importance). Studies done from each point of view have looked at whether creativity declines with age.

Creativity as Measured by Great Works

Lehman (1953) conducted the classic work in this field. He studied the ages at which scientists, philosophers, mathematicians, painters, inventors, and other creative people produced their greatest works. He selected for his sample people who had already died (because someone still alive could still produce a great work). Lehman found that past and present scientists produced their greatest creative work between the ages of 30 and 40. Most great writers produced their foremost work before

● Exhibit 6.3

WISDOM IN LATER LIFE

Plato, in The Republic, *says that he likes to talk to older people. They have gone along a path that all of us will one day follow. So they have a unique perspective on life and aging. Some might call it wisdom. Consider the following thoughts on aging by some thoughtful older people.*

Art Blake, a retired judge from Jamaica, says that he recently attended the funeral of a friend. He flew back to Jamaica and went directly to the church from the airport. His plane had arrived early, so he reached the church before anyone else. "I watched as the people arrived," he says. "Many of them I knew from my childhood, we went to school and grew up together. These are all old people, I thought. Then I thought, I too must look like this. But I couldn't see it in myself. I shave everyday and I don't see my age. But I could see it in them.... The mind plays tricks on you."

Art serves as the legal adviser to an education program for older people and sits on the advisory board of a university certification program. "We want to be young," Art says. "We use creams to smooth out the wrinkles. But this is the most natural process. We cannot help but get old."

Bertrand Russell developed new interests as he aged. He began his career as a mathematician, moved on to philosophy, then in late old age he turned to political and social issues. At age 80, he said,

> The best way to overcome it [old age]—so at least it seems to me—is to make your interests gradually wider and more impersonal, until bit by bit the walls of the ego recede, and your life becomes increasingly merged in the universal life. An individual human existence should be like a river—small at first, narrowly contained within its banks, and rushing passionately past boulders and over waterfalls. Gradually the river grows wider, the banks recede, the waters flow more quietly, and in the end, without any visible break, they become merged in the sea and painlessly lose their individual being (quoted in Puner 1979, 270).

John Holt, an educator who wrote about children and their untapped potential, turned to reflect on education for adults later in his career. Holt took up the cello in late middle age. In his book *Never Too Late* (Holt 1978, 185), he wrote about his experience learning the instrument and about his own potential as a person.

> If I could learn to play the cello well, as I thought I could, I could show by my own example that we all have greater powers than we think; that whatever we want to learn or learn to do, we probably can learn; that our lives and our possibilities are not determined and fixed by what happened to us when we were little, or by what experts say we can or cannot do.

the age of 45, and most poets produced theirs in their late 20s and early 30s. Painters peaked between ages 30 and 45. In most fields, Lehman found that achievement steadily decreased after age 45.

Lehman (1968) went on to study athletes, chess champions, orators, politicians, businessmen, and atomic scientists. He found that still-living atomic scientists, for example, showed a peak in achievement between ages 25 to 29 and a sharp drop in achievement from age 35 on. He also found that older atomic scientists (aged 60 to 64) made only one-tenth the number of contributions as the younger scientists (25- to 29-year-olds). Lehman found the same pattern for still-living astronomers, mathematicians, and botanists.

Lehman's research set off a wave of controversy. Dennis (1968), for example, challenged Lehman's conclusions about the decline in creativity with age. First, he said, Lehman's research combined people with different lengths of life. Fewer people live to old age, so there will be fewer people to create great works in later life. Lehman's findings, therefore, might reflect a demographic fact rather than a decline in creativity. Second, Dennis questioned Lehman's approach to the study of creativity. Lehman used the works of critics, historians, and experts to decide on the quality of his subjects' work. Dennis argued that experts may favour the early, groundbreaking work of great people and could find it harder to judge more recent work by a great master.

Dennis (1968) conducted his own research on creativity. He used a measure different from Lehman's to compensate for these errors. First, while Lehman studied the age when creators produced their greatest work, Dennis studied the creative output (the number of works produced) of 738 people. Second, he selected long-lived subjects, all of whom had lived past age 78, to control for the effects of mixed longevities.

Dennis measured the output of a variety of creative people: artists, scientists, scholars, and dancers. He found that each group produced the least amount of work in their 20s. In almost all fields, creativity (measured by output) peaked between ages 40 and 49, about 10 years later than Lehman's finding. Dennis, like Lehman, found that people in different fields peaked at different ages. Artists (dramatists, librettists, architects) peaked earliest and showed the sharpest decline in their 70s. Dennis found that scientists also experienced declines in middle age, but they showed a sharp decline only after age 60. Scholars showed little decline with age. They produced as much in their 70s as in their 40s, and they added to their former number of books by 25 percent between ages 70 and 79.

Dennis's work expands on Lehman's, rather than contradicting it. Dennis shows that differences in the peak age of creativity may depend as much on the social structure of a discipline as it does on a creative person's age. Scholars reach a peak later than artists and stay productive longer. Dennis explains that the arts, such as painting or composing, depend more on individual creativity. An artist's output declines if he or she loses strength or becomes ill. Scholars and scientists can get younger colleagues (such as graduate students) to help them with their work. They can stay productive even if their strength declines (Dennis 1968).

Later studies by Simonton (1977) on great composers partly supported the idea that creativity declines with age. Simonton found that total productivity peaked between ages 45 and 49 and then declined. Total themes (musical ideas) in composers' works also decreased after ages 30 to 34, although they did not decrease to a point below the totals of the composer's younger years. Studies of Nobel Prize winners (Zuckerman 1977) and high-level chess players (Elo 1965) also report peaks in creativity for people in their mid-30s.

More recently, Simonton (1988a, 1990) reviewed the research on creativity and aging. He concluded that in the last decade of a creative person's career, his or her productivity equals about half his or her peak output (given a normal life span). In general, Simonton (1990, 322) says, "if one plots creative output as a function of age, productivity tends to rise fairly rapidly to a definite peak and thereafter tends to decline gradually."

Does the quality of the work also decline with age? In other words, do the creative works of a person's later career decline in quality? Simonton (1990) says that creative people can produce great works at every age. But across an entire career he proposes a **constant-probability-of-success model** (323). This model states that within a career, the larger the number of creative works a person produces in a given period, the more great works he or she produces during this time (Simonton 1988b).

Why does creativity decline with age in some people? A decline in health, a decrease in energy, changes in a profession, and different goals and motivations later in life all explain the decline in creative output (Simonton 1988b). But even with this general decline, creativity can continue into late old age. Sophocles, Michelangelo, Goethe, Picasso, Winston Churchill, Grandma Moses, and Georgia O'Keefe, for example, all remained creative past the age of 80. Lehman reported many cases of creativity in old age. He found that 20 percent of atomic physicists made contributions to their field after age 65 (Lehman 1968, 100).

Simonton might have argued that most of these people had created their greatest works at younger ages. Still, they continued to contribute to society and culture

● Exhibit 6.4

CAN OLDER PEOPLE BE CREATIVE?

Cato learned Greek at eighty; Sophocles
Wrote his grand *Oedipus*, and Simonides
Bore off the prize of verse from his compeers,
When each had numbered more than fourscore years.
And Theophrastus, at fourscore and ten,
Had just begun his *Characters of Men*.
Chaucer, at Woodstock with the nightingales,
At sixty wrote the *Canterbury Tales*;
Goethe at Weimar, toiling to the last,
Completed *Faust* when eighty years were past.

Source: Henry Wadsworth Longfellow, 1928, "Morituri Salutamus," reprinted in *The Poetical Works of Longfellow,* London: Oxford University Press.

as they aged. And some types of creativity, like comprehensive historical studies, may be possible only in old age. It may take a historian a lifetime to amass the knowledge and gain the perspective needed to make a great contribution.

Creativity as Measured by Psychological Tests

Lehman (1953, 1968) and Dennis (1968) studied unique groups of people—people famous enough to have their work noted in history. But what about "average" people—those who carry out most of the work in society? Does creativity change with age? Creativity studies of the general population often rely on psychological tests. Like memory and intelligence studies, most creativity studies show a decline in test scores with age, with a peak around age 30 (McCrae, Arenberg, and Costa 1987; Simonton 1990). None of these studies shows an increase in creativity in later life (Cornelius and Caspi 1987), although a study by Jacquish and Ripple (1981) found a complex pattern of change in creativity with age. They studied 218 men and women 18 to 84 years old. They found that the oldest group (61 to 84) had lower fluency and flexibility scores, but scored as well as the youngest group (18 to 25) on originality. The middle group (40 to 60) scored best on all measures. This study suggests that some measures of creativity may decline more than others with age.

A study by Crosson and Robertson-Tchabo (1983) suggests that a person's background and experience may also influence creativity in later life. The study compared two groups of women, one of which included 271 women artists and writers aged 23 to 87. The second group included 76 women aged 26 to 74 who had not had careers in the creative arts. The study found that the non-creative career subjects over 60 scored significantly lower than the non-creative career people under age 50. But the study found no significant correlation between age and creativity in the creative group. Crosson and Robertson-Tchabo suggest that continued creative work may help a person stay creative longer.

Studies that use creativity tests suffer from a number of problems. First, they often use cross-sectional designs that confuse differences between age groups with changes due to aging (Collins and Tellier 1994). These studies may measure differences in educational background and test-taking ability as much as creativity. Second, the measures used in these studies have low validity, which means that results may bear little relation to real-life creativity (Simonton 1990). We must remember that creativity can take forms other than great works and scores on tests.

Creativity as Personal Expression

Creativity can refer to a great achievement, a test score, or a form of personal expression. This last perspective treats creativity as a source of individual satisfaction regardless of how other people judge the works produced.

Kenneth Koch, a professional poet and teacher, reported on the value of creative expression for personal well-being. Koch agreed to teach poetry writing to 25 people in a nursing home in New York City. He said that on the first day the people looked "old, sick, tired, uncomfortable. Some seemed to be asleep or almost so" (1982, 210). Other people in the class gazed around the room or showed signs of pain. Koch began with a collaborative poem. In this case he asked each person for a line about his or here childhood. Some people refused to contribute, but most did, and Koch put their lines together in a poem.

He reported that the group members became "excited at the unaccustomed pleasure of hearing what they said read aloud, and excited at hearing it admired by me and by other students" (1982, 211). Koch (1977) collected these poems in a book titled *I Never Told Anybody*. These poems represented the first formal creative works produced by the participants, but it only hints at the joy writing poetry brought to their lives. Koch's report shows that older people often lack an opportunity to express themselves creatively.

Crosson and Robertson-Tchabo (1983) believe that if older people had more opportunity to express their creativity they would show more creative behaviour. Engelman (2000) led a creativity class for six years with a group of women at a senior centre. The class solved puzzles, engaged in brainstorming, and invented poems and stories. Engelman concludes that people at any age can display creativity and that the act of creation brings joy to older people's lives. A mental fitness program in Canada called "Fitness for Life" included a creative thinking module. Researchers compared baseline mental fitness scores with outcomes after an eight-week program. The researchers found that at the end of the program depression scores had declined while mental fitness and self-esteem scores had improved (Cusack, Thompson, and Rogers 2003).

Unfortunately, few people have access to programs like this. Butler (1974) says that older people have to become autodidacts—self-teachers. These kinds of people take charge of their own learning, transforming their world in response to their own concerns, and, in

● Exhibit 6.5

PORTRAITS OF THREE CREATIVE OLDER CANADIANS

Doris Finta

Doris Finta, 86, discovered a passion for art after she retired. She explains to Marg Langton of *The Hamilton Spectator* how this happened.

> I retired at 63 and finished my degree the next year. I started in French, then English literature but I got seduced into art. Art ended up being the air I breathe.
>
> I got my honours degree when I was 71. It was 50 years after I started university. I did a two-year project on [artist] Joyce Wieland. I got to know her quite well. I used to meet her at the art gallery [Art Gallery of Ontario]. We'd go up to the modern section and she'd know everybody....
>
> Art is my life now, it gave me back joy—rich, rich possibilities. It's coloured everything.
>
> I was a founding member of the Burlington Fine Arts Association. I'm still carrying on with an art appreciation program that I lead at the Burlington Art Centre. I'm doing printmaking, watercolours and drawing. I take summer courses in Haliburton.
>
> My degree was a gate into a whole new world.

Helen Dougher

Helen Dougher, 89, began writing poetry at age 11. Suzanne Bourret profiled her for *The Hamilton Spectator*.

> Helen Dougher ... has good friends but her closest friend is the poetry she writes. It keeps her company when she cannot sleep and it soothes and comforts her when she misses loved ones. Her reflective verses project lovely and vivid pictures of nature and the seasons, her favourite cats, the European cities she has visited, and thoughts about those close to her who have passed on.
>
> When you read [her poetry], you find an intelligent, gentle soul who hears and sees from a different level and who shares her pictures of a different age and a quieter time. When her poetry is read, it smoothes away rough edges, it consoles and soothes the soul....
>
> She had her first poem printed in *Chatelaine* when she was 11 or 12 and was paid $3.... She says, "I think people thought it was very queer to write poetry in a town like that [Dunnville, Ontario] in those days."
>
> Dougher kept writing poetry through[out her life. She] joined the Tower Poetry Society in the early 1960s.

It's a group that meets monthly to discuss their poetry at Carnegie Gallery in Dundas. Her first book of poetry, *This Golden Fire*, was published by the Tower Poetry Society Press in 1977. Her second book, *Homecoming*, was published in 1986 by Potlatch Publications. She did much of the distribution herself.... Her poetry ended up in schools and libraries across Canada and once while vacationing in Providence, R.I., she found a copy of her verse at Brown University.

Elena Turroni

Elena Turroni, 90, began her career by teaching cooking and sewing at local high schools. She also made wedding cakes and cooked for family and friends. Her sister suggested that she start a small business. Over the years she became a well-known caterer and cookbook author. She told her story to Diane Ujfalussy of *The Hamilton Spectator*.

> When you've made strawberry shortcake for Eleanor Roosevelt, have been asked to cook dinner for the Queen and rustled up grub for former prime minister John Diefenbaker, you get a pretty good idea you can cook. Elena Turroni has spent decades inventing and reinventing all kinds of recipes. She ran her own lucrative catering business in Welland for years and raised funds for charitable organizations through local cooking shows.
>
> "I would cook what anyone asked me to. I did a lot of research at the library," Turroni said. "I read books on the cooking of most every country. I love to improvise. I find it challenging and rewarding to create different tastes or textures."
>
> The influx of Italian immigrants in the '50s made the Turroni name synonymous with fine Italian catering. She would be called upon to cater Italian weddings and some Saturdays she would have anywhere from four to seven. "There was always a book and pencil in my hand. Even in bed, I had to have my book nearby in case I got an idea," she said.
>
> She recalls creating fabulous fare for original parties—events on the beach, gardens and even an Indian party complete with dancers and women in saris....
>
> She is still involved in the community and coming up with new mouth-watering recipes. Turroni ... will soon be releasing her fourth cookbook—*Italian Regional Cooking, Elena Turroni Turns 90* (and is still turning out cookbooks).

Sources: M. Langton, "Seniority: In Their Own Words: Doris Finta, 86," *Hamilton Spectator*, September 23, 1999; S. Bourret, "Poet Evokes Images of Times Past," *Hamilton Spectator*, February 15, 2000, E2; D. Ujfalussy, "Terrific Turroni Still Turning It Out," *Hamilton Spectator*, October 13, 1999 (online). Reprinted with permission of The Welland Tribune.

the process, creating something new. This view of creativity makes later life a time of potential discovery and self-renewal rather than a time of decline.

PSYCHOLOGICAL DISORDERS: ABNORMAL AGING

Studies of memory, intelligence, and creativity describe the normal changes that come with aging, but some people show abnormal changes as they age. They may suffer from psychological problems such as paranoia, anxiety neuroses, and schizophrenia. Experts call these functional disorders because they interfere with how a person functions. These problems have no clear organic cause, and some older people may have suffered with them throughout their lives. Other people suffer from organic disorders. At least two different types of organic disorders show up in old age. First, some people enter old age with an existing developmental disability (e.g., Down syndrome). Second, some people get a disease of the brain such as Alzheimer's disease, Parkinson's disease, or stroke. These illnesses arise from a deterioration of the brain.

Organic Brain Disorders

Developmental Disability

Developmental disability (DD) refers to the effects of diseases such as Down syndrome. These illnesses usually begin at birth and affect a person's function in society throughout their life. Better treatment and medical care have led to longer life expectancies for people with developmental disabilities. Sparks and his colleagues (2000) report that average life expectancy for people with DDs rose from 11 years in the 1930s to more than 50 years today. These advances have led to an increase in the number of people with such disabilities in later life. Salvatori and her colleagues (1998) report that the number of older people (aged 55 and over) with developmental disabilities will double by 2028 to between 26000 and 60000. Many of these people now live in the community, a trend that will increase in the future.

People with these disabilities face unique issues as they age. First, they frequently age prematurely. They may in their 40s need to be supported as if they were an older person. Second, they rarely have children or a spouse to give them support. Third, they will rarely have a pension, savings, or other economic resources.

People with a developmental disability will rely heavily on social services and public support. But Salvatori and her colleagues (1998) say that social services and government policies often fail to serve their

needs. Their relative youth (most need help before age 65) often makes them ineligible for programs open to older people. Also, current housing and recreation options for seniors often fail to meet the needs of a person with a developmental disability.

These people need a wide choice of social support and housing options, including group home living and supported independent living. They also need special programs to support retirement, leisure, and work. These programs should focus on their individual needs and should promote social integration, autonomy, and economic independence.

Sparks and his colleagues (2000) surveyed agencies that provided services to people with DD. Agencies that served DD clients reported that their staff needed training in general aging and dementia care. Service providers also felt the need for health and medical information. They "expressed concern about the lack of well trained medical specialists available to serve aging adults with DD" (215). Sparks and his colleagues propose a number of actions to serve adults better with DD. These include better education for service providers, integration of adults with DD into existing programs, and help for DD clients with finding recreation and activities in retirement. This relatively small but growing number of older people will pose new challenges to current policies and to current social services.

Cognitive Impairment in Later Life

Organic brain syndrome, senile dementia, and dementia are general terms used to describe a variety of organic brain disorders. Organic disorders lead to confusion, forgetfulness, and sometimes anti-social behaviour. Some individuals with these disorders wander, strike out, or resist help from their caregivers. Dementia cases create stress for both professional care providers and family caregivers. As more people live into late old age, dementia will show up in greater numbers. "Those managing to stay on till well beyond 85 will form a group with very much higher than average risk of severe dementia" (Stone 1986, 31).

Canada began its first nationwide study of dementia in 1990—the Canadian Study of Health and Aging (CaSHA), the largest of its kind. The study included more than 10000 older people in five Canadian regions and included institutionalized seniors as well as people who live in the community. The study had four objectives: (1) to report on the prevalence of dementias among older Canadians; (2) to assess the risk of someone's getting Alzheimer's-type dementia; (3) to describe patterns of care for dementia patients and to measure caregiver burden; and (4) to create a uniform database (Gauthier, McDowell, and Hill 1990). The study also included a number of add-on projects that focused on topics such as the genetic origins of Alzheimer's disease.

This study has provided the best estimate yet of the prevalence of dementia in Canada. For example, the researchers found that 253 000 people or 8 percent of people aged 65 or older in Canada in 1991 had some form of dementia. The study found a dementia rate of 2.4 percent among people aged 65 to 74 and 34.5 percent among people aged 85 and over (cited in Tierney and Charles 2002; see also Conn 2002). The research projects a threefold increase in the number of dementia cases by 2031 (double the rate of total population growth) (Burke et al. 1997; CaSHA 1994; National Advisory Council on Aging [NACA] 1996c, 1996d).

Cases of Alzheimer's disease make up about two-thirds of all dementia cases and the prevalence of the disease increases with age (CaSHA 1994). Carswell-Opzoomer and her colleagues (1993) studied the prevalence of dementia in nursing homes in the Ottawa-Carleton region. They found that 52 percent of residents (women with an average age of 84, and men, 78) suffered from dementia. In the future, nursing homes and hospitals will have to care for more and more cognitively impaired patients.

About a third of older people with dementia live in the community (CaSHA 1994). Shapiro and Tate (1997) found that community-dwelling older people with dementia tend to use more formal services than healthy older people or people with other forms of cognitive impairment. They found that the health care system spends more than twice as much to care for dementia clients as for non-impaired older people. But Shapiro and Tate report that, compared to people with other cognitive impairments, people with dementia use less expensive services (such as home support and personal care services). This group also tended to use respite care more than any other group. Still, the CaSHA advises that the cost of care for dementia patients in Canada comes to more than $3.9 billion per year (Tierney 1997). The cost for each community-dwelling dementia patient came to more than $8000 per year and for each institutionalized dementia patient more than $28 000 per year.

None of the research so far has produced a method to treat Alzheimer's disease (the most common form of dementia). Physicians often cannot make a certain diagnosis of the disease's presence. They first try to rule out other causes of confusion and personality decline such as brain tumours, blood pressure problems, or hyperthyroidism. Dozens of other illnesses must be ruled out before an illness can be diagnosed as Alzheimer's (Hermann 1991). Caution prevents doctors from quickly reaching a conclusion of Alzheimer's because a patient might have a treatable illness or a problem such as overmedication or infection. Tierney and Charles (2002) report on the development of the Alzheimer Predictive Index. Physicians can use this index to assess people who have some memory loss. Research shows that 89 percent of the time the index can predict the

---

● **Exhibit 6.6**

THE PREVALENCE OF DEMENTIA IN CANADA

Age	Dementia (%)	Alzheimer's (%)
65–74	2.4	1.0
85+	34.5	26.0
All 65+	8.0	5.1

The Canadian Study of Health and Aging reported the above estimates for the prevalence of dementia in Canada. "These Canadian estimates of the prevalence of dementia," the report says, "fall towards the upper end of the ranges in other studies, whereas the estimates for Alzheimer's disease fall in the middle of the ranges. This may suggest an unusual balance between Alzheimer's and other forms of dementia in the Canadian population."

Source: Adapted from Canadian Study of Health and Aging Working Group, 1994, "Canadian Study of Health and Aging: Study Methods and Prevalence of Dementia," *Canadian Medical Association Journal* 150(6): 899–913. Online at http://www.uottawa.ca/academic/med/epid/csha1.htm (October 24, 2003).

onset of Alzheimer's disease within two years. This index and other new methods will lead to quicker diagnosis. Early diagnosis helps families cope with the disease's progress. Research on early treatment may develop ways to slow or stop the progress of the disease.

Organic disorders pose problems for the affected individuals and their families. Family caregivers often feel despair because their care receiver does not recognize them anymore. This can add to their burden. A better understanding of memory loss might help these caregivers cope with their care receivers' illnesses.

Sainsbury and Coristine (1986, 99) studied patients with cognitive impairment. They found that patients often could not recognize a relative's picture, but these same patients could choose the relative's picture from a set of four pictures. The researchers said that even though a person loses "recognition memory," "affective memory" remains intact. This finding suggests that cognitively impaired patients may have good feelings toward their relatives, even if they do not seem to recognize them.

● Exhibit 6.7

DIRECT INTERVENTIONS IN THE CASE OF ALZHEIMER'S DISEASE

Tierney and Charles (2002) and Roberts and her colleagues (2000) reviewed the literature on interventions that help patients and families cope with Alzheimer's disease. The points below list some of the most common problems patients and families face and some successful interventions.

Functional Behaviour

- Urinary Incontinence—behaviour modification, scheduled toileting, and prompted voiding routines (work best in community settings).
- Activities of Daily Living—graded assistance, verbal prompts, physical demonstrations, home help.

Disruptive Behaviour

- Verbal Disruption—music, family-generated videotapes, one-to-one social interactions, audiotaped phone conversations.
- Aggression, Agitation, Mood Disturbance—daily walking program, light exercise, music preferred by the patient, dim lights, drug therapy. The authors caution that drug therapies (such as the use of anti-psychotic drugs) should begin only after other interventions have failed. Even then, such interventions apply best to problems such as delusions, anxiety, and agitation. The authors further caution that drugs should begin at a low

dosage, and caregivers should monitor drugs for effectiveness and side effects.
- Emotional Disturbance—homelike atmosphere, small-sized units, increased lighting, gardens, low stimulation, and limited relocation.
- Acting out—specialized care units.

Memory Loss

- Time/Space Disorientation—reality orientation, remind person of time and place.
- Forgetfulness—reminiscence therapy (minor improvements in memory, but improved staff–patient relations); AchE-Is (acetylcholinesterase inhibitors, which show small but statistical and clinical improvements in patients with moderate Alzheimer's disease). (Long-term treatment may delay nursing home placement and death—but this is only a preliminary finding.)

Caregiver Stress

- Lack of Social Support—counselling and support group membership; weekly support group and available counsellors.
- Conflict with Care Receiver—home-based training where caregiver and care receiver practice working together on tasks.
- Lack of Knowledge—educational training (e.g., a multi-week program of information sharing).

Sources: Adapted from M.C. Tierney and J. Charles, 2002, "The Care and Treatment of People with Dementia and Cognitive Impairment: An Update," in National Advisory Council on Aging, *Writings in Gerontology: Mental Health and Aging* 18: 97–113; and J. Roberts et al., 2002, "Specialized Continuing Care Models for Persons with Dementia: A Systematic Review of the Research Literature," *Canadian Journal on Aging* 19(1): 106–26. Reprinted by permission of Canadian Gerontological Association (www.utpjournals.com/cja).

The researchers added that "the subject may be aware that he knows the visitor but not recall the relationship. Awareness of this fact in conjunction with the knowledge that severely impaired people can yet possess strong affective associations can be of considerable comfort to concerned relatives" (Sainsbury and Coristine 1986, 103). Harrison (1993, 436) says that caregivers can focus "on those positive interests, characteristics and abilities which remain and may be strengthened through thoughtful and personalized interventions."

Still, people with Alzheimer's disease pose practical problems for their families. Patients sometimes suffer from depression or may sleep all day and wander all night. Sometimes they leave home and lose their way. All these behaviours create stress for caregivers. McShane and his colleagues (1998) found that families tended to institutionalize a cognitively impaired family member if the person tried to get through locked doors, wandered, and got lost. In partnership with the Royal Canadian Mounted Police, the Alzheimer Society of Canada (2004) established the Safely Home—Alzheimer Wandering Registry, a national database of people with Alzheimer's disease. Police can use the database to help find and return a lost person home. In addition, the Ministry of the Solicitor General has funded the creation of a police handbook to advise police on how to deal with Alzheimer's patients (*Seniors Today* 1995).

Families often feel committed to keeping their care receiver at home. Nahmiash (1995) reports that families supply 70 to 80 percent of the care given to older relatives in North America. Smale and Dupuis (2003a, 2003b) conducted a study of dementia caregivers in Ontario. They found that caregivers most often reported that (among supports currently provided) they needed home health care, in-home respite care, and adult day-away programs. They also reported a need for support groups, homemaker services, and transportation services.

But when a care receiver's behaviour becomes too difficult to handle, even the best family supports and community care cannot relieve caregiver burden. For example, Lévesque and her colleagues (2000) studied the use of services by caregivers in Quebec. They found that some family members with dementia resist day-care programs and won't cooperate with in-home helpers. This made it hard for family caregivers to get the day care or the attendant help they need. Family caregivers risk burnout unless they get some relief. One woman in Ontario, who cared for her husband with dementia, described her feelings.

> Many times I've locked myself in the bathroom, not because I was afraid of what [my husband] might do but just to get away from the constant barrage.... I'm very exhausted.... I'm on my own and I'm getting very down, I've done more crying in the past two years than I ever thought I had in me.

Another woman who cares for her husband says, "I haven't had any peace of mind or rest for years. [My doctor] said I had a high rate of burnout, caregiver burnout and he said you can't go on like this anymore" (Dupuis and Smale 2004).

Professional caregivers can also feel burdened by the demands of dementia patients. A study by Novak, Chappell, and Miles-Tapping (1990) found that nursing assistants who were distressed by patient behaviour felt most burdened. In the coming years, service workers will care for more and more clients with these illnesses and will need to understand the basis of the illness and how to treat these clients.

Functional Disorders

Functional disorders disrupt normal life. They include emotional upset, depression, and anxiety. The Canadian Medical Association (1987, cited in MacCourt et al. 2002) says that about 30 percent of older people in Canada need mental health care services. Health and Welfare Canada (1991, cited in MacCourt et al. 2002) puts the need at 25 percent. Studies report rates of mental disorder between 10 percent and 25 percent among institutionalized older people (Préville et al. 2002).

Still, the majority of community-dwelling older people today report generally good mental health. In 2002, the Canadian Community Health Survey (CCHS) asked a sample of 30 000 people aged 15 and over from across Canada to report on their mental health. The study found that, compared to the population aged 15 to 64, the group aged 65 and over reported about the same level of very good or excellent mental health (66 percent). Older people, compared to younger people, report the least contact with services and support associated with mental health. And only about 1 percent of older people report having an unmet mental health care need (the lowest of any age group). They also reported the lowest rate of barriers to getting mental health care (Statistics Canada 2003c).

Depression

Depression refers to a state where a person feels sad, helpless, irritable, and hopeless (Normand 2000). In general, studies have found that the risk of depression decreases in later life. People aged 65 and over have a lower risk than

Exhibit 6.8

THE STAGES OF DECLINE DUE TO ALZHEIMER'S DISEASE

Health and Welfare Canada (1984) has described the three stages that an Alzheimer's patient goes through. Some people may go through these stages in a few months; for others, it may take years. The changes that come with Alzheimer's disease begin slowly. Often family members recognize the first signs only when they look back over a year or two of caregiving.

Stage I: A person first shows changes in memory. They forget their keys or their wallet more frequently. They may also forget recent events or forget that they did a job around the house. The forgetfulness gets worse over time. The person forgets more often, takes longer to do simple jobs, or begins to recheck work already done.

One woman recalls that her husband, an engineering professor, would spend three or four hours writing a 50-minute lecture that used to take him an hour to write. Another woman recalls that she first became worried when her husband, a physician, lost his way home from work one night. He planned to stop at a patient's house for a short house call around 5 p.m. The patient lived only a few blocks away from their house, so his wife expected him home by 6 p.m. She began to worry at 8 p.m. when she still hadn't heard from him. An hour later he came in exhausted. He had spent the last three hours driving around their neighbourhood looking for their house.

Stage II: The second stage of the disease includes more memory decline, loss of speaking ability, and an end to normal daily activity. The ill person may wander at night, lose control of his or her bowel and bladder, and threaten others. One woman left a knife in her garden after she used it to weed the flower bed. Her husband picked it up and stalked through the bushes into a neighbour's yard, saying to the neighbour, "I'm going to kill you." The neighbour ran inside and called the police. When the man's wife came outside to finish weeding, she found the police wrestling her husband into a squad car.

In another case, a man walked into a new car dealer and signed a contract for a $20 000 car. His wife found out only after the salesman called her to check on the financing. The owner of the dealership agreed to void the contract, but only after she pleaded and explained about her husband's illness.

This stage of the disease can put stress on the family. Caregivers—most often spouses or children of the ill person—can feel tense, trapped, and exhausted. Family members have to take on new roles: Wives become chauffeurs or nurses; children become parents or police; and husbands become homemakers (Novak and Guest 1985). Mace and Rabins (1981, 63) report one case of a burdened husband who had to bathe his wife. "She screams for help the whole time I am bathing her. She'll open the windows and yell, 'Help, I'm being robbed.'" One man confessed to Mace and Rabins, "There was a time when I considered getting a gun, killing my wife, and then killing myself" (179).

Stage III: The person in the last stage of Alzheimer's disease needs institutionalization and often 24-hour nursing care. The person can no longer speak or communicate. He or she may wander or move constantly unless restrained. Seizures may occur. Death occurs between two and nineteen years after the disease starts (Health and Welfare Canada 1984). Death often comes from an illness such as pneumonia or heart disease, but death certificates rarely mention Alzheimer's disease as a cause of death, making it impossible to know the exact number of deaths caused by Alzheimer's.

Not all Alzheimer's patients show all the above-mentioned symptoms. Some show other symptoms of confusion such as depression and crying. But these stages give a general picture of the disease. They also give only a faint idea of the stress that Alzheimer's disease puts on the primary caregiver.

any other age group (Normand 2000). The CCHS found that only 1.8 percent of older people reported a major depressive disorder (Statistics Canada 2003c). Those aged 75 and over had a rate less than 1 percent. Cohen (1990) notes that controversy over prevalence rates exists for most mental disorders in later life. He reports that depression can appear as vague physical decline or complaints about more than one physical symptom. These cases would increase the estimated proportion of depressed older people in the community.

● Exhibit 6.9

RATES OF HOSPITALIZATION FOR ONE OF SEVEN MENTAL ILLNESSES* IN GENERAL HOSPITALS PER 100 000 BY AGE AND SEX, CANADA, 1999/2000

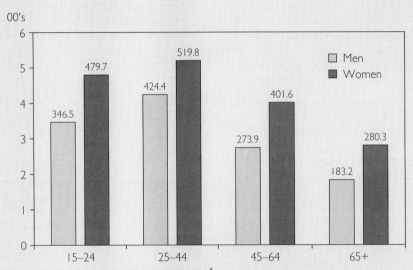

Note that hospitalization due to mental illness (for functional disorders) decreases with age for both men and women. The oldest age group shows the lowest rate of hospitalization for this type of mental illness.

*The seven diagnoses most responsible for hospitalization are anxiety disorders, bipolar disorders, schizophrenia, major depression, personality disorders, eating disorders, and attempted suicide.

Source: Adapted from Health Canada, 2002, *A Report on Mental Illnesses in Canada*, Ottawa: Health Canada Editorial Board, p. 18.

People with resources such as social skills, problem-solving ability, and emotional support from family and friends will less likely feel depressed (Antonucci 2001). A person who appraises a situation as non-threatening or who copes actively to improve situations will also show less depression (Cappliez 1988). This perspective shows that social as well as psychological conditions influence depression (Reker 1997).

Social support buffers the effect of poor health and protects a person from feeling depressed. A study of depression among elderly Chinese Canadians supports this conclusion. Lai (2000) studied a sample of older Chinese people in Calgary. He found that 9.4 percent of his sample reported mild depression and 11.5 percent reported moderate to severe depression. This sample had higher rates of depression than did the general population of older people in Canada. He says that depressed Chinese elders often lack access to mental health supports. Their inability to speak English creates

a barrier to support. Also Chinese elders may not understand the Western approach to mental health. We will look in more detail at the influence of social conditions on psychological well-being in Chapter 7.

Préville and his colleagues (2002) studied psychological distress in institutionalized and frail community-dwelling older people. They found that nearly 47 percent of their total sample showed psychological distress (three times the rate of the Quebec general older population). They found that, compared to institutionalized older people, frail older people who lived alone had more than twice the rate of psychological distress. Also, people with functional limitations reported more psychological distress.

The "unhappy" Canadian, the Canada Health Survey reports, is likely to be old, female, widowed, low income, in poor health, and without much education (Health and Welfare Canada and Statistics Canada 1981). The inability to get out and the loss of social supports can also lead to unhappiness or depression. Gilbart and Hirdes (2000) studied institutionalized older people in Ontario hospitals. They found that many of these residents reported sadness and some anxiety. And people with the least social engagement reported the least happiness. A study of depression in nursing home patients by Laprise and Vézina (1998) supports this idea. They used two scales and found depression rates in a nursing home of 56 percent and 46 percent. People in the best health get the most out of social engagement. A decrease in social supports in later life puts the mental health of infirm and isolated older Canadians at risk. Gilbart and Hirdes (2000) say that care planning should take a holistic approach. It should include attention to patients' psychosocial as well as physical needs.

Treatment and Intervention

Mental health experts sometimes ignore the needs of older people. Eaton, Stones, and Rockwood (1986), for example, found that physicians often failed to detect cognitive impairment in older patients. The researchers suggest that doctors, during their medical school training, should receive more knowledge about the care and treatment of mental disorders in older people. Continuing medical education could also include this training. Doctors need to understand the causes and treatment of mental disorders in later life (MacCourt et al. 2002).

A range of treatments can help older people cope with psychological problems. Smyer, Zarit, and Qualls (1990) believe that the individual's characteristics (including age), the diagnosis criteria used, the older person's adaptation patterns, and the intervention setting (community or institution) all influence the choice of treatment. Some reversible organic brain syndromes can be treated with chemical therapies. Physicians can treat alcoholics in the early stages of Wernicke-Korsakoffs dementia (a neurological disease) with large doses of thiamine.

Many therapies exist for older people with functional problems—problems related to a person's personality or social life. Drug therapy can help older people cope with anxiety and depression; behaviour therapy can help with insomnia; and psychotherapy can help the person who has a personality disorder (Gatz and Smyer 2001). Katz (1999, cited in Gatz and Smyer 2001) says that problem solving, interpersonal and brief psychotherapy should form the first line of treatment for depression. Life review (Butler and Lewis 1982) can help with adaptation to loss, and milieu therapy, where a person makes changes to his or her environment, can help a person deal with stress-related problems.

Some clinicians suggest the use of pets to help relieve loneliness. Goldmeier (1986) found that older people who had pets reported less loneliness, and that older people who lived with other people, even without pets, showed the least loneliness. Goldmeier says that pets cannot fully substitute for human companionship, but pets can create non-threatening relationships for people who might otherwise reject therapy or other human contact.

A recent policy statement by the Canadian Association on Gerontology (MacCourt et al. 2002) points out the need for specialized training for health care providers and special services to meet the needs of older people. Special services would include day programs, outpatient assessment units, and community outreach programs designed to serve psychogeriatric patients. The association's policy statement supports a social model of care. This model looks at the social and environmental (as well as the psychological) needs of the older person. It also proposes a multidisciplinary response to these needs. Chapter 8 will discuss in more detail this general shift toward a comprehensive health care model.

The Loss of Competence

Psychological intervention can sometimes protect the older person from harm. It can also lead to making decisions for people who can no longer decide for themselves. A person with a cognitive impairment may lose the ability to understand his or her situation and make decisions. But when should another person step in to make decisions for someone else? Checkland and Silberfeld (1993) say that this should occur only after a careful assessment of a person's **competency**.

Saint-Arnaud (1993, 35) defines competency as the ability to "understand information relevant to the decision to be taken, weigh the pros and cons in terms of his/her goals and values" and to be "capable of communicating decisions" (see also Silberfeld 1994). Competency differs from **legal capacity**, "the exercise of rights by all citizens" (Saint-Arnaud 1993). Legal incapacity refers to the loss of civil rights when a person comes into protective care. In this case, someone else (a lawyer, family member, or the public trustee) has the legal right to make decisions for the older person. This guardian attempts to follow, to the extent that he or she knows them, the wishes of the person under care.

A person's competency gets formally decided through an assessment by a professional (a physician, psychiatrist, or other recognized expert). An assessment attempts to answer the question of whether a person should lose their legal rights based on their inability to make a decision. An assessment should ensure the same assessment standards for everyone and the absence of an assessor's bias. Also, assessment should take place more than once to monitor a person's present and future ability to make decisions (Silberfeld 1992). If a person has been assessed as being incompetent, that person's ability to make choices on his or her own behalf is removed, so writers on this topic urge caution in making the judgment.

Checkland and Silberfeld (1993) say that, even after an assessment of incompetence, others should intervene as little as possible. For example, they say that a person may have lost the ability to manage money, but may still have the ability to live at home. Thus, a person can have decision-specific capacities. The researchers propose that someone else make decisions for this person on financial issues, but the person keep the right to make the decision on where to live. The authors say that competency should rest both on mental ability and on what a person can do. For example, a person may thrive at home but not have the verbal skill to say how it is done. Silberfeld (1994) says that a competency assessment should find this person competent. Also, any view of a person's decision-making ability should take into account that individual's past decisions, values, and track record (Silberfeld et al. 1996). Shidler (1998) says that in cases of decisions about life-prolonging treatment, the physician and the proxy (often a family member) should involve the older person as much as possible.

The issue of competency can often come up in cases of older people at risk. An older person may feel able to live on his or her own. The individual's children may feel this puts the person at risk. Older people who want to live on their own may minimize risk and hope all goes well. But "caregivers, who fear the worst, can magnify the risk" (NACA 1993g, 3).

The NACA (1993c, 2) presents the following case:

Mrs. X is an 86-year-old widow who has lived alone with the help of home support services for the past ten years. She is an insulin-dependent diabetic with a sweet tooth. During the past two years, she has become increasingly short of memory and confused. She often forgets to eat or eats junk food. Efforts to have her live with her only son and daughter-in-law several miles away have failed. The home care case manager is becoming uncomfortable because, even with the maximum level of home care available, Mrs. X is considered to be at risk. Following a fall, where she fractured her wrist, she was hospitalized. The son, in consultation with home care, decided to institutionalize his mother. Mrs. X is clearly unhappy in the nursing home, objecting to all aspects of her care and continually asking when she can go home.

Has the son acted in his mother's best interests or in his own? Family members may consult the family doctor for a competency assessment in order to carry out their own wishes. This assessment may go along with a desire to assume **legal guardianship** for the older person. But guardianship (where the court appoints someone to make decisions on the older person's behalf) also creates a risk. "Starting from assuredly good intentions [to keep the older person from harm], risk becomes part of an unconscious rhetoric for controlling elderly people" (Silberfeld 1992, 134).

Naglie and his colleagues (1995) point to the importance of careful competency assessment in an aging society. The label of incompetence removes a person's free choice, and experts should apply it with caution. Stelmach, Konnert, and Dobson (2001, 390) say that "competence is specific to one moment in time and one decision at a time, and therefore, does not refer to a ... [person's] ability to make all decisions." Browne and his colleagues (2002) say that interference with a person's liberty should take the mildest form necessary to ensure the person's and his or her care receiver's safety. They propose that in health care facilities, for example, staff should document problem behaviours in writing before placing limits on a person's freedom. Borovoy (1982, cited in NACA 1993a, 4) says that "when we are talking about the precious freedom to be left alone, then we should insist that it cannot be lost unless there are the most exacting criteria and the most scrupulous procedures."

CONCLUSION

Psychological well-being means more than coping with problems, stress, and loss. It means growth, learning, and a sense of purpose. The research on the psychology of aging shows that older people in good health stay alert, intelligent, and able to learn. They face stresses unique to later life, but they can get through these crises, often with the help of others. Sometimes the biggest block to older people's well-being comes from the prejudices and stereotypes other people have about old age. The research on the psychology of aging has begun to remove the basis for these stereotypes. Studies have begun to explore and describe the changes that take place in old age. They have begun to chart human potential in later life. More research and knowledge about old age and new cohorts of older people will teach us more about mental potential in old age.

Summary

1. Psychological studies of aging take three forms: the psychology of the aged, the psychology of age, and the psychology of aging. The psychology of aging studies change in individuals over time. It looks at the effects of aging on psychological abilities.

2. Early research supported the myth that intellectual ability declines with age, but recent studies show more complex findings. For example, younger people perform better than older people on memory and intelligence tests in the lab. But the pace of testing, the types of questions asked, and the way older people learn can all affect the older person's performance.

3. In general, laboratory studies show that memory declines with age, although different types of memory show different amounts of decline. Recent research suggests that a decrease in working memory accounts for poorer memory in older people. Education and background differences between older and younger people may account for some of the differences in performance in memory studies.

4. Test conditions may decrease older people's ability to remember in laboratory studies. Studies of memory in real-world (not laboratory) contexts show that older people can compensate for memory declines. Studies also show that when compared, younger and older people's recall of historical and social events showed little or no deficit for older people.

5. Early studies used cross-sectional methods to study the effects of aging on intelligence. The results confused cohort differences with age changes. Longitudinal methods show declines in fluid intelligence (problem-solving skills). But they show little change in crystallized intelligence (skills based on acquired knowledge). Research also shows that older people can improve their scores on intelligence tests through training. Willis (1990) studied intelligence scores in individuals over time. She found that some people showed stable fluid intelligence scores, and others showed decline. Training increased both types of individuals' abilities.

6. New models of intelligence have begun to look at human potential in later life. Researchers have begun to study wisdom—older people's good judgment and their expert knowledge about life.

7. Studies of both the quality and quantity of creative production show a decline in creativity with age. Comparisons of older and younger people on psychological tests also find greater creativity among younger subjects. Both of these approaches to the study of creativity emphasize the products of creative work. Reports of subjective creative development show that people can create and learn to do so at any age. Education, opportunity, and an interest in a subject can all lead to creativity in later life.

8. The number of cases of organic brain disorders such as Alzheimer's disease will increase as more people live to late old age. These disorders place a heavy burden on families, and the people with these diseases often need professional health care at the end of their lives.

9. Functional mental disorders (e.g., anxiety and depression) show up less often in old age than people commonly believe. Older people with these problems can benefit from drug therapies, psychotherapy, or milieu therapy.

10. Older people can lose competence to manage their lives due to organic or functional problems. Researchers, ethicists, and physicians work to clarify the concept of competency. They want to find a definition and assessment of competency that serves older people's needs and limits restrictions on their rights.

11. The research on the psychology of aging presents a balanced view of aging. Some mental faculties may decline, but others remain stable as long as a person is in good health. More research and knowledge about the process of aging will teach us more about mental potential in later life.

Study Questions

1. State the three psychological approaches to the study of aging. Discuss the benefits and limitations of each approach.
2. What approaches have psychologists taken to the study of memory in later life? State two findings that show up in most laboratory studies. How do laboratory and contextual studies of memory differ in what they conclude about memory in later life?
3. What do psychologists mean when they speak of intelligence as multidimensional? Describe the differences between fluid and crystallized intelligence.
4. Discuss the costs and benefits of longitudinal and cross-sectional studies of memory.
5. What are some of the newest theories about intelligence and aging?
6. State three ways in which psychologists measure creativity in later life. What do each of these measures find?
7. What do psychologists mean by organic disorders? Give some examples. What do they mean by functional disorders? Give some examples.
8. What treatments do psychologists propose for organic disorders? For functional disorders?
9. What issues does the loss of competence raise for the older person? For the person's physician? For the family? Discuss the tension that exists between older people's potential need for protection and their right to make decisions for themselves.

Key Terms

cognitive mechanics information-processing mechanisms that implement fluid intelligence. (113)

cognitive pragmatics culture- and knowledge-related applications of intelligence, similar to crystallized intelligence. (113)

competence the real-world skill used to adapt or respond to a challenge. (110)

competency the ability to understand information that applies to a decision, the ability to think about the consequences of the decision, and the ability to communicate a decision. (125)

constant-probability-of-success model a model that states that the greater the number of creative works a person produces in a given period within a career, the more great works are produced. (116)

contextual view of memory the idea that many conditions influence memory, including physical, psychological, and social contexts and the knowledge, abilities, and characteristics of the individual, as well as the situation in which the individual is asked to remember. (109)

crystallized intelligence intelligence that depends on stored information, acculturation, and learning. (112)

depression the emotional state of feeling sad, helpless, irritable, and hopeless. (122)

developmental disability a significant impairment in mental ability present at birth or acquired in childhood or adolescence. (119)

encoding the process whereby a person puts new bits of information together with already stored information. (107)

episodic memory memory oriented toward the past, or acquired at specific time and place, as in learning in an experimental setting. (107)

fluid intelligence reasoning, abstracting, concept formation, and problem solving, with little use for knowledge gained through reading, schooling, or work. (112)

intelligence the "ability to negotiate environmental demands successfully" (Labouvie-Vief 1985, 506), "that which intelligence tests measure" (506), or what a person taking the test can do now. (111)

latency the length of time it takes for a person to process information or respond to a question. (107)

legal capacity the right of all citizens to take part in the legal process and to have civil rights. (125)

legal guardianship process in which the court appoints someone to make decisions on another person's behalf. (126)

long-term memory the storehouse of knowledge that also includes the rules for applying knowledge. (107)

mediator a picture of a word or a rhyme or some other intermediary used to help with remembering. (108)

memory the recall of information after learning has taken place. (106)

neurofibrillary tangles a sign of Alzheimer's disease in which neuronal fibres wrap around one another and fail to function properly. (106)

non-episodic memory memory oriented toward the present or the future with no reference to the time at which the person stored the memory; includes learned skills through practice or a person's general knowledge of the world. (107)

plasticity the ability to change and adapt. (113)

psychology of age a perspective in the psychological study of aging that focuses on differences between age groups. It uses cross-sectional methods to study differences between age groups. (106)

psychology of the aged a perspective in the psychological study of aging that emphasizes the biomedical view of aging as decline or disease, supporting ageism and the view of older people as a social problem. (106)

psychology of aging a perspective in the psychological study of aging that looks at changes in individuals over time, using longitudinal methods to study both gains and losses through the life cycle. (106)

semantic memory the store of factual information. (110)

sensory memory information perceived through the senses and stored as memory. (107)

short-term memory where information is stored temporarily while it is being processed or for a short time afterward. (107)

wisdom "expert knowledge about the important and fundamental matters of life, their interpretation and management" (Featherman, Smith, and Peterson 1990; see also Baltes et al. 1990). (113)

working memory where recent acquired information is manipulated and processed at the same time as it is being stored temporarily. (108)

Selected Readings

National Advisory Council on Aging. *Writings in Gerontology: Mental Health and Aging,* No. 18. Ottawa: Minister of Public Works and Government Services, 2002.

A collection of articles by experts in mental health and aging that discuss positive mental health as well as mental disorders. Articles also deal with groups that need special attention—gay and lesbian seniors, seniors in institutions, and people with dementia. Many of the articles review the literature on interventions and propose methods of treatment.

Park, D.C., and N. Schwarz, eds. *Cognitive Aging: A Primer.* Philadelphia: Taylor & Francis, 2001.

This book reviews recent research on mental activity in later life. Topics range from a report on the underlying mechanisms of mental activity, to a summary of research on memory, to applied topics like cognitive aging and health. A well-written book that tackles complex topics. A challenge to the beginning student, but useful for a more advanced look at these topics.

Smith, Anderson. "Memory." In James E. Birren and K. Warner Schaie, eds. *Handbook of the Psychology of Aging,* 4th ed., pp. 236–50. San Diego: Academic Press, 1996.

A good review of the literature covering the major theories that attempt to account for age differences in memory. The article refers to basic topics in the field such as working memory, memory for different types of information (spatial location, nonverbal material), and issues of validity of laboratory testing.

Chapter Seven

The Social Psychology of Aging

Photo © Ariel Skelley/CORBIS/MAGMA

INTRODUCTION

What is a good old age? What social forces shape adult development? What contexts and social conditions lead to good aging? These questions have guided research in the social psychology of aging for more than 50 years. Researchers have found that many patterns of good aging exist. What follows are three cases that show the variety of forms a good old age can take.

Joe Willis, 70, worked as an engineer for an oil company until he retired. Now he spends January and February playing golf in Florida and spends the summer at his cottage in Muskoka. His company calls him back two or three times a year as a consultant; he serves on the board of directors of a seniors' centre; and he volunteers as a nursing home visitor. "I visit the old folks once a week," he says. "At Christmas I take them to a show or out shopping." Joe does not see himself as old. He works less now and has more leisure time, but he feels the same as before he retired. He stays active and involved and has found new ways to give meaning to his life.

Birdie Caldwell's husband died 15 years ago. She moved out of their house and into a two-bedroom apartment a year after his death. She also went back to work as a secretary—work she had not done since her teens. Now, at age 65, she still lives on her own. She has two daughters who live less than an hour away by car. She visits them a few times a month and sometimes stays for the weekend. She travels, belongs to a bridge group, and enjoys her freedom.

Rose Reitman, 73, also lives by herself in her own apartment. Her husband died three years ago. She has a bad case of arthritis in her legs, which keeps her indoors most of the year. On warm days she walks a few blocks to the local shopping centre. Most of the time she watches TV, knits, or talks to friends on the phone. Rose feels content in her old age. She sometimes talks to 10 or 15 friends and relatives in a week. Nieces and nephews call her from all over the country on her birthday or on holidays. Her daughter lives two and a half hours away by car, and her son lives across the country. She has six grandchildren; their pictures cover her walls and tabletops.

Three different portraits of old age: Birdie stays active; Rose lives a quiet life without social demands; Joe has found new roles to replace ones he had lost. Each of these people shows a different response to the challenges of aging, but they all report high life satisfaction. These cases show only a few of the patterns of successful aging today.

This chapter will look at (1) theories of human development in later life, (2) the social structural conditions (such as membership in an ethnic community) that influence the experience of aging, and (3) some social-psychological problems that older people face in society today.

WHAT IS A GOOD OLD AGE?

Three social-psychological theories of aging—disengagement theory, activity theory, and continuity theory—each claim to describe the ideal way to grow old. Researchers have debated the merits of these theories since the 1960s, and references to them show up in the literature even today.

Disengagement Theory

Early work by Cumming and Henry (1961) describe old age as a time of disengagement—a time to withdraw from social roles and to decrease activity. They base **disengagement theory** on a study of 279 people aged 50 to 70 in Kansas City. The study focused on people in good health and with enough money to live comfortably. They found that in this sample social roles and emotional ties decreased with age.

Cumming and Henry (1961) describe disengagement as inevitable, universal, and satisfying to both the person and society. Disengagement, they say, serves an important psychological function: It allows older people to reduce their activity naturally as their strength declines. Disengagement also serves a useful social function: It allows older people to leave social roles before the final disengagement—death. This withdrawal creates a smooth transfer of power and responsibility from one generation to the next.

Almost as soon as disengagement theory appeared, critics attacked it on three fronts. First, disengagement theory supports the stereotype of old age as a time of weakness and decline. Second, the theory assumes that the old perform less well than the young and, therefore, supports the existence of mandatory retirement based on age, rather than on a person's ability to do the job. Third, the theory assumes that all older people respond to the world in the same way—that they all disengage from social roles. More recent research shows that many older people, especially those who have good health and a good income, stay active in later life (Markides and Mindel 1987).

Activity Theory

Neugarten, Havighurst, and Tobin (1968) put forward a second major theory of aging: **activity theory**. This theory is just the reverse of disengagement theory. It holds that, as people lose social roles in old age, they stay happiest when they replace these roles with new ones. This theory, moreover, blames society for the process of disengagement. Modern society, it says, pushes older people out of social roles. The activity theory fits the North American view that happiness comes from work and activity.

Neugarten, Havighurst, and Tobin (1968) found three types of active people who reported high life satisfaction. One group started new activities to fill in for lost social roles. The researchers called them "reorganizers." Another group held on to their mid-life roles and stayed active. The researchers said these people were "holding on." A third group stayed active but narrowed the range of their activities, and this group the researchers described as "focused." Most recent studies also find that high activity correlates with high life satisfaction.

Lemon, Bengtson, and Peterson (1972b) set out to test activity theory. They asked 411 older people about their activities and their life satisfaction. The researchers found little relationship between the frequency of activities and life satisfaction. Only informal activities with friends predicted life satisfaction. They say that "the data provide surprisingly little support for the implicit activity theory of aging" (31). Today, most gerontologists feel that both disengagement and activity theories provide too narrow a view of aging.

Continuity Theory

A third theory of aging is that people feel most satisfied if they continue the roles and activities of their middle years (Atchley 1982). This theory, **continuity theory**, says that old age is a continuation of a person's past (rather than a break with it or a change in direction) and that people will choose the lifestyle in old age that is most like the pattern of life they lived in middle age. People will adapt to new situations by using successful patterns of behaviour from their past (Atchley 1999). Mildly active people in their younger years will prefer a mild level of activity in later life and will feel satisfied with this lifestyle. But active people will want to keep up their activity—although activity might take new forms in old age. Quirouette and Pushkar (1999) found that well-educated women plan to continue their activities. The women studied had a strong core identity and expected their abilities to continue into later life. Research by Smale and Dupuis (1993, 298–99) supports

"the importance of continued involvement in leisure activity throughout one's lifetime even if some activities are dropped in favour of others."

These three theories tell part of the truth about life satisfaction in later life, but all of them give too simple a picture of old age. Some people disengage from some roles and still have high life satisfaction; other people remain active and still feel little life satisfaction. Life satisfaction, in part, depends on the kind of activity a person takes part in. Smale and Dupuis (1993) say that older people find satisfaction in activities that have personal meaning. "It may not simply be hobbies and crafts which are related to well-being, but rather the opportunity they provide for freedom of choice, self-expression, and personal fulfilment" (Dupuis and Smale, 1995, 84). Lemon, Bengtson, and Peterson (1972a) found that while a decline in group activities did not lead to lower life satisfaction, a decline in social activity with friends did. Kozma and Stones (1978, 248) conclude that activity or disengagement alone do not lead to happiness, but that "people appear to be happy if most of their experiences are pleasant and their perceived needs are met."

PERSONALITY DEVELOPMENT

Stage Theories

Some psychologists who study the individual in society focus on personality development. A number of researchers describe this development as a series of stages. Erik Erikson (1963), for instance, created one of the best-known stage models of the life cycle. McCrae and Costa (1990, 11–12) call it "the single most important theory of adult personality development." Erikson's model describes eight stages of ego development. At each stage, he says, the person faces a crisis with two possible outcomes. If a person gets through the crisis successfully, growth occurs. As a result, the person reaches a new stage of development. If not, the person experiences some psychopathology that inhibits further development.

The task of late adulthood, Erikson says, is "to be, through having been, to face not being" (1959, Appendix). Wisdom is the virtue of this last stage; it comes when the person achieves "**integrity**" and overcomes the threat of "despair and disgust" (1959, 98). Like other psychoanalytical thinkers (Bühler 1951; Jung 1976), Erikson describes old age as a time of inwardness, a time when a person reflects on the past and brings closure to life. At this point, he says, a person with a healthy personality accepts his life as the product of his own actions within a particular culture. This last stage sums up the seven earlier stages, and when a person achieves

● **Exhibit 7.1**

MEN, WOMEN, AND LIFE SATISFACTION

Men and women report differences in life satisfaction and personality in later life. Connidis (1983b) asked a sample of 400 older Canadians how they felt about aging. She found that most people had a positive view of later life, although they had a realistic view of the problems that come with aging. She also found that men and women differed in how much they liked, disliked, and worried about old age. For example, 71 percent of men, compared with 56 percent of women, reported no worries about growing older. When the older people in Connidis's sample did complain about old age, men complained more often about physical restrictions while women complained more often about poor health.

Men and women also liked different things about aging. Men more often mentioned good health and freedom from work as things they liked about old age. Women more often mentioned contentment and freedom from family responsibility. These findings probably reflect the different social roles played by this generation of older men and women in their early and middle years. Most of these women had worked at home raising families, while the men had worked in the labour force. In later life they each felt a different kind of freedom—women felt the freedom from child rearing, and men felt the freedom from work. These kinds of responses may change in future studies as women today spend time on careers as well as child rearing.

integrity, Erikson says, it brings a wholeness to life. A person who displays integrity inspires the young to trust in the culture and to follow its prescriptions for action (Erikson 1963, 269; Erikson 1982, 63).

Some writers have expanded on Erikson's outline of middle and later life. Erikson began as a child psychologist, and his life-cycle model reflects his interest in children. In his classic paper "Growth and Crises of the Healthy Personality" (1950), for example, he spends 45 pages on the first 20 years of life and devotes only five pages to the next 50 to 60 years. Peck ([1955] 1968) modified Erikson's model by adding more stages to it.

Erikson's last stage, Peck ([1955] 1968, 88) said, "seems to be intended to represent in a global, nonspecific way all the psychological crises and crisis-solutions of the last forty or fifty years of life." Peck divided this last stage of life into two periods—middle and old age. He found seven crises a person had to overcome within these periods. At each stage, the person gives up the narrow commitments—to the body, to people, to concepts, and, finally, to the self—that dominated earlier stages of life. Peck's work shows that middle and later life are complex and active periods of development.

Erikson, Peck, and others (Gould 1978; Levinson 1978) propose that a stage model of development best describes middle and later life. Each writer proposes an ideal pattern of aging and development, implying that those who follow it live a successful old age, while those who deviate from it face problems and frustrations as they age. Later studies question whether a set of universal stages exists. Surveys of large numbers of people

have not found the stages these models predict. Lacy and Hendricks (1980), for example, looked for attitude changes predicted by Gould's work. They used data from a survey of more than 9000 people, but could not find attitude shifts to support Gould's stages.

Braun and Sweet (1983–84) reviewed data from four large surveys to see if passages from one stage of life to another existed. They compared personality differences within and between age groups.

They did find personality differences between age groups. But they also found that in studies done at different times and in different countries (the United States and Canada), the characteristics of each age stage differed. In addition, they found that after a passage around age 19, little developmental change took place in people's attitudes as they aged. These findings don't support the stage model of adult development. Dixon and Cohen (2001, 135) say that the research shows personality changes in adulthood. But it doesn't show "changes through particular sequences leading to specific endstates."

Butler (1975; see also Novak 1985–86) has criticized the stage model of development for another reason. He challenges the idea that people in old age can only accept who they are and what they have been. "People are locked in by such a theory," he says. They may look healthy from Erikson's point of view, but they suffer because they are trapped by their work, marriage, or lifestyle. "Excessive or exaggerated identity," according to Butler, "seems clearly to be an obstacle to continued growth and development through life and to appreciation of the future. Human beings need the freedom to live with change, to invent and reinvent themselves a number of times throughout their lives" (400–401). Blau (1973, 185) warns that adults can "become too well adjusted to society's expectation and insufficiently attuned to their own nature and needs" in old age.

Stage models create a simplistic picture of current conditions. Today, people divorce, remarry, have children, start businesses, leave careers, return to careers, and return to school at all ages in adulthood. Studies find many stages in the life cycle and different stages and patterns for men and women. These findings reflect the diversity of the life course in a time of social change (Ryff, Kwan, and Singer 2001).

SELF-DEVELOPMENT IN LATER LIFE

Current criticisms of stage models call for a more flexible model of the self in later life. Erikson's last stage of integrity versus despair and doubt points in this direction. He says that a person in later life can give meaning to past events and experiences and this can lead to integrity, a sense of wholeness and well-being. Some social psychologists put this dynamic model of the self at the centre of their studies (Ruth and Coleman 1996).

Breytspraak (1995, 93) defines the **self** as "the ability to be aware of one's own boundaries and individuality and to reflect upon these." Ritzer (1992, 202) says the self has "the ability to take oneself as an object." Thus it can act as both subject and object.

Breytspraak (1995) says that two motives shape behaviour as people age. First, people try to view themselves positively and to present a good image of themselves to others. Second, people try to maintain their sense of self in the face of a changing social environment. This makes the self a dynamic process more than a state of being. The self constantly shapes interaction and interprets events to achieve these two goals. Researchers report that self-constructs may change throughout life. Older people, compared to younger people, for example, have a more limited view of their future selves. They reported fewer hopes and fears for their future selves. And they tend to define themselves in relation to their current concerns, especially health (Blanchard-Fields and Abeles 1996).

Aging poses a number of challenges to the self. These challenges come from at least three sources: social attitudes toward older people, physical decline, and the loss of social roles. Ageism, for example, poses a challenge to everyone in later life; in our society a person must work to combat ageism. The self's sensitivity to

others' perceptions can make experiencing this bias a painful experience, as it can lower a person's self-esteem. A strong social support network will make it easier to resist and overcome ageism. For example, friends and family can give a person feelings of worth and importance that combat negative stereotypes.

Physical decline also challenges a person's sense of self. A person who derives self-esteem from playing sports may feel let down as his or her ability decreases with age. Losing the ability to drive can cause a profound blow to self-esteem because our culture links driving with maturity, adulthood, freedom, and self-efficacy. Even people with Alzheimer's disease, a radical loss of the self, resist giving up driving a car. Sports programs for older people, such as the Seniors Olympics or the Seniors Golf Tour, help people maintain their self-esteem in the face of physical decline. So do programs that refresh older people's driving skills.

Furthermore, role loss can rob a person of self-worth. Social roles give a person status, purpose, and a sense of achievement. Loss of roles threatens a person's well-being. Retirement, loss of a spouse, and the empty nest all challenge people's sense of self as they age. Most people cope with these role losses and find new sources of self-esteem. Someone may find self-worth in volunteer work by counselling others. A retired machinist may find self-esteem in a second career as a cabinet maker. Sometimes these new roles lead to a more satisfying sense of self. The challenge of role loss demands that the older person search for new meaning in later life.

Ryff and her colleagues (1999) report that higher income and more education lead to greater feelings of well-being in later life. Wealthier, better-educated people feel more purpose in life and report more personal growth in old age. This summary of the literature shows the link between the self and social conditions such as income, education, and social class. Likewise, a person's culture plays a role in self-development. How does the culture view old age? What roles does the culture offer older people? Answers to these questions shape a person's sense of self in later life. Ryff and Singer (1996, cited in Clarke et al. 2000) say that in modern society "opportunities for continued growth and development and for meaningful experience may be limited." Ryff, Kwan, and Singer (2001) call for more research on the effects of social integration on health in later life. Singer and Ryff (1999, cited in Ryff et al. 2001) found, for example, that people with a history of poverty showed less physical decline if they have strong social relationships.

McAdams (1996, 134) says that identity in later life relies on a "lifestory," and this story changes over time. Near the end of life, says McAdams (1990, cited in Ruth and Coleman 1996), the self may live in the present. Ruth and Coleman (1996, 317) review studies that describe a "spiritual Me." A person at this point may begin an inward journey. Tornstam (1994, 207–11, cited in Ruth and Coleman 1996) refers to this as "gerotranscendence"—the self begins to expand its boundaries and reflect on the meaning of human life.

SPIRITUALITY: THE SEARCH FOR MEANING IN LATER LIFE

The search for a good old age can take many forms, including religious faith, service attendance, and non-traditional spiritual beliefs. Some people see spirituality as the person's relationship to God. Others take a more philosophical view. Moberg (2001, 10) defines spirituality as a person's "ultimate concern, the basic value around which all other values are focused, the central philosophy of life." Spirituality can take place within organized religion or through personal beliefs and rituals. Some people express their spirituality outside traditional religious channels. They may feel oneness with nature or a commitment to the betterment of all life. Some older people turn to Eastern and Western meditation practices to feel a sense of wholeness. Yoga and tai chi exercises can create a sense of unity within oneself and with the environment. Studies show that spiritual practices such as these can lead to better health, improved social relations, and high life satisfaction (Chan 2003).

The diversity of Canadian life, with its many ethnic and cultural groups, leads to many different religious and spiritual perspectives. Most Canadians claim Christianity as their religious belief. Forty-four percent of adult Canadians claim Roman Catholicism as their form of Christianity and 30 percent claim Protestantism (Statistics Canada 2003s). Other faiths include Judaism, other Christian faiths, Islam, Bahai, Buddhism, Hinduism, Sikhism, Confucianism, and Taoism.

Canadian spiritual life in the past often centred on the church or synagogue. Religion gave people a common set of values, a community of like-minded people, and a meaning to life. Many older people today still feel a strong connection to their religious community and have a strong religious faith (Clark 2000; McFadden 1996).

Compared with other age groups, older Canadians report the highest rate of attendance at religious services (Clark 2000, 2003). Thirty-seven percent of seniors report that they engage in religious activity at least once a week (Baril and Mori 1991; Lindsay 1999). And older age groups have kept up their attendance even though younger age groups show a decrease in religious attendance. More than a third of the older people in one study said they would spend more time on religion if they could change their commitments (DeGenova 1992, cited in McFadden 1996).

A greater proportion of older women, compared with older men, report activity in their faith community. Older women stay active in their religious community even after widowhood. But widowers show a drop in attendance at services (Clark 2000). Seniors also report the largest financial contributions to their place of worship. Moberg (1997, cited in Schulz-Hipp 2001, 87) says that older people show the strongest religious belief "on almost all measures" and that "this has remained the same year after year when similar questions are asked."

This commitment to religion may partly reflect the past experiences of older people. In the past, religion played a bigger role in people's lives than it does today. The commitment to religion may also reflect the role that faith can play as health, income, and social supports decline in late old age. Koenig, George, and Siegler (1988, cited in National Advisory Council 1992c) say that older people use religious belief as a way to cope with stressful events. Coping methods included prayer, faith in God, and support from clergy and the faith community. Religious belief can help a person find meaning in the face of despair. Fry (2000) studied religiosity and spirituality in a community and an institutional sample of older people in Alberta. The study found that religious participation and spiritual practices predicted greater feelings of well-being. Religiosity and spirituality had more influence on well-being than measures of social resources or physical health.

Religious leaders and caregivers can help older people live their faith. It's important that professionals understand and respect the religious traditions of the people they serve. Professionals can help a religious community provide support to older members, and they can help older members take part in their religious communities. Support can take the form of arranging outreach religious services or car pools to places of worship.

Spiritual practices, whether formal religious services or quiet reflection on the past, can bring fullness to later life. Psychologist Viktor Frankl (1990, 7–10) teaches that later life provides a unique time for inner growth. He says that older people can bring in the "the harvest of their lives." McFadden (1996) says that researchers and practitioners need to learn more about the many expressions of religion and spirituality in later life. They can then apply this understanding to improve the quality of later life.

LIFE-SPAN DEVELOPMENTAL PERSPECTIVE

The **life-span development perspective** sees the individual as continually changing from birth to death (Baltes and Goulet 1970). Unlike stage models, it does not describe an end point or goal of development (such as integrity or ego transcendence). Instead, the life-span developmental model treats crisis and change as a constant part of life. "At the very moment when completion seems to be achieved," Riegel (1976, 697) says, "new questions and doubts arise in the individual and in society."

The life-span developmental model views development as a **dialectical process**. Through this process, the individual changes in response to societal demands and society changes in response to individual action and adaptation (Riegel 1975). Life-span developmental theorists find many patterns and stages of aging. They say that people's personalities differ, as do their coping styles and the resources they use in dealing with the world.

McDonald, Donahue, and Moore (2000), for example, describe the responses people make to unemployment in later life. They found at least two responses to layoffs in later life. Some people still saw themselves as workers and looked for new jobs. Other people defined the layoff as early retirement (see Ryff, Kwan, and Singer 2001). The path chosen by a person depended in part on the individual's pension benefits, the timing of the job loss, and the person's attitude. One early retiree said, "Oh, we were gearing down. We figured we'd retire at 60, so it was three years earlier." A less happy worker could barely contain his anger. He said, "Well, when I ... after all the time and never received the interviews and no answer back, I ... made up my mind, that's it. Like, that's me finished for the rest of my life for working" (McDonald, Donahue, and Moore 2000, 75).

The life-span development model proposes that older people, like these former workers, give meaning to the events that shape their lives. Some people accept events and build them into their life plan. Other people resist change and fight to hold onto their former selves. The life-span development perspective also says that older people can reshape society. For example, some older people have formed job bureaus. These agencies, often run by seniors, help retirees find work that suits their interests and abilities.

Older peoples' responses to aging differ by gender, age cohort, and social class. All of these differences create varied patterns of aging. The life-span developmental model turns the researchers' attention to the social context to explain the differences in the time of onset, direction, and duration of development in later life (Novak 1985–86).

PERSONALITY AND SOCIAL CONTEXT

Life-span development researchers study three types of environmental effects: (1) **non-normative events** (unexpected events such as illnesses, layoffs, and accidents); (2) **normative history-graded events** (historical events that shape a person's life, such as the Great Depression of the 1930s or World War II); and (3) **normative age-graded events** (socially sanctioned events that occur most often at a certain age like marriage or retirement) (Baltes, such as Cornelius, and Nesselroade 1979; Riegel 1975).

Non-Normative Events

Sociologists define norms as shared rules or guidelines that prescribe correct behaviour under certain conditions. Every society has age norms that prescribe how a person of a certain age should act. University students, for example, can travel across the country with backpacks each summer, see Europe on Eurail passes, and sleep in railway stations or open fields. People accept this behaviour from the young, and they even expect students to take time off to travel. Social scientists call this a normative life event.

People can also go through non-normative events, including accidents, sudden changes in health, or the death of a child. Social psychologists call these events non-normative because society does not prescribe that everyone experience them and because people cannot plan for them.

Non-normative events or life crises—such as the death of a close friend or a spouse or an illness—can lead to shock and fear. Novak (1985) studied the response to life events in a sample of 25 healthy, middle-class, community-dwelling older people in Winnipeg. These people all scored high on a standard test of self-actualization (a measure of personality development). Most of them had gone through at least one major non-normative event— early retirement, loss of a spouse, or an illness.

Sometimes these events came about because a person felt an inner urge to change (one subject retired early so that he could devote himself to writing and to reading philosophy). Sometimes change came from outside: death of a spouse or illness forced people to rethink their mid-life roles. Many of the subjects found the process of change painful and frightening.

Novak (1985) reports that these non-normative events had a common pattern. First, a person faced a problem or moment of crisis—a "challenge." These challenges included loss of a spouse, early retirement, and illness. Second, individuals "accepted" the challenge and interpreted it as a demand for some response. Third, they responded to or "affirmed" their lives in spite of the challenge. This response allowed them to enter a new phase of life beyond the roles and responsibilities of middle age.

These people were studied after they had passed through the life event. Did they succeed in affirming their lives because of their self-actualizing, integrated personalities, or did the life events they faced lead them to a new integrated stage of adulthood? Studies of coping styles suggest that people grow more competent at coping with challenges as they age (Ruth and Coleman 1996).

History-Graded Events

Non-normative events describe sudden changes in a person's personal life, but history-graded events change the lives of many age cohorts. The term "cohort," as stated earlier, describes a group of people born at the same point or within the same period (usually five or ten years) of time (Marshall 1983, 52).

Older people who were between the ages of 75 and 85 in 1985, for example, were born between 1900 and 1910. These people share the experiences of two world wars and the Great Depression. If you talk to one of them about their past, you will almost always hear stories about the Depression and the world wars. These historic events left their mark on this cohort, shaping their family lives, their work lives, and their values (Hagestad 1990).

Tindale (1980) studied a group of poor old men in a large Canadian city. Most of them had lived through the Depression as teenagers, rode the rails as hobos, and picked tobacco or fruit for 25 cents an hour. They had little education and few family ties.

Their lives in later life showed the effects of their past. "They were poor before the depression," Tindale says, "poorer still during it, and only a little less poor after it" (1980, 91). In later life these men lived alone on government pensions. They ate and slept in the downtown missions and Salvation Army shelters. They never had much, and they did not expect much at the time of the study.

The cohort born between 1945 and 1955 (50- to 60-year-olds in 2005) expect different things from life and from society, based on their experiences. These people belong to one of the largest cohorts in Canadian history. Canada built elementary schools for them when they were children in the 1950s and 1960s, universities for them in the 1960s and 1970s, and housing for them in the 1980s. They have lived through a relatively peaceful, affluent time in Canada's history, and they expect more from society than do older age groups.

As cohorts age (and members die), cohorts replace one another in society's age structure. Riley, Johnson, and Foner (1972) call this "cohort flow." As cohorts flow through the age structure, they change the size of particular age groups (e.g., the size of the group 20 to 30 years old will differ in 1940 and 1970 and 2010). New cohorts also bring new experiences with them as they age. Older cohorts today, for example, have less education than younger ones. The 1981 Canada Census reports that almost 60 percent of the cohort born between 1897 and 1906 had less than a Grade 9 education (Statistics Canada 1984b). Younger Canadians have more schooling; in 1981, 80 percent of the population under 65 had more than grade 9, and almost 40 percent had between nine and thirteen years of school (Statistics Canada 1984b). Younger, more educated groups will probably demand more educational opportunities when they reach old age.

The model of aging used by Riley, Johnson, and Foner (1972) omits a few important concepts about aging and age grading. Historical events, for example, also get filtered through the age stratification system, the system of age grades a society uses (e.g., child, adolescent, young adult). The 1900–10 cohort went through the Great Depression of the 1930s in young adulthood, and the Depression affected their decision to marry, and it affected the early years of their careers. The Depression also affected the cohort born between 1920 and 1930, but it had a different effect on these people. They lived through the Depression as children. Some of them may not remember the Depression at all; others may simply have accepted the hard times as "the way things are."

Gerontologists use the term "generation" to describe people who share an awareness of their common historical or cultural experiences, but who may come from different cohorts. The baby boom cohorts born between 1945 and the early 1960s form a generation; they have all lived under the threat of nuclear war, and they have lived in a relatively affluent time in Canadian history.

Braun and Sweet (1983–84) found that a "generational event" theory of personality better explained the differences between age groups than did a theory of life stages. **Generational event theory** says that attitudes form for a generation in their teens. People who grow up at the same time in the same society share the same attitudes. These attitudes stay fairly stable throughout life because of what Neugarten (1964, 198) calls the "institutionalization of personality." People respond in the same ways to life's demands; others expect the same responses of them; and people choose their friends and contacts to support a stable sense of self.

These studies all show the effect of social and historical events on individual personality. Like non-normative events, history-graded events happen without warning, and sometimes the changes they bring about do not show up until years later. Society also shapes personality growth more directly through normative age grading.

Normative Age-Graded Events

Anthropologists report that all societies move people through a series of age grades. Age grades define certain rights and responsibilities for their members. They give order to the life course and help people judge their own development.

Males of the Nandi tribe in Kenya, for example, belong to one of seven age groups—two for boys, one for warriors, and four for elders. These groups give males their status and allow them to play certain roles at given times in their lives. Likewise, pre-industrial societies recognized three stages of life—infancy-childhood, mature adulthood, and old age.

Industrialized society today includes the stages of infancy, childhood, adolescence, young adulthood, middle age, and old age. Some writers have now added a new stage, the young-old, after middle age and before late old age. This new stage makes sense in a society where people can expect to live in good health for 10 or 15 years after age 65.

Neugarten, Moore, and Lowe (1968) say that people internalize the age-grade system and know the proper time for a life event to occur. A Canadian middle-class girl who falls in love today at the age of 14 will feel it is too early to marry. A woman graduate student in her early 20s may also feel it is too early to settle down. A single career woman in her late 40s who wants to get married may feel it is too late.

Someone for whom major life events come early or late—a teenaged mother or a newlywed octogenarian—may feel out of sync with the age-status system. Gerontologists call this **age-status asynchronization**.

Neugarten and Moore (1968) say that people can be on time in certain ways and late or early in others. They can feel on time when they choose to marry, but late in advancing in their profession. Gee (1990) reports that women judge the success of their lives by how closely their lives match idealized models of life events. Research shows that occupation, ethnic background, and social class affect the timing of life events.

For example, Canadian women with less education, compared to women with more education, tend to marry earlier and have children earlier (Kobayashi et al. 2001). Neugarten and Moore (1986) found that female professionals had their first child an average of six years

later than unskilled working-class women. The researchers also report that women go through different life events than men. They found, for instance, that women enter a new phase of life in their late 40s. The last child leaves home, menopause occurs, and many women re-enter the labour market. This produces "an increasingly accentuated transition period in the lives of women, one that men do not face" (1968, 13).

Neugarten and Moore (1968) conclude that the social groups people belong to regulate their life cycles. Groups expect certain behaviour from their members, and members rely on these expectations to guide their actions. Members also observe the transition times of others and get a sense for when changes should occur (Hagestad 1990). These normal transition times and expected behaviour differ by historical period. Women in the past, for example, fit a traditional model of the life course. Today, women show more diverse life course patterns (Kobayashi et al. 2001). For example, more women than ever before have children before they marry. This reflects an increased acceptance of common-law partnerships.

Hagestad (1990) reviewed the literature on the life course and found that researchers have increased their interest in life events, life transitions, and life trajectories. This increased interest may reflect recent changes in the timing and sequencing of life events. For example, many women today delay having their first child until after age 30. More women than ever before enter the workforce and stay at work after they have children. Also, many women find themselves back in school in their 40s and 50s in order to prepare for new careers. The National Advisory Council on Aging (NACA) (1993f) says that women show more diverse patterns of development than ever before. Changing social values, new career options, more education, and the need for two earners in a family account for this change, which has led to a more flexible life course.

The life-span developmental model accepts the idea that maturation and psychological change affect human development, but it says that a more complete picture of human development requires knowledge of a person's life events and social context. It shows that society and history play important parts in shaping individual development.

ETHNICITY AND SOCIAL SUPPORTS

A person's cultural background, language, and country of origin also affect how he or she will adjust to aging. Immigrants to Canada, especially people who come to Canada in later life, face unique challenges as they age.

● **Exhibit 7.2**

JIM TRAGER: A CASE STUDY IN LIFE-SPAN DEVELOPMENT

Consider the case of Jim Trager, 85 years old. Jim's story illustrates the effects of non-normative, history-graded, and age-graded events on a person's life.

Jim was born in 1920. He grew up in a small town on the Canadian Prairies during the Great Depression. His parents owned a small farm and they lived in poverty during his early years. Often his dad had to do odd jobs and his mom had to take in laundry just to pay their bills. They had little to eat, and Jim went to work at the lumber mill as soon as he graduated from high school. He had little chance for a university education, given the economic pressure on the family.

Jim joined the army at the start of World War II. He enlisted in the infantry and once the war started in Europe he shipped out. He fought with the Canadian forces in France and Germany. He returned home, in 1946, uninjured. But the war and the hardship of the Depression affected him for the rest of his life.

Jim returned to his hometown and got a job working for the federal government. He met his wife-to-be, Elsie, at a local dance. They dated briefly and then got married in 1947. They had two sons almost immediately. Their sons went to the local university. One became an accountant, the other a salesman. Jim stayed with the government through his entire career. He retired at age 65 in 1985.

Jim enjoys his retirement. He leads a local seniors political action group, he takes classes for seniors at the university, and he makes miniature furniture for his grandchildren. But he and Elsie recently got some bad news. Elsie's doctor told her she had to have an operation on her back. Elsie suffered for years with back pain due to a birth defect. The wear and tear on her bones over the years meant that she would soon lose the ability to walk. She needed an operation soon or she would have to use a wheelchair for the rest of her life. The operation would require surgery twice and would take place in a city nearby. Elsie came through both operations safely. She now

takes long walks for exercise and she enjoys her active, pain-free life.

This brief life history illustrates the effects of non-normative, age-graded, and history-graded events in Jim's life. Elsie's back problem is a *non-normative event*. Neither she nor Jim expected that she'd need these operations. And they were both scared that it might leave Elsie bedridden or that she might not come through the operation. Still, Elsie decided to take the risk and Jim supported her decision.

Jim's decision to marry Elsie in his early 20s and the birth of their two sons soon after is an *normative age-graded life event*. Clearly, history (World War II) played a role in the timing of Jim's decisions. For example, the war probably delayed by a few years his decision to marry, start a family, and begin his career. But his generation normally married in their 20s and had children soon after marriage. Likewise, his decision to begin his career in his 20s fits the normal pattern for someone in Canada at that time. Society expected people in that age grade (age 20 to 30) to do these things on time. And people like Jim and Elsie acted according to this social clock.

The Great Depression and World War II are both *normative history-graded events*. These events shaped the lives of an entire generation. They caused people like Jim and Elsie to follow the same pattern of events as did others, at about the same time. Jim's return from the war, his marriage, and the start of his family, multiplied hundreds of thousands of times, led to the baby boom in Canada. The Great Depression shaped Jim's and Elsie's view of money into later life. Today, they spend their money carefully. And they both feel well-off and secure because they have a steady (if small) government pension and a subsidized apartment.

Non-normative, age-graded, and history-graded life events shaped the lives of Jim and Elsie Trager. This case study shows how society and historical events affected their lives.

Sociologists define an ethnic group as a group of people who see themselves as being alike because of their common ancestry and who are seen as being alike by others (Hughes and Hughes 1952). Culture and ethnicity form a backdrop for psychological development in old age. Ethnic culture gives meaning to life events and can buffer life crises. The size and age composition

of an ethnic community also determine the number of social supports a person has available in old age.

Gerontologists in Canada have done relatively little research on ethnicity, aging, and social supports. But studies done so far show that older people from different ethnic groups (including those from British and French backgrounds) experience old age differently. Kobayashi

(2000), for example, says that in 1996, 90 percent of Chinese elders were born in China, while only 15 percent of Japanese elders were born in Japan. For this reason, compared to Japanese elders, Chinese elders may have less access to a Canadian government pension. Newly arrived Chinese elders may also rely more on family supports because they don't speak English or French (Pacey 2002). Even within one group, differences exist. Matsuoka (1993) says that group members can differ by gender, social class, geography, religion, and political beliefs. Some group members have lived in Canada for many years, others have just arrived. Matsuoka says that most surveys miss this diversity. She proposes qualitative as well as quantitative studies in order to describe the texture of ethnic elders' lives.

Most of the Canadian research so far has explored three theories that attempt to explain the ethnic elders' experiences: levelling theory, buffer theory, and multiple jeopardy theory.

Levelling Theory

According to **levelling theory**, age levels ethnic differences. A decline in health or loss of a spouse will lead all older people (regardless of their ethnicity) to depend more on their families and on social services for help. These changes outweigh cultural differences in family structure or differences in cultural values of parent–child relations.

Rosenthal (1983) found support for the levelling theory of aging and ethnicity. She studied Anglo- and non-Anglo-Canadian older people in Ontario (Anglo-Canadians here are people who report a British background). Modernization theory predicts that Anglo-Canadian families will show weaker family ties compared with non-Anglo-Canadians and that non-Anglos will show more traditional family structures and more support for older people. Rosenthal (1983, 1986a) did not find support for this theory. Instead, she found that older Anglo-Canadians and non-Anglo-Canadians in her study reported similar family structures, similar views of family life, and similar family relations. She did find that slightly more non-Anglo-Canadians lived with their middle-aged children, but this difference disappeared in older age groups. Rosenthal (1983, 14) says "there is a strong suggestion that age levels these differences [between groups]."

Buffer Theory

Buffer theory says that ethnic identity buffers people from role loss as they age (Holzberg 1981), and a number of studies have found support for the buffer

theory of aging and ethnicity. Kobayashi (2000), for example, studied third-generation Japanese adult children and their parents. A large majority of the adult children felt a commitment to support their parents. Children provided emotional, financial, and service support. This helped buffer the challenges of aging, such as death of a spouse or poor health. Pacey (2002) found that Chinese seniors between the ages of 80 and 85, compared to non-Chinese seniors, showed nearly four times the likelihood of living with their children. This buffered the effects of lower income and inability to speak English or French.

Strain and Chappell (1984) compared the social supports of older Aboriginal people with those of non-Aboriginal people in Winnipeg. They found that Aboriginal people had larger numbers of friends and relatives than non-Aboriginal people. Aboriginal people also reported having two and a half times as many relatives outside their household and six times as many friends as did non-Aboriginal people. (Strain and Chappell point out that Aboriginal people may have a broader definition of friends than non-Aboriginal people.) Aboriginal people also have more weekly contact with their friends and relatives than do non-Aboriginal people.

A third of the Aboriginal people studied and only 6.4 percent of those who were non-Aboriginal lived with their grandchildren. Strain and Chappell (1984) trace this difference to Aboriginal culture. For example, "one native person explained that it was the duty of her grandparents to raise her. She lived with them and was taught the native way of life, thereby freeing her own parents for other responsibilities" (12).

Gold (1980) supports this finding. She describes the start of a small senior recreation program that was meant to serve a dozen or so Aboriginal seniors. But the planners found that they also had to include the rest of the senior's family. "The culture demanded that the young serve the old," she says, but it also required that the old look after the very young. "So the food was prepared and served to the old, while the old tended youngsters" (3). This program for 12 Aboriginal elders became a program for 50 to 100 people of all ages. These elders had a role to play in their culture, even if they had low status in non-Aboriginal society.

Frideres (1994, cited in Wister and Moore 1998, 105) says that many Aboriginal elders face a "double alienation." They stand outside mainstream Canadian society and they have lost their role in their own communities. Some programs work to reverse this trend. Vanderburgh (1988) reports that, in Ontario, the Ojibwa Cultural Foundation began an elders' program to revive the Aboriginal elders' role as mentors. The program arranges for elders to teach language skills, crafts, and healing methods to the young, and, with other programs, encourages elders to speak with authority at public gatherings about their experience. The mandate to speak with authority and play a guiding role in community life, rather than chronological age, is what defines elderhood. An Aboriginal person who achieves this status has a buffer against the stress of aging.

Holzberg (1982) also found support for the buffer theory. She started an ethnic history program for Eastern European Jews at the Baycrest Centre in Toronto. These older people believed that they had to preserve their memories of the past for their children and grandchildren, so they decided to write and publish a book of their memoirs. This undertaking gave them a purpose in life and increased their self-worth. Holzberg says that "it was the value of ethnic history to the group rather than the value of life history to the individual as a reaffirmation of self that was the rallying point of collective effort" (253). Working for a higher cultural purpose can buffer people from the threat of meaninglessness that sometimes comes with old age and death.

Multiple Jeopardy Theory

Multiple jeopardy theory says that aging makes life worse for members of an ethnic group. Minority members have low status to begin with, and they often have low incomes too (Markides and Mindel 1987). Aging may add to their troubles (Havens and Chappell 1983).

Wong and Reker (1985) found support for the multiple jeopardy theory. They compared a sample of 40 Chinese Canadians and 40 Anglo-Canadians in Ontario. The average age of the members of both groups was 68. Wong and Reker asked each group about the kinds of problems they faced and the methods they used to cope with these problems. They found that both groups had about the same number of problems, but the Chinese Canadians viewed their problems as being more serious than those of the Anglo-Canadians. The Chinese Canadians also felt that they coped less well than the Anglo-Canadians, and they had lower well-being scores. Wong and Reker say that these findings support the multiple jeopardy theory (see also Lam 1994). They say that stress due to living in a foreign culture and minority status add to the problems of physical aging.

Moore (1995) compared Aboriginal and non-Aboriginal older people. She found that Aboriginal men tended to have higher unemployment rates and lower incomes than non-Aboriginal men. Aboriginal men and women, compared with non-Aboriginals, had about one

and a half times the low-income rate. Low income leads to poor health and poor housing. Wister and Moore (1998) report that Aboriginal elders often lack opportunities for work and they have poor preventive health care services. Older Aboriginal people (aged 45 and over), compared to the total Canadian population aged 45 and over, have higher rates of diabetes, arthritis, heart disease, stroke, and other chronic illnesses. Older Aboriginal people compared to non-Aboriginal elders have higher rates of disability. And studies estimate that older Aboriginal people have a hospitalization rate twice that of the national average (Wister and Moore 1998). These findings show that older Aboriginal people face multiple jeopardy. Older people in visible minorities (non-Caucasian, non-white, non-Aboriginal) show similar characteristics and also face multiple jeopardy (Chard 1995).

Havens and Chappell (1983) also found support for the theory. They studied the cumulative effects of being old, female, and a member of a minority group. They found that on a standard psychological measure of mental function "old-elderly women of Polish, Russian, and Ukrainian descent are significantly more disadvantaged ... than any of the other groups" (129). Havens and Chappell found less support for multiple jeopardy when they asked this group whether they felt personally disadvantaged. It seems that older ethnic people do not feel (or do not report feeling) worse off than non-ethnic elders.

Statistics Canada also reports multiple jeopardy for ethnic elders. Statistics Canada (1984a), measuring economic well-being, found that older immigrants have a greater chance than non-immigrants of living in low-income families (see also National Council of Welfare 1998). Specifically, the study found that 10 percent of non-immigrants aged 65 and over lived in low-income families, compared with 11 percent of immigrants who had come to Canada before 1961, 14 percent of immigrants who arrived between 1961 and 1970, and 22.5 percent of the most recent immigrants. This study also found that immigrants get more of their income from the Old Age Security and the Canada Pension Plan than do non-immigrants (Statistics Canada 1984a). Older members of Asian, African, and Latin American ethnic groups show some of the lowest economic well-being on measures of labour force activity, retirement income, and investment income (Wanner and McDonald 1986). These studies show that being old and an immigrant, especially a recent immigrant from a developing country, increases the chance that a person will have a low income. Bagley (1993) also found that recent older Chinese immigrants reported more depression and anxiety than established older Chinese residents of Canada.

● Exhibit 7.3

THE CHALLENGE OF AGING AMONG ABORIGINAL PEOPLES

Buffer theory says that a culture can buffer the effects of physical decline and loss that come with age. Aboriginal culture, under the best conditions, buffers elders from some of the effects of aging. But Aboriginal culture cannot always buffer people from the lifelong inequalities and conditions that lead to problems in old age.

Margaret Labillois (1994), elder and former Micmac chief, describes the decline in status of older Aboriginal people in her own lifetime. "When I was growing up," she says, "elders were always respected for their knowledge and their experience. They were our teachers, our books, our education, our baby-sitters, our story tellers, and our special helpers—in short, a way of life.... Today elders are no longer elders, but just old people" (15; see also d'Anglure 1994). She goes on to say that many Aboriginal older people today live in poverty. They have few housing options on reserves, and older people who live off the reserve may live in poor-quality housing. A report by the Ontario Advisory Council on Senior Citizens (1993) says that not one of Ontario's 128 First Nations has a full hospital. Their communities have few nursing homes and few counsellors to help people cope with diseases such as diabetes.

Modernization accounts for part of this decline in status of Aboriginal older people. Young people get formal education and the mass media provide information that makes older people's knowledge seem obsolete. But ageism and racism throughout life also account for the decline in Aboriginal elders' well-being. Chipperfield and Havens (1992), for example, studied Aboriginal elders' own sense of respect at two points. They found that in both the mid-1970s and mid-1980s Aboriginal elders gave themselves the lowest rating of respect of any ethnic group in Manitoba.

Frideres (1994) says that Aboriginal older people suffer from more health problems than non-Aboriginals. They also have twice the average length of time with a disability in life, compared with non-Aboriginals. He traces ill health in Aboriginals in old age to poor nutrition, poor living conditions, and poverty throughout life (see also Armstrong-Esther 1994). He adds that racism and exclusion kept Aboriginal people outside mainstream society.

Professional care providers may assume that Aboriginal older people get the support they need from their families. But Armstrong-Esther (1994) questions the Aboriginal family's ability to care for older family members today. For example, do older Aboriginal people choose family support? Or do they turn to the family as their only option because formal supports do not exist? And how well can Aboriginal families meet the needs of their older members?

Older Aboriginal people, Frideres (1994, 30) says, "have experienced a double alienation, as they have remained outside the mainstream Canadian institutional structure as well as outside the changing Native community." A recent revival of interest in Aboriginal culture and tradition has restored some older people to the status of elder. But Mussell (1994) reports that most older Aboriginal people do not fill leadership roles or feel that they can help with community issues (see also Tasse 1993). He calls for the development of older Aboriginal people as a resource for their communities. They represent "a wonderful resource that has hardly begun to be explored" (Mussell 1994, 58).

Limitations of Ethnicity and Aging Theories

Each of the theories discussed gives some clues about how ethnicity affects social and psychological well-being as a person ages. But each theory has its limits. Levelling theory, for example, may hold true only for people in late old age. At that point, almost everyone turns to government-run services such as home care or institutions for help. Buffer theory describes aging in a culture that holds the old in high esteem. But an ethnic group with a different belief system, or a group with few members in Canada, may find that ethnicity does not buffer the effects of aging.

Hall (1993) studied 16 elderly Vietnamese immigrants in Lethbridge, Alberta. These people (most of them women who lived with their children) reported dissatisfaction with their living arrangements. They also said they felt isolated and rarely met with other relatives. Sixty-nine percent of them reported dissatisfaction with their relationships at home. Hall found that for many of

Exhibit 7.4

OVERCOMING BARRIERS: TELLING IT LIKE IT IS

Elvira Herrera, of the Centre for Spanish Speaking People in Toronto, composed the letter below. Five seniors in the centre's English as a Second Language program contributed to the letter. The letter shows the tensions that can exist in families that sponsor the immigration of older members in Canada. In particular the letter points to the language barrier that keeps older immigrants from living a normal life. The letter ends on a note of hope for a better life in their new country.

My dear family:

How happy I felt coming to Canada to live with you! I thought all my dreams would come true: Enjoying the company of my children, watching my grandchildren grow up, learning English, having a job, making new friends.... Look at me now....

Oh! if you knew how many times I have tried to write this letter, my dear son, my dear daughter, my beloved grandchildren. But I preferred to hide my feelings in order not to make you suffer, too. Did you ever think of the consequences when you sponsored me to come to this country? Then I could have thought twice before deciding to make this enormous change in my life. Now it's too late. I don't have my house, my friends, my independence, I don't have money I can spend freely, and I think I'm also losing my family!

Please do not think I don't value your efforts. I know you have to work hard and don't have much time for housekeeping or taking care of your children. But I did not know you wanted such help from me. It's my pleasure to babysit my grandchildren from time to time, but I didn't think this would be a daily obligation. When I told you that I wanted to learn English so I could go out by myself and feel more secure, your answer was, "Mama, you are very old, you cannot learn English. Beside that, I need you here." For years, I didn't venture to ask again. I thought the least I could do was help you, since I was already a burden on the family. But, to tell you the truth, I cannot stand it any more! I couldn't even go to church on Sundays, if your husband was tired or not in a mood to drive me

there, because you were afraid that I could get lost if I went by bus.

You came to this country very young. You have already adapted to the culture and customs here. For me, as a senior, the process is very difficult. I cannot even communicate with my grandchildren because they haven't learned to respect the old ones. When I ask the eldest to go with me to a store, he refuses, because he doesn't want anyone to know that we speak Spanish. He's ashamed to go out with his grandma. I feel so lonely and frustrated.... When I lived in my homeland I used to go everywhere, saying hello to everybody, solving problems, helping people, receiving friends in my home. Now, when your friends come over, I prefer to go to the basement and cry silently in my room, because your friends aren't mine and I do not feel welcome to join you. You don't seem to care about talking in English, although you know I don't understand. And I don't have the confidence to invite over some people I have met at church. This is not my house. I just have a dark little room in the basement....

However, things are going to change now. A friend opened my eyes. She asked me, "Why don't you go to school? Why don't you have coffee with us when we invite you? Why do you seem so sad?"

I know you were very surprised when I told you about my registration in a seniors' English class. I know you were mad at me because I wouldn't have lunch ready for the family, or be home to babysit your daughter until you returned from work. But dear one, I need to have a life, too. I can help you. As your mother, I am willing to do that. But you know I need my own activities and friends, too. I know now that I'm capable of learning English, although you laugh at me and try to convince me not to go back to classes because I'm "wasting my time." Now I ride the bus, I have joined a seniors' club and I don't need anyone to take me to church. Certainly I am old, but I have rediscovered the valuable person inside me. I hope you'll understand.

I want to lead my own life, a life worth living, as long as I am alive. Let me live.

Your loving mother.

Source: "Growing Older, Growing Bolder," *The Moment* 21 (1994): II. Courtesy of Jack Costello, director of the Jesuit Centre for Social Faith and Justice.

them, life in Canada meant boredom, a lack of social contacts, and clashes with children and grandchildren.

The case of Aboriginal people in Canada also calls into question buffer theory. Compared with non-Aboriginal people, Aboriginal elders have a lower life expectancy, less formal education, and lower income, and they are more likely to live in poor-quality housing (Bienvenue and Havens 1986; Senior Citizens' Provincial Council 1988; Statistics Canada 1984b). Blandford and Chappell (1990) found that older Aboriginal people reported lower life satisfaction and more loneliness than non-Aboriginal people. Further research revealed that poor health and lack of help accounted for Aboriginal people's lower life satisfaction and loneliness. This example again shows that membership in an ethnic group may not buffer aging even when a group values its elders. Social-psychological well-being in later life also depends on objective conditions like health and social supports.

Research on multiple jeopardy theory shows that ethnic elders rate less well on objective measures of well-being than non-ethnic older people. But Gibson (1988) argues that the theory oversimplifies the effects of ethnicity on aging. It ignores the personal meaning of aging, the social context, and the availability of personal supports. It also fails to explain some of the findings from health research, such as the possibility that ethnic differences in mortality lessen in late old age. Worst of all, the multiple jeopardy theory compares ethnic group members with those in the majority group and focuses on the negative effects of ethnic membership. Gibson points out that ethnicity alone does not predict a decrease in well-being in old age.

What can we conclude about the effects of ethnicity on aging from these conflicting theories and research reports? What seems certain is that the effects of ethnicity on aging depend on many things other than membership in an ethnic group. The age distribution of the ethnic group's population (the ratio of younger to older people in the group), the geographic closeness of the group (how easily members can pool their resources), the degree of assimilation of the group into Canadian society (how well members can use available resources), and the time of immigration (recent immigrants have less access to public pension funds) all influence the experience of aging for ethnic elders. These conditions differ for each ethnic group, so that "ethnicity" or membership in an ethnic group can mean many things.

Rosenthal (1986b) points out that many studies of ethnicity fail to take into account the differences between ethnic groups. Eastern and Southern European ethnic groups can differ as much from one another as they do from the British ethnic group. This observation also applies to immigrants from Asian countries such as China, Japan, or Vietnam. Asian immigrants come from different societies and have different cultural traditions and religious beliefs. Also, some older immigrants have lived in Canada for many years. Others arrived only a few years ago. Studies of ethnicity need to specify the social and economic conditions of the groups under study.

The next section discusses a model for understanding the social causes of individual problems in later life. It also describes some of the ways in which social breakdown can be avoided or reversed in the case of immigrant seniors.

SOCIAL BREAKDOWN

Kuypers and Bengtson (1973) say that older people often suffer from psychological breakdown due to inadequacies in the social environment. They call this a **social breakdown syndrome**, and they describe it as having the following seven steps (see also Exhibit 7.5):

1. Role loss, lack of norms to guide behaviour, and the loss of friends and relatives as reference groups (i.e., groups that support one's values and behaviour) all make a person susceptible to breakdown.

2. The person begins to depend on external labels for a sense of self. These labels sometimes have negative connotations (e.g., widow and retiree).

3. Society may view the older person as incompetent. Middle-aged children may begin to take responsibility away from an aging parent. Institutions often leave nothing for older residents to do for themselves.

4. The older person may assume a dependent role in response to this treatment.

5. The older person develops skills that fit the dependent role. People learn to live down to the expectations others have of them.

6. The person loses previous skills. People in nursing homes may lose the ability to make their bed or chop vegetables because they never get the chance.

7. People label themselves as sick and inadequate. This fits the social definition of older people as incompetent and creates a further turn in the cycle of breakdown. It also makes the older person more susceptible to negative labelling.

The case of Carl Teicherow will show how this syndrome can lead to breakdown. Teicherow, 71, worked for Canada Manpower until he took early retirement at age

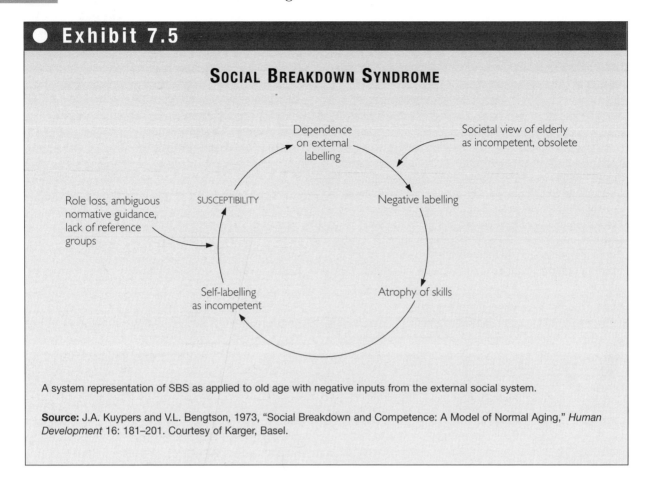

● **Exhibit 7.5**

SOCIAL BREAKDOWN SYNDROME

A system representation of SBS as applied to old age with negative inputs from the external social system.

Source: J.A. Kuypers and V.L. Bengtson, 1973, "Social Breakdown and Competence: A Model of Normal Aging," *Human Development* 16: 181–201. Courtesy of Karger, Basel.

63. He says he retired because his department began to hire college graduates to fill new jobs. Carl had only a high-school diploma and felt that his new co-workers looked down on him. As his older co-workers retired and more young people joined his division, he felt increasingly isolated. He began to feel that the young workers got all the credit and the promotions. "Those young people they hired didn't know as much as they thought," he says. "Sure, they had university degrees, but they had no common sense. They didn't know anything about people. I said, 'The hell with it, if the government doesn't care about this department, why should I?' So I quit as soon as I had the chance."

Carl still feels bitter about work and the young people who joined his department. He doesn't work now, or do much of anything else. He had leadership skills during his working years; his wife says he got elected president of any group he joined. But he quit most of those groups after he retired. Now he watches TV or reads, but these activities give him little pleasure. He had a bad bout of depression a year ago and threatened suicide. His doctor gave him some pills and told him to find something to keep busy.

His wife worries about his depression, but she does not know how to help him.

Kuypers and Bengtson (1973) suggest a way to reverse the social breakdown syndrome. They propose a **social reconstruction syndrome**. This syndrome reorganizes the social system to provide older people with new ways to feel worthwhile. This approach includes (1) a new value system that bases social worth on a person's basic humanity, not on what he or she produces; (2) greater self-reliance; (3) a strong internal sense of control; (4) learning new problem-solving strategies; (5) better-quality services, such as housing and transportation, and better income; (6) maintaining coping skills; and (7) a reduced susceptibility to external judgments. An improvement in any of these areas would increase the older person's quality of life.

THE SOCIAL ROOTS OF PROBLEMS IN OLD AGE

Studies of how history and culture influence aging show that successful aging as well as maladjustment and psy-

Exhibit 7.6

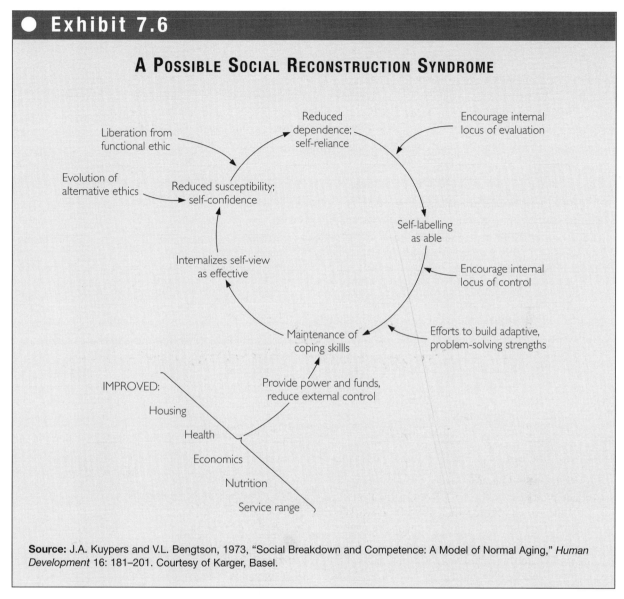

A POSSIBLE SOCIAL RECONSTRUCTION SYNDROME

Liberation from functional ethic

Reduced dependence; self-reliance

Encourage internal locus of evaluation

Evolution of alternative ethics

Reduced susceptibility; self-confidence

Self-labelling as able

Internalizes self-view as effective

Encourage internal locus of control

Maintenance of coping skillls

Efforts to build adaptive, problem-solving strengths

IMPROVED:

Provide power and funds, reduce external control

Housing

Health

Economics

Nutrition

Service range

Source: J.A. Kuypers and V.L. Bengtson, 1973, "Social Breakdown and Competence: A Model of Normal Aging," *Human Development* 16: 181–201. Courtesy of Karger, Basel.

chopathology can have social roots. Some maladjustment in later life comes about because society gives older people fewer guides to define correct behaviour than it gives the young. In the case of seniors newly arrived from another country, for example, the norms of Canadian culture may not fit their understanding of old age.

Researchers say that older people in modern societies occupy a tenuous status—a status or position in the social structure that does not have a role associated with it. A retiree occupies a status—that of a retired person—but does not have a role to play in society, since retirees are expected not to work, and nothing else is expected of them. The loss of roles in later life, through retirement, children growing up, or arrival in a new culture, excludes older people from taking part in society. It also signals a problem older people have today: finding meaning in later life.

Loneliness

Gerontologists distinguish between social isolation and loneliness. **Social isolation** refers to the decrease in social contacts that often comes with age (Hall and Havens 2002). Widowhood, the deaths of friends, or children moving away can lead to social isolation.

Loneliness comes about when people feel a "relational deficit" or a gap between the number of relationships desired and the number they have (Sermat 1978; Weiss 1973). Loneliness refers to a dissatisfaction with the quantity or the quality of social relationships (Hall and Havens 2002). A person may feel lonely despite having many social contacts. For example, a widow may play an active part in her bridge club, but she may feel lonely because she misses the company of her husband. Hall and Havens (2002, citing Holmen et al. 1992) say that some older people who live with their children or with siblings report high levels of loneliness.

Delisle (1988) found rates of loneliness between 25 percent and 54 percent among seniors in his research in Quebec. Hall and Havens (2002) found that, in Manitoba, 45 percent of people aged 72 and over reported strong feelings of loneliness. The oldest group in the study (aged 90+) reported the most loneliness.

Researchers finds that a drop in the number of social contacts and a feeling of loneliness often go together (Hall and Havens 2002). For example, people who live in an institution risk loneliness. Ryan (1998) studied hospitalized older people. She found that people who reported decreased social contacts with family and friends reported more loneliness. Delisle (1988) found that single older people, those without children, people in poor health or bedridden, people with poor education, introverts, timid people, or those with low self-esteem face the greatest risk of feeling lonely.

The Fredericton 80+ Study looked at healthy people aged 80 and over in rural New Brunswick (Miedema and Tatemichi 2003). About one-third of the people in this study said they felt lonely sometimes or regularly. Women made up the majority of these cases. The researchers found that living alone and feeling dissatisfied with child contact best predicted feelings of loneliness.

Most studies agree that a good old age means more than the acceptance of loss or isolation. But older people often feel they can do little about their loneliness (Abrahams 1972; Gordon 1976). Perlman, Gerson, and Spinner (1978) suggest two ways to combat loneliness. First, older people should maintain their social contacts with friends and neighbours. A project in England arranged for volunteers to visit frail and isolated older people. The older people reported satisfaction with the visits. Some friendships grew beyond the original program (Andrews et al. 2003). Moen and her colleagues (2000) say that church work and volunteering can decrease loneliness and isolation.

French and her colleagues (2000, 69) found that helping others gave older people a purpose in life. As one woman told the researchers, "if there's nothing to get up for in the morning, what's the use of getting up? What's the use of living?" The prevention of loneliness should include broader changes in society that would help older people stay involved in social life.

Second, older people need a supportive social setting to grow old in. Modern life can break up families and communities. Social resources can help older people keep in contact with their social network. Better transportation, well-designed housing, and more recreational facilities can help older people combat loneliness. They give older people a choice of activities and a stronger sense of control over their lives.

Some institutions have used animal-assisted therapy (visits by a pet to the facility) to combat loneliness (Banks and Banks 2003). The researchers found that visits of 30 minutes once a week reduced loneliness for patients who enjoyed the presence of animals. A controlled study found a significant decrease in loneliness among the group that received visits from a pet (Banks and Banks 2002).

Technology can also help older people combat loneliness. Cellphones and the Internet can help people to stay in touch with relatives and friends. A study of "cybersenior empowerment" (McMellon and Schiffman 2002) found that the Internet can help older people combat loneliness. The researchers conducted a survey of Internet use by a sample of older people. They found that nearly all of the people in the study (91 percent) used the Internet to keep in touch with friends through e-mail. People with physical limits or those who lived in social isolation felt more in control of their lives.

Older people run the risk of loneliness as they age. Some people adapt to social isolation and enjoy being alone. But other people prefer a more active and engaged social life. Awareness of this preference can help family members and social service providers respond to seniors' needs.

Suicide

What do current findings tell us about older people and suicide? Men aged 65 to 74 had a suicide rate of 24.3 per 100 000 population in 1996, while men aged 75 to 84 had a rate of 27.4 and men aged 85 and over had a rate of 36.8. These figures show that the suicide rate for men increases with age. Also, men aged 75 and over had the second highest rate of suicide (after men aged 20 to 59) (Langlois and Morrison 2002). Women's rates are much lower than men's at all ages. Women aged 65 to 74 had a rate of 5.4 per 100 000, while women aged 75 to 84 had a rate of 3.6 and women aged 85 and over had a rate of 3.3. Women's rates, in contrast to those of men, show a decline in older age groups (Lindsay 1999).

Why do people commit suicide in old age? Durkheim (1951) proposed that a lack of social integration led to high rates of suicide in modern society.

Normlessness or anomie, a lack of connection between the person and society, puts a person at risk. Current research on suicide in later life supports this view. Older people often lose the contacts and links that prevent suicide. Researchers rank "death of a spouse" as the most negative life event. Retirement, the deaths of friends, and a move to a nursing home also weaken the older person's social network (Osgood, Brant, and Lipman 1991). As this network shrinks, the person may lose a sense of purpose and meaning, which increases the risk of suicide. Mireault and de Man (1996) report that people tend to think about suicide if they live alone or in a nursing home, abuse alcohol, or feel dissatisfied with their health and their social supports. Men may face a higher risk than women if they lose a spouse or lose their social network as they age.

Reker, Peacock, and Wong (1987) found that older people, compared with middle-aged people, reported stronger feelings of lack of purpose and meaning in life. The researchers say that loss of social roles and social relations may lead people to feel suicidal. Also, loneliness and isolation, widowhood or divorce, retirement, and serious illness all increase the risk of suicide (Lapierre et al. 1992; Trovato 1988). Health Canada (1994) reports that older people who commit suicide often feel depressed.

Lenaars and Lester (1992) call for some response to the high rate of suicide among older people (especially older men) in Canada. The National Advisory Council on Aging (2003, 3) says that "the consistently higher suicide rates for men aged 85 and older ... is a longstanding problem that has not yet drawn the attention needed." Studies (Richardson, Lowenstein, and Weissberg 1989,

cited in Health Canada 1994, 22) report that "in the month before committing suicide, three-quarters of elderly suicides visited their physicians, and during the week before, one-third visited their physicians." More awareness by physicians of the signs and symptoms of suicide might prevent some deaths. Also, older people should have better access to psychiatric services, should they need them. The media should make people more aware of the signs of potential suicide in older people.

CONCLUSION

Older Canadians face a number of threats to their social-psychological well-being. But, in general, they report high life satisfaction. They know about the problems of old age, such as loss of a spouse, illness, and physical decline, but they also see many good things about old age. Connidis (1983b) found that older people enjoyed their personal freedom and the chance to do the things they want to do. These advantages, she found, outweigh the problems that come with age. Northcott (1982) found similar results in a study of 440 people in Edmonton. "The elderly," he says, "are more likely than the nonelderly to report no area of life as a major source of pressure and the older the respondent the less pressure reported from all areas of life except health. As pressure falls, satisfaction tends to rise.... In short, the picture one gets of old age is that it is a period of relatively low pressure and relatively high satisfaction, though not without its problems." Each stage of life has its good and bad points, but "old age," Northcott (1982, 77) concludes, "looks far more attractive than stereotypes suggest."

Summary

1. Social psychologists describe at least three models of good aging: disengagement, activity, and continuity. Research shows that each of these patterns can lead to high life satisfaction.

2. Men and women adapt differently to aging, but most older Canadians of both sexes report high life satisfaction. They report that they feel less pressure and enjoy more personal freedom in old age than they did in their middle years.

3. Theories of personality development state that people go through a series of predictable stages as they age. Erikson described three stages for middle and old age. Other theorists describe more stages. These theories predict that people go through many changes in adulthood. Some studies question the universality of these stages. But nearly all researchers and theorists see later life as a time of challenge and change.

4. The life-span developmental perspective sees crisis and change as an essential part of life from birth to death. This view states that as people age, they make choices in response to social demands. This perspective allows for many patterns of aging.

5. Self-development takes place throughout life. At least two motives shape development: the desire to present a good image of oneself and the desire to maintain a sense of self in the face of change. People face a number of challenges to the self in later life, including ageism, physical decline, and role loss.

6. Spiritual development can also take place in later life. Many older people today come into old age with strong religious beliefs. The diversity of Canadian society ensures a diversity of beliefs among older Canadians. Some people express their spirituality outside traditional religious faiths.

7. Life events shape human development. These include non-normative events, normative history-graded events, and normative age-graded events. Studies of history-graded and age-graded events show the effects of social structures on personal development.

8. An ethnic group's culture and structure both shape the experience of aging. The group's values, beliefs, and degree of assimilation in part determine how young people treat older members. The group's structure, size, geographic closeness, and age structure also determine the treatment of older members.

9. Kuypers and Bengtson (1973) say that if society views older people negatively, older people can lose confidence in themselves. This can ultimately lead to dependence and psychological distress. They call this process a social breakdown syndrome and conclude that society should judge people by more than their productivity. A change in society's value system, they say, can reverse this syndrome, as can adequate social supports.

10. Members of different ethnic groups will need different forms of social support. Proper support can reverse or avoid social breakdown and lead to a high quality of life. Policymakers need to keep ethnic differences in mind when they plan programs for older people.

11. The way society treats older people can lead to personal problems like loneliness, suicide, and the breakdown of competence. Social psychologists trace these problems to the lack of social supports for older people today.

Study Questions

1. Name and briefly state three of the major social psychological theories of aging.

2. Name and briefly describe the last stage of adult development in Erikson's theory of the life cycle. State some of the criticisms of stage models of adult development.

3. What are three challenges that face the self in later life? How can individuals cope with these challenges?

4. What role does religion play in many older people's lives? How and why might religiosity in later life change in the future?

5. Name and describe three types of environmental effects that influence people throughout life.

6. What three theories attempt to explain ethnic elders' experiences? Explain these theories in detail.

7. Briefly describe the social breakdown and reconstruction syndromes. What role does society play in each of these processes? Why can someone's ethnicity put that person at risk of social breakdown?

8. Discuss the sources of loneliness in later life and state at least two ways to combat the condition.

9. What does current research tell us about older people and suicide? How do suicide rates differ between older men and women? What might account for the differences in rates between older men and women?

Key Terms

activity theory a theory that people need to stay active to live a satisfying old age by replacing old activities with new ones as they age. (135)

age-status asynchronization the discomfort a person can feel when some life events happen later or earlier than for other people. (141)

buffer theory a theory that membership in an ethnic group buffers the effects of aging. (143)

continuity theory a theory that people age best when they continue to do the things they have always done. (135)

dialectical process the process of the individual changing in response to societal demands and society changing in response to the individual's action and adaptation. (139)

disengagement theory the theory that people naturally disengage from activity as they age. (134)

generational event theory the theory that attitudes form for a generation in their teens, so people who grow up at the same time in the same society share the same attitudes, which stay fairly stable throughout life. (140)

integrity the state of fulfillment and self-knowledge achieved in a good old age, according to Erikson. (135)

levelling theory the theory that aging levels out the differences among people in different ethnic groups. (143)

life-span developmental perspective the view of the individual as continually changing from birth to death, with crisis and change considered a constant part of life. (139)

loneliness an emotional state that occurs when a person feels a "relational deficit" or a gap between the number of relationships desired and the actual number that exist; also refers to a dissatisfaction with the quality of social relationships. (149)

multiple jeopardy theory the theory that membership in an ethnic group increases a person's troubles in later life. (144)

non-normative events unexpected events such as illnesses, layoffs, and accidents. (139)

normative age-graded events socially sanctioned events that occur most often at a certain age, such as marriage or retirement. (139)

normative history-graded events historical events that shape a person's life, such as the Great Depression of the 1930s, the invention of the personal computer, or the terrorist attacks of September 11, 2001. (139)

self "the ability to be aware of one's own boundaries and individuality and to reflect upon these" (Breytspraak 1995, 93); "the ability to take oneself as an object" (Ritzer 1992, 202). (137)

social breakdown syndrome a pattern of attitudes and behaviour caused by inadequacies in the social environment and ultimately resulting in psychological breakdown. (147)

social isolation refers to the decrease in social contacts that often comes with age; the death of a spouse, the deaths of friends, and children moving away can all lead to social isolation. (149)

social reconstruction syndrome interventions intended to offset the negative effects of social breakdown and reconstruct a supportive social environment to restore psychological well-being. (148)

Selected Readings

National Advisory Council on Aging. *Aboriginal Seniors' Issues.* Ottawa: Minister of Supply and Services Canada, 1994.

A collection of articles that range from a demographic study of Aboriginal people to a personal account of aging by a Micmac elder and former chief. The papers present some of the problems, such as poor health care services, faced by Aboriginal elders. Some of the papers also discuss the important roles that elders played in the past and, in some cases, still play in their communities. Well-written articles that give many insights into aging among Aboriginal people.

Nichols, Barbara, and Peter Leonard, eds. *Gender, Aging, and the State.* Toronto: Black Rose Books, 1995.

A look at how gender, class, and ethnicity shape the experience of older people. The book makes a strong case for the impact of economic resources on freedom and choice in later life. The contributors often let older people tell their own stories in order to support this view.

Ryff, Carol D., and Victor W. Marshall, eds. *The Self and Society in Aging Processes.* New York: Springer, 1999.

A collection of articles by authors from Canada and other countries who link the individual experiences of aging to the larger society. The book includes theoretical and empirical studies on identity and adaptation, social class and self-concept, and retirement. A challenging book for the person new to gerontology, but a good resource for a more in-depth study of social-psychological issues.

Part Four

Four

Institutional Change

Chapter Eight
Health Care

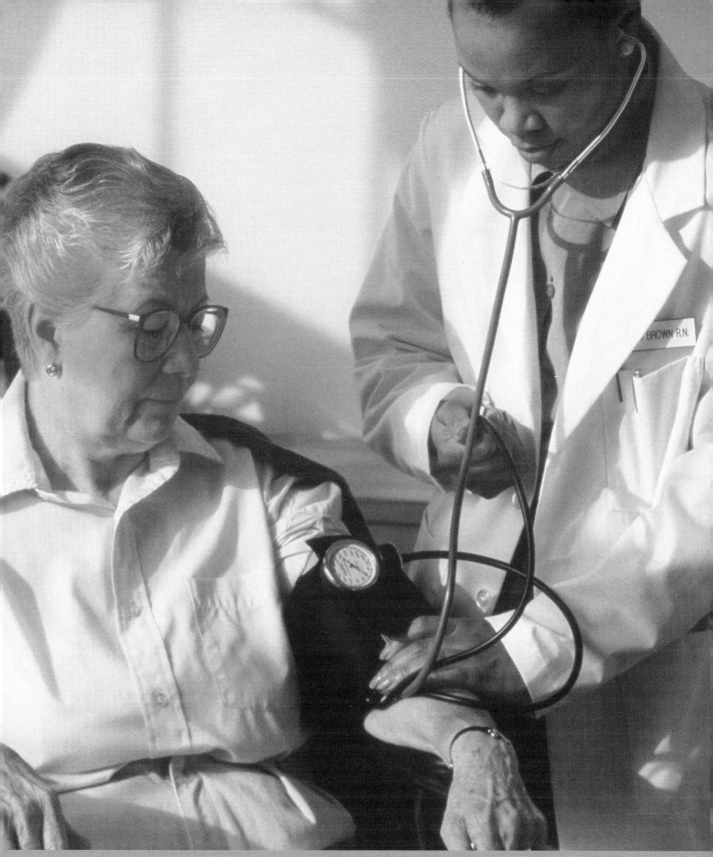

INTRODUCTION

Mrs. Granovetter, 72, lives by herself in a three-room apartment. Until six years ago, she worked as a supervisor in a nursing home, but poor health forced her to quit. She says she has an aortic aneurysm that "looks like a bicycle tire with a bubble in it." She also has arthritis, and her joints get so stiff during the night that, she says, it sometimes takes her until noon to get out of bed. Still, she manages to live on her own. Her daughter, who lives on the other side of town, calls her every day; she talks to or visits with her next-door neighbour daily, and she can still drive. A few times a week, she drives to a nearby shopping centre to sit and watch the people go by. She knows just where to park and how far she has to walk to the nearest bench. Last year, her children took her on a trip to England. She says they didn't get to walk through the castles, but they toured around in the car and she saw the countryside. With help from family and friends, Mrs. Granovetter stays active and enjoys life.

Like Mrs. Granovetter, a majority of older women suffer from arthritis and almost a quarter of them have heart trouble. And, like her, most of them cope well with some help, and they say they have good health (Lindsay 1999). Even among people aged 75 and over, nearly three-quarters of those who live outside institutions report good to excellent health (Lindsay 1999; Roberge, Berthelot, and Wolfson 1995). A Canadian policy statement defines health as "a resource which gives people the ability to manage and even to change their surroundings" (Epp 1986, 3). By this definition, more than 90 percent of people aged 65 and over have enough good health that they can live on their own in the community.

Health care refers to the support needed for people to maintain optimum health. The health care needs of Canada's older population range from health promotion, to health maintenance, to long-term chronic care.

This chapter looks at (1) the structure and function of the health care system today, (2) how the present system fits the needs of older people, and (3) how the system is changing to meet the needs of an aging society.

THREE MODELS OF HEALTH CARE

Social scientists use models to simplify and describe complex social systems. A model does not perfectly represent the system, but it describes the system's basic structures, functions, and values. Three models of health care have shaped the development of the health care system in Canada: the medical model, the social model, and the health promotion model.

The Medical Model

The **medical model** focuses on the treatment of diseases and injuries. Treatment most often takes place in the physician's office, in a hospital, or in other health care institutions. The medical model favours surgery, drug therapy, and rehabilitation through physical therapies. Within this model, "medical care and treatment are defined primarily as technical problems, and the goals of medicine are viewed in terms of technical criteria, such as validity, diagnosis, precision of disease-related treatment, symptom relief and termination of disease process" (Chappell, Strain, and Blandford 1986, 101). Physicians control both the organization of health care and the work of other health care professionals. They learn this approach to medicine in medical school and often get little training in other forms of health care such as counselling or long-term community care.

The Social Model

The **social model** sees medical care as only one part of a complete health care system. This model sees personal and family counselling, home care, and adult day-care programs as part of the health care system. This model of health care tries to keep older people in their own homes. Care often takes place in the community—in a person's home, at a drop-in centre, or in a counsellor's office. In this model, the doctor works as part of a health care team that includes nurses, physiotherapists, counsellors, social workers, and other professionals. The social model has grown in importance as more older people need continuing care or long-term care.

Long-term care (LTC) serves people with functional disabilities and few informal supports (Shapiro 1994, 1995). Béland and Shapiro (1994, 245) define long-term care as "all the social and medical services dedicated to the aged who have functional limitations." LTC combines formal services in the home or an institution with family care. It attempts to make up for functional problems and give people as much autonomy as possible. LTC often takes place in the community as an attempt to keep people out of institutions. Home care, for example, offers a range of services that allow people to stay in their homes. Services include Meals on Wheels, homemaker visits, volunteer visits, and physiotherapy (Federal/Provincial/Territorial Subcommittee on Continuing Care [FPT Subcommittee] 1992; see Béland and Arweiler 1996a and 1996b for a detailed discussion of Canadian long-term care).

Béland and Shapiro (1994) reviewed provincial reports on long-term care. They found a number of proposals common to nearly all provinces: (1) decentralized decision-making; (2) a coordinated, single-point-of-entry system; (3) a shift from institutional to community services; (4) integration of health and social services; and (5) a continuum of care that includes institutional and community care. Health and Welfare Canada (FPT Subcommittee 1992) projects a shift from the medical to the social model of care in the future.

The Health Promotion Model

The **health promotion model** focuses on prevention and self-care. It aims to prevent disease through lifestyle change, increased knowledge about healthy behaviour, and environmental improvement. Programs that promote fitness and those that warn about the dangers of smoking or excessive drinking follow this model. The model also includes actions that most people do not associate directly with health care, such as workplace safety regulations, seatbelt legislation, and pollution control for factories.

Each of these models plays a part in the Canadian health care system today. The social model has gained acceptance as a possible alternative to institutionalization. The health promotion model may save the health care system money in the long run by keeping people healthier longer. Recent decreases in heart disease, for example, may have come about through health promotion programs that encourage low-fat diets and discourage smoking. One study found that arthritis health education led to decreased visits to doctors and a cost saving to the health care system (Clarke 1997). Still, the medical model dominates the system today. Canadians spend more money (much of it through taxes and health insurance programs) on physicians and hospital care than on any other kind of health care (Shapiro and Roos 1986).

CHALLENGES TO THE HEALTH CARE SYSTEM TODAY

In 1957, the Canadian government put in place a hospital insurance system that covered the entire population (Chappell 1988). In 1968, the government insured physician services, and by 1972 all provinces belonged to a national medical insurance program. The provincial and federal governments shared the costs for this system of health care, with the federal government matching provincial contributions to the program dollar for

dollar. The *Canada Health Act* of 1984 described the principles of the Canadian health care system (Canada 1984). The system had the following characteristics: (1) universal coverage; (2) access to services; (3) portability (people could get the benefits in their new location when they moved); (4) comprehensive services that include outpatient and hospital care; and (5) administration of the system by a nonprofit public agency.

Sullivan and Baranek (2002) state a core value of the Canadian health care system. They say that "all citizens in Canada ... are entitled to the same quality, timeliness, and level of medically required service, based on their health care needs and not their ability to pay" (5). The National Forum on Health said that "the vast majority of Canadians [in this study] were immensely proud of the type of health care system that has been built in Canada. They had an abiding sense of fairness and equality" (cited in Conference of Deputy Ministers of Health 1999, 135).

But the Canadian national health care system faces some new challenges. For example, current health care reforms have shifted care from institutions to the community. This policy has decreased institutionalization, but it has placed more burden on women, families, and communities (Forbes 2001). Funding has not always followed this shift to community care. Also, waiting times for services have increased, leading to some loss of confidence in the system (Shapiro et al. 2000). In one international study, Canadians and people in the United Kingdom most often complained about waiting times (Chen and Hou 2002; Chen et al. 2002; Donelan et al. 2000). The proportion of the public who rated Canada's health care system as excellent or very good fell from 61 percent in 1991 to 25 percent in February 2000 (Angus Reid 2000, cited in Sullivan and Baranek 2002). And only 62 percent of Canadians in 1999 felt that the health care system met the needs of all the people in their province (Chen et al. 2002, citing the Canadian Institute for Health Information 2001). The proportion of people aged 65 and over who reported unmet health care needs rose from 5.1 percent in 1998–99 to 8.1 percent in 2000–01 (a statistically significant difference) (Sanmartin et al. 2002). Recent data reflect an "increasing concern about the state of the health care system" (Chen et al. 2002, 18).

Although most provinces provide some long-term care insurance, the current system does not fully insure LTC. Users often have to pay for programs such as adult day care or homemaker services. Also, the system emphasizes medical and institutional care, the two most expensive types of services (Shapiro 2003).

● **Exhibit 8.1**

THE CANADIAN AND AMERICAN HEALTH CARE SYSTEMS: A COMPARISON

Canadians value their health care system. It stands as a point of national pride and it embodies many of the values Canadians hold dear—fairness, equality, and service for the good of all. Americans have a much less positive view of their system. The U.S. looks at the Canadian system with both envy (at the universality of service and relatively low cost) and curiosity (how can a "socialist" system of medicine exist in such an otherwise decent country?). The Canadian system seems to have the edge on the American health care system. Below we present a brief comparison of the two systems based on the work of Barer and his colleagues (1992).

- **Attitudes:** Only 10 percent of the U.S. population in 1989 thought their health care system worked "pretty well." In the same year, 56 percent of Canadians thought their system worked pretty well. Among people aged 65 and over, 15 percent of Americans said their system worked "pretty well." But 66 percent of older Canadians thought their system worked "pretty well." Sixty-eight percent of older Americans said they felt "very satisfied" with their most recent hospital stay compared to 93 percent of older Canadians.
- **Universality of Coverage:** The Canadian health care system covers all older people without cost to the individual. The system allows no private insurance (except for extras such as single-room hospital coverage) and charges no user fees or co-payments. Medicare in the U.S. does not cover everyone; it covers only some hospital or physician services, and it requires co-payments. About 77 percent of the older population buys supplementary health insurance.
- **Cost of the System:** The Canadian system (although more comprehensive) costs less than the U.S. system. Canada insures 100 percent of its population. The U.S. insures only 84 percent. Administrative costs by insurers account for the greatest difference in expenses between the two countries. About 26 of every 100 insurance premium dollars for private insurance go to administrative costs and profit. Canada's universal system spends only 1 percent of its total budget on administrative overhead. In short, Canada's universal health program costs less to administer than the fragmented U.S. system of state and private providers.

- **Coverage:** Health care coverage in Canada improves when a person turns age 65. All provinces provide free or low-cost pharmaceutical services for older people. Provinces all have long-term institutional and community care programs. Some user payments exist for some LTC programs. But the programs link costs to a person's retirement benefits. Medicare in the U.S. covers only hospital and medical care. States may offer some long-term institutional care or community care. But most use a means test (based on income) to decide a person's eligibility for a program. Medicaid covers nursing home stays only for poor older people. Access to Medicaid support can require that a family spend down all of their non-housing assets, and this can reduce a family to poverty.
- **Cost to the Individual:** Estimated yearly costs for medical care for an older person in Canada (in 1991) range from zero (for about two-thirds of the country) to about $545 in British Columbia. Very high users of pharmaceutical care in some provinces may go above this amount. But these people account for a tiny percentage of older people in Canada. The U.S. system of Medicare Part A involves a complex calculation of user costs for hospital stays. Older people who want more coverage also subscribe to Medicare Part B (98 percent of older people choose this option). People pay a monthly premium, a deductible of US$200 for services and at least 20 percent of physicians' charges beyond the deductible. Most older Americans buy additional and costly insurance to cover these Medicare service costs. Barer and his colleagues estimate that the average American senior spent about US$1215 (in 1992) on hospital, medial, and pharmaceutical services each year. (This figure underestimates the true average because of the problem of assessing the costs of co-payments.) Older people in the U.S. now spend as much of their own income on health care as before the institution of Medicare (Wiener and Illston 1996).
- **Catastrophic Illness Protection:** The Canadian system protects older people from financial ruin due to catastrophic illness (such as Alzheimer's disease). Hospital, medical, long-term care, and pharmaceutical services come either free or at a

● Exhibit 8.1 (cont.)

low cost to Canadian seniors. Barer and his colleagues (1992, 151) say that, "in marked contrast, elderly Americans without comprehensive private health insurance face potential economic ruin from hospital, medical, and pharmaceutical costs ... [To get coverage beyond Medicare] "they must first deplete both income and assets to pay such costs." Wiener and Illston (1996, 439) say that in the U.S. "long-term care still imposes a substantial financial burden that can be financially crippling." This system can put at risk a lifetime of savings, home ownership, and the hope of leaving a legacy to one's children. The middle-class person, neither rich nor poor, can suffer the greatest loss under this system.

The Canadian health care system provides an umbrella of care for individuals and families. It provides a sense of security for older people and reduces the fear of illness that can come with age.

The U.S. system consists of a patchwork of private and public insurance systems. The quality and amount of insured service depends on one's ability to pay for acute and long-term care. People who buy private LTC insurance, for example, will get only the amount of service (number of days at a specific rate) that they pay for. This system can place older people and their families at financial risk. The system requires that individuals look out for their own interests, buy the most insurance they can afford, and hope for the best.

The number of hospital beds in Canada declined from about 177 000 beds in 1992 to 132 000 in 1997. The decrease in hospital beds has reduced the number of overnight admissions and the average length of a hospital stay (Statistics Canada 2003l). And this has lowered the cost of hospital care. But the change in hospital practices has also led to more need for home care and, in some cases, longer waits for hospital services (Rosenberg and James 2000; Shapiro and Havens 2000). Canada had about 6000 other health care facilities (including nursing homes) and 56 000 physicians in 1998 (up from 31 000 in 1970) (Statistics Canada 1999a). Some researchers link the increased cost of medical care to the increase in the number of physicians (Evans et al. 2001).

In 1999, Canada spent $86 billion or 9.2 percent of its gross domestic product (GDP) on health care (Statistics Canada 2003l). This worked out to about $2800 per person. Nearly 70 percent of health care expenses came from public sources (the federal and provincial governments), while private health expenditures accounted for about 30 percent (Hicks 1999, cited in Sullivan and Mustard 2001). Hospital and other institution costs came to $32.4 billion in 2001. Hospitals accounted for 30.6 percent of total health care costs in 2001. The proportion of health care dollars spent on hospitals fell during the 1990s (Canadian Institute for Health Information 2003). Still, both private and public spending on health care increased each year during the

1990s and early 2000s. From 1998 to 1999, for example, public health care expenses rose by more than 5 percent (double the national inflation rate) (Simpson 1999). The Canadian Institute for Health Information (2003) projects increases of over 4 percent per year for 2002 and 2003. Still, compared to the other member countries of the Organization for Economic Co-operation and Development (OECD), between 1990 and 2000 Canada had the smallest increase in health care spending as a share of GDP (Anderson, Petrosyan, and Hussey 2002).

These facts show both the strengths and weaknesses of the health care system today. Canadian medical and hospital insurance matched the most complete coverage in the world, with almost 100 percent of Canadians covered (Statistics Canada 1990a). Older people, for example, receive free hospital and surgical care as well as free access to a range of programs that include chiropractic and optometric services (Health and Welfare Canada 1982a). Also, all Canadians have access to some form of public support for pharmaceuticals. Public programs pay for about half of Canada's $8 billion drug costs (Sullivan and Mustard 2001). But Canada also ranks among the nations with the greatest per capita expenditures for health care (Commission on the Future of Health Care in Canada 2002; Rosenberg 2000).

The cost of Canada's medical care system grows each year. Denton and Spencer (1995) project that health care expenses will more than double between

● **Exhibit 8.2**

THE MEDICAL MODEL AND THE SOCIAL MODEL IN LONG-TERM CARE

Medical Model	Social Model
patient	resident, consumer
acute patients	chronic client
physicians and hospitals	community settings and home
patient fits organization	organization fits client, changes to fit client if necessary
rigid system boundaries	open system boundaries
high priority to short-term need	high priority to long-term need
serves long-term care if it has excess capacity	serves long-term care first
diagnosis/treatment/cure model	assessment of functional capacity, service needs identified, services delivered
organizationally inflexible	organizationally flexible and creative
institutional care	community-based and home care
excludes people in the community	includes community members and may include institution
institution-centred	person-centred
makes little use of informal network	includes informal support
medical/physical assessment	multidimensional assessment (physical, psychological, social needs)
meets patients' medical needs	helps clients to meet their own needs
patient accepts professional treatment	client plays role developing treatment plan
professional has most power in relationship	client and professional share power
hierarchical organization	flat organization, team approach
expensive resources	lower-cost resources
major share of health care budget	small share of health care budget

These two approaches see and treat the older person differently. Each has a role to play in the Canadian health care system. Some critics feel that the system today relies too heavily on the medical model, and that an older population needs more services based on social model principles.

Source: Adapted from B. Havens, 1995, "Long-Term Care Diversity within the Care Continuum," *Canadian Journal on Aging* 14(2): 245–62. Reprinted with permission from the *Canadian Journal on Aging*.

1986 and 2041. In part, these higher costs are explained by the fact there are more older people in the population. Other sources show that older people as a group use hospitals more often than younger people and that they use them for longer periods (Denton and Spencer 1995). Some people fear that an aging population will cause a breakdown in the health care system.

A closer look at the health care system shows that older people account for only a small part of past increases in health care costs (Barer, Evans, and Hertzman 1995; Black et al. 1995; Evans et al. 2001). Denton and his colleagues (2001), for example, studied physician services in Ontario. They projected increases in costs over the next four decades. They found that population aging did lead to increased costs in the future, but it had only a moderate effect by past standards. General population increases had a greater effect than population aging on doctor costs over the next four

● Exhibit 8.3

SELECTED NATIONS WITH PERCENTAGE OF POPULATION AGED 65 AND OLDER AND PERCENTAGE OF GROSS DOMESTIC PRODUCT (GDP) SPENT ON HEALTH CARE, 1996

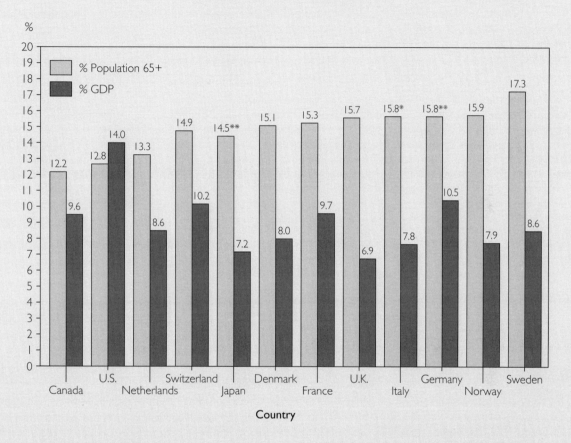

* Based on 1994 data
** Based on 1995 data

Canada has the youngest population among the developed nations presented here, but ranks among the top five nations in spending. Also, the percent of GDP spent on health care bears no direct relationship to the proportion of older people in a country. Binstock (1993) concludes that the propor- tion of older people in a country does not explain high health care costs. Instead, public policies that encourage or discourage health care use affect how much money gets spent on health care. So does the increased use of high-tech medical care treatment.

Source: M.W. Rosenberg, 2000, *The Effects of Population Ageing on the Canadian Health Care System,* Social and Economic Dimensions of an Aging Population Research Program (SEDAP), Paper No. 14, Tables 6 and 8, Hamilton, ON: McMaster University.

decades. The researchers also say that changes in technology, medical knowledge, and doctors' treatment choices will affect costs.

Evans and his colleagues (2001) studied the link between population aging and health care use. They looked at acute inpatient hospital days, physician services, and drug use. In each case, they report that population aging has little effect on the rates of use or on costs. For example, drug use by older people increased by 147 percent (per capita) from 1985 to 1999. But the increased number of older people accounts for only 2 percent of this increase. Instead the researchers found that increases in specific costs for specific treatments account for over three-quarters of the rise in costs.

They trace most of this increase to shifts in doctors' choice of more expensive drugs. The researchers conclude that "demographic trends *by themselves* are likely to explain some, but only a small part, of future trends in health care use and costs, and in and of themselves will require little, if any, increase in the share of national resources devoted to health care" (Evans et al. 2001, 166). Evans and his colleagues say that non-demographic conditions account for most of the increases in health care costs.

A study by Carrière (2000) supports this conclusion. Carrière projected hospital use in the future based on past trends. He found that population aging does not affect the total number of days that Canadians stayed in hospitals per year. But population aging does lead to an increased proportion of older hospital patients. It could also lead to a large majority of hospital beds occupied by older patients in the future. Carrière says that in the future we will need different types of care for older patients.

This will require more training in geriatric care for doctors, nurses, and staff. For example, Canada had 144 geriatricians in 2000. But the population needed as many as 481. The country will have 198 geriatricians by 2006, but projected need will rise to 538. Canada has 0.44 geriatricians per 100 000 population. The Royal College of Physicians in England set a standard of 2 per 100 000 (nearly five times the Canadian level) (National Advisory Council 2003). Canada needs more specialists who can provide care that suits the needs of older people.

Increased drug costs, more doctors, rising costs for complex treatments, unionization of hospital workers, and more tests to diagnose disease account for most of the increases in the cost of health care (Feeny 1994). Chappell and her colleagues (1997) found, for example, that the budget for the drug reimbursement system in British Columbia (Pharmacare) increased by 2200 per-

cent from 1974 to 1994. They say that increased drug prices accounted for most of this increase. Drug-related illnesses also add to the cost of medical care (Tamblyn and Perrault 2000). Kozyrskyi (2003, 26) says that "almost 50 per cent of drugs prescribed for the elderly have been reported to be either inappropriate or unnecessary. Drug-related problems in the elderly not uncommonly lead to hospitalization." These practices drive up the cost of drugs and of health care in general.

Some critics of the system today question whether older people need more done to them, or whether they need done to them what currently gets done. Critics question whether the medical model fits the needs of an aging society (Chappell 1988). They argue that for the same cost Canadians could buy care that more closely fits their needs (Evans 1984). "As a society," Chappell, Strain, and Blandford (1986, 112) say, "we have not yet dealt with the issue—especially during old age—'When is health care servicing inappropriate or too much?'"

THE HEALTH CARE SYSTEM AND OLDER PEOPLE'S HEALTH CARE NEEDS

By any standards, older people have more health problems than younger people and use more health care services. Lindsay (1999) reports that people aged 65 and over, compared with younger people, see specialists and general practitioners more often. They also have more hospital separations[1] than younger people and they spend more days in the hospital during each stay. Hospital use increases with age from middle age on. Women aged 75 and over have a separation rate more than three and a half times the rate of women aged 45 to 64. They spent 23.1 days in the hospital on average during each stay, compared with 9.2 days for the 45- to 64-year-old group. Men aged 75 and over had a rate almost four and a half times the rate of men aged 45 to 64. They spent 17.1 days in the hospital on average during each visit, compared with 8.6 days on average for each stay for the 45- to 64-year-old group (Lindsay 1999).

Statistics Canada reports that older people have higher surgery rates than younger people (Maclean and Oderkirk 1991). Between 1975 and 1987, the surgery rate for older people increased at more than triple the rate for people under age 65. Barer, Evans, and Hertzman (1995) report that surgical rates increased for older people by 45.6 percent between 1971 and 1985–86.

---

1. "Hospital separations" refers to the discharge or death of an inpatient; a person discharged more than once in a year counts as more than one separation.

Older surgery patients also stay in the hospital more than 10 days longer on average than younger surgery patients (Maclean and Oderkirk 1991).

Barer and his colleagues (1986) studied the reasons older people use more health care services today than in the past. They wanted to find out whether this increase in costs reflects changes in the diseases older people have today, or whether it reflects the way the system cares for older patients. If the costs reflect older people's increased need for treatment, population aging could lead to a sharp increase in health care costs. But if changes reflect the way the system operates, new approaches to treatment could contain costs. Barer and his colleagues found that little data existed to test the first possibility (that older people have different diseases or more diseases today than in the past). They do suggest that the way the system responds to older people's needs leads them to make heavier use of the medical care system today than in the past.

Studying consultation visits to specialists, Black and her colleagues (1995) analyzed Manitoba data to see why older people use more health care now than in the past. They found that a decrease in the health of older people accounted for only a tiny increase in consultation visits (one-tenth of 1 percent). Instead, they traced increases in consultations to doctors' increased tendency to make referrals. This practice, they say, accounts for at least half of added visits to specialists by older people. They go on to say that people in good health account for at least one-third of this increase in visits to specialists. These findings have led researchers to link physicians' choice of treatment to health service use.

Chappell, Strain, and Blandford (1986, 100) report that physicians "control approximately 80 percent of health care costs." Only a quarter of this percentage goes directly to physicians; the rest goes to hospital use (half of all health care costs), drugs, tests, and other medical expenses. Doctors control these expenses through the decisions they make about treatments and through their reliance on high technology in hospital settings.

Data from Ontario estimate that each doctor costs the system $500 000 a year. Half of this goes to pay for the doctors' services and half goes to other expenses such as drugs, lab tests, and hospital admissions (National Advisory Council on Aging [NACA] 1994c). Some researchers propose that fewer doctors would lead to lower health care costs (Evans et al. 2001). Some provinces have cut medical school admissions for this reason, and some provinces limit the number of doctors who can practice and others have capped doctors' billings to the provincial system. Other researchers suggest that doctors need more knowledge about how to care for older people. More appropriate care might lower health care costs.

Shapiro and Roos (1986, 165) say that hospital-based care uses "about 60 percent of all health care dollars," but they determined that individual need cannot explain older people's pattern of hospital use. Looking at physicians' "hospitalization style," Shapiro and Roos found that patients of hospital-prone doctors spent, on average, twice as much time in the hospital as patients of non-hospital-prone doctors. These doctors also accounted for 73 percent of high users who had repeated hospital stays.

The federal government began to insure hospital care in 1957, 10 years before it insured the cost of visits to doctors' offices. This policy encouraged doctors to admit patients to hospitals for treatment, since doing so saved patients money. Gross and Schwenger (1981, 129) blame the high cost of the health care system on "a heavy reliance on institutional care."

Drug Use by Older Canadians

Appropriate use of prescription and over-the-counter drugs can help older people maintain or improve their health and well-being. However, the misuse of drugs can create or intensify existing health problems (Bergob 2004). Most drug use among older Canadians is by prescription, typically medications for the heart or blood pressure. Older people use more prescription drugs than younger people. Older people represent approximately 12 percent of the Canadian population, yet they use 20 to 30 percent of all prescription drugs. Prescription drug use is higher among older women than older men and tends to increase with advancing age for older women. Drug use tends to decline for older men as they age.

While most older Canadians report good to excellent health, a significant minority of older people report using three or more drugs during a one month period. Multiple-drug use is more common among older women than older men. And, as with prescription drug use overall, multiple-drug use tends to increase with advanced age for women but decrease for men. Older people in fair or poor health tend to use more than one drug. This applies particularly to those who report greater stress in their lives and to those without family or friends to provide social support (Bergob 2004). Older Canadians, compared to younger people, tend to use more prescription drugs and to be multiple-drug users. In a Quebec study that examined the use of mood-altering drugs among young adults (those age 18–64) and older adults (those 65 years of age and older), 22 percent of the older adults used this type of drug compared to 5 percent of younger adults (Préville et al. 2001). Women and those with lower incomes were more likely to use these medications than were men or those with a higher income. A Montreal study found that older people who used mood-altering drugs were more likely than nonusers to report feelings of loneliness and to feel they lacked social support (Perodeau and du Fort 2000).

The proportion of older Canadians who use mood-altering drugs to treat depression has risen from 9.3 percent in 1993 to 11.5 percent in 1997 (Mamdani et al. 2000). This represents a cost increase of 150 percent, from $10.8 million to $27 million in that period. Part of this increase (about 20 percent) is a result of population shifts and an increase in the use of antidepressants among the older population. However, a more significant factor, accounting for approximately 60 percent of the increase, is related to changes in prescribing practices, with a greater use of more expensive antidepressant medications.

In a study that examined the over-the-counter drug use of older adults (Amoako, Richardson-Campbell, and Kennedy-Malone 2003), 90 percent of older adults used pain medicine, two-thirds took high blood pressure medication, more than one-half used caffeine daily, and about 10 percent used alcohol. The researchers caution that older adults may be unaware of the potential adverse effects that could result from combining these substances.

Graham and Braun (1999) found that married seniors could influence their partner's behaviour related to alcohol and other substances. In their study, older couples were very similar in their use of caffeine, tobacco, and antidepressants, and in whether they drank alcohol, as well as in the frequency and quantity of alcohol consumption. The researchers suggest these findings could shed light on the relationship between gender and widowhood and late-onset problem drinking.

A study that examined the nature and extent of medications stored in the homes of older Canadians found the number of medications ranged from 3 to 48, with an average of 20 medications per home (Poirier and Barbeau 1999). About one-half of the medications were prescription medications, while the others were over-the-counter drugs. Approximately one-quarter of these medications were past their expiration date. This raises concerns related to the effectiveness and safety of expired medications in the homes of older Canadians. The large number of medications in each home raises the problem of adverse drug reactions due to the misuse or inappropriate combining of medications. Health professionals, family members, and older adults themselves can help ensure the proper use of prescription drugs. In particular, older people who use more than one drug or who have more than one physician face the risk of adverse reactions (Bergob 2004).

The present and future costs of prescription drugs for older adults is a concern for individuals and for society as the population continues to age. Some researchers believe that, as younger Canadians move into later life, their use of prescription drugs may be different than for today's older people. Bergob (2004, 6) says that "increased public awareness and adoption of lifestyles and behaviours that promote good health may result in tomorrow's seniors being healthier and less dependent on medical interventions."

Complementary and Alternative Medicine

Interest has grown in the use of complementary and alternative medicine for the treatment of a wide range of health concerns. In the older population, these include *qigong* (an ancient Chinese therapy) for the treatment of depression (Tsang et al. 2002), aromatherapy for the treatment of sleep problems (Connell et al. 2001), and herbal and homeopathic remedies, chiropractic services, and acupuncture for the treatment of health conditions such as depression, chronic pain (Dello Buono et al. 2001), and arthritis (Loera et al. 2001).

One study found that 58 percent of older Americans living in an urban centre had used some type of complementary or alternative medicine in the past year (Cherniack et al. 2001). Those most likely to have used these treatments were women, those with a higher education, and those with thyroid disease or arthritis. Another American study found that 41 percent of their sample used at least one complementary or alternative medicine (Astin et al. 2000). The most frequently used remedies were herbs (24 percent), chiropractic services (20 percent), massage (15 percent), and acupuncture (14 percent).

Research has documented some success with alternative and complementary therapies. For example, Connell and colleagues (2001) report that aromatherapy brought about a modest but significant improvement in sleep for hospitalized older patients. Griffin and Vitro (1998) report a number of positive results from the use of therapeutic touch with people with Alzheimer's disease. Therapeutic touch is a modern approach to an ancient technique of the "laying on of hands" to rebalance an individual's life energy. Griffin and Vitro report that following a therapeutic touch treatment, patients were more relaxed and better able to sleep. This technique was also an effective way to build an emotional connection with Alzheimer's patients who could not communicate verbally.

Complementary and alternative therapies still remain on the fringe of mainstream Western medicine. Astin and his colleagues (2000) found that although 80 percent of people who used complementary or alternative medicine reported receiving significant benefits from these treatments, most of these people (58 percent) did not discuss these therapies with their physicians. As alternative and complementary medicine gains greater acceptance, particularly among medical professionals, its value as an alternative to, or in combination with, more accepted Western medical practices will also increase.

INSTITUTIONAL CARE

The 1995–96 National Public Health Survey reports that seniors make up 81 percent of people living in institutions. Most of these seniors (73 percent) were women (Health Canada 1999b). Institutionalization rates vary from province to province. In Quebec in 1996, for example, 9.7 percent of seniors lived in institutions. Manitoba, Ontario, New Brunswick, Nova Scotia, and Newfoundland report that between 6 and 7 percent of seniors live in institutions. British Columbia has the lowest rate, with 5.4 percent of seniors living in institutions (Health Canada 1999c). Canada's national rate of institutionalization of seniors was 7.3 percent in 1996. This is higher than that of the United States (4.6 percent) and of the United Kingdom (4.1 percent), but lower than other developed countries such as Holland (11 percent) (Health Canada 1999c; NACA 1996a).

Some institutions house only older people. On any given day, 7 percent of older people live in these institutions (NACA 1999a), and most of them live in nursing homes. These homes go by a variety of names: special care facilities, homes for special care, and personal care homes. The term "nursing home," as it is used here, refers to any institution (that is not a hospital) that offers medical care for chronically ill older people.

Each province has its own system for classifying patients. The government allocates funds to institutions based on the level of care needed by each patient. Charles and Schalm (1992a, 1992b) describe the development of a seven-level system in Alberta. Most provinces define four levels of nursing home care. In Manitoba, people in levels three and four need 3.5 hours of nursing care per day and need help with at least two basic activities of daily living such as bathing, dressing, and eating. People in level two need 2 to 3.5 hours of nursing care per day and need moderate care and help with at least one basic activity of daily living. People in level one need 0.5 to 2 hours of nursing care per day and need personal help only to wash or attend activities (Forbes, Jackson, and Kraus 1987; Shapiro and Tate 1988b).

A detailed analysis of institution admission calculated the odds of entering an institution given certain conditions in a person's life. Shapiro and Tate (1988b, 238) found that people in Manitoba with the specific characteristics—age 85 or over, living without a spouse, "recent hospital admission, living in retirement housing,

having one or more [problems with activities of daily living] ... and having a mental impairment"—had more than a three-in-five chance of entering an institution within two and a half years. Montgomery, Kirshen, and Roos (1988) report that the chance of residing in a nursing home increases dramatically over the four years before a person's death. Trottier and her colleagues (2000) found that health problems such as Alzheimer's disease, urinary incontinence, and stroke led to institutionalization. These problems (and the chance of institutionalization) increase with age. These studies suggest that as the population ages, the numbers and percentages of older people who spend some time in an institution will increase.

Such increases would be unfortunate. Institutionalization can lead to decreased well-being and even death for older residents. Bravo and her colleagues (1999, cited in Dubois, Bravo, and Charpentier 2001) studied institutions in Quebec. They found that in 25 percent of the institutions at least one person received below-standard care. This occurred most often in smaller institutions (40 people or less), where up to 20 percent of older people got below-standard care. The researchers found that only a few homes reached these high percentages of below-standard care. But in these cases the older people suffered from a low quality of life.

Gutman and her colleagues in British Columbia (1986) found a high percentage of deaths among patients within the first six months of admission to a personal care home. They concluded that admission to a LTC institution in itself causes severe stress to older people. Shapiro and Tate (1988a) also found high mortality rates right after admission to a nursing home. They suggest that clinical instability or relocation may account for this high rate (see also Hirdes and Brown 1996). Also, the sickest older people enter institutions. This, in part, accounts for the high death rate for new patients. Still, Chappell and Penning (1979) found that, after matching for levels of health, people in institutionalized settings showed lower well-being than those in the community.

Most people, including government leaders, doctors, nursing home staff, and older people themselves, agree that we should keep older people out of institutions when we can. And provinces use community care programs to keep people in the community as long as possible. Still, institutions play a useful role in the continuum of health care services. For example, LTC institutions reduce the use of hospitalization for residents (Montgomery, Kirshen, and Roos 1988; Shapiro, Tate, and Roos 1987). And this reduces the cost to the health care system if hospitals close some of their beds.

Sometimes a person needs to live in a nursing home. Kelly, Knox, and Gekoski (1998) asked middle-aged and older women whether they would choose a nursing home setting for themselves or someone else with severe cognitive or physical problems. They found that women chose institutional care most often if the older person lived alone or had little informal support. Only one-third of the people in this study had negative views of institutional care. People with Alzheimer's disease may also benefit from institutional care. Institutions can have design features (such as circular hallways, colour-coded walls, or a secure garden) that make life easier for people with memory problems (Lovering et al. 2002; Passini et al. 1998). Canada's long winters, the great distances between older people and hospitals, the need for constant care, few informal supports, and poverty sometimes make institutional life the only way for people to get the care they need.

Brillon (1992) notes that some provinces have no special laws to protect the rights of older people in nursing homes, and some institutions have no clear policies that protect residents' rights. Poirier (1992) proposes three types of rights that institutions should protect: the right to take care of one's own things, the right to respect for one's rights, and the right to manage one's own life. This last right poses some of the greatest problems. An institution has to serve the collective good as well as ensure the right to manage one's own life. For example, the institution may infringe on the right to privacy as staff enter and leave patients' rooms or provide personal care.

MacLean and Bonar (1983; see also Coons and Mace 1996) say that institutions can and should make life in the institution as much like life outside as possible. They call this the **normalization principle**.

First, people should feel the normal rhythm of the day, week, and year. They should get dressed each day, have a weekly routine, and celebrate holidays, birthdays, and anniversaries. Institutions should also include programs that keep residents active. This can include outdoor as well as indoor activities. A garden, for example, can provide a safe environment for outdoor programs (Heath and Gifford 2001; Lovering et al. 2002). Activity can increase the quality and length of patients' lives (Stones, Dornan, and Kozma 1989).

Second, people should get a normal amount of respect. Sometimes staff forget that patients have a right to decide things for themselves. Buzzell (1981) reports that in one home the staff decided that Edna, a 74-year-old patient, should begin walking again after a hip fracture. Buzzell calls the attempt a "nightmare." First, the staff took Edna's wheelchair away so she would have no

choice but to walk. Then, when she tried to walk, the nurses on staff called her "lazy" and threatened her if she moved too slowly. Edna suffered dizzy spells, but an aide tried to force her to walk "non-stop to the end of the corridor, sixty feet," until "Edna pleaded for rest." But the aide refused to let her rest in her wheelchair and threatened to take her off the active treatment program.

MacLean and Bonar (1983) say that staff should treat the older patient as an adult. They should avoid using baby talk, talking down to the person, or making decisions without consulting the patient. Penning and Chappell (1982) found that older residents who felt they had freedom and the ability to make choices showed improved mental health. People showed high levels of psychological adjustment when the institution offered freedom of choice (O'Connor and Vallerand 1994).

Third, people should lead as normal a social life as possible. This can include day outings, camping trips, and garden boxes for outdoor activity (Bonifazi 1998; Cott and Fox 2001). Gilbart and Hirdes (2000) found that most residents in the institutions they studied faced the risk of feeling sad or anxious, but people who engaged in social activity and had a good relationship with a key person in their lives reported the most happiness. The Index of Social Engagement used in this study contained items on activity participation and involvement in facility life. The researchers say that social engagement was "the most important variable for explaining variation in well-being among residents" (62).

Normalization should also include sexual contact and sexual intimacy if a person has a willing partner. Institutions often allow married couples to live together. Gladstone (1992) reports that when both members of a married couple live in an institution, the couple will likely live in the same room. This can improve a person's quality of life. An 87-year-old man says that when his wife had a stroke she spent a year in a hospital. "I lived alone and was terribly depressed," he says. "When we both got accepted here [in a nursing home] I was really glad to be with her again. At least I'm not lonely for her anymore" (NACA 1993g, 24).

People should also have access to their money, and they should have their own pictures, small pieces of furniture, or pets to make the institution more like their home. MacLennan (1983) says that the institution should also expect patients to socialize and to do as much for themselves as they can. Rattenbury and Stones (1989) found, for example, that reminiscence and current-topic discussion groups increased residents' psychological well-being. Forbes, Jackson, and Kraus (1987, 92) say that older people in institutions "have the right to make decisions about issues which affect them, and to maintain contact with their past life."

Some groups have special needs. Wister and Moore (1998) describe a number of institutional settings for Aboriginal elders that attempt to normalize the environment. The North Thompson Band in British Columbia, for example, offers a public lunch in its senior health care facility on the Chu Chua reserve. This lunch draws other elders from the community as well as family and friends. This creates a community involvement in the life of the home. Tsawaayuus (Rainbow Gardens) in Port Alberni houses both Aboriginal and non-Aboriginal elders. The setting provides Aboriginal elders with Aboriginal cultural activities and foods. The home also employs Aboriginal

workers. Both of these programs attempt to buffer the effects of isolation caused by institutionalization.

A normalized environment should also include a weekly staff meeting. Meetings allow staff members to talk about problem patients and help them to channel frustration into methods for helping patients function better. Devine (1980) found that normalizing encourages nursing staff "to become leaders and teachers of the residents" instead of just caretakers. She found that staff stopped stereotyping older people as senile and useless because it worked against the goals of the program.

Keating and her colleagues (2001) say that some nursing home settings have moved toward a social model of care. They hire more non-nursing staff and they include

---

● Exhibit 8.4

HOW TO MAKE VISITS COUNT

A person with an older relative or friend in an institution may come to dread visiting day. If the relative has a cognitive impairment or few verbal skills, a well-meaning visitor can find the visit unpleasant and disturbing. Below, Pat Gibbs, consultant to the Ministry of Health in British Columbia, gives some helpful advice on how to make the most of a visit.

Q: My husband is glad to see me when I visit him at the Extended Care Unit, where he has lived for the past two years since I could no longer look after him at home. But he doesn't talk or respond much, and I run out of things to say. Sometimes it's hard to come up with ideas to pass the time during our visits.

A: You have raised a concern that many other caregivers share. Perhaps some of these suggestions might help.

- Bring in photograph albums from home—many pleasant hours can be spent in reminiscing using old photographs.
- Bring in a small tape deck and cassette tapes of music that the two of you enjoyed, and spend a visit listening to music together.

- Include other residents, room-mates, or visitors in social interaction during the visit. For example, if you turn on the T.V. so that your husband can watch a game, invite someone else to join in. This may facilitate your husband's forming relationships with others in the Extended Care Unit.
- Simple grooming activities are relaxing, do not require conversation, provide the soothing contact of touch, and may be things that the staff have limited time to do for your husband, such as a manicure, or even a massage!
- Try reading out loud—clips of interest from the newspaper, or letters from relatives. Some letters can be read more than once—it doesn't have to be a new one each time.
- Capitalize on all the amenities and resources that the facility has to offer. If possible, change the location of your visits from time to time. Take your husband in his wheelchair down to the chapel, the library corner, the lounge for tea, out to the courtyard for fresh air.
- Incorporate special events going on at the residence into your visiting time with your spouse, such as a family barbecue, or happy hour.
- If appropriate, bring in a pet from home.

Source: P. Gibbs, 1996, "How to Make Visits Count," *BC Caregiver News* 1(5): 4. Reprinted with permission.

family members on the caregiving team. Family support can reduce the cost of care. But family members also provide unique supports to the older resident. For example, family members monitor the effectiveness of professional care, they advise professionals on the older person's preferences, and they provide emotional support.

This research project found that some family members engaged in housekeeping activities. But most often they spent their time enhancing the older person's well-being. Family members averaged between 30 and 50 hours of support per month (depending on the older person's condition). The researchers say that partnerships between informal and formal caregivers show promise. But they caution that both patient and staff need an orientation to this partnership approach. And the institution needs to monitor the work load and expectations placed on family members (Keating et al. 2001).

Nursing homes and other institutions will never take the place of a person's own home or apartment. But the changes suggested here make a nursing home more comfortable for older people who have to live there.

● **Exhibit 8.5**

CONTROVERSY: THE USE OF RESTRAINTS IN NURSING HOMES

Many institutions use restraints to cope with residents' behavioural problems (Eaton, Stones, and Rockwood 1986). Restraints include bed rails, belts, geriatric chairs, jackets, and medications. A nursing practice conference in 1980 compared Canadian and British use of restraints. In one Canadian study of 136 patients aged 70 and over, almost 85 percent of patients had a restraint. A similar study of 172 patients in England found that only about 20 percent of patients had restraints (cited in Bogaert 1980). The conference members concluded that Canada uses restraints more often than necessary.

Roberge and Beauséjour (1988) studied the use of restraints in a sample of 35 Quebec nursing homes and chronic-care settings. They found that both types of institutions used restraints on 47 percent of all residents. Institutions that used restraints used bed rails 56 percent of the time; belts and geriatric chairs 16 percent of the time; and jackets 8 percent of the time. Physicians had prescribed some of these restraints (63 percent for the nursing homes and 46 percent for chronic-care institutions). In some cases (18 percent), the institutions had policies that required restraints.

But many health care professionals disagree with the use of restraints. Mitchell-Pedersen and her colleagues (1985) removed 97 percent of the physical restraints in a hospital setting in one year. They found no significant increase in accidents; they also found that staff attitudes toward their work improved. "Staff became highly creative in looking after patients without the use of restraints and a feeling of pride developed as they were able to provide care that honoured the autonomy of their patients" (Mitchell-Pedersen et al. 1985, cited in Forbes, Jackson, and Kraus 1987, 73).

The use of restraints raises ethical issues. Many institutions say that patients need restraints for their own safety. But patients pay the price for this supposed safety. Forbes, Jackson, and Kraus (1987, 72), for instance, say that physical and chemical restraints disturb older patients and rob them of their comfort and autonomy. Healey (cited in Bogaert 1980, 22) asks, "Do we ... have a right to act against their will because we think it's in their best interests? Could it be we are more often than not selfishly protecting our own interests?" The National Advisory Council on Aging (1993g) says that institutions must get informed consent before they restrain a mentally competent resident. A person who refuses restraints would then sign a waiver that absolves the institution of liability.

Roberge and Beauséjour (1988) say that institutions should use non-coercive methods to care for patients. They suggest that methods such as occupational therapy, music therapy, and more family contacts would help staff reduce behaviour problems. Some institutions use electronic methods to keep track of patients. These include electric locks, tags on patients' clothing that alert staff, and pressure-sensitive strips on chairs that sound an alarm if a person begins to wander (Watzke and Wister 1993). Technologies such as these can allow people freedom to move and still provide the safety they need.

The NACA (1993g) supports the older person's right to choose or refuse treatment. NACA supports this right even if a choice increases a person's risk of illness or accident. "An ethical course is to restrict individual freedom only if necessary and only as much as necessary" (7).

THE NEED FOR CHANGE

Canada's commitment to the medical model accounts for much of the increase in health care costs today. In 2001, for example, the largest contributors to health care expenditures were hospitals (30.6 percent), physicians (13.2 percent), and drugs (15.7 percent) (Canadian Institute for Health Information 2003).

Some signs suggest that change in the system has begun. British Columbia, for example, created several programs to control the rising cost of drugs. One program gave patients a 10-day trial of a new drug (rather than a 90-day supply) to cut down on the cost of wasted medicines. Another program targets drug fraud and medication abuse. It links pharmacies throughout the province via computer so pharmacists can review a person's entire drug use pattern to ensure the best treatment. A third program attempts to cap the cost of expensive medications by proposing preferred (less expensive brands) of the drug. Closer monitoring of drug use can also reduce hospital admissions (Chappell et al. 1997).

In 1997, Alberta's health minister called for a review of the province's long-term care system. The government set out a plan to reduce costs and to give responsibility for health services to regional health authorities (RHAs). The plan also called for decreases in acute hospital beds and increases in community care. Saunders and his colleagues (2001) report that in part this plan succeeded. During the 1990s, in Alberta acute hospital stays decreased and use of home care and doctors' services increased. But the plan did not reduce costs. Also, the researchers say that their report didn't study the quality of care that patients received. New systems and policies try to contain costs. But continued reliance on doctors, hospitals, drugs, and expensive treatments will drive up the costs of medical care in the future. Shapiro (1992) says that nursing homes rely too heavily on the medical model. They hire costly registered nurses to give care when most patients need help with activities of daily living (such as bathing). "Except for residents who require specialized resources," she says, "even the heaviest care residents are in this category because their heavy dependency on others is primarily for ADL [activities of daily living] help or for supervision due to their cognitive impairment" (208). Reliance on the medical model also sometimes leads to inappropriate care for the older patients in the community. Chappell (1993b, 495) reports that between 25 and 60 percent of doctors' services to older people "are not necessary and do not increase the quality of life."

These and other issues led the federal government to review the national health care system. In April 2001, Prime Minister Jean Chrétien commissioned a study of Canada's health care system. He appointed Roy Romanow, Queen's Counsellor, to chair the Commission on the Future of Health Care in Canada. The prime minister charged the commission to study the current system and propose reforms to meet Canada's future health care needs. The commission met with citizens and groups across the country, held televised forums, and received reports from researchers. The commission handed down its report (often called the **Romanow Report**) in November 2002 (Commission on the Future of Health Care in Canada [Commission] 2002). It contained 47 proposals for change. This forms what the report calls a "roadmap for a collective journey by Canadians to reform and renew their health care system." Many of these proposals respond to the needs of older people. Below is a sample of the recommendations that speak to older people's needs.

Recommendation 1: A new Canadian Health Covenant should be established as a common declaration of Canadians' and their governments' commitment to a universally accessible, publicly funded health care system (Commission 2002, 247).

Recommendation 5: The *Canada Health Act* should be modernized and strengthened by:

- Confirming the principles of public administration, universality, and accessibility, updating the principles of portability and comprehensiveness, and establishing a new principle of accountability;

- Expanding insured health services beyond hospital and physician services to immediately include targeted home care services followed by prescription drugs in the longer term;

- Clarifying coverage in terms of diagnostic services;

- Including an effective dispute resolution process;

- Establishing a dedicated health transfer directly connected to the principles and conditions of the *Canada Health Act* (Commission 2002, 248).

Recommendation 7: On a short-term basis, the federal government should provide targeted funding for the next two years to establish:

- a new Rural and Remote Access Fund,
- a new Diagnostic Services Fund,
- a Primary Health Care Transfer,
- a Home Care Transfer, and

• a Catastrophic Drug Transfer (Commission 2002, 248–49).

Recommendation 26: Provincial and territorial governments should take immediate action to manage wait lists more effectively by implementing centralized approaches, setting standardized criteria, and providing clear information to patients on how long they can expect to wait (Commission 2002, 251).

Recommendation 34: The proposed new Home Care Transfer should be used to support expansion of the *Canada Health Act* to include medically necessary home care services in the following areas:

• Home mental health case management and intervention services should immediately be included in the scope of medically necessary services covered under the *Canada Health Act.*

• Home care services for post-acute patients, including coverage for medication management and rehabilitation services, should be included under the *Canada Health Act.*

• Palliative home care services to support people in their last six months of life should also be included under the *Canada Health Act* (Commission 2002, 252).

Recommendation 35: Human Resources Development Canada, in conjunction with Health Canada, should be directed to develop proposals to provide direct support to informal caregivers to allow them to spend time away from work to provide necessary home care assistance at critical times (Commission 2002, 252).

The report concludes by stating that "the immediate priorities must be to strengthen medicare's legislative and institutional foundations, to stabilize funding, and to address the critical concerns that are eroding Canadians' confidence in the system" (Commission 2002, 254). These changes will take place over time. The implementation plan extends to 2020.

The Canadian Geriatrics Society's response to the Romanow Report proposes an increase in the number of physicians who choose to specialize in geriatrics. It also proposes more geriatric expertise for general practice physicians (MacKnight et al. 2003). This group also calls for more home care services for those with chronic illness, more assistance to family caregivers, and an increase in qualified staff in long-term care facilities. The changes proposed in the Romanow Report and responses to this report will improve the health care system overall. But the implementation of these changes will depend on the government's ability to fund reform.

LONG-TERM CARE: NEW APPROACHES TO COMMUNITY CARE

The *Canada Health Act* of 1984, the basis of Canada's health care system, ensures hospital and physician care for all Canadians. One important benefit of the system is that it protects acute and chronically ill older people from financial ruin in case of a long-term illness. However, Chappell, Strain, and Blandford (1986, 108) say the health care system focuses on "institutional care rather than community care, on acute care rather than chronic care and on medical care rather than health care broadly defined." Older people who need other types of long-term care, including homemaker help, Meals on Wheels, or transportation, must often turn to the social welfare system for help. These programs and services fall on the border between health care and social service (Chappell 1993c). The availability of these services varies by province and region (Clark 1999). Some communities have a wide range of services, others have few. Havens (1995c, 84) says that "community based long term care is both less universal and less uniform across the country than any other form of health care." Havens and Bray (1996, 34) say that community-based long-term care gets "limited funding from the federal government" compared to other forms of health care.

An aging population "requires a qualitative as well as a quantitative change in the health care system. An aging population requires a fundamental restructuring of health care and a redefinition of what constitutes health care" (Myles and Boyd 1982, 274–75). The federal and provincial governments have begun to consider an insured national home care program because home care looks like a way to cut health care costs and provide quality services to older people. Most provinces have already begun to shift health care services away from institutions (Canadian Home Care Association 1998; Havens and Bray 1996).

This change has led to an overall decrease in hospital beds, a move from short-stay to long-stay beds, and hospital and nursing home bed closures in some provinces (Barer, Evans, and Hertzman 1995; Saunders et al. 2001). It has also meant fewer doctors in some provinces and more review of doctors' practices (King 1994). Finally, it has meant the growth of community care services. Williams and his colleagues (1999, 126) say that in Canada "home care has grown at more than 21 per cent per year over the past two decades."

The greatest increases in the use of home care were by older women and people who live alone. Also, people with chronic conditions and a need for activities of daily living support tend to use home care services (Wilkins and Beaudet 2000). Home care use rises dramatically with age. People aged 85 and over, for example, show a usage rate five to six times greater than people aged 65 to 69 (Coyte 2000, cited in Sullivan and Baranek 2002). Nursing and housekeeping were used more than any other home care services. By 1997, public spending on home care in Canada had reached $2.1 billion (up from only $62 million in 1975. Researchers estimate that people privately spend another $500 million on home care (Sullivan and Baranek 2002).

Most provinces have taken steps to decrease the use of institutional care. King (1994) reports that New Brunswick has allotted $6.6 million to expand its single-point-of-entry community care program, which allows access to all community social and health care services from one point in the system. This program will serve older people throughout the province. Manitoba has had a similar system for many years. Other provinces also use this approach.

Ontario expanded its commitment to community-based LTC between 1996 and 1998. The government set up 43 **Community Care Access Centres (CCACs)** across the province. Volunteer boards run these centres, which buy services from providers who compete for contracts. CCACs award contracts based on quality and price. For-profit and not-for-profit organizations (such as the Victorian Order of Nurses) compete for the contracts. This system creates managed competition of community care. Williams and his colleagues (1999) point out a number of challenges this system will face. How will CCACs decide the quality of a service? Who will service providers account to for the quality of their service? How much should CCACs monitor quality? The CCACs will feel increasing pressure as the population ages and as budgets remain capped. However, this system has moved community care to an important place in the health care system.

Quebec has also set up a community health network. Its network has 161 **Centres locaux de services communautaires (CLSCs)**. CLSCs combine the work of professionals and volunteers to deliver home care services (Nahmiash and Lesemann 1993). The system tries to direct health needs away from hospitals and toward community care. Quebec has also regionalized the hospital sector. This change decentralizes authority. "The basic purposes of regionalization are to minimize the duplication of services and facilities, to increase access to services, to permit the establishment of efficient referral channels and mechanisms, and to allow communities to become more involved in decision making over their

priorities and program development" (Manga 1993, 197). Manitoba has done roughly the same thing.

The use of regional health boards or councils has spread to other provinces as well (NACA 1995a). Regional boards manage and finance institutional and community health care services. They control costs in a time when the federal government has cut funds to the provinces and are thus responsible for tough decisions about where to cut services (Deber, Mhatre, and Baker 1994). Some of these boards or councils have seniors advisory committees or the boards consult with local seniors' groups (Seniors Advisory Council 1999).

Critics of these boards fear that administrators and health care professionals will have most of the power on the boards. Also, community control may lead to unequal access to services and varied standards of service. Skinner and Rosenberg (2002), for example, say that rural communities often have smaller tax bases due to aging populations. This can lead to lower levels of health care service. Supporters of regional boards say they are familiar with local needs and can work for the best interests of the community, but health care experts disagree about the value of the boards.

Many provinces intend to shift health services from institutions to community care. But in many cases the development of community care lags behind hospital bed closings. Montigny (1997, 139) studied long-term care reform in Ontario. He reports that the Ontario government in 1993 had promised $640 million to enhance long-term care. But by May of that year, he says, "only $100 million had been provided and only $26 million had actually been spent on the expansion of home-care services…. It seemed that families would either be forced to provide the services that were not being offered within the community or aged people would go without."

Chappell (1993b, cited in National Advisory Council 1995a, 14) warns that "if medical care is cut back without an expansion of community care, seniors are left not with a new health care system, simply a less adequate one." Morris and his colleagues (2000) point out that community care has grown more technical and demands more knowledge of medical practice as older people leave hospitals sooner. A lack of funding puts more pressure on community services. And in some cases community care simply means more stress for an elderly spouse or an overworked child caregiver—usually a woman (Gregor 1997; Saunders et al. 2001). Some critics of health care reform say that it covers up the government's plan to have family members take on more health care work (Montigny 1997). Neysmith (1993, 162) says that underfunding community care "tip[s] the dependency scale" toward family and kin;

Exhibit 8.6

COMPONENTS OF THE CONTINUING CARE SYSTEM

The Federal/Provincial/Territorial Subcommittee on Continuing Care (1992, 25) proposed a list of "major categories of services and settings" that make up the long-term care system. The list below presents programs most often used by older people. It gives a flavour of the mix of services, some medical and some social. This mix can cause confusion for people who need long-term care. Many providers offer these services (government, not-for-profit, for-profit); provincial health insurance pays for some services, and other services charge a user fee. Case managers can help make sense of this system and get people the services they need.

Meals on Wheels

Meals on Wheels delivers hot, nutritious meals to a person's home. Volunteers deliver the meals. These programs supplement diet to maintain health.

Adult Day Care

Adult day care provides personal help, health care services, and recreation in a group setting. People attend for half or full days.

Homemaker Services

Non-professionals help with personal care or housekeeping. Services may include help with bathing, cleaning, and cooking.

Home Nursing Care

A nurse visits someone's home to provide care. This service may cover day and evening care seven days a week and usually requires a doctor's referral.

Community Physiotherapy and Occupational Therapy

Physiotherapy and occupational therapists provide direct treatment and advice on illness prevention, arrange for equipment for home use, and teach family members how to help clients.

Assessment and Treatment Centres and Day Hospitals

Short-term services are available for diagnosing and treating health problems, including physical and psychological assessments, usually in an acute-care hospital.

Nursing Home Care

A nursing home provides institutional care for people who cannot remain at home because of health problems. Nursing homes provide long-term care for chronically ill people.

Chronic Hospital Care

An institution that provides special care for people with a chronic illness and functional limits and who do not need all the services of an acute-care hospital.

Other Services

Other services include programs that provide people with assistive devices, nutrition counselling, and social workers' services.

Source: Copyright © Minister of Public Works and Government Services Canada, 2000.

puts more burden on women, who are usually the primary caregivers; and leaves poor older people without health care resources.

The NACA says that too little community care leads to poor care for patients after they leave the hospital. A study in Saskatchewan, for example, found that 60 percent of people discharged from the hospital with home care needs did not get formal services (Saskatchewan Health 1998, cited in NACA 2000b). The NACA goes on to say that unmet needs for home care exist throughout Canada. Older people in rural settings sometimes found themselves without ongoing care. Shapiro and Havens (2000) say that poor discharge planning can lead to a person's re-admission with worse health problems.

● **Exhibit 8.7**

THE ROMANOW REPORT AND HOME CARE

The Romanow Report (Commission 2002) proposes federal funding for home care. The report recognizes the importance of community care within the health care system. And Canadian gerontologists, who have studied home care, generally praised the report. In particular, they praised its support for community care and home care programs, and the increase in federal funding for the health care system.

But some of these same researchers (Hébert 2003; Shapiro 2003) say that the report's home care recommendation excludes some of the most important needs of older people. For example, it targets home care support for mental health patients, post-acute patients, and palliative care patients. But older people rarely need these services (or need them for only a short time). Older people more often need combined medical and social services. And their home care needs include long-term care for chronic illnesses that limit their activities of daily living (MacKnight et al. 2003).

The report places home care support within the *Canada Health Act*. This focuses its application on medical problems (e.g., post-acute care support). Shapiro (2003) points to caregivers' need for non-medical support (such as housekeeping and respite care) when they give care over a long time. The report sees this need but fails to provide federal funding for this support.

This issue (and others) call for rethinking of some of the report's recommendations as they relate to older peoples' needs. The report calls for full implementation of its proposals by 2020. The process of dialogue and debate will continue as the report moves from recommendation to reality. Gerontologists will help shape this debate as they conduct research on health care needs in later life.

Wells (1997) found that hospital staff often began the discharge planning process early in the person's treatment—too early for the patient or the family to make a good discharge planning decision. Also, she found that discharge plans often reflected the hospital's concern for shorter stays, rather than the clinical condition of the older person. Early discharge planning often caused patients and their families distress. A hospital's desire for shorter stays sometimes led professionals to make discharge decisions for patients. Patients were sometimes left out of the decision-making process, leading to their dissatisfaction with the decision. Wells points out that this policy also raises ethical questions as health care professionals face a conflict between the hospital's goals and the patient's best interests.

Typical Community Care Programs

The social model of health care looks for ways to keep people out of institutions. A health care system based on the social model of care would "have at its core a broad definition of health and would make adequate provision for non-institutionally based chronic care" (Chappell, Strain, and Blandford 1986). Community care programs include hospitals, nursing homes, doctors' services, and community-based services such as geriatric day hospitals, adult day care, and home care.

The programs discussed below, beginning with geriatric day hospitals, form a **continuum of care**—from more institutional contact to little or no institutional contact at all. They show how the Canadian health care system has applied some of the principles of the social model of health care to meet older people's needs.

Keep three points in mind as you read about these programs. First, the same people who run the programs have done some of the evaluations of programs presented here, and this could bias their reports. Second, few evaluations use control groups to see what would have happened to a similar group if they had not used this kind of program. A program that claims to save money by keeping people out of institutions should compare its costs to service for a similar group of people who were in an institution. Third, evaluation studies often report short-term changes, which makes it hard to judge the long-term effects of a program.

Even with these shortcomings, however, evaluations and reports often provide the only available information about new programs and give some idea of what these programs do and how well they work.

Exhibit 8.8

PROPOSAL FOR A NATIONAL HOME CARE SYSTEM

The National Advisory Council on Aging reports that in 1998, 84 percent of people in a national poll favoured a national home care system (Queen's Health Policy 1999). The current system provides uneven service and often lacks coordination. The current system also leads to private funding for many services (e.g., out-of-pocket payment by families). The NACA calls for the following:

1. A National Home Care System. This system would share "Common Home Care Objectives." The provinces and the federal government would agree on how best to deliver services, as well as on what services make up the home care system. The NACA proposes that provinces integrate national objectives into their health care systems.

2. Public Administration with a Single Payer. This would decrease the cost of services and eliminate the tendency for private sector providers to provide only the most profitable services. And it would decrease the out-of-pocket costs to families.

3. Portability of Home Care Services. This would allow older people to move more freely throughout the country and get similar services wherever they live.

4. Improved Accountability. A national system would provide reports on the system's costs and effectiveness. It would judge these costs and benefits against the nationally agreed-on goals.

5. Delivery of Home Care Services. A national system would decrease costs due to the complex of service providers. The government as well as private companies now offer services. This can lead to extra costs for accounting and paperwork. A national system would create the best mix of public and private service providers.

6. Standardization of Human Resource Issues in Home Care. Standards are needed to guide the work and hiring of home care workers. The current workforce often gets low wages and may have little training.

7. Leadership Role of the Federal Government. The federal government should serve as a role model for the country. The NACA cites the Veterans Independence Program as an example of a strong program. This program provides a full range of health care services to veterans (and in some cases to spouses and children).

The NACA sees home care as a part of the health care system that will grow in importance with an aging society. Canada's home care system today grew without clear goals or a plan. Often the programs responded to local needs for services and expanded as those needs grew. The NACA calls for a more systematic approach that would serve older Canadians throughout the country.

Source: Adapted from the National Advisory Council on Aging, 2000, *The NACA Position on Home Care. No. 20*, p. 8, Ottawa: National Advisory Council on Aging. Reprinted with permission.

Geriatric Day Hospitals

Geriatric day hospitals offer a full range of hospital services to people who live in the community. A day hospital will assess an older person's needs and plan a rehabilitation and care program. Services include physical checkups, drug monitoring, dental clinics, diagnosis, treatment, and rehabilitation. Day hospitals can also keep an eye on older patients at risk in the community and ease older acute-care patients back into the community when they leave the hospital.

Eagle et al. (1987) say that day hospitals can improve patients' physical and emotional well-being. But they add to the cost of the health care system. To contain costs, day hospitals should not offer care to a patient for more than two days per week, or for more than six to eight weeks. The day hospital should operate at full capacity to make best use of the facility. And the day hospital must take in patients who would otherwise enter an institution.

Adult Day Care

Adult day-care programs "provide non-institutional support for those unable to remain in the community without it" (Chappell, Strain, and Blandford 1986, 121). These programs include hot meals, recreation programs, and a chance for the older person to socialize. The programs also give family caregivers time off to rest, shop, and maintain their own social life. Adult day care offers fewer medical services and more social and recreational services than day hospitals. Some provinces require that people pay for day-care services themselves, while other provinces include the service as part of the provincial health program (Weeks and Roberto 2002).

As yet, research has not shown a conclusive improvement of function or a reduction in the use of other services due to adult day care (or day hospital care) alone (Baumgarten et al. 2002; Chappell and Blandford 1987). However, studies do report an increase in participants' well-being (Chappell 1983). A study in Quebec found that two-thirds of adult day-care clients said they felt less lonely and half said they felt less anxious and depressed (Baumgarten et al. 2002). Likewise, a study of the first day-care centre for handicapped older people in Victoria showed that most clients improved their social skills and their self-esteem, and some improved their physical skills. Families reported better family relationships and better health for the client's spouse (Jackson 1983).

Home Care

Home care is one of the most important parts of a comprehensive health care system. Chappell (1999b, i) calls it "a cornerstone of a comprehensive, appropriate health care system for seniors." A NACA report (1986b) defines community support or home care services as "a co-ordinated and integrated range of services designed to help people live as independently as possible in the community." Home care includes medical care, such as a visiting nurse, housework, personal care, and meal delivery. A federal government report describes three goals of home care: (1) substitution for more costly care in institutions; (2) maintaining a person at home at a lower cost to the system; and (3) prevention of functional breakdown that could lead to institutionalization (FPT Subcommittee 1990).

In 1977, the Canadian federal government started the Extended Health Care Services program to support provincial home care programs. Home care programs differ from province to province, but all the provinces and territories in Canada have some public home care and nursing services. Some provinces have extensive home care programs that include Meals on Wheels, home repair services, laundry and cleaning help, emergency alert services, friendly visitors, nutrition counselling, and transportation.

Chan and Kenny (2001) say that all provincial home care programs assess clients, coordinate services, and manage cases. Case coordinators in Manitoba, for example, use an assessment interview to identify client needs. They then set up a system of supports to help the older person stay in his or her home (Berdes 1996). Ontario provides case managers to assess a person's needs and link them with public and private services. Case managers set up personalized care plans and try to protect clients from decreases in care services (Aronson 2002; Aronson and Sinding 2000). Hall and Cotye (2001) found that older people (aged 75 and over) and people in poor health who needed help with instrumental or ordinary activities of daily living (IADL) tended to use home care the most. McWilliam and her colleagues (2000) say that in-home assessments and care management lead to more physical independence for seniors at home.

Paré (2000, cited in NACA 2000d) reports on a Montreal program called SIPA (a French-language acronym for integrated care for seniors). This program uses hospitals and long-term care settings to serve frail seniors in the community. It offers nursing services around the clock. Paré reports a 50 percent drop in LTC admission rates and fewer seniors in hospital beds waiting for care.

Private for-profit and nonprofit home care agencies also exist. They most often provide "homemaking, in-home attendance, home health care, nursing and palliative care" (Nahmiash and Reis 1992). Liu and Lazaruk (1998, 298) call home care "the first step in long-term care." Shapiro and Tate (1997) found that a wide range of older people used home support and personal care services to maintain themselves in the community. People with dementia and other kinds of cognitive impairment used more home care services than any other group of older people. Home care along with respite care, adult day care, and nursing helped keep these people out of institutions. These programs encourage independence and well-being among older people (Shapiro and Havens 2000).

In the past, home care played a relatively small role in the Canadian health care system. A government study of home care in 1990, for example, said that "home care remains a minor component of the health budget" (FPT Subcommittee 1990). A policy statement by the Canadian Association on Gerontology said that in

1997–98 Canada spent $2.1 billion on public home care. This came to only 4 percent of the total spent on public health care (Chappell 1999b).

But home care programs have grown in recent years. Hollander and Chappell (2002) say that public spending on home care in Canada grew by 11 percent per year from 1990–91 to 1997–98. Ontario, for example, increased its home care budget from $177.4 million in 1984 to more than $1 billion in 1999 (more than a fivefold increase) (Hall and Coyte 2001). Hollander and Chappell (2002, 1) say that "the amount of spending on home care by private individuals needing care, and their families, is not known at this time but may be substantial."

Today, home care supports the move away from institutionalization. It provides the resources to keep a growing number of older people in the community. Krueger and his colleagues (2000) studied the health care needs of seniors in the community. Seniors reported the following five needs in this order: caregiver support, community long-term care, services for people with dementia, palliative care, and cancer patient care. People considered community long-term care the single most important health issue for the next five to ten years.

Until recently, governments supported home care in the belief that it lowered costs. A national study of home care costs in Canada supports this belief. This study took place across Canada in a number of sites. The British Columbia sub-study compared home care to institutional costs. Hollander (2001) reports that "the overall health care costs to government for clients in home care are about one half to three quarters of the costs for clients in facility care," depending on the type of care.

The study goes on to report that the more stable the person's type and level of care, the better the savings to the system. Home care costs came to less than institutional costs even when the study included informal caregivers' costs. The amount of savings depends on whether the study assumed a cost for informal caregivers equal to a professional caregivers' wage or equal to a minimum wage (Hollander and Chappell 2002).

The more hours of home care used, the closer costs approach those of institutional care. At 120 hours of home care, for example, the costs equal those of an institution (Hollander and Chappell 2002). An increase in the number of oldest-old people (85 and over), who have the most health problems and the most functional decline, will increase the use of home care in the future (Crowell et al., 1996; Finlayson and Havens 2001). This will create more demand for home care and will increase the need for home care funding. Chappell (1999, ii) says

"there are real reasons to be concerned about underfunding of home care in Canada."

A move to increase home care will require a change in the funding priorities of the health care system. The Romanow Report proposes such a change (Commission 2002). It proposes federal funding for home care and makes home care a legitimate program within the health care system. This may slow the shift of home care costs from the government to the family (Aronson 2002). But the report proposes to support home care only for mental health care, post-acute care, and palliative care. This recommendation needs to broaden its definition of home care to include the social services that older people want and use. Hollander and Chappell (2002) say that home care now exists as a part of the health care system in Canada. The national study of home care costs has shown the cost savings due to home care. These researchers propose that policy discussion now turn to the integration and coordination of all continuing care services (including long-term care and case management). "[I]ntegration and coordination will make it easier to substitute home care services for residential services and acute care services" (Hollander and Chappell 2002). A coordinated and integrated system will provide the most appropriate care for the lowest cost.

HEALTH PROMOTION

So far, this chapter has focused on illness rather than health, but there is no other way to talk about the health care system. We call it a health care system, but it is actually a sickness treatment system. It serves people who are already sick, and it focuses on curing disease. This approach has its limits. Hospitals, doctors, nursing homes, or home care do not prevent disease, but only treat illness after it occurs. The health promotion model puts health in a social context. The World Health Organization ([WHO] 1984, 101) defines health promotion as "the process of enabling people to increase control over, and to improve their own health.... [It is] a mediating strategy between people and their environments, synthesizing personal choice and social responsibility in health to create a healthier future."

Canada's interest in health promotion predates this WHO definition by a decade. In 1974, Marc Lalonde, then the federal minister of health, discussed this and other approaches to Canada's health care system in a report called *A New Perspective on the Health of Canadians* (Lalonde 1974). There he proposed the concept of the **health field**. The health field includes the usual health services, but within it the health care system is one way—not the only way, or even the best way—to

● Exhibit 8.9

VICTORIA'S SHORT-TERM QUICK RESPONSE TEAM: A BRIDGE BETWEEN THE MEDICAL AND SOCIAL MODELS

Many older people enter acute-care hospitals through the emergency department (Manitoba Health Services Commission 1985). And most older people use emergency care appropriately (Parboosingh and Larsen 1987). A fall, a broken bone, or a stroke, for example, can lead to an emergency admission. After the emergency passes (the medical team sets the bone or the first phase of the stroke passes), the acute-care hospital can do little for the older patient (Eakin 1987). Still, the patient may not be able to return home. Some patients live alone and lose the ability to care for themselves after a stay in the hospital. Some may need more help than a family member can give. Others give up their apartment and sell their furniture because they assume they will never go home again. While they wait in the hospital for a nursing home bed, their health may get worse (Aronson, Marshall, and Sulman 1987).

A report of the Manitoba Health Services Commission (1985) said that acute-care hospitals ought to pay more attention to discharge planning and involvement of home care professionals (see also Fisher and Zorzitto 1983). Such a policy might avoid unnecessary admissions. In 1987, the Capital Regional District in Victoria, British Columbia, instituted a special program to decrease the number of acute admissions of older people from emergency departments. The Capital Regional District calls this program the Short-Term Quick Response Team (QRT).

The QRT arranges for community supports at the right time to help the older person return home. A QRT liaison nurse assesses the emergency room patient at a physician's request. Criteria for admission include the following: acute medical condition, but hospitalization not required; a patient aged 60 years old or over; home support possible; and patient nursing needs not more than three hours per day.

When a patient meets the QRT criteria, the QRT liaison nurse sets the team in motion. The QRT social worker and home care nurse call the patient's family

doctor and arrange live-in homemaker services, transportation, and home nursing as needed. The social worker and nurse assess the patient's home support network and arrange follow-up support such as Meals on Wheels where needed. The QRT turns the case over to the regular LTC program after a maximum of five days.

Olive Ross, 86, is one of the QRT's success stories. Mrs. Ross broke her leg and arm in a fall. The QRT moved in a 24-hour homemaker for a month and arranged daily physiotherapy and occupational therapy. As Mrs. Ross improved, services were cut back. Mrs. Ross says, "I don't know what I would have done if I had to stay in hospital.... When I broke my hip a while back, I was in hospital for three weeks and ended up losing 15 pounds" (Paterson 1989).

Marion Candy, 89, also benefited from the QRT's services. She had blacked out and fallen in her apartment. When she came around, she dragged herself to the door and screamed for help. She had cut her scalp and needed seven stitches. After she was stitched up at a hospital, she returned home the same day, but kept losing her balance. "I lurched a lot and grabbed on to anything I could to keep my balance," she said. Her family doctor called the QRT, and the team arranged for an array of services and supports that included a homemaker, Meals on Wheels, a walker, a bath seat, and a handrail near the toilet. These supports have allowed Mrs. Candy to stay in the community (Kelk 1989).

The QRT offered the first service of this kind in North America. A report says that "this clearly indicates the QRT is a genuine alternative to hospital admission, and is not simply delaying the inevitable" (Quick Response Team n.d., 6). More than a decade and a half later, this program still serves seniors in Victoria. Rachlis (2000) reports that the program has spread to Alberta and Saskatchewan. Montgomery and Fallis (2003) found that a rapid community-response program also led to faster rehabilitation and delayed institutionalization.

improve health. In addition to traditional medical services, the health field also includes improvements in human biology (through basic research), improvements in lifestyle, and improvements in the environment as ways to better health.

An international conference on health promotion that took place in Canada produced *The Ottawa Charter on Health Promotion* in 1986. The charter focuses on the conditions that give rise to health. These conditions include "peace, shelter, education, food, income, a stable eco-system, sustainable resources, social justice and equity" (Hamilton and Bhatti 1996, 2). The charter also proposes actions that (1) build healthy public policy; (2) create supportive environments; (3) strengthen community action; (4) develop personal skills; and (5) reorient health services. Hamilton and Bhatti say that this model challenges researchers and policy planners to link change in underlying social conditions to health. Research, for example, has linked low levels of income and education to poor health. Likewise, studies of the environment have linked pollution to poor health. These studies support the idea that health promotion must deal with the environment, society, and personal habits.

This model makes sense in Canada today. Studies show that "the majority of the aged remain functionally well until an advanced age" (Health and Welfare Canada 1982a, 43; Statistics Canada 1990a). A study of community-dwelling older people in Canada, for example, found that among respondents only 4.8 percent of the 65- to 74-year-olds and 10.8 percent of people aged 85 and over reported poor health. A large majority of older people aged 65 and over (78 percent) reported good to excellent health. Even among those aged 85 and over, 71 percent reported good to excellent health (Lindsay 1999).

Health promotion programs in general work to keep older people well (Clark 1995). Some of these programs even take place in hospitals. Sulman and Wilkinson (1989) report on a hospital-based geriatric activity group. The staff started the group to help patients who were waiting for placement. The staff had found that the longer these patients stayed in the hospital, the worse they functioned, so the program set out to decrease this decline. It involved 45 minutes of activities at each session, including seated exercises, social interaction, gardening, and more passive pursuits such as watching movies.

The program highlights the value of health promotion activities in an acute-care hospital setting. "Such programming also contains the possibility of moving these patients to lighter levels of care, and, in some cases, might prevent the need for placement altogether" (Sulman and Wilkinson 1989, 46).

The NACA (2000a, citing Rachlis 2000) reports on a program in Edmonton called CHOICE (Comprehensive Home Option of Integrated Care for the Elderly). This program promotes good nutrition, exercise, and contact with others. CHOICE staff go to clients' homes, help people get ready for a day at the CHOICE centre, and help clients home again at night. The centre provides medical, dental, and foot care, as well as rehabilitation aid. Health professionals monitor clients who have chronic conditions to prevent further illness. The centre serves healthy meals and provides activities.

Health Canada now has an Internet site called Health Promotion Online (HPO) that offers health promotion information. Developed by Health Canada's Health Promotion and Programs Branch (HPPB), HPO gives older people and health professionals the resources they need in an easy-to-use website. Resources include information on the latest health issues, online discussion forums, a list of health organizations in Canada, and a calendar of health-related events happening in Canada and around the world (http://www.hc-sc.gc.ca/english/for_you/hpo).

The Future of Health Promotion

Canada now recognizes the health promotion model as a model for the development of future health policy. When Jake Epp (1986) was Canada's minister of health and welfare, he produced a report titled *Achieving Health for All: A Framework for Health Promotion*. This report defines health as a "basic and dynamic force in our daily lives, influenced by our circumstances, our beliefs, our culture and our social, economic, and physical environments" (3). The report provides a framework for health policy in Canada and includes a description of the challenges to health in Canada, health promotion mechanisms, and implementation strategies to achieve health for all (see Exhibit 8.10).

Older people can benefit from improvements in all parts of this framework. For example, some older people already engage in self-care (Segall 1987). Some people eat breakfast regularly and engage in regular exercise (Penning and Chappell 1993; Schoenborn 1993). But, more often than younger people, people aged 60 and over said they had no plans to improve their health (Penning and Chappell 1993).

Improvements in self-care through the proper use of medication, a good diet, and exercise can improve older people's quality of life. McWilliam and her colleagues (2000) found, for example, that low-intensity aerobic exercise improves physical and mental well-being. A more educated older population may have a better understanding of how to prevent illness (Clarke 1997; Parboosingh, Stachenko, and Inhaber 1997; Segall 1987). Mutual aid programs can give people social and emotional support (Fedorak and Griffin 1986). Furthermore, a healthy environment will include community health services, transportation, and home care.

But will the government support changes in social structures, policies, and allocation of funds? Epp's 1986 report makes no promises. But it does recognize the need

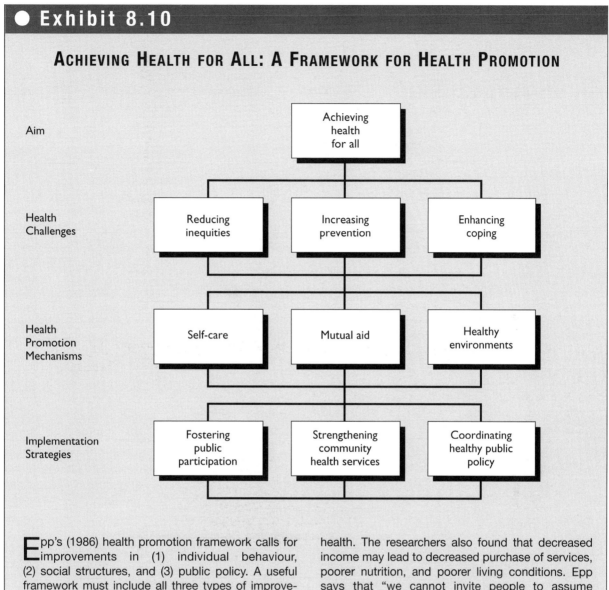

● **Exhibit 8.10**

ACHIEVING HEALTH FOR ALL: A FRAMEWORK FOR HEALTH PROMOTION

Epp's (1986) health promotion framework calls for improvements in (1) individual behaviour, (2) social structures, and (3) public policy. A useful framework must include all three types of improvement. Changes in individual behaviour, for example, may not be able to overcome health conditions due to income inequities (such as poor diet due to poverty). Hirdes et al. (1986) found that a loss in income led to a perceived decrease in self-reported health. The researchers also found that decreased income may lead to decreased purchase of services, poorer nutrition, and poorer living conditions. Epp says that "we cannot invite people to assume responsibility for their health and then turn around and fault them for illnesses and disabilities which are the outcome of wider social and economic circumstances" (12).

Source: Health Canada, 1986, *Achieving Health for All: A Framework for Health Promotion*, p. 8. Reproduced with the permission of the Minister of Public Works and Government Services Canada, 2004.

for the government to support health promotion. It also gives a good reason for this support. "We believe," the report says, "that the health promotion approach has the potential over the long term to slow the growth in health care costs" (Epp 1986, 13). Research at present cannot easily show the direct link between most health promotion programs and decreased health care costs. Strain (1991) found that older people with strong beliefs in health maintenance used more health care services. They may not use a large amount of service, but they use a variety of services.

Glor (1991) reports two problems faced by health promotion programs. First, no agreement on quantitative measures of health exists. Second, few programs produce a measurable effect on health where scientists have tried to measure it. Shapiro and Havens (2000) say that some programs go on even when they show little effect. Other programs that show promise close for lack of funds. These authors call for better decisions about funding based on careful evaluations. Some writers even question the value of helping people to live longer. Evans (1984) says that these programs may lead to higher costs because they keep more people alive long enough to get chronic illnesses in later life.

Still, disease prevention and health promotion have caught on in Canada among seniors. For example, 30 to 40 percent of older men and women reported eating fewer foods with high fat content and less fried food (Stone and Fletcher 1986). A report on Canada's Health Promotion Survey found that, compared with younger people, seniors less often skipped breakfast, smoked cigarettes, drank alcohol, or used illicit drugs. Also, compared with younger drivers, a smaller proportion of older drivers said they drink and drive, and a larger proportion of older drivers said they used seatbelts (Health and Welfare Canada 1988). Some of these health promotion behaviours reflect the values and lifestyles, such as little use of illicit drugs, that seniors have brought with them into old age. But in other cases, as in the use of seatbelts, seniors have responded well to health promotion policies.

Ward-Griffin and Ploeg (1997) used critical feminist theory to assess health promotion programs today. They found that these programs focus too much on the individual and the body. Instead, they say, health promotion programs should focus on the economic and social conditions that limit an older woman's health promotion options. For example, many older women live in or near poverty. Also, many older women spend time and energy as caregivers. These conditions put limits on health promotion choices. Ward-Griffin and Ploeg propose that health promotion move beyond fitness and diet programs focused on the body to programs that improve income, housing, and equal opportunity for women at all ages.

Researchers will continue to study the health promotion model. They will look at the effects of health practices, programs, and policies on older Canadians' health. This research, if it supports recent findings, will show the usefulness of this model in an aging society.

ISSUES FOR THE FUTURE

Neysmith (1993, 148) says that "Canada can be described as a country with ten provincial and two territorial systems of long-term care." The provinces often agree on the same values and principles of LTC, but each province has its own commitment to services, its own policies on access to care, and its own funding arrangements.

This means that the principle of universality that underlies acute health care does not apply as well to LTC (Havens 1995, 1995c). First, clients often must pay for long-term care. Government health benefits may not cover day hospital, respite, or homemaker costs. This can leave the poorest older people without help. Second, long-term care can lack coordination. Deber and Williams (1995) say that as many as 2000 small agencies deliver services in Toronto. This makes it hard for people to find the help they need. Third, many people fall through the cracks. They may not know about services or may not have access to a service (for example, a religious-based service may serve only people who share that faith). Health professionals refer to this as the care gap—the difference between what care could or should be and what usual care is. The care gap leads to missed clinical benefits and higher costs for payers (Canadian Association on Gerontology 1999).

The health care system of the future will need to respond to these problems in the LTC system. Three areas of the present system will have to be revised to meet older people's needs: the availability of services, access to services, and coordination of services (Sturdy and Tindale 1985).

Availability

The ability to stay in the community depends in part on the availability of services that support a person at home. Some provinces or parts of provinces have a continuum of care—from home care to acute hospital care—for older people. Other parts of the country, such as many rural areas, offer only a few home care options. Skinner and Rosenberg (2002) say that government policies now make local communities responsible for managing health care. This has led rural areas to rely on informal and volunteer home care programs. But the aging of rural populations puts pressure on these informal services. These communities have more older people and fewer young people to provide volunteer services.

One rural community care worker described the workings of the Meals on Wheels program in her community. She arranges with a local restaurant to pick up a half-dozen to a dozen meals each day at noon, then delivers them during her lunch hour to people on her caseload. She marvels at the good luck of city-based community workers, who can refer their clients to existing Meals on Wheels programs. Rural parts of Canada will need more community programs in the future.

Accessibility

A program is accessible if an older person can get to it and make use of it. Havens (1980) studied the unmet needs of older people in Manitoba. She found that in each age cohort both men and women reported that the accessibility of services was more of a problem than their availability. In other words, even where a range of well-designed services existed, older people still found it hard to make use of them. The older the person, the more problems they had with access. Better access requires better transportation and more home-based care for very old seniors.

The NACA (1989; see also Shapiro and Havens 2000) says that new immigrants and seniors from many ethnic groups may need special help to get services. Special dietary requirements, cultural differences, and food preferences can limit ethnic group members' use of community services. Culturally sensitive professionals can help overcome some of these barriers. Wister (1992) reports that people who know about home supports tend to use them. Better information for seniors not fluent in English would provide them more access to services.

Evans (1996) says that the Canadian health care system sometimes intentionally limits access to care. He says that the system makes services scarce and delays treatment in order to control costs. The system uses waiting lists to ration services for older people. This policy makes it harder for older people to get the treatment they need, when they need it. In the case of life-threatening illnesses such as heart disease, it may risk a person's life (Pringle 1998). In the case of less threatening illnesses, such as a hip replacement, a person may wait in pain for a year or more. Pringle says that if the Canadian system is going to use waiting lists, they should function predictably (21). Today, she says, a person's wait may depend on the number of other people on the list, the surgeon's judgment about the urgency of treatment, or how the surgeon's secretary manages the list. Pringle calls this "a manageable problem that we have chosen not to manage."

Coordination

The health care system needs better coordination and integration (Health and Welfare Canada 1982b; NACA 1990a). This need will increase with the growth of community care, because community programs decentralize care. They bring together nurses, social workers, and therapists, who often work for different agencies and whose views on how to care for a client will vary.

The NACA (1995a, 13) says that a **single-point-of-entry model** best coordinates services for older people. It improves "flexibility, continuity and quality of care for clients." It also controls costs. A single-point-of-entry model gives personalized help to each client. Staff from a single agency assess clients' needs, coordinate service delivery, and monitor clients' progress. A staff member may arrange for meal delivery, a visiting nurse, and homemaker help in one case. In another case, the staff member may arrange for respite care and day hospital use. Many provinces, including Manitoba, Alberta, and New Brunswick, already use this approach. The NACA supports further development of single-point-of-entry systems throughout the country.

Coordination avoids overlapping between services, and integration unites health and social services into one system. The principle of universality in the *Canada Health Act* ensures that everyone has access to the same services. A more coordinated system will also save time and may save money. Hébert and his colleagues (2001) looked at the costs of care for disabled older people. They found that home care cost more than intermediate facility care when they took informal caregiver costs into account. For very disabled person, home care cost more than nursing home care. Hébert and his colleagues propose an increase in the number of intermediate care facilities. These would best serve older people with disabilities who had little informal support. This study shows the need to provide careful and ongoing assessment of the older person's needs, which will keep costs down and will provide care that best suits the older person's needs. The NACA sums this up: "health reform means more than controlling costs to achieve an affordable health care system. It means providing appropriate and effective care that is responsive to the changing needs of Canadians" (NACA 1995a, 20). Responding to older people's needs should be at the core of a reformed health care system.

CONCLUSION

The changes taking place today suggest that the health care system will look different in the future. Government concerns with efficiency and costs have led to proposals for reform. Health care professionals have proposed a shift from a biomedical model to a social, community-based model (Church and Barker 1998; Mhatre and Deber 1992). In 1997, all provinces except Ontario introduced regional structures for health care services. Regionalization involves a shift in responsibility for public health. It moves power from the government to regional authorities. This approach allowed each province to restructure its system to best meet its needs.

The Ministry of Health in each province remains responsible for broad health priorities and ensures that regional authorities comply with provincial standards. Developers of this system believe that it will lead to more efficient, fair, and responsive health services.

Closer studies of older people's health care needs will allow the system to fine-tune its programs and treat-

---

● **Exhibit 8.11**

CONTROVERSY: USER FEES FOR HEALTH CARE

Concern about the rising cost of health care has led some writers to call for new ways to finance health care. Some of these writers suggest that fees for service would improve the health care system (see Béland 1995). A number of health care researchers disagree.

Evans, Barer, and Stoddart (1995; see also Evans et al. 2001) say that user fees will shift the source of funding health care from taxes to individuals. A shift to user fees benefits people in good health and with high incomes. They will pay less in taxes for the health care system and will pay only for care they use. Evans, Barer, and Stoddart put it simply: "The wealthy and the healthy gain, the poor and sick lose" (362).

Evans, Barer, and Stoddart (1995, 370) go on to say that Canada's health care costs have not gone out of control. Health care costs have gone up more gradually since the start of Canada's national health care system. Public funding in Canada and in other countries has led to more cost control. Studies of other countries show that user fees create higher costs through higher prices and more service providers. Effective control of costs comes about through limits on the number of hospital beds or the number of physicians. Also, a government-sponsored national system saves administration costs that drive up the cost of health care.

Some supporters of user fees say that fees will create more health care options and would allow people to buy more services if they chose. People may want this as an option to a waiting list for public services. Also, some supporters of fees say they will encourage new services to develop that might improve the public system some day (NACA 1995b).

But critics of user fees say that such fees will create a second health care system. People who used and paid for services themselves might withdraw support for the public system. People who paid a fee would have a high standard of care. Poor people who could not afford to pay a fee would have to make do with underfunded services. User fees challenge the principle of universality in the *Canada Health Act*. This principle states that everyone should have access to the same package of health care services. But people with more money would clearly gain by being able to afford user fees.

Finally, supporters of user fees say they will discourage overuse or abuse of the system. They will make people think twice before they use a health care service. Studies show that user fees do discourage use. But most people do not know in advance that they do not need a service (Béland 1995). So people get poorer treatment for illnesses they do have, and the quality of health care falls. Also, Evans, Barer, and Stoddart (1995) say that individual decisions account for only about 10 percent of health costs. Hospital stays and visits to specialists account for 90 percent of costs. And doctors, not individuals, decide on these treatments. User fees will have little effect on the total health care budget.

The Romanow Report on the future of health care in Canada comes out against user fees and a two-tier system (Commission 2002). It supports Canada's commitment to a sound publicly funded health care system. It also proposes more funding for specific programs. Many of these programs will help older people (e.g., more home care, improved rural and remote services). Future changes to improve the health care system should focus on appropriateness of treatment (community care to help people stay out of institutions), good management of resources, and accountability to the community. "Health care reforms and cost control are legitimate needs," Béland (1995, 410) says. "But neither should jeopardize access to medical care, which is an accomplishment of Medicare."

ments (Barer, Evans, and Hertzman 1995). The critique of the medical model and growing interest in social models of health care will lead to more community-based services. Also, as the population ages, more people will show an interest in disease prevention and health promotion. More comprehensive models of health care, such as the social and health promotion models, will lead to better health care for older people as well as better health at all ages.

Summary

1. Health care needs for the elderly range from maintenance programs for the well elderly to long-term institutional care for those who have severe health problems.

2. Three models of health care exist in Canada today: the medical model, the social model, and the health promotion model. The medical model that dominates the health care system today is concerned with the treatment of illness.

3. The Canadian health care system consists of five basic principles: universal coverage, access to services, portability, comprehensive services, and administration by a nonprofit public agency. The provincial and federal governments share the cost of this system.

4. Canada has one of the most comprehensive health care systems in the world, but it spends proportionately more of its gross national product on health care than do some countries with more comprehensive systems.

5. Research shows that the commitment to the medical model may account for higher than necessary health care costs. Complex medical procedures, increased salaries for medical personnel, and high institutional costs all lead to increasing health care costs.

6. Canada has one of the highest rates of institutionalization in the world. Institutions serve the needs of many older people, and programs exist that can improve the quality of life of institutionalized patients. But sometimes people enter institutions because they cannot get the support they need to stay in the community.

7. The Romanow Report on the Canadian health care system proposes reform to the system. The report repeated Canada's commitment to its universal medical care system. It also rejected the use of user fees. Some reforms, such as support for palliative care and long-term care, will improve care for older people. Other reform proposals, such as the limitation of home care to post-acute, mental health, and palliative care patients, need expansion to include seniors' needs.

8. The social model of health care supports a continuum of services from institutional care to home care. It calls for health care programs that help older people stay in their own homes. These programs include geriatric day hospitals, adult day-care programs, and home care.

9. Home care programs tailor services to fit the needs of the older person. They provide families with help to relieve caregiver burden. These programs may or may not save money, but they do achieve one goal: they allow people to stay in their homes as long as they can.

10. The health promotion model of health care supports healthy lifestyles and a better environment. It takes a broad view of health care that recognizes a need for changes in the workplace and improvements in socio-economic status.

11. The government will have to deal with three service issues in order to meet the needs of an aging population: availability of services, access to services, and coordination of services.

12. The health care system will change in the future. It will evolve to meet the needs of older people. This will include more community-based care and more health promotion programs. The system has already begun to make some of these changes.

Study Questions

1. List and describe the three major approaches to health care that exist in Canada today.

2. Explain why the cost of health care in Canada grows each year. How might the government control costs?

3. Discuss three ways in which doctors directly help keep the cost of health care high. How can doctors take steps to lower these costs?

4. Describe the normalization principle. How can institutions use this principle to provide higher-quality care for patients?

5. How does the government propose to restructure the current health care system? How will this provide better service to an aging society?

6. Describe at least two alternative health care programs that exist today.

7. Explain two of the major approaches to health promotion and give an example of each.

8. Discuss three types of improvements in health care that would improve service to older people.

Key Terms

adult day-care programs programs that provide non-institutional support for people who are otherwise unable to remain in the community. (177)

Centres locaux de services communautaires (CLSCs) Quebec's local centres for community services combine the work of professionals and volunteers to deliver home care services and direct health needs away from hospitals toward community care. (173)

Community Care Access Centres (CCACs) Ontario's system of volunteer-run community care centres that provide a single point of entry into the health care system and services such as the Victorian Order of Nurses. (173)

continuum of care the array of services that range from institutional care to little or no institutional contact. (175)

geriatric day hospital a hospital program that offers a full range of hospital services to older people who live in the community, and that assesses individuals' needs before setting up a health care plan. (176)

health care refers to the support needed for people to maintain optimum health. The health care needs of Canada's older population range from health promotion, to health maintenance, to long-term chronic care. (158)

health field the realm of health services, including the health care system, traditional medical services, improvements in human biology, improvements in lifestyle, improvements in environment, as envisioned by Marc Lalonde (1974). (178)

health promotion model a health care model that focuses on self-care and preventing disease through lifestyle change, increased knowledge about healthy behaviour, and environmental improvement. (159)

home care a range of social and medical services designed to help people live independently in the community. (177)

long-term care social and medical services, including formal services, home or institutional care, and family care, for people who have functional limitations. (158)

medical model a health care model that favours surgery, drug therapy, and rehabilitation through physical therapies with a focus on the treatment of diseases and injuries, usually in the physician's office, in a hospital, or in other health care institutions. (158)

normalization principle the idea that institutions can and should make life in the institution as much like life outside as possible. (168)

Romanow Report the 2002 Canadian federal government report of the Commission on the Future of Health Care in Canada, led by Roy Romanow, which underscores Canada's commitment to its health care system and makes several proposals for improving the delivery of health care to seniors. (171)

single-point-of-entry model a single agency that assesses clients' needs, coordinates service delivery from multiple sources, and monitor clients' progress. (183)

social model a health care model that includes personal and family counselling, home care, and adult day-care programs as part of the health care system, and that tries to keep older people in their own homes. (158)

Selected Readings

Béland, François, and Evelyn Shapiro. "Policy Issues in Care for the Elderly in Canada." *Canadian Journal on Aging* 14(2), 1995.

This special issue of *Canadian Journal on Aging* contains writings on current issues in Canadian health care. Articles range from a discussion of population aging and its impact on health care costs to the role of long-term care in the continuum of care. The collection attempts to answer many questions about the future of the health care system by looking in detail at the use of the system today.

Cousins, S. O., and T. Horne, eds., *Active Living among Older Adults: Health Benefits and Outcomes.* Philadelphia: Brunner/Mazel, 1999.

This book summarizes a large body of literature on physical activity in later life. The authors find that most studies look at exercise and fitness programs. The book shows that during the 1990s researchers and practitioners came to value physical activity for older adults. They also began to promote less intense activities preferred by older people (such as yoga and walking). A good summary that shows the benefits of activity in later life.

Haber, David, *Health Promotion and Aging,* 2nd ed. New York: Springer, 1999.

This book emphasizes the active role that older people can play in shaping the care they receive. Haber promotes collaboration between the older person and the health care professional. The book contains thorough information on exercise, nutrition, weight management, and health education, as well as resource lists and health education material.

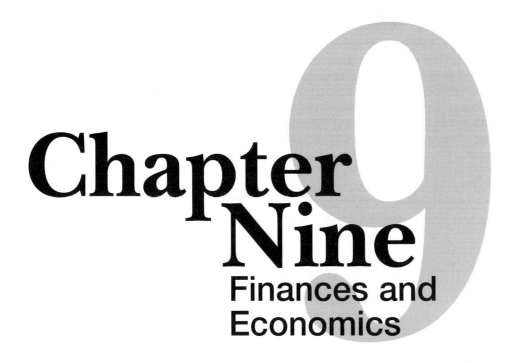

Chapter Nine
Finances and Economics

Photo © Kindra Clineff/Index Stock Imagery

INTRODUCTION

J ack Bruckner, aged 65, took early retirement two years ago. He gets a pension from his job and an Old Age Security cheque each month. His wife, Betty, 59, never worked outside the home, so she gets no pension.

They live in a small government-subsidized apartment. Last spring, Jack and Betty decided to travel east. Jack knew their old car would never make the trip, so he went to the bank for a car loan. "I never thought they'd give me a loan," he says. "I went in thinking they'd just laugh at the idea. But the bank manager looked at my pension income and approved the loan. I can't believe it—I never thought, with the little we make, that we'd be able to buy a new car."

Like many older people, Jack and Betty do not have much, but they feel satisfied with what they have. Both of them lived through lean times when they first got married. They worry less about money now than in the past, and, Jack says, when Betty gets her pension from the federal government in a few years, their financial worries will be over.

Canada's pension system can take most of the credit for the Bruckners' financial well-being. The income of older people adjusted for inflation increased faster than that of younger people (15 to 64) from the early 1980s to the present. Lindsay (2000b) says that between 1981 and 1997 the average annual income of women aged 65 and over increased by 17 percent (compared to 14 percent for younger women). Over the same period, older men showed an increase in income of 19 percent (compared to a decrease for younger men).

Cheal (1985a, 1985b) looked at intergenerational family transfers—the amount of money that passes from one generation of family members to another—to assess older people's financial well-being. He found that older people gave more (in net value) than they got and that there was a larger difference between what they gave and what they got than for any other age group. Later work by MacDonald (1990) shows the same trend. This study of almost 10 000 people in the United States shows that younger people received more gifts and loans from older people than they gave. On average, the young received eight times more from their parents than they gave to them. Cheal (1985a) concludes that older people have more money to spend than earlier studies suggested.

A number of studies and reports like these show that, as a group, older people have better incomes than many people imagine. Prus (1999), for example, says that the poverty rate for seniors has decreased since the early 1980s. They now have a rate similar to the rest of the population. Compared with other age groups, they show the least **depth of poverty**—the distance between their income and the poverty line (National Council of Welfare 1996b). Older people below the poverty line, on average, have incomes that come to about 85 percent of the poverty line.

Myles (2000, 288) says that Canada has one of the best income security systems in the world. He calls the cost of the public system "modest by international standards." But he says that Canada has one of the lowest rates of seniors' low income among the developed nations. "In short," he says, "like Baby Bear's porridge, Canada seems to have gotten it 'just right' when measured against these international benchmarks."

Still, the retirement income system has its flaws, some of them serious. While income has risen in the past few years for older people in general, certain groups still have incomes below the poverty line in old age. Older people from lower-income backgrounds, people who cannot speak English or French, people without much education, and people who live in small towns tend to have lower than average incomes. Very old people, women, and unattached individuals (a term used by Statistics Canada to describe a "person living alone or in a household where he/she is not related to other household members") often live below the poverty line (National Council of Welfare 1996b). Older women, compared with older men, also show a greater depth of poverty and a smaller proportion of people living well above the poverty line (National Council of Welfare 1996b). In 1996, for example, unattached women aged 65 and over had poverty rates of 45.4 percent while men in this age group had a 29.3 percent poverty rate. In contrast, the poverty rate for married couples aged 65 years and over was 8.6 per cent (National Council of Welfare 1998).

Even reports of average family incomes show lower incomes for older people. For people who earned an average wage before retirement, the Old Age Security (OAS) will make up about 14 percent of their pre-retirement income. The Canada Pension Plan (CPP) will make up another 25 percent. Therefore, the average wage earner will have to find other means to make up lost income in retirement. People who earn above the average wage will need to make up even more income in order to maintain their standard of living, and those on fixed pensions (i.e., not indexed to the cost of living) get poorer every year because of inflation. Most people, except the very rich and the very poor, will feel a drop in their standard of living when they retire.

Many individuals and groups, including the federal and provincial governments, the National Council of Women, and the Royal Canadian Legion, have suggested changes to Canada's pension system. Their concerns led to the **great pension debate** in the 1980s and more recently to a debate over the **universality** of Canada's public pension system (Myles 1988). The results of these debates have begun to influence the retirement incomes of older Canadians and will also influence the pensions of future retirees.

This chapter looks at (1) the structure of the Canadian pension system and how it works, (2) the flaws in the system and suggestions for pension reform, and (3) the future of Canada's retirement income system.

HISTORICAL DEVELOPMENTS IN CANADA'S PENSION SYSTEM

Until the 1920s, Canadian pension policy reflected the "market ethos" (Bryden 1974, 19). According to this thinking, individuals should take responsibility for themselves in old age and those who need help should get it from their families (Bryden 1974; Snell 1996). Bryden reports that city life and industrialization in Canada made this ethos hard to practice. The *Labour Gazette*, for example, stated in 1924 that "high rents, [and] overcrowding in houses, make it difficult for the poor to provide for their aged parents. It has been the

● Exhibit 9.1

LOW-INCOME RATE,* PEOPLE 65 AND OLDER, 1980–1997, SELECTED YEARS

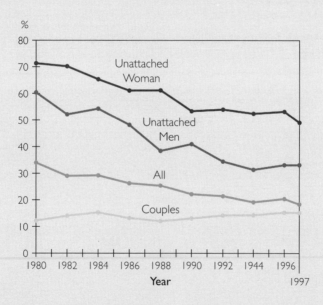

The graph shows the general downward trend in the poverty rate for all older people. The couples group aged 65 and over has the lowest proportion of low income throughout this period. Unattached men show the most dramatic decline in low income.

Improved public pensions account for most of the improvement. Unattached women show a decline in low income, but a less dramatic decline than for unattached men. They still have a higher proportion of low income than any other group.

* Based on Statistics Canada's low-income cut-offs, 1992 base.

Source: Adapted from C. Lindsay, 1999, *A Portrait of Seniors in Canada,* 3rd ed., Cat. No. 89-519, Tables 7.7, 7.9, and 7.10, pp. 108–10. Reprinted with permission from Statistics Canada.

experience of social agencies that many of the old men and women in their districts are suffering from the lack of the necessities of life" (*Labour Gazette* 1924, cited in Bryden 1974, 42).

The federal government decided to act to relieve the poverty among older people. A House of Commons committee issued a report in 1925 that called for a $20 pension to people aged 70 or older who passed a residence requirement and a means test (a test of financial need). The committee proposed that the federal government and the provinces should each pay half the cost of pension benefits. The plan did not require pensioners to pay anything into the program. The committee saw the program as a supplement to income more than as a pension. The *Old Age Pension Act* became law in 1927, and all the provinces and the Northwest Territories agreed to the plan by 1936. This plan, for the first time, defined pensions as a right due to all older Canadians. Snell (1993) shows that men, compared with women, had greater access to these pensions. A woman with a younger, employed husband could have her claim rejected. The state expected her husband to support her. Snell traces this type of discrimination to the state's assumption about male dominance in families.

In 1951, the federal government passed the *Old Age Security Act* and the *Old Age Assistance Act* to replace the *Old Age Pension Act*. The *Old Age Security Act* set up a pension plan run solely by the federal government. The new plan paid up to $40 a month at age 70 without a means test. The federal government increased this pension to $55 a month in 1961. The *Old Age Assistance Act* set up a means-tested pension for people between 65 and 69 years old who could demonstrate financial need. The provinces and the federal government shared the cost for this program. The plan required no contributions and paid the same pension to all poorer pensioners, including homemakers.

These early programs supplemented the incomes of older people (they offered basic income security). The federal government kept payments low, so people would have an incentive to provide for their own old age (National Health and Welfare 1973, cited in Chappell 1987). In the 1960s, the federal government broadened the pension system by setting up the Guaranteed Income Supplement program to supplement Old Age Security. This program was designed to help the poorest older people. In 1966, the federal government and the government of Quebec started the Canada and Quebec Pension Plans. Today, all wage earners in Canada pay a part of their incomes into these plans.

By the 1970s, Canada had two types of programs in place: **income security programs** (the Old Age Security and the Guaranteed Income Supplement) and **income maintenance programs** (the Canada and Quebec Pension Plans). These programs form the basis of the Canadian pension system today. The federal government designed the first type of program to help people meet their basic needs in retirement and the second type to help people maintain their pre-retirement income and lifestyle.

By the early 1980s, federal government transfers (the Old Age Security and the Guaranteed Income Supplement and other transfers paid for from tax revenues) and the Canada Pension Plan accounted for 47 percent of older Canadians' retirement incomes. By 1997, this figure had increased to 54 percent of their incomes (Lindsay 1999). Occupational pensions (those from former employers) made up 21 percent of older people's total income in 1997 (up from 12 percent in 1981), and assets (investments and savings, not including registered retirement savings plans, or RRSPs) made up 12 percent of retirees' income in 1997 (down from 27 percent in 1981) (Lindsay 1999). Federal government transfers and the CPP have made up increasing proportions of seniors' income over the years.

Myles (1984) reports that federal government transfers also make up increasingly larger portions of individuals' incomes as they age. "As each year passes," he writes, "the number of wage earners declines, savings are spent and inflation erodes the real value of both savings and private pensions" (22). This means that older people depend more on public policy and programs for their well-being than ever before, so the study of pensions is vital to an understanding of old age today.

THE CANADIAN RETIREMENT INCOME SYSTEM TODAY

Canada's complex system of pension plans and programs, along with earnings from work, should create a decent old age for all Canadians, but it does not. Some older people still suffer a sharp loss in income and a shocking change in lifestyle when they retire. Almost every tier and subsection of the Canadian pension system needs improvement to address this problem. The following discussion will look at the structure and the limits of the Canadian pension system today.

Tier One: Government Transfers

Canada has a three-tiered pension system shaped like a pyramid (see Exhibit 9.2). The Old Age Security (OAS), the Guaranteed Income Supplement (GIS), and the Allowance (ALW)—called federal government transfer

---

Exhibit 9.2

Canada's Three-Tiered Pension System

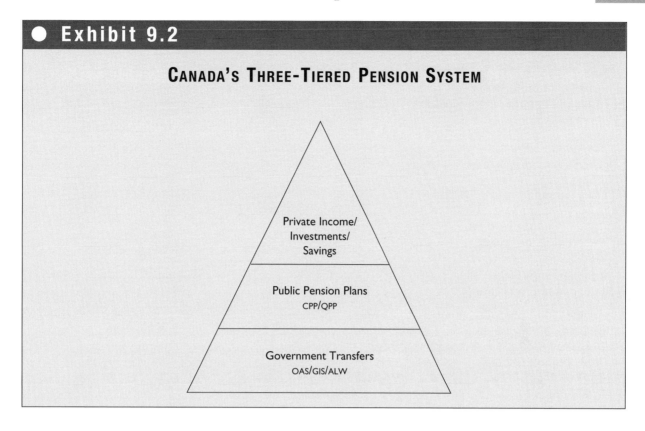

Private Income/
Investments/
Savings

Public Pension Plans
CPP/QPP

Government Transfers
OAS/GIS/ALW

---

programs—make up the first tier. Nearly all Canadians aged 65 or over, rich or poor, get the same OAS pension. But in 2004 people who earned over $59 790 had to repay their OAS at a rate of 15 percent of their income over this amount. So, for example, someone with a net income of $96 972 or more repaid their entire OAS benefit (Social Development Canada 2004).

The GIS goes to people with a low income or no income other than the OAS. ALW payments go to spouses or common-law partners or survivors of OAS pensioners. The ALW helps survivors aged 60 to 64 and couples with only one income. People do not directly contribute to OAS, GIS, or ALW pension funds; the federal government pays them out of tax revenue. The GIS and ALW accounted for about 23 percent of government transfer costs in 2000 (Maser and Begin 2003).

The federal government estimates that it spent more than $26.6 billion on government transfers in 2002–03 (up from $11 billion in 1984) (Human Resources Development Canada 2003a). This first tier of programs accounts for over one-fifth of the income of senior families and over one-third the income of unattached older people (Lindsay 1999). These programs protect older people's incomes—especially those of the very poor—from falling below a specified level. Among unattached older women, for example, more than one-half of their

income on average came from federal government transfers (National Council of Welfare 1999). Prus (2000; see also Prus 2002) found that income inequality drops in later life because of the help poorer seniors get from public pensions (CPP and OAS/GIS). Myles (2000, 305) says that even "small proportional increases from all public income sources, including CPP/QPP [Canada's and Quebec's pension plans], tend to reduce inequality."

Not surprisingly, poorer people depend on transfers most. These transfers (OAS/GIS) reduce low-income rates also increase income equality (Myles 2000). Unattached older women, the poorest group of older people, received 37 percent of their income from transfer payments in 1997. Older men received only 25 percent of their income from these sources (Lindsay 1999). Men, compared with women, receive nearly twice the proportion of income from private pensions (Lindsay 1999).

In the third quarter of 2003, the OAS went to 3.9 million people. Maximum payments came to $461.55 a month per person (Human Resources Development Canada 2003a). The federal government taxes the OAS as income, so pensioners with enough income to pay taxes will pay some or all of their OAS back to the government. The poorest older people, who pay no tax, keep all their OAS benefits. The federal government indexes

---

● **Exhibit 9.3**

SOURCE OF INCOME FOR PEOPLE AGED 65 AND OVER IN CANADA, 1999

Source	Men	Women
Private pensions	35.1	22.0
OAS/GIS	20.0	35.3
CPP/QPP	20.6	19.6
Other government transfers	2.8	3.0
Investments	11.2	14.7
Employment	8.4	3.9
Other money income	2.0	1.6
Total*	100	100

*Totals of more than 100 percent due to rounding.

Source: Created from K. Maser and J. Begin, 2003, *Canada's Retirement Income Programs: A Statistical Overview (1990–2000)*, Tables 1-5 and 1-6, pp. 23–24. Ottawa: Minister of Industry.

OAS payments to the consumer price index or cost of living, and adjusts the rate four times a year, but the high cost of the program (over $20 billion in 2003) makes it an obvious target for federal government cutbacks.

The GIS goes to the poorest seniors. In 2003, more than 1.4 million OAS pensioners (37 percent) received full or partial GIS (Human Resources Development Canada 2003a). GIS benefits in 2003 went to single older people who received less than $13 176 that year from sources other than the OAS and GIS. It also went to couples in 2003 with a combined (non-OAS and non-GIS) income of $17 184 or less. The federal government does not tax the GIS, and it indexes GIS payments to the consumer price index, so that they go up quarterly as the cost of living rises.

A person (or a couple) gets either full or partial GIS payments based on a yearly income test. In the third quarter of 2003, a single person could receive a maximum GIS of $548.53 per month, while a married couple could get a maximum of $818.85 per month for the two of them (Human Resources Development Canada 2003a). Single pensioners, more often than married pensioners, have low enough incomes to need the GIS. Women, many of them widows, make up about 80 percent of all single people poor enough to get the GIS. Eighteen percent of single older people and 13 percent of couples who receive the GIS are so poor that they get the full amount (National Council of Welfare 1999).

The federal government added the Spouse's Allowance (SPA) program (now called the Allowance (ALW) to tier one of the system in 1975. The ALW goes to a low-income pensioner's spouse who is aged 60 to 64 years old. It pays an amount equal to the OAS and the maximum GIS at the married rate. This couple gets the same transfer payments as a poor couple with both spouses aged 65 and over. If the GIS pensioner dies, the spouse continues to receive payments. When the survivor reaches age 65, the federal government stops ALW payments and the person then gets an OAS/GIS pension.

The vast majority of ALW payments go to women. All widows or widowers aged 60 to 64 in need can get the ALW. About 95 000 older Canadians get the ALW; the program costs about $414 million a year. Without GIS and ALW benefits, almost half (47 percent) of all older Canadians would live below the poverty line. However, the ALW, like the GIS, fails to bring the poorest recipients above the poverty line for a large city (Human Resources Development Canada 2003b; National Council of Welfare 1999).

Newfoundland, Ontario, Manitoba, Saskatchewan, Alberta, British Columbia, Yukon, the Northwest Territories, and Nunavut also have provincial or territorial supplement plans to help the poorest seniors. More than 300 000 seniors get provincial or territorial supplements. These benefits total about $250 million per year. Most provinces and territories do not index payments to

● Exhibit 9.4

THE CANADA PENSION SYSTEM

Pension	Maximum Benefits per Month
Old Age Security	$461.55 (single, July 2003)
Requirements and program details: 65 years or over; residence requirement; Canadian citizen or legal resident; non-contributory; indexed quarterly.	
Guaranteed Income Supplement	$548.53 (single, July 2003) $818.85 (couple, married, or common-law with one pensioner, July 2003)
Requirements and program details: low or no income other than OAS; non-contributory; indexed quarterly.	
Partner's Allowance	$818.85 (July 2003)
Requirements and program details: equal to the sum of OAS and maximum GIS at married/common-law rate; partner of OAS pensioner who gets GIS; partner between 60 and 64; must satisfy other OAS requirements; non-contributory; indexed quarterly.	
Widowed Partner's Allowance	$904.03 (July 2003)
Requirements and program details: paid to any low-income widow or widower (60 to 64 years old); non-contributory; indexed quarterly.	
Canada Pension Plan Retirement Pension (max.)	$801.25 (monthly, 2003)
Requirements and program details: 9.9% of income paid into plan; half by worker, half by employer (minus a basic exemption: 2003—$3500). Up to Year's Maximum Pensionable Earnings (YMPE) 2003—$39 900; indexed yearly.	
Canada Pension Plan Survivor Benefits	$480.75 (CPP 2003, partner 65 and over) $444.96 (CPP 2003, partner under 65)
Canada Pension Plan Death Benefit	$2500 (CPP, max. lump sum, 2003)
Program details: paid to estate of deceased contributor.	
Canada Pension Plan Disability Benefit	$971.26 (max. 2003)
Program details: paid to contributors with severe and prolonged disability.	
Canada Pension Plan Children and Orphan Benefits	$186.71 (CPP 2003)
Program details: paid to each child or orphan of contributor.	

Source: Figures from Human Resources Development Canada, 2003, *Income Security Programs Information Card,* http://www.sdc.gc.ca/asp/gateway.asp?hr=/en/isp/statistics/julsep03.shtml&hs=ozs, accessed on August 22, 2004.

the cost of living, but some provinces increase the amounts from time to time (National Council of Welfare 1999). All provinces also reduce taxes for older property owners or give rent rebates to seniors. These programs play a further role in keeping very old people and even people with occupational pensions at a decent income level.

The National Council of Welfare reviewed the federal government transfer system and concluded that the system keeps many older people out of poverty. Still, the council says, "it is clear that the government programs that make up the first level of Canada's retirement income system are not generous enough to keep all pensioners out of poverty" (National Council of Welfare

● Exhibit 9.5

AVERAGE AFTER-TAX INCOME OF INDIVIDUALS AGED 65–69, 1971 AND 1997 (IN 1997 $)

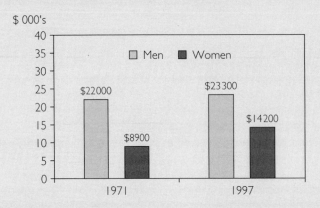

The after-tax income of the younger old women (aged 65 to 69) increased by 60 percent over this period (compared to only about 6 percent for men). This reflects the trend toward women working in the labour force, and paying into the CPP, private pension plans, and RRSPs. In June 2000, for example, almost 60 percent of women aged 65 to 69 received CPP benefits (compared to only 30 percent of women aged 85 and over). Note that, in spite of this increase, men still have incomes on average more than one and a half times those of women.

Source: Data from National Advisory Council on Aging, 2001, *Seniors in Canada: A Report Card*, Ottawa: Minister of Public Works and Government Services Canada, p. 21. Reprinted with permission.

1996a, 16). In 2002, for example, the OAS and GIS together guaranteed a single older person an income of $11 800. But that amount came to $7461 below the poverty line for single seniors living in a large city. OAS and GIS payments to couples in large cities in 2002 fell nearly $3000 below the poverty line (Canadian Council on Social Development 2003).

Some policies weaken the universality of the OAS pension. In 1977, the federal government introduced new residence requirements for government pensions. Until 1977, an older person who had lived in Canada for at least 10 years qualified for an old age pension. After 1977, a person earned one-fortieth of his or her pension for each year in Canada after age 18. Anyone with fewer than 10 years in Canada got no benefits. Many immigrants to Canada will now get less than a full OAS when they turn 65. This policy will erode the universality of the old age pension system (National Council of Welfare 1990a).

A new policy has further weakened the universality of the OAS. The federal budget speech of April 1989 introduced a **clawback** of OAS benefits from wealthier

seniors. The effect was that seniors who had a net income of more than $59 790 per year (in 2004) had to pay back a portion of their OAS pension for every dollar they receive in income over this amount (Social Development Canada 2004). In 2004, a senior with an income of over $96 972 would lose all of his or her OAS pension. The government phased in the policy over three years from 1989 to 1991. This measure has turned the OAS into a means-tested pension plan. Myles and Street (1995, 346) conclude that the "OAS will gradually lose its status as the first tier of the retirement pension system and, along with GIS, become part of the social assistance program for low income seniors."

Tier Two: The Canada Pension Plan and the Quebec Pension Plan

The Canada Pension Plan (CPP) and the Quebec Pension Plan (QPP) form the pension system's second, smaller tier. Virtually 90 percent of the labour force between ages 18 and 70, their employers, and self-employed people paid about $30 billion into the plans in 2001–02 (Human Resources Development Canada 2003a). The CPP/QPP paid a maximum retirement benefit in 2003 of $801.25 per month (or $9615 per year) and paid out over $20 billion in 2003 to 3.9 million retirees.

The CPP allows a province to opt out of the plan. Quebec chose to do so and set up its own plan. The QPP differs from the CPP in a few details, but in most ways it mirrors it. This text will use the term CPP to refer to both plans.

The CPP does two things. First, it ensures that workers have some pension beyond the OAS/GIS/ALW when they retire, and, second, it saves the federal government money in GIS and ALW payments in the future. The CPP combines two types of pension plans: a savings plan and a transfer plan. It works like a **savings plan** because each worker pays a percentage of his or her salary into it each month. In 2003, for instance, the law required workers to pay 4.95 percent of their wages into the plan. Their employers paid a matching amount. Self-employed people paid 9.9 percent of their incomes into the plan. The government expects that investment of the surplus in the plan will allow it to freeze the contribution rate at 9.9 percent until at least 2014 (National Council of Welfare 1999). The payments are credited to individual workers and, when they retire, their pension will depend on how much they paid into the plan.

The CPP also works like a **transfer plan** because the money paid in today does not go into a private account for each person. It goes to pay the pensions of retired plan members today. Pension experts also call this a pay-as-you-go plan. Today's workers will receive their CPP pensions from workers' contributions in the future. This type of plan does not require that a person spend many years saving for a pension. But it does require that each generation pay for the pensions of the past generation.

The CPP does some things well. First, it protects people from inflation. Personal savings can decrease in value over time, but the CPP promises that a person will get a pension in the future geared to the cost of living at that time. Second, the CPP covers almost all workers, so most workers will enter retirement with some CPP benefits. Third, the plan is **portable**, which means it moves with workers when they change jobs. In a fluid job market, where people change jobs often, this can mean the difference between having a pension or not.

Fourth, the plan locks in both workers' and employers' contributions from the start. This is called **vesting**. Workers get credit for their total payments (their own and their employer's contributions) even if they move from one employer to another.

Fifth, the CPP promises to pay workers up to 25 percent of their pre-retirement pensionable earnings (to a maximum of 25 percent of the year's average industrial wage) for life.

Sixth, the plan applies the same rules to men and women. Women pay in at the same rates as men, and the plan entitles them to the same benefits. Some occupational plans (also called employer plans or registered pension plans—RPPs) base benefits on different mortality tables for men and women, so women in some plans get smaller payments because on average they live longer than men.

Seventh, all CPP members get survivor and disability benefits, a vital point because in Canada women often outlive their husbands and many women have no pensions of their own.

Eighth, the CPP calculates a person's pension by adjusting pensionable earnings from past years to bring them up to current wage levels. This adjusts for the fact that inflation makes earlier wage levels a poor basis for calculating a pension today and makes the CPP better than occupational plans that use lifetime earnings to calculate pension payments (National Council of Welfare 1989b).

Ninth, the CPP allows contributors to choose early or late retirement. A contributor can receive benefits as early as age 60 or as late as age 70. The CPP decreases or increases by 6 percent per year for each year a person begins receiving benefits before or after his or her 65th birthday. A person who retires at age 60 would receive 70 percent of his or her normal CPP pension. The retiree will get this lower rate even after the age of 65. A person who retires at age 70 will get a 30 percent larger pension than he or she would have got at age 65.

Tenth, and not least, the federal government indexes the CPP to the cost of living. It goes up as the cost of living increases, so people do not fall behind each year as they do with a fixed-income pension.

The CPP now pays benefits to more older people than ever before. In 1967, it paid benefits to less than one-half of 1 percent of older people, but in 2003 the CPP retirement benefit went to more than 10 percent of all people 65 and over (Human Resources Development Canada 2003a; National Council of Welfare 1999). The number of people who receive CPP pensions, the size of their pensions, and the total paid out in CPP pensions will all increase in the years ahead.

Still, the CPP has its limits. For instance, it does not help people maintain their pre-retirement income—the second goal of the Canadian pension system. For many older people today—those who never worked for a wage—the CPP offers no help at all, and some people who get the CPP find that it does not pay enough. In 2004, for example, the OAS/GIS and CPP paid a maximum of $15 274 to a single person. But the poverty line (called the low-income cut-off by Statistics Canada) for a single person in a city of 500 000 or more people came to $19 261 in 2004 (Canadian Council on Social Development 2003). This means that the combined OAS/GIS and CPP for a single person in a large city left him or her $3987 below the poverty line. Recipients who earn less than the maximum CPP fall even farther below the poverty line.

These low CPP payments do not replace much of the average person's income. Also, the plan pays low survivor benefits ($9465 per year in 2002) (Social Development Canada 2002), and the poorest older people, who receive the GIS, lose $1 of their benefits for each $2 they receive from the CPP. As a result of these low rates, most people face a drop in living standards when they retire. People need private pensions or savings to maintain their pre-retirement lifestyles.

The CPP may also face future problems. Today, Canada has five workers to pay the pension of each CPP retiree. By 2030, this will drop to three workers. Canada has responded to this change by raising contribution rates (to a total of 9.9 percent of a person's wage). And Canadians have accepted this increase.

Higher CPP payments will help more people than retirees. The increase in the older population accounts for only about a third of the higher projected increase in CPP costs. About 45 percent of the increase in future payouts comes from higher payouts for disability and enriched benefits. Higher-than-expected payouts of disability pensions would threaten the CPP reserve fund. Other proposed reforms include cutting back benefits, better administration of the program, and investment in the stock market (Battle 1997; Lam, Prince, and Cutt 1996; Robson 1996). Some people propose raising the retirement age or limiting cost-of-living increases (Brown 1995; Freeman 1994; Gee 1995a). The CPP has taken some of this advice. The program began investing surplus funds in the financial markets in 1998. In 1999, for example, the CPP invested nearly $2 billion in the financial markets (Maser and Begin 2003). This entails some risk. But good management of these funds will add to the CPP's ability to meet future demands.

Tier Three: Private Pensions, Savings, and Work

Private income makes up the third tier of the Canadian pension system. The OAS/GIS and CPP alone cannot provide a comfortable income for most older people. The National Council of Welfare (1999, 27) says that "a person spends a lifetime working at the average wage or better, retires with the maximum possible CPP or QPP pension, and still cannot escape from poverty without other major sources of income or major government assistance." Because of this shortfall, all workers need private pensions and savings to make up the difference between federal government pensions and pre-retirement income.

How many workers can count on occupational pension plans to help them in retirement? Maser and Begin (2003) report that 5.3 million workers belonged to occupational pension plans in 2000. In that year, pensioners in total received $21 billion in pension income. Nearly all (85 percent) public sector workers (such as government workers, teachers, nurses, people who work for a Crown corporation) belonged to a plan, compared to about a third of private sector workers (people who work for privately owned companies) (Statistics Canada 1996).

Most pension plans pay a pension of 2 percent of a person's salary times the number of years of service. But less than half of all plan members have their incomes indexed to inflation (Battle 1997). Occupational pension benefits in 1999 made up 35.1 percent of the income of males aged 65 and over, but only 22 percent of the income of females aged 65 and over (Maser and Begin 2003).

Most older people rely on savings to make up some lost pre-retirement income. Investment income in 1999 made up 11.2 percent of the income of males aged 65 and over and 14.7 percent of that of females aged 65 and over. These sources ranked as the fourth major source of income for males and females (Maser and Begin 2003).

The federal government has encouraged more savings through **registered retirement savings plans (RRSPs)**. An RRSP is a government plan that allows people to save money for their future pension without paying income tax on it until they withdraw it in retirement. This defers the taxes to a time when they have a lower income and a lower tax rate. Statistics Canada (2003t) reports that since 1995 Canadians have invested more in RRSPs than in registered (occupational) pension plans (RPPs). The maximum contribution to an RRSP for 2005 is set at $15 500 (Hudson 2003). Individuals who belong to a private pension plan can contribute to an RRSP up to this maximum after adjusting for their contribution to their private pension plan. The number of RRSPs grew from 206 000 in 1969 (2.3 percent of tax filers) to 6.3 million in 1999 (40 percent of the labour force) (Maser and Begin 2003). In 1999, contributors saved a total of more than $25 billion in RRSPs, an increase from $6.2 billion in 1983 (Frenken

1995; Maser and Begin 2003). Proposed higher limits for RRSP contributions could make them even more attractive to middle- and upper-income earners in the future.

Other income received in retirement includes earnings, rent subsidies, and tax exemptions. In 1997, employment income accounted for 21.8 percent of family income to households with a head aged 65 and over (Lindsay 1999). Also, many corporations offer subsidies for their goods and services, such as reduced prices on theatre tickets or reduced air fares for older people. These indirect subsidies add to older people's average total income. And this does not count other benefits such as subsidized health care costs and home care services.

How well does the private pension system help most people cope with retirement? Not very well on three counts. First, coverage is low: only 39.3 percent of female paid workers and 41.8 percent of male paid workers in 2000 had private pension plans (Statistics Canada 2003q). The rate of coverage decreased for females by 1.5 percent from 1991 to 2000, and decreased for males by 7.4 percent over this same period (Maser and Begin 2003). Less unionization, pressure on companies to lower costs, and more workers in low-paid industries all help account for this decrease.

These figures include workers in the public sector and workers in the private sector. But the rate of plan membership for men and women differs in each sector. Women made up more than half (57 percent) of public pension plan members at the end of 2000. But men outnumber women in private sector RPPs by nearly two to one (Maser and Begin 2003). Only about 30 percent of private sector workers in Canada have a RPP (National

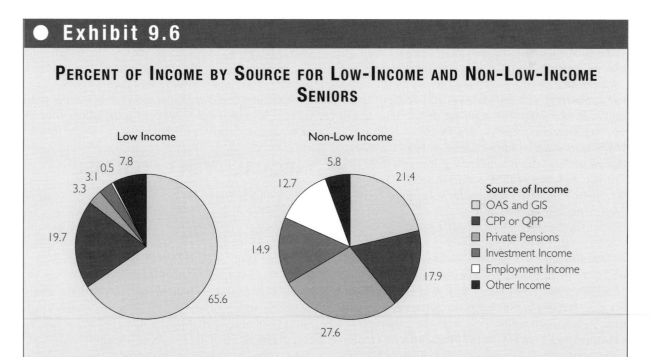

● **Exhibit 9.6**

PERCENT OF INCOME BY SOURCE FOR LOW-INCOME AND NON-LOW-INCOME SENIORS

Low Income

Non-Low Income

Source of Income
- ☐ OAS and GIS
- ■ CPP or QPP
- ▨ Private Pensions
- ▨ Investment Income
- ☐ Employment Income
- ■ Other Income

Low-income seniors rely almost entirely for their income on public sources (OAS, GIS, CPP). The OAS/GIS/ALW makes up the single largest source of the low-income senior's income. Most low-income seniors are widows who had no private pensions and little opportunity to save for retirement. Public pensions account for most of the improvement in low-income seniors' financial status. Prus (2002) says that without these programs a greater income gap would exist between low- and high-income seniors.

Non-low-income seniors get a large share of their income from private sources such as private pensions and investments. This income keeps these seniors out of the low-income category.

Source: Adapted from the Statistics Canada website "Low Income," http://www12.statcan.ca/English/census01/products/analytic/companion/inc/canada.cfm#4, accessed on September 15, 2004. Reprinted with permission.

Council of Welfare 1999; Statistics Canada 1996). Most of these people work for firms with 1000 or more employees. People who work part-time, who are seasonal workers, and who work for small businesses and at low-paying jobs rarely have an RPP.

Also, the poorest people have the least chance to get a private pension. In 1996, only 4 percent of people with incomes under $10000 per year belonged to an RPP that they paid into. On average, these people paid only $253 into their plans. On the other hand, 49 percent of people with incomes more than $50000 paid into occupational plans in that year. They paid on average $3121 into their plans. According to the National Council on Welfare (1999, 39), "it seems unlikely that occupational pension plans will ever be an important source of retirement income to people in low-wage jobs. Coverage by contributory pension plans increases sharply as incomes rise."

Second, in 1997, 74 percent of public sector RPP members had some inflation protection. But only 17 percent had some inflation protection (National Council of Welfare 1999). In an inflationary economy, people on a fixed pension—even a good one—become poorer as they age. At 3 percent inflation, a pension will lose about 25 percent of its value over 10 years and nearly half its value after 20 years (National Council of Welfare 1999).

Statistics Canada reports that in 1999 the average annual income from occupational plans came to $14593 for men and only $8452 for women (Maser and Begin 2003). In sum, "occupational pension plans play an important, but limited role in providing retirement income to Canadians" (National Council of Welfare 1999, 42; Statistics Canada 1996).

Third, only a small percentage of people who belong to occupational pension plans ever collect a full pension (Senate of Canada 1979). Two things account for this. The first is that few plans in the past have had early vesting. Early vesting locks both the employer's and the employee's payments in the plan soon after employment begins. The second is that most plans lack portability. When workers leave a company today, most of them get either a deferred pension (if their money is vested and locked in) or they get their own (but not their employer's) pension contributions back—sometimes with no interest. The employer's share stays in the fund when workers get their pension contributions back, so a person who changes jobs loses half of the fund and has to start again. Even if the whole labour force belongs to occupational pension plans, as long as workers change jobs often (as they do today), only workers with fully vested contributions will ever collect a full pension.

The government started the RRSP program to help people cope with gaps in the private pension system and to encourage more savings for retirement, as discussed earlier. Anyone with an income can start an RRSP and gain benefits from the program. But, in practice, the program helps people in higher income brackets the most.

First, the higher a person's income, the more likely it is that he or she will pay into an RRSP (Palameta 2001).

Second, people with higher incomes can pay in the most and tend to make the maximum contribution. Poorer people simply do not have this much money to put aside.

Third, people in higher tax brackets get more money back through the tax deductions received through the program. The higher their tax bracket, the more they receive through tax deductions. For instance, a tax filer in the highest tax bracket got a tax saving of $447 for an RRSP contribution of $1000. But a filer in the lowest bracket got a tax saving of only $255 for a $1000 contribution. The richer person's higher tax rate leads to more tax savings (National Council of Welfare 1999). So people with more money do better than poorer people under the current system. And wealthier Canadians take more advantage of the system.

Exhibit 9.7 shows the proportion of people from selected income levels who paid into RRSPs and the average amount they contributed.

INEQUALITY IN LATER LIFE

Older people as a group have more income security today than ever before. Relatively few older people have incomes in the lowest income group (less than $5000 per year). Nevertheless, most older people live on modest incomes.

Myles (1981) uses a political economy perspective to look at the structural reasons for inequality in old age. He shows that education and former occupational status largely determine income in later life. A person with a high level of education and a high-status occupation stands the best chance of a high income in retirement. These people also stand the best chance of maintaining their status after retirement. Norland (1994) shows that, as a group, older people have less education and engage in less work activity than younger people. This condition largely accounts for their lower incomes in later life. Older people who have access to work, investments, and occupational pensions will have higher incomes. These benefits go to people with higher levels of education and higher job status.

Also, some groups face more financial problems than others in old age. Membership in a non-European ethnic group leads to lower income in retirement. Asian, African, or Latin American ethnic group members tend to retire later and have less chance of getting OAS, GIS, or CPP benefits. Minority seniors also have less chance

Exhibit 9.7

RRSP CONTRIBUTORS, BY SELECTED INCOME CLASS, 1999
ALL TAX FILERS

Income Class	Percentage of Tax Filers	Average Contribution
Under $10 000	3	$1050
$10 000–$19 999	13	1670
$20 000–$29 999	31	2250
$30 000–39 999	46	3000
$40 000–$59 999	59	4120
$60 000–$79 999	70	5830
$80 000 and over	72	9920
Total	29	4090

This table shows a clear pattern. The higher the income bracket, the greater the proportion of people who paid into an RRSP. Also, the higher the income bracket, the larger the amounts of money that people in that income bracket paid into a plan. The average contribution for people who earned $80 000 and over came to more than nine times the amount on average contributed by people who earned less than $10 000 a year. Increases in contribution limits will increase the use of RRSPs by wealthier Canadians and will increase the gap between the contributions of the rich and the poor. The poorest Canadians cannot afford to save in an RRSP.

Source: Adapted from the Statistics Canada publication by K. Maser and J. Begin, 2003, *Canada's Retirement Income Programs: A Statistical Overview (1990–2000)*, Cat. No. 74-507, Table 4-7, p. 90. Reprinted with permission.

of getting an occupational pension and thus have lower incomes. Trends in public pension policies also lead to lower incomes for immigrants. Recent immigrants, for example, receive only partial public pensions. Brotman (1998) reports that it can take 10 to 20 years for a recent immigrant to reach an income level equal to the average in Canada.

Chard (2000) reports that, compared to older men or other older women, older visible minority women have the lowest incomes. Brotman (1998) reports that older people who belong to a visible ethnic minority and Aboriginal older people had the highest rates of poverty among the seven groups she studied. She goes on to say that Chinese and black older people had a rate of poverty one and a half times the rate of senior poverty. Racial discrimination throughout life in part accounts for these high levels of poverty.

People who live near or below the poverty line in Canada before they retire will stay there in old age. Older women have higher rates of low income than any age group in Canada. Almost one-quarter of women face low incomes in later life. Unattached women show the highest rates of low income (49.1 percent). Older women have lower incomes and show higher rates of poverty than older men, a situation that reflects differences in men's and women's work careers, salaries, and pension options (Lindsay 2000a).

Women and Pensions

The National Council of Welfare (1984, 24) says that "one conclusion stands out from all the facts and figures [about aging and poverty]: Poverty in old age is largely a women's problem, and is becoming more so every year." In 1997, women aged 65 and over earned only about two-thirds the income of men in that age group (Lindsay 1999). The low-income rate of all elderly women was 24 percent in 1997, more than double the poverty rate of elderly men (11.7 percent). In that same year, 49.1 percent of unattached women aged 65 and over (who lived alone or with non-relatives) lived in poverty, compared to only 33.3 percent of unattached senior men. Unattached older women had more than nine times the low-income rate of elderly women who live in families.

The low-income rate has declined for all older women from the 1980s to the present. But older women still have lower incomes than older men. Why do women have such low incomes in old age? First, traditional expectations about women and work lead women to have different work patterns than men. Women often leave a first job to raise children. Due to family responsibilities, they spend three times longer than men between jobs, and they tend to work at each job for a shorter time than men (Connelly and MacDonald 1990). When women work outside the home, they often take part-time, low-paying jobs. Many working women say they cannot find full-time work. Also, the traditional expectation that women will place family before career leads to part-time work and keeps women from getting high salaries and from storing up pension credits (Street and Connidis 2001).

Second, the structure of public and private occupational pension plans discriminates against women— sometimes in hidden ways. Women have begun to increase their presence in the workforce. In 1999, 54.6 percent of women worked outside the home (up from 42 percent in 1976) (Maser and Begin 2003). This should lead to more and better occupational pensions for women. But women often work for smaller, non-unionized companies with no occupational pension plans, and, as pointed out above, they also tend to work part-time (Ginn, Street, and Arber 2001). Not only do women in part-time jobs often get a lower hourly pay than women who work full-time, but they also get no fringe benefits. Women in such jobs often fail to qualify for private pension coverage (National Council of Welfare 1990b).

Third, women in general are paid less than men and hold lower-status jobs (Connelly and MacDonald 1990; Lavoie and Oderkirk 1993). Statistics Canada (1995) reports that younger, never-married, well-educated women earn about the same incomes as similar men. But women more often than men work in low-wage jobs that are defined as unskilled and offer little chance for advancement. Statistics Canada (2003b) produced a report on earnings for all men and women (in full- and part-time work) in 2001. The report shows that women earned only 64.2 percent of men's incomes (a figure almost unchanged since 1992).

Women who work in service jobs often work part-time, and many of the firms they work for have no pension plans. Only 39.3 percent of women in paid labour in 2000 belonged to an occupational pension plan (compared with 41.8 percent of men), and most of these women work for government or for Crown corporations. In private industry, a smaller percentage of women belonged to a pension plan (Maser and Begin 2003).

Even within relatively low-paying fields, women find themselves in the poorest-paying jobs. For instance,

● **Exhibit 9.8**

GENDER DIFFERENCES IN INCOME, AGE 65+, 1998

This chart compares the incomes of married and unattached senior men and women. Senior men have higher incomes than senior women regardless of marital status. Married men had nearly twice the income of married women. Unattached men had incomes 30 percent greater than those of unattached women. Gender differences in income and work opportunities throughout the life course explain most of the income differences in later life.

Source: Adapted from Statistics Canada, 2003, "Gender Differences in Low Income," No. 15, http://www.hc-sc.gc.ca/seniors-aines/pubs/factoids/2001/no15_e.htm, accessed on August 10, 2004. From *A Portrait of Seniors in Canada,* 3rd ed., Cat. No. 89-519, October 1999. Reprinted with permission.

women tend to work as salaried clerks. Men tend to sell expensive products such as cars or appliances. These jobs often pay a commission in addition to a base salary. Women work in service jobs such as waitress, hairdresser, or child-care worker. Men tend to work at services such as police officer, security guard, or soldier. Even when women work at the same job as men, they often get lower pay.

Low pay means that women pay a smaller amount into the CPP than men, resulting in a smaller CPP pension when they retire. Women received only 56 percent of the average CPP benefits received by men in 1999. In 1999, most women got less than 60 percent and many got less than 40 percent of the maximum CPP. In that same year, most men received between 80 percent and 100 percent of the maximum CPP. Low incomes and short careers at paid labour explain this gap (National Council of Welfare 1999).

A look at younger retired workers (i.e., those aged 65 to 69) found that women received an average annual pension of $3588. Men in this age group received on average $6396 or 56 percent more than women (National Council on Welfare 1999). In 1997, a woman on average earned only 62 percent of a man's income so that even in the future women will have a lower proportion of the maximum CPP than men (Lindsay 2000a; National Council of Welfare 1996a).

The National Council of Welfare sums up these findings: "[Women] become the prime victims of the built-in injustices of our labour market, which excludes women from the best positions, pays them less than they are worth and segregates them into a narrow range of low-wage occupations with few fringe benefits and limited chances for advancement" (National Council of Welfare 1990b, 2).

Widows

Widows make up the largest group among women 65 and over, and, of all women, they benefit least from Canada's pension system. "After fifty years or so of unpaid, faithful service," the National Council of Welfare (1979, 32) says, "a woman's only reward is likely to be poverty." In 1997, 49.1 percent of unattached women (most of them widows) lived below Statistics Canada's low-income cut-off (compared to 33.3 percent of unattached men).

Why do older widows have such low incomes? First, only 42 percent of all workers belonged to an occupational pension plan during their working years (National Council of Welfare 1999). About half of these plans in 1997 paid a lump-sum survivor pension to the surviving spouse of a retired worker. Another 26 percent paid a survivor pension of only 50 to 60 percent of the plan

member's pension. Nine percent of plans offer only a refund of contributions to the surviving spouse of a retired worker. Many private sector plans provide for only five years of survivor payments. "A woman who loses her husband when she is 65," the National Council of Welfare (1989b, 39) says, "and lives until age 85 could be in dire straits for the last 15 years of her life."

Second, only 69 percent of members of public sector plans and 27 percent of members of private sector plans provided a survivor pension if the plan member died before retirement. Even when a survivor plan exists, sometimes a woman gets nothing because her spouse had opted for higher benefits in retirement while he was alive. Many plans refund only the worker's contributions with interest if a plan member dies before retirement. Some plans return nothing to the surviving spouse.

Third, the public pension system also lets widows down. The CPP sets the benefits for a surviving spouse aged 65 and over at 60 percent of the deceased spouse's pension. The maximum amount payable came to $5412 a year in 1999. The average survivor's pension came to only $3092 in January 1999. The OAS in that year for a single person came to about $4902. Combined, these payments came to only about two-thirds of the poverty line for a single person living in a large Canadian city (National Council of Welfare 1999). Carey and Yamada (2002) say that a woman will see a 20 to 30 percent fall in economic well-being if she becomes a widow. Davies and Denton (2001, 2002) report a similar outcome for divorced and separated older women. These women rely for almost 40 percent of their income on the OAS/GIS system. Davies and Denton (2002, 487) speak of the "grave economic situation of women who have experienced a divorce or separation late in life" (see also Ballantyne and Marshall 2001).

Women coming into old age in the near future will do a little better. More of them work. For example, women between ages 35 and 54 have the highest earnings for women (Lindsay 2000a). Many of these women will get CPP pensions in the future. Maser and Begin (2003) report that 44.2 percent of women contributed to the CPP in 1990. This figure rose to 45.5 percent in 1999. Also, the average contribution of women to the CPP rose from 37.3 percent of the total to 39.9 percent. In other words, more women now contribute to the CPP and with higher contributions than ever before. Smith and her colleagues (2000) say that the CPP/QPP accounts for most of the rise in income for older women. This especially applies to women aged 60 to 75.

Still, many women will get only small pensions. Homemakers will have no employer pensions; they will get no CPP pension of their own; and if their husband's pension plan pays no survivor benefits, they will get no pension at all. Younger women will do better in the future because more of them work. Women who leave work to raise a family today tend to return to work more quickly than women did in the past. Women with higher education tend to have fewer interruptions in work (Fast and Da Pont 1997). They also have begun to enter male-dominated occupations and more of them belong to private pension plans (Connelly and MacDonald 1990; Statistics Canada 1996). Also, more women than in the past paid into RRSPs. In 1999, 2.77 million women paid into an RRSP (compared to only 1.9 million in 1991).

Nevertheless, the large majority of women have no RRSPs. And those who do, compared with men, pay less into their RRSPs (Maser and Begin 2003). Lower incomes for women may account for this difference. Also, low wages and part-time work will leave most women without occupational pensions and they will have small CPP pensions. McDonald (1997a) also reports that women have few chances to find work in later life.

The system needs reform. McDonald and Robb (2003, 14–15) say that "the current pension system does not mirror the complexity of women's lives in terms of their multiple transitions in and out of the labour force, their institutionalized lower earnings, their unpaid work and the changes in individual and family life styles." Women and men need better occupational pension plans, and women need better survivor and homemaker benefits and more help from the OAS/GIS/ALW (McDonald 1997a). By proposing some changes to the system, the federal government sparked what some people call the great pension debate in the early 1980s. The debate was about whether a public pension plan such as the CPP or whether private pension plans would best serve Canadians. More recent debates have been concerned with universality of the OAS.

PENSION REFORM

Canada has debated pension reform since the early 1980s. A series of conferences, task forces, and papers at that time all proposed changes in the pension system (Government of Canada 1982; House of Commons Canada 1983). Some changes did indeed take place. By the late 1980s, for example, all provinces except British Columbia and Prince Edward Island had some legislation covering occupational pensions. Also, new rules have improved the public pension plan system. What follows are some of the highlights of these reforms.

First, the federal government income security system has made three important improvements over the years: (1) improvements in GIS have led to decreased poverty rates for single older people; (2) as of 1985, all widows and widowers with low incomes would get the ALW; and (3) the federal government continues to index the OAS to the rate of inflation, although it has not increased the OAS to bring it closer to the average industrial wage (AIW).

Second, beginning in June 1984, the CPP also allowed women and men to deduct the years they spent child rearing from their pensionable years. (Until 1984 these years counted as zero income and lowered a person's average lifetime salary.) People who take time off to care for their children can now deduct from their work record 15 percent of the years with the lowest earnings. Also, the CPP now provides for **credit splitting** if spouses divorce. Each spouse gets an equal share of the credits accumulated during their time together. This provision, however, includes a hitch: It requires an application for credit splitting. It is likely that not all eligible people apply for or arrange credit splitting. Between 1978 and January 1996, for example, only 65 709 people applied for and received approval for credit splitting (National Council of Welfare 1996a).

Third, in May 1985 the federal government announced changes in the *Canada Pension Benefits Standards Act*. These changes set minimum standards for one million federal government workers and workers in federal government industries such as Crown corporations. The federal government asked provinces to change their rules to meet the new standards. They include the following:

1. Locked-in vesting mandatory after two years in an occupational plan;

2. Improved portability by transfer of vested pensions to locked-in RRSPs;

3. The right of all full-time workers to join a private plan after two years of work; all part-time workers must have the right to join if they have earned at least 35 percent of the yearly maximum pensionable earnings ($37 400 in 1999);

4. Payment of survivor benefits worth at least 60 percent of the amount the couple would have received had the contributor lived; these benefits will continue if the survivor remarries;

5. Division of pension credits and payments 50–50 if a couple divorces, unless the couple or the courts choose a different option.

These changes serve as a model for the private sector as it considers pension reform.

Fourth, the federal government and the provinces have agreed that all occupational plans shall provide a joint life/last survivor benefit. A spouse will receive at least 60 percent of the occupational pension the couple would have received if both had lived (Maser and Begin 2003). The pension continues even if the survivor remarries. This provision has one drawback: Both spouses must agree to lower pension payments in the present. If the couple chooses a higher pension today, they forgo survivor benefits in the future.

These changes balance some of the inequities in the system. The poorest older people on the GIS will benefit from these changes, and so will widows and women who work part-time. But the federal government will still have to tackle some tough issues in the future. These include homemakers' pensions, the rising cost of indexed OAS pensions, and **indexation** of private pension plans (this increases the pension according to the cost of living). Women face many disadvantages in old age that current pension reform only partly addresses. But "the whole income-security debate," Neysmith (1984, 18–19) writes, "has been defined in terms of pensions that are related to one's track record in the paid-labour force [and] occupationally based pensions by definition cannot meet the needs of most women." Canadian society will need to deal with this larger issue through broader reforms that will have to include increasing opportunities for women in the labour force.

THE FUTURE COST OF REFORM

Changes in private and public pension plans will mean one thing: Pensions will cost more money. CPP rates have increased to 9.9 percent of workers' earnings (from 3.6 percent in 1986). Better occupational plans will also cost more. So will better survivor benefits. In 2001, Canada's Chief Actuary reported that current reforms will lead to a sustainable CPP system in the future (Health Canada 2002a). Assets will grow in the coming years and they will absorb economic and demographic changes in the future. But as Canadian society ages, more people will begin to draw pensions. And younger people will have to pay for most of these costs.

How will people feel about these changes? Will younger people revolt at the high cost of pensions for the older generation? The state of Canada's economy will partly determine how younger people will feel about pension costs. A strong economy and low inflation will make it easier to pay more for pensions; increased costs and low wages will make it harder. A weaker economy could lead younger people to balk at the high cost.

Some people predict trouble ahead for pay-as-you-go social security programs (like Canada's). They say that the current system cannot support a growing older population and a shrinking workforce (Oderkirk 1996). The system will crumble, critics say, when the baby boom reaches old age and looks to a smaller workforce to fund its pensions. A longer life expectancy for future generations will only increase the size of the older population and make the burden of pension payments greater on the young. Brown (1997, citing the Canadian Institute of Actuaries 1993) says that the next generation may not agree to fund the social security program now in place.

The vision of economic crisis in the future has led to many reform proposals. One plan would privatize the Canada Pension Plan. Under this proposal, each person would invest CPP funds in private sector assets. Each person would manage his or her own fund and would get back the money he or she managed to accumulate. This plan could serve all Canadians much as the CPP does today. But Brown (1997) points out that this approach has many drawbacks. Each worker would bear the risk of a poor investment or of inflation. Also, the plan would include no death or disability benefits. Women would lose child-rearing drop-out provisions. Furthermore, based on other systems, the cost of managing a privatized plan would run about 10 times that of the CPP. Still, some people believe that privatization would solve many future pension plan problems.

Other proposals fit more easily into the current system. They include a later age for retirement. Myles (2002, 325) says that "keeping current and future generations in the labour force longer (i.e., later retirement) is widely seen as the most painless and cost-effective cure for the expected impact of population aging." He goes on to say that a small increase in the retirement age has a large impact on the cost of retirement benefits. For example, a 10-month increase in the retirement age would lead to a 10 percent cut in the cost of benefits. Older workers delay taking money from the system and they also add to the national wealth and government revenues.

Myles predicts more labour demand for older workers and better pay in the future. So healthier and better-educated workers may choose to stay at work longer. Policies in Canada have also put a higher tax on social security benefits so that wealthier seniors keep less of their payments. Battle (1997) says that the OAS has already evolved from a universal program to a means-tested plan (by taxing back OAS payments from wealthier Canadians). This change fits a trend in government policy (including health care policy) to limit programs to people most in need. Myles and Teichroew (1991, 91) project a "withering away" of the OAS and more emphasis on public support through the GIS in the future. They also project growth in subsidized private savings through RRSPs and workplace pensions.

Plans to privatize the CPP or to means-test the OAS would achieve what Myles and Teichroew (1991, 85) call "the main project of both the Liberal and Conservative parties throughout the 1980s—to make the welfare state more efficient by targeting scarce transfer dollars to those most in need." These policies also support the trend to shift responsibility for financial well-being in later life from the state to the individual. Such trends will not help the neediest older people, in particular, older women. And they will place more pressure on middle-class Canadians to look after their own well-being in old age.

Myles (1982) offers two reasons why Canadians will support a stronger public pension system in the future. First, he says, without state support the young would have to help care for their parents themselves, and younger people will prefer to pool their risks through a central pension system. Second, he says, middle-aged people, because they will be old soon themselves, have a self-interest in supporting a strong pension and social security system for the elderly.

In the end, a strong publicly supported pension system—given the longer life expectancy today—makes sense for everyone. As long as taxpayers see this they will continue to support improvements in Canada's retirement income system.

CONCLUSION

Myles and Street (1995) sum up current trends in pension policy reform. The government, they say, will reduce its role in pensions and other benefits to middle-income workers. It will cut back on "social insurance" that provides income security in retirement. Instead, it will turn to "social assistance" to help needy older people. "Providing income security above poverty levels will be up to the private sector, individuals and families" (352).

Pension policies over the past 20 years, including the most recent changes in pension laws, have created a dual pension system. The public system in the form of the OAS and GIS will give support to the most needy older people. This system Myles and Teichroew (1991, 99) call "a welfare state for women." It serves people who work outside the labour market. The private system in the form of RRSPs and private pension plans gives state support to pensions for middle- and upper-income earners. This system serves "organized workers and the predominantly male occupations of employed professionals and managers" (99).

The shift in policy to self-reliance for middle-income earners may not produce the end product that the government wants. Current and future policies encourage middle-aged, middle- and upper-income earners to save more money in RRSPs, a practice that will cost the government money in lost taxes and will counteract some of the savings made by cutting OAS payments to middle- and upper-income retirees (Myles and Street 1995). Myles and Street conclude that a larger retired population will cost society more money one way or another. Policies simply shift the cost of a retired population from one group to another (from young taxpayers to retirees who have to live on their own resources).

A new view of retirement could help solve this problem. Some studies project a shortage of young workers in Canada in the future (McDonald and Chen 1995). This shortage could create potential jobs for older workers and reduce the cost of retirement pensions to the state. But, so far, older workers have shown little interest in staying at work. Retirement rates have increased and people now leave work earlier than ever before. All of this suggests that Canadian society will continue to debate and reshape its pension program in the years ahead.

Summary

1. Canada's pension system has a sound structure, but the current system needs improvement. Some people— very old women, people from lower-income brackets, people with low levels of education, widows, and homemakers—all run a higher than average risk of poverty in old age.

2. Canada has a three-tiered system: the OAS, GIS, and ALW make up tier one, the CPP and QPP make up tier two, and private pensions and savings make up tier three.

3. The Canadian retirement system has two goals: (1) to keep all older people out of poverty; and (2) to replace pre-retirement income. At present, it meets neither goal for many Canadians.

4. Poorer Canadians, the people who need private savings the most in retirement, have the least chance of having any. Private pension plans cover fewer than half of Canadian workers. The CPP at best replaces only 25 percent of a person's income up to the average industrial wage, and the OAS/GIS/ALW leave the poorest older people in poverty.

5. Women, compared with men, face a higher risk of poverty in old age, because unequal coverage by pension plans, lower-paying jobs, and different work patterns due to child rearing often leave women with lower pensions.

6. Widows run a high risk of poverty in old age. The CPP pays a relatively small survivor pension. Private pension plans offer only about a 60 percent pension to survivors.

7. The federal government has recently made changes to the system. Reforms include higher GIS/ALW payments, a more secure CPP pension system, rules that encourage RRSP contributions, and rules that strengthen private pension plans.

8. Proposed reforms to the CPP and to private plans try to ensure that more Canadians, including homemakers, get pension coverage. Better public and private pensions for these people may reduce the costs of federal government transfers in the future. This will save the government money and give more people a better income in retirement.

9. The government will probably reduce its role in providing pensions to middle-income workers in the future. Individuals, families, and the private sector will have to provide income for people over the poverty line.

10. Canadians will pay for pension reforms as long as people support the notion that everyone—young and old—gains from a strong pension system.

Study Questions

1. Name and describe the parts of Canada's three-tiered retirement income system.

2. Explain how the Canada Pension Plan funds pensions today.

3. List two strengths and two weaknesses of the private pension system. Why does the private system fail to help most people in retirement?

4. Present the social-structural causes of financial inequality in old age. What groups face the most financial problems as they age? Why?

5. How has the Canadian government changed the public pension system to provide better coverage for older Canadians? How will reforms affect middle-class Canadians? How will they affect poorer Canadians?

6. What changes have writers proposed in the current public pension system to provide better retirement incomes for older people in the future?

Key Terms

clawback required repayment of Old Age Security benefits from wealthier seniors to the government. (196)

credit splitting a plan by which each spouse gets an equal share of pension credits accumulated during their time together. (204)

depth of poverty the distance between a person's income and the poverty line. (190)

great pension debate the debate in the 1980s over how to fund public pensions for older Canadians in the future. (191)

income maintenance programs income supplement programs such as the Canada and Quebec Pension Plans that help people maintain their pre-retirement income and lifestyle. (192)

income security programs income supplement programs such as the Old Age Security and the Guaranteed Income Supplement that help people meet their basic needs in retirement. (192)

indexation a method of increasing pensions linked to increases in the cost of living. (205)

portable describes a pension that moves with workers when they change jobs. (197)

registered retirement savings plans (RRSPs) a government plan that allows people to save money for their future pension without paying income tax on the money protected within the RRSP. The pension is taxed when it is withdrawn in retirement. The taxes are deferred to a time when the person has a lower income and is in a lower tax rate. (198)

savings plan a payment plan to which each person contributes a percentage of his or her salary each month. In the case of the CPP/QPP, the payments are credited to individual workers; when they retire, their pension will depend on how much they paid into the plan. (197)

transfer plan also called a pay-as-you-go plan—money paid into the plan goes to pay the pensions of retired plan members today. The CPP/QPP also works like a transfer plan. (197)

universality the idea that everyone in Canada has a right to a public pension regardless of his or her income. (191)

vesting workers with a fully vested pension have credit for their total pension contributions (their own and their employer's contributions) even if they move from one employer to another. (197)

Selected Readings

Denton, F.T., D. Fretz, and B.G. Spencer, eds. *Independence and Economic Security in Old Age*. Vancouver: UBC Press, 2000.

This book looks at the relationship between economics, health, and independence in later life in Canada. It includes articles on income and savings, retirement, women, and the future economic well-being of older people. The articles contain many original analyses of Canadian data. The book also contains comparisons of Canada with other countries. This book serves as a good source of current information on economics and aging.

J. Ginn, D. Street, and S. Arber, eds., *Women, Work, and Pensions: International Issues and Prospects*. Buckingham: Open University Press, 2001.

This book takes a critical look at women, work, and pensions in several countries, including Canada. It allows for a rare cross-cultural comparison of aging policies related to older women.

National Council of Welfare, *A Pension Primer*. Cat. No. H68-49/1999E. Ottawa: Minister of Public Works and Government Services Canada, 1999.

This report on Canada's pension system presents facts and information in an interesting, readable style, and includes a glossary of terms. The report argues that the pension system needs improvement.

Chapter Ten
Retirement and Work

INTRODUCTION

Claude Rioux retired six months after his 65th birthday. He had worked as a warehouseman for an electronic supply company. Claude never thought much about retirement in his middle years. But a year or two before he retired, he began to feel he had nothing in common with his fellow workers. Most of his friends had retired, and most of his new co-workers had just left high school. They talked about girls and motorcycles and listened to loud music. He had always liked work, but he began to enjoy it less each day. After he turned 65, his boss came by to ask if he had any retirement plans. Another time, the boss called him into his office and asked him when he planned to leave. "I said I didn't know," Claude says. "Why give him the satisfaction of thinking he could push me out? Hell, I still do a good job. Better than some of the kids who work here now. Oh, I planned to leave in January, but I wouldn't tell him. I thought, 'I'll leave when I'm good and ready.'"

No one forced Claude to retire and he left work just about on schedule. He had little reason to keep working past age 65—he had a small pension from work as well as his Canada Pension Plan (CPP) and Old Age Security (OAS), and he planned to open a small electronics repair shop at home. He stayed on until January only to show that no one could push him around.

Statistics Canada reports that a smaller proportion of men and women work past age 65 than ever before. In 2002, only 10.5 percent of men and 3.7 percent of women aged 65 and over continued to work in the labour force (Statistics Canada 2003h). These figures show that retirement has become a normative life event. Some people will spend a quarter or more of their adult life in retirement.

Gerontologists view retirement today from two points of view: first, as a social institution and, second, as a process of personal adjustment. This chapter will look at retirement from each of these perspectives. It will look at (1) the origin and role of retirement in modern society, (2) the forces that lead a person to retire, and (3) the effects of social structures and social class on retirement options.

RETIREMENT AS A SOCIAL INSTITUTION

The Origins of Retirement

Myles (1984) traces old age today to two developments. The first is the **retirement principle**—the idea that a person leaves work at a fixed age, regardless of mental or physical ability. The second is the **retirement wage**—a pension paid by the state to support older people. Myles says that a new group of people grew out of these two developments: "a population of elders still fit for production who do not engage in economic activity" (7).

Employers and employees have both supported the retirement principle in North America. Industry supported it for two reasons. First, retirement allowed companies to retire older, skilled workers and hire younger, less-skilled workers at lower wages; and, second, companies, using a philosophy of "scientific management," sought to speed up production and get more out of their workers. Unions offered to have workers work faster if companies reduced the workday, but a faster pace of work made it hard for older workers to compete with younger workers (Atchley 1985). Retirement gave older workers a graceful way to leave work.

The Canadian government supported the retirement principle for a number of reasons. Canada's first civil service commissioner, Adam Shortt, said in 1922 that "retirement relieves the government of the embarrassment and extravagance of retaining the services of officers who have outlived their usefulness; creates a proper flow of promotions; renders the service more mobile; deters efficient workers from leaving the public service for private employment [and] in general tends to promote efficiency in every way" (quoted in Bolger, 1980, 8, cited in Myles 1984, 13).

Canada introduced the *Old Age Pension Act* in 1927 to promote the goals outlined above and to solve a social problem created by retired workers. Matthews and Tindale (1987) give three reasons for this act. First, more people lived to old age. Second, many old people lived in poverty. Third, employers needed to reduce unemployment and increase productivity. The *Old Age Pension Act* encouraged retirement and provided a basic income to the poorest older people.

Unions in North America supported retirement for their own reasons. They wanted companies to use seniority (first hired, last fired) as a method for deciding layoffs or cutbacks. Seniority gave workers a right to a job, and it gave the oldest workers the most job security. But companies resisted the seniority system because older workers cost them more and seniority rights made it hard for them to fire inefficient older workers. Retirement served both unions and employers. It limited seniority rights to people under the age of retirement and allowed companies to let older workers go. The unions traded the older worker's right to a job for job security in middle age (Haber 1978, cited in Atchley

1985, 54). Snell (1996, 6) says that the new "mandatory, continuing unemployment [program that emerged] would be known by the euphemism 'retirement.'"

Still, compared with today, few people retired in the past. First, in Canada many people worked on farms or in small businesses, types of work with no retirement age. Second, and most important, a lack of retirement income kept most people working as long as they could. Only with the increase in public pensions and social supports for older people after World War II did retirement spread (Gratton 1993; Myles 1984).

The U.S. Social Security program led the way for this change. The United States designed Social Security as a way to get people to retire (Myles 1984, 16). Until then governments had given social assistance to older people, but this assistance, like Canada's early old age assistance program, gave only the poorest older people a small amount of money to help them survive. The government based the program on the English poor law

notion of "less eligibility." This rule held that assistance should relieve poverty, but should come to less than the lowest working wage.

Social Security, and later Canada's public pension system, set a new goal for public pensions. These programs promised to make up for a retiree's lost income. "By 1980, the institution of retirement had been consolidated and old age had become a period in the life cycle defined and sustained by the welfare state" (Myles 1984, 21).

Government now plays the major role in guaranteeing pensions to older retirees. Public pensions and transfer payments act as a deferred wage because people pay into the programs through taxes and payments to the CPP and the Quebec Pension Plan (QPP) while they work. In Canada, though, the amount a person gets does not depend only on how much he or she paid in. People today get "a share of the social product over and above any claims they may have possessed in their capacity as wage earners" (Myles 1984, 29). Myles calls this a citizen's

● Exhibit 10.1

DECLINE IN EMPLOYMENT AMONG MEN AGED 55–64, 1976–2000

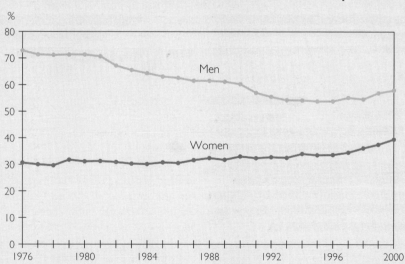

Workforce participation of men aged 55 to 64 shows a dramatic decline from 1976 to 2000. Between 1976 and 1995, the participation rate for men in this age group fell from 74 percent to 54 percent. It rose to 58 percent by 2000. But the rate remains far below the rate of 1976. Women aged 55 to 64 show an increase in workforce participation over this time. Their participation rate rose from 30 percent in 1976 to 39 percent in 2000. Women, compared to men, are still less likely to work outside the home.

Source: Health Canada, 2001, "Canada's Seniors. No. 9: Decline in Employment among Men Aged 55 to 64," http://www.hc-sc.gc.ca/seniors-aines/pubs/factoids/2001/no09_e.htm, accessed August 11, 2004. From the Statistics Canada publication *Profile of Canada's Seniors* (Focus on Canada series; analytical products: 1991 Census of Population), Cat. No. 96-312, August 1994, p. 6. Reproduced with permission.

wage. This wage makes retirement a time of economic security and freedom for many older people.

Schulz (1985) estimates that, without government support, workers would have to save 20 percent of their income each year just to get a pension equal to 60 to 65 percent of their earnings during the last five years before retirement. Few people could afford to save this much on their own. With government help, retirement has become an option for many more people than ever before. Statistics Canada reports that in 1976, for example, 9.3 percent of men and women aged 65 and over took part in the labour force. This figure dropped to 7 percent in 1986 and 6.4 percent in 1998 (Lindsay 1999).

Men aged 65 to 69 showed the greatest decrease in labour force participation during the 1980s (the rate of decrease has levelled off since then). Their participation rate fell by almost 27 percent from 1979 to 1989. Men aged 55 to 64 showed the second-largest drop. Lindsay (1999) says that between 1976 and 1998 their participation rate fell by 18 percent (from 74 percent to 56 percent). (See Exhibit 10.1.) During this time, the dollar amount of government income security payments increased and more people received CPP pensions. The retirement trends for the past decade support the idea that people tend to retire early if they have a good pension.

However, the tendency to retire early applies more to men than women. Women, compared to men, have a different pattern of labour force participation in later life. In 2002, for example, only 3.7 percent of women aged 65 and over worked for pay compared to 10.5 percent of men in that age group. First, women have different work careers than men. In 1998, 22 percent of women aged 65 and over had never worked outside the home (Lindsay 1999). Second, women in the labour force have fewer private pensions and smaller public pensions. This gives them fewer retirement options.

In Canada, more women than men retire early. Many women retire because their spouse has retired, and, because women often marry older men, they retire at an earlier age on average than men. A Canadian study (Matthews and Tindale 1987) compared the reasons men and women retire. The researchers found that women, more often than men, retire because of the ill health of a spouse or a family member. A later Statistics Canada study found that family responsibilities ranked third as the most common reason for women to retire (Lindsay 1997). This item barely ranked at all for men. Zimmerman and her colleagues (2000) found similar results among women retirees. These findings show the effects of non-work pressures on women's decision to retire. These findings also caution against using data

based on male retirement patterns to draw conclusions about retirement for women.

WHY DO PEOPLE RETIRE?

A number of personal conditions lead people to choose retirement. These include a person's expected income, job opportunities in retirement, their health, a spouse's decision to retire, and attitudes toward work (Human Resources Development Canada 2001; Tompa 1999). Social forces can also lead a person to choose retirement. These forces include (1) mandatory retirement rules, (2) better pensions that start at age 65, and (3) a more positive societal attitude toward retirement.

The Debate over Mandatory Retirement

No federal law in Canada forces a person to retire at age 65, and no statute requires a worker to leave work at a certain age. The federal public service ended mandatory retirement in 1986 (Guppy 1989). Still, two-thirds of collective agreements have mandatory retirement clauses and mandatory retirement rules affect half of all workers (Goodman 1999b).

The debate over mandatory retirement concerns two principles: (1) that of individual equality and justice, and (2) that of group rights (Guppy 1989). The first principle says that society should prohibit discrimination against a person on the basis of race, religion, gender, or age. The Croll Commission report, *Retirement without Tears*, used this principle in its argument against mandatory retirement, which, it said, violates the older worker's human rights (Senate of Canada 1979). "Discriminating against people in employment because they are no longer young," the report says, "[is] clearly objectionable on social grounds. [It is] no more justifiable than discrimination because of religion" (128). The second principle says that groups have the right to a fair share of social opportunities. Affirmative action regulations are based on this principle. The debate often focuses on specific issues like the need for older workers to allow younger workers a chance to work. But beneath this and other issues lurk the conflicting principles of individual versus group rights.

The Canadian Charter of Rights and Freedoms appears to outlaw mandatory retirement based on age. The Charter states in Section 15(1) that "every individual is equal before and under the law and has the right to the equal protection and equal benefit of the law without discrimination and, in particular, without discrimination

● **Exhibit 10.2**

LABOUR FORCE PARTICIPATION RATES BY AGE AND SEX, CANADA, 1991

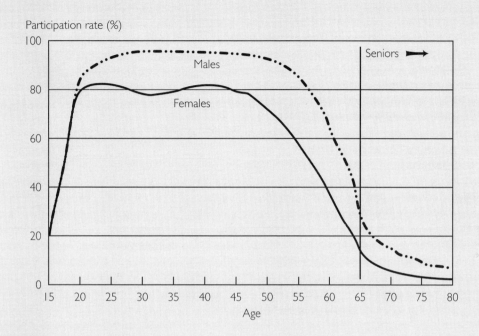

Note that labour force participation rates increase between ages 15 and 24 for both men and women. By age 24, more than 90 percent of males and 80 percent of females are in the labour force. For men, high rates of participation hold until around age 55. Then a gradual drop occurs (from 84 percent of 55-year-olds in the labour force to 42 percent of those age 64). A sharp (12 percent) drop occurs at age 65. By age 75, only 10 percent of men remain at work.

The pattern of labour force participation for women mirrors that of men with some differences. First, women have lower rates of participation throughout adulthood. Second, women begin to leave the labour force earlier. Their rates drop from 77 percent at age 47 to 20 percent by age 64. Third, women show a less sharp decline at age 65 and they leave the labour force more slowly in later life.

Source: Adapted from J.A. Norland, 1994, *Profile of Canada's Seniors* (Focus on Canada series; analytic products: 1991 Census of Population), Cat. No. 96–312, p. 6. Reprinted with permission from Statistics Canada.

based on race, national or ethnic origin, colour, religion, sex, age or mental or physical ability" (cited in Guppy 1989). But the Charter contains other sections that make this passage unclear. For example, it does not regulate private conduct, so it may not apply to private sector retirement agreements. Also, the Charter protects the good of society from individual freedoms. Guppy concludes that "the Charter does not offer a clear formula to follow in deciding the future of mandatory retirement" (175).

On December 7, 1990, the Supreme Court of Canada ruled on a challenge to mandatory retirement

brought by seven professors and a librarian in Ontario. The court ruled by a five to two vote in favour of mandatory retirement. The decision upheld the "constitutional viability of public service employers, including government, hospitals and universities, requiring employees to retire at age 65" (Guppy 1989). The decision shows the kind of contradictions in the Charter that Guppy described. The majority position, written by Justice Gérard LaForest, stated that mandatory retirement constitutes age discrimination and that age discrimination violates individual rights. But it allowed mandatory

● Exhibit 10.3

Functional versus Formal Criteria for Retirement

Mandatory retirement uses a formal criterion (a specific age) to decide when a person should retire. Critics of this approach say that people should be judged on their functional ability. Shephard (1995), for example, reports that decreases in physical ability do not necessarily lead to a loss of work ability. Salthouse and Maurer (1996; see also Park and Gutchess 2000) reviewed the literature on age and work ability. They conclude that "there is little or no relation between age and work performance or job proficiency" (355). Gibson, Zerbe, and Franken (1993) studied older and younger workers' views of employees. Both younger and older workers rated older workers as higher on initiative, stability, and experience. And people can overcome many of the changes that come with age. People who can still do their jobs should not be forced to retire.

Employers can adapt the workplace to help workers do their jobs. Workplace design often fits a young male in ideal physical condition. Gaullier (1988, cited in National Advisory Council on Aging [NACA] 1992b) says that about 70 percent of today's work-force do not fit this ideal. Shephard (1995) suggests introducing job redesign and ergonomic supports to help older workers do their work. Some manufacturing companies provide hydraulic lift supports to aid older workers and non-slip floors to prevent accidents. They also provide fitness classes and space for workers to exercise. Such programs take advantage of older workers' abilities and their lifetime of experience and skill.

retirement under Section 1 of the Charter as a reasonable limitation and a "minor" infringement that will add to "the greater public good" (Canadian Association of University Teachers [CAUT] 1991).

Employers swayed the court by claiming that an end to mandatory retirement would lead to problems in the labour force and would limit the opportunities of younger workers. The ruling did not clearly apply to the private sector, but can serve as a precedent for application to the private sector. Also, the ruling will apply in provinces such as Ontario that allow mandatory retirement, but not in provinces such as Manitoba, Quebec, and New Brunswick that prohibit it.

Justice Claire L'Heureux-Dubé wrote a dissenting opinion that pointed out the negative effect of mandatory retirement on women. Working women often have fewer years in the workforce than men and so have less pension coverage if they have to retire at age 65. She also pointed out that in places that have ended mandatory retirement, the new policy has had no proven negative effect; universities have kept their tenure systems, retirement plans have stayed in place, and there is no evidence of rising unemployment among young workers (CAUT 1991).

Later court rulings in 1992 and in 1995 continue to support mandatory retirement. Klassen and Gillin (1999) expect that the court will maintain this position in the near future. The concern in the Supreme Court rulings about opening positions for the young through mandatory

retirement curiously comes at a time when a shortage of younger, skilled workers will appear throughout Canadian society. Employers may find that they have to entice older workers to stay at work (McDonald and Wanner 1990). Tindale (1991, 19; see also Gee 1995b) says that while "mandatory retirement will not disappear with a bang, by means of precedent-setting judicial decisions, it may well disappear with a whimper of attrition as the labour force shortage grows."

Better Pensions

Workers often retire as soon as they can afford to. For most Canadians this means before age 65. Méthot (1987) concludes that if mandatory retirement ceased to exist, its absence would have little effect on the number of older workers.

At least three economic forces lead workers to retire at age 65 today. First, some workers with good pension plans may earn more money in retirement than if they keep on working. Taxes and the cost of commuting, clothes, lunches, and other work-related expenses may make work an expensive option.

Second, most private pension plans begin to pay full benefits at age 65. Quinn and Burkhauser (1990) report that many occupational pension plans penalize a person for staying on past retirement age. These plans provide many people with a strong incentive to retire at 65.

Third, OAS payments start at age 65, as do CPP/QPP payments and Guaranteed Income Supplement (GIS) payments. A person who works past age 65 will still get these benefits, but will lose a large portion of them through higher taxes. The GIS program also discourages older people from working. The federal government reduces the GIS by $1 for each $2 a person earns; a person who earns a provincial supplement loses the other $1 from his or her supplement benefits. Government policies such as these result in a 100 percent "**taxback**" on the poorest people, who get nothing for work up to the amount equal to their GIS and provincial supplements. Also, the taxback takes money from the older person's income next year for money earned this year. This means that low-income older people who work risk losing next year's income supplements (as well as their salary) if they get sick or cannot find a job. These rules create a strong incentive for retirement.

Better pensions and decreased incentives to work have increased the trend toward retirement. In addition, increased leisure and recreational opportunities have also changed social attitudes toward retirement.

New Attitudes toward Retirement

Atchley (1976, 87) says that "everyone seems to know people who carefully planned for retirement only to become sick and die within six months after leaving their jobs." He goes on to say that, no matter what their job, he has "yet to encounter an occupational group for which retirement is related to a decline in self-reported health. It is true that many people expect retirement to adversely affect health, but very few realized their expectations."

A Canadian study by Shapiro and Roos (1982) supports this view. They studied retirees' use of health care services in Manitoba and found that retirees and workers visited the doctor for minor and serious problems at about the same rate. They conclude that "there is no evidence that retirement per se is associated with increased utilization of ambulatory physician services or admission to the hospital" (192). Other studies show that, in general, Canadians adjust well to retirement (Gee and Kimball 1987). Matthews et al. (1982) found that the effect of retirement came in at 28 on a scale of 34 life events ranked from greatest effect to least effect. This study suggests that retirement has relatively little impact on most people.

Early Retirement

Statistics Canada (Gower 1995; see also Tompa 1999) reports a 15-year trend toward early retirement for workers aged 55 to 64. Labour force figures show that the number of men in this age group who had left the labour force increased by almost 200 percent from 1975 to 1985. During this same period, the total number of men in this age group increased only 23 percent. Human Resources Development Canada (2001) reports that "age 55 replaced age 65 as the most common planned age of retirement for younger persons." On average, Canadian workers now retire at about age 60 (Kieran 2001).

Two types of workers tend to take early retirement: workers in poor health and those who expect a good income in retirement (Statistics Canada 2001f). The 1994 General Social Survey (GSS) (cited in McDonald and Donahue 2000) found that 25 percent of men and 22 percent of women gave health as their reason for retirement. This group made up the single largest proportion of retirees. McDonald and Donahue report that, compared to healthy people, people who retired for health reasons retired at an earlier age. This group also tended to have lower education, to come from lower-status occupations, and not to have a private pension. They faced handicaps at work throughout their lives.

Retirement due to poor health affected men and women differently. Women who retired due to poor health did not show a drop in income. The researchers say that for these women, the "starting point on the income ladder is so low to begin with and their work patterns so limited, none of their work history much matters when it comes to retirement income. It is marriage that has the largest and most positive effect on women's household retirement income" (McDonald and Donahue 2000, 516). But men who retired due to poor health faced significant drops in income. They often had no private pension or investment income, and they often got few transfer dollars. McDonald and Donahue ask whether the government ought to make special pension arrangements for this large group of older retirees.

People also retire early because they want more leisure time and less work. These people have a positive image of retirement (Gower 1995). Neugarten (1980) says that only a small percentage of workers (about 8 to 10 percent) fit the stereotype of the faithful worker who is forced out of work. "The evidence shows that as one gets older, the desire to continue working is clearly not as strong as it was once thought to be by many sociologists" (Schulz 1980, 199).

Some private pension plans encourage people to choose early retirement. Many large companies, the government, and universities sponsor early retirement plans. Early retirement allows companies to hire less costly young workers or to leave jobs empty after a retiree leaves. Bell Canada, which had an average retirement age of 55 in the early 1990s, used retirement to trim its labour force.

Almost all retirees in that period left the company before age 65 through an incentive program that encouraged early retirement (Marshall 1995c).

Robertson (2000) studied the reasons older people left work with an incentive package. Reasons included timing, the financial incentive, and changes in corporate culture. The early retirement package helped workers make up their minds to leave. One woman said, "I had planned to retire at 60 ... and I thought, well, at 59 they're offering a package that would probably equal my year's salary ... And if I hadn't taken it, I may have been still sitting there today working ... it kind of made my mind up for me" (70). Another worker said, "they came and offered me over a year's wages to leave ... which I thought was just fantastic ... And I said, well, okay. Thirty-eight years. And I thought, that's long enough" (70).

Schulz (1991) says that retirement policies in developed countries serve as a way to adjust the labour supply. These programs "intentionally ... discourage people from working" (303). Companies use retirement as a buffer against economic change. McGoldrick and Cooper (1988) found that managers referred to incentive programs as voluntary, but workers more often saw them as coercive. Marshall (1995c, 46) calls this the "retirement incentive game." Management tries to offer the fewest incentives possible to produce the desired effect: downsizing. The

Exhibit 10.4

Planned Retirement Age of Employed Persons Aged 45 Years and Older and Aged 16 to 44

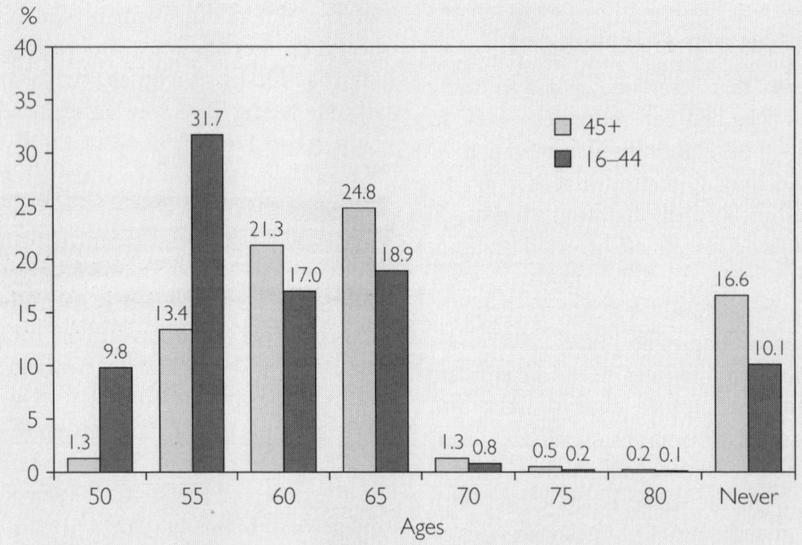

This chart shows the preference for early retirement among both younger and older workers. The largest proportion of older workers choose age 65, probably because their pension plans provide incentives to retire at that age. The largest proportion of younger workers plan to retire at age 55. The chart shows a shift in the planned retirement age to younger ages for all workers. This reflects the options available through private and public early retirement programs. The chart shows that retirement plan incentives shape retirement decisions. Note also that 16.6 percent of older workers and 10.1 percent of younger workers said they never planned to retire. Workers make choices based on their personal circumstances—expected income in retirement, savings, and health.

Source: Adapted in part from the Statistics Canada *General Social Survey,* Cycle 9: Education, Work and Retirement—Custom tabulation service, Cat. No. 12C0013, April 2003, 1994. Adapted from Human Resources Development Canada, 2001, *Income Security Programs Evaluation of Public and Private Financial Incentives for Retirement,* Exhibit 5.1, SP-AH087-05-01E, http://www11.hrdc-drhc.gc.ca/pls/edd/EPPFI_221000.htm, accessed on October 19, 2003. Reprinted with permission.

worker needs to make a decision: take the offer, wait for a better one, or risk a layoff. Marshall says that playing this game requires that workers know the cost of taking the plan, the benefits of early retirement, and their own life expectancy. No one wants to retire and then live in poverty for another 20 years.

Canada's *Public Service Superannuation Act* allows retirement as early as age 55 with 30 years' service (Health and Welfare Canada 1979). Statistics Canada (2001f) says that in the 1990s many public sector industries encouraged workers to take early retirement. Between 1997 and 2000, for example, 63 percent of public sector employees retired before age 60 (twice the rate of the private sector) (Kieran (2001). Kieran reports that public sector employees with 30 years at work can get a pension at age 55. This made age 55 the most popular age for public sector employees. Private sector employees tended to stay on until age 65, and self-employed workers retired even later. Some private sector pension plans in Canada allow early retirement on a reduced pension. Some private plans even include a special rule allowing early retirement on an unreduced pension for a certain number of years of service or age plus service (Marshall 1995c).

Changes in the CPP in 1987 also encourage a more flexible retirement age. The plan now allows payments to begin as early as age 60 or as late as age 70. People who retire early get decreases in their basic pension equal to 0.5 percent for each month between the date the pension begins and the month after their 65th birthday. Retirees cannot earn more than the current maximum annual CPP pension at age 65. Those who retire after age 70 receive an increase of 0.5 percent on their basic pension for every month between the date the pension begins and the month after their 65th birthday.

Results from the 2002 GSS in Canada show an increase in flexible thinking about retirement (Statistics Canada 2003f). About a fifth (22 percent) of workers aged 45 to 59 said they planned to retire early (before age 60). Another 45 percent said they planned to retire between age 60 and 64 or at age 65. Only 3 percent said they planned to stay at work after age 65. But a large proportion of people, 31 percent, said they either didn't know when they would retire or that they would never retire. These last two groups represent about 1.4 million Canadians.

These findings show that many older workers (about 44 percent) plan on early retirement—before age 65. Relatively few workers plan to work past age 65. These findings support trends toward early retirement that began in the late 1970s. The GSS found that poorer people, people without pension plans, and recent immigrants showed the greatest likelihood to report that they would never retire. These workers expressed concern about their income in later life.

Women more often than men expected to have low incomes in retirement. Unattached workers (widowed, divorced, or separated) also reported concerns about low income in retirement. McDonald, Donahue, and Moore (2000a) studied widows and found that they tend to retire later than married women. They also tend to plan less for retirement, have less information about retirement, and save less for retirement. They also tend to have low incomes and this affects their retirement options.

Will the trend toward early retirement continue into the future? Or will people tend to stay at work longer? The GSS data suggest that the timing of retirement depends in large part on a person's work history. People with more education and a higher income tend to retire early. These people have more choices and a better attitude toward retirement (Kieran 2001).

ALTERNATIVES TO A FIXED RETIREMENT AGE

Workers today can choose early or delayed retirement instead of mandatory retirement at age 65. They can also choose a number of other options. NACA (2000c, 5) reports a "blurring of the line between work and retirement." Marshall, Clarke, and Ballantyne (2001, 379) report on a study of workers at Bell Canada in Ontario. They found that many retirees return to work in "**bridge jobs.**" They take on a job that might not be in their former career before they retire for good. For example, 46.5 percent of the men and 25.3 percent of the women worked for pay after retiring. Human Resources Development Canada (2001) reports that a growing number of older men (aged 55 to 64) are looking for work. Options for retirees today include flexible retirement, part-time work, and second careers.

Flexible Retirement

Atchley (1985, 192) predicts that in the future "the small proportion [of people who do] not want to retire can expect to find it increasingly easier to stay on as long as they can still do the job." Some of these workers may choose **flexible retirement**, an option that allows them to slowly cut back the number of hours they work each week.

Older Canadians tend to work if they have occupations that allow for choice in their retirement age and if they can work at their own pace. People in religious professions and farm workers, for example, make up the highest proportion of people employed after age 65 (Lindsay 1999). Kieran (2001) says that farmers (who are mostly self-employed) may need to work in order to earn money and to run the family business. Snell and Brown (1987) report that people who find meaning in work and consider their work important also tend to work after retirement. This applies best to older men who work in managerial jobs. Also, many older male workers who continued working tended to be in the fields of agriculture, manufacturing, construction, and transportation (Lindsay 1999). Older women who work after the traditional retirement age most often work in service professions.

Stryckman (1987) also proposes work sharing as an alternative to either retirement or full-time work. Work sharing spreads the available work for a position over a number of workers. Paris (1989) reports that in a Canadian study 19 percent of 375 companies offered formal job-sharing programs. Another 10 percent of these companies said they allowed informal job sharing. This option, which fits a trend in the labour force toward more temporary jobs, would allow workers to work part-time in their current positions and might entice some older workers to stay at work after retirement age. Work sharing can benefit employers by giving them more flexibility in responding to labour demands (David 1993). It also opens opportunities for people who want part-time or temporary work.

Part-Time Work

A 1998 study found that 46 percent of Canadians expected to work after retirement (Ekos Research Associates 1998, cited in Goodman 1999b). McDonald (1997b) reports that 17.1 percent of retirees do return to work and the majority of them move to a new employer. Most people who work past age 65 choose to work part-time instead of full-time as an alternative to full retirement (Quinn and Burkhauser 1990). Stone (1994) reports that retired men in good health often work, but they do so for fewer hours per day than before retirement. In 1998, 34 percent of employed men and 57 percent of employed women aged 65 and over worked part-time (Lindsay 1999). Méthot (1987) found that most older people who worked (85 percent of men and 79 percent of women) said they did not want full-time work. The figures for part-time older men and women have increased by about 10 percent since 1975.

Professionals and people on the margin of the economy show the greatest tendency to take up part-time work. Many of these people retired due to mandatory retirement or because they could not find full-time jobs (McDonald 1997b). Part-time bridge jobs can ease a worker's move to full retirement. Examples of bridge jobs include security guard, hardware store salesman, and department store clerk. These jobs pay less than the retiree's former salary and the work often has little to do with their former career job, but workers take these jobs to stay active and to earn extra money.

A report by Health and Welfare Canada (1982a, 3) says that "opportunities to work part-time are very important to the employment of senior citizens." Some people (women without pensions, widows) want to work part-time because they need the money. Others like to work because it gives them a chance to meet new people. Sometimes people who retired because of bad health find that their health improves enough that they can manage a part-time job. A Canadian study found that 35 percent of men and 63 percent of women who retired due to ill health (about 25 percent of all retirees retire for this reason) said their health had improved (Health and Welfare Canada 1979). Some of these people may want to work part-time.

Some workers turn to part-time work because they cannot find full-time jobs. For example, Rowe and Nguyen (2003) say that the chance of finding a new job nears zero at age 65. In 1997, for example, about 20 percent of unemployed men aged 55 and over and 22 percent of unemployed women in this age group had been out of work for more than a year. This comes to about twice the rate for younger people (McDonald, Donahue, and Moore 2000b, citing Statistics Canada 1998). The older the person, the more difficulty he or she will have finding work (David 1993). Foot and Gibson (1993, 64) believe that unemployment among older workers will remain "an important policy issue" in the years ahead.

Gibson, Zerbe, and Franken (1993) studied employers' views of older workers. They found five barriers to older workers' re-employment. Employers felt that older workers lacked the skills to do the job, they cost more to employ, and they had a harder time fitting into the company's culture. McDonald, Donahue, and Moore (2000b) also report sexual discrimination (against women) and racism as causes of unemployment among older workers.

McDonald and Wanner (1990, 108; see also McDonald, Donahue, and Moore 2000b) report that older Canadian workers with a record of unemployment tend to get "discouraged out" of the job market. Some workers who lose their jobs may not find work that suits them, so they give up looking and retire early (McMullin and Marshall 1999). Schellenberg (1994) found that older workers lacked job search skills. He reports that older unemployed men and women (age 45 and over), compared with younger people, tended not to check directly with employers for new jobs.

Part-time work can help workers cope with job loss. Statistics Canada (2003r) reports that 27 percent of people aged 45 and over said they worked part-time because of business conditions or because they could not find work. Part-time work can also help workers maintain their standard of living until they can collect a government pension.

Twelve Seniors Employment Bureaux (SEBs) operate in Canada today. The government, foundations, and local agencies fund these offices. They help retired workers find part-time work or other working arrangements that suit their needs. The SEBs began by defining an older worker as someone aged 60 and over. They now help people aged 45 and over. McDonald, Donahue, and Moore (2000b) say that unemployed older people can benefit from counselling. The counsellor can encourage an older person to improve his or her job skills, go back to school, look for part time work, or work as a volunteer in order to get a new job. The researchers also report retirees' need for social support from family and self-help groups.

Part-time work serves a number of functions for older people. Some older people work part-time to stay busy, others work because they need the money. Still others work part-time because they cannot find full-time jobs. Moen and her colleagues (2000) found that work after retirement led to greater life satisfaction for men. But it led to lower life satisfaction for women. Older men may choose to work for personal fulfillment, but older women may have to work to pay their bills. Part-time work means different things to different people, but it plays an important role in the transition to full retirement.

Second Careers

Some people retire to a **second career**. Job bureaus for seniors report that former teachers may want to work as cabinetmakers, former accountants may want to work as painters, and former homemakers may want to work in an office or a retail store. Neugarten (1980, 74) says that "many business executives become engaged in community affairs in the last years of their employment and find it relatively easy to move into those areas after they retire." These people work at second careers for more than the money. A second career allows them to develop skills they could not use when they worked full-time.

Tournier (1972, 129) calls a second career a "free career." A second career, he says, differs from leisure and from the kind of work a person does in middle age. "It has a goal, a mission, and that implies organization, loyalty, and even priority over other more selfish pleasures—not in the line of duty, since professional obligations are not involved, but for the love of people. It is, therefore, not an escape, but a presence in the world" (130). A second career, Tournier says, grows out of interests that lay dormant or undeveloped in middle age. A saleswoman at The Bay, for example, spent her weekends cooking traditional Ukrainian food for her family. When she retired from work, she began a career as a volunteer kitchen director at her local senior centre. The work gave her a sense of purpose and allowed her to use her talents in a new way.

Tournier (1972, 136) also calls a second career a "personal career" because "one has to formulate one's

---

● **Exhibit 10.5**

PROFILE OF A SECOND CAREER

May Ebbitt Cutler started a new life—several new lives, really—after she turned 65. In 1987, the founder of the children's book publishing company Tundra was elected to a four-year term as mayor of Westmount, in greater Montreal. Since then, she has mounted theatre productions in Montreal, Detroit and New York City. She kept her hand in politics: the grandmother of six was deeply involved in Westmount's battle against the Quebec government's plan to merge Montreal with neighbouring municipalities. She found time to travel abroad, to China, India and Brazil, among other destinations. And she has survived a battle with breast cancer. "I love being a senior," says the 77-year-old Cutler. "I have so much freedom after raising a family for 35 years. I am happy to be alive and to be able to contribute."

Source: Susan McClelland, 2001, "The Costs of an Aging Population," *Maclean's*, July 9, p. 18. Reprinted with permission.

own aim, choose one's own method of work, set one's own daily task and assert one's identity in one's work." One bus driver began a second career as an actor when he joined a seniors' theatre group, and an electrician began a second career as a public figure when a seniors' club elected him president. They became resources in their communities, and their second careers brought meaning and purpose to their retirement.

Disrupted Careers

Many older workers who leave the workforce today do so involuntarily. Corporate downsizing and globalization have led companies to retire or lay off older workers (He, Colantonio, and Marshall 2003). The 1994 GSS found that for workers aged 45 to 64, nearly one-fifth (18.6 percent) reported at least one job interruption in the past five years. And 14 percent say they lost their jobs. These workers gave "shortage of work" or "out of business" as the most common reasons for job loss. Women reported a higher rate of job loss than men and for the same reasons—layoff, lack of work, company closure. Workers also list poor health, mandatory retirement, and early retirement policies as reasons for involuntary retirement.

Rowe and Nguyen (2003) studied cohorts of workers as they lost and gained jobs from age 50 to 65. They found that only 51 percent of men and 30 percent of women said that they had retired from their job by age 65. The large majority of job losses (84 percent for men and 88 percent for women) came from other sources—layoffs, illness, or family needs. About a quarter of the workers in this study, who appeared to retire between ages 50 and 65, went on to take new jobs. The researchers say that only about 20 percent of men and 10 percent of women fit the traditional model of retirement (work at a single job until age 65 and then retire). About 60 percent of job losses for men and women were involuntary.

McDonald, Donahue, and Marshall (2000) report that among people aged 55 to 64 who retired, 68 percent of men and 66 percent of women said they retired unexpectedly. Marshall, Clarke, and Ballantyne (2001) see later life work disruption as a shift away from stable work careers that lead to retirement. "Retirement is taking on new meanings for men and women: It is not a discrete event marking secession of paid employment, nor is it a stable state following exit from the paid employment. Rather, it is a process that varies in its timing and duration" (180).

McDonald, Donahue, and Marshall (2000, 289; see also McDaniel 1997) found that unexpected early retirement led to low incomes in retirement. Those who

retired due to unemployment had the lowest incomes in retirement. These younger retirees cannot qualify for government pensions yet. This creates a "retirement gap" that leaves them with low incomes. Schellenberg (1994, 1) says that "many Canadians age 45 and over are facing severe economic hardship due to joblessness."

McDonald, Donahue, and Moore (2000b, 78–79) report the effects of this hardship. One retiree said, "I've never been as poor, having worked all these years, as I am today." Another retiree said, "I'm coping, I'm coping. But I have to dip into my RRSP. I cannot survive on what I receive ... and now I'm planning to move out of my apartment to look for cheaper accommodation."

Some workers will adapt to this new world of retirement by using strategies such as flexible retirement, part-time work, and second careers. Other workers will try to find new jobs. They will often have to work in lower-status jobs, at low pay, and they will face further job disruptions. Researchers have just begun to study this new pattern of retirement.

WOMEN AND RETIREMENT

McDonald (2002) says that the concept of retirement rarely applied to women in the past. Retirement occurs when a person leaves the paid workforce. But, until recently, relatively few women had a work career that led to retirement. McDonald (2002) reports that in 1931, for example, only about 20 percent of women worked in the paid labor force (compared to about 60 percent in 2000). Even today, Connidis (1982) says, women follow different career paths than men. Some take up careers after raising a family; others work during their child-rearing years; some never enter the labour force; and many single women show unbroken work records (Keating and Jeffrey 1983). This variety makes it hard to describe a typical pattern of retirement for women.

Few studies have looked at how women adjust to retirement or at what retirement means to them. The studies that have focused on women show diverse patterns among women subjects and large differences between women and men. Atchley (1982) says that different factors shape male and female attitudes to retirement, and different factors lead to life satisfaction for each group. He concludes that "women's retirement is indeed a separate issue compared to men's" (165). In the past, Beeson (1975) says, researchers treated women's retirement as a non-event. Szinovacz (1982) says that until 1975 the annual meetings of the Gerontological Society of America contained almost no discussion of women's retirement.

This has begun to change as more women have started working outside the home. Statistics Canada (cited in McDaniel 1995) reports that 69 percent of women with husbands and children under six worked outside the home in 1991; this was an increase from 49.4 percent in 1981. Researchers have begun to study women's transitions to retirement as a normative event.

Szinovacz (1983) believes that changes in the work patterns of women will make their retirement experience similar to that of men. Marshall (1995b) reports that women show an increase in labour force participation from the 1950s to the present. In 1999, for example, 89 percent of women between the ages of 55 and 64 said they had at some time worked in the labour force (compared to only 78 percent of women aged 65 and over). Ninety-five percent of women aged 25 to 54 say they had at some time worked in the labour force (Lindsay 2000b). Gauthier (1991) reports that more women today have occupational pensions than in the past. And he expects the proportion of women with occupational pensions to grow in the future. Szinovacz (1983) observes that many women now have long, continuous work records (15 or more years) and a strong commitment to work, and they may feel a sense of loss when they retire. Retirement for a woman means the loss of work colleagues, the loss of contact with customers and clients, and the loss of a social role.

It may also mean a big drop in income, because many women have no pension plan. Ballantyne and Marshall (1995) report that retired women aged 45 to 64 had 27 percent less family income than full-time working women. Women with a strong work commitment, who have many social contacts at work, and who have low incomes, have the most negative views of retirement and the strongest incentive to work (Nishio and Lank 1987). Older women who work tend to work part-time or are self-employed. Those who work for others tend to work as non-managers in clerical, sales, or service jobs (Lindsay 2000b).

Marshall (1995c) says that older women are more likely than older men to say they do not know when they will retire. One woman said, "If we've had children and had to stay at home for periods of time, we don't have pensions that we can live on.... If and when we retire, the pension I've earned you couldn't live on" (Marshall 1995c, 38–39). A woman in another study (McFadgen and Zimmerman 1995, 108) said, "It is hard to plan for retirement if you don't have the means to support yourself."

Szinovacz (1983) reports that women also have different retirement needs than men. McFadgen and Zimmerman (1995) found that women need more knowledge about their pension plans. Women also say they prefer to reduce their hours rather than retire all at once. In response to the dearth of information about women and retirement, McDaniel (1989) and Johnson and Williamson (1987) call for more research on the subject.

NEW DIRECTIONS IN RESEARCH

Retirement research has taken some new directions. O'Rand (1990), for example, reports that dual-career couples fall into several categories with regard to retirement. In most cases, one spouse retires before the other; only 20 percent of the time do they retire together. Longitudinal research on two-earner couples should study the retirement decisions couples make in response to pension eligibility and economic conditions.

New studies are looking at how life changes in other family members (sickness of a spouse or parent, marriage of children, or widowhood) affect women's careers and retirement patterns. As more women enter the labour force, as more single women enter old age, and as better pensions make retirement an established part of adult life, social structures and individual responses to retirement will change. These changes will lead to new research approaches and new ideas about later life.

CRITIQUE OF THE RETIREMENT LITERATURE

McDonald and Wanner (1990) review a wide range of theoretical perspectives on retirement. Micro-level theories such as disengagement, activity, and continuity theory each prescribe a different model for a good old age—namely, disengage from activity, stay active in new pursuits, or maintain middle-aged activities. But these theories have some common themes. All of them (1) assume that retirement will bring a decrease in social activity, (2) focus on individual responses to retirement, and (3) assume that retirement will cause problems and that people need to adjust to live a happy life. "Most importantly," McDonald and Wanner (1990, 9) say, each of these theories views retirement "as a problem caused and solved by individual behavior."

Macro-level theories such as modernization theory (Cowgill 1974) and age stratification theory (Riley, Johnson, and Foner 1972) take social structures into account. Modernization theory explains that retirement arises when a society industrializes and technology puts older people out of work. Older people then have lower incomes and lower social status. Age stratification theory describes retirement as a role that a person plays in later life. This theory assumes that members of each age cohort will enter retirement and play this role. Like the micro theories, these theories take a functionalist view of retirement. They see it as an inevitable part of modern social life, and they assume that the individual must move through this role as a normal part of the life course (McDonald and Wanner 1990).

Both micro- and macro-level theories place responsibility for coping with the retirement role on the individual. They take the social structure as given and unchangeable and expect the person to adapt. A failure to retire well amounts to a personal failure. Programs such as pre-retirement education (PRE) can help a person plan for retirement (McDonald, Donahue, and Moore 2000b). But PRE programs seldom question the social structures that create or shape retirement, and they do not criticize the social structures that allow some people to retire easily, while others struggle in old age.

Political economy theory, on the other hand, looks at the sociocultural conditions that shape aging. This perspective sees retirement as the outcome of "economic, political, and social structures" that existed before retirement (McDonald and Wanner 1990, 14). These include beliefs about older workers, the kinds of jobs people have, their salaries, gender discrimination, economic conditions, and opportunities for workers to save or take part in a pension plan.

Gee and Kimball (1987) apply this perspective to a review of a study by Kaye and Monk (1984) on male and female university retirees. The study found that women did more volunteer work in retirement; men did more teaching and research. Kaye and Monk (1984) interpreted this finding to mean that men have greater opportunity or interest in continuing to work after retirement. Gee and Kimball emphasize that personal motivation explains only part of the difference in male and female retirement activities. More of the women in this sample had worked as university administrators, more of the men had been professors. Gee and Kimball say that the women in this study may have had little opportunity to continue their administrative work except as volunteers, whereas the men could carry on their research and teaching after retirement within the university structure. The difference in male and female retirement activity probably reflects the different structural opportunities open to these two groups.

Marshall (1995b) found that corporations often use early retirement plans to cope with shifts in the economy, corporate restructuring, and downsizing. Restructuring has hit many older manufacturing industries. These companies have a high proportion of older workers. Retirement incentives encourage these workers to retire. Corporations then avoid layoffs and salary freezes. Marshall and Marshall (1999) say that corporate restructuring affects both when older workers retire and the benefits they get. "The golden handshake of a retirement incentive plan," Marshall says (1995b, 57), "seems to be the most readily available way to reduce staff complement, so it is increasingly used."

This interpretation emphasizes the social forces that affect individual behaviour. Studies of national retirement systems, for example, show that government policies affect the decision to retire. Gruber and Wise (1999b) studied retirement policies and outcomes in 11 countries. They found that early retirement policies in many national pension plans encourage people to retire. In France, for example, 60 percent of workers who reach the early retirement age of 60 decide to retire. The CPP also allows for retirement at age 60. And this has increased early retirements (Baker and Benjamin, 1999).

Guillemard (1997) used the political economy perspective to study retirement policies in 12 European countries. She found that a shift in social policy has begun to reshape the retirement process in Europe (see also Gruber and Wise 1999a). Her research shows that in many European countries rising unemployment has forced older workers to leave work before the official retirement age. These countries have then expanded their unemployment and disability programs to cover the unemployed older workers until they reach retirement age.

Workers may work part-time, get retraining, or return to unemployment several times before officially retiring. Schellenberg (1995) and LeBlanc and McMullin (1997; see also Tompa 1999) report on a similar trend in Canada. For example, twice as many people now receive CPP/QPP disability pensions as 10 years ago. (These people made enough CPP contributions and cannot work due to a disability). Still, Canada lags behind Europe in the development of programs for displaced workers.

Guillemard (1997, 454) concludes that unemployment and disability policies have begun to reshape later life. Until 1997, Canada had the Program for Older Worker Adjustment (POWA) that offered financial help to laid-off workers aged 55 to 64 (LeBlanc and McMullin 1997). This type of program, along with disability insurance and social assistance programs, keeps the older worker in a semi-retired state and makes the end of a working career less clear. Campolieti (2001) reports that the CPP disability program accounts for about 66 percent of the decrease in labour force participation for men aged 45 to 64. Guillemard says that social policies lead to more varied patterns of retirement and work in later life. "Retirement" begins whenever an older worker cannot get back into the workforce. Guillemard shows how economic conditions and social policies shape individual decisions and the life course.

The political economy perspective links large-scale social policies, structures, and economic trends to individual life. It uncovers the sometimes hidden forces that shape individual decisions and life chances. McDonald and Wanner (1990, 14) say that this perspective offers "a very useful adjunct to individual explanations and holds considerable promise for expanding our understanding of retirement."

RETIREMENT AND SOCIAL STRUCTURES

Social Class and Retirement Options

Tournier says that before some people can take up a second career they will need "sufficient resources for them no longer to have to earn their living" (1972, 134). Guillemard (1977) agrees, arguing that second careers and other options such as volunteer work best fit the lifestyles and backgrounds of middle-class workers (executives, technicians, or engineers). These people form a new privileged group in society. They have good pensions, good health, and higher aspirations than working-class retirees. They may also have the verbal or technical skills that volunteer organizations or community groups value and need.

Discussions about retirement preparation obscure the issue of pension adequacy. Studies show again and again the link between pension benefits and the decision to retire. Luchak and Gellatly (2001), for example, found that workers showed a high commitment to staying at work if the company based their pension benefits on their highest salary. Workers with a lot of seniority reported a greater tendency to stay at work in order to increase their retirement benefits. Studies also show that people will retire if they have a good pension. A study in Quebec (Baillargeon 1982), for example, found that men with indexed pensions in both the public and private sectors had a good attitude to retirement. Baillargeon (1982) reports that half of higher-level workers look forward to retirement.

Studies show that a person with a good income and a middle-class or upper-middle-class occupation stands a good chance of being satisfied with retirement. People with money have more of a chance to take part in leisure activity, while people with poor pensions and no savings may be unable to retire at all. Middle-class and upper-

middle-class workers (white-collar workers, managers, professionals) with orderly work careers (few layoffs or job changes) report high satisfaction in retirement. Gall and Evans (2000, 193) studied a sample of 224 men in London, Ontario. They found that pre-retirement expectations shaped quality of life in retirement. Retirees who expected satisfaction in "activity, finances, health, and interpersonal relations" had a high quality of life six to seven years after they retired.

Studies also show that people with the most education and the highest incomes, married men and single women, tended to find or keep work after age 65 (McDonald and Wanner 1990). Quinn (1981) studied men 58 to 63 years old. He reports that about a third of the men on salary or wages worked part-time, while 60 percent of self-employed men (many of them professionals) worked part-time. Health and Welfare Canada (1982b) reports that older men with university degrees have four times the labour force participation rate of older men with less than grade 5 education. Older women with university degrees have five times the participation rate of older women with less than grade 5. Professionals such as doctors, lawyers, and professors can work as consultants or work part-time at their careers (Goodwin and Chen 1991; McDonald and Wanner 1990). Norris (1993) studied retired and working professionals. She found that both groups lived meaningful lives and reported high life satisfaction. The working professionals enjoyed the prestige and challenges of their work. They often delegated work to younger colleagues and used their social networks to maintain their status at work.

Statistics Canada (1986, 104) says that in high-income families people worked "well beyond the normal age of retirement." Even at age 75 and over, almost half of the high-income men and more than 10 percent of the high-income women still worked. The fact that they work puts these people in the high-income group, but also the kinds of work they do—running their own companies or working as independent professionals—allow them to ease out of work at their own pace. In sum, good income predicts that a person can and will retire. But independent professionals, even though they have a good income, often choose to continue working.

Social Structures and Retirement Options

Dowd (1980) says that social structures and economic conditions, more than personal preferences, explain why people retire when they do. Dowd divides the economy into two sectors, the **core** and the **periphery**: "One sector [the core] is highly organized and characterized by high wages and pension systems, and the other [the periphery] is marked by low wages and few, if any fringe benefits" (77). Exhibit 10.6 shows the effect of social structure on the chances of getting a private pension. It shows that workers in the core sector stand a better chance of getting a private pension than workers on the periphery (see also McDonald and Wanner 1987). Calasanti (1988) found that, due to this inequity, periphery retirees have a greater concern about satisfac-

tion with finances. This reflects "the monetary struggles they have experienced throughout their lives" (22).

In Canada, women more often than men work in the peripheral sector—45.8 percent of all women workers provide services, 17.9 percent are in trade occupations, and 2.9 percent work in agriculture (Labour Canada 1986). These occupations often have no mandatory retirement rules, and they allow for easy entry, flexible hours, and part-time work (Robinson, Coberly, and Paul 1985). At the same time, these occupations pay less than core occupations, and in general they offer fewer

Exhibit 10.6

PRIVATE COVERAGE OF EMPLOYEES AGED 35–54, BY INDUSTRY AND OCCUPATION, 1997

Pension Plan Members as % of Paid Workers

Industry	Men	Women
Manufacturing	66.0	43.7
Distributive Services	62.4	50.8
Business Services	54.2	45.0
Consumer Services	31.4	21.8
Public Services	90.2	70.9
Occupation		
Professional and Managerial	61.6	58.9
Natural and Social Sciences	79.2	71.3
Clerical	72.7	49.1
Sales	39.5	33.2
Service	62.9	24.1
Primary and Processing	60.9	29.4
Construction	59.6	20.2

A higher proportion of men compared to women belong to pension plans. This holds true for every industry and occupation reported above. Professional and managerial positions show the most similar rates of coverage for men and women. This reflects the higher incomes and better benefit packages that employees of both sexes get. But men occupy a greater proportion of these positions. By contrast, consumer services and sales have low coverage rates for both sexes. But women hold more of these positions. These facts lead to lower rates of private pension coverage for women.

Source: Adapted from R. Morrissette and M. Drolet, 2001, "Pension Coverage and Retirement Savings," Table 4, in *Perspectives on Labour and Income* 13(2): 43. Citing the Survey of Labour and Income Dynamics, 1997. Statistics Canada, Cat. No. 75-001-XPE. Reprinted with permission.

private pensions. These conditions give women fewer choices than men when it comes time to retire. McDonald and Wanner (1984) found that single women have one of the lowest rates of early retirement in Canada. They say this probably reflects their concentration in occupations with lower incomes and poorer pensions (108). They go on to show that poorer people of either sex tend not to retire early (114).

The variety within the older population based on differences in gender, social class, age, and so on leads to varied responses to work in later life. People can have full- or part-time work, full retirement, second careers, and so on. This variety suggests that retirement needs further study and that "the term 'retirement' may well conceal more than it reveals" (Quinn and Burkhauser 1990, 320). Today, not all Canadians have an income or occupation that produces a satisfactory retirement. Greater equality in retirement opportunity will come only with a decrease in the social inequities based on class and gender.

CONCLUSION

Some people retire today with private pensions, CPP benefits, and RRSP savings. Other people (many of them women and people who have worked at low-wage jobs) will never retire. A comfortable retirement depends on public support and private wealth. Some writers project that changes in the labour force and the economy will make retirement less common in the future. Taylor (1995, 18) says that "retirement as we know it—ten or twenty years of fun, partly at public expense, as a reward for showing up at work during our adult lives—is doomed. The happy coincidence of generous governments and the postwar economic and population boom that made it possible has come undone." He predicts that few Canadians can save enough to fulfill their retirement dream, and government pensions will fail because too few workers will exist in the future to support the baby boom retirees.

Some changes to Canada's pension system and economy suggest that Taylor may have a point. First, the government has already begun to focus government pension programs on needy older people. A few years ago the government began to tax back OAS payments from wealthier Canadians. New proposals may limit OAS payments to people with low incomes. Second, CPP contribution rates have begun to climb. They will increase more in the future in order to prepare for the baby boom retirees. Third, the labour force has begun to change. More seniors work part-time and share jobs today than ever before. People change employers many times as corporations downsize and new technologies

open up new industries. These changes will mean fewer private pensions even for people with a full work record.

Because of these changes, people in the future might work to a later age. And they may work in a job unrelated to their first career. Part-time work, second careers, and self-employment trends in later life already point in this direction. Schulz (1991) points to a growing tension between older people's desire for leisure and the future need for more workers. McDonald and Chen (1995) point to a labour shortage in the future.

Current data support this concern (Statistics Canada 2003u). Statistics Canada reports that the fields of education and health care will soon feel the "retirement crunch." About half the workforce in education will reach retirement age in 12 years, and half the managers in education will reach retirement age in nine years. Health care has a little more breathing room. About half the health care labour force will reach retirement age in 20 years. Statistics Canada goes on to say that the forestry, mining, oil and gas, and utility industries will face a wave of retirement in the next two decades.

A shortage of managers may likely develop in the near future. And this will take place throughout the workforce. Robson (2001) warns that employers and the government may need to revise policies that now encourage older workers to retire. McDonald and Chen (1995) argue for finding ways to keep older people in the workforce. This could include retraining workers for service-sector jobs and increased education so that older people can take on more administrative and management jobs.

At present, few opportunities exist for older worker retraining. Marshall (1995c) says that, compared to younger workers, older workers in Canada took fewer courses and got less training. Only Ontario and Manitoba have training programs for unemployed older workers. The federal government has no policy on training older workers and no training program targeted to them. This will have to change if Canada wants to keep older workers productive and in the labour force.

Myles (1984) notes that retirement as we know it depends on the **citizen's wage**, a government pension tied to age. Limits to this pension and on other government supports (such as free prescription drugs) would encourage older people to work. Likewise, flat incomes and many job changes during a work career will make it harder for a person to save for retirement. All of these trends suggest that people may work to later ages in the future.

But not everyone agrees with this prediction. Schulz (1991) warns that fewer younger workers may not produce more jobs for older people. For example, employers may turn to workers in other countries for many tasks. These employers can ship and receive data from the new workers electronically (Sheppard 1991). Also, employers may still see retirement as a way to decrease the labour force. "Given also the current rigidity of personnel practices, a lack of educational and training opportunities, and assumptions of declining productivity, the future may see these factors combine to create powerful barriers to employment of older workers" (Schulz 1991, 301). Schulz sees negative atti-

tudes of employers and workers' desire for retirement as the greatest barriers to work in later life. McDonald and Chen (1995, 87) see a "seemingly unwilling labour force engaged in a stampede to early retirement." Sheppard (1991, 293) believes that early retirement "may increasingly become a valued end in itself, a life goal." The desire to leave work and the existence of public and private pensions make retirement an attractive option for more people than ever before.

Summary

1. Most people want to retire, and they retire as early as they can if they have a good pension.
2. Some people want to continue working, and they have challenged compulsory retirement rules in court. The Supreme Court of Canada has supported compulsory retirement, except in provinces that prohibit it.
3. Arguments over mandatory retirement may suggest that most workers want to work past age 65, but studies show that if their health is poor or a good income awaits them, most people will leave work before age 65. People now accept retirement as a reward they have earned for years of work, and they want to collect that reward as soon as they can.
4. Canadians now have more choice about when they retire and what pattern of retirement they will follow. Some people take full retirement at age 65, others work part-time, and still others start second careers. In the future, older workers may have the option of flexible retirement. Social conditions (such as the economy, the availability of jobs, or a person's occupation) affect a person's retirement options.
5. A good income gives retirees the most options and the best chance to plan for and enjoy retirement. Professionals and people with good private pensions or savings have the most options.
6. The larger number of women in the labour force will lead to new theories of retirement and new research approaches. Women have different work careers than men. They often face social-structural barriers (such as low pay and broken work records) that lead to low incomes and few retirement options.
7. Retirement research has focused in the past on how individuals cope with retirement. A broader view of retirement links individual behaviour to social and economic inequities in society. More research needs to be done on the effects of gender, educational background, and socioeconomic status on retirement.

Study Questions

1. List the two perspectives that gerontologists use to study retirement.
2. Explain how the retirement principle and the retirement wage give rise to the social institution called retirement.
3. What conditions lead people to choose retirement?
4. Explain the two principles involved in the debate over mandatory retirement.
5. Why does the practice of mandatory retirement affect only a small number of people?
6. What developments have made early retirement possible for older people today?
7. Describe two alternatives to a fixed retirement age.
8. What social groups stand the most chance of being satisfied with retirement? What social groups usually opt to continue working past the normal retirement age?

9. Discuss the different effects of social and economic structures on men and women. How do social structures discriminate against women and lead to fewer options for women in retirement?

10. What social forces will shape retirement in the future?

Key Terms

bridge job a job that a worker takes on the path to retirement (often in work outside the individual's former career). (219)

citizen's wage a government pension tied to age. (227)

core sector the sector of the economy that includes the most stable, high-paying jobs and usually provides workplace pensions. (226)

flexible retirement an option that allows workers to slowly cut back the number of hours they work each week. (219)

free career a second career in a field that allows a person to explore previously dormant or undeveloped interests. (221)

periphery sector the sector of the economy that offers less stable, low-paying jobs with few, if any, fringe benefits, rarely including workplace pensions. (226)

retirement principle the idea that a person leaves work at a fixed age, regardless of mental or physical ability. (212)

retirement wage a pension paid by the state to support all older people. (212)

second career work that allows people to develop skills they did not use in their pre-retirement career. (221)

taxback taxes paid on earnings by recipients of the Guaranteed Income Supplement and provincial supplements, which can amount to a 100 percent reduction in supplement payments for the poorest older people who work. (217)

Selected Readings

Denton, F.T., D. Fretz, and B.G. Spencer, eds. *Independence and Economic Security in Old Age.* Vancouver: UBC Press, 2000.

A collection that contains articles on current issues and trends in retirement. Articles look at unexpected retirement, the role of the economy in retirement decisions, and options to traditional retirement.

McDonald, P. Lynn, and Richard A. Wanner. *Retirement in Canada.* Toronto: Butterworths, 1990.

This book discusses theories of retirement and the social history of retirement. The authors also look at how people respond to retirement. This is an excellent discussion of the way social structures influence individual experience.

Tindale, Joseph A. *Older Workers in an Aging Work Force.* Prepared for the National Advisory Council on Aging. Cat. No. H71-2/1-10-1991E. Ottawa: Minister of Supply and Services Canada, 1991.

This study begins with a look at demography and labour force trends. It then looks at a series of important issues related to retirement: the timing of retirement, the relationship of performance to age, and alternatives to a fixed retirement age. The author gives examples of innovative retirement options.

Chapter Eleven

Housing and Transportation

Photo © Ariel Skelley/CORBIS/MAGMA

INTRODUCTION

L ydia Wosk, 73, lives alone in her own home—a one-and-a-half-storey wood-frame house just outside the downtown core. She has only a half-block walk to the bus, and she goes downtown almost every day. Three times a week, she rides out to the university for classes. Lydia's husband died suddenly seven years ago of a heart attack. The loss left Lydia in shock. One Sunday, about six months after the funeral, her three sons and their wives came over for dinner. "Mom," her oldest son said, "we've been thinking. You don't need a house this big. And you're all alone. Why not move in with us? You could live part of the year with each of us so you wouldn't have to worry about being a burden on anyone."

"I knew what they were planning," Lydia says. "So I was ready. 'This is my house,' I told them, 'I own it. I paid for it. And this is where I'm going to stay.'"

Lydia's house gives her more than just a place to live. It gives meaning to her life. The wall over the TV, for example, holds pictures of her children and grandchildren. The couch and chairs all have hand-crocheted covers she made herself. She says the couch reminds her of the times she and her husband used to watch hockey together on Saturday nights.

A home allows older people like Lydia to feel more independent. Rutman and Freedman (1988, 24) studied older apartment dwellers and found that home meant "comfort, familiarity, security and independence." It was also a place where they had control and where they could express their individuality. "I love my home," one woman said simply in a letter to the Ontario Advisory Council on Senior Citizens (OACSC). "I live alone," another woman said, "but I am never lonely. I like baking, and my door is always open to visitors. I am never too busy to make them a cup of tea with a scone and black currant jelly" (OACSC 1978, 1980–81).

Not all older people need or want to live in a single-family house. Some older people live in apartments; others live with their children; still others live in enriched housing (where they can get help with meals and cleaning); and some live in rooming houses. The kind of housing that older people need and can afford depends on their health, marital status, income, and ability. A single-family house, for example, presents the most challenges (Kerr and Normand 1992). It demands good health, knowledge about home repairs, and enough income to pay for heat and taxes. An apartment demands less know-how and fewer worries about heating costs. People who are too frail to prepare their own meals can live in an apartment building with meals served in a common dining room. A nursing home cares for people too ill to care for themselves.

Canada's housing system today allows older people many choices about where to live. Housing options include private houses, apartments, congregate housing, homes for the elderly, and nursing homes. All these housing options have a place in the housing market.

This chapter will look at (1) the housing options available to older people, (2) the programs and policies that exist in Canada to help older people meet their housing needs, and (3) transportation systems that enable older people to keep in touch with their community and use the resources available to them.

AN ECOLOGICAL MODEL OF HOUSING

Lawton and Nahemow (1973) created an **ecological model** that describes the relationship between the older person and his or her environment. Their model describes the interrelation of two variables: individual capability (competence) and the demands of the environment (**environmental press**). Lawton and Nahemow define capability as the aggregate of a person's abilities, including health, psychological adjustment, and intelligence. They define environmental demand as environmental forces that, combined with need, lead a person to make a response (659).

People feel the most comfort when their capability matches the demands of the environment and they can fulfill their needs. Too great or too little environmental demand leads to a decreased feeling of well-being and a maladaptive response (see also Schooler 1990). A healthy person in a hospital bed, for example, will feel bored and lethargic because the environment demands too little. A person recovering from a stroke may feel fatigued after a 10-minute conversation because the conversation demands too much from him or her. The Lawton–Nahemow model says that people try to find a comfortable fit between what they can do and what they need to do to meet their needs (see Exhibit 11.1).

Parmelee and Lawton (1990) propose an updated version of the person–environment model. This revised model redefines the competence dimension as "autonomy" and redefines the environmental press dimension as "security." An autonomous person (one with high competence) can pursue goals with his or her own resources. He has freedom of choice and action. If a person has some disability, a secure environment (one with little press) can help that individual achieve his goals. A secure environment offers dependable physical

● **Exhibit 11.1**

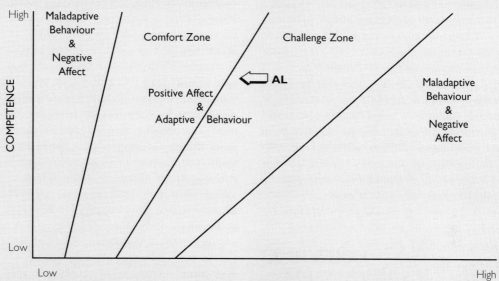

THE LAWTON-NAHEMOW ECOLOGICAL MODEL

The ecological model states that "when a person of a given level of competence behaves in an environment of a given press level," the result could be placed on a chart like the one above (Lawton 1980, 11). The chart shows the results of the fit between a person's competence and environmental press in terms of the person's behaviour and affect (feeling). The model shows that varied combinations of competence and press can lead to adaptive behaviour and positive affect. Likewise, the model shows that improvement in person–environment fit can take place on two dimensions: the person can move to or create a less demanding environment; the person can improve his or her competence; or the person can do both.

The chart also illustrates the following points:

1. The mid-point of the chart (AL) represents average press at a given level of competence. To the immediate left of the mid-point is the "comfort zone" where a person feels most at ease.

2. As press increases, adaptation takes place until the press goes beyond the person's ability to adapt (the right diagonal).

3. If a press decreases below the adaptation level, a person will feel bored and anxious (the left diagonal).

4. The "challenge zone" represents the points where press encourages the maximum use of a person's ability.

5. The greater the competence, the greater the adaptive ability; the lower the competence, the lower the adaptive ability.

6. No matter how high the level of competence, at some level of press the person will lose the ability to adapt. No matter how low the level of competence, the person still has some adaptive ability.

7. A person with low competence can be easily upset by even a small increase in press. But a person with low competence can benefit from even a small improvement in the environment (Lawton 1980).

Source: M.P. Lawton and L. Nahemow, 1973, "Ecology and the Aging Process," in C. Eisdorfer and M.P. Lawton, eds., *Psychology of Adult Development and Aging.* Washington: American Psychological Association. Copyright © 1973 by the American Psychological Association. Reprinted with permission. Courtesy of Lu Nahemow.

and social resources. Autonomy and security "form a dialectic that lies at the heart of person–environment relations in late life" (466). An increase in security—for example, a move to a nursing home—puts limits on a person's autonomy. Likewise, greater autonomy, such as driving a car, entails some risk.

Housing and transportation should maximize autonomy but provide enough security for a feeling of comfort. Loss of a spouse, changes in a person's informal supports, and illness may all lead to changes in a person's autonomy. And this in turn may lead to changes in housing needs. Some people will need help in order to feel secure. Help can include home maintenance, financial aid, and changes that adapt the environment to fit the person's level of autonomy. Housing options offer different balances between autonomy and security. The most suitable choice will depend on the older person's ability, which will also change over time.

The current approach to housing for older people in Canada focuses on **aging in place** (Haldemann and Wister 1992). This policy attempts to provide older people with environmental, social, and economic supports so that they can stay in their own homes. A recent study found an increased concentration of older people in suburban settings (Smith 1998) and advised that social planners should take this trend into account when they plan social services for older people. Planners may need to provide special transportation and services to people who age in place in suburbs. As Parmelee and Lawton (1990) point out, a move from one type of housing to another may offer the best autonomy–security balance.

This chapter uses the ecological model to look at the housing and transportation options that exist for older people. An ideal housing system would allow people to match their ability to the environment's demands. It would help them to stay where they are as long as they want to stay there, and it would allow a smooth movement from one setting to another when a change in a person's ability or needs makes a move necessary.

LIVING ARRANGEMENTS

Living arrangements refer to the type of household a person lives in.[1] These arrangements can include living in an institution, living with a spouse, living with grown children, living with relatives or non-relatives, or living alone. Older Canadians live in all of these arrangements,

but the proportion of people in each type of accommodation differs by age and gender.

Couples who live without children make up more than half of all senior households. Women who live alone make up another 33 percent of senior households (Canadian Mortgage and Housing Corporation [CMHC] 2002a). Three-generation households (many of them immigrant households) made up only 3 percent of all households in Canada (Che-Alford and Hamm 1999). Lindsay (1999) reports that, in 1996, 84 percent of men aged 65 to 74 lived with family members compared to 68 percent of women in this age group. Among people aged 85 and over, these figures drop to 69 percent of men and only 40 percent of women who live with family members. About 6 percent of people aged 65 to 74 live with relatives other than a spouse or child (Zukewich Ghalam 1996). About 7 percent of men and women aged 65 and over in 1996 lived in institutions. Of men aged 65 to 74 in 1996, 14 percent lived alone compared to 30 percent of women in this age group. For those 85 and over, 29 percent of men and 58 percent of women live alone (Lindsay 1999).

One of the most dramatic changes in living arrangements over the past several decades in Canada has been the increase in the proportion of older people, particularly women, who live alone (Lindsay 1999). Wister and Gutman (1997) report that between 1961 and 1991, the proportion of older women who live alone more than doubled. Wister (1985, 127) calls this an "unprecedented rise in single-person living among seniors." Béland (1987) reports that in Quebec the number of older people who lived alone more than tripled between 1956 and 1976, going from 5.6 percent to 19.1 percent. This change corresponds to a drop in the proportion of older people who lived with family members. Béland says that a decrease in the number of children older people might move in with may account for this trend. He also links the increase in people living alone to the norms of independence and autonomy. People who live with their children, he says, "are mostly women, very old, widowed, ill, and suffering from some functional incapacities" (797; see also Béland 1984b).

Hamilton and Brehaut (1992, 8–11) studied 75 single older women on Prince Edward Island who lived alone. These women report their desire for independence. "I mean, if you're independent," one woman says, "you want to stay independent." Many of the women in this study also report that they rely on family and friends to support them in their independence. "I feel quite independent," one woman says, "and that's due to my own family's care."

A study by Doyle (1994) in British Columbia also found that older women who lived alone enjoyed their

---

1. Statistics Canada defines a household as "a person or persons who occupy the same dwelling and do not have a usual place of residence elsewhere in Canada" (Norland 1994, 31).

● Exhibit 11.2

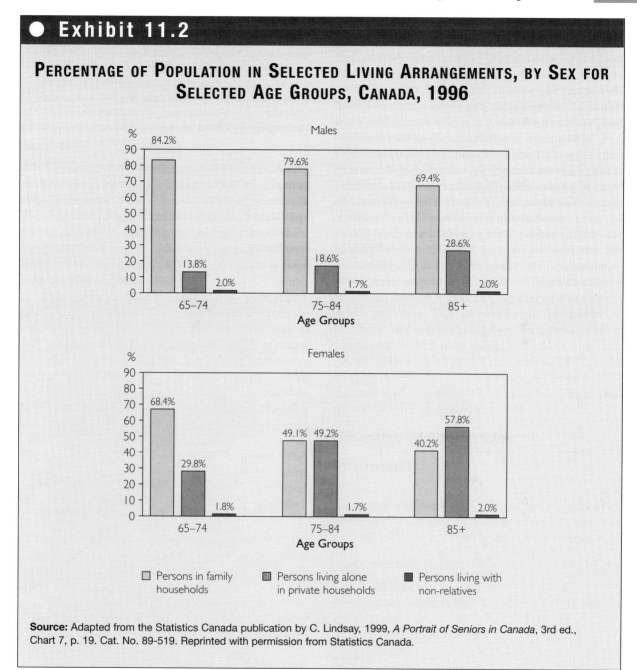

PERCENTAGE OF POPULATION IN SELECTED LIVING ARRANGEMENTS, BY SEX FOR SELECTED AGE GROUPS, CANADA, 1996

Males

Age Groups	Persons in family households	Persons living alone in private households	Persons living with non-relatives
65–74	84.2%	13.8%	2.0%
75–84	79.6%	18.6%	1.7%
85+	69.4%	28.6%	2.0%

Females

Age Groups	Persons in family households	Persons living alone in private households	Persons living with non-relatives
65–74	68.4%	29.8%	1.8%
75–84	49.1%	49.2%	1.7%
85+	40.2%	57.8%	2.0%

☐ Persons in family households   ☐ Persons living alone in private households   ☐ Persons living with non-relatives

Source: Adapted from the Statistics Canada publication by C. Lindsay, 1999, *A Portrait of Seniors in Canada*, 3rd ed., Chart 7, p. 19. Cat. No. 89-519. Reprinted with permission from Statistics Canada.

freedom. More than 88 percent of these women said that living alone allowed them to do what they want, when they want to do it. Doyle says that these women cared for others throughout their lives and now enjoyed caring only for themselves and felt "it's my turn now!" (43).

Men and women aged 85 and over who live in the community show even more dramatic differences in the tendency to live alone. Twenty-seven percent of men aged 85 and over lived alone in 1991. But 58 percent of women aged 85 and over (double the rate of men) lived

alone (Lindsay 1999). Between 1971 and 2001, the 85-and-over group showed the greatest increase in the tendency to live alone (Clark 2002).

Three things explain this trend toward women living alone. First, demographic changes and social norms make it more likely that a woman, rather than a man, will live alone in old age. In 1996, only 10 percent of senior men, compared to 46 percent of senior women, were widowed. And fewer widowed women remarry than widowed men (Lindsay 1999).

Social pressure works against remarriage for women. Also, social norms say that a woman should choose a man her own age or older when she remarries. At the same time, it is more socially acceptable that a man remarry a younger than an older woman (Veevers 1987). This convention leaves older women with a small pool of potential mates.

Second, better government pension plans and subsidized housing make living alone in a private household a viable option for more women today. Older women who live alone make up the largest group in subsidized housing (Blakeney 1992). Community-based health care supports also make it possible for older women with health problems to stay in their own homes, rather than move to a nursing home.

Third, a change in attitudes and values explains this trend. Connidis (1983a) found that most older people say they would rather not live with their children, and Wister (1985) found that older people prefer the privacy and independence that come with living alone. They prefer what Rosenmayr and Kockeis (1963) call "**intimacy at a distance**." (See Exhibit 11.3.)

A Statistics Canada report on women aged 55 to 64 shows that more older women may live alone in the future (Burke and Spector 1991). This study found that increases in divorce rates, low remarriage rates, and declines in the mortality rate have led to more women in the 55 to 64 age group living alone. These women, as they age, will increase the proportion of older women who live alone in the future.

● Exhibit 11.3

INTIMACY AT A DISTANCE

Many children and their elderly parents now share what Rosenmayr and Kockeis (1963) call "intimacy at a distance." Young people keep in contact with their parents. Parents and children visit each other, help each other, and keep in touch by phone and e-mail, but they rarely live with each other.

The National Advisory Council on Aging (1986) asked seniors living in a seniors' residence why they prefer to live alone. Here are some of their comments:

Albina Tenner:
When my doctor advised me that I shouldn't be living alone, my daughter was willing to have me move in with her, but I prefer the independence we have here.

Violet Smith:
My son lives in Toronto, and he used to worry about me, but now he knows that someone looks in on me every day. I looked after my mother-in-law for 14 years, and I decided that no one was going to go through that with me.

Hilda Tickell:
My son-in-law and grandsons are very supportive, but they respect my independence. They're only a phone call away if I need them, but I wouldn't want to be waiting around for them to call, nor would I ever want them to feel that they have to call. I have my own life to live.

Velma Would:
I lived with my granddaughter and her husband and that would have worked out except that I began to feel isolated because they were away at work all day. We didn't live close to public transportation, and I began to feel I couldn't get out, especially in winter. I decided to move here because I'm the kind of person who likes to have other people around.

These comments raise some important questions. How much of older people's desire for independence comes from their feeling that they do not want to become a burden on their children? And how much of their desire for independence reflects the fact that in modern society older people have no place in their children's busy lives? Intimacy at a distance helps to solve this cultural dilemma. It allows older people to keep in touch with their children, but without living with them.

Source: Excerpted from National Advisory Council on Aging, 1986, *Expression* 3(1): 3. Ottawa: National Advisory Council on Aging. Courtesy of the National Advisory Council on Aging, Health Canada, 2000.

This trend has policy implications. The Canada Mortgage and Housing Corporation (CMHC) says a person has core housing need if the housing is too small or in poor repair, or if the household spends more than 30 percent of its total income on housing. The CMHC (2002a) reports that 38 percent of women aged 65 and over who live alone have core housing need. This figure jumps to 55 percent of senior women who live alone in rented housing. The CMHC says that "the incidence of core housing need for these female-led households was higher than that for male-led households. The central difficulty in female one person ... households appears to be income, as the household incomes of each of these groups were well below the average for all comparable households" (7).

Unmarried older people also have smaller support networks than married people, and they rely more on formal health care services (such as home care) than do married couples. They may also neglect their health. Niewind, Krondl, and Lau (1988) report that people who live alone have less varied diets than people who live with others. People with less social contact also showed less use of nutritious foods such as vegetables. "The findings on dietary quality come as an additional argument for special attention to dental health and to the housing arrangements for the geriatric population" (45).

More single older people living alone will increase the demand for suitable apartment housing and better public transportation. Many older women who live alone have low incomes (Silver and Van Diepen 1995), and they will need housing alternatives such as supportive housing and home-sharing programs.

TYPES OF HOUSING

Single-Family Houses

Most homeowners want to stay in their own homes after they retire. In 1997, 84 percent of families with a head aged 65 and over owned their own home. And a large majority (71 percent) of these older homeowners live mortgage free (Lindsay 1999).

Home ownership differs across the country. Of all the provinces and territories, the Northwest Territories has the lowest proportion of seniors who own homes: 34 percent of those aged 65 to 74, and 42 percent of people aged 75 and over. Newfoundland, compared with the other provinces, has the highest proportion of homeowners among its seniors. Eighty-eight percent of people aged 65 to 74 and 83 percent of people aged 75 and over own their own homes in that province. Seniors have a higher proportion of condominium ownership

than any other age group. About 8 percent of seniors owned condominiums compared to 5 percent of people aged 45 to 64. People who live alone or couples without children find condominiums a good housing option because they offer an affordable alternative to a single-family home (Lo 1996).

Most older homeowners take good care of their houses. Only about 6 percent of families with a head aged 65 and over say their houses need major repairs. About 83 percent of these families say their houses need only regular maintenance (Lindsay 1999).

Older men, more often than older women, tend to live in single-family houses. Connidis and Rempel (1983) say that fewer women own their own homes because a woman often has to move out of a single-family home as she ages. First, when her husband dies she may have less money to spend on housing. Increased heating costs, maintenance, and taxes can all force a woman to sell her home and move into an apartment. "If I had the money, I would gladly stay here for the rest of my days," a woman in Prince Edward Island says, "but now that he's gone it's going to be a burden" (Hamilton and Brehaut 1992, 19). Another woman told Hamilton and Brehaut (1992, 21): "I don't heat all the house in the winter. I close all but one bedroom in the winter time and the bathroom. And I don't heat my dining room ... because your oil is so expensive and can't heat it all."

Second, women give up their homes because they know less about how to care for a home. "This is not to say that women are incapable of such tasks but rather that their patterns of socialization have not typically included the knowledge and practice necessary for a comfortable sense of mastery over them" (Connidis and Rempel 1983, 10). Older women say they lack knowledge about repairs, lack experience hiring trades people, and can't afford to hire people to do the work (Hamilton and Brehaut 1992). A number of programs in Canada work to help men and women stay in their homes.

Tax and Home Maintenance Programs

Older homeowners without mortgages live rent free, so they should have the most financial assets and they should have the least trouble paying for housing. But many older people have trouble keeping up their homes. They own large, older houses—most of them single-family, detached—that cost a high proportion of the owner's income to heat and maintain.

The federal government and the provinces help older homeowners through grants, loans, and tax rebates. British Columbia, for example, allows seniors who have lived in the province for at least one year to defer payment

● **Exhibit 11.4**

ALTERNATIVE TYPES OF HOUSING

The Canada Mortgage and Housing Corporation (CMHC) studied five alternative types of ownership for seniors' housing—life leases, equity co-ops, leaseholds, shared equity, and cohousing. These alternatives can help make housing for seniors more affordable. A CMHC report describes each of these options.

Life Leases. A life lease allows a person to live in a dwelling for life in exchange for an entrance fee (a one-time payment, usually about 30 percent of the total cost of the unit). Residents also pay a monthly payment to cover project maintenance and operating costs (Mancer and Kosmuk 1999). Non-profit community groups such as service clubs often sponsor life-lease projects. These groups often help with the ongoing management and operation of the project.

Life-lease projects admit people aged 55 and over. The first projects opened in Manitoba and Saskatchewan in the 1980s. About 200 life-lease projects exist in Canada today, most of them in Ontario and Manitoba (Mancer 2003). No life-lease projects exist east of Ontario. The Manitoba government has enacted legislation that protects the investment of seniors in life-lease housing. Other provinces, such as British Columbia, apply other real estate legislation to life-lease projects. Life-lease projects allow the resident to recover all or part of their payment when they leave the project.

Equity Co-ops. Members finance an equity co-op housing development. They use no government subsidies to finance their project. This type of housing began in the late 1980s. Eighteen equity co-ops exist in Canada—all of them in B.C., Alberta, and Quebec. Two-thirds of these equity co-ops serve the 55 and over housing market. This housing option works best where each owner has responsibility for their unit only (a condominium arrangement). That way if one member defaults the others are not responsible for the debt. This arrangement has encouraged the

development of equity co-ops in Alberta and Quebec.

Leaseholds. A leasehold gives a tenant right to use of the property, but the landlord holds ownership of the property. The property goes back to the landlord when the lease ends. Local governments often use the leasehold option to develop affordable housing for groups such as seniors. The land still belongs to the government, so that it can redefine the use of the land in the future. Private sector retirement communities also use the leasehold method. Leaseholds can lower housing costs because the landlord pays for and owns the land. The tenant then gets higher-quality housing for a lower cost (but has to give up the housing at the end of the lease).

Shared Equity. Shared equity offers another form of co-op housing. It provides affordable housing to lower-income seniors. These programs often take place in the inner city. Buyers can earn equity in their homes over a period of time. They can get this equity through a good payment record and by taking part in managing their project. The CMHC says that co-op members report extreme satisfaction with this type of housing. This stable housing option has allowed some people to move from social assistance to employment.

Cohousing. Cohousing refers to Collaborative Housing. People in this type of housing have their own self-contained unit, but share common areas such as a kitchen, laundry room, and children's playroom. Only five of these projects exist in Canada—four in B.C. and one in Ontario. People who choose this option report satisfaction with their choice.

Most people in these alternate types of housing say they feel very satisfied with their choice. They especially felt a strong sense of community. And in some cases the housing alternative allows them to own a home even though they may have a low income.

Source: Adapted from Canada Mortgage and Housing Corporation, 2003, "Alternate Tenure Arrangements," Socio-Economic Highlight 65, http://www.cmhc-schl.gc.ca/publications/en/rh-pr/socio/socio065.pdf, accessed on December 6, 2003. Reprinted with the consent of CMHC. All other uses and reproductions of this material are expressly prohibited.

of property taxes until they sell their home. At that time, they pay the outstanding taxes with interest (at below-market rates) out of the money they get for their home.

The federal government's **Residential Rehabilita-tion Assistance Program (RRAP)** offers loans to homeowners of up to $16 000 for people who live in southern Canada and $24 000 for people who live in far northern areas. Landlords can receive between $24 000 and $36 000 depending on a house's location. These loans help home-owners and landlords improve run-down housing. The government will forgive these loans if an owner remains in the home and if a landlord keeps rents low (CMHC 2003e).

The government also grants forgivable loans to land-lords and homeowners to adapt a building to seniors' needs. The loans cover costs up to $3500. Improvements include additional handrails, lever handles on doors, bathtub grab bars and seats, walk-in showers, and easy-to-reach storage areas. The CMHC (2003b) calls this the Home Adaptations for Seniors' Independence (HASI) program. The National Advisory Council on Aging (NACA) (2002b) proposes that the federal government increase this amount to $25 000 (part loan and part grant) to encourage the development of housing for seniors.

Some provinces also sponsor home repair programs that offer low-interest and forgivable loans to low-income older people. Many provinces also offer older people a rebate or tax credit on school property tax. These programs help some older people stay in their own homes. The programs focus on the neediest cases and on people with health or safety needs. They also focus more on home repairs, rather than on mainte-nance or structural adaptation to help people stay in their homes. Dunn (1997) reports that during the 1990s the federal government capped growth on social housing costs. It also reduced its commitment to new housing, including RRAP programs. These cuts limit housing supports at a time when the number of older people in the community continues to grow.

Home Adaptation

Studies show that the proportion of people with disabili-ties increases with age. Most older people in private house-holds report some limitations in mobility (walking and carrying) and agility (bending and stretching). Because climbing stairs can become difficult, some people close off the upstairs of their home and live only in the downstairs rooms (Hamilton and Brehaut 1992). People who want to age in place may need to adapt their current housing to support independent living. Fox (1995) reviewed findings from the Canadian Health and Disability Survey of people aged 55 and over. She found that about 38 percent of dis-

abled older people needed at least one design change to their homes, but 40 percent of them did not have the change they needed. People with higher incomes had a greater likelihood of having a needed design change.

The CMHC says that private and nonprofit housing companies have responded to older people's needs. Housing adaptation can take many forms. Universal design, for example, aims to serve people of all ages. Designers use lever door handles, low-threshold tubs, and temperature limits on hot water tanks to improve living for children as well as older people. Trickey et al. (1993) studied the modification needs of a group of older people in Montreal. The researchers found that almost half the modifications took place in the bath-room. They included grab bars and shower seats, the modifications most used by the people in the study.

Life-span housing, begun in Norway, puts all essen-tial rooms (the living room, dining room, kitchen, and bathroom) on the ground floor. The United States calls it "universal housing" and the United Kingdom refers to it as "Lifetime Homes." Canada uses the term "**FlexHousing**" to describe this kind of housing. This type of housing has no thresholds or steps. It provides easy access to all rooms of the house and can adapt to the needs of a person in a wheelchair. Details include easy-to-reach light switches and sockets, accessible furniture, non-slip flooring, and kitchen cabinets and appliances that can move up and down as needed on a wall bracket.

FlexHousing is based on four principles: adaptability, accessibility, affordability, and healthy housing (energy and resource efficiency) (CMHC 2003c). Older people can stay in their homes longer because a FlexHouse adapts to the older person's needs at a reasonable cost. The home can change again to meet the needs of a younger family when the older person sells the home.

Reverse Mortgages

Some older homeowners are asset rich but cash poor. They have equity in their homes but may find them-selves in a situation where they have, say, $150 000 in equity but not enough cash income to pay the gas or water bill. Reverse mortgages, known about but almost ignored in Canada, could give some of these older homeowners enough income to stay in their homes.

Several types of reverse mortgages exist. The most common plan is called the **Reverse Annuity Mortgage (RAM)**. In this plan an older person uses the house to secure a loan from a bank. The person then buys a life-time annuity from an insurance company with the loan. The insurance company pays the bank loan and pays the older person a set amount to live on for life. The older person can stay in the home as long as he or she wants. The bank takes over the house when the last survivor of a couple dies. This plan has at least one major limitation. The interest payments to the bank will go up if interest rates rise, thus reducing the older person's income.

Interest in reverse mortgages has grown. The Ontario Chamber of Commerce sees RAMs as "one of the hottest products around" (Kormos and Horton 1994). But not everyone will benefit from a reverse mortgage. For example, a reverse mortgage can add interest charges of 25 to 40 percent to the original loan. A $55 000 loan could pay a 70-year-old single man almost $6000 per year as an annuity (a yearly payment for life). This would amount to about $90 000 over 15 years. But at 11 percent, the RAM over 15 years would produce a debt of $274 117. The loan company would deduct this money from the sale of the house. In other words, the RAM would cost $274 117 less $90 000, or $184 117.

Some people will agree to this cost. They will choose to have more money now. Other people will find the cost too high. They may want to leave a larger estate to their children. People need to know the benefits and the costs of RAMs so that they can make informed decisions.

Apartment Living

The CMHC (2002c) reports that in 1996, 42 percent of seniors who lived in senior-led households lived in multiple dwellings (including apartments, semi-detached houses, row houses, and apartments in duplexes). This figure increases to 48 percent among people aged 75 and over. About 9 percent of men and 18 percent of women aged 65 to 74 and about 14 percent of men and 25 percent of women aged 75 and over live in high-rise apartment buildings (i.e., five or more storeys) (Wister and Gutman 1997). The proportion of older people who rent has increased from 23 percent in 1951 to 34 percent in 1991 (Silver and Van Diepen 1995). Older people often choose to move into an apartment when they can no longer care for a house.

People with good incomes can choose from a wide range of apartments: a high-rise or a low-rise, a two-bedroom suite with a balcony and a view, or an apartment near a bus route and shopping. Other older renters have to settle for less. Many people move to rental housing due to low incomes.

The CMHC (2002c) reports that seniors who rented their housing made up 64 percent of senior-led households in core housing need (i.e., the housing falls below a standard of adequacy—in good repair—or suitability—in size—and the household spends more than 30 percent of its total income on housing). And renters make up 70 percent of senior-led households that report affordability need. Lo and Gauthier (1995) say that 85 percent of older people with affordability problems received government payments as their main source of income. These figures show that many older people need rent support to ease the burden of housing costs.

The provincial governments offer several kinds of help to renters: property tax credits, school tax rebates, subsidized low-income housing, and shelter allowances.

● Exhibit 11.5

CASE STUDY OF REVERSE MORTGAGES

Few companies offer reverse mortgages in Canada, and few people know about them. But they may become more common in the future.

James Rogers, president of a company in Vancouver that offers one of the few Reverse Annuity Mortgage (RAM) programs in Canada, calls them a "reverse insurance policy." People collect the policy's payment in installments while they live and make one lump-sum payment (their house) when they die. Two examples will show how this plan works.

A man aged 65 who owns a $135 000 house joins the reverse mortgage plan. The plan allows him and his wife to live in the house rent free, and it also pays him $350 a month for life. If he dies before his wife, she continues to receive payments. The company gets the house after they both die.

What about younger people with less equity in their homes? A 60-year-old woman who has $100 000 in equity and joins the program is able to live in her home rent free until she dies. She also gets $260 a month for life. The house goes to the mortgage company when she dies. Lower interest rates and rising house prices today make this an attractive plan for mortgage companies.

Source: Mark Novak's notes, based on a Canadian Broadcasting Corporation production telecast in 1986.

Most provinces have built subsidized apartments for low-income seniors. Provinces have also built supportive housing. This type of housing provides social support services, safety, and a sense of community. Services include Meals on Wheels, housekeeping, and emergency response. It appeals to older seniors (aged 75 and over) with moderate to severe disabilities (NACA 2002b). Support for tenants with dementia, for example, may include social services (provided by local agencies) and education for staff and other tenants (Schiff and Gnaedinger 1997).

Some years ago, Ontario took the lead in supportive housing (sometimes called social housing) for older people in need. The province defines **supportive housing** as housing for people who need minimal to moderate care. People in supportive housing use services such as homemaking, personal care, and social support programs. This allows them to live independently (Ontario Ministry of Health and Long-Term Care 2004). Supportive housing can take many forms, from bungalows to high-rise apartments. The CMHC says that supportive housing should have five characteristics: (1) it should look and feel residential; (2) the physical environment should support seniors' needs; (3) it should offer access to needed services; (4) management should have a progressive philosophy; and (5) it should offer choice at a reasonable cost (Davis et al. 2000).

Supportive housing helps older people stay independent and in the community. It helps frail or disabled older people feel more secure. One tenant in Sydney, Nova Scotia, said, "It's like home. I have my own bedroom and furniture. My family doesn't have to worry." A resident in a Montreal high-rise complex said, "Everyone helps each other even if it means going to the corner store to buy a loaf of bread for someone" (Davis et al. 2000, 24–25).

Most of the other provinces, along with the federal government, offer aid to renters in low-income housing. These programs keep a person's rent at or below 30 percent of his or her income. Some provinces offer **shelter allowances** to older people. British Columbia, for example, sponsors a program called Shelter Aid for Elderly Renters (SAFER). The program provides help with rent to low- and middle-income seniors (NACA 2002b). Shelter allowances subsidize the person, not the housing project. They allow older people to choose their own apartment from those available in the marketplace. This policy frees people from having to move into government housing.

Zamprelli (1985) compared shelter allowances and low-income housing programs in Canada. He concluded that (1) shelter allowances offer an easy-to-use system to support older people. They give people more freedom to

choose the housing they want; and (2) low-income housing offers more control of housing quality, and government-subsidized housing can offer health and social services where people live. This can help many older people live in an apartment on their own, even if their health declines.

Both shelter allowances and subsidized apartments for seniors give low-income older people more opportunity to choose an apartment that meets their needs. These programs allow low-income seniors to live in affordable, high-quality housing.

Preferences in Apartment Living

No single type of housing fits all older people, but older people do prefer some types of apartments and neighbourhoods over others. Studies have looked at seniors' preferences for age-segregated versus age-integrated housing, high-rise versus low-rise housing, and normal versus special design.

Age-Segregated versus Age-Integrated Housing

A survey in Ontario found that 66 percent of senior respondents wanted neighbours without children, and that more than 64 percent of senior respondents preferred to live in a building among people their own age (Hough 1981).

A study by Lawton (1982) of 150 housing sites in the United States found that older people who lived in age-segregated housing showed more feelings of well-being. Hough (1981) reports that seniors accept age-integrated or mixed-age housing if the majority of tenants are seniors and if each age group lives in its own building. This allows the seniors to choose when and how often they want to interact with families.

Kaill (1980) concludes that people prefer building segregation because it gives them more control over their social contacts with other age groups. He adds that "this interpretation does not necessarily imply that older people do not wish to be in contact with younger members of the population, but simply that they wish to retain choice in the matter" (85).

High-Rise versus Low-Rise Housing

Canadian studies show that older people can and do adapt to high-rise housing. Gutman (1983) reports in one study that 52.8 percent of people living in a high-rise building preferred this type of building. She says that "where a trade-off is required between a high-rise in a 'good' location (i.e., close to public transportation and to community facilities and services) and a low-rise in a 'poor' location, the high-rise should be the structure of choice" (193).

Normal Design versus Special Design

Appropriate design can help people stay in their apartments even if they lose some abilities. It also creates a safer, more secure environment. "Design," a CMHC guide says, "can be a positive factor in stimulating effective employment of leisure time, the development of new roles, and a sense of purpose for those of advancing years" (CMHC 1978, 2). Gutman (1983, 187) says that "greater compliance with such guidelines would do much to improve the quality of units built for seniors while not substantially increasing construction costs." She found that older residents liked having easy access to public transportation and downtown services.

Older people also need space for meetings, lounges, coffee shops, places of worship, greenhouses, beauty parlours, and exercise rooms. Apartment housing in the past often ignored this need, but some new buildings now include extra public space. They also include recreation and entertainment programs that help people use the space.

Studies show that seniors choose the kind of housing that gives them both security and freedom. Béland (1984a, 184) says that "senior housing represents for [the] elderly a place where some protection is available, while enabling them to preserve personal autonomy."

Enriched Housing

Enriched housing, sometimes called sheltered or congregate housing, builds extra protection for the older person into the housing design. This type of housing gives people more social and health care support than they get in a normal apartment building. Minuk and Davidson (1981, 55) describe enriched housing as "a housing facility where supportive services (meals, housekeeping, medical services) are available on-site on a regular basis for a moderate fee." Baker and Prince (1990), in a review of the literature on enriched housing, conclude that all enriched housing includes a resident warden and an alarm system, and that most also include communal facilities such as a dining room and laundry rooms (citing Harper 1984).

The term "enriched housing" can apply to any type of housing. In Canada, it ranges from converted hotels that offer rooms and hot meals for single men to campus-like settings with high- and low-rise housing and many levels of health care. Havens and Bray (1996) report that 6274 non-certified facilities for older people existed in Canada in 1986 (about 8 percent of all resi-

dential care facilities). These settings go by varied names, including adult foster homes, board-and-care homes, and lodges. They offer little or no health care services. They provide meals and some supervision. Sometimes enrichment means only a lounge with a television set in an apartment building. More elaborate enriched housing includes lounges, shops, and, in some cases, clinics. Some buildings employ activity workers and program planners who show films and organize exercise programs and field trips for residents.

Alberta has a system of lodges run by senior citizen foundations. These lodges house from 15 to 122 people. A person in a lodge has his or her own living space, but shares space for meals and recreation. Residents may also share bathroom space. Lodges do not provide nursing care but do provide meals and housekeeping to residents. Lodge residents get home care services as they would if they lived in a single-family home or apartment—nearly half of all lodge residents get home care services (Borden and McGregor 1994). Lodges provide people with the freedom to live on their own and the supports they need to cope with decreased abilities.

In Great Britain, the Abbeyfield Society created a model of enriched housing that has spread to Canada (NACA 2002b); several towns in Ontario and British Columbia have Abbeyfield houses. The Abbeyfield model attempts to combat loneliness and serve people who live at risk in their homes. Most Abbeyfield houses, which often exist in large older homes in residential neighbourhoods, have six to ten residents and a housekeeper. Residents have their own rooms with a bath, but share in chores such as cooking. Some Abbeyfield houses provide extra care for people who cannot fully care for themselves. This type of housing appeals to older people who need support, but want to live in a home-like setting.

Hallman and Joseph (1997) studied rural residents' attitudes toward the Abbeyfield model. They asked key informants—local officials, housing managers, and seniors—to assess the Abbeyfield model. Key informants in small communities (under 5000 people) generally felt positive toward the model. Those in larger communities (over 5000 people) generally felt moderately supportive. Most of the informants thought it would be difficult to set up Abbeyfield housing in their community. The researchers say that Abbeyfield supporters would have to sell rural seniors on this option by convincing them that the Abbeyfield model would give them an alternative to staying put. Abbeyfield might succeed, the researchers say, in the smallest rural communities. In these communities, "small congregate housing projects are the only viable means of expanding housing choice" (101).

Critics of enriched housing say that it can lead to early dependency by giving people too many services and that it attracts sick or less able people. But studies have found more benefits than drawbacks to this kind of housing. Lawton (1976) found that people in enriched housing reported high morale and high life satisfaction. He says that proper planning can discourage dependence. In some cases, enriched housing can even foster independence, because it allows individuals to live on their own rather than in institutions. An alarm system for each apartment gives people a sense of security and can save a person's life in an emergency. But something as simple as "I'm okay" signs for door knobs in apartment buildings encourages neighbourliness. Enriched housing offers an important alternative to people who need support but who do not need the high levels of care given in a nursing home or hospital.

This type of housing can lead to unique problems, however. For example, the average age of residents increases over time as residents age. Some buildings that began with a mixture of age groups among residents 10 or 15 years ago now house a markedly older group, whose average age is 80 or older. This may compromise the self-government that exists in these buildings. (Enriched housing complexes could become high-rise nursing homes over time—see Exhibit 11.6.)

Wister and Gutman (1997, 31) report that the government built many apartment buildings during the 1960s and 1970s for "shelter only." These buildings contained mostly bachelor apartments with few amenities. Today, these buildings contain many very old and frail people. The emphasis on community care tends to keep them in the community. But these buildings and their apartments no longer suit their needs. And many of them lack space to allow for communal kitchens and other amenities. Today, Wister and Gutman (1997, 32) say, "it is unrealistic to think that a project can offer only shelter."

Apartment housing comes in many packages: high-rise, low-rise, public, private, nonprofit, age-segregated, age-integrated, without services, or enriched with services. Older people need this variety because their needs and abilities differ. They also need tax rebates, shelter allowances, and subsidized housing so that they can freely choose the housing that best suits their needs.

Rural seniors have special needs. About 41 percent of older people in Canada live in rural settings and small towns (Lindsay 1999). Joseph and Fuller (1991) say that while rural communities often have programs for young and frail older people, they lack a range of options for people who have varied needs for supports. Joseph and Fuller (1991) report that rural communities often lack options such as enriched housing for semi-independent seniors. Hallman and Joseph (1997) say that the small number of older people in rural communities limits the variety of housing options available. Zimmer and Chappell (1997) studied urban and rural older people in Manitoba. They found that both groups of older people valued three types of neighbourhood amenities: necessities (e.g., bank or food nearby); social interaction (e.g., friend or senior centre nearby); and life enrichment (e.g., park or library nearby). Rural older people, more often than urban older people, ranked social interaction as very important.

Hodge (1987) observes that where seniors' housing does exist, it often fails to meet design standards. He studied seniors' housing blocks in nine Ontario rural communities and found that "only two of the projects have more than 50 percent of the physical and architectural features considered desirable for senior citizen shelter care facilities" (149). The best project he studied had only 60 percent of the recommended desirable features. Projects lacked consistency in design, and many lacked safety features and aids to help people with their daily activities. Hodge also found that designers had placed many of the buildings in out-of-the-way locations, making it hard for seniors to use community resources. Some of the criticisms of design and location in this study would apply to urban housing for seniors too.

Keating (1991) reviewed the literature on rural older people in Canada. She found that, compared with all older people, they tend to live in older homes, have fewer services such as hot and cold running water and an indoor toilet, and face high maintenance costs. Joseph and Martin-Matthews (1993) report that rural households often lack housing basics such as piped water or amenities such as freezers and cars. The poorer the province, the more likely rural older people will live in poor conditions. Elders on Aboriginal reserves have some of the poorest facilities. Poor housing leads to poor health and decreased life satisfaction. Keating concludes that "rural elders are ... badly served. By all objective measures, rural elders have fewer amenities in their near environments than do their urban counterparts" (Keating 1991, 47).

NEW IDEAS IN HOUSING

Garden Suites

Granny flats, or **garden suites**, offer elderly parents a chance to live near, but not with, their children (CMHC

● **Exhibit 11.6**

THE SVENGALI OF SENIORS' HOUSING

Lions Place opened in August 1983 in Winnipeg. It has 18 storeys—16 for apartments and two for recreation space. When you come into Lions Place from Portage Avenue, you enter an open, sunlit two-storey foyer. A hotel-style front desk stands in front of you. Hanging plants filter the light from a glass-enclosed walkway above. On the right, stairs ascend to the second-floor balcony overlooking the entry hall. Behind this lounge stretches more than 5000 square feet of lounge space with card tables, soft chairs for reading or relaxing, and more plants. At the back of the lounge stands a two-storey humidified greenhouse where tenants can take classes in gardening and care for their own plants. The second floor includes a coffee shop, an exercise area, a glass-roofed walkway, a carpeted bowling alley, an arts and crafts room, and a billiard room. The exercise area has a whirlpool, sauna, and changing rooms.

The building houses people with a wide range of incomes. No one pays more than 25 percent of his or her monthly income for rent. Provincial rent subsidies help the poorest tenants. Other government subsidies help to run the building.

Lions Place looks and feels like a simple but well-equipped hotel. How do you build this kind of high-rise for older people in a time of government restraint and when the Canada Mortgage and Housing Corporation (CMHC) no longer has an interest in senior housing? And when the government allots only 200 new senior suites a year to the entire province of Manitoba? "You negotiate," Jake Suderman says with a smile.

Jake is Winnipeg's Svengali of senior housing, turning empty lots into comfortable high-rises for older people. Until he retired, he managed three buildings for the local Lions Club. And he is a master at outmanoeuvring bureaucrats and goading politicians to take action.

"We started out with $80 000 from the Barbara Bell estate," Jake says. He convinced the Lions Club board of directors to buy an empty downtown lot for $1 million. He then went to the CMHC to arrange a loan. Lloyd Axworthy, former member of Parliament and of the provincial legislature from Winnipeg's core area, also supported the project, which became part of Winnipeg's Core Area Initiative. The federal government allowed the Lions Club to build a 287-suite building by giving it suite allotments not used by other provinces.

With the basic plan approved, Jake started a new round of negotiations, this time over the size of the suites and the amount of lounge space. "What you can build," he says, "is dictated by land cost. The CMHC allowed $3500 per suite at that time, and then so many square feet for amenity space. Sometimes you have to embarrass them into changing the rules. I said, 'You're going to build three hundred apartments with *three* lounges? You're kidding? You're going to build a morgue here.'"

In the end, Jake got the lounge space he wanted. He also got bigger apartments and 12 empty rooms in the building just for future use as tub rooms. The building includes a geriatric and dental clinic that serves tenants and older people in the community.

Jake also added a staff that runs arts and crafts programs, physical fitness programs, day trips, guest lectures, theatre productions, gardening classes, and discussion groups. These programs keep people physically and psychologically fit. At least one staff member is there to deal with medical and other emergencies 24 hours a day.

"Tenants like their suites," Jake says. "But more than anything else they like the staff. In their old apartments, they only had a landlord or maybe a family that didn't care much for them. Around here we say, 'We're here just for you.' They know they can approach us. We get them involved—like in the auction or in the annual tea. And we make them feel at home. We let them have something to say."

1987). A granny flat most often exists as a separate building on the child's property. The building will sit in the backyard and will use the utilities attached to the child's home. A converted garage may also serve as a granny flat. This arrangement solves one of the dilemmas that some older people face as their physical abilities decline.

Connidis (1983a, 361, 363) asked 400 older people in an Ontario community a simple question: "If circumstances were to change and you had to choose between living with a child or in a facility for seniors, which would you prefer?" She found an "overwhelming tendency to choose a facility for seniors rather than living with children." A study in Regina supports Connidis's findings. It found that "only 8% of the sample indicated that they would move in with a child if they needed 'someone to keep an eye on them' (no health care) suggesting that the majority of seniors 'draw the line' at placing this type of demand on a younger family member" (Senior Citizens' Provincial Council 1981, 47; see also Okraku 1987).

The design of modern houses may have influenced these findings. Most modern houses have only two or three bedrooms and no room for another kitchen, bedroom, or bathroom to house an aging parent. In Australia, the state of Victoria created a housing option for older people that overcomes the problems of modern house design. They call this alternative a granny flat. It consists of a portable modular cottage for a parent. The government arranges to move the cottage onto a son's or daughter's property, then the government connects the flat to the electricity, sewer, water, and telephone services of the house. When the older person dies or moves to a nursing home, or if the family moves, the government takes the cottage away. This plan allows children to care for their parents as long as they can.

Lazarowich (1986) says that almost all moves to a granny flat start with an invitation from the older person's children. When a family does agree to set up a flat, the family—parents and children—need to talk about what they expect from one another. Most older people do not want to become 24-hour babysitters.

Australian-style garden suites may face trouble from local zoning laws and neighbours' attitudes. The suites increase population density in neighbourhoods and neighbours may feel that the units will lower property values. For this reason, these houses may work best in rural settings. The CMHC funded a pilot project to explore the issues that garden suites raise in Canadian communities. This study also suggests policies and methods for developing garden suites (Kinnis 1997).

In Vancouver, some families use duplexes and four-plexes the way garden suites are used. This overcomes some of the city's zoning and building problems. The older person sells his or her home and uses the money to help buy a duplex that houses both generations. The older person and younger family members share the taxes, repair costs, and any mortgage costs for the new property (Evans and Purdie 1985).

These new housing arrangements will lead to new social interdependencies and new challenges to family relations. What will happen if the older person's child

separates from or divorces his or her spouse? Or if the child moves to another city? Studies of these options will have to show that they make social as well as financial sense, and trial projects can answer only some of these questions. Only longer-term studies will show whether garden suites and granny flats can work in Canada.

HOMELESSNESS

Homeless older people stand at the far end of the housing continuum. They often live on the street and use shelters for night-time rest and some meals. Researchers consider homeless people over age 50 as seniors. Homelessness creates stress and leads to a poor diet and untreated health problems. A CMHC report (2003b, 1) says that "homelessness results in premature aging, with those at 50 looking and acting 10 to 20 years older." Homelessness also leads to lower life expectancy.

In 2002–03, two researchers studied homeless older people in Quebec, Ontario, Manitoba, British Columbia, and Yukon for the CMHC (CMHC 2003b). They found that people aged 50 and over make up 20 to 30 percent of homeless people who use shelters. Many of these shelter users suffer from alcoholism and addiction. But they also show a high rate of dementia, stroke, heart conditions, and incontinence. The researchers say that drug addiction leads to other problems such as hepatitis C, HIV/AIDS, and brain damage.

Older homeless people make demands on shelters that the shelters cannot meet. For example, shelters cannot offer help with activities of daily living or the need for bed rest. Also, many shelters cannot meet the needs of people with mobility problems. But the limited number of nursing home and hospital beds leaves the shelter as the only option. Many homeless older people also have antisocial behaviour (such as poor hygiene and the use of foul language) that makes it hard to move them to other care settings.

Supportive housing and assisted living programs sometimes serve homeless seniors. These programs provide a room, meal services, recreation, and health care programs. They do not offer 24-hour nursing care. Many professionals who serve homeless seniors say that downtown locations would serve this type of senior best. A downtown setting puts them close to day-care programs, food services, and health care centres. These settings should support healthy aging, reduce harm, and provide client-centred care. The CMHC (2003b) study provides a number of case studies of shelters in Canada that support the needs of homeless seniors.

TRANSPORTATION

A home has to suit an older person's abilities and meet his or her needs, but a house or an apartment becomes a prison if the older person cannot get to services, friends, and recreation. The Ontario Advisory Council on the Physically Handicapped (OACPH 1987) goes further. It says that "a community without transportation handicaps its residents. A transportation system which is not accessible or available to all residents handicaps the community" (1).

Public Transportation

Only a few studies have looked at the transportation needs and use patterns of older people in Canada. Most of these studies report that current systems fail to meet older people's needs (Joseph and Fuller 1991). The National Advisory Council on Aging (1985, 2) says that 11 percent of people aged 55 to 64 are "transportation handicapped"—either they have no public transport or they have trouble using it. This figure jumps to 34 percent for people aged 80 and over. And those who rely on others for transport often feel that they cannot meet their transportation needs (Cvitkovich and Wister 2001).

Rural and urban seniors have different transportation problems. Cities have services, but older people often cannot use them. A survey by the United Senior Citizens of Ontario (1985) found that seniors placed inconvenience first on their list of transportation problems. Rigid routes and schedules make it hard for older people in the suburbs to travel. In the winter, long waits for buses, icy sidewalks, or snow mounds at bus stops keep people housebound.

Rural areas often lack public transportation. Grant and Rice (1983) describe many rural seniors as "transportation disadvantaged." This group includes (1) people who feel lonely, dissatisfied, and without a confidant; (2) physically frail people over age 74 who never socialize outside their homes; and (3) low-income widows without a car or someone to drive them (see also Finlayson and Kaufert 2002). Enman and Rogers (2002) found that in Atlantic Canada a lack of transportation programs and professional care increases depression and decreases the ability to get help.

Hamilton and Brehaut (1992) interviewed women in Prince Edward Island who lived in rural settings. They complained about the lack of public transportation and about their dependence on others. One woman in a small town said, "I don't like the idea that you got to bum somebody to take you uptown now. As long as I had my eyesight I could walk. It's just down and up

around the corner. But now I can't walk and in order to go to get your medications, to get your cheques cashed ... you got to get somebody to take you." Another woman said, "I got no way of going anywhere. I gotta wait 'til some of the rest of them is ready to come and take me. It's too far off the main highway" (51–52). The researchers say that people who had their own transportation reported a higher quality of life.

Hodge and McKay (1992) observed that very few small towns have public transportation such as buses or taxis. But even seniors in towns that have a bus service seldom use it. When older people in five small British Columbia towns were asked about their use of the local bus service, only 22 percent of the seniors used the bus regularly and only 37 percent used it once a week or more. People in the study said the bus did not run on weekends or in the evening, it needed advance booking, and they had to wait a long time for the bus. People in these towns said they preferred a fixed bus route or a dial-a-bus option.

People in rural areas need more options. First, designers can place seniors' housing close to the downtown in small towns. Seniors could then walk to the services and shops they need. Second, in small towns transportation programs might include volunteer-run shuttle buses or car pools for seniors. Hodge and McKay (1992) found that about a quarter of older people in towns without buses said they would consider using a taxi voucher system (where a service agency pays the taxi fare for the senior). About a fifth said they preferred a shared taxi ride or a mobility club (a volunteer group where older people provide rides to other seniors—see below). Hodge and McKay (1992) say that rural older people need more options that include night and weekend bus services, volunteer drivers, and mobility clubs.

In the cities, most older people do not need special transportation services; instead they need to have existing services improved. Ninety percent of the transportation disadvantaged said they could use services that already existed if the services changed slightly. Suggested changes include well-lit subway stations, buses that adjust their height to suit passengers when they enter and leave, and clearer signage. These modifications would help people of all ages.

Finlayson and Kaufert (2002) studied the community mobility patterns of older women. They found that even in a city with good public transportation older people can feel limited in their mobility. For example, older women perceived buses and transfer points as risky. These women mentioned their fear of confrontation with beggars, vagrants, and teenage gangs. This led them to cope by carrying extra change for beggars or

● Exhibit 11.7

A TYPOLOGY OF TRANSPORT LIFESTYLE GROUPS

A   Independent, Own Auto—people with the money and physical ability to drive their own car and live alone; most mobile seniors. Finances and physical ability impose major limits on car use. This group may switch to other means of transportation as they age.

B   Dependent, Access to Auto—people who live with others (mostly for financial reasons) with their own car; less mobile.

C   Independent, No Auto—have money and independence but may not be able to afford many options such as car rental, taxis, or buses.

D   Dependent, No Access to Auto—live with others; no auto; much less mobile.

E   Sheltered or Group Housing—some physical and economic dependence; can meet transportation needs because of group setting.

F   Disabled—all income types; have some physical disability and need special transit programs such as those used by disabled non-seniors.

G   Institutionalized—poor health; others care for needs; have the least unmet mobility needs (because the institution meets their needs).

Individuals vary in their physical ability, their income, and the support they get. Each lifestyle group has its own transportation needs. More transportation options will give all older people more freedom and independence.

Source: Adapted from Ontario Ministry of Municipal Affairs and Housing, Research and Special Projects Branch, 1983, *Towards Community Planning for an Aging Society,* Toronto: Queen's Printer for Ontario, 7. Copyright © Queen's Printer for Ontario, 1983. Reproduced with permission.

avoiding travel at night. Some women also mentioned their fear of falling on ice or snow. The researchers say that "community mobility is dependent to some degree on risk perception, and ... this perception is closely associated with time of day and weather" (82). Limits to mobility (whether due to lack of transport or fear of trouble) can reduce an older person's independence. One woman described her own view of mobility independence:

> Woman: "Well, really a car is independence to me. And independence is important to me because independence is power."
> M.F. "How is independence power?"
> Woman: "Because then you do what you want to do. It's doing what you want to do, when you want to do it. And that's power. It's the power to move around when you want to." (82)

Private Transportation

Older people, like younger people, prefer auto travel to other forms of transportation (Atkinson 1991). Approximately 70 percent of Canadians aged 55 and over have a driver's licence (NACA 1999d). Ninety per-

cent of people in older families and 49 percent of older unattached people own their own vehicle (Lindsay 1999). And more older people will drive in the future as lifelong drivers reach retirement age (Bess 1999).

People in rural areas rely heavily on cars and trucks. Small towns often lack other forms of transport and people often live far from friends and shopping. Statistics Canada reports that almost 20 percent of rural seniors live more than a half-hour from a grocery or convenience store; only 5 percent of urban seniors live this far from shopping. Sixty percent of rural and small-town seniors drive their own vehicles compared to 46 percent of urban seniors. Most older people wherever they live use their vehicles for daily needs such as shopping and personal appointments (Bess 1999a).

This increase in senior drivers raises some new transportation issues. First, older people who drive will have to include the rising cost of auto insurance and maintenance costs in their budgets. Statistics Canada's 1996 Family Expenditure Survey found that urban seniors spent between 8 percent and 12 percent of their total budget on their cars (Bess 1999a). Rural seniors spent about 17 percent of their total budget on their cars. Second, older people in high-rises and downtown apartments will need parking spaces for their cars. Third, older people have health problems that may affect their driving. For example, about 16 percent of people between the ages of 65 and 69 have pain severe enough to interfere potentially with their driving. Arthritis and rheumatism may limit a person's ability to steer and respond to emergencies. Research shows that older people take multiple medications that may interfere with their driving ability (Bess 1999a).

Many older people take their health condition into account when they drive. They may drive less often, avoid night driving, and stay off highways. Some people stop driving before functional problems lead to an accident or injury. Still, people over age 60 have more accidents and more fatalities per distance driven than middle-aged (40- to 60-year-old) drivers (Evans 1988). Also, older drivers (aged 60 and over), compared with younger drivers, have more multi-vehicle accidents and stand a greater chance of a serious or fatal injury (MacDonald 1989). This has led the Canada Safety Council to set up a program called the "**55 Alive Mature Driving Program**." This program helps seniors improve their driving skills and teaches them how aging affects driving.

Some people have suggested special driver's licenses for daytime-only drivers and non-highway driving. Charness (1993) suggests that smart cars (with automatic guidance systems), head-up instrument displays projected on the windshield, and night vision technology make driving easier. Transport Canada has sponsored research to test infrared monitors and audio warning systems in cars. These systems may help older drivers keep track of other cars, traffic lights, and pedestrians (Blackwell 2002). Research needs to see whether they also reduce accidents.

The rising number of older people with Alzheimer's disease also poses problems. The Alzheimer Society of Canada (1990, cited in National Advisory Council 1993d) reports that 30 percent of people with Alzheimer's disease still drive. More than three-quarters of these drivers said they had no problem with driving. And over one-quarter of their caregivers thought they had no problem. Still, the Alzheimer Society reports that, over a five-year period, 47 percent of these drivers had an accident. Families often agonize over when to stop a person with dementia from driving. Doctors play a key role in helping a family to make this decision. The Dementia Network of Ottawa produces a Driving and Dementia Toolkit. This toolkit helps doctors assess a person's ability to drive if he or she has some dementia. It also provides doctors with information about referral centres and other help for families (Byszewski 2002).

Some provinces monitor the ability of older drivers. Ontario requires that drivers aged 80 and over take written and road tests each year. Alberta requires drivers aged 75 and over to produce a medical report that says they can drive. Drivers have to renew this medical clearance at age 80 and every two years after that.

An aging population raises new issues about the right to drive. For example, some studies show that accident rates increase with age (especially past age 74) (Daigneault, Joly, and Frigon 2002). But this same research shows that age alone cannot predict a person's driving ability. Millar (1999, 68) says that "decisions about licensing people with age-related disorders should be based on functional measures rather than on diagnostic labels. Older drivers are not a homogeneous group, and there does not appear to be a predictable pattern of risk." Regular testing of the older person's abilities (past age 75) can help keep unsafe drivers off the road. Education and training can improve older drivers' abilities. Technology can make roads and cars safer for drivers of all ages. Policies and practices need to balance safety concerns and the older person's need for mobility (NACA 2002–03).

New Transportation Needs and Programs

Transportation needs for older people in the future will go beyond current use patterns. New programs may rely on technological change and on new forms of social organization. Older people will run some of these programs themselves. One program in Edmonton, referred to as a **transportation brokerage**, matches passengers with services that meet their needs. In Moncton and the Acadian peninsula, a **mobility club** helps people in small towns and rural areas. This club formed a nonprofit, self-help transport service. People with cars call in to tell a dispatcher about trips they plan to make in the next week or so. People who need rides call a day before they have to take a trip. A dispatcher matches riders with drivers. Drivers also volunteer for up to one emergency trip per month (Grant and Rice 1983).

Joseph and Martin-Matthews (1993) see volunteer programs as a response to decreases in government support and expect there will be more reliance on volunteer transportation programs in the future. Some model programs already exist. Rural communities may need to combine a number of options to serve their older people.

THE FUTURE OF HOUSING AND TRANSPORTATION

Given the choice, older people say, they want to live in the community. But low income, poor health, and a lack of support often make community living hard. Older people see the loss of ability as the greatest threat to their independence and to their personal growth (Mack et al. 1997).

New technology will improve housing for older people and allow more people to age in place. New technologies include low-tech solutions such as countertops that can move up and down to suit the user and barrier-free floor plans. More sophisticated technologies include robotic arms that respond to a user's voice. They can take food out of a cupboard, pour a drink, or put food on the table. Other countries have developed electronic homes with electric door-openers and locks, remote-control window shades, and voice-activated appliances (CMHC 1992). Some of these devices already exist in Canadian homes and may become standard in the future.

Studies of supports for older people suggest ways to improve housing and transportation. For example, often different providers deliver housing, transportation, and social and health care services to older people. Different policies govern these systems, and they sometimes lack coordination. A number of studies suggest that seniors would benefit from an integration of these systems (Baker 1994; Brink 1994). Kelley and MacLean (1997) say that, compared to city dwellers, rural older people face greater challenges in meeting their home maintenance and transportation needs. These researchers propose increased case management services to help older people get and manage resources.

Blandford, Chappell, and Marshall (1989) describe a program that links seniors' housing to existing community services. In this program, tenant resource coordinators (TRCs) were placed in seniors' housing. The TRC provided tenants with information about community services and also coordinated services for tenants (e.g., grocery delivery or friendly visitors). The researchers found that the TRC placements led to improvements in services for seniors and increased dissemination of information about services to tenants. This type of support can help older people get the services they need at a modest cost to owners and managers.

A report titled *Freedom to Move Is Life Itself* presents a variety of proposals that would improve transportation services for older people. The proposals range from changes in technology (easier automobile entry, better bus shelters, special traffic lights) to supportive social arrangements (use of volunteer drivers, developing

transportation regions with varied services in each region, conducting research on transportation needs and options) (OACPH 1987). Joseph and Fuller (1991) call for an integration of housing, service, and transportation policies to meet the needs of seniors (especially those in rural settings). This type of integration would help seniors maintain their autonomy and receive the type of support that best meets their needs.

Haldemann and Wister (1992) reviewed the literature on housing in Canada over the past 30 years. They found that government policies play a large role in creating housing options for older people. Policies range from tax relief, to rent subsidies, to support for reverse mortgages. These policies often provide support that makes it possible for rural older people to stay in "small, difficult-to-service communities" (Joseph and Martin-Matthews 1993). Public policy has tried to provide available, high-quality programs to both rural and urban older people. But cutbacks in funding could change these policies. Joseph and Martin-Matthews (1993) say that cutbacks in services could leave rural older people without the support they need. Research on housing and transportation policy can track the effects of policy changes on older people. This research would look at ways in which government policy can support housing for different older people, including policies targeted to help married and single, middle- and low-income, and urban and rural seniors.

What will the future of Canadian housing for seniors look like? No one can say for sure. But current trends suggest some new developments in seniors' housing. First, members of the baby boom generation will redefine seniors' housing needs as they enter old age. This group, unlike past generations of seniors, will enter old age with pensions and housing equity. They have already surprised housing pundits. People expected baby boomers to downsize their housing (to condominiums and townhouses) as they aged. But many of them have taken the equity from their mid-life homes and bought bigger homes. Likewise, many have bought vacation homes that may serve as their retirement homes in the future. Baby boomers often buy new homes, which may create a demand for new construction (CMHC 2002b).

Second, as this group ages, people may eventually move into condos and townhouses. This could lead to a decline in the need for single-family housing. This decline could affect different parts of the country differently. The Prairies, for example, may see a decrease in their younger populations, with fewer young people available to buy the homes of downsizing baby boomers.

Third, new types of housing options have begun to emerge. FlexHousing, for example, provides a multi-generational option. An older couple or person could help finance the home and would live in the home (in a separate apartment) with their adult children. Other options such as a prefabricated apartment that fits into a garage may offer another option to multi-generational living. Baby boomers have many housing options available to them as they age. These options will range from smart homes, to retirement communities, to supportive housing.

CONCLUSION

People can cope with environmental demands in several ways as they age. They can maintain or improve their abilities (through self-help or rehabilitation). Or they can change their environment (by modifying their homes, moving, or getting help through changes in social policy). Most older people live in a few types of housing. Younger old people, couples, and widows and widowers tend to live in their own houses and apartments. As people age, they need more support to maintain their independence. This chapter has focused on the policies and programs in Canada that help older people live in an environment that suits their abilities. This review shows that with some help most older people can live high-quality lives in their own homes and apartments into late old age.

Summary

1. Research on housing and transportation shows that older people enjoy old age most when they feel in control of their environment. People can maintain this control by changing their environment (for example, moving to an apartment from a single-family home or getting help through social policy reform).

2. A good match between a person's ability and environmental demand leads to high life satisfaction. An ideal housing system offers older people a range of housing choices because people's needs differ. People should be able to move from one type of housing to another—from a house to an apartment or enriched housing—as their needs change. Or they should be able to get support to help them stay where they are.

3. Most older people want to stay in the kind of housing they now occupy. Government policies and programs—such as rent subsidies, tax rebates, and repair loans—help older people stay where they are. Other programs—such as loan guarantees, new building programs, and shelter allowances—allow older people to move to the kind of housing that suits their needs.

4. Canada offers older people a wide range of housing options. These include single-family homes, apartments, enriched housing, and multi-level enriched housing. New types of housing—like garden suites and multi-generational housing—will increase seniors' housing options in the future.

5. More older people than ever before, especially women, live alone. Fewer older people live with family members. People who live alone may need more formal supports to live on their own as they age. This could put more pressure on formal services in the future.

6. Both urban and rural older people value three types of amenities: necessities, social interaction, and life enrichment. Compared with urban older people, rural older people have the poorest facilities and fewest amenities available. Rural older people also ranked social interaction as very important.

7. Good transportation links older people to their communities—to services, recreation, and friends. But both urban and rural transportation systems need improvement. Most older people in cities could use the transportation that exists if it were modified to suit their needs. Poor lighting in subways, snow along bus routes, and rigid schedules make urban transportation systems unsuitable for many older people.

8. Rural seniors often have no available transportation, but new programs in rural settings include bus services shared by a number of small towns, volunteer bus services, and people who pool their resources to help one another get around. Older people in rural settings have begun to set up the transportation services they need.

9. Good housing and transportation lead to increased life satisfaction for older people. An environment that fits the person's abilities helps keep older people satisfied, active, and in touch with their community.

Study Questions

1. Describe the ecological model of housing. When does a person feel the most comfortable according to this model?

2. Explain the current government policy regarding housing for older people in Canada. How does the government's policy differ from the ideal housing system?

3. Define the term "living arrangement." What types of living arrangements are available to older Canadians?

4. Why do many older women opt to live alone rather than with other family members? What conditions make this trend possible?

5. Explain the different types of housing that are available to older people today. What kind of people are likely to live in each type of housing?

6. What types of housing designs do seniors prefer? Why? What are the benefits of appropriately designed houses for seniors?

7. List and describe some of the new alternative types of housing that older people can choose today.

8. Describe the major transportation issues raised by an increase in senior drivers.

9. Describe two programs now available to help older people meet their transportation needs.

Key Terms

aging in place the situation of older people living into late old age in the same place they lived in their middle years. (234)

ecological model the Lawton–Nahemow model of interaction between the individual and the environment that holds that a person's ability and the demands of the environment influence that person's life satisfaction and ability to function. (232)

enriched housing housing that provides services such as meals and cleaning services to help people live on their own. (242)

environmental press the demands of the environment on a person. (232)

55 Alive Mature Driving Program a program that helps seniors improve their driving skills and teaches them how aging affects driving. (248)

FlexHousing a housing concept that designers and builders use to make future changes in housing easy and affordable in order to meet the changing needs of people as they age. (239)

garden suite or **granny flat** part of a house made into a self-contained unit for an elderly relative. In Australia, a granny flat refers to a small, portable cottage erected in the garden of an adult child's house. (243)

intimacy at a distance the desire of many older people to live near, but not with, their children. (236)

mobility club a volunteer group of older people who provide rides to other seniors. (248)

Residential Rehabilitation Assistance Program (RRAP) a federal government program offering loans to low-income people to help them improve run-down housing. (239)

Reverse Annuity Mortgage (RAM) a type of reverse mortgage whereby a person buys a life annuity and gets an income while living in the home and the mortgage company takes over the house when the person dies. (239)

shelter allowances government allowances that subsidize the person, not the housing project, and allow older people to choose their own apartment. (241)

supportive housing housing for people who need minimal to moderate care and use services such as homemaking, personal care, and social support programs (241)

transportation brokerage a program that matches passengers with transportation services that meet their needs. (248)

Selected Readings

Gutman, Gloria, ed. *Shelter and Care of Persons with Dementia.* Vancouver: Gerontology Research Centre, Simon Fraser University, 1992.

This collection describes a variety of programs and housing designs for people with dementia. Some of the authors describe and evaluate special-care units for dementia patients in institutions. Other authors describe innovative designs—such as wandering tracks—that respond to the needs of dementia patients. Finally, a number of authors discuss ways to care for dementia patients in the community. This collection provides insights into the needs of dementia patients and provides many examples of creative responses to their needs.

Rodriguez, Luis. *Canada's Response to the Housing Needs of Its Aging Population.* Ottawa: Canada Mortgage and Housing Corporation, 1997.

The author prepared this report for the World Congress of Gerontology in 1997. It reviews housing policies and programs that serve older Canadians. The author also summarizes the Canadian government's housing research and demonstration projects. A good overview of senior-related housing activity in Canada.

Chapter Twelve
Leisure, Recreation, and Service

INTRODUCTION

Dan Kreske worked as an insurance agent until he retired six years ago. He had a good income from his investments, savings, and Canada Pension Plan. He heard about free university classes and started to attend. Now he goes to class two or three afternoons a week (depending on the courses offered). He has also renewed his interest in athletics. He played golf all through his working years, and he jogged and swam, but in retirement he found he had more time to develop his ability. Recently, he competed at Lake Placid, New York, in the Masters Division of the North American Speed Skating Championships. He made two third- and two fourth-place finishes and won 10 points for his team. "I lost to guys 25 years younger than I am—it was one of the greatest thrills of my life," he says.

Many older people like Dan Kreske continue to develop established skills and talents in retirement. Other older people discover new interests when they retire, or they discover a talent for poetry, acting, or art. Still others turn to community service, or they may start to do volunteer work in a hospital or senior centre part-time.

Seniors today have more opportunities for self-development and community service than ever before, and many of them have a great desire to develop themselves and give to others as they age. For many older people, the years after retirement become a time of search, discovery, and fulfillment. This chapter will review some of the programs and activities that help seniors live a satisfying old age. This chapter will look at (1) how seniors today spend their time, (2) new personal development programs for seniors (recreation, fitness, and education), and (3) seniors' community involvement.

WHAT DO OLDER PEOPLE DO?

Only a handful of studies in Canada have looked at what older people do every day. Mostly they show that, in the absence of work, older people use their time for leisure and recreation.

Retired men and women, for example, report more free time than any other age group (Harvey, Marshall, and Frederick 1991). Older people use this time to engage in a variety of social activities, including participation in political or charitable organizations, or in neighbourhood, community, and school groups. They also eat in restaurants, take walks, and visit family and friends (Lindsay 1997). Older men and women say they spend about two hours per day socializing (about the same amount as younger people). Unmarried older people, who live alone, report spending the most time socializing (Lindsay 1997).

Nearly half of older people (over 1.5 million seniors) say they take part in a religious activity at least once a month (Lindsay 1999). But research shows that compared with younger people, they spend more of their time on solitary activities and at home (Harvey, Marshall, and Frederick 1991). Statistics Canada's General Social Survey found that people aged 65 and over spent about 14 percent more time on personal care (including sleep) than people aged 15 to 64 (Lindsay 1997).

The General Social Survey reported that, of people who watched television, men and women aged 65 and over watched more than younger age groups (Lindsay 1999). Women aged 60 and over, in 1997, watched TV an average of 5.2 hours per day and older men watched an average of 4.6 hours per day. McPherson (1983) says that TV helps structure time for people who live alone. An older person may watch a morning talk show over breakfast, eat supper with the evening news, and go to sleep after the national news. Some people schedule their days around the afternoon soap operas.

Statistics Canada also reports an increase in VCR ownership. In 1983, 2.3 percent of households headed by someone aged 65 and over owned videocassette recorders. This figure increased to 79 percent of senior-headed households by 1997. About 28 percent of senior-headed households in 1997 owned a compact disc player (Lindsay 1999).

Older people also spend a lot of time reading. Statistics Canada (1989b) reports that over 90 percent of senior couples and about 80 percent of unattached seniors buy reading material. Kinsley and Graves (1983, cited in McPherson and Kozlik 1987) found that people aged 65 and over spent almost an hour and a half per day reading—compared with only 22 minutes for 15- to 17-year-olds and 45 minutes for 25- to 44-year-olds.

All studies on leisure activities show the same trend: Older people spend most of their time on passive, media-related leisure. They spend a lot of this time alone. Men aged 65 and over in 1998 said they spent on average 6.5 hours a day alone. Women in that year said they spent 8 hours alone. Widowed seniors spent on average over 10 hours a day alone (about twice as much time alone as married people) (Clark 2002). The 1998 Canada General Social Survey found lower rates of reported happiness among seniors who live alone and who spend more time alone. Seniors also spend a lot of time indoors with friends and relatives (Horgas, Wilms, and Baltes 1998). When older people do take part in outdoor activity, the activities usually demand little exertion (such as walking or gardening).

Compared to younger age groups, seniors spend more of their time resting during the day. Lefrançois and his colleagues (2001) studied the leisure activities of 224 people aged 80 to 85 in Quebec. They found that this group engaged less in physical and intellectual activities. They most often engaged in emotional, spiritual, and social activities. A decrease in their physical condition during the year of the study had the greatest negative effect on their activities. Decline in instrumental activities of daily living affected all types of activities (not just physical activities). The researchers found that people substituted less demanding activities as their ability declined.

Strain and her colleagues (2002) conducted one of the few longitudinal studies of seniors' leisure activity. They studied 380 people aged 60 to 85 in Manitoba. Two-thirds were women and two-thirds were married. They looked at whether a person continued or dropped an activity between the years 1985 and 1993. In 1985, they found the most participation in watching television (99.5 percent), reading (95.8 percent), and shopping (93.2 percent). They found the least participation in church services/activities (66.1 percent), playing cards (64.7 percent), and going to the theatre/movies/ spectator sports (58.9 percent). They found that over the eight-year period of the study nearly all people in the study continued to watch television (93.1 percent) and read (91.2 percent). More than half (55.4 percent) of those who went to the theatre, movies, or a spectator sport had stopped that activity.

Strain and her colleagues (2002, 220) found that "being younger, having more education, rating their own health as excellent/good, and having no ADL/IADL limitations in 1985 were associated with a greater likelihood of continuing more activities." People who maintained their health and who remained married also showed the greatest likelihood of continuing their activities. This study supports the findings of other research (Lefrançois et al. 2001).

Strain and her colleagues say that a change in functional ability over time has a strong impact on whether a person continues participating in leisure activities. People may reduce their activity as their function declines. They may adapt their leisure activity to their declining ability. Or they may focus on fewer activities (Horgas, Wilms, and Baltes 1998). Menec (2003) studied people over a six-year period. She found that people who took part in solitary activities (such as reading or handiwork) or in social activities (such as visiting friends)

reported feeling happy and interested in life. But those who took part in social activities also showed decreased mortality rates and less functional decline.

Seniors are also travelling within Canada more often than they did in the past. In 1997, seniors made an average of just under three trips per person within Canada—this is almost a full trip more per person than in the early 1980s. Furthermore, seniors made an average of 0.6 international trips per person in 1999 (Health Canada 2001d). Lehto, O'Leary, and Lee (2001) found that older travellers look forward to good weather, new foods, and shopping for local crafts. The researchers found that travellers fit into three clusters—eco-tourists, female enthusiasts who wanted to meet people, and people on a budget who want relaxation.

Older people as a group show some common approaches to the use of their time. They often engage in socially satisfying, non-demanding, non-strenuous activities. Foot and Stoffman (1998) agree. They project a declining interest in vigorous sports (hockey, downhill skiing) among older people in the future. This appears to support the disengagement theory of aging.

Other research questions this pessimistic conclusion. Studies show different activity preferences among different types of seniors. Income, region, and social status all influence what an older person chooses to do. Those with low income and little education and those with high income and a university degree show the lowest involvement in popular culture activities (such as watching TV, listening to music, going to movies, engaging in crafts, and reading newspapers). People with middle incomes and either a high-school diploma or some secondary education show the most involvement in popular culture activities. People with university degrees tend to read more books than other groups (McPherson and Kozlik 1987). "Even within the same age cohort life chances and lifestyles vary because of differences in social status" (115).

Other studies in Canada show that, compared with seniors in Eastern Canada, those in the West report more physical activity and more involvement in sports (Curtis and McPherson 1987). Also, higher income and more education lead to more active leisure. Mobily and his colleagues (1995) found that older people's activities varied by season. Not surprisingly, cold weather led to decreases in outdoor activities.

Studies also show that gender influences activity level. Zuzanek and Box (1988) report that women, more than men, say they take part in visiting, religious activities, reading, bingo, sewing, and shopping. Men, more than women, say they take part in sports, outdoor activity, gardening, visiting pubs, do-it-yourself projects, and auto repairs (see also Lefrançois, Leclerc, and Poulin 1998). In general, women spend their free time on expressive social activities, while men spend theirs on passive media consumption and competitive or repair-related activities (Harvey, Marshall, and Frederick 1991). Researchers say that traditional male and female roles shape leisure activities in later life.

Strain and her colleagues (2002) found that the loss of a spouse (more common for women than for men) led to a decrease in activity over time. "By late life only a small minority of women are active at a health-maintaining level" (Cousins and Keating 1995, 340–41). Cousins (1995, 74) refers to "the almost universal withdrawal of North American women over their life-course" from vigorous, health-promoting activity. Later work by Cousins (2000) found that older women (aged 70 and older) had "sensational" negative views of strength and flexibility training. For example, they thought that strength training would lead to serious injury and illness. Cousins gives four reasons for this response. These women felt frail due to inactivity, lacked experience with exercise, felt age and gender stereotyping, and believed public warnings about the risk of exercise.

This same difference between men and women shows up in sports' participation. Corbeil (1995) reports that at all ages men are more active than women in sports. The low participation in sports by women may reflect the fact that fewer women than men have spouses with whom to share sports activity.

Low participation in sports by women may also point to the lack of opportunity women have had to participate in sports in the past. A study by Curtis, McTeer, and White (1999) found that participation in high-school sports predicted sport participation in adulthood. They found that women participated less in high-school sports and less in sports in later life. Low participation in sport reflects a lifelong trend for these women.

The difference in activity level between men and women may disappear in the future. Longer life expectancy means that couples will live together and stay active together longer. This could lead to more active lifestyles. Also, more options for an active lifestyle exist today. For example, the growth of fitness clubs and programs will give women more chance to live physically active lives. Cousins (1996) reports that the most active women today believe they have social reinforcement for their activity and the skill to take part. And Lalive d'Epinay and Bickel (2003, 161) report a change in traditional patterns of sport and exercise participation

"from one in which sports and physical exercise were a mostly male, urban, and upper- (middle-) class activity, to a more generalized, democratic pattern."

This research shows that health, education, income, and social status all shape leisure in retirement. Also, McPherson and Kozlik (1987) say that age cohorts may develop leisure subcultures. Older cohorts today may prefer more passive leisure, while younger cohorts may live a more active old age. Each cohort will have its preferred way of spending leisure time, in part based on members' past experience. Future cohorts of older people will also bring their own interests with them into old age. And they will probably enjoy a wide variety of leisure activities.

LEISURE

What theory of aging best describes leisure activity in later life? Most of the research on aging and leisure supports the continuity theory of aging. Cousins (1993) studied older women who take part in exercise programs and found continuity in their pattern of fitness activity. These women often report that they behaved as "tomboys" as young girls. Cousins (1995) found that childhood encouragement in sports led to social support for exercise in later life. Also, women who developed physical skill and mastery in childhood maintained positive beliefs about their physical ability later in life (Cousins 1997). Studies find that people often keep the leisure preferences in retirement that they had in middle age (Corbeil 1995; Singleton, Forbes, and Agwani 1993). People who enjoyed athletic activity, socializing, or travelling will continue to do these things when they retire (unless something such as poor health prevents them).

A study by McGuire, Dottavio, and O'Leary (1987) suggests that we need at least two theories to account for older people's leisure patterns: continuity theory and the life-span developmental perspective. These researchers looked at data from a nationwide recreation survey in the United States and found two patterns of leisure involvement in older adults. One pattern fits the continuity theory of aging. People who fit this pattern were called **contractors**. This group had stopped at least one outdoor activity in the past year and had not learned any new activity since age 65. A second pattern fits the life-span developmental perspective. The researchers called the people who fit this pattern **expanders**. This group had not stopped any activities in the past year and had added at least one new outdoor activity since age 65.

The study found that contractors had continued the same activities they had learned in childhood. Expanders, on the other hand, continued to add activities throughout life. The researchers could not predict group membership by the use of income, age, race, or gender, and concluded that leisure service providers should create many options for older adults today. At least one type of older person, the expander, will take advantage of these new opportunities. Cousins and Keating (1995) support this view. They found that women remain active throughout life by starting new activities at turning points in their life cycles.

Can people learn to make better use of their leisure time? Zuzanek and Box (1988) found that people restructure their time after retirement. They maintain some activities, but they also trade old activities for new ones. These findings show that people can change and expand their repertoire of activities, and they can develop new interests as they age.

Leisure education can play a role in rehabilitation settings such as day hospitals. One program included the development of self-awareness, leisure awareness, attitudes, decision-making, social interaction, and leisure skills (Searle and Mahon (1991). Searle and his colleagues (1995, 1998) report that leisure education leads to increased leisure control, more **leisure competence** (the ability to make use of leisure time), less boredom, and increased self-esteem.

Research supports the relationship between leisure activity participation and improved physical and psychological well-being. Smale and Dupuis (1993) say that participation in leisure activities contributes to psychological well-being throughout life. They conclude that "involvement in activities that promote creativity, self-expression, and a sense of accomplishment may be most strongly related to the re-establishment of a sense of purpose and/or self-worth" (Dupuis and Smale 1995, 84).

● Exhibit 12.1

TWO-WHEEL ADVENTURES BROOK NO COMPLAINTS

Continuity theory says that people will continue in later life the activities that they enjoyed in their middle years. The article below shows that older people can get great satisfaction from continuing their leisure interests into retirement. They may also bring a unique blend of enthusiasm and ease to their activities.

The repartee comes fast and furiously when members of The Geritols pack their motorcycles and meet for a coffee in a different part of Victoria every day. The loose-knit group of 38 biking enthusiasts, an offshoot of the Victoria Motorcycle Club, range in age from 60 to 85.

The group shares more than a passion for motorcycles. They also share a love of travel, a keen sense of humour, and an appreciation of the camaraderie that comes with shared interests.

Each year they take three or four road trips around the Pacific Northwest and many also take part in three motorcycle enduros west of Sooke on 2400 acres of land that Timber West lets them use. In this context, the enduros are a type of off-road orienteering on trail bikes.

The road trips are often spiced up with practical jokes, such as the time one member videotaped Bonge Noesgaard in the bath for the souvenir travelogue and another put a For Sale sign on Les Blow's bike and sat back to watch his consternation when people kept coming up to him with offers to buy his bike.

... There has been the odd brush with the law. "We've never been stopped for speeding, but we did get hauled in for riding on the shoulder near Tacoma once," says Noesgaard. "The first thing we did was take our hats off so the officer could see how old we were.

"Then we asked him if it was true that we would get steak three times a week in jail. When he told us it was just bread and water, we said, 'No thanks, we'd rather pay the fine.' By the time we got finished we had him feeling guilty for stopping us and he didn't give us a fine."...

Listening to their good-natured banter, it's easy to see what keeps this group of bikers coming back for more. They welcome new members to their kafeeklatsches and riding adventures. There's just one rule.

"We don't like to hear complaints. We like riders who take things as they come," says Noesgaard.

Source: "Two-Wheel Adventurers Brook No Complaints," *Fifty Plus, Victoria Times Colonist* advertising feature, October 5, 1999. Reprinted courtesy of *Victoria Times Colonist*.

NEW ACTIVITIES IN OLD AGE

Fitness and Health

Some decline in physical function is due to aging (for example, the slowdown in cell metabolism or a decrease in lung elasticity). Research shows that aerobic capacity and peak performance decline with age even in trained athletes (Ericsson 1990). But researchers still do not know how much of this decline is due to aging and how much is due to past health problems, past habits, and underuse of the body. Studies of fitness training show that exercise can slow and even reverse some of this decline (Buckwalter 1997; DiPietro and Dziura 2002).

DeVries (1975), one of the first researchers to study the effects of exercise on older people, says that declines in physical function have as much to do with decreased

activity as with aging (see also Buckwalter 1997). Kraus and Raab (1961) call this the **hypokinetic disease**. They say that the lack of activity can lead to mental and physical problems, while increases in activity can prevent or reverse these problems.

Many studies find clear signs of improvement in physical and mental well-being as a result of exercise. Lalive d'Epinay and Bickel (2003) report on a study of exercise and well-being among young-old (aged 64 to 74) men and women. They found that long-term exercisers and new exercisers reported greater feelings of well-being (less depression and better self-reported health) than those who quit or did not exercise. They found that those who quit exercising had the lowest well-being scores. Spirduso and MacRae (1991) report that aerobic exercise can improve information-processing speed. Aerobics can also lead to improve-

Exhibit 12.2

ACTIVE CANADIANS,* 1996–1997

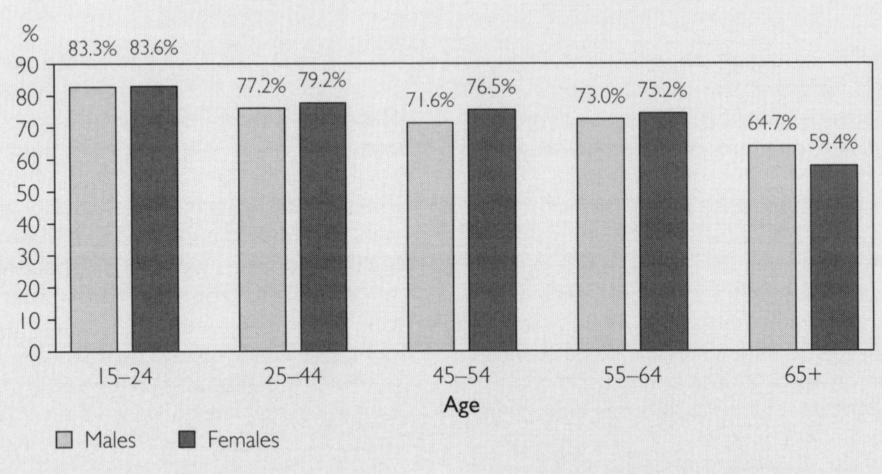

* People living in a private household who participated in regular or occasional physical activity in 1996–97.

Compared to men, women report greater rates of involvement in physical activity in all younger age groups. Only at age 65 and older do women show a slight decrease below male rates. This may be due to

increased rates of arthritis in later life for women. Also, the loss of a spouse and companion may lead to less engagement in physical activity outside the home for older women. Note that compared with middle-aged people, older people show only a small decline in the proportion who engage in regular or occasional physical activity. They also show a relatively high rate of physical activity.

Source: Reproduced from the Statistics Canada publication by Colin Lindsay, 1999, *A Portrait of Seniors in Canada*, 3rd ed., Table 8.1, p. 116. Cat. No. 89-519. Reprinted with permission from Statistics Canada.

ments in memory, intelligence, and cognitive speed (O'Brien and Vertinsky 1991; Stones and Dawe 1993). Studies show improvements in arterial and muscle flexibility. Cunningham et al. (1987) conducted a controlled study of a clinical training program for retired men. The researchers found significant improvements in the exercise group in maximum volume of oxygen, ventilation, and grip strength.

Iso-Ahola (1993) says that an **active leisure lifestyle** does at least two things. It directly benefits health and it helps to buffer the influence of life events and illness. Other studies support this view. Brooks (1994) reports that physical activity reduces the incidence of diabetes and hypertension and increases bone density (see also Shephard 1990). Caspersen, Powell, and Christenson (1985) note that improved fitness leads to greater endurance, agility, and speed. O'Brien and Vertinsky (1991) found that aerobics improves memory, intelligence, and cognitive speed (see also Arbuckle et al. 1994).

These benefits in turn lead to better functioning in daily life for older people. Active people even in their ninth decade, according to Diamond (1984), stayed interested in their professions and remained physically healthy. Coleman and Iso-Ahola (1993) report that leisure produces self-determination and social support that buffers stress. Iso-Ahola (1993) says that millions of people each year would avoid illness and extend their lives by adopting healthier lifestyles. This, in turn, might reduce medical costs. He considers prevention of sedentary lifestyles an important social issue.

Fitness and Well-Being

Fitness programs can improve the psychological well-being of older people as well as their health (Lalive d'Epinay and Bickel 2003). Studies show that exercise reduces depression and at low intensity leads to feelings of exhilaration (Steptoe and Cox 1988). Eighty percent of individuals in exercise programs report that exercise makes them feel better (Morgan and O'Connor 1988). Studies also show that exercise leads to improved social life and increased happiness (Myers and Hamilton 1985; Stacey, Kozma, and Stones 1985). "This finding

---

● **Exhibit 12.3**

WHAT THEY'RE BUYING TO GET FIT

A Globe and Mail *article begins, "Aging boomers are trading in their aerobic equipment for sporting goods that offer a more relaxed route to fitness." Reporter John Heinzl uses the sporting equipment people buy as a guide to their changing lifestyles. He details the trend toward activity that puts less strain on aging muscles and bones.*

Getting fit used to mean breaking a sweat. But more and more aging boomers seem to be frowning upon physical exertion.

The fitness movement has shifted into slower gear, largely a reflection of the greying boomer population. And that's dramatically changing how people spend their money on sporting goods, sales figures show.

Golf—roughly equivalent to an intense round of croquet for sheer aerobic benefit—is coming on strong. In the United States, sales of golf clubs and accessories are expected to rise 7 per cent this year to more than $1.4 billion (U.S.), according to the U.S.-based National Sporting Goods Association. While the association tracks sales south of the border only, the trends are similar in Canada, industry experts say.

Camping, another leisure activity masquerading as a sport, is also attracting hordes of aging athletes who are exchanging their Rub A-535 for cans of mosquito repellant. The NSGA is projecting an 8-per-cent jump, to $1.02 billion, in sales of tents, canteens and other camping gear.

If it involves running and jumping, people just aren't doing it as much as before. Sales of aerobic wear and tennis equipment, which have been dropping faster than a topspin lob, are projected to continue their decline in 1995.

More people are gliding instead of running. David Marcus, executive vice-president of sporting retailer Forzani Group Ltd. of Calgary, says in-line skates continue to be the top-selling product across Canada.

Do you think this trend toward more relaxed leisure will continue as the baby boomers age? How would you suggest that the sporting goods and leisure industries respond to an aging population?

Source: John Heinzl, 1995, "What We're Buying," *Globe and Mail,* July 8, B19. Reprinted with permission from *The Globe and Mail.*

alone," Stacey, Kozma, and Stones (1985, 73) say, "provides sufficient justification for enrolling in an exercise program." Moderate exercise can even postpone death (Blair et al. 1989). Iso-Ahola (1993; see also Bravo et al. 1996b) reports on a variety of other psychological benefits of leisure, including happiness, self-actualization, and life satisfaction.

Active leisure also leads to increased social interaction, and it allows people to maintain and develop friendships (Coleman and Iso-Ahola 1993; Iso-Ahola 1989). Many people report that their most enjoyable leisure experiences take place with friends. Social interaction during leisure can serve as an important resource for older people, especially widowed and single seniors. Bravo and her colleagues (1996a; see also Estabrooks and Carron 2000) found that people in a group exercise program outperformed those in a home-based program.

Other fitness programs show similar results. Mittelman et al. (1989) studied 33 seniors who bicycled from Victoria, British Columbia, to St. John's, Newfoundland. The group bicycled six days a week, averaging about 90 kilometres per seven-hour day, and made the trip in 100 days. The researchers studied the seniors at three points: before they started, at the midpoint of the trip, and two days before the end of the tour. (Eleven seniors dropped out during the tour.) The seniors filled out questionnaires that asked about their background (age, marital status, etc.), health, exercise habits, expectations for the trip, their psychosocial condition, and anxiety. The researchers also gathered data on the seniors' physical condition (weight, height, etc.), strength, heart rate, blood pressure, blood chemistry, and food intake.

The study found that the seniors increased their flexibility during the tour, showed improved cardiovascular response to work, and had blood samples that suggested bone-mineral turnover (a sign of bone mass growth or maintenance). Eighty-five percent of the seniors rated the tour as enjoyable or extremely enjoyable. About a quarter of the group reported that they felt stronger and felt increased well-being. Members also reported increased self-confidence, better fitness, and a sense of accomplishment. The researchers conclude that "bicycle touring has a generally positive effect on the initially fit senior citizen" (Mittelman et al. 1989, 154).

Even in institutions, exercise programs can improve participants' sense of well-being. People in an activity program in a nursing home reported that they felt better, slept better, and did more of their own personal care (LaRocque and Campagna 1983).

The Challenge to Fitness Programs

All fitness programs for older people face two hurdles: getting older people involved and keeping them involved. Chen and Millar (2001), for example, found that compared to younger people seniors showed the least tendency to start moderate physical activity, the least tendency to maintain moderate physical activity, and the greatest tendency to stop moderate physical activity.

The continuity theory of aging supports this view. It says that in old age people will tend to do the things they have always done or try to find substitutes for these activities. This, in part, explains the lower participation rates of women in sports. O'Brien and Vertinsky (1991) say that women take part in sports to a lesser degree than men from adolescence on (see also Gauthier and Haman 1992). Older women also avoid exercise and exertion. The stereotyping that labelled sport as male activities in the past helps explain this decrease in female physical activity with age.

Other factors that lead to decreased activity for women in old age include arthritis, chronic heart disease, caregiving demands, cost, and fears about injury (O'Brien and Vertinsky 1991). Wister and Romeder (2002) say that people with a chronic illness (such as arthritis or hypertension) may need an exercise program. But their illness (for instance, pain or stiffness due to arthritis) may make it hard for them to join or stay with a program. The researchers suggest that program directors take disease symptoms into account when planning a program. They say that "programs should be fun and easy" (532). Also, programs should include self-care and self-help education. Zimmer, Hickey, and Searle (1997) found that many people with arthritis quit activities due to their illness, but they also found that some people—those with a strong social network, more education, and fewer mobility problems—replaced lost activities with new ones. The researchers say that, given support, older people with chronic illness can find substitute leisure activities and maintain an active life.

Mittelman et al. (1989) found that one-third of the seniors in the cross-country bicycle tour already mentioned dropped out before the end. Six of the eleven seniors who left the tour did so because of conflict with the tour leader. Only one senior left the tour because of the level of physical exertion. Stacey, Kozma, and Stones (1985) report that the people who drop out may need the programs most. They say that older, less happy, and more anxious people tend to drop out of programs.

Leaders also need to choose programs that fit seniors' approach to exercise. Research shows that the best training program consists of high-intensity and high-frequency exercise (Sidney and Shephard 1978), but seniors tend to drop out of this type of program. Myers and Gonda (1986) say that most seniors can improve their physical condition with a less strenuous exercise program. "Walking, dancing or swimming can also be used to enhance aerobic capacity and may be more appropriate for older adults than such activities as jogging-running, skating or cross-country skiing" (177). Less strenuous programs fit the needs of more seniors today and they encourage people to attend the programs more often.

Cousins and Burgess (1992) describe a number of ways to attract sedentary seniors to activity programs. First, they say, program leaders must minimize risk. Shephard (1990) presents a good discussion of the physical risk that exercise poses for people in their 70s and older. This risk includes injury, extreme fatigue, and, in some cases, sudden death. But programs also present a psychological risk. Psychological risk includes fear of embarrassment, ridicule, and failure. People may fail to meet their own or others' expectations. This attitude can even be found in former athletes who set unrealistic goals for themselves.

Second, program leaders must be aware of diversity. Older people vary in their health, ability, and commitment to activity. Cousins (2001) found that women in one study differed in their views on the value of physical activity. Active people saw the benefits in better health and better physical function. Semi-active people had doubts about the value of activity. Inactive women felt committed to an inactive lifestyle. These women felt that keeping busy with other activities such as volunteer work better met their needs.

Professionals who work with older people need to listen to people who join a program. Good communication between a program leader and participants creates the most successful program. Program leaders can then set individual goals for clients, with realistic expectations. Education, income, gender, and personal background influence people's knowledge about exercise and their attitude toward it. Older people need varied types of programs to suit their varied needs and interests (Grant 2002).

Third, program leaders must make programs enjoyable and rewarding. Tudor-Locke and her colleagues (2000) studied frail older people in a home exercise programs. They found that some of these people got bored with the program. Bocksnick and Hall (1994) studied recreation programs in six nursing homes. They found that half the residents who took part in the programs felt that they merely filled and killed time. Residents also

said they felt pressure to take part in activities. Program leaders had a more positive view of the programs. To avoid this kind of discrepancy, leaders need to keep in close touch with what members define as an enjoyable and rewarding program. Shephard (1986) reports that as many as one-half of participants quit exercise classes in the first six months. Older people need to play an active role in planning, assessing, and developing activity programs. This builds commitment to the program and leads to ongoing participation (see Losier, Bourque, and Vallerand 1993).

Waldron and Moore (1991) say that older people often take part in physical activities in order to be with others and for self-actualization. Programs should give people a chance to socialize before and after classes. Leaders of these programs need to support and encourage participation (O'Brien and Vertinsky 1991). Rhodes, Martin, and Taunton (2001) studied women in a strength-training program over six months. They found that a feeling of improved ability as well as social support helped people stay in the program for the first three months. After that, they tended to stay with the program if they felt that they improved their ability. Leaders of exercise programs need to use varied methods to help people stay in the programs. A country line dancing program can provide as much aerobic effect as a walking routine, and older women, for example, may find line dancing more fun (Gordon, Overend, and Vandervoort 2001).

SENIOR CENTRES

Most cities and towns across Canada have senior centres. They form the closest thing to a nationwide recreation system for older people. People drop in to their local centre, meet other seniors, play cards, take classes, and in some cases get medical help. About 20 percent of older Canadians say they have used a senior centre (Statistics Canada 1987; Strain 2001). Few studies have looked at who uses senior centres and why they use the centre. The studies that do exist (mostly done in the U.S.) report contradictory findings.

Strain (2001) conducted one of the few Canadian studies. She found that centres tend to serve rural low-income women who live alone and have a friendship network. Further analysis showed that centres served people with few limitations on their instrumental activities of daily living (IADLs). About a third of the people in the study (30 percent) said they visited a centre five or fewer times in the past six months. About a fifth (21 percent) said they visited a centre 48 or more times in that same period. Compared to those who lived with others, people who lived alone tended to make more visits to a centre. Most people who participated in a centre in 1991–1992 still belonged in 1995.

Strain (2001) says that senior centres attract a relatively small proportion of older people (about one in five). Her research shows that centres meet the needs of some seniors more than others. Strain says that in rural settings senior centres "may reflect a broad community appeal and acceptance of the senior center/drop-in centre as a meeting place" (486).

In small communities, the centre sometimes offers the only opportunity for social contact. Some centres offer social and health care services as well as recreation. The Regina Native Elders Incorporated runs a centre that offers Meals on Wheels, crafts, and health checkups. Other Aboriginal people's centres offer help with letter writing, filling out forms, and transportation to activities.

In Manitoba, senior centres belong to the Services for Seniors program. The government has identified this as a core health service. Senior centres create and develop resources to help older people stay active and independent in their communities (Manitoba Health 1997, cited in Strain 2001).

In Winnipeg, a nonprofit agency called Age and Opportunity, Inc. (A & O) runs six full-service centres as part of Manitoba's system of centres. These centres meet the strict standards set by the National Institute of Senior Centres in the United States. A & O centres offer programs such as bingo, billiards, and folk dancing, but they also offer members financial and personal counselling and health care. The staff and the members of A & O centres share the work. While the staff ensure that the centres have programs for counselling, education, health clinics, and so on, the members decide on recreation programs, fundraising, and centre maintenance. Each centre has a unique program that reflects members' interests and needs. At one centre, classes might include English as a second language, at another conversational French. Centres also offer lunch and supper. Seniors at A & O centres also give to their communities. Members plan programs and help prepare meals, sing in centre choirs, and visit local schools to perform for the students.

● Exhibit 12.4

GRANDMA'S LEAP OF FAITH (FROM A PLANE)

One week after her 85th birthday, Olive Thompson was soaring with the eagles. While her grandchildren watched from the ground, she threw herself from an aircraft, falling a few hundred metres before her parachute snapped open.

"It was a feeling like nothing else in the world," she said, after her first experience with skydiving.

"I think it could become quite addictive. I've already booked next year's jump."

There could be a difference next year. She's thinking of going solo.

"I wanted my first jump to be solo but the training is quite vigorous. They make you jump from a picnic table about 20 times and I wasn't sure my knees were up to it."

In last week's dive, she was hitched to Scott Borghese, an instructor at the Borghese Parachute Centre in Simcoe.

With the plane three kilometres above the ground, she put on her helmet, pulled down the goggles and took the plunge.

"I'm not sure how long the free fall lasted, but it wasn't long enough. It was such a spectacular sight. I could see all the way to Port Dover and the line of cars crawling along the highway."

She even managed a smile for the photographer who joined her leap of faith.

"I wasn't the least bit nervous. Maybe that's because I'm at peace with my world. I have a wonderful family and I've had a wonderful life. If anything went wrong, it couldn't have happened at a better time."

She won $20,000 in a lottery last Christmas and decided to treat herself to a new stove and a parachute jump.

"I thought skydiving would be a great way to celebrate my birthday ... certainly more exciting than sitting around the house drinking tea."

Source: Mike Hanley, 1999, "Grandma's Leap of Faith (from a Plane)," *Hamilton Spectator*, July 7, A12. Reprinted with permission of *The Hamilton Spectator*.

Wagner (1995), in the United States, describes two models of senior centre membership: the social service agency model and the social club model. The first type offers services to frail older people in poor health. People attend for lunches and for health maintenance services. Healthier seniors use the centre as a voluntary organization or social club. Strain (2001) found that in her longitudinal study young-old seniors began to use senior centres. But still she notes that fewer than 10 percent of people joined a centre over the four years of the study. This finding highlights the challenge that senior centres face from other recreational programs.

Education programs at universities and colleges now attract many seniors who might once have been satisfied with the programs at a senior centre. Also, more mobile, younger seniors may prefer to attend an art gallery or fitness program across town that meets their needs better. This leaves less well, less mobile older people to use neighbourhood centres. People who see the senior centre as a voluntary organization take a less active role in leadership and tend to use the centres for a shorter time. A concentration of less healthy seniors in the senior centre of the future may move centres more toward the social agency model.

Ouellette (1986) studied the recreation preferences of French and English senior citizens' club members in New Brunswick. The findings from this study suggest that Canadian senior centres need to take into account members' sociodemographic and ethnic background. Ouellette found that marital status, gender, and ethnicity all influence leisure enjoyment and participation. The French-Canadian women in this study, for example, said they enjoyed spiritual activities more than physical ones, while the English-Canadian men said they enjoyed mass media activities (e.g., television, radio) more and spiritual activities less. Ouellette traces the difference in spiritual interest to gender, but also to traditional cultural differences between the French and English. He says that leisure education and counselling need to take gender and ethnicity into account. He concludes that "there is some justification to develop and offer programs or services that would differ in orientation and/or content" for particular ethnic groups (226). Senior centres will need to take ethnicity into account as they alter their programs to fit the needs of a changing older population.

EDUCATION

Most schools today serve the same basic function they did a century and a half ago, when they first began: teaching children to become adults and preparing young

---

● Exhibit 12.5

HANGING AROUND THE MALL

Some older people choose not to join a senior centre or other organized group. Researchers Sijpkes, MacLean, and Brown (1983; see also Graham, Graham, and MacLean 1991) of McGill University studied older people who spend their days at the Complexe Desjardins mall in Montreal. They found that many older people use the mall as a drop-in centre. Here they describe a typical case:

An old man who lives in a twenty dollar a week room on Sherbrooke Street in Montreal leaves his room at eleven in the morning of a cold windy day. The streets are treacherously slippery. He carefully negotiates the two blocks to the Jeanne Mance entrance of the subway system. There he takes the escalator down to begin a long subterranean walk, occasionally enlightened by a glimpse of the outdoors, past the metro station, through the Place des Arts complex; he nips under Ste. Catherine Street to finally end up in the main space of Complexe Desjardins. By now he is quite warmed up from his cold outside walk, and he sits down on one of the many benches in the space, talks to some of the older people he knows, reads a newspaper that one of them has bequeathed him, and carefully smokes a cigarette.

Around noon he wanders over to the very centre of the space where he stands for a while watching the daily production of a live TV show for a French local channel. He splurges on a coffee which is available from a variety of little shops in the complex. On his way home he talks to some more people he knows and winds his way back through the underground system.

Source: Excerpted from P. Sijpkes, M. MacLean, and D. Brown, 1983, "Hanging around the Mall," *Recreation Canada*, February, pp. 44–46. Reprinted with the permission from the Canadian Parks and Recreation Association.

people for specific jobs in society. This system offers little to the older person, who is already an adult and retired from a job.

Statistics Canada says that in 1996 almost 20 000 seniors were enrolled in some kind of formal educational program. Of these, about 25 percent were registered as full-time students, 75 percent enrolled on a part-time basis. A Statistics Canada (1989b) study found that 9 percent of couples aged 65 and over said they spent some money on education. The study gave no figures for unattached seniors because so few of them reported spending anything on education. Devereaux (1985) says that, of the people aged 65 and over who enrolled in adult education courses, more than three-quarters of men and over 90 percent of women took hobby courses (e.g., woodworking, painting, cooking) or personal development courses (e.g., history, music appreciation).

Results from the Winnipeg Area Study support Devereaux's findings. In 1992, the study found that more than half of adults under age 50 had enrolled in classes since 1988, compared with less than one-third of adults aged 50 and over. Of those who took classes, nearly three-quarters of adults under age 50 reported taking classes to improve their careers. But less than 40 percent of adults over age 50 said they took career-related classes. People aged 50 and over showed the greatest tendency of any adult group to enroll in hobby or interest courses (Novak and Percival 1993). People aged 50 and over also showed the greatest tendency to take a course or workshop, rather than a degree or diploma program.

These findings support the idea that older people have less interest in credentials than younger learners. They want shorter, more focused programs. Also, older people most often take education programs for personal growth rather than career development (Lemieux 1997). Older people enjoy convenient programs that suit their schedule, income, and learning styles (Williams and Montelpare 1998).

Chené (1994) studied the meaning of learning in later life through interviews with 55 older people in Quebec. These people came from seven learning contexts, including a senior centre, a dance course, and a volunteer training program. Older learners emphasized the family spirit, friendship, and sense of belonging that they got through their learning group. One group member said, "It is a group where one comes regularly. There is a spirit of ... almost a family spirit. You know, we get to know each other, and I like it very much." Another member says that classes give her a purpose in life. "When you wake up in the morning, you say to yourself: 'Oh good, this morning we have a class' ... because our children are all gone, and life is sometimes very empty"

(770–71). Chené's work shows that older people value the social contacts as well as the knowledge that comes from learning in later life.

The school system, with its emphasis on testing, grading, and credentials, does not appeal to most older learners. Standard theories of aging, such as disengagement theory and activity theory, cannot explain older adults' interest in education. The growth of education programs for seniors today shows that seniors stay engaged. Some older people enroll in formal university and college classes, but many more older people engage in less formal kinds of education, such as programs at senior centres and community clubs. Few seniors take up middle-aged types of education that lead to degrees and credentials as activity theory predicts they would (National Advisory Council on Aging 1990b).

Continuity theory gives one explanation for older people's choice of education; it says that a lifetime of experiences leads a person to certain choices in later life. For example, people with many years of formal schooling will tend to return to school in old age. Also, people who have enjoyed learning as a form of leisure will opt for this type of learning experience. This observation fits with some of the facts about aging and education today. For example, older people with higher levels of education tend to return to school. But continuity theory cannot account for the older person who attends university for the first time in retirement, or for the person who takes up a new interest in theatre, film, or music in later life.

The life-span developmental perspective or a life course approach offers another theory of why older people keep learning. These perspectives say that growth and change take place at every stage of life, and that people grow and change in many dimensions. For example, a woman may have severe arthritis that keeps her housebound. But she can still learn and grow intellectually. These perspectives emphasize the uniqueness of later adult life stages and the need for a flexible educational system to serve older people. This view fits with current theories of lifelong learning. Adult educators say that the needs of older learners differ from those of younger learners. Older learners most often come back to school for personal development and to find meaning in later life. Older learners ask: Is the knowledge useful? Does it help me make better sense of my life and the world around me? Does it help me live more fully and enjoy my life more?

Schools will have to change their ideas about education and educational settings to meet the older student's needs. Myles and Boyd (1982, 271), for example, describe the experience of an older person who walks onto a university campus today.

Mrs. Smith arrives ... and finds classes dispersed over a large campus with limited facilities for getting around. The principles of credentialism which lead to the organization of academic activity around exams and the accumulation of credits are of little relevance to her. When she attempts to relax in a recreation area she is subjected to loud music which she finds noxious.... In effect, what Mrs. Smith is encountering is a social institution designed and organized for the young.

To meet the needs of older learners like Mrs. Smith, universities will have to give older students more options about class times, subject choices, and testing methods. They will also have to increase the kinds of social supports—such as counselling or pre-registration assistance—that they give to older students. Some of these changes have begun, and others will take place as more older people come back to school.

Universities, in fact, have begun to adapt their programs to older learners. Many offer free tuition and special classes for seniors. They give library cards to seniors and involve them in the planning and design of senior education programs. Teachers learn that they need to change their teaching style to fit older students' learning styles. Studies on learning and memory show that older people take more time to learn something new, and that anxiety, fatigue, and a lack of practice at school tasks make it harder for older people to succeed.

Also, older people will drop out of a program if they cannot link what they learn to what they already know. Instructors need to take more time to present material, allow time for students to ask questions or state their views, and match the pace of their instruction to students' abilities. Instructors who adjust their style to the older learner's needs will find that they get as much from their teaching experience as they give (Chené and Sigouin 1997).

The use of appropriate teaching methods along with more flexible schedules and open enrollment will encourage more older students to take secondary or postsecondary courses.

Distance education methods open education to older people. Toronto's Ryerson Polytechnic University offers courses by radio through its Open College. Other innovative delivery methods, such as Internet-based programs and homebound learning, will increase educational opportunities for older people (see Exhibit 12.6).

Lifelong learning has become a part of Canadian society. Moody (1988) gives several reasons for this development. First, schools show a greater concern for the older student today. They offer more flexible schedules, advice on courses, and in some cases special orientation programs for mature students (Thacker and Novak 1991). Second, career changes and new demands at work lead people to return to school. Almost three-quarters of men and half of women (of all ages) in the labour force take job-related or academic education programs (Devereaux 1985). Third, studies show that people with more education tend to keep taking classes (both academic and recreational) as they age (Denton, Pineo, and Spencer 1988; Vigoda, Crawford, and Hirdes 1985).

Already, more people go to school for more years than ever before. Younger age groups have more education. Statistics Canada says that in 1996 only 8 percent of all Canadians aged 65 and over had a university degree, compared with 17 percent of people between the ages of 25 and 64. Cyr and Schnore (1982) project a 15 percent increase between 1971 and 2011 in young-old men (65 to 74 years) with postsecondary education and an 8 percent increase in young-old women with postsecondary education. Denton, Pineo, and Spencer (1988) make a similar projection. They estimate that the increase in the number of older Canadians, along with an increase in educational level for older people, will lead to more than 200 000 older people enrolled in courses in 2010, a 141 percent increase over 1985 course enrollments. This increase in older students will require new educational models and new programs to meet their needs.

Educational Alternatives

Elderhostel

As more older people continue their education, new programs like **Elderhostel** will emerge to meet their needs (see Exhibit 12.7). Elderhostel is the largest education and travel program in the world for people aged 55 and over. About 200 000 older people enroll each year in 10 000 Elderhostel courses in 90 countries (Elderhostel 2003). Elderhostel combines formal learning with the European concept of hostelling (travelling from place to place and staying in inexpensive, safe lodgings).

Classic Elderhostel programs take place on a university campus. Most programs last one week—from Sunday afternoon until the following Saturday morning. A one-week program typically includes three courses. Elderhostel programs also take place in cities, national parks, and famous locations. Students may stay at a downtown hotel, a retreat house, or other simple lodgings (including safari tents when appropriate). Course choices include such options as whitewater rafting trips, touring Venice, and African safaris. The program also offers "homestay programs," where students live with a host family. These programs give hostellers a chance to travel, meet new people, and learn things in a variety of settings they might not otherwise see.

● **Exhibit 12.6**

HOMEBOUND LEARNING

Education programs have begun to attract more older people. Most take place in schools or in other community centres. But what about the homebound senior? Frail older people, people with disabilities, or people who must stay in because of bad weather—all of these people miss the chance to take part in community-based education programs.

A program in Winnipeg called Homebound Learning Opportunities (HLO), sponsored by Creative Retirement Manitoba, meets the needs of homebound seniors. The program serves people aged 50 and over. Participants range in age from 50 to 94 and have a variety of educational backgrounds and health problems. A facilitator visits a senior at home to offer a course once a week for four to eight weeks. The program also serves groups in hospitals and personal care homes (Penning and Wasyliw 1992).

In one case, a woman had always wanted to learn to paint. But she had a continuous oxygen feed, and others told her that paint fumes would interfere with her breathing. A Homebound Learning consultant suggested the use of acrylic paints and then arranged for her to take a painting course (Kelly 1987). In another case, a woman said she'd always wanted to learn to tap dance. But she now had arthritis in her legs and could barely stand. Could Homebound Learning help? The program arranged for another senior, a dance instructor, to visit this woman. The instructor arranged for the woman to learn tap dancing while sitting on a kitchen stool.

Creative Retirement Manitoba, a nonprofit seniors' learning organization started the program, which began in 1988 with $35 000 from a local foundation. By 1989, a program review found that 232 people had taken part in 151 individual or group courses for a total of 1334 class hours. In addition, 27 people had subscribed to an audio-visual lending library and 70 people had taken part in an eight-part educational sampler series. By 1992, the program had offered a schedule of 125 topics for one-to-one or group learning. Nearly 600 people took advantage of this program.

The program also expanded to include an audio and video library, peer counselling, and televised classes through a local public access station. The most popular individual courses included portable computer operation, a distinguished lecturer series, and armchair fitness exercise. The most popular group topics included armchair fitness, tai chi, and acrylic painting (Penning and Wasyliw 1992). In 1992, Creative Retirement offered its "first computer programming course to an 80 year old post-stroke shut-in" (Creative Retirement 1992, 5). The oldest computer student that year was 84 years old. In 1994, the program offered its first course on how to use the Internet. "Shut-ins," a flyer for the program says, "can use their computer or ours to learn how to access a local, national, or international computer 'community' from the comfort of their own home." The program opens a window on the world to people otherwise cut off from their community.

Do people enjoy the program? Reports from students show that they do (Homebound Learning Opportunities 1989). A husband and wife, for example, began guitar lessons through the HLO program. "We played our first duet the other day," they say. "We hugged each other and laughed, feeling grateful for the opportunity to learn to play guitar at our age. [I have] even practised as much as three hours a day on my guitar since starting this course."

Another participant says that he has gained benefits from his relaxation training course. "My wife even listens in on my course and has learned from it. It's doing me good. I think it's a great thing for homebound seniors. It was a God-send for me because I can't get out much anymore. I hope this program stays around."

A guest-home owner says that "the frail residents in our facility definitely show a difference as a result of participation in armchair fitness classes.... Residents are clearly more talkative and cheerful both during and after these classes. Residents in particular appreciate being led by a facilitator who is an older adult herself. If she can do it, they feel they should be able to."

This program shows that people want to learn throughout life, even if they have a physical problem. It also shows that in an aging society educational programs need greater flexibility than ever before. Kelly, Steinkamp, and Kelly (1987) say that the types of leisure activities people need will change with age. They found that as people age, many social and leisure activities decline. But social and home-based activities show little decline and in some cases an increase. These activities lead to the highest subjective well-being. A homebound learning program fits the social and home-based preferences of many older people. As the older population ages, this type of program will grow in importance.

● **Exhibit 12.7**

ELDERHOSTEL

A few samples from the U.S. and Canada online catalogue for Winter 2004–05 will give you some idea why this program has grown so fast:

- The Fur Brigade Trails and the Cariboo Wagon Road. In this exciting program, we explore British Columbia's historic and contemporary trade routes, communities, and spectacular landscape. Our route follows the Fur Brigade Trails that became the Cariboo Wagon Road during the 1858 Gold Rush. We venture up the lush Fraser River Valley by riverboat, along the sheer cliffs of the Fraser Canyon, and return through the Coast Mountain Range by motor coach.

- Nova Scotia's Cultural Heritage. We immerse ourselves in the history and cultural diversity of Canada's East Coast, and visit two distinct areas of Nova Scotia. Halifax, Nova Scotia's capital, is a modern port city with 18th-century elegance and is steeped in the history of its origins as the prime fortress in British North America. Then we journey by train to Cape Breton Island, an area rich in Scottish and Acadian heritage. The natural beauty of the Cabot Trail in Cape Breton Highlands National Park is reminiscent of the Scottish highlands. Enjoy miles of rugged shoreline and stunning vistas.

- Music on the Mississippi. As the song says, "the Southland gave birth to the blues" and much more. Aboard a unique passenger river barge, we cruise from Memphis to New Orleans, Beale Street to Bourbon Street, learning about America's indigenous music—blues, jazz, spirituals, gospel, Civil War tunes, Dixieland, country, rock 'n' roll, bluegrass, zydeco, soul, and Cajun. We also study life connected to the mighty Mississippi, including its people, their ethnic identities, musical expressions, and stories behind the music. Performances onboard and in historic settings bring the music alive.

- Great Art Centres in New York City. Join us for this All-Art Week in New York. We will explore the world-class Metropolitan Museum of Art, the largest art collection in the Western Hemisphere; Frank Lloyd Wright's Guggenheim Museum, famous for modern and contemporary art; and the serene Frick Collection, with its Renaissance masterpieces housed in the stunning Fifth Avenue mansion of Pittsburgh steel magnate Henry Clay Frick. Slide lectures by scholars will illuminate the history of art and of museums and gallery districts in New York.

This selection of programs from across the continent gives a glimpse of the options Elderhostellers can choose. Each program has its own character and charm. Elderhostel also offers international programs to England, Indonesia, Hungary, and many other countries. These programs cost more than those in Canada and often require good physical condition. Elderhostel students can choose the courses and the ambiance that suit their interests.

Source: Adapted from Elderhostel, 2004, "About Us," http://www.elderhostel.org/about/default.asp, accessed on August 28, 2004.

Elderhostel began in 1975 in the U.S. The University of New Brunswick offered the first course in Canada in 1980 and Canadian programs expanded quickly. From 1980 to 1981, the number of participants in Ontario more than doubled, and in the Maritimes the number of programs grew from one program in 1980 to programs in all four provinces by 1981 (Elderhostel 1981).

Today a program called "Routes to Learning Canada" (formerly Elderhostel Canada) offers programs similar to those of Elderhostel. But Routes to Learning emphasizes environmental and cultural awareness and sensitivity. Programs take place throughout the country. They range from the strenuous to the sedate. One program offers a 10-day Fraser River expedition in Voyageur canoes. This multi-generational program encourages grandchildren to attend with their grandparents. Another program offers a weekend at the opera in Toronto. This program takes members backstage to learn about the staging and choreography that go into an opera performance.

Arsenault (1997) studied 154 older adults at 10 Elderhostel sites in Canada. She found that Elderhostel programs met the needs of at least six types of older learners. "Activity-oriented people" joined because they liked the field trips, "geographical gurus" take the program to learn about a specific part of the country, "experimenters" want to explore new ways of learning, "adventurers" will try anything new, "content-committed" attend to explore a special interest, and "opportunists" attend to get reduced travel costs. Others took the program to explore new ways of leisure learning. Organizations such as Routes to Learning and Elderhostel clearly meet a wide range of seniors' interests. This in part accounts for the growth in enrollments and in students' satisfaction.

Institutes for Learning in Retirement

Institutes for Learning in Retirement (ILRs) have met with success at a number of Canadian universities. These programs offer a variety of formats from lectures, to seminars, to travel courses. In most cases older people decide together on the topics they will study. The ILR model uses peer teachers and group self-management.

These programs have grown rapidly in number throughout North America over the past few years. The New School for Social Research in New York started the first ILR in 1962 (Beck et al. 1991). Elderhostel has set up a network of Life Long Learning Institutes (the Elderhostel Institute Network) throughout North America. And the network continues to expand. By 1997, the network had 200 affiliate members. ILR courses have no grades or tests. They often take the form of study groups where students teach one another. Students in the ILRs, some of them retired professionals, often lead the classes. But they may teach subjects far from their specialties. A retired engineer might lead a course in Shakespeare. A professor of adult education might teach a course on French cuisine.

Unique Canadian institutes have developed across the country. Grant McEwan Community College in Alberta, for example, developed a "Minerva Senior Studies Institute." The Minerva Senior Studies Institute (2003) today provides learning opportunities for older adults over age 50. The institute sponsors a theatre program called the "Minerva Theatre Group," and also offers courses on topics such as history, art, and computing, as well as a "Walk-About" series of local tours.

McGill University has one of the largest and most active institutes in the country. It began with 197 people registering for courses in 1989. The McGill Institute for Learning in Retirement (MILR) uses peer learning in small groups. Member volunteers act as moderators. Many of the moderators come from executive, manage-ment, and leadership positions in the community. The members and moderators plan about 30 nine-week courses on academic topics that interest group members. Courses have included "A Comparative Study of a Rumanian Shtetl and a French-Canadian Parish in the 1930s," "Poetry: The Voice of Love," and a current events course in French. A seniors' council coordinates the program with the support of the McGill University Centre for Continuing Education.

Clark and her colleagues (1997) studied the McGill students' satisfaction with peer learning. They interviewed 315 students enrolled in the program and 106 people who had not attended for at least a year. The responses showed a high degree of satisfaction with peer learning. Students said that the quality of the experience depended on the ability of the moderator and the participation of fellow students. Students also said they wanted to take part in planning programs as well as in attending them. The researchers say that older adults in this ILR want to set their own educational directions.

Some people say that programs such as Elderhostel or ILRs segregate older people. They say that these programs offer less mental challenge than university courses. Van der Veen (1990), for example, calls for "inter-age universities" that serve mixed age groups. These universities would take into account the special needs of older adults, but would mix older people with younger people in classes. Some older people might prefer this kind of education. In either case (age-mixed or age-segregated programs), older people enrich campus life. They challenge faculty in new ways, bring fresh interest and ideas to the classroom, and create role models for younger students. Schools that offer the programs mentioned above have found that they benefit when they include older people in their vision of the campus (Scholz 1993).

Older people will want more education in the years ahead. They will come into later life with more education than past groups of seniors, and they will want to keep up with the world around them. Computer technology has attracted the interest of some seniors (see Exhibit 12.9). Lindsay (1997) reports that, in 1994, 6.9 percent of women and 12.4 percent of men aged 65 and over said they had taken a computer course. Twice the proportion of men, compared to women, say they use a computer. About 9 percent of men and 6 percent of women aged 65 and over say they have a computer at home. Older computer users mostly use their computers for word processing, data entry, and record keeping. But Statistics Canada (2001d) reports that 13 percent of older people used the Internet in 2000.

● Exhibit 12.8

A PERSONAL ODYSSEY: AN EDUCATIONAL ADVENTURE

Education for older people can take place outside the classroom. More older people than ever before now take adventure travel holidays. These programs combine travel, learning new skills or information, and some physical challenge. Adventure travel programs range from whitewater raft expeditions to mountain climbing treks. Rod Dawson describes an educational program that challenged him physically and emotionally.

Once more to dip my paddle and spin the world beneath my keel. A nine-day Canadian Outward Bound Wilderness School canoe trip, 100 miles northeast of Thunder Bay. Be there such a thing as heaven, it will surely include lakes, rivers, forest trails and campfires from northern Ontario.

A million reasons not to go.

At age 66 would I be able to keep up? I didn't feel old—on the other hand—neither did I feel young. Three major surgeries for cancer had taken a lot of the zip and vinegar out of me. I feared walking that lonesome road to another year—a year that might not be there for me. Maybe I can do it? Maybe I can't?

In the end I went because in my heart I really wanted at least one more trip.

We were all to meet at the airport in Thunder Bay. I opted to travel by bus from Belleville. When two other Outward Bounders boarded the bus in Toronto I knew I wasn't the only economy traveller. We shared a taxi from the bus depot to the airport.

Outward Bound policy states: "It is best that no one in your group has any preconceived ideas about your capabilities, therefore we do not allow spouses or partners to be in the same brigade." There are a few rules with Outward Bound. No alcohol, no smoking and no exclusive relationships. The expectation is that members will come with an open mind. The goal is to build confidence and self-esteem. A self-affirming experience, not a survival school....

Monday morning. We were scheduled for cold water immersion experience and this was September. We were taught canoe strokes and canoe over canoe rescue.

Then off to the Upper Kopka River, our first portage and my moment of truth. I asked to carry the first portage. If I could do this I could handle my share of the trip. When I put the canoe down at the water's edge I knew I had crossed my Rubicon.

Our canoe expedition had begun. Thirteen people, six canoes, five tents and all of our equipment. We travelled and worked together as a group, yet I think for everyone it was a very unique personal experience.

Wednesday. Just before dinner, we were dropped off for our "solo." Each participant was given a plastic tarp, rope, food, matches, sleeping bag and mattress to spend 24 hours alone on an isolated piece of shore. A steady drizzle kept me close to shelter and fire. Without watch or sun to mark the time the solitude was magnificent. Wrapped in a garment of morning mist, time marched forward with an immeasurable cadence and before I was ready 24 hours had passed.

It is said that adult participants in Outward Bound are often at a transition point in their life, reaching an age plateau, leaving an old job, ending a relationship or wondering about the wheres and whys of life. I had no grand expectations, I went only to canoe. But something happened.

On the solo and while paddling the next day, I met myself, my regrets, my hopes, my fears. It was Friday afternoon, paddling bow in the lead canoe I dipped my cup into the lake, drank, looked around and breathed deeply. One year ago this very day I lay in a hospital bed, alive because of surgeons' skills and a frightening array of painful medical technology. The contrast between then and now was so overwhelming that tears ran down my cheeks.

Source: Rod Dawson, "A Personal Odyssey," *Maturity,* January/February, pp. 26–27. Reprinted with permission of Rod Dawson. Publisher: *Maturity Magazine,* CYN Investments Ltd.

Compared to older women (aged 60 and over), a higher proportion of older men use the Internet (17 percent to 9 percent). But older women show some of the greatest increases in Internet use of any age group.

Still, a generation gap exists in computer use. Among the oldest old people (aged 75 and older), for example, only one person in twenty had used the Internet. And older people felt less need for universal

● Exhibit 12.9

PERCENTAGE OF HOUSEHOLDS USING COMPUTER COMMUNICATION, BY AGE OF HOUSEHOLD HEAD, 1997

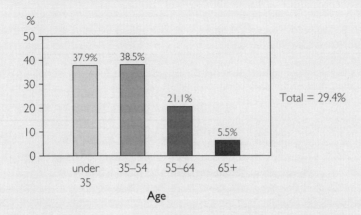

Total = 29.4%

Source: Reproduced from the Statistics Canada publication by Colin Lindsay, 1999, *A Portrait of Seniors in Canada*, 3rd ed., Table 5.3, p. 85. Cat. No. 89-519. Reprinted with permission from Statistics Canada.

access to the Internet. By contrast, nearly all people (90 percent) aged 15 to 17 said they used the Internet in 2000. Older people who use the Internet tend to use e-mail to stay in contact with family. They also used it for financial management, to get information on goods and services, and to get the news (Statistics Canada 2001).

Lindsay (1999) reports that few older households report using computer communication services such as the Internet. Only 4 percent of older households reported Internet use compared to 15 percent of households with heads under age 65. Still, the proportion of senior households with an Internet connection doubled between 1996 and 1997. The use of the Internet will continue to grow. Studies of frail and institutionalized older people, for example, found that with some training they began to search the Internet, use e-mail, and play computer games (Malcolm et al. 2001; Namazi and Mclintic 2003). Older women (aged 65 to 74) in one study reported that use of the computer made them feel less isolated from their families and better informed about health issues (Malcolm et al. 2001). Nearly all studies point to the need for instruction and support as older people learn this new technology. Hendrix and Sakauye (2001; see also Larkin-Lieffers 2000) say that trainers should set up a non-threatening environment and give people time to practise.

Computer clubs for seniors have also sprung up around the country. Johnston (1999) surveyed 170 seniors (between aged 51 and 81) who belonged to Canadian computer clubs. These members most often used their computers for word processing and to search for information from bulletin boards and on the Internet. They got the most satisfaction from using their knowledge to help others, sharing their knowledge face-to-face, and keeping up to date. Only 30 percent of these seniors said they often or very often used their computers to communicate with family and friends. These findings differ from studies of frail or institutionalized older people. Those studies report the importance older people place on e-mail as a way to keep in touch with family and friends.

Future cohorts of older people will enter old age computer literate. Many of them will use computers to surf the Internet. The Internet opens up worlds of information to active and housebound older people. The growth of the Internet into a worldwide information and communication tool happened almost overnight. It has begun to change the way all of us, including older people, keep up with new ideas. Internet sites include everything from online pharmacies, to health advice, to online shopping. These services will help housebound seniors. Also, the use of e-mail, chat rooms, and discussion groups will open new social outlets for all older people (Jaberg 1996). Furlong (1997) sees the Internet as an opportunity to build new communities among older people. It may even lead to romance. She says she has witnessed 10 marriages due to meetings online.

Education institutions have begun to offer courses on the Internet. The government offers information to seniors through the Seniors Canada On-line website. And older people use the Internet to keep in touch with one another. A study of 333 Internet users from the United States, Canada, and New Zealand found that they used the Internet about 10 times each month for an average of three hours per week (Trombo 1995). Seniors in the future will make even more use of the Internet. But seniors may have problems viewing the computer screen, reading small font sizes, and using a mouse. Education programs and improvements in technology will make computer use easier in the future. A program sponsored by Creative Retirement Manitoba teaches older people to use the Internet and provides them access to Internet services (see Exhibit 12.10).

COMMUNITY SERVICE THROUGH VOLUNTEER WORK

Exercise, recreation, and education lead to increased life satisfaction for older people. So does community service work or volunteer work—through the chance to give to others. O'Brien and Conger (1991) report that active older people take great satisfaction in their ability to help others. "It is possible that the giving of social support may be as important to the integrity of today's aging women as is the taking" (86).

Stone (1988) reports that seniors gave at least seven types of assistance to others: donations of money, transportation help, personal care, babysitting, housework, yardwork, and volunteer work. Rates of giving differed for each activity. Less than 10 percent of people aged 55 and over engaged in personal care. But more than half of people aged 55 and over donated money to an organization or to other people outside their household. And more than 15 percent of people aged 55 and over reported doing volunteer work.

● Exhibit 12.10

SENIORSCAN: AN INTERNET PROGRAM

Creative Retirement Manitoba (CRM), an education program run by and for seniors, offers more than 100 courses to more than 2000 older people each year. The most popular courses include a program on computers that teaches older people to surf the Internet.

The computer program began in 1993 when CRM placed computers in six senior centres throughout Manitoba. Seniors can use the computers for free. CRM has trained coaches to help beginners. SeniorsCan, also called the SCIP system (Seniors Computer Information Program), is the oldest Canadian seniors online information system. The SCIP website (http://www.crm.mb.ca) has information for seniors on such topics as health, housing, law and consumer issues, and lifestyles.

A report on the program says that almost one-third of the people in the program had no prior experience with computers. Another 41 percent had only "some experience." Only half the program users had computers. The report goes on to say that a large majority of people "found computers exciting,

became more interested in them with use, wanted to learn more about them and would use them in the future" (Trombo 1995, 2).

Seniors from around the world, including Europe, Australia, and New Zealand (as well as Canada), have logged onto the SCIP site. SCIP also features a web discussion group where seniors can discuss topics of interest. It has a CyberPals (e-mail pen pals) option. It has an option called "Ask a Great-Granny," where grandparents and parents go for advice on family problems. And it includes links to the Manitoba Seniors Handbook, the Elderhostel catalogue, and other sites on the Internet.

The government hopes that SCIP will lower health care costs as people have increased access to information about self-care. Jon Gerrard, federal secretary of state for Science, Research and Development, said that SCIP "is empowering the people to look after their health better, at a lower cost" (Pihlchyn 1995).

SCIP shows that seniors themselves can lead the way in the development of new computer uses.

Older volunteers make an important contribution to Canadian society (Chappell et al. 1999d). Lindsay (1997) reports that 19 percent of men and 22 percent of women aged 65 and over work in charitable or service organizations as volunteers. Seniors say they average 3.9 hours per week on volunteer work (more than any other age group) (see Exhibit 12.11). Robb and her colleagues (1999) say that unpaid informal and formal help given by seniors amounts to over $4.5 billion per year. Gottlieb (2002) goes on to report that nearly one older person in four volunteers (about three-quarters of a million people). About a third of older volunteers provide support to others through programs like friendly visiting. About 27 percent help with meal delivery. Older people give more time to volunteering than any other age group—about 202 hours per year. This amounts to the equivalent of 96 000 full-time jobs.

Chappell and Prince (1997) found that seniors tend to volunteer out of social obligation or for social value.

They also tend to provide service to others. One program, for example, trained older volunteers to act as health advocates for discharged older hospital patients (Dulka et al. 1999). The volunteers learned interviewing skills and made home visits after discharge. Volunteers often detected patient needs (such as transportation or meal service) that the discharge planners had missed.

The higher a person's education level, the greater the chance that he or she does volunteer work for an organization. In general, compared with people who live alone, those who live with a spouse also tend to volunteer more (Stone 1988). Prince and Chappell (1994, 1) report that volunteers have "slightly higher household incomes, and better self-assessed health than non-volunteer seniors."

Research suggests that more older people would work as volunteers if they had the opportunity. A study of people aged 60 and over in Northumberland and Newcastle, Ontario, found that many older people

● Exhibit 12.11

GIVING BACK TO THE COMMUNITY: AVERAGE HOURS PER WEEK VOLUNTEERS SPEND ON FORMAL ACTIVITIES, BY AGE, 2000

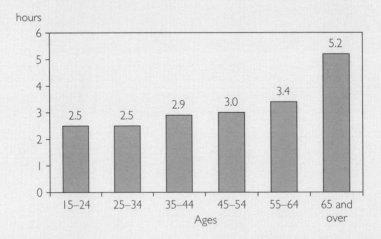

Canadian seniors stay active by volunteering in their communities. In 2000, 18 percent of the total senior population took part in some formal volunteer activity. The majority of older people (58 percent in 1997) took part in informal volunteer activities outside their homes.

● Exhibit 12.12

CANADIAN EXECUTIVE SERVICE ORGANIZATION: PAT AND DAVE REDEFINE RETIREMENT

TORONTO—Volunteering with the Canadian Executive Service Organization (CESO) gave Toronto couple Pat and David Evershed an opportunity to do something they had never done before—work professionally together.

Despite the fact that they both have degrees in social work, their areas of expertise are different. "It was interesting; we bring similar skills to a project, but we have different strengths," says David, 69.

"We have the ability to discuss things together. And even though we weren't used to it, we could play things off one another," adds Pat, 65. "We have an understanding of each other's work." ...

David began his career as a Family Services social worker before moving into management positions. "My father was a farmer and I was expected to be the same, but I knew that it wasn't the job for me. I wanted to work with people," he says.

Pat was a Justice of the Peace in Newmarket. She saw a need for qualified counsellors within the Family Court system and decided to go to night school to obtain her social work degree.

Both have been CESO VAs [Volunteer Advisers] since 1999.

"When David encouraged me to put in my application to become a VA I didn't think that I had any skills that CESO would need. I was surprised to be the first one to get an assignment," says Pat.

Together, they travelled on their first CESO assignment to Peru where they worked on a national program that serves victims of family violence.

"David was going to come with me as a spouse but I knew that his organizational expertise would be an asset, so he was put on the assignment as well," says Pat.

The Eversheds were also sent to Armenia where they worked on separate assignments, but both made a connection with the people. David helped two NGOs [non-government organizations] improve their management structure. Pat helped to establish a Family Court and worked on another project involving women's programs.

"The people were so wonderful. I will never forget the conditions and poverty they had to overcome," recalls Pat.

David agrees but notes: "They had a spirit and a generosity that I find gives me a lift. We really got to know the people. In Armenia they like learning about your family and they make you a part of theirs. It's an added bonus to be treated that way."

The Eversheds' work with CESO did cause some concern amongst family members.

They have four children and 11 grandchildren. "Our kids were upset because we weren't playing the role of the grandparent," adds David. "I think they are gradually getting used to our travels."

The Eversheds enjoy travelling together, because as David puts it: "It's just more fun!"

However, David has completed two assignments in Armenia by himself and Pat says she would travel without David "but only if it is to a place I know, or a big city."

Both believe that volunteering with CESO is important, "you get to use your skills where they are valued."

Not wanting to waste their retirement years sitting around the house, the Eversheds decided that they would also volunteer at the CESO Operations Centre in Toronto. Both work with Roster Services.

"I like working with people. I love going to new places. I have a real fear of having nothing to do. I'm not ready for the rocking chair," David says.

Source: Adapted from CESO News Release, November 20, 2003. Reprinted with permission.

would like to work as volunteers in schools (Hawkins 1980). Many of the subjects in this study said they would start work right away if they had the chance. Seventeen percent said they would work in a library; 14 percent said they would listen to a child read; and 14 percent said they would teach students about seniors' hobbies and skills. Prince and Chappell (1994) say that more than 80 percent of people in the 1987 National Survey on Volunteer Activity said they would give more time to volunteer work.

A program for seniors was started in Montreal to enrich the school curriculum and to bridge the generation gap. In this program, a worker from the Centre local de services communautaires arranged for a group of seven older people in the downtown core to work with children in a local school. The seniors, who ranged from 55 to 90 years of age, worked with a class of 27 students for 10 weeks. Classes included attending a performance of the Montreal Symphony, a slide show on Venice organized by the seniors, and a play put on for the seniors by the students. The classes ended with a bus trip to Canadiana Village and a picnic lunch (Nahmiash 1985).

Burden and Lee (1992) studied 141 agencies in Victoria, British Columbia, that use older volunteers. Nearly all of the agencies said they would like more older volunteers. About a third of the agencies found that office work suited older volunteers. About one-quarter of the agencies said that older people did well in one-to-one relationships. Agencies found older people patient, available, and committed to their volunteer role. Agencies agreed that they enhance volunteering by providing flexible hours, job sharing, and vacations.

A later study by Gottlieb (2002) found that agencies faced new challenges as they relied more and more on volunteers. Gottlieb studied 19 not-for-profit agencies in Ontario. These agencies relied on volunteers to carry out some of the agencies' work. Agencies reported three types of problems they faced when they used volunteers. First, clients today make heavier demands on volunteers than in the past. Staff has to take more time to supervise these volunteers and volunteers find the work stressful. Second, agencies have trouble recruiting volunteers. And older volunteers themselves often need help due to physical disabilities and lack of social support. Older volunteers also prefer short-term commitments and specific types of work. Third, agencies worried about the risk of sending volunteers to meet clients without supervision. They worried about volunteers' physical safety and their psychological well-being. Gottlieb asks whether agencies expect too much from volunteers. Today, he says, "the twin challenges are to find ways of increasing the societal contributions made by older volunteers, and recipro-

cally, the contribution that volunteering makes to the health and well-being of Canada's older adults" (8).

Senior volunteers can have a global as well as a local impact. The federal government sponsors a program called **Canadian Executive Service Organization (CESO)** (pronounced "kesso"). The program began in 1967. It recruits experienced volunteers and assigns them to work in underdeveloped countries in Africa, Asia, the Caribbean, and Central and South America. The program also works with Aboriginal groups in Canada. Volunteers, many of whom are retired people between the ages of 60 and 70, give technical and management advice to businesses, undertake feasibility studies, and help train workers and managers. The program now has 3500 volunteer advisers in 22 underdeveloped countries and 16 new market economies in central Europe. The program pays travel and maintenance expenses. This year, CESO's volunteer experts will take on about 1200 assignments. These will include about 600 in Canada with Aboriginal and non-Aboriginal individuals and communities (CESO 2003).

Volunteering, whether at a local school or in a foreign country, can give an older person a sense of purpose in life. Bond (1982) studied 323 older volunteers and found that people who volunteer their services have higher life satisfaction than people who do not. He suggests that counsellors prescribe volunteer work for clients who feel dissatisfied with their lives.

CONCLUSION

Older people engage in a wide range of leisure, educational, and community service activities. Government, nonprofit, and for-profit organizations have developed new programs and activities to engage and challenge older people. Future cohorts of older people will have more education than older people in the past. They will bring new interests in education, travel, and service. These people will help define old age as a time of personal growth and community enrichment.

Summary

1. Older people spend a great deal of their time on passive media-related activities such as reading the newspaper and watching television. Older people often spend their time alone, but they also enjoy spending time with others.

2. Income, lifestyle, gender, and health influence what people do and how active they remain in old age. Older people in good health have shown one of the highest rates of increase in sports and exercise activities in the past few years.

3. Physical functions do decline with age, but fitness training can reverse some physical decline. Fitness training can also lead to better sleep patterns, a better self-image, more social contacts, and increased happiness. Even in institutions fitness programs can improve residents' health and well-being.

4. Older people will join and stay in fitness programs if they have control over program content and feel relaxed and unthreatened by competition. More and more older people now value fitness and exercise.

5. An active leisure lifestyle provides physical, psychological, and social benefits in later life. This leads to better functioning and greater life satisfaction.

6. Senior centres across the country offer education, counselling, and recreation for older people. They form the closest thing to a network of recreational programs in Canada. Centre activities will need to change in the future to meet the needs of younger, more active seniors.

7. People with many years of schooling will keep on learning as they age. Universities often sponsor special programs for seniors. Programs such as Elderhostel and Creative Retirement Manitoba offer alternatives to traditional schooling. These programs are designed to fit the older person's interests and learning styles.

8. Computer technology has attracted the interest of many older people. The Internet, for example, has provided new sources of information to both active and housebound older people. It has begun to change the way in which older people have access to new ideas, information, and people.

9. Many older people volunteer to help others. More older people might offer their skills and services to the community if they had the opportunity. New programs help older people find ways to use their skills. Studies show that volunteers report an increase in life satisfaction.

Study Questions

1. How do most older people spend their time in retirement, according to studies on leisure activities? What activities do retired people enjoy most?

2. How and why do the lifestyles of older people vary in retirement? What conditions influence how active a person remains in old age?

3. Research suggests that two theories account for older people's leisure patterns. Name these theories and describe how they account for leisure choices in retirement.

4. Describe some of the programs and services available that can help older people stay active. What special needs must recreational planners consider when they design programs for older people?

5. List some of the physical and psychological benefits of regular exercise and fitness programs for seniors.

6. How can recreational planners attract sedentary seniors to activity programs?

7. What services do senior centres provide for older people? What other types of programs compete with senior centres for older people's participation?

8. Why do older people attend educational programs? What types of courses do they prefer when they go back to school?

9. How will universities and colleges have to modify their programs if they want to attract older students?

10. List and describe the major educational alternatives that are available to older people today. How has home computer use benefited older people?

11. Summarize the major types of activities that lead to increased life satisfaction in later life. Why does volunteer work, in particular, lead to high life satisfaction?

Key Terms

active leisure lifestyle a type of lifestyle that directly benefits health and helps to buffer the influence of life events and illness by regular participation in physical activities. (261)

Canadian Executive Service Organization (CESO) a federal government program that recruits volunteers, many of whom are retired executives, to serve as advisers and mentors in underdeveloped countries or with Aboriginal groups in Canada. (276)

contractors people who have stopped at least one outdoor activity in the past year and have not learned any new activity since age 65, in keeping with the continuity theory of aging. (258)

Elderhostel a not-for-profit company that promotes lifelong learning by organizing educational and cultural tours aimed at people in their 50s and older (originally based on a combination of university life and the European concept of hostelling). (267)

expanders people who have not stopped any activities in the past year and have added at least one new outdoor activity since age 65, in keeping with the life-span development theory of aging. (258)

hypokinetic disease the idea that the lack of activity can lead to mental and physical problems, while increases in activity can prevent or reverse these problems. (260)

Institutes for Learning in Retirement (ILRs) programs that offer older people a variety of educational formats from lectures, to seminars, to travel courses, with topics usually decided upon by the group. (270)

leisure competence the ability to make use of leisure time for life satisfaction. (259)

Selected Readings

Cusack, S.A., and W.J.A. Thompson. *Leadership for Older Adults: Aging with Purpose and Passion.* New York: Brunner/Mazel, 1999.

This is one of the few books that looks at the potential for leadership through senior centre participation. The authors promote a dynamic model of later life, in which the older person takes charge of the organization and creates an empowering environment. The authors describe leadership styles and opportunities in later life. They also propose practical tips on how to develop leadership within seniors' organizations.

Health and Welfare Canada. *Ageing and Independence: Overview of a National Survey.* Cat. No. H88-3/13-1993E. Ottawa: Minister of Supply and Services Canada, 1993.

This report of a national survey that studied people aged 45 and over presents people's assessment of their physical activity and satisfaction with activity. The report presents some optimistic findings about older people's attitudes toward physical activity. The results on middle-aged people suggest that these people will bring positive attitudes toward activity into old age.

Chapter Thirteen
Family Life and Social Support

Photo © Paul Barton/CORBIS/MAGMA

INTRODUCTION

Rising divorce rates, blended households, and high residential mobility all point to major changes in the modern family. Add to this the fact that more older people live alone than ever before, and it seems as though families have abandoned their aging members. Shanas (1979) called this the "hydraheaded myth" of family breakdown. People continue to believe it, even though studies show over and over again that it is not true.

Research shows that older people keep in contact with their families, that they turn to family members for help when they need it, and that they themselves provide support to family members (Connidis 2001; Townsend-Batten 2002). It is estimated that more than 80 percent of informal support received by older adults comes from family (Merrill 1997). After spouses, children are their most important source of social support. However, support between older parents and children flows in both directions (Connidis 2001).

Today, most older people, even widowed older women, prefer to see their children, but not to live with them. Better incomes, government rent supports, and health services allow more people to choose this option than ever before. This chapter will look at family life and social support. Part One will look at three topics related to family life: (1) marital status (including marriage, widowhood, divorce, and lifelong singlehood), (2) sexuality and aging, and (3) gay and lesbian older adults. Part Two of this chapter will examine four topics related to social support: (1) older people as a source of support, including their role as grandparents, (2) informal support given to older people from family members and friends, (3) family caregivers, and (4) abuse against older people.

PART ONE: FAMILY LIFE

MARITAL STATUS IN LATER LIFE

The life course perspective takes a dynamic view of family life and social relations. It shows how events and conditions that occur early in life affect roles and relationships in later life (George 1996; Price, McKenry, and Murphy 2000). This perspective sees family life as a scene of both stability and change. For example, some people will marry young and stay married to the same spouse throughout their lives. They experience the continuity of marriage. But many of these same people will experience changes in their sex lives, in their relationship with their spouse, and in the development of new roles such as grandparenthood. Gerontologists view some of these changes, such as widowhood, as normative or expected life events. Other changes, such as divorce, may come suddenly and affect only a few people. Changes in marital status often lead to change in a person's social status and a change in that individual's social network. The following sections will focus on life events and issues related to marital status in later life: marriage, common-law unions, divorce, lifelong singlehood, and widowhood.

Marriage

Nearly all Canadians get married (Milan 2000). In 2001, 90 percent of men and women aged 50 to 69 had married at least once (Statistics Canada 2001b). In that same year it was estimated that 73 percent of men and 78 percent of women aged 30 to 39 would marry at some point in their life. Overall, Canada's marriage rates have been declining. At the same time, the average age at first marriage has risen over the last decade from 27 to 29 years of age for men and from 25 to 27 years of age for women (Statistics Canada 2003m). With these changes, and an increase in common-law unions, particularly among the young (Statistics Canada 2001b, 2004a), more men and women may postpone or forgo marriage in the future. Still, most Canadians marry, and about half of those who do marry stay married to the same person until their spouse's death.

Lindsay (1999) reports that 57 percent of people aged 65 or older live with a spouse. (A small percent—1 percent—live with a common-law partner.) Married older adults have some advantages over their unmarried peers. First, married couples tend to have more financial resources than unmarried people aged 65 and over. Couples tend to be younger than unmarried older people, and often one or both members of the couple work. Even among people the same age, married couples have more money. This may be because they had a higher lifetime income than unmarried people, more savings, and a family home. Men are more likely than women to be married in later life (Lindsay 1999). Older women are more likely to be widowed.

Second, married people report higher life satisfaction and well-being (Cotten 1999) and greater happiness (Stack and Eshleman 1998) than do the separated, divorced, or widowed. The majority of married older adults say they are happy, particularly those in good health (Crompton and Kemeny 1999). Most older couples also report high marital satisfaction, especially married men (Bogard and Spilka 1996). Satisfaction in marriage tends to be higher for those recently married and those in long-term marriages. It tends to be lower

● Exhibit 13.1

NEVER TOO OLD FOR LOVE

The following excerpt shows that people can find love at any age. It also shows Canadians' desire to marry even late in life.

Sherman Browning, a 90-year-old bachelor, and Jean Goodbrand, 89, are getting married today at Trillium Villa Nursing Home, where both are residents.

Sherman Browning's fiancée thinks he's the cat's pajamas.

In fact, Jean Goodbrand, 89, is so in love with her 90-year-old husband-to-be that she invited all the residents at Trillium Villa Nursing Home to watch them tie the knot today.

"A diamond in the rough, that's what Sherman is," Goodbrand said in the Villa's library Tuesday....

....When asked why he finally decided to get hitched, [Browning, a bachelor] said, "I'm getting married because I love her. Ninety years is not really a long time. If you think back, it's nothing. Time doesn't wait for nobody."....

....The couple is looking forward to married life.

"I think we'll get along fine," said Goodbrand. "He's got a lot of good points."

Source: Excerpted from Dawn Cuthbertson, 2003, "Never Too Old for Love," *Sarnia Observer*, December 20, pp. A1–2. Reprinted with permission.

among those in their child-rearing years. Older spouses, particularly men, are more likely than younger couples to feel an increased satisfaction with their marriage over time. Affection and companionship, rather than emotional intensity, often become important in later-life marriage (Goodman 1999a).

Increased satisfaction in long-term marriage may be due in part to children growing up and moving away from home. Couples with children often enjoy a new freedom in later life. They live adult-centred lives that allow them to travel, visit with friends, share work at home, and do things together. Researchers report increased marital satisfaction for many couples in the "empty nest" stage of marriage (Heidemann, Suhomlinova, and O'Rand 1998). This is often a time for couples to focus more of their time and energy on themselves and each other. The empty nest stage of marriage has been called a "period of euphoria in marriages that have survived the demands of childraising" (221).

Third, research shows that married people tend to adjust better than non-married people to aging. A good marriage gives the couple intimacy, mutual support, and high life satisfaction (Cotten 1999). It also provides a sense of security and emotional stability (Fitzpatrick and Wampler 2000). Marriage is linked to longer life (especially for men) and better health (Rowe and Kahn 1998; Schone and Weinick 1998; Statistics Canada 2003x). Married partners monitor each other's health.

Marriage also helps reduce stress and it provides people with social support. All of this leads to better health (Miller, Hemesath, and Nelson, 1997). Married people also stand the best chance of staying out of nursing homes if they get sick, because they have someone to care for them. Marriage gives a person a live-in support system (Connidis 2001). Older married couples tend to rely more on each other than on outside social relations (Barrett and Lynch 1999). They also report a greater likelihood than non-married older adults of having sexual relations.

Research shows that the positive benefits of marriage apply only to good marriages. Constant bickering and dissatisfaction in a marriage can lead to depression and illness. Peters and Liefbroer (1997) say that researchers need to look at the quality of a marriage to understand the impact of marriage on well-being. They say that marriage does not guarantee happiness. And a person can enjoy the benefits of a close and committed relationship with a partner even if they live in separate households.

Common-Law Unions

The number of people in Canada choosing to live in common-law relationships has increased over the past two decades (Milan 2000). In 2001, 16 percent of all Canadian couples lived in common-law unions, compared to only 6 percent in 1981. More younger people

● **Exhibit 13.2**

MARITAL STATUS OF OLDER CANADIANS BY AGE AND SEX, 1996

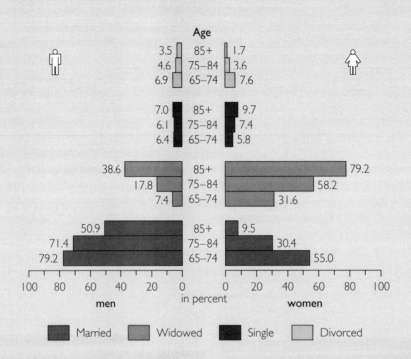

Source: Reproduced from the Statistics Canada publication by Colin Lindsay, 1999, *A Portrait of Seniors in Canada*, 3rd ed., Table 2.3, p. 41. Cat. No. 85-519. Reprinted with permission from Statistics Canada.

Note that more men than women are married at every age presented here. Note also that the difference in rates of marriages between men and women increases with age. More than half of men age 85 and over are married compared with only 10 percent of the oldest women. Widowhood rates for men and women differ as well. Very few men compared with about a third of women are widowed at ages 65 to 74. By age 85 and over, women have double the proportion of widows compared with men. These figures point to the different life experiences of men and women in later life due to mortality and the tendencies of each sex to remarry.

than older people choose this form of relationship. But some older people choose to live together and not marry. Research in Canada and the United States shows that the rate of cohabitation among the older population has gone up in the past few decades. In the United States, the rate went from nearly zero in 1960 for people aged 60 and older to 2.4 percent of this group in 1990 (Chevan 1996). In 2001, in Canada, 5 percent of those aged 55 or older were in common-law unions (Statistics Canada 2003k).

Common-law relationships serve different purposes for different age cohorts. For younger people, living common-law tends to precede or replace a first marriage. For older people, living common-law more likely precedes or replaces a remarriage (Statistics Canada 2001b). Most older adults who establish a relationship after the end of a first marriage enter a common-law union (Statistics Canada 2003k). These older people desire a close and intimate relationship, but not necessarily one within marriage (Leigh 2000).

Chevan (1996) finds that more older men than women cohabit (these older men tend to live with younger women). Fewer available partners for older women may explain this fact. Also, Chevan reports that poor men and women show the greatest tendency to cohabit. Living together (outside of marriage) may make good economic sense for the poorest older people. Cohabitation is also more likely among those who are separated or divorced, and among younger seniors. Researchers expect that the number of older adults who form common-law unions will increase in the future as the baby boom cohorts enter old age (Hatch 1995).

Older adults now and in the future will have greater choice in the type of intimate relationships they form (Cooney and Dunne 2001). For example, today many unmarried couples live in committed relationships while they maintain separate households. These non-resident couples are known as **LAT ("living apart together") couples**. In 2001, 8 percent of Canadians 20 years of age or older lived in such relationships. Eleven percent of people in these relationships were 50 years of age or older (Milan and Peters 2003). A LAT arrangement offers some older adults a way to have their own home and an intimate and committed partner.

Divorce

Divorce rates in Canada have increased significantly since the early 1970s. This followed the liberalization of divorce laws. Statistics Canada (2003j, 2004a) reports that 38 percent of married couples can expect to divorce before celebrating their 30th anniversary. Divorced older adults are the least prevalent of all older marital groups. About 5 percent of men and 6 percent of women aged 65 to 74 in 1996 reported that they had divorced (Lindsay 1999; Moore, Rosenberg and McGuinness 1997). However, the rate of divorce among older people has increased significantly (Gee 1995). Research also shows that more men and women are divorcing later in life (Statistics Canada 2004a). This represents a shift toward greater acceptability of divorce among older people. Moore, Rosenberg, and McGuinness (1997) project an increase in the number of divorced older people in the future as younger cohorts enter later life. Yet little research exists on divorced older people.

Most people who divorce in middle or later life rarely remarry (Cohen 1999; Wu and Penning 1997). But older divorced men are twice as likely as older divorced women to marry again (Gee 1995a). Divorce in later life often means economic insecurity, particularly for women (Miller, Hemesath, and Nelson 1997). For men, it often means loss of social contact with children and relatives (Barrett and Lynch 1999).

Davies and Denton (2002) compared the economic well-being of older women who divorced in middle or later life with divorced men and with women and men who remained married. They found that being divorced, for both men and women, meant greater economic hardship. But women, compared to divorced men or married people, more often lived below the poverty line. This study supports other Canadian research that finds very high rates of poverty among older unmarried women (McDonald 1997a; McDonald, Donahue, and Moore 2000). And because these older women are unlikely to remarry, they often feel the economic effects of divorce for many years.

Divorced older people tend to have smaller social networks than married or widowed older people (Connidis 2001). Divorced older men have the smallest social networks, the weakest ties to their families, and the lowest life satisfaction of any marital group. They are also less likely to receive support from their adult children (Barrett and Lynch 1999). But older men, compared to women, tend to remarry after divorce. This trend leads to more divorced older women than divorced older men (Moore, Rosenberg, and McGuinness 1997). Divorce can lead to disruption in family celebrations such as Thanksgiving and Christmas and the need to renegotiate or re-create family rituals and traditions. Divorced older parents may also no longer have the financial resources to provide assistance to their adult children (Downs, Coleman, and Ganong 2000).

Longer life expectancies in the future could increase the number of marriages that last 50 years or more. But the increased rate of divorce means that a third of marriages will end within 30 years (Statistics Canada 2004a). Researchers predict a higher divorce rate and more divorced older people in the future. This will make the economic well-being, mental health, and family life of divorced older people more important in the future.

Lifelong Singlehood

A small proportion (about 7 percent) of older people have never married. The proportion of singles increases in older age groups from 6.1 percent for people aged 65 to 74 to 8.9 percent for people aged 85 and over (Lindsay 1999). This may reflect the different social and historical conditions that people in each of these age groups live through. Singles have made unique adaptations to aging. They play vital and supportive roles in the lives of siblings, older parents, and others. They also form friendships and other social relationships to provide themselves with supporters, confidants, and companions.

Little research exists on the lives and social relationships of lifelong single older people (Barrett 1999; Davies 1995; Dykstra 1995). Older singles often face both the stereotypes of aging as well as those associated with people who are seen as "un-marriageable." One common and enduring belief is that older never-married people are lonely, socially isolated, and disconnected from family. But most older singles, particularly single women, develop strong and diverse social networks and have active ties with siblings, friends, and other family members (Barrett 1999; Campbell, Connidis, and Davies, 1999; Dykstra 1995).

Stein (1981), in some of the earliest work on singlehood, developed four categories of singles based on whether people viewed their singlehood as voluntary or involuntary, and as temporary or stable. Those who see their singlehood as voluntary, whether short-term or permanent, have made a conscious choice to stay single. Research shows that people who choose singlehood feel more life satisfaction, less loneliness, and greater well-being (Dykstra 1995).

Overall, never-married older people report that they lead active lives and feel happy, in good health, and satisfied with their standard of living. Many singles feel that they have greater freedom and control over their life. In general, single women are more satisfied with their lives than single men (Barrett 1999). Davies (1995) finds that older single women report greater psychological well-being than younger single women or older single men. And while older single people report more loneliness than married seniors, single people, particularly single women, tend to feel less lonely than divorced and widowed older people (Dykstra 1995).

Never-married older people, compared to married and widowed older people, tend to rely more on siblings and friends for social support (Campbell, Connidis, and Davies 1999). They also have strong relationships with parents, aunts, uncles, nieces, and nephews. Connidis and Campbell (1995) report that families with at least one never-married sibling have greater in-person contact. Never-married older people, especially women, report good emotional support and good help in everyday life (Campbell, Connidis, and Davies 1999). The literature, in general, suggests that most never-married people have good support networks (Connidis and McMullin 1999). Still, never-married older people lack spousal and child support in later life, so they may use more formal supports than married older people (Barrett and Lynch 1999). Older single people who need care are more likely to require institutional care because they lack a spouse or children.

Researchers project an increase in the proportion of older single people as baby boomers enter later life. These singles as they age may play a significant role in helping to change societal attitudes about permanent singlehood. Researchers say that future studies should look at the coping strategies that never-married people use to maintain their high quality of life (O'Brien 1991).

Widowhood

In 1996, 80 percent of older widowed Canadians were women (Statistics Canada 2003n). In the older population, rates of widowhood increase with age for both men and women. But women have a higher rate of widowhood at all ages. For people aged 65 to 74, 7 percent of men compared to 32 percent of women are widowed. For those aged 85 or older, 39 percent of men are widowed compared to 80 percent of women (see Exhibit 13.2). This means that most older men, particularly those younger than age 85, can expect to end their lives with a spouse. Older women, particularly those aged 75 and older, are more likely to live their final years in widowhood, most often living alone (Bess 1999b).

After 30 years of marriage a woman, compared with a man, runs more than three times the risk of widowhood. Men and women also differ in their tendency to remarry after the loss of a spouse. Older widowed men are seven times more likely than older widowed women to remarry (Cohen 1999). Widows outnumber widowers for three reasons: (1) women live longer than men; (2) women marry older men; and (3) men, more than women, tend to remarry after widowhood. Exhibit 13.3 shows the outcome of these three trends.

Today, almost 70 percent of widows are over age 65. Seventy-five percent of widowed women 65 years of age or older live alone (Bess 1999b). The average age of widowhood for women is 66 years. For men, it is 69 years of age. Based on the gender gap in longevity, this means that men can expect to be widowed for six years of their lives compared to 15 years for women (Martin-Matthews 1996). A woman widowed at age 80 can expect to live almost nine years after her spouse dies. In early research in Canada, Matthews (1987) called widowhood an "expectable life event," one that creates a great deal of stress (Lopata 1996; Martin-Matthews 1999). Many men and most women will go through the pain of the death of a spouse. Widows report that widowhood stripped them of their identity. Van den Hoonaard (1997) calls this "identity foreclosure." It signals the end of a woman's former identity (as a wife) and the need to build a new identity. MacDougall (1998, 1–2), a widow, says that "part of the pain has to do with our sense of self; without our life-long partner, it becomes necessary to redefine our place in the world. When one has been part of a couple for a very long time, the adjustment can seem impossible."

Studies of widowhood have focused on two themes: the social supports that buffer the widowed person's

● Exhibit 13.3

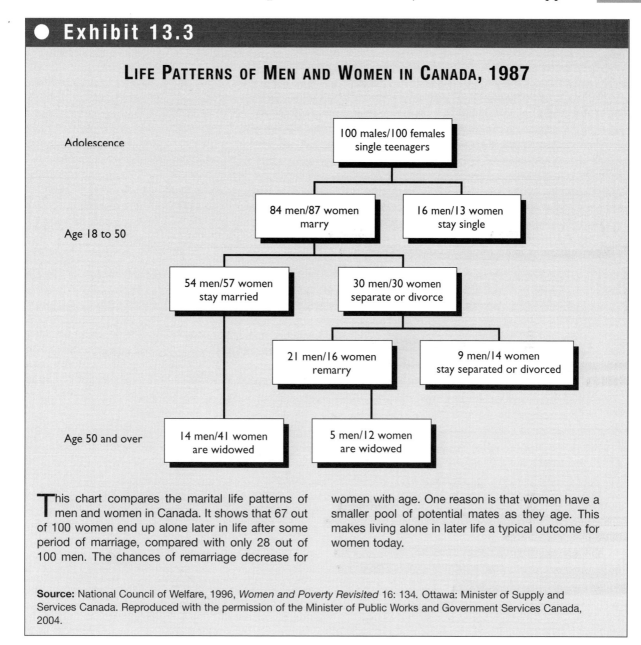

LIFE PATTERNS OF MEN AND WOMEN IN CANADA, 1987

Adolescence

100 males/100 females
single teenagers

Age 18 to 50

84 men/87 women
marry

16 men/13 women
stay single

54 men/57 women
stay married

30 men/30 women
separate or divorce

21 men/16 women
remarry

9 men/14 women
stay separated or divorced

Age 50 and over

14 men/41 women
are widowed

5 men/12 women
are widowed

This chart compares the marital life patterns of men and women in Canada. It shows that 67 out of 100 women end up alone later in life after some period of marriage, compared with only 28 out of 100 men. The chances of remarriage decrease for women with age. One reason is that women have a smaller pool of potential mates as they age. This makes living alone in later life a typical outcome for women today.

Source: National Council of Welfare, 1996, *Women and Poverty Revisited* 16: 134. Ottawa: Minister of Supply and Services Canada. Reproduced with the permission of the Minister of Public Works and Government Services Canada, 2004.

stress and the differences between men and women in their responses to widowhood.

Gender Differences in Widowhood

Most studies of widowhood contain too few men to compare with women, but a few studies show how the loss of a spouse affects each gender. First, studies of family supports, friendship, and **confidants** (someone in whom one confides) show that widowed women have more social supports than widowed men (Campbell, Connidis, and Davies 1999; Connidis and Campbell 1995). Most older men spent their lives focused on their careers, while older women spent their lives focused on people. As a result, women have more close relationships than men in old age. Because men have fewer supports than women, they more often experience loneliness after their spouse dies. They may also experience a decline in their social functioning and mental health status. Chipperfield and Havens (2001) say that while life satisfaction declines for both men and women following the death of a spouse, men show a greater decline.

Second, wives link men to wider social networks. Women more often than men say they have close relationships with family and friends besides their husbands.

They often name these friends, relatives, and children as their confidants, and they keep up these relationships when their husband dies (Campbell, Connidis, and Davies 1999; McCandless and Conner 1997). A widower loses a wife, a companion, and his link to other family and social ties. This may explain why many men rush into another marriage after they lose a spouse. Wu (1995) found that widowed men remarry sooner than widowed women. After five years, less than 6 percent of widowed women have remarried. But more than 22 percent of widowed men have remarried. Within 10 years, 35 percent of men have remarried (compared with only 11 percent of women).

Third, widowed men, compared to women, find it harder to make new friends or to join self-help groups. Studies show that widowers suffer from isolation and loneliness after the loss of their spouse (Lopata 1996). This in part reflects their low involvement in relationships outside marriage over the life course (Patterson 1996). Compared with women, widowers run a higher risk of suicide. Men also have a higher risk of dying within the six months following the death of their spouse (Lee, Willetts, and Seccombe 1998). Moore and Stratton (2002) found that, in spite of these challenges, some older widowed men bounce back from widowhood. The men in their study re-established a meaningful life after the loss of their spouse. Many of them found companionship and got involved in social activities. Chipperfield and Havens (2001) found that widowers' life satisfaction increased with remarriage (something that did not occur for women). Social supports and family roles buffer the stress of widowhood for both men and women.

Men typically name their spouse as their confidant. But women, compared to men, more often have confidants other than their spouse. Widows, for example, often chose a sister or friend as a confidant (Campbell, Connidis, and Davies 1999). Campbell and her colleagues (1999) found that siblings, particularly sisters, provide emotional support to their widowed sisters. Sisters also serve as confidants and companions, especially if they live nearby. Siblings can connect individuals to their past while being a source of support in the present. Confidants can contribute to good morale and lessen anxiety, tension, and depression.

Relatively few widows remarry. This, in part, reflects the larger number of eligible women compared with older men. Those who do remarry say they want companionship and the feeling that they add to another person's happiness. Talbott (1998) found that many older widows reported an interest in men, but they also

reported negative attitudes toward remarriage and an increased enjoyment in their independence. Older women may want to avoid the role of caregiver in a new marriage. Research finds that women stay socially active in mother and grandmother roles after their husbands die. Many women also hold onto their wife role. They remain committed to being a wife many years after the death of their husband. Van den Hoonaard (1999) says that the opportunity for widowed women to talk about the last days of their husbands' lives can give them comfort. These stories can also act as bridges on their journey from being a wife to being a widow.

Older women's greater life expectancy and the tendency to remain widowed lead to many of the problems that older women face. These often include financial difficulties (Martin-Matthews 1999). Inflation, for example, will eat away at a survivor's pension, if the widow has one. A widow may have to move from her home if her health declines (Bess 1999b). And she runs a greater risk of institutionalization than a married person because she will lack spousal support if she gets sick. Widowhood, in spite of good social supports, puts a woman at greater risk as she ages. Supportive relationships with family and friends help widowed women deal with the challenges they face.

SEXUALITY AND AGING

Stones and Stones (1996) begin their book *Sex May Be Wasted on the Young* with a discussion of ageism and sexuality. Young people in their teens and 20s, they say, thought of their grandparents as "way past it.... The idea of their own relatives making love with passion evoked reactions from giggles at the improbable to horror at the unimaginable" (Stones and Stones 1996, x).

But studies show that most older people have an interest in sex throughout life and that, given good health and a partner, older people can (and do) have sexual relations into late old age (Schlesinger 1996). Researchers at Duke University conducted one of the earliest studies of sexuality in later life. This study, the Duke Longitudinal Study of Aging, included data on 254 people between the ages of 60 and 94 (Pfeiffer, Verwoerdt, and Wang 1968; see also Verwoerdt, Pfeiffer, and Wang 1969).

Cross-sectional analysis showed a drop in sexual interest and activity with age, but longitudinal data showed many patterns of sexual change. About 20 percent of the men showed an increase in sexual interest and activity with age. The researchers found that on average men stopped having intercourse at age 68, but the age when men stopped ranged from 49 to 90. Masters and Johnson (1970), in their classic study, reported that men stopped having sex because of boredom, interest in outside activities, fatigue, eating or drinking too much, illness, or fear of failure. More recent research finds that the best predictors of men's continued sexual activity are good physical health, level of sexual activity earlier in life, and a healthy and interested partner (Metz and Miner 1998).

Women tend to stop having sexual relations earlier than men—on average at age 60. This reflects the higher rates of widowhood for women in old age. Research shows that whether a woman maintains an active sex life or not depends on good health and the presence of an active sexual partner (Metz and Miner 1998). Being married is key to women's continued sexual activity (Matthias et al. 1997). Jacoby (1999, 41) refers to a "partner gap." She reports that, compared to older women, more older men have sexual partners, and this difference between women and men in the proportion with a partner increases with age. Widowhood or a husband's decision to stop having sex often puts an end to a woman's sexual activity (Loehr, Verma, and Séguin 1997). "The saddest truth ... is that for most (though not all) older widows, the loss of a husband translates into the end of sex"(Jacoby 1999, 43).

The Duke University research found that sexual activity in old age depends most on a person's pattern of sexual activity in the past. Men and women who have a partner and who enjoyed sex in the past will continue to enjoy it as they age (Metz and Miner 1998). The Duke study also found that sexual activity leads to high life satisfaction and good health for people between ages 45 and 70. Many older couples say that sex is more satisfying now than when they were younger. Sexual expression often evolves with age to include other forms of intimacy beyond just sexual intercourse, such as touching, hugging, and holding hands (Cooley 2002).

Older people can have a satisfying marriage without an active sex life. But research supports the idea that continued sexual activity can lead to happiness and well-being for older couples (Matthias et al. 1997). Thomas (1982) expressed it well and with humour more than 20 years ago, when he compared sexuality in later life to eating popcorn: "It is not harmful, nor is it essential, but it is one of the pleasures of life" (cited in Ade-Ridder 1990, 64). Twenty years later, "while expressing our sexuality isn't as essential for survival as food or water, it fulfils a need for affection and belonging. This in turn has a positive impact on our self-esteem and quality of life"(Cooley 2002, 2).

Adaptations in Sexuality Due to Aging

Sexually active older people have to adjust to changes in their bodies as they age. A man, as he ages, takes longer to get an erection, takes longer to feel ready for intercourse again, and may have shorter, less intense orgasms. A woman, as she ages, may find that her vagina loses elasticity and opens less fully, and that she may have shorter orgasms. Older couples may need to use vaginal lubrication. Many books and videos exist that can help couples explore ways to adapt to these changes (Cooley 2002).

People can accept many changes as they get older—changes in strength, the senses, and athletic ability. But a change in sexual function can often damage a person's self-concept and psychological well-being. Sexual performance remains an integral part of what it means to be "manly" or "womanly" in our society (Stones and Stones 1996). Almost 30 years ago, Butler and Lewis (1976) talked about a **second language of sex** that could overcome the negative feelings that come with changes in sexual functioning. This language focuses on responsiveness, caring, and affection.

Sometimes a couple will need medical help or counselling to cope with changes in sexual performance (Cooley 2002). This can take the form of a medical checkup, information about changes in the body with age, or sex therapy. Lifestyle changes can also improve sexual desire and functioning. This includes reduced alcohol consumption and smoking, good nutrition, and increased exercise. Studies show that older people can (and many do) make these adjustments as they age.

Drugs (such as Viagra) now exist to restore or enhance sexual performance in older men. The American Association of Retired Persons (AARP) conducted a study of sexual behaviour and found that 10 percent of men used a new drug treatment or other therapy to overcome impotence (Jacoby 1999). But half of the men in the study who took some form of medication took Viagra. The majority of men and their partners in this study who used the drug said it increased their sexual enjoyment. The success of Viagra and similar products in the marketplace will lead to new forms of drug therapy for impotence. This option and a greater interest in sexual activity among baby boomers will lead to more active sex lives among older adults in the future.

Changing Attitudes to Sex in Later Life

Many researchers say that negative individual and societal attitudes toward sexuality may inhibit sexual activity in later life. Myths, stereotypes, and ageist jokes imply that sex is socially unacceptable or inappropriate for older people. This can lead older people to feel embarrassed about their own sexual desires and behaviour. Hillman and Stricker (1996, 544) found that negative views of sexuality in old age held by younger people "appear to have a direct impact on elderly persons' expressions of, and attitudes toward, their own sexuality." These negative attitudes can cause some people to withdraw from sexual activity, even though it gives them pleasure and benefits their health and well-being.

Older people in institutional settings face unique problems and barriers when they try to express their sexuality. The structure of life in a facility allows them little privacy and little control over their time and activities. The views of the staff and facility policies can limit a person's sexual activity. Even married couples who share a room can feel inhibited (Connidis 2001). Walker and colleagues (1998) studied staff and older residents' attitudes toward sexual activity of older people. They found that staff, more than older residents, considered sexuality very important. But older residents, more than staff, felt that sex improved their quality of life and well-being. Walker and Ephross (1999) found that current nursing home residents had a somewhat positive view of sexuality. They reported that sexuality and intimacy played an important or very important role in their lives, and they felt that sexual activity benefited their health and well-being.

Fairchild, Carrino, and Ramirez (1996) studied 29 U.S. nursing homes. They report that 28 had no formal program to train staff about residents' sex-related issues. And almost one-half of the facilities did not address sexuality at all within their staff training programs. Furthermore, social workers described staff attitudes toward residents' sexuality as "mixed" or "largely negative." They used terms such as "intolerant," "humorous," or "condemning." They also reported that they had "intolerant" or "condemning" attitudes toward homosexuality and lesbianism.

Research supports the need for more formal staff training programs that teach workers about the sexual needs and feelings of older residents (Fairchild, Carrino, and Ramirez 1996; Walker and Ephross 1999). Staff members need to consider residents' need for privacy. Also, the increased number of residents with Alzheimer's disease (AD) or other forms of dementia raises the issue of consent to sexual relations. Staff may need to assess a confused resident's ability to consent to sexual relations, and they may need to protect dementia patients from sexual exploitation or abuse (Lichtenberg 1997).

Attitudes of staff and older people toward sexuality will continue to change for several reasons as new cohorts of people enter old age. First, gerontology courses teach younger people and professionals the facts about sex in old age. This knowledge can change the attitudes of those who work with older people. Second, books that give advice to older people now, more than in the past, encourage sexual activity. In the past, such books typically spoke to middle-aged children about caring for their aging parents, but, more recently, these books give advice directly to older people. Third, cohorts differ in their views on sexual relations. Older cohorts have tended to take a more conservative view of sex, and to discourage sex outside of marriage. But younger cohorts have more open attitudes to sex, and if they bring these attitudes with them into old age, there will be a more positive view of sex and more sexual activity among older people. Johnson (1997) already finds evidence of this trend. This research found a more positive and accepting attitude toward sexuality among older people, particularly the young-old.

Older people in the future will take a more positive attitude toward sex. But, as in the early 1980s, Weg (1983) warned that older people will only face a new stereotype if they feel they must have a partner and stay sexually active as they age. Weg's words remain relevant more than 20 years later: "There is no one way to love or to be loved. There is no one liaison that is superior to another. No one life-style in singlehood or marriage, heterosexual or homosexual, will suit all persons. Self-pleasuring, homosexuality, bisexuality, celibacy, and heterosexuality are all in the human sexual repertoire" (76).

Gay and Lesbian Older Adults

Most studies of sexuality in later life have focused on married or single heterosexuals. Few studies report on older gay and lesbian adults (O'Brien and Goldberg 2000; Schwartz and Rutter 1998). Do these people face unique problems as they age? Do older gays and lesbians adapt better or less well than heterosexuals to sexual changes with age? Like heterosexuals, gays and lesbians decrease their sexual activity with age (Schwartz and Rutter 1998). Gay men typically have more partners than lesbian women, but for both, sexual activity diminishes as they grow older. Most gay men have sexual relations with only one partner in later life (Berger 1996).

Lee (1987) conducted the first study of gay aging men in Canada in the late 1980s and found that men who had partners in the past—a wife, lovers, or a combination of both—reported life satisfaction even if they now lived alone. Lee found that homosexual men with lovers tend to report high life satisfaction, but he also said that having a lover in later life "is not easy to achieve" (Lee 1987, 147; see also O'Brien and Goldberg 2000).

Lee also found that men who preferred other gay men as friends, those who knew an older gay man as a role model, and those involved in a gay social life showed higher life satisfaction. Lee's findings showed that older gay men get satisfaction from many of the same things as heterosexual men—companionship, sexual fulfillment, and friendship. They also have unique sources of satisfaction and face unique challenges as they age. Lee's early study showed that gay men can adapt to the changes that come with age and that, as Lee said, "it is possible to achieve happiness alone or by sharing life with a lover, even one found late in life" (151).

Research suggests that older gay men and lesbians are concerned about the same things as many other older people—health, finances, and loneliness. For example, having a committed partner increases life satisfaction and decreases loneliness for older gay men and lesbians (Brown et al. 1997). But some concerns of older gay and lesbian adults relate to their sexual orientation, including worrying about discrimination in health care, housing, long-term care, and rejection by children or grandchildren.

One theme appears in nearly all the studies of homosexuality in later life. Societal attitudes toward homosexuality have shaped and continue to shape the lives of gay and lesbian older people. The double social stigma of being gay and being old may increase the challenges that older gays and lesbians face in later life (Grossman 1997). Many older gay and lesbian people have had to adapt their lives in order to live in a heterosexual world. Societal homophobia led many gay and lesbian older people to hide their homosexual relationships (Grossman 1997). They feared that exposure might cost them their jobs. Gay working-class men, for example, have a difficult time disclosing their homosexuality (Chapple, Kippax, and Smith 1998).

Friend (1996) says that gay and lesbian adaptations to a hostile society may improve their ability to cope with the challenges of aging. First, he says that gays and lesbians have experience in constructing a positive image of themselves in spite of social definitions. This may help them construct a positive image of themselves as they age. Second, gays and lesbians have experience in creating supportive relationships, which may help them create the support networks they need as they age. Third, many gays and lesbians have experience with political advocacy and will be better able to defend their rights as they age. This activist experience may help aging gays and lesbians provide the social supports they need in later life (Brotman, Ryan, and Cormier 2002).

Like older heterosexual adults, older gays and lesbians need a broad range of social supports and services.

Researchers report that gays and lesbians can best meet these needs by planning and implementing programs for their community (Beeler et al. 1999; Jacobs, Rasmussen, and Hohman 1999). Informal supports also play a significant role. Long-term relationships with a committed partner provide both gay men and lesbians with companionship, acceptance, and support (Berger 1996). Ties to other family members and friends also provide support (Fullmer 1995).

Research on homosexuality in later life has only begun. A number of research topics still need study (Grossman 1997). These include the longitudinal study of aging gay and lesbian couples (O'Brien and Goldberg 2000), ethnic and cultural issues faced by gays and lesbians, gay widowhood (Shernoff 1997), and aged gays and lesbians in the homosexual community. Researchers also need to study the relationships between gay older parents and their adult children and grandchildren (Connidis 2001). Studies of gay and lesbian aging show that societal influences and past experiences shape a person's life in old age. They also show that sexuality plays an important part in homosexual as well as heterosexual aging.

PART TWO: SOCIAL SUPPORT

Social support refers to help and assistance we give to and receive from others. Older people benefit from the support they receive from family members and friends in the form of emotional support, companionship, help with household chores, and a range of other help. But older family members also give help to family members through financial support and help with child care. They also provide a home for unmarried, divorced, or unemployed adult children. Part Two of this chapter looks at (1) older people as a source of support, including their role as grandparents; (2) informal support given to older people from family members and friends; (3) family caregivers; and (4) abuse against older people.

OLDER PEOPLE AS A SOURCE OF SUPPORT

Most of the writing on older people in families focuses on their needs and on what other people do for them. But older people also give help to their families (Keefe and Fancey 2002). Very early work by Shanas (1967) found that, contrary to the belief that older parents are passive recipients of their children's support, reciprocal help was given in the form of household chores, financial aid, and assistance during illness and other crisis situations. Older parents also provided child-care assistance. Research finds that reciprocity within supportive relationships leads to well-being and higher morale.

Robb and her colleagues (1999) found that, compared to younger people, older people provide more informal unpaid help. The researchers estimate that this unpaid help by older adults in 1992 came to $5.1 billion (including travel time). Older people give at least three kinds of support. First, they help their spouses and children with health care and daily chores; second, they give their children financial support; and third, they give emotional support to and serve as role models for younger family members.

Daily Help Given by Older People

Research has focused on the care and support given to older parents. But research has paid less attention to the help that older people give to family members and others. The research that does exist shows that older people give varied forms of help to younger people.

For example, older people help with housework or yardwork. And they do so most often for their children, or for a friend or neighbour. Also, older people help with personal care. This care most often goes to help a friend, neighbour, or relative (not living with them) (Lindsay 1999). Some older parents provide daily and lifelong care to children with disabilities (Joffres 2002). Many parents also share their home with adult children. These are children who delay leaving home or who return home in adulthood. Adult children who live with older parents often do so because they have no spouse, attend school, or have no job. The number of adult children (those in their 20s and 30s) who live with parents has increased since the 1980s (Boyd and Norris 1999).

Stone, Rosenthal, and Connidis (1998; Government of Canada 1999) studied seven kinds of help given by older parents to their children, including financial support, child care, and help with daily chores. The researchers found that overall support from older parents to adult children peaks between ages 55 and 64, with 47 percent of these parents saying that they give help. Still, a quarter of parents aged 65 to 74 give medium or high levels of help. And even at age 75 and older, nearly a fifth (18 percent) of parents say they give some help to their children.

These researchers say that older parents aged 45 to 74 probably give most of their support as unpaid work such as child care. Later in life (age 75 and over), parents may offer more financial support as their own physical ability declines. The researchers suggest that parents give the most support to the children they feel have the most need. The authors find that the give and take of support

remains relatively balanced between parents and children until around age 70. Then children begin to give more help than they receive.

Still, these researchers and others find that although support within families flows both ways, over a lifetime parents give more support than they receive. Furthermore, older people provide some support to their children throughout their later years. Stone, Rosenthal, and Connidis (1998, 24) say that "if we had included the monetary value of services provided informally by one generation to another we would increase markedly the relative size of the figure for flows that benefit the young."

These findings overall show that most older people live interdependently with family, neighbours, and friends. They give and receive help with practical activities, finances, and advice throughout their lives.

Financial Support

Older people give younger members of their family financial support. The amount and kind of support given differs by social class and ethnic group, but studies show that even middle-aged people think of their parents as givers. Other studies show that the elderly give more money to their children than they get from them (Ploeg et al. 2003; Stone, Rosenthal, and Connidis 1998). A study in the United States by McGarry and Schoeni (1995, cited in Stone, Rosenthal, and Connidis 1998) found that parents tended to give the most money to children with the least financial resources. Older people report that they get pleasure and satisfaction from giving money to younger family members (Bass and Caro 1996; Ploeg et al. 2003).

Ploeg and her colleagues (2003) found that most parents gave financial assistance to their children because of the love and commitment they feel to individual children and to their family overall. Some parents gave money as an early inheritance, when children could benefit from it most, and when they themselves could enjoy the experience of giving. Many parents saw their financial support as a way to help adult children "build" their lives as they began their careers or families. Others gave to help children "rebuild" their lives after difficult life events such as a divorce or the loss of a job (Ploeg et al. 2003). These parents saw a financial need and had the financial resources to help.

Emotional Supporters and Role Models

Research shows that adult children rely on their parents as role models throughout their lives. Many adult children turn to their parents for emotional support and help during and after a divorce (Hamon 1995). Parents can also act as role models for their adult children as they experience important later life transitions such as grandparenthood, widowhood, and retirement (Connidis 2001). Older family members derive great satisfaction from the help they give to their children and to other younger family members.

In early research from the 1980s, Rosenthal, Marshall, and Synge (1980) found that older people play many roles in their families. These include the "occupational sponsor" (the person who helps others find jobs or get started in business), the "comforter" (the person to whom people turn for personal advice and support), the "ambassador" (the person who represents the family at ceremonies), the "head of the family" (the person who makes choices that others go along with), and the "kin keeper" (the person who keeps people in touch with one another). Women generally occupy the kin keeper role. Families with kin keepers tend to get together more often. Men in families with kin keepers benefit by having stronger ties to their siblings.

Older parents bring their families together on special occasions, fostering increased contact among family members. Older women often serve as advisers and confidants to their widowed daughters. Older men often give financial help to their children and grandchildren. Parents appear to give help to their adult children according to their children's needs.

Family roles can give meaning and purpose to an older person's life. Research finds that older people have the highest emotional well-being when they give as well as receive support. Reciprocity makes older people feel useful, independent, and worthwhile. Older people's supportive roles can strengthen intergenerational ties and create more fulfilling relationships between parents and their children, as well as their grandchildren.

Grandparenting

Grandparenthood is a common experience for older Canadians (Kemp 2003). More people will take on the grandparent role today than ever before, and many of them will assume this role in late mid-life. In 2001, there were about 5.7 million grandparents in Canada (Milan and Hamm 2003). According to the 2001 General Social Survey (GSS), 65 percent of Canadian women and 53 percent of Canadian men aged 55 to 64 are grandparents (Milan and Hamm 2003). Women make up 80 percent of grandparents. This reflects the fact that more women live into old age than men. On average, grandparents have between four and five grandchildren. And most

grandparents have regular contact with at least one grandchild. Researchers expect the number of grandchildren per grandparent to decrease in the future as couples have fewer children.

In the 1980s, Hagestad (1985, 48) called grandparents of the time "demographic pioneers." Grandparents now play complex roles in the lives of their grandchildren (Kemp 2003). Some grandparents feel that they do enough by simply being present; but others play a more active role as family arbitrators, watchdogs, or family historians. Grandparents often look out for the well-being of younger relatives, help them when they can, and create links between family members. The grandparent role offers older people one of the most satisfying and enjoyable ways to give to other family members.

Some grandparents involve themselves in the daily lives and care of their grandchildren. In 2001, 4 percent of Canadians lived in households with at least three generations (grandparents, parents, and grandchildren) (Milan and Hamm 2003). A small but significant number of grandparents live with grandchildren without the presence of the middle generation. In 2001, 1 percent of all grandparents raised their children's children (Statistics Canada 2003g). Researchers call these arrangements **skip-generation households** (Milan and Hamm 2003).

Grandparents often care for their grandchildren because their own children can't provide the care. This can occur because of divorce or separation, mental health difficulties, substance abuse, or the death of an adult child (Waldrop and Weber 2001). Grandparents feel rewarded when they raise their grandchildren, but they also face challenges. These can include worries about their own health, problems with social isolation, and financial difficulties (Roe and Minkler 1998). At a period when older people expect more time and freedom in their retirement years, these grandparents take on unanticipated child-care responsibilities, often with high-risk grandchildren (Minkler 1999a). Caring full-time for a grandchild can create a close emotional bond, particularly for grandmothers (Bowers and Myers 1999). But it can also increase grandparents' stress (Sands and Goldberg-Glen 2000).

Research shows that grandchildren value their grandparents. An eight-year-old in a Quebec study (Grand'Maison and Lefebvre 1996, 83) said that he enjoyed visiting the garden at his grandfather's house. "He shows me things. He has lots of imagination, and he's very clever. We look at the mushrooms and imagine what kind of shapes they look like." A 12-year-old girl says, "I really love my grandparents. If I skip a week seeing them, I miss them. They've looked after me so many times.... My grandmother is a terrific teacher.... She taught me about cooking and I can make great muffins. With my grandfather, I learned about using tools and about the value of work well done" (Grand'Maison and Lefebvre 1996, 88).

The grandparent–grandchild relationship has become more common in the lives of adult grandchildren. The majority of young adults in Canada have at least one living grandparent (70 percent of adults in their 20s and 32 percent of adults in their 30s) (Kemp 2003). Holladay et al. (1998) studied granddaughters in their teens and early 20s. The researchers found that sharing activities and going through family crises (such as a death or illness) led granddaughters to feel close to their maternal grandmothers. Boon and Brussoni (1998) found that undergraduates who had the closest relationship with their own grandparent saw the grandparent role as loving and supportive.

Studies show that children's feelings about their grandparents also depend on the relationship between the grandparents and the parents. Holladay et al. (1997), for example, found that parental attitudes influenced teenaged granddaughters' feelings of closeness to their grandmothers. An absence of criticism of the grandmother by the parent and parents' comments on the importance of the grandmother led to greater feelings of closeness. Older grandchildren have closer ties with their grandparents if they see the relationship between their parents and grandparents as close (King and Elder 1997).

Gender can also influence the quality of the relationship, with closer ties in general for female family members. For example, grandchildren tend to be closer to their maternal grandparents (Chan and Elder 2000). Grandparents are closer to granddaughters than to grandsons, and grandmothers have closer and more active ties with both granddaughters and grandsons than do grandfathers (Silverstein and Long 1998). What a grandparent makes of the grandparent role also depends on the older person's gender, age, marital status, and relationship with his or her adult children.

Very early work by Neugarten and Weinstein (1964) studied styles of grandparenting. They describe five styles: a formal style, a fun-seeker style, a surrogate-parent style, a reservoir-of-family-wisdom style, and a distant-figure style. Only a few of the grandparents (most of them grandfathers) in their study showed a reservoir-of-family-wisdom style; this type of person had special skills or resources to give.

A few of the people in that study (all of them grandmothers) showed a surrogate-parent style; this type of person looked after grandchildren while parents worked. About one-third of the grandfathers and one-fifth of the grandmothers showed a distant-figure style; this type of

person had friendly feelings for their grandchildren, but did not see them very often. About a quarter of the grandfathers and a third of the grandmothers showed a fun-seeker style; this type of person spent leisure time with their grandchildren and had fun with them. About a third of both grandmothers and grandfathers showed a formal style; this type of person left parenting to the parents and did not offer advice on child rearing. The researchers found that older grandparents (aged 65 or over) more often took on a formal style, while younger grandparents tended to take on a fun-seeker style.

Twenty years after the work by Neugarten and Weinstein, Cherlin and Furstenberg (1985) looked at the grandparenting styles of 510 U.S. grandparents with teenaged grandchildren. They report five styles of grandparenting: detached, passive, supportive, authoritative, and influential. Detached and passive grandparents were usually older than grandparents in the other groups and tended to take a more hands-off relationship to grandparenting. One woman summarized this attitude simply: "I don't think the grandparents should interfere with the parents" (Cherlin and Furstenberg 1985, 107). Detached grandparents also tended to see their grandchildren less often and to live farther from them than did grandparents in other groups. This is comparable to Roberto and Stroes's (1995) more recent category of "remote" grandparent.

Influential grandparents tended to be younger. They were apt to get more involved in their grandchildren's lives. One grandfather said, "If he has some problem, he'll come over to see me.... And if I need some help, like getting some screens down ... for the summer, I'll get him to help me bring those down" (Cherlin and Furstenberg 1985, 108). The influential grandparents lived closer and saw their grandchildren more often than grandparents in other groups. Roberto and Stroes's (1995) "companionate" style of grandparenting shares features with the influential grandparent. The companionate grandparents feel close to grandchildren, offer advice and assistance, but do not take on a parental role.

At about the same time as Cherlin and Furstenberg's work, Hagestad (1985) conducted a study of grandmothers and grandfathers in Chicago. She found that both men and women talked with their grandchildren about practical life in adult society. The grandfathers took an instrumental or practical view of their role. They gave advice on job hunting, education, and managing money. The grandmothers more often dealt with family life and relationships.

Jerrome (1996, 91) gives an example of this support. A young man says about his grandmother that "it is great to be able to go round and complain about home or about dad being ridiculous or whatever. She will always be lovely and agree how stupid he is." Hagestad (1985) reported that grandmothers more often than grandfathers changed their own view on social issues, dress, and education due to their grandchildren's opinions on them. Hagestad (1985, 41) called this "reversed socialization." Hagestad's early work, and other research that has followed, shows that grandchildren and grandparents have an influence on one another's lives (Kemp 2004).

Research findings suggest that aging and decreased activity may lead to decreases in grandparents' influence on their grandchildren. Some of the grandparents in Cherlin and Furstenberg's study, for example, used "selective investment" to focus their energy on some of their closer or more personable grandchildren. In general, research shows that while the bond between adult grandchildren and their grandparents remains high across the life course, the relationship involves continuity and change over time. Mills (1999) finds that as grandchildren age, they grow closer to grandmothers but less close to grandfathers. Other research suggests that a gradual decline takes place in the relationship over time, with some increased closeness in the grandparents' later years (Silverstein and Long 1998). Hodgson (1995) finds that grandchildren feel a continued closeness to grandparents over time, with some grandchildren reporting an increased appreciation for their grandparents as they themselves age. The literature shows that the grandparent role allows room for personal expression and that older people can use it as a source of emotional satisfaction.

Research by Kemp (2004) looks at the expectations grandparents and grandchildren have of themselves and each other within what she terms these "grand" roles. Kemp finds that while the roles and relationships are diverse, grandparents and grandchildren do have expectations related to behaviour and responsibilities within the relationship. For example, both grandparents and grandchildren feel that grandparents should provide love, support, encouragement, and assistance to grandchildren, but should not interfere in their lives unless asked for help or advice. As one grandmother says, "I think being a grandparent is to listen and not to criticize" (11). A granddaughter says "grandparents are just supposed to be there when you need them and they always are ... they don't give advice unless you ask for it" (15). Grandparents were also seen as role models, teachers, and sources of family history and lived experience.

Grandchildren felt they should be respectful to grandparents and give them their time and attention. They felt an obligation to "give back" to grandparents for all the love and support grandparents had given to the family. This came in the form of spending time with grandparents and doing things to make grandparents proud of their accomplishments. Grandparents also hoped that their grandchildren would spend time with them and be an important part of their lives. However, for both grandchildren and grandparents, independence was important. Grandchildren sought to establish their own independence and grandparents wanted to maintain their independence (Kemp 2004).

Other research finds that grandparents' relationship to their grandchildren relies in part on the mediation of their children and children-in-law. In the late 1980s, Gladstone (1989) studied 110 grandparents in non-intact Canadian families (where parents had split up). He found that adult children and children-in-law act as mediators between grandchildren and grandparents. They can obstruct or arrange visits. Children-in-law can inhibit contact by keeping the former spouse from seeing children. This would, in turn, keep the grandparent from seeing the children. Contact with grandchildren of divorced or separated children depends on the grandparent's relationship to the former child-in-law, whether the child or the child-in-law has custody of the grandchild, and geographical closeness. More recent work by Hilton and Macari (1997) finds that maternal grandparents stay more involved in the grandparent role than paternal grandparents when their daughter gains custody of her children. The reverse takes place when a son gains custody of his children. Kruk (1995) found that denial of access by a child-in-law (often in the case of divorce) accounted for most cases of contact loss.

Gladstone (1989) concluded in his study that grandparents can negotiate relationships with their children and children-in-law in broken marriages to enhance contact with their grandchildren. This can present a challenge to the grandparent when emotions erupt during separations and divorces. Family practitioners can help to enhance grandparent–grandchild relationships during these times. Kruk (1995) says that family therapists should include grandparents in their work with post-divorce couples. This inclusion recognizes the grandparents' role in the post-divorce family. It also allows them to support their grandchildren during this stressful time.

A self-help group with chapters across the country called **GRAND (Grandparents Requesting Access aNd Dignity)** helps grandparents who cannot get access to their grandchildren. The group, which started in 1983, provides education and support, and lobbies for changes in laws to protect grandparents' access to their grandchildren. After GRAND collected 10 000 names on a petition to change the *Divorce Act*, they presented the petition to the House of Commons. The petition asks that the act include a statement such as the one in the Quebec Civil

Code that says "in no case may a father or mother, without serious cause, place obstacles between the child and grandparents." This petition, however, was not successful. The federal *Divorce Act* does allow for access applications from people other than parents, but does not explicitly identify grandparents (Goldberg 2003).

Kruk (1995) reports that grandparents who used legal means to get access to grandchildren had some success. One Toronto lawyer reports that he handled 40 cases for grandparents between 1992 and 1995. He won every case and got the grandparents custody or access (Davis 1996). However, not all access cases are successful. In March 2001, in *Chapman v. Chapman*, the Ontario Court of Appeal decided in favour of the parents and their right to limit the grandmother's access to their children (Goldberg 2003). The parents had a poor relationship with the grandmother and felt she had a negative influence on their two children. The Ontario Court of Appeal ruled that competent parents are presumed to act in the best interests of their children and should therefore decide who the children see and spend time with.

Grandparents who go to court risk increasing the tension with the child-in-law. Kruk (1995) says that legislative support for grandparent rights would decrease the need for legal action. Today, grandparents have to show the courts why they should have access to their grandchildren. They also have to show that denying access would be harmful to grandchildren (Goldberg 2003). A change in the law would guarantee grandparents' rights of access.

INFORMAL SUPPORTS FOR OLDER PEOPLE

Life course events and sociocultural conditions influence the quality of life in old age, but they do not determine it. Older people can and do respond actively to the changes that aging brings. Their response depends on their personality, past experience, and social resources, including social supports. This section will look at the social supports that help older people cope with aging and improve their quality of life and well-being.

Researchers study two types of social support: formal and informal. The 2002 GSS reports that one million older Canadians who live in the community need support due to a chronic health problem (Cranswick 2003). This assistance comes from informal support, formal support, or a combination of both. **Informal support** refers to the unpaid help given by friends, neighbours, and family. Informal support includes everyday help such as rides to the doctor or to a shopping centre, help with yardwork, or just a visit from a neighbour. Informal supporters can also help an older person cope with a personal crisis, adjust to a change in health, or locate a formal service. In 2002, 39 percent of women and 46 percent of men received all of their support from informal, unpaid sources (Cranswick 2003). Women provide the majority of informal support. In 1996, 61 percent or 1.3 million informal caregivers were women (Frederick and Fast 1999).

The term **formal support** refers to professional caregivers such as doctors, nurses, and social workers as well as paid homemaker and health care services. People pay for formal supports either from their own resources or through their taxes. Studies find that few older people who need help with daily chores or health care use only formal care. More often people use both the formal and informal support systems. Keating and her colleagues (1997, 24) call this a "caring partnership." They say that social policies now favour this mix of informal and formal care. Studies show that people usually turn to the formal system only after the informal system no longer meets their needs. Penning (2002) finds that even those who make extensive use of formal care services still rely on their informal care network.

In the early 1990s, Snell (1990) studied the legal history of family support in Canada in the 1920s and 1930s and found that laws of the time held families responsible for caring for their older members. The federal Criminal Code still requires children to provide their parents with the basic necessities of life if the parents cannot provide for themselves. All provinces have legislation that requires a child to support needy parents if the parents cannot support themselves. However, although the *Parents Maintenance Act* has been a legal statute in Ontario since 1921, only a few times have parents sued adult children for support (the 1993 *Godwin v. Bolsco* case, cited in Parsons and Tindale 2001).

Today, most older people get voluntary informal support from their families. Keating and her colleagues (1999) report that 90 percent of older people in the community who get help with household tasks get help from family and friends. Only 10 percent of this group gets help from a paid helper. Informal caregivers also provide about two-thirds of all care. People continue to get support, especially from the nuclear family, even after they face a health care crisis. Informal supports can also buffer stress from life events such as widowhood or illness. A greater proportion of older women, compared with older men, get emotional support from children or friends (Campbell, Connidis, and Davies 1999). Older men, compared with older women, have smaller support networks.

In the late 1980s, Stone (1988, 14) found that the availability of **primary potential support groups** changed as people aged. He defined this type of group as family and close friends who give help to the older person and who can expect help from the older person. Stone reported that about a third of people aged 65 to 79 lived with a spouse and had family and friendship ties. Men more often than women had this kind of support group structure. Past the age of 80, community-dwelling older adults tended to live alone, but they still had links outside their household to children, close friends, and other relatives. Women more often than men had this kind of support group structure. Very old people in institutions had smaller support structures or none at all.

Stone's research described the "potential" support group available to older people. Other studies have looked at how older people choose their informal supporters out of this potential group. Studies have also looked at the tasks informal supporters undertake. Four models describe the way people use informal supports:

1. The **task specificity model** says that different groups (family, friends, neighbours) have different abilities and offer different types of support (Litwak 1985). Each group plays a specific role in supporting the older person.

2. The **hierarchical compensatory model** of support states that people choose all types of support first from their inner family circle. This typically means their spouse and children. They then move outward to get support from less intimate people if more intimate ties can't meet their needs (Cantor and Little 1985). This model says that a married older person will get help first from a spouse, and a widow or widower will get help from a child (most often a daughter). The older person will then turn to friends, neighbours, and formal supports in that order.

3. The **functional specificity of relationships model** (Simons 1983–84) recognizes that "one tie may provide one type of support or a broad range of support, dependent on how that particular relationship has been negotiated" over the life course (Campbell, Connidis, and Davies 1999, 118). For example, the gender, marital status, parenthood, and proximity of helpers all influence the amount and type of support a person will get.

4. The **convoy model of support** sees people as having a dynamic network of close ties with family and friends (Kahn and Antonucci 1980). This model uses concentric circles to position close relationships around the individual, with the closest ties in the closest circle. Outer circles show ties that are less close (Haines and Henderson 2002). These ties form a "convoy" that travels with individuals throughout life, exchanging social support and assistance. The nature of this convoy can grow and change over time with changing life circumstances.

In the early 1990s, Penning (1990) compared the ability of the first two models (the task specificity model and the hierarchical compensatory model) to explain older people's use of informal supports. She found only limited support for each model. Older people tended to use a variety of formal and informal supports at the same time and not in a specific hierarchical order. She also found that groups did a variety of tasks that overlapped. For example, relatives and neighbours both helped with household tasks. Penning (1990, 227) said that "it is unlikely that assistance is provided routinely and uniformly on the basis of a set order of preference." She concluded that "the issue of who provides assistance to whom, of what type, and under what conditions is complex."

More recently, Denton (1997) used data from Canada's General Social Survey to study the use of formal and informal supports. She found that formal supports compensate for the lack of informal supports. But she did not report any hierarchical compensation. Use of formal supports in this way most often applies to single older people who live alone and have no children. She also found that in a smaller proportion of cases caregivers used formal supports to supplement their informal support. This study builds on Penning's earlier work from 1990. It shows that formal care both compensates for and supplements informal support.

Campbell, Connidis, and Davies (1999) found support for the functional specificity of relationships model. They found that siblings provide a range of social support for certain groups, including single women, the childless, single men, and widowed women. But siblings provide little support for divorced and married men. In general, siblings give support when they live nearby. Siblings also tend to serve as companions and confidants, and they more often provide practical support to sisters than to brothers. These findings show that particular groups of older adults develop supportive ties with siblings, "not as substitution or compensation for lost ties but based on a lifetime of negotiating unique ties with siblings" (144).

Haines and Henderson (2002) assessed the convoy model of social support. They found that while the model helps to identify significant supportive relationships, not all strong ties provide support. They also found that weak ties, typically ignored in the convoy model of support, do provide instrumental support, emotional support, and companionship.

Other research findings add another dimension to this complexity. Whether or not older people live with someone strongly influences the type of support they get. If an older person lives with someone, that person will likely give him or her support for the activities necessary to daily living (Boaz, Hu, and Ye, 1999; Campbell and Martin-Matthews 2000b). It seems that shared living arrangements (between siblings or friends) may help widowed or childless older people live in the community. Strain and Blandford (2003) find that caregivers who live with an older parent provide daily help with meal preparation and household chores. Family members often relocate to give or receive care (Cranswick 1999). In 1996, 470 000 Canadians moved closer to family members either to provide care or because they needed care. Many of these people (130 000) moved into the same home with these family members.

Studies find that men get less informal support than women from non-spousal supporters. This shows up most clearly in the case of less serious illnesses. Chappell (1989) concludes that women's stronger emotional bonds with friends and family lead to greater support. Chappell, Segall, and Lewis (1990) found the same trend toward greater support for women regardless of the type of illness (common ailments, health emergencies, or functional disability). Compared with men, women tend to consult more family and friends regarding common ailments. Women, more often than men, say they would consult a relative outside the house for a health emergency. And women, compared with men, report support from more helpers and more help from daughters and relatives for functional disabilities. Older people who have a helping network feel greater subjective well-being.

Two conditions lead to the use of formal supports along with informal supports. First, some older people have incomplete informal networks and need specific kinds of help (such as someone to shop for them). Second, some older people who have intact networks have high health care needs. For example, caregivers who care for older family members with dementia use more personal care services and in-home services than other caregivers (Hawranik 2002). The informal and formal systems work together in these cases to share the overall load.

Ward-Griffin (2002) found that both formal and informal care providers perform physical and emotional care work. Formal care providers, specifically nurses in this study, have professional knowledge and skills that differentiate them from family care providers. However, as Ward-Griffin says, the boundary between professionals and family caregivers blurs when family members develop caregiving skills and knowledge. In other related work, Ward-Griffin (2000) found that in caregiving situations, where nurses and family caregivers worked together, nurses gradually transferred the caregiving labour to the family caregiver. She found that family caregivers did most of the physical and economic care, but got little practical assistance. Ward-Griffin argues for a more equitable sharing of responsibility between family and professional caregivers.

Policy often speaks of partnerships between state programs and informal supports. But a number of researchers ask whether this new focus on the family will provide better care or simply shift the burden of care to families (Keating et al. 1997; Rosenthal 1997). Ward-Griffin and Marshall (2003), for example, see a growing imbalance as the state withdraws formal supports and expects more from informal supporters. Keating and her colleagues (1999) say that the emphasis on family and community care can place a heavy burden on **informal caregivers** who are typically family members. Harlton and her colleagues (1998) found that older people and policymakers differed in their view of care to older people. Policymakers thought that family and neighbourhood (informal) supports gave older people more control over their lives. But older people felt that family support made them more dependent and a burden on their families. They did not feel that family members should provide housing, financial support, or personal care (Kemp and Denton 2003). They preferred state-funded supports, believing that these supports gave them the most control over the services they received. Policymakers need to learn more about the views of older clients and their families in order to create programs that meet older people's needs. Kunemund and Rein (1999) find that generous state-funded social and health care supports strengthen rather than weaken family solidarity.

Rosenthal (1997) sees some further issues related to care of older people. She describes a conflict between the policy to shift care to the family, the increase in the number of older people, and the decrease in available women to provide family care. Middle-aged women (traditional caregivers) have entered the labour force in large numbers. They now have to juggle work and care for older parents. This added demand leads to stress, absenteeism, and sometimes withdrawal from work. Rosenthal recommends that the government fund programs and resources to support the policy shift to family care. Caregiver problems (such as juggling multiple responsibilities) remain personal troubles. Rosenthal says that the government needs to see them as public issues. And the government needs to provide formal supports to help family caregivers fulfill their roles.

Children as a Source of Informal Support

Adult children stay in touch with older parents. Among adult children 25 to 54 years of age, 7 out of 10 contact their mothers at least once a week by telephone, letters, or through visits (Townsend-Batten 2002). Six out of 10 of this age group stays in frequent contact with their fathers. Daughters, compared to sons, have more contact with their mothers. And both daughters and sons have more frequent contact with mothers than with fathers. This may reflect the kin keeper role that mothers often play in families (Rosenthal 1995). Contact between adult children and parents leads to greater feelings of life satisfaction and well-being for older people (Rowe and Kahn 1998).

Adult children provide much of the support needed by their parents. Research finds that even older adults who reside in long-term care facilities receive informal help from their children (Dupuis and Smale 2004). Keefe and Fancey (2002) report that strong feelings of attachment to a parent and recognition of past help and support lead to caregiving. Other studies report that daughters, compared with sons, provide more care to parents. Daughters (compared to sons) also report greater feelings of stress (Penning 1998). Daughters-in-law often provide care to their husband's parents. They may feel responsible to give care even if they don't feel affection for the parent (Guberman 1999). Single women provided more care than any other type of caregiver (Connidis, Rosenthal, and McMullin 1996). Walker (1996) traces this fact to cultural pressures on women to give care. One woman put it simply: "Who else is going to do it?" (Aronson 1992; Walker 1996).

Keefe and Fancey (2003) looked at reciprocity in the caregiving relationship between older mothers and their employed daughters. Four findings come from their work. First, parents and children each tend to focus on the period of time when they most needed assistance. For the daughter, this means focusing on the past when her mother provided most help and support. For older mothers, this means focusing on the present and the assistance she now receives from her daughter. Second, older mothers tend to minimize and downplay the importance of their past help to their daughters. Third, the daughters' recognition of past help and support

from their mothers was critical for understanding the daughters' present commitment to parent care. Fourth, the daughters' employment affected how much support she could give to her mother.

Studies show that adult children and their parents see the amount of support provided by the children differently. Many studies report that older people feel they receive less support than their children say they give. Early work by Bengtson and Kuypers (1971) referred to this as differences in the **developmental stake**. Older people have a greater stake in the relationship with their children. They have invested more in the relationship and they have more to lose if it fails (Jerrome 1996). So older people tend to emphasize the existence of family harmony and solidarity. They may de-emphasize the amount of support they receive in order not to see themselves as a burden on their children. This difference in perception can create tensions in the family. Adult children may feel that their parents do not appreciate how much they do for them, even though the children may feel they do as much as they can.

Research shows that intergenerational interaction has grown in intensity and complexity in recent years. Older people and their children live longer lives and spend more years interacting with one another. Gee (1988) reported that in Canada from the 1830s to the 1950s, the number of years spent parenting declined for women, but the time spent as an adult child increased. Today, people spend more years as an adult child of living parents than as parents of young children. This trend will continue in the future. In some cases, child caregivers of older parents will also need support as they grow older.

Three provinces—Nova Scotia, Ontario, and Quebec—offer programs that provide financial support to caregivers of older family members. These programs have one of two goals: (1) to reward caregivers for their efforts or (2) to help with the cost of caregiving to delay institutionalization of the older person. Controversy exists over this approach to providing care. Some writers argue that payment to family members strengthens family values. Others claim that payment (at generally low wages) exploits family members who have little choice but to accept the job. Finally, policymakers worry that payment will lead to fraud and abuse of the program and the older person (Blaser 1998). Payment to family members (who now give care for free) may also lead to an increase in the cost of caring for older people.

Keefe and Fancey (1997) studied a financial support program in Nova Scotia. They compared three groups of family caregivers (mostly daughters). One group received home care support (homemaking and nursing support), a second group received financial support to provide care, and a third group received both types of support. Keefe and Fancey found that paid caregivers tended to be younger women who live in a non-urban setting with the care receiver. Those who received home care support tended to be sons or spouses who live in an urban setting. The paid caregivers felt more burdened by caregiving. They spent more time and energy and felt more tired and anxious than the caregivers receiving home support.

The researchers conclude that financial support buys the time and services of family caregivers when they have access to few formal supports. But the findings suggest that financial support helps caregivers cope only with the economic costs. Paid caregivers still experience more personal cost than caregivers who get home help. Some writers feel that financial support programs give public recognition to caregivers' efforts. Other writers fear that these types of programs will lead to increased costs to the system and to a decrease in the natural tendency of families to care for older members. Keefe and Fancey (1997) show that both types of support (home help and financial support) benefit caregivers. And, in the case of rural caregivers (with few formal services available), financial help makes the most sense. They propose that future programs combine financial support with home help services. This dual program would help caregivers cope with the stress of caregiving and might also lead more families to care for older relatives in the community.

Researchers say that changes in the family may limit informal caregiving in the future. For example, geographic mobility, immigration, greater numbers of young adult children living at home, smaller modern homes, multi-generational help needs, more pressure on fewer children, women in the workforce, caregiver burnout, and conflicting demands on caregivers may all put pressure on the informal care system. A lower birth rate and smaller numbers of children per family mean that middle-aged children will have fewer siblings to help support their aging parents.

Sources of Informal Support for Childless Older People

Adult children are a primary source of support and well-being for older parents. But who provides this support to older adults who are without children? Studies find that childless older people create a network of supportive family and friends. Those who have chosen to remain childless report high life satisfaction and happiness (Connidis and McMullin 1999). They have about the same satisfaction with life as married older people who have close relations with their children and higher satisfaction than parents with distant ties to children. McMullin and Marshall (1996, 356) report that "compared to parents, childless individuals experience less life stress and similar levels of well-being." Connidis and McMullin (1999) also find that childless older adults report financial benefits, greater freedom, and career flexibility.

Still, the social networks of older childless people offer less support when the older person becomes sick (Rubinstein 1996). Childless older people who report disadvantages point to lack of companionship, missed experiences and incompleteness, and lack of care in old age (Connidis and McMullin 1999). This group tends to be disadvantaged in other ways as well. They tend to be unmarried, older, female, less financially secure, in poorer health, and living alone. Widows in particular feel less advantage to childlessness. Because childless older people may lack informal support, they may need more formal supports than do older parents. They also face a greater risk of institutionalization than do people with children (Giranda, Luk, and Atchison 1999).

Friends as a Source of Informal Support

Studies find that people enjoy friends most in youth and in old age. High-quality friendships in later life lead to high life satisfaction (O'Connor 1995). Studies show that many older people get more enjoyment out of visits with friends than with family. Researchers say that people in a family may visit one another as a matter of routine or because they feel obliged to see one another. But when older people see their friends, they do so out of choice. Most older people choose friends from their own age group. Older people may have more in common with their friends than with younger family members, and shared interests and experiences lead to greater warmth and good feelings. Women tend to have closer ties to friends than men (Connidis 2001). MacRae (1996) studied older women in a small Nova Scotia town and found that the women (aged 65 to 98) had active friendships. Almost all of them had a close or intimate friend. MacRae says that friendships can last over many years and play a vital part in helping older people maintain their identity.

De Vries, Jacoby, and Davis (1996) studied friendship patterns and satisfaction with friendship among older people from different ethnic groups. They found that compared to people of French origin, people of British origin reported more friendships. French older people tended to form friendships in their neighbourhood and through family. The French lived closest to their friends. The British, compared to other ethnic groups, tended to live farther from their friends. The authors suggest that for French older people, their geographic closeness, unique definition of friendship, and familial orientation may account for these differences. Ethnicity plays a role in shaping the size and pattern of friendship networks in later life.

Researchers say that friendships can help older people overcome problems caused by lost work roles and the lost spouse role in old age (Field 1999). Older people use friends for social and emotional support (MacRae 1996). Friends help each other cope with life difficulties and stressful events. Friends who are the same age often share the same physical limits, the same interests, and the same historical background. Lifelong friends also share cherished experiences and memories. Research shows the importance of close and supportive friendships in the lives of older adults (Adams and Blieszner 1995; MacRae 1996). A variety of relationships, including friendships, create a full and satisfying support network.

Siblings as a Source of Informal Support

Eighty percent of older adults have at least one living sibling; the sibling bond often lasts throughout a lifetime. Siblings can serve as an important source of social support for older people. But their importance often gets overlooked (Campbell, Connidis, and Davies 1999). The supportive role of a sibling will vary by individual need and circumstance. For example, a married older person with many children nearby may make little use of sibling support. Campbell, Connidis, and Davies (1999) found that single people and women make the most use of sibling supports (Barrett and Lynch 1999; Connidis and Campbell 1995). Childless older people, compared with people with children, set up more supportive ties with their siblings (Connidis and Campbell 1995). They tend to get more support from siblings when they get ill. Childless siblings also tend to give support to their brothers and sisters (Barrett and Lynch 1999). Rubinstein (1996) reports that childless women often build relationships with siblings' children or the children of non-relatives.

In general, older women tend to have more active sibling ties than older men, with ties between sisters stronger than ties between brothers or a brother and sister (Connidis 2001). Geographic proximity influences some types of support but not others. For example, while companionship requires in-person contact, con-

fiding and emotional support between siblings can occur over a greater distance (Campbell, Connidis, and Davies 1999). Siblings more often provide emotional support than practical support, even for those who live close by (Miner and Uhlenberg 1997).

Informal Support and Caregiver Burden

Research shows that older people often use informal supports and that these supports succeed in keeping people out of institutions. Married people have a built-in caregiving system—most older Canadians reported their spouse as their main source of support. Even old and frail people continued to give care to their cognitively impaired spouses. In late old age, when people have serious functional disabilities, married people have half the institutionalization rate of unmarried older people.

Many studies report that giving care to a physically disabled or cognitively impaired older person can lead to feelings of **caregiver burden**. This refers to problems and stress due to caregiving. Some research suggests that spouses of those receiving care suffer a greater burden from caregiving than do adult children. They may feel the strain more as they see their partner decline (especially if the person shows mental as well as physical decline). Lévesque, Cossette, and Lachance (1998) found that a negative view of dysfunctional behaviour led to psychological distress and negative feelings about caregiving. O'Rourke and his colleagues (1996) found that caregivers felt subjective burden (for example, a feeling of hopelessness) apart from specific caregiving demands.

Research suggests that the caregiver's interpretation of the situation may lead to greater or lesser feelings of burden. For example, Chappell and Reid (2002) found that the caregiver's perception of social support was related to their feeling of well-being. O'Rourke and Wenaus (1998, 385) found that spouses who show an "inordinately positive appraisal of their spouse and marriage" suffer the least burden. They propose that spouses may reconstruct their marriage as positive in the past to balance the stresses they face in the present. "Provision of care thus serves as perceived payment or appreciation for the privilege of sharing their lives in better times" (396). Caregivers who can identify some positive feelings about caregiving have lower depression, less burden, and better self-reported health (Cohen, Colantonio, and Vernich 2002).

Spouses may have health problems themselves that make caregiving difficult and add to the feeling of burden. They may also have fewer resources (financial and social) to call on than would a middle-aged child. Jutras and Lavoie (1995) report that people who lived with an impaired older person (many of them spouses), compared with those who did not, felt stress and reported poor psychological well-being. Family caregivers feel a loss of control and autonomy. One caregiver reports, "I feel like, like now, I'm all on tenterhooks. I feel like I'm on a treadmill, all the time, all the time, and I can't get off this thing" (cited in O'Connor 1999, 226). Kin caregivers also report stress due to tasks like cleaning, doing laundry, and shopping. Still, O'Connor reports that many spouse caregivers refuse to use outside help. They feel an obligation to their spouse and they feel that they can give the best care.

Even after a spouse enters an institution, a caregiver spouse feels caregiver burden. Loos and Bowd (1997) found that caregiver spouses felt guilty after institutionalization. Spouses of institutionalized older people, compared with adult children, feel more physical and developmental burden. Physical burden referred to the strain of long visits and travel to the institution. Hallman and Joseph (1999) found that women, compared to men, spend more time travelling to give care. Developmental burden referred to spouses' feelings of being unable to get on with life. One wife told Gladstone (1995, 56) that "when you're apart after never being apart it has an effect on you. You seem to be in a turmoil. We'd known each other since we were 14 years old so we were together a long, long time."

In the early 1990s, Rosenthal and Dawson (1991) identified the concept of **quasi-widowhood.** Ross, Rosenthal, and Dawson (1994) studied 40 wives who had placed their husbands in nursing homes. These women said that they felt relief after placement. But they also felt failure, "anger, guilt, sadness, depression and grief" (40). Most women over time adapt to living with a spouse in an institution (see also Loos and Bowd 1997). Overall, they express satisfaction with the care their husbands receive (Dawson and Rosenthal 1996). Some women accept the loss of their spouse as a friend and companion and restructure their lives outside the institution.

Other spouses keep close ties to the institution. Ross, Rosenthal, and Dawson (1997a, 1997b) found that more than 80 percent of the wives in their study visited their husbands at least several times a week. About 20 percent visited every day. This pattern continued over the nine-month period of the study. Most wives said they visited out of love, devotion, and duty. Active visitors over this period, the researchers said, were "holding on to the past." They often had husbands with physical impairments. Active visitors took on a variety of tasks, including planning birthday parties, personalizing their husband's room, and bringing in special foods. Overall, active visitors provided care as a way to maintain their attachment to their husbands and as a way to maintain their role as a wife and supporter. Wives felt most satisfied if they felt useful. But the researchers found that active visitors felt more depressed at the end of nine months and felt dissatisfied with the care their husbands got.

This study suggests that wives who begin to give up the caregiver role do better after their husbands are institutionalized. The researchers found that about two-thirds of spouses gave up some of their caregiving responsibility. These wives had cognitively impaired spouses. They visited less and allowed staff to take on the job of caring. The process this group began going through is called "embracing new realities." They felt less depressed and said they felt "sort of like a widow" (Ross, Rosenthal, and Dawson 1994, 29). Healing began to take place as wives gained distance from the caregiver role.

Some caregivers report feelings of satisfaction and accomplishment. Greater commitment to and enthusiasm in the caregiving role can lead to greater feelings of well-being (Pierce, Lydon, and Yang 2001). Cohen, Colantonio, and Vernich (2002) found that 73 percent of caregivers could identify at least one positive thing about caregiving. An additional 7 percent identified more than one positive thing. Caregivers enjoyed helping their care receiver feel better. They also felt duty and love toward their care receiver (Ross, Rosenthal, and Dawson 1997a). Chappell and Kuehne (1998) studied caregiving spouses. They found that most couples expressed positive feelings about caregiving. Campbell (2002) found that many adult sons said their relationship with their parent improved after they began caregiving.

But many family members pay an emotional and psychological price when they take on informal caregiving. Caregivers of cognitively impaired older people, particularly those caring for relatives with Alzheimer's disease or other forms of dementia, many of them spouses, feel the most stress (Keefe and Medjuck 1997). MacRae (1999) found that a majority of caregivers at some time felt shame and embarrassment at a care receiver's behaviour. Spouses often tried to cover up the problem of memory loss. Children prepared situations in advance or avoided situations where a parent's memory loss would prove embarrassing. Many family members caring for a person with AD conceal the illness from others to protect the person from negative labelling (MacRae 2002). Many caregivers of persons with dementia feel stress associated with the illness (O'Rourke and Cappeliez 2002). Caregivers often feel isolated, fatigued, and overwhelmed by the strain of care.

Caregiving leads to a variety of tensions for middle-aged children. They often feel both intense pressure in trying to meet the demands on their time made by work, their children, and caregiving, and emotional upset at having to deal with an ill parent (Keating et al. 1999). A respondent in one study of middle-aged children said, "I have looked after both parents for twenty-seven years and they have become very dependent on me. We are very tied down and I don't know how much more my nerves and health can stand" (Marshall, Rosenthal, and Synge 1983). In another study, a woman said, "[Mother] has been getting more and more forgetful and confused and can't be alone at all. I'm depressed, and I don't sleep well. How can I go to work when she needs constant supervision?" (Brody 1990, ix).

Rosenthal and Matthews (1999) find that many caregivers combine managerial care (that is, orchestrating care, managing finances, arranging formal services, and providing financial assistance) with other types of assistance. Providing managerial care, particularly organizing and coordinating the care that is needed, contributes to stress for women and to personal and work-related costs for both men and women. Joseph and Hallman (1996) found that adult children feel stress due to travel time to their care receiver. The researchers found that some older adults moved closer to their caregiver to relieve some of this stress. Other care receivers moved into their caregiver's home, a move that may lessen stress due to travel but also create new tensions.

Caregiving can bring up the inherent tension between the adult child's personal autonomy and his or her interdependence within a family. Joseph and Hallman (1996) report that caregivers sometimes used vacation time to manage their caregiving tasks. Caregivers report conflicts between family and work responsibilities (Gignac, Kelloway, and Gottlieb 1996; see also Cranswick 1997). For women, this shows up as job dissatisfaction and absenteeism. For men, it shows up as job costs and absenteeism. Many caregivers feel they are unable to take a vacation because of their caregiving responsibilities (Campbell 2002). These feelings can lead to disappointment, resentment, and frustration.

Even adult children who do not consider themselves primary caregivers feel concern about their parents. Those who have parents living in long-term care facilities often continue to play a significant role in the parent's care (Gladstone and Wexler 2000, 2002a; Keefe and Fancey 2000; Ross, Carswell, and Dalziel 2002). Research finds that 70 percent of family members visit at least weekly (Ross, Carswell, and Dalziel 2002). Family members often feel responsible to monitor the care their older relative receives in the facility. Ross, Carswell, and Dalziel (2002) found that family members provide both direct and indirect care in the facility, including making their relative's environment more home-like (33 percent), providing personal care (26 percent), and acting as advocates for their relatives and watching over their care (40 percent).

Keefe and Fancey (2000) report that more than half of family members saw no change in their perceived responsibility after their care receiver moved to a facility. People who reduced their caregiving tended to cut back on direct supports such as transportation, meals, or laundry service. Some family members felt their responsibility had increased after a relative entered an institution. They said they spent time at the facility visiting or dealing with their relative's affairs.

This increased responsibility often came from changes in the older resident's health. One daughter in Keefe and Fancey's study said about her mother that "as her confusion is getting worse I'm finding myself called upon more to sort out the messes either by phone [to the facility] or leaving our jobs [her husband accompanies her] and going up [to the facility] for the afternoon" (240). This change from direct responsibility to indirect responsibility took time and energy from other responsibilities.

Research shows that a good relationship between family members and facility staff enhances the well-being of residents and family members. Gladstone and Wexler (2002b) found a more positive relationship between families and nursing staff in long-term care facilities when the nurses felt their care was recognized and appreciated by family. Family members who created friendly and open relations with staff, who appreciated the difficulties faced by staff, and who recognized the nurses' expertise and experience tended to have better relationships with nursing staff. Family members felt that having a good relationship with staff could mean an extra hug or pat on the shoulder for their family member. It also improved the quality of family visits (Gladstone and Wexler 2002a). In good family–staff relationships, family members expressed appreciation to the staff and assisted them with instrumental tasks (Gladstone and Wexler 2000). Iwasiw et al. (2003) say that nursing staff in long-term care facilities can benefit from listening to family members about older residents' experiences and needs. This can improve the level of care and the quality of life for residents.

Most studies show that females report more strain from caregiving than males. These women suffer more physical strain, lower morale, and greater psychological burden than men. In the early 1980s, Brody (1981) proposed that women could get caught in the middle—

sandwiched between care for their children and care for their parents. "Such women are in middle age, in the middle from a generational standpoint, and in the middle in that the demands of their various roles compete for their time and energy" (471). But recent studies question this view of middle age. They find that relatively few women get caught in the middle like this (Rosenthal, Martin-Matthews, and Matthews 1996).

Rosenthal (2000) examined this sandwich generation. These people have at least one living parent and at least one child living in the household. Based on data from the 1990 General Social Survey, Rosenthal, Martin-Matthews, and Matthews (1996) found that 71 percent of women aged 35 to 39 had the structural potential to be sandwiched between parents and young children (having both an older parent and a child living at home). This number dropped to 51 percent for those aged 45 to 49, and to 24 percent for women aged 50 to 54. But the proportion of women in this sandwich generation who actually provide care to an older parent at least monthly and who have a child living at home was very low. The highest percentage in any age group was only 13 percent of women. Most daughters who cared for older parents had grown children who had moved out of the house. Most were also not in the paid labour force. Rosenthal, Martin-Matthews, and Matthews (1996) conclude that relatively few Canadians get "caught in the middle." But they say that when it does occur, it can create a heavy burden.

Does this mean that middle-aged children feel little caregiver burden? First, a large minority (about one-third) of sandwich generation members do face demands from children and very old parents. Hirdes and Strain (1995) looked at the balance of exchange in support (such as housework and personal care) between young, middle-aged, and older people in Canada. They found that children and older people tend to get more support than they give. But middle-aged people tend to provide more support than they get. Second, the need to give care to an older parent alone may create tensions for middle-aged children. Third, middle-aged women do more caregiving than men. Many of these women work outside the home and face demands at work that make caregiving for a parent more stressful.

Myles (1991) called the trend toward more women working outside the home and having less time available to provide care to older parents a "caregiving crunch." But research finds that employed women provide as much care to parents as non-employed women (Rosenthal et al. 1999). Rosenthal (2000) says that this "crunch" does not lessen the informal care working women give to older parents. Instead, working women feel the "crunch" because society expects women to serve

as caregivers. Research shows that these women experience more stress and greater absenteeism from work (Matthews and Campbell 1995). Researchers say that caregivers need to work out family strategies to cope with stress. They also need job flexibility and community supports to help them stay at work. Social policies and services need to provide options to family care (Rosenthal 2000).

Unless some reform takes place, however, women will continue to absorb the cost of caregiving in the community. Myles (1991) said that changed workplace norms and more sympathetic personnel practices could help ease this crunch. But he also called for more radical reform, saying that "nothing short of a revolution in gender relations and in the sexual division of caregiving work is required to solve the problem" (84).

Men as Caregivers

Women provide the majority of care to older family members (Hallman and Joseph 1999; Keating et al. 1999). But men also provide care, particularly adult sons (Campbell and Martin-Matthews 2000a; Campbell and Martin-Matthews 2003; Harris 1998) and older husbands (Miller and Kaufman 1996; Rose and Bruce 1995). And men may take a more active role in caregiving in the future. Demographic changes, changes in family size and structure, and women's increased employment outside the home all increase the chances that a man will provide care to an aging parent or spouse.

Research finds that husbands play a significant role in caring for their wives in later life (Rose and Bruce 1995; Russell 2001). Husbands make up about 40 percent of spousal caregivers. Studies also find that husbands and wives provide about the same amount and types of care (Miller and Kaufman 1996). Research suggests that husbands feel committed to the care of their wives. They often see caregiving as an extension of their work role—a "new career," or a continuation of their authority in the family (Rose and Bruce 1995). But some men do not feel comfortable providing care that involves "traditionally female" tasks, such as domestic work and personal care. These men report "role incongruence." Still, they feel satisfaction and a sense of accomplishment in being able to provide care to their spouse (Bamford et al. 1998).

Younger men, like younger women, often must balance multiple roles (Campbell 2002; Martin-Matthews and Campbell 1995). They care for an older parent, but still fill the roles of spouse, employee, and parent. This balancing act can create a strain and feelings of burden. Adult sons make up 15 to 40 percent of adult child caregivers. Care by adult sons, in general, tends to fit with "traditional" roles for men within families. They take on finan-

● **Exhibit 13.4**

CAREGIVING SONS TALK ABOUT THEIR EXPERIENCES

In Campbell's (2002) study, sons talked about their experiences caring for an older parent. The following comments reveal their commitment to care, the importance of caregiving in their lives, and the emotional journey they experienced in this caregiving role.

- "I owe her because she spent a lot of years bringing me up but I wasn't all that great as a kid. She did a lot for me and I just figure at this time in her life that she needs me there, and I am dedicated."
- "I feel pride, and being satisfied that I'm doing something good. So it has given me, one might say, value in my life."
- "I'm looking after him 24 hours a day, 7 days a week and it gets a little stressful sometimes. But our relationship is so close, that's why I do it."

- "Everything is all mixed together. You feel everything. You just put one foot in front of the other and whatever hits you hits you. If you want to sit down and cry then you sit down and cry and then you kind of carry on."
- "It slowly evolved and it's just like you're adding another brick onto the pile, so you don't notice it all that much. It's easier when it comes gradually because if it was sudden, I'm sure it would have floored me."
- "I used to be very outgoing, very happy-go-lucky, you know. Not a lot of things used to bother me. Now I find myself, some days, if I have a bad day, sort of short with people, sort of sad and, you know, sort of edgy, that's in a negative way. But in a positive light, it's opened my eyes that there are people that need help."

Source: Lori D. Campbell, 2002, "Men Who Care: Exploring the Male Experience in Filial Caregiving." Paper presented at the International Symposium Reconceptualising Gender and Ageing, University of Surrey, Guildford, U.K., June 25–27.

cial and managerial work, home maintenance chores, and yardwork (Campbell and Martin-Matthews 2000a; Keating et al. 1999). Adult daughters, compared to sons, more often take on the care of both mothers and fathers. Daughters also tend to provide assistance with domestic tasks or personal care, such as bathing, dressing, and toileting. A number of factors influence sons' level of involvement in caregiving—how close the son lives to his parents, the age of the children in his own family, whether he has siblings, and feelings of obligation (Campbell and Martin-Matthews 2000a). For example, living farther away and having young children at home appears to limit a man's involvement in parental care (Campbell and Martin-Matthews 2003). However, a man who has no brothers or sisters and who feels an obligation toward his parents may provide more assistance.

Matthews and Heidorn (1998) studied brothers-only sibling groups. They found that sons kept in contact with their parents and engaged in gender-typical services—yardwork or financial advice. They also accepted both informal and formal services as ways to meet their parents' needs. Sons attempted to keep parents as independent from them as possible.

The gendered nature of the care tasks also tends to influence sons' involvement in care (Campbell and Martin-Matthews 2003). For example, men with a higher income do less traditionally female care (such as domestic chores and personal care), while men with a higher education do more traditionally male care (including financial management). Campbell and Martin-Matthews (2003, S356) suggest that "men who possess more resources (education and income) may be able to use these resources to take on the role expected for men in care, and to limit or resist care that is more nontraditional care for men."

Qualitative research shows the greater complexity that exists in sons' care to older parents (Campbell 2002; Parsons 1997). Sons provide a wide range of support, including assisting with domestic and personal care (Campbell 2002; Harris 1998). Campbell (2002) collected data on 60 adult sons who provide care to older parents. She finds some common themes in the experiences of these sons. For example, most men provided care out of a sense of commitment to family. They felt a strong bond to their parent and a desire to repay them for past support. Many sons talked about how providing care had brought them emotionally closer to their parent. For most, the caregiving role evolved as a gradual process. Men experienced a mixture of emotions, including feelings of love, compassion, responsibility, as well as sadness, frustration, and guilt. They also talked about how caregiving had changed their lives. It helped them to develop greater patience, compassion, and tolerance.

Campbell (2002) also reports differences between married and never-married sons in their involvement in care. In general, married sons more often worked, less often lived with their parent, and more often gave care in limited and traditional ways (visiting, providing help with transportation, home maintenance). These sons saw their caregiving role as only one role that had to fit into their family and work lives.

In contrast, never-married sons more often lived with their parent, did not work or had marginal work, and were more involved in care (including domestic and personal care). For these sons, caregiving played a central role in their lives. It gave their lives meaning and purpose. Never-married sons often had little or no social support, few financial resources, and intense caregiving responsibilities. This made them particularly vulnerable to caregiver stress and burden.

Many men feel stress and burden in caregiving. Some husbands may need care themselves, and sons may juggle multiple responsibilities in order to provide care. But sons say they feel good about caregiving and that caregiving gives them "a chance to pay their parents back for their care, a sense of purpose and personal growth, and the importance of being a role model for their children" (Harris 1998, 347; see also Campbell 2002).

Care for the Caregiver

A number of researchers have proposed ways to ease caregiver burden (Chappell and Reid 2002; Chappell, Reid, and Dow 2001; Gottlieb and Johnson 2000; Hebert et al. 2003). Some of these proposals are listed below.

1. **Family counselling** can help ease the burden of caregiving. Counselling works best when it takes into account the entire family system—the caregiver's spouse, children, and siblings, as well as the older person. Counselling can help caregivers deal with moral conflicts about how much protection to give a care receiver. Counselling or psychotherapy can help a caregiver deal with stress and depression. Gendron and her colleagues (1996) report on the value of skill training. They found that assertiveness training and cognitive restructuring (taking a more positive view of caregiving) led to a feeling of less caregiver burden. Hébert and his colleagues (2003) studied caregivers who attend weekly psycho-educational group sessions. These sessions focus on stress appraisal and coping. Group members

showed improvements in their reaction to behavioural problems.

2. **Support groups** give caregivers information about how to cope with caregiving demands. They also give caregivers emotional support. The Alzheimer's Society, hospitals, and churches offer support groups. Some groups offer support based on a specific disease (e.g., dementia or cancer). Some of these groups have a professional leader; others work as self-help groups. Only a small percentage of older caregivers (about 4.5 percent) use support groups (Colantonio, Cohen, and Corlett 1998, citing the Canadian Study of Health and Aging Working Group 1994). But a report on a small sample of registered caregivers in Toronto found that 26 percent of the sample said they would like to use a support group (Colantonio, Cohen, and Corlett 1998). People in support groups often report feelings of relief and greater ability to manage as caregivers (Gallagher and Hagen 1996; Hagen, Gallagher, and Simpson 1997). Demers and Lavoie (1996) found mixed results in a study of support groups. They found that caregiver burden increased among support group members, but depressive symptoms remained stable. Other forms of support that may benefit caregivers include telephone support (Ploeg et al. 2001) and online supports (including e-mail correspondence and support groups).

3. **Respite services** in the community give caregivers a break from the demands of caregiving (Chappell 1997). These services range from friendly visitors who stay with the care receiver for a few hours to full-day adult day care, to longer institutional respite. Institutional respite programs can last from several days to several weeks, allowing caregivers to take vacations, deal with personal needs like medical treatment, or simply rest.

Chappell (1997) conducted an evaluation of respite services. She found that regulations created barriers that sometimes prevented caregivers from getting the help they needed. Barriers included a minimum two-night stay for respite admission, slow processing of respite requests, and failure to link the need for respite to the caregiver's condition. Lack of funding also limits the availability of respite care. Some research finds that behaviour problems decrease after respite. But caregivers still feel some burden. Other studies of respite have also found mixed results.

Gottlieb and Johnson (2000) reviewed the literature on centre-based respite programs for dementia caregivers. They found that the services, when offered, appear to be "too little, too late." They said that between one-third and one-half of caregivers did not use the service. Those who did often began the programs two to four years into their caregiving career. Many dropped out soon after they began. Gottleib and Johnson (2000) report little measurable benefit from these respite care programs. Yet many family caregivers value and want respite. One caregiver, who got in-home respite, said, "I kept my sanity. I could breathe again, and I wasn't spinning in circles.... I was more patient, happier, and more caring" (Chappell 1997, 26).

In a study by Dupuis and Smale (2004), caregivers of persons with dementia identified a number of issues related to respite services and programs. These include the need for immediate and readily accessible emergency respite to deal with crises, more hours of in-home respite care, and more flexible respite programs such as short-term and overnight respite care. As one wife caring for her husband said, "I use to just pray that there was a hotel or something you could take them to just so you could sleep one night" (26). Caregivers also identified the need for meaningful social and recreational respite programs for the persons with dementia.

Other work by Chappell, Reid, and Dow (2001) suggests that the meaning of respite differs among caregivers and may not just be related to services or organized programs. Almost half of the caregivers in their study defined respite as "stolen moments." This involved activities or situations that for a short time took them away from the worries of caregiving. These stolen moments could be a few hours spent with family or friends. None of the caregivers in the study talked about respite in terms of services. Dupuis (2000) finds that caregiving daughters who experienced "leisure moments" in the institution-based caregiving context felt more enjoyment in care. People in the middle phase of caregiving (ten months to two years of care) enjoyed leisure moments, compared to those in earlier or later phases of care (Dupuis and Smale 2000). These stolen or leisure moments may provide caregivers with a form of respite that is more a state of mind than a tangible service.

4. **Eldercare programs** at work can help family caregivers cope. These programs include counselling

services, information on community services and support, and flexible work schedules. Some research shows that children who provide care, particularly middle-aged caregiving daughters, may quit their jobs to take care of their parent. Other women reduce their work hours. Employed daughters feel increased stress trying to balance caregiving and paid employment (Keefe and Fancey 2002). Research finds that mothers of working women get the same number of hours of care (formal and informal) as mothers of non-working women, but the working women often have to pay for personal care and meal services. These paid services fill in for them while they work.

A study done in the 1990s by the Canadian Aging Research Network (CARNET) asked more than 5000 employees in eight organizations about their caregiving responsibilities (Gottlieb and Kelloway 1993). The researchers found that 46 percent of workers gave some care to an older person. Types of care fell into three groups: help with activities of daily living (ADLs), such as bathing and grooming; help with instrumental activities of daily living (IADLs), such as help with shopping and transportation; and management help, such as managing money or arranging for services. Management help created some of the greatest stress on workers. Twenty-six percent of the people who provided care to older parents also cared for a child under age 19. Gottlieb and his colleagues (1994; see also Martin-Matthews and Campbell 1995) found that women with young children at home who provided care to older parents faced a high risk of personal and job costs. One-quarter of workers who cared for older parents averaged nine hours per week helping with activities of daily living as well as general care. The rest averaged three hours per week of general help such as household chores.

Caregiving for many workers leads to stress and time away from the job. About one-third of working caregivers in the CARNET study said that caregiving disturbed their work. Barling, MacEwen, and Kelloway (1994) found that caring for older parents led to absenteeism from work and psychological strain. Compared with other workers, people who cared for young children and an older parent had four times the proportion of absences from work. Caregiving also leads to fewer special projects at work, less business travel, and fewer promotions (Keefe and Medjuck 1997; Martin-Matthews and Campbell 1995). Guberman and Maheu (1999) found that caregivers had to juggle their responsibilities to manage both work and caregiving. They face the constant threat of a breakdown in their support system (e.g., a home care worker may call in sick). Some caregivers have to cut back on leisure, education, and volunteer activities.

Some companies have responded to this problem. More than a decade ago, in 1992, the Royal Bank began an eldercare program that offered counselling and referred workers to community supports (Nemeth and Howse 1994). Research at that time (Gottlieb and Kelloway 1993) found that flexible work schedules for caregivers led to less stress and more job satisfaction. Dual caregivers (those who cared for children and older parents) made the most use of Employee Assistance Programs and part-time employment. Still, companies could do more to implement these programs and inform workers about eldercare options. Medjuck, Keefe, and Fancey (1998) studied 37 workplaces in Nova Scotia. They found that only half of the human resources documents they studied contained a family leave policy. Those that had leave policies often had restrictions that limited their usefulness. Less than a third of the documents referred to an employee assistance program to help employees cope with stress and social issues. Current research shows that companies should make eldercare information and programs more available to workers.

Good programs and other interventions cannot completely do away with all feelings of burden, nor should they be expected to. Spouses and children feel loss, anger, and frustration as they see a person close to them suffer through an illness. These feelings reflect a legitimate response to a parent's or spouse's suffering. But interventions can help caregivers understand caregiving; they can help caregivers cope with the everyday demands of care; and they can give caregivers social and emotional support.

Few of the proposals to ease caregiver burden address the large-scale issues of gender inequality or the changing role of women in the labour force. For example, current programs and policies that are meant to help caregivers take family caregiving for granted, putting the burden on female family members. Too often help for caregivers comes into play only when family care breaks down. And the rhetoric about family care suggests that the state will try to shift more caregiving to family members. Guberman and Maheu (2002) say that practitioners and policymakers must move to a more community-oriented approach to caregiving. This will remove primary responsibility for care from families and family caregivers and shift to a more collective responsibility where families are only one of many available resources. Caregiving demands will increase in the future. Researchers propose more studies of caregiving policies.

The Future of Informal Support

Informal supports play a vital role in the well-being of older people. But the availability of informal supports may decrease in the years ahead. At least three changes in Canadian society point to this likelihood.

First, changes in demography may decrease the amount of informal support older people will get in the future. Family size has shrunk, so older people in the future will have fewer children to call on for help. A decrease in the availability of nuclear family supports will increase the risk of institutionalization. Also, the number of children over the age of 65 who care for their parents will increase in the future as more people live longer. Some of these children will be unable to care for their parents, and some may need health care help themselves.

Second, as people live longer, their support groups suffer from cohort attrition. Peers die off over time, leaving members of some support networks without help. This makes children a vital source of support for most older people as they age.

Because married women typically live longer than their spouse, they have to turn to children for support. Few studies have looked at how older women feel about relying on their children. Keefe and Fancey (2002) find that older mothers tend to overstate their present dependency on their caregiving daughters and diminish their own past support to daughters. Research needs to look more closely at older women who receive care. This will give family members and policymakers a better idea of what kind of support the older person wants. Research also needs to examine the support that older parents give to their caregivers and families over time to gain a better understanding of reciprocity and interdependency in family relationships.

Third, expressive ties for older people tend to decline because of the death of a spouse and cohort attrition. This change leads older people to use their remaining ties to meet expressive needs, potentially causing problems for the baby boom generation in the future. They have had fewer children of their own than did older people today. In the second or third decade of this century, the middle-aged children of baby boom parents may find themselves swamped by their parents' care needs.

These trends suggest potential problems with the availability of informal supports in the future. But other trends might lead to stronger informal supports. First, because of longer life expectancy, spouses will live together longer than ever before. This increased longevity will give married couples more informal support as they age. Greater longevity will also mean the parent–child relationship can endure long into the adult child's middle and later years. This may strengthen the bond within these relationships and the exchange of social support.

Second, current trends in health promotion (better diet, exercise, and a decrease in smoking) may lead to better health in old age. If these trends continue, older people in the future may need less long-term health care support.

Third, new types of groups based on the mutual needs of older people may develop. In the 1980s, Novak and Stone (1985) called these **semiformal structures** because they fall between the informal (voluntary) support structures of the family and the formal (professionalized) structures of the health and social service systems. Semiformal structures include car pools, groups of people in the same building who shop together, friendly visitors, or "daily hello" phone calls. These groups and relationships do not rely on informal kinship, friendship bonds, or the fee-for-service bond of formal supports. Instead, they are based on a bond of reciprocity and on the fact that they bring mutual benefit to users. More of these groups in the future could make up for losses in older people's networks.

Both trends—the decrease in informal supports and the increase in alternative forms of support (including home care and semiformal structures)—could get stronger in the future. The well-being of older people in the future will depend on how well alternatives to traditional supports meet their needs.

Researchers caution that current trends in policy may lead to future problems in long-term care. Current policy supports a shift in responsibility for care of older adults from institutions and professionals to "the community." This most often means a shift to the family and, typically, to the middle-aged or older woman (National Forum on Health 1997, cited in Pederson 2002). Government policy views formal support as an aid to family support. Armstrong (2002, 17) says that this approach of "'sending care to communities' most often means sending care to families and, within families, to women." Armstrong and others worry that this lack of government support for community services to meet the needs of these caregivers could damage personal networks, relationships, and families' ability to care. Women, as well as men, who choose to care for older

family members need support at work, good community supports, and institutional care when their care receiver needs it. Fewer institutional beds will leave families without this option.

A decade ago, Rosenthal (1994) said that formal support should play the central part in social support. Families (middle-aged women) could then decide how much or how little of this support they need. "We should not overestimate the availability or quality of family care," Rosenthal (421) said. "Some older people do not have family members who are able to provide care." Others may have family members who do not have the time or energy to give more than emotional support. Still others may prefer professional help to family care.

More recently, Rosenthal (2000) restated her belief in the need for society to take more responsibility in caring for older Canadians: "Whether families are or will be capable of providing needed support to older relatives must take second place to the question of who should be responsible for the care of older people. My position, one that is growing stronger over the years as I continue to learn more about older families, is that the care of the elderly is a public, not a private, issue and that responsibility lies with the state. Within that framework, we may then examine the role families might play if they are able and willing" (61).

ABUSE AGAINST OLDER PERSONS

Most older people get support and comfort from their families, but some people face exploitation and abuse. No single definition of abuse against older persons exists. But a broad definition refers to abuse and neglect as "any action or inaction by ANY person, which causes harm to the older or vulnerable person" (Council against Abuse of Older Persons 2002). Abuse against older persons includes physical abuse, psychosocial abuse, financial abuse, neglect (active or passive), institutional abuse, and domestic violence. Research shows that most abuse against older persons comes from family members. In this situation, many abused older people suffer in silence, making the rate of abuse hard to estimate and harder to eliminate. A number of studies of abuse against older persons in Canada discuss research findings, policy issues, and best practice.

Canadian Research Findings

Most Canadian research on abuse against older persons has used convenience samples, sometimes with low response rates. This makes it hard to generalize from these findings. Fifteen years ago, Podnieks et al. (1990) conducted Canada's first random-sample survey on abuse against older persons. The researchers conducted telephone interviews with a sample of 2008 people aged 65 and over who lived in private households. These people presented a statistically reliable picture of the 91 percent of seniors who lived on their own in the community. The survey asked about abuse carried out by family members and other intimates.

The sample contained about two-thirds women; 73 percent of respondents owned their own homes and 52 percent were married. About a third of the respondents received the Guaranteed Income Supplement (the federal government pension that goes to the poorest seniors); 63 percent reported good or excellent health, and the large majority shopped, cooked, and cleaned for themselves. Relatively few respondents reported feeling lonely, bored, or downhearted. The majority by far (92 percent) said they felt fairly happy or very happy.

The researchers defined four categories of abuse: material abuse, chronic verbal aggression, physical violence, and neglect (Podnieks et al. 1990). The study counted only the most serious and obvious cases. Because of this, the researchers cautioned that their findings probably underestimated the number of abused older people.

The study estimated that about 4 percent of all older people (about 98 000 people) in private dwellings in Canada had experienced abuse since turning age 65. This was similar to the rate (3.2 percent) that Pillemer and Finkelhor (1988) reported at about the same time for a random sample study in the United States. Most of these cases involve passive, verbal, emotional, and financial abuse, rather than physical violence or neglect. This fits with the findings of other research (Wolf 1996). More recent data from the 1999 General Social Survey (GSS) in Canada finds that 7 percent of older Canadians report some type of emotional or financial abuse, the most common types of abuse (Dauvergne 2003). These findings are significantly higher than earlier work suggested.

Podnieks and her colleagues (1990) found that about 2.5 percent of older adults in the Canadian study had experienced material abuse; about 1.4 percent of older adults experienced chronic verbal aggression; about 0.5 percent of older adults experienced physical violence; and about 0.4 percent of older adults experienced neglect. The study also found a fifth common form of abuse: denial of access to grandchildren. About 4 percent of older adults reported denial of access at least once since they turned age 65. If the researchers had included this category at the start of their study, the overall rate of abuse would nearly have doubled to 7 per-

cent of older adults. Nearly 0.8 percent of older adults in the study suffered from more than one form of abuse. The 1999 GSS finds this to be almost 2 percent of older Canadians (Dauvergne 2003). Rates in the 1999 GSS study run nearly twice as high as the earlier study by Podnieks and her colleagues (1990) reported.

Podnieks and her colleagues (1990) found that female victims of abuse outnumber male victims by almost two to one. Also, some types of people faced a higher risk for some types of abuse than for others. For example, people who reported material abuse tended to live more isolated lives and to have poor health. These people faced abuse from varied sources, including spouses, friends, children, and distant relatives. People who reported neglect were most often women with poor health, low morale, and a dependence on others for functional help. They faced abuse from spouses, children, and non-family caregivers.

Research in Quebec supports these findings (Lithwick et al. 1999). The researchers looked at 128 mistreatment cases involving older adults (aged 60 or older) in three community service agencies. The researchers found psychological abuse in 70 percent of cases, financial abuse in 41 percent of cases, neglect in 32 percent of cases, and physical abuse in 20 percent of cases. The majority of victims in this study were women (75 percent) while the majority of abusers were men (65 percent). Most abuse came from spouses (48 percent of cases) or adult children (30 percent of cases). More than one-half of these older victims suffered from two to four types of abuse.

Research has often focused on cases where a child caregiver abuses an older person he or she cares for. But recent studies show that often the abusing child relies on the abused person for financial support. Financial dependence can lead to resentment, anger, and abuse. Pittaway and Gallagher (1995) found that in 56 percent of cases of abused older people (aged 55 and over in their study) the abuser partly or wholly depended financially on the abused person. Bond and his colleagues (1999) studied cases of suspected financial abuse in a sample of mentally incompetent older Canadians. They found that the abused person was more likely to be female, to live in a long-term care facility or to own her own home, and to have a high monthly income. Often the nonpayment of bills in the long-term care facility signalled possible financial abuse.

People who report chronic verbal abuse and physical violence have some things in common. They tend to be married, and they report that the abuse came from their spouse. Beaulieu, Gravel, and Lithwick (1999) found that spouses differed from other people in their

● **Exhibit 13.5**

OLDER ADULT SUFFERS ABUSE OF TRUST

Dr. Peter Ingram, a psychogeriatric specialist in Winnipeg, describes a case of material abuse. He goes on to explain the options open to him and his patient once he detects the abuse.

Anastasia Kowalchuk (not her real name) is angry. She can't understand why the bank took $12 000 of her money, more than half the 87-year-old woman's savings.

Her niece, who had been visiting from Toronto, took her to the bank where Anastasia hoped to withdraw some money to donate to her community's nursing home, where she plans to move this year. She was shocked to see how little money she had left. With the help of her niece, she asked the bank to find out what had happened.

On a return visit, the bank manager showed her the transaction slip with her signature, authorizing the withdrawal. Although Anastasia's vision is dim from cataracts, she had to agree the signature looked like her own.

Anastasia has had trouble remembering things for some time. She forgets to pay her bills and deposit her pension cheques. When her friend Mary offered to help her with cooking meals and housekeeping two years ago for a small salary, it seemed like a good way to stay out of the nursing home.

When Mary more recently suggested she also help with the banking, Anastasia agreed. Now Mary is acting strangely; she has been shouting at Anastasia and told her not to talk to Sophia or Kateryna, her neighbours. As Anastasia speaks only a little English, she feels isolated without her daily chats in Ukrainian with her two elderly friends. She wishes her husband were alive to explain things. Anastasia's family doctor asked Dr. Ingram and his staff to assess her and look into the situation. A community nurse interviewed Anastasia's niece, neighbours, and someone from the bank. Dr. Ingram concludes that Anastasia may suffer from dementia and material abuse. Dr. Ingram will decide whether Anastasia can manage her finances or whether he should apply for an Order of Supervision. This order allows the Public Trustee to take over Anastasia's finances and ensures the safety of her savings.

Dr. Ingram may find that Anastasia has enough cognitive ability to look after her own affairs. In this case he can only warn her to take more care in managing her finances. If the abuser comes from Anastasia's family, Dr. Ingram says, "often nothing changes."

"This is very frustrating," he says, "and I find it hard to walk away from these people without helping them."

Source: P. Ingram, 1996, "Senior Suffers Abuse of Trust," *Winnipeg Free Press*, January 11, A6. Reprinted with permission.

pattern of abuse. They found that spouses "exercise strong psychological control, and they are the least reluctant to use physical force.... They are neglectful in a quarter of the cases of mistreatment" (8).

Both men and women report violent abuse. Both men and women also cause the abuse, but men more often than women engage in violent abuse in families. Police-reported data from 2000 show that men made up 80 percent of those accused of violence against older family members. Adult children and spouses account for about 70 percent of family violence against older adults (Dauvergne 2003). Older men face the highest risk of victimization by their adult children. Older women face the same risk of victimization from their children or from a spouse. Researchers have developed several theories to explain the causes of abuse against older persons

(McDonald and Collins 2000). One theory holds that caregiver stress leads to abuse. A second theory says that abuse exists as part of a larger pattern of violence in some families. Family members who suffered abuse or who witnessed abuse in childhood become abusers themselves. A third theory sees abuse against older persons within marriage as a continuation of spousal abuse into later life. Finally, some theorists say that abuse against older persons fits into a larger societal pattern of ageism and the devaluation of older people (Harbison 1999a).

Aronson, Thornewell, and Williams (1995; see also Harbison 1999b and Neysmith 1995b) take a feminist approach to the study of abuse against older persons. They say that the term "elder abuse" masks the link between abuse against older women and the relative powerlessness of women throughout life. They prefer the term "wife assault in old age" to describe the physical abuse of older women. Beaulieu and her colleagues (1999) support this point. They found that in 40 percent of domestic violence cases the violence had gone on for more than 25 years. Aronson and her colleagues say that studies of abuse against older women must link current abuse to structured social inequalities. Pittaway, Westhues, and Peressini (1995) say that Western society has undervalued women's work as caregivers in the family. This made most older women dependent on men for financial support throughout their lives. "From a feminist perspective," Pittaway and her colleagues (1995, 42) say, "the societal inequities which exist for women may just continue into old age unless these issues are addressed."

Policy Issues

Policy refers to regulations and guidelines on how to deal with abuse against older persons (MacLean and Williams 1995). Abuse policies attempt to help the older abused person. Policies can include criminal court action, mandatory reporting, guardianship and power of attorney, and mediation to resolve disputes. But these methods use public means (by a social worker or police) to improve a family relationship, a course of action that often fails. The law assumes that two people in a dispute have only a limited relation to each other, but an abused spouse or parent often has a long-term relationship with his or her abuser and he or she may want to maintain this relationship (sometimes at personal risk). For example, a study of the effectiveness of adult protective legislation (Bond, Penner, and Yellen 1995) found an unwillingness by both the alleged abuser and the victim to cooperate during investigations, and a general reluctance to report cases of abuse. The researchers found that few cases get to court. Legal action may do little to improve the abused person's life. A legal outcome, such as removing the abused person from a setting, may cause more stress to the abused person. Likewise, the abused person may reject legal remedies such as jailing an abusing child or spouse whom they depend on for help. Pittaway and Gallagher (1995) found that nearly a fifth (18 percent) of abused older people in their study said they feared reprisal.

Researchers support the need for intervention strategies for both the abused older people and their abusers (Lithwick et al. 1999; Nahmiash and Reis 2000). Judith Wahl and Sheila Purdy (2001), at the Advocacy Centre for the Elderly in Toronto, have written a guide to assist victims of abuse. This publication discusses the types of abuse against older persons, signs that may indicate abuse, com-

munity resources that are available, and what others who are concerned about abuse can do to help.

Nahmiash and Reis (2000) examined the effectiveness of intervention strategies in cases of abuse in Canada. The most successful strategies involved concrete help from nurses and other medical professions as well as homemaking services. Other successful interventions helped to empower older people. These included support groups, volunteers who acted as advocates, and information about a person's rights and available resources (see also World Health Organization/ International Network for the Prevention of Elder Abuse 2002). The most successful interventions for caregiver abusers involved individual counselling to reduce stress, as well as education and training (Nahmiash and Reis 2000). Barriers exist to implementing these changes. For example, Wolf (2001) finds that many victims of family violence refuse to join a support group. She suggests that support groups have an older group leader or co-leader, someone familiar with issues these older people face. Other research (Lithwick et al. 1999) finds that many abused older people refuse services that might reduce stress. These included medical services, home care assistance, day-care centres, and respite programs.

A study in British Columbia and the Yukon looked at the use of emergency shelter services available to older women who are victims of domestic violence (Hightower et al. 1999). The researchers found that only 2 percent of the women in these shelters were age 60 or older. Only 4 percent of these programs had services especially geared to older women. Hightower and her colleagues (1999) say staff at shelters need to recognize and understand the special needs of elderly abuse victims.

Future Issues in Abuse against Older Persons

Abuse and neglect against older persons has existed throughout history. What then accounts for the sudden interest in abuse and neglect? Four social changes account for this interest: (1) the growth of the older population, (2) the increased political power of older people, (3) the women's movement and a critical analysis of the family, and (4) the state's willingness to intervene in family life.

Some authors (Callahan 1986; Crystal 1986) argue that formal service agencies have adopted the cause of abuse against older persons in order to expand their influence and get more funding. This view links the sudden interest in abuse to the expansion of the welfare state. Other authors says that special programs aimed at reducing abuse reinforce negative stereotypes of older

● **Exhibit 13.6**

WHAT ARE YOUR ATTITUDES AND BELIEFS ABOUT ABUSE AGAINST OLDER PERSONS?

Researcher Michael J. Stones created a research tool, the Elder Abuse Aptitude Test (EAAT), to study attitudes and beliefs about elder abuse. Fill out the EAAT below and total your score to assess your attitudes and beliefs. The EAAT will also sensitize you to the many types of abuse that older people can face.

The following statements refer to how people sometimes act toward older adults. They refer only to behaviour by someone an older adult has reason to trust. That person could be a relative or someone who takes care of the older person. That person could also be someone paid to help or look after the older person's affairs, such as a doctor, nurse, homemaker, or lawyer. The questions do not refer to how strangers treat older people. Do you understand the kinds of people the questions refer to?

Please indicate whether the actions below are (1) not abusive, (2) possibly abusive, (3) abusive, (4) severely abusive, or (5) very severely abusive toward an older person if done by someone that person has reason to trust. Remember that the questions don't apply to an act by a stranger. Circle a number next to each statement, given that:

[1] means Not Abusive
[2] means Possibly Abusive
[3] means Abusive
[4] means Severely Abusive
[5] means Very Severely Abusive

A person a senior has reason to trust who

1.	Steals something a senior values	[1]	[2]	[3]	[4]	[5]
2.	Makes a senior pay too much for things like house repairs or medical aids	[1]	[2]	[3]	[4]	[5]
3.	Pushes or shoves a senior	[1]	[2]	[3]	[4]	[5]
4.	Lies to a senior in a harmful way	[1]	[2]	[3]	[4]	[5]
5.	Opens a senior's mail without permission	[1]	[2]	[3]	[4]	[5]
6.	Pressures a senior to do paid work when that senior doesn't want to	[1]	[2]	[3]	[4]	[5]
7.	Doesn't take a senior places that senior has to go (like a doctor's appointment)	[1]	[2]	[3]	[4]	[5]
8.	Withholds information that may be important to a senior	[1]	[2]	[3]	[4]	[5]
9.	Unreasonably orders a senior around	[1]	[2]	[3]	[4]	[5]
10.	Doesn't provide a senior with proper clothing when needed	[1]	[2]	[3]	[4]	[5]
11.	Tells a senior that he or she is "too much trouble"	[1]	[2]	[3]	[4]	[5]
12.	Fails to provide proper nutrition for a senior	[1]	[2]	[3]	[4]	[5]
13.	Disbelieves a senior who claims to be abused without checking that claim	[1]	[2]	[3]	[4]	[5]

Add the numbers you circled and divide the total by 13. How did you score? How did your classmates score? Stones reported average scores of 4.07 for 22- to 40-year-olds, 3.83 for 41- to 64-year-olds, and 3.50 for 65- to 93-year-olds. How do you think people from other backgrounds or with little knowledge of abuse against older persons would score? Research using an expanded version of this test (the Elder Abuse Survey Tool— EAST) (Stones and Bédard 2002) found that older respondents and rural residents rate fewer items as severely abusive and more items as not abusive compared to other respondents. This reflects a greater tolerance for abusive behaviour among older people and those who live in rural areas.

Sources: M.J. Stones, 1994, *Rules and Tools: The Meaning and Measurement of Elder Abuse: A Manual for Milestones* (Newfoundland); M.J. Stones and D. Pittman, 1995, "Individual Differences in Attitudes about Elder Abuse: The Elder Abuse Attitude Test (EAAT)," *Canadian Journal on Aging* 14 (Suppl. 2): 61–71, reprinted with permission from *Canadian Journal on Aging*; M.J. Stones and M. Bédard, 2002, "Higher Thresholds for Elder Abuse with Age and Rural Residence," *Canadian Journal on Aging* 21(4): 577–86.

people as feeble and helpless (Harbison 1999a). Wolf and Pillemer (1989) take a different view. They see health and social service professionals' intervention in child abuse and in abuse against older persons as parallel. In both cases, professionals, on behalf of the state, set out to protect a vulnerable minority (Otto 2000). Through this process, abuse against older persons has become a legitimate social problem. They see this attention as a first step in creating social policies to protect abused older people.

The research on abuse against older persons supports the idea that older people suffer from varied forms of mistreatment. Some subgroups may have a higher-than-average risk of abuse and may need special attention. This includes older women, those who are physically or cognitively frail, and those who depend upon their abuser for financial security or caregiving (Brandl 2000).

Professionals need more education about abuse and the tools to assess and detect abuse (Reis and Nahmiash 1997, 1998; Trevitt and Gallagher 1996). Still, the research shows that the vast majority of older people do not experience abuse. These findings should make us more aware of abuse and also help keep the issue of abuse in perspective.

Canadian researchers have explored the causes, theories, and responses to abuse against older persons. Research is needed on the role of ethnicity or culture in the abuse and neglect of older Canadians (Kozak, Elmslie, and Verdon 1995). More research is also needed on abuse against older persons in residential settings. Glendenning (1999), for example, reviewed the literature on abuse and neglect in long-term care settings. This review found that the facility environment, the characteristics of the resident, and the characteristics of the staff (including the problem of staff burnout) all influenced the existence of abuse. Future studies need to propose policies and practices to help ensure the safety of a growing and diverse older population within the community and residential settings.

FUTURE RESEARCH

In the 1980s, research on the family and social supports in later life focused on what Abu-Laban (1980, 196) then called "the 'normal' (or at least the research worthy) aged—[the] gray-haired, Anglo-Celtic, heterosexual, life-long marrieds, who have produced children and grandchildren." Studies reported how this ideal family coped with the normal crises of growing older. These studies then turned to "the support ties of the white-

haired, Anglo-Celtic, widowed mother and grand-mother" (196).

More recently, researchers (Connidis and Campbell 1995) have also criticized this narrow view of family life. First, the literature idealizes marriage and the caregiving spouse, but it says little about the dysfunctions that marriage and the use of informal supports can create. Married couples, for example, make less use of formal services. The caregiver spouse sees care as a normal and expected part of marriage (Davidson, Arber, and Ginn 2000). The failure to use available supports can make life harder for both spouses. Also, when spouses rely on each other for support, they can lose contact with friends and relatives. This situation can lead to feelings of burden, isolation, and depression for both spouses. More research on marriage in later life should focus on both the benefits and the problems that marriage can bring. Peters and Liefbroer (1997) suggest the need to look beyond marital status. They propose studies of partner status, marital history, and individuals' views of marriage.

Second, the structure of the family has changed. Sociodemographic changes related to family size and structure, patterns of marriage and divorce, changing roles for women, increased life expectancy, and greater diversity in the timing of life course events and transitions means that more families will include older family members. "The dynamic aspect of this is," Rosenthal (2000, 45) says, "a much increased overlap of lives between familial generations." Many older people today have living siblings, adult children, and grandchildren. Families will have more generations alive at one time than ever before. This means that older people today have large reservoirs of potential informal support. We know little about the lives and relationships of older people in these new family structures.

Older people in the future (around 2025), compared with older people today, will have fewer children and fewer siblings. This will give them a smaller pool of close relatives to call on for support and could lead to increased reliance on **fictive kin**. This term refers to close relationships with non-relatives such as friends, neighbours, and home care workers.

Third, research on older people's family life has almost ignored the lives of certain types of people. Little research has been done on never-married older people (Siegal 1995), divorced older people (Barrett and Lynch 1999), or the childless elderly (Connidis and McMullin 1999). We also know little about gender differences in the social support needs of different marital status groups, including those who remarry in later life (Wister and Dykstra 2000). Further research should also look at the social support needs and experiences of older gay and lesbian couples and individuals (Beeler et al. 1999; Jacobs, Rasmussen, and Hohman 1999; O'Brien and Goldberg 2000).

Fourth, few studies have compared the family life of older people from different cultural and ethnic backgrounds. More research on ethnicity in old age should look at family relations (Mitchell 2003), informal supports (Keefe, Rosenthal, and Béland 2000), and the use of social services by different ethnic groups. Kobayashi (2000) looked at intergenerational support in Japanese-Canadian families. She found that filial obligation (the obligation to care for a parent) had a significant effect on children's provision of emotional support to parents. But it did not affect the amount of financial or service support children gave. She says that researchers need to study parent–child exchanges and the differences in support given by sons and daughters.

Buchignani and Armstrong-Esther (1999) examined the informal care needs of older Native Canadians in Alberta. They found that while many had fair or poor health, very few had the financial resources to pay for formal services or to live independently in old age. Adult children, spouses, and sisters provided support. The researchers say that institutional barriers and a lack of available services lead these older Canadians to rely extensively on family care.

Fifth, although research during the 1970s, 1980s, and 1990s focused mostly on older women, making up for the absence of research on women in other parts of the social science literature, few studies on family and social relations have looked at older men. Researchers need to look at male friendships, lone-father families

(McQuillan and Belle 2001), widowers, grandfathering, gay men as they age, male remarriage, as well as men involved in caregiving to family members, particularly adult sons (Campbell and Martin-Matthews 2003) and older husbands. Studies that have described men show that they face special challenges in old age.

Sixth, some researchers suggest that marriage is becoming increasingly fragile. Current low marriage rates among younger people, increases in common-law and living-apart-together relationships, high divorce rates, and fewer remarriages in middle and later life will lead to new and more diverse patterns of family life for older people. These trends may produce more unmarried older people, both men and women. They may also lead to more older people with children from several marriages.

An older person in the future may have several sets of children and grandchildren from several marriages. Their children too may have children from several marriages. The study of these family structures in the future will give a more complete picture of family life in old age.

CONCLUSION

Older people live rich social lives. They interact with family members, friends, and neighbours as well as with their spouses. Most older people rely on these networks of family and friends for social, emotional, and health care support. Older people also give to their families and serve as role models for the young. Old age is a time of change—the death of a spouse, for example, creates one of life's greatest stresses. But research shows that most older people cope with the challenges of aging and experience satisfying and rewarding social lives.

Summary

1. The myth persists that middle-aged children abandon their elderly parents, but studies show again and again that children maintain contact with their parents, provide them with help, and get help and support from them when they need it.

2. A good marriage provides support for both partners as they age. Married older people use less formal care, rely less on children and friends for support, and have a lower institutionalization rate than unmarried older people. Older women run a higher risk than older men of losing this support due to widowhood.

3. Never-married older adults play vital and supportive roles in the lives of siblings, older parents, and others. They also form friendships and other social relationships to provide themselves with supporters, confidants, and companions.

4. Older divorced men are more likely than older divorced women to remarry. Being divorced in later life often means economic insecurity, particularly for women, and loss of social contact with children for men.

5. Older adults now and in the future will have greater choice in the type of intimate relationships they wish to form. These will include common-law and living-apart-together relationships for those older people who want a close and intimate relationship, but not necessarily one within marriage.

6. Widowhood has become an expected life event for women in Canada, although it still creates stress in a woman's life. Researchers disagree about the impact of widowhood on men. Some studies show that men have fewer social supports and that they suffer from isolation, loneliness, and a high risk of suicide. More recent studies suggest that men may need less social support than women and that they adapt in different ways to widowhood.

7. Older people have an interest in sex throughout life. Most people will need to adjust their expectations about sexual performance in later life. But, given good health and a willing partner, older people can enjoy sexual relations into late old age. New attitudes toward sexuality may encourage more sexual activity in later life.

8. Long-term relationships with a committed partner can provide both older gay men and lesbians with companionship, acceptance, and support. Other social network ties with family members and friends also serve an important social support function in their lives.

9. Most older people keep up social contacts with relatives and friends as they age. They also give support as well as receive it. They help their children socially, financially, and emotionally. They help their peers by acting as confidants. Older people, like younger people, get esteem and a sense of purpose from helping others.

10. Grandparenting offers older people one of the most enjoyable roles in old age. It has few responsibilities attached to it, so older people can shape the role to suit their personality, lifestyle, and interests.

11. Older people often depend on informal support networks for emotional and health care support, but informal support can place a burden on family members (particularly women). These burdened caregivers may lose their income from work, their pensions, and even their health due to caregiving demands. Government financial support for caregivers would make caregiving a less burdensome option for many people and would recognize their valuable service to the community.

12. Adult children, most often daughters, provide most of the informal support needed by their older parents. Research shows that strong feelings of attachment to a parent lead to caregiving, and that feelings of closeness between parents and children lead to satisfaction and happiness. Older adults, particularly those without a spouse or children, receive support from sibling and friends as well.

13. Abuse against older people most often takes the form of material abuse and chronic verbal aggression. A smaller proportion of older people face physical aggression and neglect. Education for police, counsellors, family members, and older adults themselves may help reduce the incidence of abuse. Legal services, mental health services, and shelters could help older people to cope with the aftermath of abuse.

14. Some trends, such as cohort attrition for very old people and smaller families for baby boomers, suggest that informal supports will decline in the future. Other trends, such as longer life expectancy for spouses and the development of semiformal structures, suggest that older people will still rely on informal supports in the years ahead. These two trends may counterbalance each other, and older people in the future may develop new types of social supports.

15. Many gaps still exist in the literature on family life in old age. Research on atypical groups of older people— for example, older gay men and lesbians, permanently single and divorced older people—will increase our understanding of family and intimate relations in later life.

Study Questions

1. What are the benefits of marriage in old age? How does divorce affect people in old age? Why do some older people choose to live in common-law or living-apart-together relationships?

2. What types of people form the social support networks of older divorced and never-married people? Compare and contrast the networks of divorced and never-married people.

3. Explain why widows outnumber widowers in the aging population. Why do men seem to suffer more than women socially and psychologically when they lose a spouse?

4. Explain the difference between formal and informal support. What kind of support do most older people get? Describe the benefits of this type of support. How do older people choose their potential support groups?

5. In addition to family, where else do older people look for informal support? How do support networks differ by marital and parental status?

6. What types of help and support do older people provide to family and friends?

7. Explain the term "sandwich generation." What are the major difficulties that arise when people take on the role of caregiver to their aged parents?

8. Discuss several things that may ease the burden of caregiving on spouses or adult children.

9. Why do demographers project that the availability of informal supports may decrease in the future? In the absence of informal support, what other types of support are available to the older population?

10. What are the different types of abuse against older persons? How common is this abuse and who is often responsible for abusing an older person? Suggest some ways that abuse against older persons can be prevented, both in the community and in institutions.

11. Explain the different styles of grandparenting.

12. Why do some gerontologists believe that researchers could expand the scope of studies in aging and the family? What types of issues and trends should this research address?

Key Terms

caregiver burden refers to problems and stress due to caregiving. (301)

confidant someone in whom one confides. (287)

convoy model of support a network of close family and friends who travel together throughout life, exchanging social support and assistance. (297)

developmental stake the idea that, compared with their children, older people have a greater investment in the relationship with their children. (299)

eldercare programs workplace programs that can help family caregivers cope with care for an older family member. (307)

family counselling counselling with a social worker or psychotherapist that includes parents, children, and siblings. (306)

fictive kin the close relationships that an older person develops with non-relatives such as friends, neighbours, and home care workers. (314)

formal support paid support from professional caregivers such as doctors, nurses, social workers, and home care workers. (296)

functional specificity of relationships model a family or friendship tie may provide one type of support or a broad range of support, depending on the particular relationship between the caregiver and the care receiver. (297)

GRAND (Grandparents Requesting Access aNd Dignity) a group that helps grandparents who cannot get access to their grandchildren. (295)

hierarchical compensatory model people choose their supports first from their inner family circle and then move outward to get support from less intimate people as they need more help. (297)

informal caregivers unpaid care providers with a tie of kinship or affection toward the care receiver. (298)

informal support unpaid support from family members and the community. (296)

LAT (living apart together) couples couples that have a committed relationship but maintain separate households. (285)

primary potential support groups family and close friends who give help to the older person and who can expect help from the older person. (297)

quasi-widowhood experiencing feelings of grief, depression, and loss after a spouse is placed in a nursing home. (302)

respite services services ranging from friendly visitors who stay with the care receiver for a few hours, to full-day adult day care, to longer institutional respite to give caregivers time off. (306)

sandwich generation people in mid-life who have at least one living parent and at least one child living in the household. (304)

second language of sex the "language of sex" that develops in a long-term intimate relationship and focuses on responsiveness, caring, and affection. (289)

semiformal structures forms of organized support, such as car pools, groups of people in the same building who shop together, friendly visitors, or "daily hello" phone callers, that fall between the informal and formal support structures. (309)

skip-generation households grandparents living with grandchildren without the presence of the middle (parent) generation. (293)

social support the help and assistance people give to one another. (291)

support groups groups that give caregivers information about how to cope with caregiving demands and provide emotional support. (306)

task specificity model different groups (of family, friends, neighbours) have different abilities and offer different types of support, each playing a specific role. (297)

Selected Readings

Connidis, I.A. *Family Ties and Aging*. Thousand Oaks, CA: Sage, 2001.

This book provides a comprehensive and well-integrated examination of research on family ties and aging. It discusses relationships with spouses, children, and grandchildren, as well as those that are often neglected in the literature, such as the family ties of single, divorced, and childless older adults, as well as older gay men and lesbians. The book highlights the diversity that exists within family relationships based on gender, ethnicity and race, socioeconomic status, and sexual orientation. A resource for undergraduate and graduate students, academics, practitioners, and policymakers.

Hall, C.M. *The Special Mission of Grandparents: Hearing, Seeing, Telling.* Westport, CT: Greenwood, 1999.

This book describes the diversity of challenges and satisfactions experienced by grandparents from different cultural and family backgrounds. The book addresses a number of ways grandparents can influence their grandchildren's lives as friends, confidants, and support providers. The author shows that grandparents can have a positive influence on their families.

Stones, L., and M. Stones. *Sex May Be Wasted on the Young.* North York, ON: Captus, 1996.

Two gerontologists look at sex in later life. They describe many of the well-known studies of aging and sexuality, but more often they present case studies, examples of people they know, and some of their own thoughts on aging and sexuality. Their well-written, witty, and informative book works to overcome ageism and stereotypes about sex in later life.

Van den Hoonaard, D.K. *The Widowed Self: The Older Woman's Journey through Widowhood.* Waterloo, ON: Wilfrid Laurier University Press, 2001.

The author discusses her research on a sample of older Canadian widowed women in a book that combines symbolic interactionist theory and qualitative methods with autobiographical accounts of these women's experiences. The book presents widowhood in the women's own voices.

Chapter Fourteen
Death and Dying

INTRODUCTION

Draw a line across a piece of paper. Put the word "birth" at the left end of the line. Put the word "death" at the right end of the line. Now put a dot for today's date. Put the date of your birth under the "birth" dot. Now put the date you project for your death under the dot that says "death."

How did you feel about fixing a date for your death? How did you come up with a date? Do people of different ages think the same way about death? Do you look forward to your next birthday? Or do you think about how few years you have left to do the things you want to do? How do older people think and feel about death?

This chapter will look at death in old age. It will focus on (1) attitudes toward death and on where death takes place, (2) ethical questions about death and dying, and (3) mourning and grief.

DEATH AND SOCIETY

Aiken (2001) says that attitudes toward death fall on a continuum. Some societies see death as an enemy, something we fight with all our power. Other societies welcome death and even see it as a transition to a better, even blissful, world. Still others, in the middle, see death as a mystery.

Kastenbaum (1999, xv) says that he misses the old days—"the really old days." In the ancient past, he says, people saw death as a mysterious transition. They created myths and stories to explain death to themselves. The Greek Hades, the Christian Heaven or Hell, or the Muslim Paradise all show humans grappling with the meaning of death. For some societies, death meant an eternity of darkness and shadow. For others, as Dante describes in his Inferno, it could mean punishment for an evil life. And for Muslims, death means a life of ease and pleasure for believers. As Kastenbaum says, "death was clearly something BIG." The power of the stories and their central role in religion and culture tell us that people have always wondered about death.

But times have changed and we have a new view of death and dying (one that coexists with some of our traditional views). Science and technology extend life and push death and dying to late old age. Death in Canada today most often takes place in a hospital or nursing home. We rarely have a direct experience of death. We see graphic scenes of death in the movies or on TV. But these images distance us from death (Aiken 2001). They have little impact on our daily lives. We can turn off the TV or leave the theatre if the images scare or depress us.

Today, death challenges our moral and ethical codes. Our legal system grapples with the issue of physician-assisted suicide, our health care system deals with the long trajectory toward death that we call long-term care, and families cope with institutions such as hospitals and nursing homes where death most often occurs. Death may still fill us with fear. But more often it confronts us with practical choices (to die in an institution or at home? to prolong care or end treatment? to opt for burial, cremation, or freezing of the body until science finds a cure?). We still hear the old stories through our religious traditions and literature. But they lack mystery and sound more like fantasy. Discussions of death and dying today often focus on death and dying in old age.

DEATH IN OLD AGE

In the past, high infant mortality rates, childhood diseases, and high female death rates during childbearing years made death among all age groups a common event. Today, most infants will live to old age. Life expectancy at birth in 2001 stood at 77.1 years for males and 82.2 years for females (Statistics Canada 2003c). Even in old age, life expectancy has increased. A man aged 65 in 1996 could expect to live another 16.3 years, a woman 20.2 years (Lindsay 1999).

Longer life expectancy today means that death often takes place in old age. Northcott and Wilson (2001) say that in 1996, for example, people aged 18 or under accounted for less than 2 percent of all deaths in Canada. In that same year, people aged 65 and over accounted for 75 percent of deaths. Today, most people die of the diseases of old age—cancer, heart disease, stroke, and lung disease (Lindsay 1999). These diseases result from a lifetime of accumulated stress on the body.

The trajectory of death from these diseases differs from dying in the past. People died earlier in the past and they often died quickly of an acute illness (e.g., influenza, pneumonia) or accident. Today, people die in old age from more than one chronic illness (e.g., cancer, heart disease, diabetes). Death comes slowly and unpredictably. People often experience a slow decline along with intense crises that lead to death. Dying can include pain, delirium, swallowing problems, loss of mental function, and other forms of discomfort (Ross et al. 2002). Dying in old age makes special demands on health care providers, family members, and older people themselves.

Only a small number of studies have looked at how older people feel about death. Marshall (1975) says that the major theories of aging avoid the subject. According to activity theory, people want to stay active throughout their lives. They substitute new roles and activities for ones that they lose as they age. When people retire, activity theory says that they will have the highest life satisfaction if they find new things to do. This theory says nothing about death.

Disengagement theory says that people want to disengage from social roles as they age. This theory also says that retirement and withdrawal from social responsibilities leads to high life satisfaction. According to this theory, an awareness of impending death starts the process of disengagement. People know that they will die soon, so they ease their way out of social life. Disengagement produces a smooth transition of power from one generation to the next. Death has a less disruptive effect on society if older people disengage from social roles as they age. This theory focuses on the social effects of dying, but it says little about death as a personal experience or about how older people feel about death.

Erikson's (1963) theory of ego development says that the last stage of life leads to a life review. A person looks over his or her life, ties up loose ends, and prepares for death. Erikson describes this as **ego integrity**. "It is the acceptance of one's one and only life cycle as something that had to be and that, by necessity, permitted of no substitutions" (1963, 268). The integrated person accepts his or her biography and culture, and with this acceptance "death loses its sting" (268). Peck ([1955] 1968) says that in the last part of this last stage a person can achieve **ego transcendence**. People in this stage feel a deep concern for others and for the culture they will leave when they die.

These theories say that older people respond to death in more than one way: Some people deny it, some accept it, and some embrace it. The few studies that have tested these theories have found complex combinations of acceptance and rejection of death.

A study conducted by University of Toronto researchers (cited in Koster and Prather 1999) found that people at the end of life had five concerns: avoiding a drawn-out death, getting pain relief, having control of treatment options, staying in touch with loved ones, and becoming a burden. People feared that they would burden family with physical care, that family members would have to witness their death, and that family members would have to make decisions about life-sustaining treatment.

Studies that compare older and younger people find that older people think about death more, but feel less afraid of death than the young. Lavigne and Lévesque (1992) studied older people in long-term care centres in Montreal. They found that about a third of the people in the study thought of their own death when they heard of the death of a peer. A Canadian study by Gesser, Wong, and Reker (1986) studied the fear of death and three kinds of death acceptance among old and young people. They found that older people showed less fear and more acceptance of death than younger people. They also found that as fear of death decreased, hopelessness decreased and happiness increased. They say that people who get over the fear of death feel satisfied with life. These people find meaning and purpose in the time they have left, and they feel in control of their lives.

Religion plays a smaller role in society today than in the past. But people often turn to religious leaders and institutions at the time of death. Church groups, for example, arrange visits to dying church members. Religious leaders spend time with dying people at their bedsides and they lead religious services after a person has died. People with different religious beliefs differ in their attitudes to death. Gesser, Wong, and Reker (1986) found that older people more than younger people accepted life after death. "It may be that belief in the afterlife helps the elderly to find meaning and purpose in life, as well as in death.... Older people overcome their fear of death because they feel that life after death goes on" (20). Most religions teach that people get the kind of afterlife they deserve. Studies show that people with mild or uncertain religious belief fear death most, while those with strong religious beliefs or no belief at all deal with death best (Gorer 1967; Kalish 1963). People with a mild belief may accept enough of religion to believe in an afterlife, but not enough to feel they will have a good one.

INSTITUTIONAL DEATH

Religious belief and a sense of purpose can help buffer the fear of death, but how and where a person expects to die also affects how he or she feels about death. In the past, most people died at home, surrounded by family, friends, and neighbours. Some cultures still ensure this kind of death (see Exhibit 14.2). But, in Canada, a large majority of deaths (for people of all ages) take place in hospitals.

A study at the Baycrest Centre for Geriatric Care in Toronto compared the death rate in the centre's hospital, nursing home, and apartment complex. The study found that the hospital had a death rate more than 20 times greater than that of the nursing home and more than 130 times greater than that of the apartment complex. Shapiro (1983) studied hospital use by a group of more than 3000 patients aged 68 and over and found that about two-thirds of the sample entered the hospital in the year they died.

● Exhibit 14.1

SENIORS TALK ABOUT DEATH AND DYING

Researchers Jacques Grand'Maison and Solange Lefebvre studied older people in the Laurentian region of Quebec from 1988 through the 1990s. They spoke with dozens of older people individually and in groups. They conducted long interviews on social, cultural, moral, and spiritual issues. Their report, *Sharing the Blessings* (1996), contains many excerpts from these interviews. Below you will find reflections on death and dying from their study. These excerpts show the variety of ways that older people think about death and dying. They also show that older people remain committed to a satisfying life even in the face of death.

"For me," a woman, age 59, says, "death is a happy end after a full life. I can't think it's true that you have to suffer when you die. My grandfather died at ninety-four, and he died singing. I've always remembered this. It shows you can be happy, have a beautiful, healthy old age, and don't have to go through all sorts of stages to realize you're happy."

"I try to fight against the anguish of death...," a woman, age 66, says. "But you can't avoid it; one day you'll die, and I hope there's something on the other side. I'm working at accepting the end."

"I believe in life," a man, age 68, says. "Nothing but Life with a capital L. Life is perhaps God.... I don't know anymore.... Death is emptiness, it has no meaning. If you can't enjoy life, you might as well pack and go."

"Death? It's a nagging question," says a man, age 68. "I believe in another life, but I don't know what form it will take. I must say that questions about death become more urgent when someone close to you dies.... To be honest ... I'm getting older, and it's coming."

"Death has no meaning for me," a woman, age 55, says. "It's a return to nature. Unfortunately this isn't very profound. I saw my parents die, but they continue to live in me. It wasn't so terrible. They're still alive. When I've got troubles, I call on my mother and ask her to do something. But death doesn't affect my existence. I love life, love being alive, I'm content just to be on this earth. It's simply the pleasure of being."

Source: J. Grand'Maison and S. Lefebvre, 1996, *Sharing the Blessings: The Role of Seniors in Today's Society,* trans. from the French by Jane Brierley, Sherbrooke, QC: Mediaspaul. Reprinted with permission of Mediaspaul.

Hospitals will take in more and more dying patients as the population ages, but studies show that many doctors and nurses in hospitals feel uncomfortable with dying patients. Ross and her colleagues (2002) say that acute-care hospitals often marginalize older dying patients. Staff see them as practical problems or "bed blockers." The medical model, based on technology and cure, often fails to meet the needs of the dying older person. A study in the 1970s at the Royal Victoria Hospital in Montreal found that patients wanted to know their diagnoses and their chance of recovery, but doctors did not want to speak openly about death and had little interest in patients' emotions. Social workers also tended to play down patients' problems (Mount, Jones, and Patterson 1974). Shedletsky and Fisher (1986) replicated this study 12 years later. They found that almost all staff (97 percent) felt that patients should be told about their terminal illness, but only 80 percent said that patients on their units were told, and 70 percent of staff members said

that discussions of death and dying never or infrequently took place. Nearly all staff members (97.6 percent) felt that hospitals should meet patients' emotional needs, but 41 percent felt that these needs are never or infrequently met.

Skelton (1982) reports that medical staff sometimes feel guilty or angry about dying patients. Because they have spent all of their professional lives learning to keep people alive, they think of death as a failure and avoid dying patients or respond less quickly to their needs. Health and Welfare Canada (1982b) says that the dying patient does not fit the model of health care of the acute hospital. "Skills of investigating, diagnosing, curing and prolonging life [the goals of an acute-care hospital where people have short-term, curable illnesses] are not relevant to the care of the dying" (4). Health care professionals need ongoing training in the care of dying patients. This should include knowledge about pain management and about the unique needs of minority older people (Ross et al. 2002).

● **Exhibit 14.2**

DEATH AND DYING AMONG THE HUTTERITES

In an article on aging and death, Joseph W. Eaton reprinted the following letter from a Hutterite farmer to his sister. The letter describes the death of their younger brother.

Dear sister, our dear brother came home on September 8, on a Wednesday morning about 5 o'clock. He said that he had a fairly nice trip. He cried a great deal because of pains. He stated that distress teaches one to pray. I went immediately the following day to visit with him. I could hardly look at him, it was so painful to me; he looked so terrible that it made my heart almost break. However, I remained with him until he died, and until the funeral was over.

Two evenings before his death, his home was full of people, approximately 25 were there. He expressed a heavenly pleasure when he saw them all and said he could not express his pleasure in seeing them. It struck me almost as a miracle when I saw this starved and weak body lying there, telling us such a strong story. We listened to him, warned him not to talk so much because it may do him harm. However, he stated, "while I am still alive, I can speak. When I will be dead, then, of course, I won't be able to tell you what I have to say." ...

He stated that dying does not cause him any difficulty; he said that he had a clear conscience and is in peace with God and all people. He asked many people in my presence whether they had something against him. However, everybody replied in the negative. They said to him that they themselves were in peace with him....

[Just before his death] his children stood around him with a sad heart, and all realized that his departure will be soon. He called his oldest son, gave him his hand and pressed a kiss on his forehead, and advised him how he should behave in the future. Among other words he told him he should obey his preacher, the boss and the field boss, and if the community entrusted a position to him, he should execute same as well as he could, and not only superficially....

[He then calls to his side his daughter, the colony business manager, his wife and his brother.] He said, "I am at peace with God and with all people. I have a clear and good conscience. I am ready to depart, but now everything goes so slow. I have only one desire and that is to go to my Lord." He said quite frequently how good it is to have a clear and peaceful conscience. He advised us also that we should prepare ourselves, because the pleasure was inexpressible.

So I have described to you the events and experiences which I have seen with my own eyes, and it is my request and my wish that we all should prepare ourselves. Blessed by God.

Source: Joseph W. Eaton, 1964, "The Art of Aging and Dying," *The Gerontologist* 4: 94–112. Reproduced with permission of The Gerontological Society of America, 2000.

CHANGES IN THE TREATMENT OF THE DYING

The health care system has begun to change its approach to dying patients of all ages. Two doctors more than any others—Elisabeth Kübler-Ross in the United States and Dame Cicely Saunders in England—started this reform.

Stages of Death and Dying

Kübler-Ross (1969) described five stages that her patients went through before they died. First, she says, people deny that they are dying. They say, "Not me." They may believe that the doctor has the wrong X-rays or someone else's tests. They may go from specialist to specialist looking for a new diagnosis. They may not even hear the doctor tell them they have a fatal illness.

Second, she says, people feel angry. They begin to believe that they will die. "Why me?" they ask. At this point, people blames the doctors or their spouse or God for their illness.

Third, they begin to bargain. They say, "Yes, me, but ..." and try to make deals with the hospital staff. They may promise to be a good patient and to follow doctor's orders, if only they will get better. They may bargain with God, promising to go to worship or to live a more pious life. They may bargain with God for one more summer at the cottage, or for enough time to see a child married, a grandchild born, or their next birthday.

Fourth, they feel depressed. Their illness gets worse, and they know they will die. They say, "Yes, me," and they feel a great sadness. Kübler-Ross says that depression has two stages. In the first stage, people mourn present losses—the loss of family, career, and the things they love, such as a home, car, or cottage. In the second stage, they mourn future losses—the loss of good times to come, the chance to see children or grandchildren grow up, and other future events. People begin to say goodbye in this stage.

Fifth, people accept death. They say, "My time is close now ... it's okay." They say goodbye to family and friends and die in peace.

Kübler-Ross says that at every stage a person holds on to hope. At first, a person may hope the doctor made a mistake; later there may be hope for a remission if the person has cancer, and later still there may be hope for a painless death.

Some writers question the number of Kübler-Ross's stages or their order. Shneidman (1984, 199) rejects Kübler-Ross's stage theory—"the notion that human beings, as they die, are somehow marched in lock step through a series of stages of the dying process"—on clinical grounds. He reports a wide range of emotions, needs, and coping methods that dying people use. "A few of these in some people, dozens in others—experienced in an impressive variety of ways" (199). Kübler-Ross (1969) herself says that patients can skip stages; stages can overlap; and people can go back over the same stage many times. Some responses, such as anger, come up again and again.

Also, different illnesses create different trajectories of death or different patterns of response. Kübler-Ross based her model on cancer patients in a hospital, but cancer patients who have remissions may go through these stages more than once. People with other illnesses show other trajectories. Sometimes, a person can have long plateaus between times of decline. However, someone who dies shortly after an auto accident may not go through any of these stages. Northcott and Wilson (2001) say that the dying process depends on many things—a person's age, the illness, the individual's will to live, and the treatments used to fight or manage the disease. Lawton (2001, citing Institute of Medicine 1997), for example, says that "sudden death, steady decline, and episodic decline" all have described unique death trajectories.

All sides of this debate share one thing: They have brought discussion and thinking about death into public life. People who have to cope with death and dying—patients, their families, and medical staff—now have a number of ways to think, and talk, about death. This has helped free many people from the silence that surrounded death and dying only a few years ago.

The Hospice Movement

The idea of a **hospice** dates back to at least the Middle Ages in Europe. Hospices at that time took in travellers who needed food, shelter, and care. Hospices today meet the special needs of dying patients. Dame Cicely Saunders opened the first modern hospice, St. Christopher's, in London, England, in 1967.

St. Christopher's has 52 beds, in-patient and out-patient services, a home visiting program, a day-care centre for the children of staff, and private rooms for older people. The hospice welcomes visitors, including children, and allows families to cook for their dying relatives if they want to. There are also rooms for relatives who want to stay overnight. St. Christopher's does not attempt to extend life; it tries to relieve symptoms and to help the patients enjoy their last days.

Hospice Program Goals

Saunders says that a "hospice is a program, not a place" (cited in Canadian Medical Association 1987, 34). First, a hospice controls pain. People fear death for many reasons, but often they fear the pain that may accompany death more than death itself. Pain relief ensures that the person will die in comfort, thus relieving much of the fear and anxiety. St. Christopher's pioneered the pain relief techniques now used by hospices around the world.

St. Christopher's created the Brompton mix—a mixture of heroin or morphine, cocaine, Stemetil syrup, and chloroform water—to relieve chronic pain. Medical staff base pain control on two techniques: First, they adjust drug dosage until it relieves a patient's pain. "The aim," Saunders (1984, 268) says, "is to titrate the level of analgesia against the patient's pain, gradually increasing the dose until the patient is pain free." Then, the nurses give the next dose before the previous one has worn off. Hospitals often wait until a person shows signs of pain before they give the next dose of pain reliever. By giving the analgesic "before the patient may think it necessary [usually every four hours] ... it is possible to erase the memory and fear of pain" (268). Patients cared for by this method need lower dosages to maintain a pain-free state because the drug does not have to overcome the pain that has begun. Lower dosages mean that patients stay more alert. Skelton (1982) says that 90 percent of people can get complete pain relief in a hospice setting, and all but 1 to 2 percent can get some help.

Second, a hospice allows a person to die a simple death. The hospice does not use respirators or resuscitators to keep someone alive. Staff members make dying a part of life in the hospice. They leave the curtains open around a dying person's bed so that patients can see that their roommates have died. Patients also know they have a say in their treatment; they can ask for medication when they feel they need it, and they can ask to die at home. Saunders (1984) reports that people who die at home often feel more pain than people who die in the hospice, and caregivers often feel burdened by the demands of care. St. Christopher's (and other hospices) agree to re-admit patients whenever the patient or the family needs more support.

Third, a hospice gives people love and care. Staff members focus on the comfort of the patient, taking the time to touch patients and hold them. The hospice will serve special foods that patients like or give them soothing scented baths. The hospice also helps patients do as much for themselves as they can; this increases patients' well-being by giving them a sense of control over their treatment. The family members of dying patients also receive care. The Family Service Project at St. Christopher's offers help to families who find it hard to cope with their grief (see also Levy 1987). Saunders (1984, 269) says that "staff and volunteers visit to assess the need and to offer support, and if more specialized help is indicated, this can be arranged."

Hospices spread to North America during the 1970s and early 1980s. More than 1000 hospices opened in the United States between 1974 and 1984. Angeli (2001) reports that by 2001 the U.S. had 2500 hospices. In Canada, hospice organizations exist in Quebec, Ontario, British Columbia, and Manitoba. Most provinces also have palliative (terminal) care units, palliative care teams, or a palliative care expert on staff in hospitals. The National Hospice Organization in the U.S. studied family satisfaction with several hundred hospice programs in the U.S. The study found high levels of family satisfaction with services (Connor 1998). Taylor (1999) reports rapid growth in hospice care in Canada. She says that "a recent Angus Reid survey found that 91% of Canadians support hospice care services" and 84 percent "strongly agree that it is important for terminally ill people to be able to spend their final days at home" (4).

Palliative Care

Palliative care is "a program of active compassionate care primarily directed towards improving the quality of life for the dying" (Subcommittee on Institutional Program Guidelines 1989, 1). A complete program of palliative care includes symptom control and spiritual support as well as bereavement support and education. Palliative care units do the same work as hospices, but they most often exist within a large acute-care hospital. Mori (1991, 10) says that the Canadian health care system prefers the term "palliative care" to the term "hospice" "because of the negative connotations associated with the word *hospice* in French and Spanish."

The Canadian Palliative Care Association began in 1991. But little reliable information on palliative care programs across Canada exists. Mori (1991, 11) reports that many settings offer palliative care services, including "free-standing hospices, home-based palliative care, hospital-based palliative care, and nursing-home-based palliative care." Workers in palliative care programs include nurses, physiotherapists, psychologists, and volunteers.

Some provincial home care programs also offer palliative care. Ninety-five percent of the people who used these programs had terminal cancer. There were about 231 community-based and hospital and community combined palliative care programs (programs to help people stay in their homes) in Canada in 1990 (Ajemian 1990). The Canadian Medical Association (CMA) (1987) estimates that people aged 65 and over make up about 70 percent of palliative care patients in Canada.

The Royal Victoria Hospital in Montreal opened Canada's first in-patient palliative care unit in 1975. The 12-bed unit offers music therapy, counselling, and physiotherapy as well as care by doctors and nurses. The unit's staff works as a team and practises "whole person medicine" (Doutre, Stillwell, and Ajemian 1979). This means that they care for the spiritual, emotional, psychological, and physical needs of the patient. The program also offers a seven-day-a-week, 24-hour home care service. The unit's staff keeps patients pain-free in their homes through drug therapy and gives family members advice and support in caring for the dying person. The unit ensures that a patient can come back to the hospital at any time. This allows dying patients to leave the hospital and, in some cases, to die at home. The unit also has a bereavement follow-up team that visits and supports families after the patient dies.

One early study at the Royal Victoria Hospital compared the palliative care unit with a surgical ward. Buckingham had himself admitted as a cancer patient to both types of units (Buckingham et al. 1976). He dieted for six months and lost 10 kilograms, exposed his skin to ultraviolet rays to make it look as if he had received radiation treatment, stuck himself with needles, and had a doctor do minor surgery to make it look as if he had had intravenous injections and a biopsy. He learned how patients with cancer of the pancreas behaved, and he imitated their behaviour. He also grew a stubbly beard and failed to bathe for several days.

Buckingham reports that he got more personal attention and kinder treatment on the palliative care ward. On the surgical ward, he found, doctors spent less than 10 minutes per day with him and less than five minutes per visit. Also, doctors travelled in groups, a habit that discouraged patients from talking to their doctors about their feelings. Buckingham reports that staff on the surgical ward avoided eye contact with patients; called patients by their disease, not their name; dwelt on the worst things about a patient's illness; and showed little good feeling toward dying patients. His staff contacts lasted on average less than six minutes per visit.

The palliative care unit showed more interest in him as a person. The nurses looked him in the eye when they talked to him and asked him personal, friendly questions, such as what food he enjoyed eating. Buckingham reports that when families wanted to talk to their doctor, the staff got the doctor on the phone as soon as possible. Families also spent a lot of time helping to care for patients: They fed patients, brought urinals, and fixed patients' pillows. The staff supported family members as they helped care for their dying relatives. Buckingham's staff contacts averaged 19 minutes on the palliative care unit. Compared with the surgical ward, on the palliative care unit he spent almost 400 percent more time talking to staff, patients, and their families.

A study by Thompson (1985–86) supports Buckingham's findings. Thompson compared palliative care, surgical, and pediatric nurses' attitudes to death. He found that palliative care nurses "approach their work with the dying with greater ease, may enter into more personal relationships with dying patients ... and come away from their work with the feelings that the work itself is rewarding and that they have been useful" (240). Thompson concludes that the values of the palliative care setting (more than nurses' past experiences) explain this positive attitude to dying patients and their needs.

Buckingham also reports that patients supported and comforted one another on the palliative care unit. "The palliative care unit facilitated this powerful support system by allowing more patient–family freedom and mobility, with open visiting and encouragement of family participation in the care of the patient" (Buckingham et al. 1976, 1214). A study by Kane and others (1984) found that, compared with conventional care, palliative care created more family and patient satisfaction and less family anxiety. Buckingham concluded that palliative care units meet the dying person's special need for emotional and social support as well as physical care.

Palliative Care for the Elderly

Palliative care units take in patients of all ages. Patients at Royal Victoria Hospital, for example, ranged from 20 years old to over 90. Studies show that palliative care can help older people as well as younger people, but some older patients have unique needs.

Shedletsky, Fisher, and Nadon (1982) studied the records of 40 older patients (average age 80.6 years) who had died in the extended care wing of a hospital. Extended care hospital settings take in many older people with long-term illnesses who need constant medical care. These units often have a palliative care treatment philosophy. The researchers found that older extended care patients differed from younger palliative care patients. First, older patients averaged more diagnoses than the younger patients. Second, the younger patients typically had cancer, while the older patients typically suffered from circulatory and respiratory diseases. Third, relatively few younger patients died from respiratory failure, while respiratory failure caused about 50 percent of all deaths in the older group.

Shedletsky, Fisher, and Nadon (1982) found that drug treatment helped about 80 percent of the people with pain and skin problems. The staff reported that just before death, 75 percent of the patients felt no pain or distress and 75 percent were conscious or semiconscious. The staff found, however, that patients with respiratory problems got the least benefit from drug treatment, and this group made up the largest portion of people with discomfort before death. The researchers concluded that some groups of older extended care patients may have special palliative care needs.

Mori (1991) points out that palliative care turns some assumptions of the health care system on their head. First, palliative care acknowledges the limits of curative medicine. It accepts death as part of life. Second, palliative care takes time. It follows the natural course of an individual's death. Palliative health services adjust to suit each person's needs. They put the individual's need for comfort first. Third, palliative care treats the whole person, which is deemed to include the person's caregivers and social support system. Palliative care calls for a different kind of health care practice, one that broadens the health care options for dying patients.

Mori (1991) describes a number of challenges that face palliative care programs. First, funding of the health care system limits some palliative care services. For example, hospitals cannot claim reimbursement for services to caregivers. So only two-thirds of palliative programs cover bereavement counselling. Also, physicians get low pay for home visits, a condition that limits

● Exhibit 14.3

THE BENEFITS OF PALLIATIVE CARE

Margaret Murray describes the difference between dying on an acute-care hospital ward and on a pallia- tive care ward. She shows the benefits of palliative care to the patient and to the patient's family.

My Aunt Harriet was an attractive, intelligent busi- nesswoman who lost a four-year battle with cancer when she was in her mid-sixties. The initial surgery and radiotherapy gave her a few more years to play tennis and pursue her other interests, but the final year with more surgery and various experiments with chemotherapy was almost straight downhill for her.

About five weeks before she died, Harriet was admitted to a large downtown hospital after her bowel and bladder function failed. Up until her admission, she had been living with my parents, spending her days in the living room with her family, and getting about the house in a wheelchair. After less than two weeks of hospitalization, her change was startling.

One Sunday afternoon, we visited her in hospital and found her slumped in a large chair, her drooping head almost touching the bare overbed table appar- ently to prevent her from falling. With some difficulty we roused her, and she began to report a conversa- tion with her husband who had been dead for 30 years. We tried to make her as comfortable as pos- sible and to bring her back to the present with quiet conversation. This was only moderately successful. She continued to doze and awaken only enough to plead with us to put her back to bed. Eventually, I

approached her nurse for help, and was told that my aunt should stay up because she "needed the stimu- lation"! Since she had been alone before our arrival, without company and in no position to look out a window or watch television, this was a remarkable concept.

Although the nurse was never impolite, she left me with the feeling that her care was given with gritted teeth—she did not know how to care for the "difficult" patient, who did not know what was good for her. I wanted to say "She's dying! The complica- tions of immobility are not as important as her need for comfort, dignity and peace." But I felt she wouldn't understand....

A few days later, "Auntie Harry" was transferred to the Palliative Care Unit at the [Salvation Army's] Grace Hospital [in Toronto]. On my first visit I found her in a sunny four-bed room, sitting up and brightly awaiting the arrival of her dinner. She had been up once that day, gently lifted into a wheelchair and taken to the lounge where she was introduced to some of the other patients. She enjoyed the brief social interaction, and was returned to bed before she became too tired. Now, she was looking forward to another excursion after supper. Her conversation was relevant and lucid; she was appreciative of her sur- roundings and had many compliments for the staff. That day I left with the feeling that an enormous burden had been lifted from my shoulders—my aunt was still dying, but somehow it was alright now, for her and for the rest of the family.

Source: M.E. Murray, 1981, "Palliative Care," *Canadian Nurse/l'infirmière canadienne* 77(5): 16–17. Reproduced with per- mission from *The Canadian Nurse*.

their interest in palliative home care. Northcott and Wilson (2001) say that the system tends to underfund palliative care programs. Only four provinces (British Columbia, Alberta, Saskatchewan, and Manitoba) fund palliative care as a core service. But an Angus Reid poll found that almost three-quarters of Canadians thought the government should fund palliative care (Sewell 2003). Canadian Hospice and Palliative Care Association reports that only 5 to 15 percent of Canadians have access to palliative care programs.

Second, health care workers and the public need more knowledge about palliative care. The public needs to know

what this option offers. Professionals need to know how to work effectively on a palliative care team. They need better primary training and more frequent continuing education (Senate of Canada 1995). Balfour Mount, one of the founders of palliative care in Canada, says that "most physicians are not trained to deal with death. Even the basics of pain control are not routinely taught at medical school" (Sewell 2003). A 2002 survey found that only two of Canada's sixteen medical schools said they felt satisfied with their course work on palliative care (Sewell 2003).

Third, Northcott and Wilson (2001) say that pallia- tive care also challenges some core beliefs that people hold today. People believe in the curative power of modern medicine. And they may feel that palliative care gives up on the patient. They may feel guilty about choosing palliative care for a dying parent. Northcott and Wilson refer to the "California daughter syndrome" (68). A child, who may not have seen a parent for many years, refuses to accept the death of the parent and demands maximum medical treatment. Northcott and Wilson call for the gradual use of palliative care measures as a person approaches death. This, they say, may avoid the appearance that treatment has ended when palliative care has begun.

Fourth, nurses in one study said that the health care system often made it hard for them to deliver palliative care at home (Ross and McDonald, 1994). They blamed bureaucracy, fragmented services, and too much focus on efficiency. These forces interfered with the quality of care they wanted to provide. It kept them from giving patients the emotional support they wanted to give. This study points to the tension between the values of palliative care and the curative model that dominates the health care system.

Fifth, many older people will have no one at home to provide palliative care outside the institution. Community-based palliative care programs favour people with a primary caregiver. One study found that most palliative care programs served married women with husbands (Levy 1987, cited in Mori 1991). Older women, many of them widowed, often lack a primary caregiver. This makes them ineligible for palliative care. Also, multiple pathologies in an older patient may make pain control more complex. Frail older people on palliative home care may need the use of respite beds and a day hospital (CMA 1987).

Caregivers of older patients in palliative care programs report feeling stressed and exhausted (Ross et al. 2002). Families need health care and social support to carry out home-based palliative care (Hollander and Chappell 2002). Home care workers can help with cleaning and shopping. Respite care can help family caregivers get the rest they need. Quality community-based end-of-life care depends on a partnership between formal and informal caregivers. It also depends on the support of institutional care when needed. In Great Britain today, for example, most care at the end of life takes place at home (Boyd 1993; Eastaugh 1996, cited in Northcott and Wilson 2001). But people often go to a hospital for a short (one- to three-day) stay before they die.

ETHICAL ISSUES

Palliative care and other approaches to the treatment of dying patients raise a variety of ethical questions. Is it ethical to stop actively treating a person's illness? Does the decision not to put someone on a respirator or not to use a heroic life-saving measure contribute to the person's death? Philosophers, physicians, and legal experts have looked at these and other issues related to dying today.

Two ethical questions come up again and again in the writing on death and dying. First, how much information should health care providers give a dying person about their condition? Second, when should a doctor allow a person to die?

Informed Consent

Some years ago, experts debated whether to tell dying patients about their condition or keep this knowledge from them. Today, most experts support an open awareness context. They agree that patients have a right to know about the choice of treatment the physician has made and about alternative treatments, including the choice of no treatment (see also Saint-Arnaud 1993). Some provinces have written the right to know into the law. British Columbia (1996) passed the *Health Care (Consent) and Care Facility (Admission) Act* in 1996. The act defines the rights of adults with respect to health care treatment. Part 2, Article 4 of the act states that

Every adult who is capable of giving or refusing consent to health care has

(a) the right to give consent or to refuse consent on any grounds, including moral or religious grounds, even if the refusal will result in death,

(b) the right to select a particular form of available health care on any grounds, including moral or religious grounds,

(c) the right to revoke consent,

(d) the right to expect that a decision to give, refuse or revoke consent will be respected, and

(e) the right to be involved to the greatest degree possible in all case planning and decision making.

The act goes on to define the responsibilities of health care workers. For example, it requires workers to respect the wishes of the patient, to communicate clearly with the patient, and to ensure that the patient consents to treatment. Patients need to know their prognosis (the likely outcome of their illness) in order to make good decisions about treatment. For this reason alone, patients have a need as well as a right to know that they are dying.

Euthanasia and Physician-Assisted Suicide

Doctors sometimes face ethical conflicts when they treat dying patients. Medical ethics says that a doctor should heal and cure patients, but the Hippocratic oath also says that a doctor should first "do no harm." What should a doctor do when machines, surgery, or drugs that extend a person's life also prolong his or her suffering? What should a doctor do when a patient asks to die? And what does the law in Canada say about **euthanasia** (actively helping someone achieve a painless death)?

First, when is a person dead? When he or she stops breathing? When the heart stops beating? Or when the brain waves stop? Harvard Medical School (1968) gives four criteria for death: the person (1) no longer makes a response, (2) no longer breathes or moves, (3) has no reflexes, and (4) has no sign of brain activity on two EEGs taken 24 hours apart. But what if a machine keeps someone breathing, or a heart pump keeps someone's heart beating? Are these people alive or dead? When does a family or a doctor have the right to take someone off these machines?

At present, a person who lacks the mental competence to refuse treatment must rely on someone else to act for them. Family members, a friend, or a medical doctor often must make this decision. Even if a person has told someone their wishes or has written a statement of their wish to end treatment at a certain point, in Canada these instructions have no binding effect on the decision.

The Law Reform Commission of Canada (1982) reviewed the question of mercy killing in a study called *Euthanasia, Aiding Suicide and Cessation of Treatment.* The commission found that the Canadian courts have never convicted a doctor in Canada for giving a patient large doses of pain-killing drugs, for stopping useless treatment, or for deciding not to treat a secondary illness (such as pneumonia in a terminal cancer patient). The courts, however, could try doctors on these grounds. This means that every doctor who decides to stop treatment risks becoming a test case in the courts. The commission feels that the Criminal Code of Canada should give doctors clearer guidance.

The commission reviewed ways to relieve doctors of criminal liability, citing the example of California, which in 1976 passed Bill 3060, called the *Natural Death Act.* This bill allows a person to write a living will that authorizes relatives or doctors to withdraw or withhold artificial methods of life support in cases of terminal illness. It also attempts to relieve doctors of responsibility for stopping treatment.

A revised policy on resuscitation in Canada supports doctors' decisions to withdraw or withhold treatment if the treatment will not help the dying person (CMA 1995; Joint Statement on Terminal Illness 1984). Northcott and Wilson (2001, 72) say that "health care professionals in Canada are not obliged either to offer or to provide futile care."

Forty states in the U.S. recognize living wills. Kelly et al. (1989) studied physicians in nine countries and

---

● Exhibit 14.4

EUTHANASIA AND ASSISTED SUICIDE: WHAT THEY MEAN

Euthanasia, sometimes referred to as mercy killing, is a term that comes from the Greek word for "good death." It means helping someone end his or her life. A distinction is often drawn between "passive" and "active" euthanasia.

Passive euthanasia means withholding or ceasing treatment of someone who is ill or injured and not expected to recover—e.g., turning off life support systems and allowing a person to die "naturally."

Active euthanasia means intervening actively to end a person's life—e.g., administering a lethal dose of sedatives to someone with a terminal illness. If performed with the consent of the person concerned, this is called "voluntary euthanasia."

Assisted suicide involves providing the means for someone to commit suicide (e.g., supplying prescription drugs) with or without direct participation in the event.

Source: Adapted from National Advisory Council on Aging, 1994, "Euthanasia and Assisted Suicide: What They Mean," *Expressions* 10(1): 2. Courtesy of the National Advisory Council on Aging, Health Canada, 2000.

found that doctors would value having specific directions on the type of care a patient wants. Using the results of the study, the researchers produced a booklet called *Let Me Decide* that offers a model of a living will and a **health care directive**. The directive gives specific information to family members and doctors about the amount of treatment the person prefers under different conditions. The person also writes out a personal statement about preferences for care as part of the directive.

Directives most often take the form of the **durable power of attorney** and the **living will**. The power of attorney gives someone (often a lawyer, but also possibly a child, spouse, or other family member) the right to make financial decisions on behalf of the older person if the person loses his or her mental capacity. The living will refers to health care wishes at the end of life. It directs the person to make decisions on the older person's behalf, if that person can't make the decision. **Advance directives** allow the older person to maintain autonomy. Directives state what medical actions a person wants under what conditions. Directives also state who has the right to make the decisions (Cramer, Tuokko, and Evans 2001). They also help family members make health care decisions and avoid court intervention in decision-making.

Some research shows that people put off making out an advance directive. They don't want to think about poor health or death (Hamel et al. 2002). Education about advance directives can increase their use. A study of 116 veterans in Canada assessed the impact of an advance directive program called Let Me Decide (Molloy, Russo, et al. 2000). The study included workshops and visits by counsellors to tell veterans about the program. The counsellors encouraged the veterans to fill out advance directive forms. Thirty-six percent of the veterans in this study completed directives. Nearly all veterans in the study felt that they benefited from the program.

Molloy, Guyatt, and their colleagues (2000) conducted a similar education program in Ontario. They paired six nursing homes in a controlled study of the Let Me Decide program's effects. They found that after the program 49 percent of the competent residents and 78 percent of families of incompetent residents had filled out advance directives. Information about advance directives increases an understanding of their value and increases their use.

Some provinces in Canada have laws that support living wills. These laws require health care workers to follow the instructions in the living will (as long as the instructions do not require illegal activity) (Northcott

and Wilson 2001). Lavoie, Blondeau, and Godin (1999) presented nurses with two treatment scenarios. In one, the patient had a living will. In the other, the patient did not. The presence of a living will led nurses to choose a level of care that provided comfort to the patient. The absence of a living will led nurses to choose an intensive treatment and aggressive therapy. The living will helped nurses choose the more appropriate level of care for patients.

Advance directives can ensure that an older person gets the care he or she wants. But advance directives pose problems that need public discussion. First, in some cases people may change their minds as they near death, but they will not get a chance to change their advance directive. Lawton (2001) reviewed studies of end-of-life preferences. He found support for this concern. The research showed that about 30 percent of people change their preferences over time. Some want more intervention (10 percent) and others less (20 percent). He concludes that people need the chance to review and, if necessary, revise their advance directive as they approach death.

Second, the Law Reform Commission of Canada (1982, 10) says that "a terminally ill patient has a right, not a secondary or subordinate right but a primary right, to die with dignity and not to fall victim to heroic measures." People should not need advance directives to protect themselves from heroic treatment. Third, subtle forms of coercion may influence an older person's instructions in an advance directive. Older people may propose an end to treatment because they feel that they will burden others with their care. These issues point to the need for better methods of communication between dying people and their caregivers (Lawton 2001).

The Law Reform Commission of Canada (1982) says that in Canada today doctors should not feel compelled to take heroic measures to keep someone alive and patients should not have to write advance directives to protect themselves from a doctor's fear of prosecution. The commission says that the law and medical ethics distinguish between killing someone and allowing someone to die. Walton and Fleming (1980, 58) say that a doctor who sets out to kill a patient—for example, by giving the patient a drug overdose—"has committed himself more firmly. He is therefore more directly accountable for the outcome." A doctor who allows death to happen—for example, by not putting a person on a respirator or by taking someone off a respirator— may or may not cause a person's death. This is **passive euthanasia**. The person may live even without the treatment. Walton and Fleming say that ethical treatment should offer the most options for the patient. "A passive course of action provides a sensible alternative to aggres-

● Exhibit 14.5

A LIVING WILL

Lawton (2001) reports that family members and physicians sometimes differ in their judgment of the person's will to live and of the person's end-of-life preferences. This potential for conflict supports the need for an advance directive. Lawton goes on to say that an advance directive allows a person to think about his or her preferences while in a sound state of mind. It allows people to control their own destiny. The courts will honour advance directives. But a person's relatives or friends need to make health care professionals aware of the directive and what it says. Cramer, Tuokko, and Evans (2001) report that most people have heard of advance directives, but relatively few people have them. In their study, they found that only 28 percent of their sample had made out a power of attorney for finances. Only 19 percent said they had a living will for health services. People with more education tended to have these documents in place. The researchers say that advance directives work best when the older person has discussed their preferences with their surrogate.

A Living Will

The living will format below appears in the California Natural Death Act. *The directive below gives an idea of what such a will should contain. Read it over and consider the pros and cons of living wills. Would you fill one out? Would you witness a friend's? Do you think Canada should allow the use of living wills?*

Directive to Physician

Directive made this _____ day of _____ (month, year). I _____, being of sound mind, willfully and voluntarily make known my desire that my life shall not be artificially prolonged under the circumstances set forth below, and do hereby declare:

1. If at any time I should have an incurable injury, disease, or illness certified to be a terminal condition by two physicians, and where the application of life-sustaining procedures would serve only to artificially prolong the moment of my death and where my physician determines that my death is imminent whether or not life-sustaining procedures are utilized, I direct that such procedures be withheld or withdrawn and that I be permitted to die naturally.

2. In the absence of my ability to give directions regarding the use of such life-sustaining procedures, it is my intention that this directive shall be honoured by my family and physician(s) as the final expression of my legal right to refuse medical or surgical treatment and accept the consequences from such refusal.

3. If I have been diagnosed as pregnant and that diagnosis is known to my physician, this directive shall have no force or effect during the course of my pregnancy.

4. I have been diagnosed and notified at least 14 days ago as having a terminal condition by _____, M.D., whose address is _____, and whose telephone number is _____. I understand that if I have not filled in the physician's name and address, it shall be presumed that I did not have a terminal condition when I made out this directive.

5. This directive shall have no force or effect five years from the date filled in above.

6. I understand the full import of this directive and I am emotionally and mentally competent to make this directive.

Signed _____

City, County and State of Residence

_____

The declarant has been personally known to me and I believe him or her to be of sound mind.

Witness _____

Source: *California Natural Death Act.* The contents of this document are in the public domain.

sive treatment and, at the same time, allows for unexplainable and unforeseen events which may be of great benefit to the patient" (60).

The current law leaves many questions open. Once treatment has begun, for instance, the law inhibits a doctor from discontinuing treatment. The doctor may know, through an advance directive, that after some time the patient would want treatment discontinued. But, by discontinuing the treatment, the doctor risks legal action. The absence of support in the law for advance directives leaves the doctor open to civil action, criminal liability, and charges of misconduct from the medical profession (Manitoba Law Reform Commission 1990).

Both the law and medical ethics reject **active euthanasia** or physician-assisted suicide—actively helping someone end his or her life either because the person asks for death or to relieve suffering. The Law Reform Commission of Canada (1982) says that a law to support active euthanasia would create more risks than benefits and might lead to new methods of euthanasia.

Skelton (1982), a pioneer in palliative care in Canada, states the experts' case simply, saying that requests for active euthanasia often hide a request for better care. "I believe most sincerely that if adequate care is given to dying patients the question of responding to requests for active euthanasia is eliminated" (558; see also Meier 1999). St. John and Man-Son-Hing (2002) agree. They say that a request for active euthanasia most often comes from someone in pain or with depression. Symptom control can make dying less painful and can reduce the request for active euthanasia. But not everyone agrees with this statement. Some studies show that women, minorities, and older people sometimes fail to get the pain relief they need (Lee 1999; Meier, Myers, and Muskin 1999). Doctors themselves disagree on how much a physician should assist a person who wishes to die.

Recent cases in the United States have (at least for now) settled the issue of the legality of physician-assisted suicide. In **physician-assisted suicide**, a doctor gives a person the means to commit suicide or gives advice on how to commit suicide. The patients take the action themselves. Controversy exists over this practice. Michigan courts acquitted Dr. Jack Kevorkian of murder three times in cases where he helped patients commit suicide. In 1999, however, a jury for the first time convicted Kevorkian of murder.

Supporters and critics of these decisions often argue about the issue of consent. Supporters of assisted suicide say that the patient's right to accept or refuse treatment will protect people from abuse of assisted suicide. Critics of assisted suicide fear that this will lead to mercy killing without patients' consent. Krauthammer (1996) reports

that this has occurred in the Netherlands (see also Senate of Canada 1995). Also, some doctors may consent to patient requests too quickly. Few guidelines exist today for doctors to follow, and medical associations have begun to review their standards in light of recent court actions and social changes (CMA 1995).

Canadian law prohibits a doctor from helping patients end their lives. A case in Canada (*Rodriguez v. British Columbia*) in 1993 supported the Criminal Code's provisions against physician-assisted suicide (Health Canada 1994). Sue Rodriguez, a 42-year-old mother, had amyotrophic lateral sclerosis (Lou Gehrig's disease). Her health decreased and she would soon lose the ability to speak, swallow, or move. She had between two and fourteen months to live. She requested a court order from the Supreme Court of British Columbia to allow her to have a physician help her end her life when she chose. She asked the court to declare the Criminal Code statute (section 241[b]) invalid. This statue prohibits assisted suicide.

The court held that Rodriguez did not have the right to have a doctor help her end her life. The court split five to four against her request. Some of the dissenting justices proposed procedural guidelines that could allow physician-assisted suicide. A court of appeal supported the majority opinion against Rodriguez's request. The outcome reflects "social divisions about how to reconcile the strongly held values of self-determination and the sanctity of life" (National Advisory Council on Aging [NACA] 1994b, 5). (Sue Rodriguez died on February 12, 1994.)

Public debate on this issue will grow. The Catholic Health Association of Canada, for example, opposes assisted suicide and euthanasia (Blouin 1995, cited in Northcott and Wilson 2001). But others support these practices (Humphry 2000). They say that medicine now has the ability to prolong life through technology. This will mean more years of pain and suffering for some patients. Also, the cost of keeping people alive on machines and with expensive medications will also increase. Some people will support active euthanasia on economic grounds. Many people see the choice of active euthanasia as a right in modern society (NACA 1994b).

Still, only a few countries allow voluntary euthanasia or physician-assisted suicide. Humphry (2000) reports that Swiss law has allowed **assisted suicide** since 1937 as long as it relieves suffering and has a humanitarian purpose. But social sanctions keep most doctors from assisting with suicide. On May 20, 1997, the Constitutional Court of Colombia approved legalized euthanasia. The court ruled that "no person can be held criminally responsible for taking the life of a termi-

Exhibit 14.6

CESSATION OF TREATMENT IN CANADA

Section 198 of the Criminal Code of Canada says that a person who gives medical or surgical treatment should act with reasonable skill and care. Section 199 says that a person has to continue an act once he or she begins if, by stopping the act, he or she endangers someone's life. These sections seem to make a doctor criminally liable for stopping useless treatment. The Law Reform Commission of Canada says that these sections do not apply to a doctor who stops treatment after careful review of a case. The commission gives an example to show why:

A doctor turns off a respirator, knowing, as he does so, that the patient will no longer be ventilated and thus will probably die. Let us suppose, in one instance, that before doing so he has assured himself, using standard medical procedures and tests, that the patient is already in a state of irreversible coma. Here the act of turning off the respirator, while technically constituting a positive act of cessation of treatment within the meaning of section 199, could not serve as a valid basis for criminal liability, and for two reasons. Firstly, the continuation of treatment is not reasonable in this case given the condition of the patient and, secondly, the cessation of treatment does not reflect wanton or reckless disregard for life on the part of the physician. But on the other hand, let us assume that this doctor performs the same act without first assuring himself of the patient's condition. There would probably then be grounds for applying these provisions, since by ceasing treatment without taking the precaution of assuring himself that such cessation will not endanger the patient, he would be showing wanton or reckless disregard for the patient's life or safety.

Source: Department of Justice, 1982, *Euthanasia, Aiding Suicide and Cessation of Treatment,* Working Paper 28. Department of Justice Canada. Reprinted with the permission of the Minister of Public Works and Government Services Canada, 2004.

nally ill patient who has given clear authorization to do so." The ruling still has to go before the country's Congress for adoption (Humphry 2000, 49).

Humphry (2000) says that in only two places does assisted suicide have societal support—the Netherlands and the state of Oregon. Oregon passed the *Death with Dignity Act* in 1994 by popular vote. This act bans voluntary euthanasia (mercy killing), but it supports physician-assisted suicide in cases of advanced terminal illness. The law lays out a detailed process for patients and physicians to follow.

The Netherlands began allowing physician-assisted suicide in 1973. In 1984, the Dutch Supreme Court allowed both voluntary euthanasia and physician-assisted suicide. These causes of death account for about 3 percent of all deaths in the Netherlands each year. Regulations exist to guide physicians' practices. In particular, doctors have to report cases where they have assisted with a suicide. However, technically euthanasia remains illegal in the Netherlands. The courts allow the process but no law exists that makes it legal (Humphry 2000).

The National Advisory Council on Aging (1994b) reports that, in 1968, 45 percent of Canadians approved of legalized euthanasia. By 1992, this figure had increased to 77 percent of Canadians. The Canadian Medical Association (CMA) conducted a study of physicians' views of physician-assisted suicide. The study found that more than 60 percent of doctors wanted to change the Criminal Code. They wanted to do away with the laws that prohibit physician-assisted suicide (NACA 1994c). In 1994, the ethics committee of the CMA supported doctors' right to assist in suicide. The committee also proposed that the CMA set up guidelines for physicians who choose to assist a patient in suicide. But CMA members voted against the committee's recommendation. They voted to ban doctors from engaging in physician-assisted suicide. Disagreement exists, even within the medical profession, over the practice. Humphry (2000, 59) says that "the medical profession almost everywhere is split down the middle on the issue of euthanasia."

This debate over physician-assisted suicide will continue as Canadians sort out the implications of changing the law. Humphry (2000, 59) says that "in every nation where there have been scientific surveys of public opinion, it has become obvious that the general *public*

Exhibit 14.7

PROPOSED CHANGES IN CANADIAN LAW

The Law Reform Commission proposes that the Criminal Code of Canada include the following statements.

1. Nothing in sections 14, 45, 198, 199 of the Criminal Code shall be interpreted as requiring a physician

   (a) to continue to administer or to undertake medical treatment against the clearly expressed wishes of the person for whom such treatment is intended;

   (b) to continue to administer or to undertake medical treatment, when such treatment is

   medically useless and is not in the best interests of the person for whom it is intended, except in accordance with the clearly expressed wishes of this person.

2. Nothing in sections 14, 45, 198, 199 of the Criminal Code shall be interpreted as preventing a physician from undertaking or ceasing to administer palliative care and measures intended to eliminate or to relieve the suffering of a person for the sole reason that such care or measures are likely to shorten the life expectancy of this person.

Source: Department of Justice, 1982, *Euthanasia, Aiding Suicide and Cessation of Treatment*, Working Paper 28. Department of Justice Canada. Reprinted with the permission of the Minister of Public Works and Government Services Canada, 2004.

want action, while the *politicians* (who actually make the laws) are either *against law reform or afraid of a religious backlash* if they follow the public's wishes." It seems unlikely that Canada will change its law to allow assisted suicide. But other approaches to end-of-life illness, such as hospice and palliative care, will get more attention. Likewise people need to learn more about advance directives so that they can get the end-of-life care that they want.

MOURNING AND GRIEF

When an older person dies, he or she often leaves behind children, sometimes a spouse, and other family members (such as grandchildren or siblings). These survivors need to adjust to the loss, and society can help with this adjustment. Funeral practices and rituals structure the grieving process. They prescribe what mourners should say, what they should wear, and in some cultures even how they should sit. Mourners in Christian cultures wear black; mourners in some Asian cultures wear white. North American society values silent, unemotional grieving; Chinese families hire professional mourners to make loud wailing noises at the funeral. Jewish tradition requires that the family "sit shiva" for seven days after a funeral. According to this custom, mourners tear their clothes, sit on low chairs to deny themselves physical comfort, cover the mirrors in their home, and light a candle that burns for one week. The mourning family accepts visitors throughout the week, and 10 men gather at the house each day for prayer. Mourning continues in less intense stages for a year until the unveiling of a commemorative stone on the grave of the deceased.

Each culture has its own funeral rituals and mourning practices, but all of them have a common purpose: to help the bereaved family cope with grief and re-establish community bonds after the loss of a community member. Regardless of the culture a person belongs to or the type of funeral he or she attends, each bereaved person has to work through personal feelings of grief.

Kastenbaum (2001, 316) calls bereavement "an objective fact." People often use this term when someone close to them dies. The fact of bereavement often leads to grief. Some research in North America shows that mourners go through stages of grief. Early work by Lindemann (1944) describes three such stages: an initial response phase, an intermediate phase, and a recovery phase.

First, the bereaved person feels shock and disbelief. He or she may report feeling cold and numb, and some people say they feel dazed, empty, and confused. These feelings protect a person from feelings of sorrow. People in this phase often fear that they will break down in public. This phase can last for several weeks.

● **Exhibit 14.8**

A FAMILY'S RESPONSE TO DEATH AND DYING

The academic discussions of the right to decide on prolonging life often focus on medical and legal issues. But every day in Canada, people, along with their physicians and nursing staff, make decisions about their older family members. These decisions, at their best, take place within a context of openness and trust between families and health care professionals. The following case shows how one family decided against aggressive treatment:

Mrs. Walker, 78, moved into an apartment in the Beth Sharon Senior Complex in early December. The complex offered her a supportive environment. It had a security system, access for a wheelchair, and a chance to socialize with other residents.

Mrs. Walker had played an active part in her community for many years as a hospital volunteer and businessperson. So, when she moved into her apartment complex, she joined the Beth Sharon Seniors Group and regularly attended their afternoon teas in a nearby centre. On January 10, as she left for the tea, she lost her balance, fell down a flight of stairs, and severely injured her head. When an ambulance arrived, she was found to be unconscious and was taken to a nearby hospital for emergency treatment.

Mrs. Walker's daughter, Phyllis, a nurse, rushed to the hospital when she was called. The neurosurgeon on staff had already completed a CAT scan and showed it to Phyllis. "I don't like the look of this," he said. "There appears to be severe bleeding at the base of the brain stem. She's not likely to be well again, or indeed function on her own."

Phyllis left the ward to talk with her sister and other family members. They agreed that they would not press for an operation to remove the blood clot. Surgery would almost certainly lead to the necessity of a respirator and other artificial means of life support. Over the next few days, as the family waited for some change in their mother's condition, Phyllis would suggest various actions or ask for another test. Each time the surgeon in charge would ask a simple question, "Would your mother like us to do that?" And each time Phyllis agreed that her mother would not want aggressive treatment to prolong her life. The decision to wait became harder to sustain as Mrs. Walker's breathing faltered. But the family stayed with its decision, based on Mrs. Walker's many discussions with them. Family members and close friends supported the family's decision to follow their mother's wishes.

Sixteen days after entering the hospital, and without regaining consciousness, Mrs. Walker died. She was cremated, in accordance with her request, and her family held a memorial service to celebrate her life.

Second, the person will begin to review what has happened. This takes three forms: (1) The bereaved person obsessively reviews one or two scenes related to the death, or may be very self-critical about something that he or she should have said or done. (2) The bereaved person searches for a meaning for the death. Religious people may find solace in knowing that God willed this death. (3) The bereaved person searches for the deceased. This may mean that a widow goes to places where she expects to see her spouse. She may also feel his presence while watching TV, eating dinner, or lying in bed. Some people even call out to their spouses and expect an answer. This phase lasts about a year.

Third, the bereaved person begins to recover. Survivors look for social contacts. They may join a club or go on a cruise. They feel that they have come through an ordeal and say they feel stronger and more competent than before. This stage begins around the second year after the death.

Kastenbaum (2001) says that grief affects a person's physical as well as psychological well-being. Some research shows that grief throws the body's neuroendocrine system out of balance. Acute grief can lead to illness and may even lead to death. Grief affects a person's entire life, including his or her social relations.

Gorer (1965) says that successful grief work includes three stages: (1) breaking bonds to the deceased, (2) readjusting to the environment without the deceased, and (3) forming new relationships. Not everyone makes a smooth trip through this process. Sometimes a person can show a delayed emotional response to a parent's or a spouse's death. The person seems to cope well, displaying lots of zest and energy, but may have internalized the grief. This delay can lead to emotional upset and physical illness later.

The case of Joanna will show the cost of morbid grieving. While her husband was in the hospital dying of brain cancer, she visited him every day. At the same time, she carried on a career in real estate and worked on a master's degree. For two years, she ran herself into the ground. She went to the hospital twice a day, at noon and at supper time, to feed her husband his meals, then she would jump in her car and show another house or run home to work on a paper.

When her husband died, she was determined that nothing was going to stop her. "I didn't allow myself time to grieve," she says. "After his death, I travelled. At Christmas I went to Spain, Hawaii, or wherever. At Easter I went somewhere. I went to Europe. There was never a day—I didn't allow myself any time at all. Do you get the picture? No time to breathe."

To keep going she used pills and alcohol. Then she started collecting pills and drinking more. "That was my way of coping, my way of standing the pain. I needed some kind of anesthetic," she says. At the end of this downward spiral, Joanna drove the front of her car through a restaurant window. She got out of her car, walked through the window frame, sat down at a booth in the restaurant, and waited for the police to take her away (Novak 1985).

Only about 25 percent of bereaved people go through morbid grieving (and few people show Joanna's extreme denial) (Schulz 1978). But research does show that people who have problems with grieving may turn to alcohol and drugs (Connor 1998). They may also feel sorrow, anger, bitterness, rage, and despair (Northcott and Wilson 2001, citing Clark 1993).

Many people deviate from the pattern of bereavement that stage models of grieving describe (Wortman and Silver 1990). Northcott and Wilson (2001) say that the pattern of grieving depends on how a person dies, whether the death takes place suddenly or over time, and the age of the person. Older people, for example, tend to show a delayed and more extreme grief reaction than younger people. Sanders (1980–81) compared the scores on a "grief experience inventory" of 45 bereaved spouses in two age groups (people over age 65 and those under age 63). She found that older spouses showed less grief than younger spouses at the time of a first interview (shortly after their spouse's death). At the second interview, older spouses showed higher scores than younger spouses on scales of denial and physical symptoms, and increases in 10 other scales compared with younger

spouses. Barrett and Schneweis (1980–81, 102) also report that life after a spouse's death "persists in being stressful for years." Martin and Elder (1993) say that grief may come and go in cycles over long periods of time. Northcott and Wilson (2001, 156) say that "grief is never truly over." These results show that an older person may need help long after his or her spouse's death.

Baker (1991) reports that spouses who have died continue to influence the living in many ways. People sometimes talk to a dead spouse, ask them for advice, or try to imagine what they would do in a situation the surviving spouse is facing. One woman said she felt her husband lie down next to her in bed some months after his funeral. Widows or widowers will sometimes decide against remarriage because of the close tie that still exists with their dead spouse. Moss and Moss (1984–85, 204) consider this a normal response to widowhood in old age and "a nourishing link to the past." More research on bereavement in old age will show how this experience differs from bereavement in younger people (Wortman and Silver 1990).

CONCLUSION

This chapter has touched on some of the complex issues related to death and dying. Each religion has its own views on issues such as euthanasia, funeral practices, and mourning. Each culture shapes its members' beliefs about the meaning of death, about life after death, and about care for the sick and dying. People will respond in unique ways to their own death and to the deaths of people they know and love. Today, changes in technology, the management of terminal illness, and the meaning of death raise new questions about death and dying.

The study of death and dying can help people to understand these issues and make better choices for themselves. An incident in the life of the lead author of this book, Mark Novak, made this clear to him.

> After my father's funeral, my mother, my sister, my father's brothers, and I got into a rented limousine and drove to the cemetery. The funeral director stopped the cars in the funeral procession at the cemetery gate. We saw the hearse pull ahead and stop a hundred yards away. I turned around to talk to one of my uncles in our car. A few minutes later, the director waved all the cars on. We stopped behind the hearse and got out. It was empty. The director led us to the graveside. We stood close to the grave, but we could not see the coffin or any earth. A blanket of fake grass covered the earth that had come from the grave. Another blanket cov-

ered the coffin. Relatives and friends gathered to the side and behind us. The director said some prayers and a few kind words. My mother, my sister, and I stood and stared at the fake grass. I think we were supposed to leave. But I motioned to the director to pull the grass back. He looked surprised. I told him to pull the grass back. He did. We saw the corner of the coffin and the corner of the grave, and we started to cry.

I tell this story because my knowledge of death and dying gave me the confidence to act. I felt I should do something, and I knew what I had to do.

Those of us in the field of aging use our knowledge of aging each day. We use it to better understand our families and friends. And we use it to understand the changes we go through as we age. Knowledge about aging allows us to plan for our future with less fear and denial. The study of aging can make old age a better time of life for each of us and for the people we love.

Summary

1. Attitudes to death vary by age, religion, and culture. Older people generally accept death more than younger people. Like younger people, older people say they want to continue living if they feel their life has meaning.

2. People with either no religious belief or a very strong one seem to cope with death best.

3. Death occurs more often in old age today than in the past, and it also occurs more often in an institution. These trends will increase as the population ages.

4. Elisabeth Kübler-Ross reports five stages of dying. Not everyone goes through all of these stages in the order Kübler-Ross describes, but her writings encouraged a more open discussion of death and dying when they first appeared.

5. Dame Cicely Saunders opened the first modern hospice in England in 1967. St. Christopher's Hospice offers an alternative to hospital care for the dying. Hospices offer pain control and a home-like setting for death.

6. Palliative care units in hospitals offer the same comfort and care as a hospice. Some of these units will help patients die in their own homes. They also assure patients that they can return to the hospital at any time.

7. Most experts and patients prefer an open awareness context for dying. They agree that patients have a right to know about the choice of treatment the physician has made and about alternative treatments, including the choice of no treatment. Doctors today need to understand their own feelings about death and dying, so they can give their patients the kind of care that their patients prefer.

8. Doctors say that proper pain control would end the fear that leads people to ask for euthanasia. The law in Canada today does not require doctors to take heroic measures to keep a terminally ill patient alive. Canada needs clearer guidelines to help doctors decide about stopping treatment for people in certain situations. Canadian law does prohibit active euthanasia. Judicial review of cases would lead to more rational decisions about termination of life.

9. Health care directives relieve doctors of criminal liability. They give family members and doctors specific information about the amount of treatment a person prefers. They also state who has the right to make decisions on behalf of the patient.

10. Death leads to grief and mourning for survivors. Culture and religion help people cope with feelings of grief. Funerals, for example, bring the community together and give mourners support. Still, each person has to work through feelings of grief in his or her own way. Researchers say that mourners go through stages of grief and that if all goes well they will emerge from grieving to carry on their life.

Study Questions

1. Researchers have proposed three theories that describe how older people respond to death. List and explain each of these theories.
2. Describe the means that older people use to buffer their fear of death.
3. How has population aging changed the context of dying?
4. Describe how Elisabeth Kübler-Ross and Cicely Saunders each influenced thinking about death and dying.
5. Explain the main function of a hospice. What methods do hospices use to help people enjoy their last days?
6. Compare and contrast palliative care units and hospices. Why do researchers think that, compared with a normal hospital, palliative care units cost less money to care for dying patients?
7. What moral issues did the Sue Rodriguez case raise? What conflict did this case raise between the medical profession and the Canadian legal system? How can Canadian society resolve this conflict for the future?
8. Describe the three stages of grief. Describe successful grief work. How do older and younger people differ in their grieving patterns?

Key Terms

active euthanasia intervening actively to end a person's life. (334)

advance directive a precise statement of the desired treatment and care, including what medical actions are to be taken under what conditions and a declaration of who has the right to decide. (332)

assisted suicide or physician-assisted suicide suicide made possible with the help of someone, who may or may not participate directly in the event; in the case of physician-assisted suicide, a doctor provides the person with the means or advice on how to commit suicide. (334)

durable power of attorney the power that gives someone, usually a lawyer, child, friend, or other family member, the right to make decisions on behalf of the ill person. (332)

ego integrity the acceptance of the notion that one's life cycle is something complete and unique. (323)

ego transcendence a late stage of psychosocial development, in which people feel a deep concern for others and for the culture they will leave when they die. (323)

euthanasia ending the life of a person suffering a terminal illness or incurable condition. (331)

grief work the process of grieving, which includes breaking bonds to the deceased, readjusting to the environment without the deceased, and forming new relationships. (337)

health care directive instructions with specific information for family members and doctors about the amount of treatment the person prefers under different conditions. (332)

hospice hospices are health care services that meet the special needs of dying patients. (326)

living will a legal document that specifies the limits of health care treatment desired in case of a terminal illness. (332)

palliative care care directed toward improving the quality of life for the dying, including symptom control and spiritual support as well as bereavement support and education. (327)

passive euthanasia withholding or ceasing treatment of someone who is ill or injured and not expected to recover. (332)

Selected Readings

de Vries, Brian, ed. *End of Life Issues: Interdisciplinary and Multidimensional Perspectives.* New York: Springer, 1999.

   This book contains articles on current issues in aging and death. Topics include preferences for place of death, bereavement, communicating life-prolonging treatment wishes, and physician-assisted suicide. An excellent collection of current thinking in this field.

Kastenbaum, R.J. *Death, Society, and Human Experience,* 7th ed. Boston: Allyn and Bacon, 2001.

   This classic text in the field, offers up-to-date information on hospice care, end-of-life decisions, euthanasia, and bereavement. The book also covers unusual topics like survival after death. Well written with good summaries of the research on death and dying.

National Advisory Council on Aging. *Ethics and Aging.* Ottawa: Minister of Supply and Services, 1993.

   A collection of articles on issues related to death and dying. The book includes a discussion of decision-making with respect to end-of-life treatment. It also includes a discussion of health care rationing. These well-written and thoughtful essays present clear and orderly discussions of many complex issues that we all read about in the newspapers.

Northcott, H.C., and D.M. Wilson. *Dying and Death in Canada.* Aurora, ON: Garamond Press, 2001.

   This book reviews the history of death and dying in Canada. The authors present current information on causes of death, gender differences in causes of death, and ages at death. The book looks at the relationship between modern medicalized approaches to death and dying in Canada and other cultural traditions (Muslim, Jewish, and Asian). The authors present case studies of how Canadians cope with and respond to death. A readable and insightful book.

References

* Numbers indicate the chapters in which the source is cited.

7* Abrahams, R. 1972. "Mutual Help for the Widowed." *Social Work* 19: 54–61.

13 Abu-Laban, Sharon McIrvin. 1980. "Social Supports in Older Age: The Need for New Research Directions." *Essence* 4: 95–209.

3 Achenbaum, A., and P.N. Stearns. 1978. "Old Age and Modernization." *Gerontologist* 18: 307–12.

13 Adam, R., and R. Blieszner. 1995. "Aging Well with Family and Friends." *American Behavioral Scientist* 39(2): 209–24.

5 Adams, R. 2003. "Strength Training: A Natural Prescription for Staying Healthy and Fit." *Gerentology Research Centre News* 22(1): 1–4.

13 Ade-Ridder, L. 1990. "Sexuality and Marital Quality among Older Married Couples." In T.H. Brubaker, ed., *Family Relationships in Later Life*, 2nd ed., 48–67. Newbury Park, CA: Sage Publications.

14 Aiken, L.R. 2001. *Dying, Death, and Bereavement*, 4th ed. Mahwah, NJ: Lawrence Erlbaum.

14 Ajemian, I.C. 1990. "Palliative Care in Canada: 1990." *Journal of Palliative Care* 6(4): 47–58.

6 Albert, M.S., and R.J. Killiany. 2001. "Age-Related Cognitive Change and Brain-Behavior Relationships." In J.E. Birren and K.W. Schaie, eds., *Handbook of the Psychology of Aging*, 5th ed. San Diego: Academic Press.

3 Albert, S.M., and M.G. Cattell. 1994. *Old Age in Global Perspective: Cross-Cultural and Cross-National Views*. New York: G.K. Hall.

5 Allen, S.M., A. Foster, and K. Berg. 2001. "Receiving Help at Home: The Interplay of Human and Technological Assistance." *Journals of Gerontology Series B* 56(6): S374–82.

6 Alzheimer Society of Canada. 2004. Introduction to "Alzheimer Care: Safely Home—Alzheimer Wandering Registry." http://www.alzheimer.ca/english/care/wandering-intro.htm, accessed on July 30, 2004.

3 American Association of Retired Persons. 1998. *Aging Everywhere*. Washington, DC: American Association of Retired Persons.

5 Aminzadeh, F., and N. Edwards. 2000. "Factors Associated with Cane Use among Community Dwelling Older Adults." *Public Health Nursing* 176: 474–83.

8 Amoako, E.P., L. Richardson-Campbell, and L. Kennedy-Malone. 2003. "Self-Medication with Over-the-Counter Drugs among Elderly Adults." *Journal of Gerontological Nursing* 29(8): 10–15.

3 Amoss, P.T., and S. Harrell. 1981. "Introduction: An Anthropological Perspective on Aging." In P.T. Amoss and S. Harrell, eds., *Other Ways of Growing Old: Anthropological Perspectives*. Stanford, CA: Stanford University Press.

3 Anderson, G.F., and P.S. Hussey. 2000. "Population Aging: A Comparison among Industrialized Countries." *Health Affairs* 19(3): 191–203.

8 Anderson, G.F., V. Petrosyan, and P.S. Hussey. 2002. *Multinational Comparisons of Health Systems Data, 2002*. Baltimore: Johns Hopkins University.

7 Andrews, G.J., Gavin, N., S. Begley, and D. Brodie. 2003. "Assisting Friendships, Combating Loneliness: Users' Views on a 'Befriending' Scheme." *Ageing and Society* 23(3): 349–62.

1 Andrews, M. 2000. "Ageful and Proud." *Ageing and Society* 20 (Part 6): 791–95.

14 Angeli, E.A.G. 2001. "Spiritual Care in Hospice Settings." In D.O. Moberg, ed., *Aging and Spirituality*, 113–24. Binghamton, NY: Haworth Pastoral Press.

8 Angus Reid. 2000. "Health Care in Canada." Opinion poll. Angus Reid Group.

6 Antonucci, T.C. 2001. "Social Relations: An Examination of Social Networks, Social Support, and Sense of Control." In J.E. Birren and K.W. Schaie, eds., *Handbook of the Psychology of Aging*, 5th ed. San Diego: Academic Press.

3   Apt, N.A. 2002. "Ageing and the Changing Role of the Family and the Community: An African Perspective." *International Social Security Review* 55(1): 39–47.

3   Araba, Nana. 1988. "Social Change: Family Role and Responsibilities of the Elderly in Africa." In *Aging around the World: A Report on the President's Symposium on Aging in Tomorrow's World: An International Perspective.* Washington, DC: Gerontological Society of America.

12   Arbuckle, T.Y., D.P. Gold, J.S. Chaikelson, and S. Lapidus. 1994. "Measurement of Activity in the Elderly: The Activities Checklist." *Canadian Journal on Aging* 13(4): 55–65.

13   Armstrong, P. 2002. "Guidelines for Examining Women, Work, and Caring in the New Millennium." *Centres of Excellence for Women's Health Research Bulletin* 3(1): 15–18.

7   Armstrong-Esther, C.A. 1994. "Health and Social Needs of Native Seniors." In National Advisory Council on Aging, *Aboriginal Seniors' Issues*, 39–48. Cat. No. H71-2/1-15-1994E. Ottawa: Minister of Supply and Services.

13   Aronson, J. 1992. "Women's Sense of Responsibility for the Care of Old People: 'But Who Else is Going to Do It?'" *Gender and Society* 6(1): 8–29.

2   Aronson, J. 1998. "Women's Perspectives of Informal Care of the Elderly: Public Ideology and Personal Experience of Giving and Receiving Care." In D. Coburn, C. D'Arcy, and G.M. Torrance, eds., *Health and Canadian Society: Sociological Perspectives*, 3rd ed., 399–416. Toronto: University of Toronto Press.

8   Aronson, J. 2002. "Frail and Disabled Users of Home Care: Confident Consumers or Disentitled Citizens?" *Canadian Journal on Aging* 21(1): 11–25.

8   Aronson, J., V.W. Marshall, and J. Sulman. 1987. "Patients Awaiting Discharge from Hospital." In V.W. Marshall, ed., *Aging in Canada: Social Perspectives.* Toronto: Fitzhenry and Whiteside.

8   Aronson, J., and C. Sinding. 2000. "Home Care Users' Experiences of Fiscal Constraints: Challenges and Opportunities for Case Management. *Care Management Journals* 2(4): 220–25.

13   Aronson, J., C. Thornewell, and K. Williams. 1995. "Wife Assault in Old Age: Coming Out of Obscurity." *Canadian Journal on Aging* 14 (Suppl. 2): 72–88.

12   Arsenault, N. 1997. "Typologies and the Leisure Learner." *Aging International* 4(2/3): 64–74.

4   Artibise, A. 1977. *Winnipeg: An Illustrated History.* Toronto: Lorimer.

5   Aschaiek, S. 2003. "Senior Idols: Annual Jubilee Put Talent Front and Centre." *Toronto Star, Comfort Life*, 22.

8   Astin, J.A., K.R. Pelletier, A. Marie, and W.L. Haskell. 2000. "Complementary and Alternative Medicine Use among Elderly Persons: One-Year Analysis of a Blue Shield Medicare Supplement." *Journals of Gerontology Series A* 55(1): M4–9.

10   Atchley, R.C. 1976. *The Sociology of Retirement.* Cambridge, MA: Schenkman.

3   Atchley, R.C. 1980. *The Social Forces in Later Life.* 3rd ed. Belmont, CA: Wadsworth.

7,10   Atchley, R.C. 1982. "The Process of Retirement: Comparing Women and Men." In M. Szinovacz, ed., *Women's Retirement.* Beverly Hills: Sage.

10   Atchley, R.C. 1985. *Social Forces and Aging.* 4th ed. Belmont, CA: Wadsworth.

7   Atchley, R.C. 1999. "Continuity Theory, Self, and Social Structure." In V.W. Marshall and C.D. Ryff, eds., *The Self and Society in Aging Processes*, 94–121. New York: Springer.

11   Atkinson, W. 1991. "Improving Transportation Systems for Seniors Benefits All." Paper presented at "Freedom to Move Is Life Itself," the FCM National Forum on Seniors Transportation, Winnipeg.

6   Bäckman, L. 1985. "Further Evidence for the Lack of Adult Age Differences on Free Recall of Subject-Performed Tasks: The Importance of Motor Action." *Human Learning* 4: 79–87.

6   Bäckman, L., B.J. Small, and A. Wahlin. 2001. "Aging and Memory: Cognitive and Biological Perspectives." In J.E. Birren and K.W. Schaie, eds., *Handbook of the Psychology of Aging,* 5th ed. San Diego: Academic Press.

6   Bäckman, L, B.J. Small, A.Wahlin, and M. Larsson. 2000. "Cognitive Functioning in Very Old Age." In F.I.M. Craik and T.A. Salthouse, eds., *The Handbook of Aging and Cognition,* 2nd ed., 499–558. Mahwah, NJ: Lawrence Erlbaum Associates.

7   Bagley, C.R. 1993. "Mental Health and Social Adjustment of Elderly Chinese Immigrants in Canada." *Canada's Mental Health* 41(3): 6–10.

10   Baillargeon, Richard. 1982. "Determinants of Early Retirement." *Canada's Mental Health* 1: 20–22.

11   Baker, J.G. 1994. "Supportive Housing for Elderly Persons in Ontario." In G. Gutman and A.V. Wister, eds., *Progressive Accommodation for Seniors: Interfacing Shelter and Services,* 85–99. Vancouver: Gerontology Research Centre, Simon Fraser University.

10   Baker, M., and D. Benjamin. 1999. "Early Retirement Provisions and the Labor Force Behavior of Older Men: Evidence from Canada. *Journal of Labor Economics* 17(4): 724–56.

3   Baker, P.M. 1983a. "Ageism, Sex, and Age: A Factorial Survey Approach." *Canadian Journal on Aging* 2: 177–84.

1   Baker, P.M. 1983. *Old Before My Time* [videotape]. Victoria: Centre on Aging, University of Victoria.

14   Baker, P.M. 1991. "Socialization after Death: The Might of the Living Dead." In B. Hess and E. Markson, eds., *Growing Old in America*, 4th ed. New York: Transaction Books.

11   Baker, P.M., and M. Prince. 1990. "Supportive Housing Preferences among the Elderly." *Journal of Housing for the Elderly* 7: 5–24.

10   Ballantyne, P.J., and V.W. Marshall. 1995. "Wealth and the Life Course." In V.W. Marshall, J.A. McMullin, P.J. Ballantyne, J. Daciuk, and B.T. Wigdor, eds., *Contributions to Independence over the Adult Life Course*, 49–83. Toronto: Centre for Studies of Aging, University of Toronto.

9   Ballantyne, P., and V.W. Marshall. 2001. "Subjective Income Security of (Middle) Aging and Elderly Canadians." *Canadian Journal on Aging* 20(2): 151–73.

6   Baltes, P.B. 1992. "Wise, and Otherwise." *Natural History* (February): 50–51.

6   Baltes, P.B. 1993. "Aging Mind: Potential and Limits." *Gerontologist* 33(5): 580–94.

6   Baltes, P.B. 1997. "On the Incomplete Architecture of Human Ontogeny: Selection, Optimization, and Compensation as Foundations of Developmental Theory." *American Psychologist* 52: 366–80.

6   Baltes, P.B., and M.M. Baltes. 1990. "Psychological Perspectives on Successful Aging: The Model of Selective Optimization with Compensation." In P.B. Baltes and M.M. Baltes, eds., *Successful Aging: Perspectives from the Behavioral Sciences*, 1–34. Cambridge: Cambridge University Press.

7   Baltes, P.B., S.W. Cornelius, and J.R. Nesselroade. 1979. "Cohort Effects in Developmental Psychology." In J.R. Nesselroade and P.B. Baltes, eds., *Longitudinal Research in the Study of Behavior and Development.* New York: Academic Press, 1979.

7   Baltes, P.B., and L.R. Goulet. 1970. "Status and Issues of a Life-Span Developmental Psychology." In L.R. Goulet and Paul B. Baltes, eds., *Life-Span Developmental Psychology: Research and Theory.* New York: Academic Press.

6   Baltes, P.B., and U. Lindenberger. 1997. "Emergence of a Powerful Connection between Sensory and Cognitive Function across the Adult Life Span: A New Window to the Study of Cognitive Aging." *Psychology and Aging* 12(1): 12–21.

2   Baltes, P.B., and K.W. Schaie. 1982. "The Myth of the Twilight Years." In Steven H. Zarit, ed., *Readings in Aging and Death: Contemporary Perspectives*, 2nd ed. New York: Harper and Row.

6   Baltes, P.B., J. Smith, U.M. Staudinger, and D. Sowarka. 1990. "Wisdom: One Facet of Successful Aging?" In M. Perlmutter, ed., *Late Life Potential.* Washington, DC: Gerontological Society of America.

6   Baltes, P.B., and S.L. Willis. 1982. "Toward Psychological Theories of Aging and Development." In J.E. Birren and K.W. Schaie, eds., *Handbook of the Psychology of Aging.* New York: Van Nostrand Reinhold.

13   Bamford, C., B. Gregson, G. Ferrow, and D. Buck. 1998. "Mental and Physical Frailty in Older People: The Costs and Benefits of Informal Care." *Ageing and Society* 18(3): 317–54.

7   Banks, M.R., and W.A. Banks. 2002. "Effects of Animal-Assisted Therapy on Loneliness in an Elderly Population in Long-Term Care Facilities." *Journals of Gerontology Series A* 57(7): 428–32.

7   Banks, W.A., and M.R. Banks. 2003. "Putting More Heart in the Nursing Home: What We Learned from the Dogs." *Geriatrics and Aging* 6(2): 66.

5,8 Barer, M.L., R.G. Evans, and C. Hertzman. 1995. "Avalanche or Glacier?: Health Care and the Demographic Rhetoric." *Canadian Journal on Aging* 14(2): 193–224.

8 Barer, M.L., R.B. Evans, C. Hertzman, and J. Lomas. 1986. "Toward Efficient Aging: Rhetoric and Evidence." Paper prepared for presentation at the 3rd Canadian Conference on Health Economics, Winnipeg.

8 Barer, M.L., C. Hertzman, R. Miller, and M.V.B. Pascall. 1992. "On Being Old and Sick: The Burden of Health Care for the Elderly in Canada and the United States." *Journal of Health Politics, Policy, and Law* 17(4): 163–82. Reprinted in M. Novak, ed., *Aging and Society: A Canadian Reader*, 152–53. Scarborough, ON: Nelson Canada, 1995.

7 Baril, G., and G. Mori. 1991. "Leaving the Fold: Declining Church Attendance." *Canadian Social Trends* (Autumn): 21–24.

13 Barling, J., K.E. MacEwen, and E.K. Kelloway. 1994. "Predictors and Outcomes of Elder-Care-Based Interrole Conflict." *Psychology and Aging* 9(3): 391–97.

13 Barrett, A.E. 1999. "Social Support and Life Satisfaction among the Never Married." *Research on Aging* 21(1): 46–72.

13 Barrett, A.E., and S.M. Lynch. 1999. "Caregiving Networks of Elderly Persons: Variations by Marital Status." *Gerontologist* 39(6): 695–704.

14 Barrett, C.J., and K.M. Schneweis. 1980–81. "An Empirical Search for Stages of Widowhood." *Omega* 11: 97–104.

6 Barrett, J.R., and M. Wright. 1981. "Age-Related Facilitation in Recall Following Semantic Processing." *Journal of Gerontology* 36(2): 194–99.

13 Bass, S.A., and F.G. Caro. 1996. "The Economic Value of Grandparent Assistance." *Generations* 20(1): 29–38.

9 Battle, K. 1997. "Pension Reform in Canada." *Canadian Journal on Aging* 16(3): 519–52.

8 Baumgarten, M., P. Lebel, H. Laprise, C. Leclerc, and C. Quinn. 2002. "Adult Day Care for the Frail Elderly: Outcomes, Satisfaction, and Cost." *Journal of Aging and Health* 14(2): 237–59.

4 Beaujot, R., and K. McQuillan. 1982. *Growth and Dualism: The Demographic Development of Canadian Society.* Toronto: Gage.

13 Beaulieu, M., S. Gravel, and M. Lithwick. 1999. "Older Adult Mistreatment: Dynamics in Personal Relationships." *Gerontology Research Centre News* (Simon Fraser University), February.

2 Beausoleil, N., and G. Martin. 2002. "Activité physiqué, santé et vieillissement chez des femmes francophones de l'Ontario." *Canadian Journal on Aging* 21(3): 443–54.

12 Beck, M., D. Glick, J. Gordon, and L. Picker. 1991. *Newsweek,* November 11, 60–63.

13 Beeler, J.A., T.W. Rawls, G. Herdt, and B.J. Cohler. 1999. "The Needs of Older Lesbians and Gay Men in Chicago." *Journal of Gay and Lesbian Social Services* 9(1): 31–49.

10 Beeson, D. 1975. "Women in Studies of Aging: A Critique and Suggestion." *Social Problems* 23: 52–59.

11 Béland, F. 1984a. "The Decision of Elderly Persons to Leave Their Homes." *Gerontologist* 24: 179–85.

11 Béland, F. 1984b. "The Family and Adults 65 Years and Over: Co-Residency and Availability of Help." *Canadian Review of Sociology and Anthropology* 21: 302–17.

11 Béland, F. 1987. "Living Arrangement Preferences among Elderly People." *Gerontologist* 27: 797–803.

2 Béland, F. 1988. "Research in Social Gerontology in Quebec: An Obscure Originality or a Deserved Obscurity?" *Canadian Journal on Aging* 7: 293–310.

8 Béland, F. 1995. "Costs of Ambulatory Medical Care over the Long Term in the Quebec Medicare System." *Canadian Journal on Aging* 14(2): 391–413.

2 Béland, F. 1997. "Editorial: Building Canadian Gerontology: A Springboard for International Recognition?" *Canadian Journal on Aging* 16(1): 6–10.

8 Béland, F., and D. Arweiler. 1996a. "Conceptual Framework for Development of Long-Term Care: Policy 1. Constitutive Elements." *Canadian Journal on Aging* 15(4): 649–81.

8 Béland, F., and D. Arweiler. 1996b. "Conceptual Framework for Development of Long-Term Care: Policy 2. Conceptual Framework." *Canadian Journal on Aging* 15(4): 682–97.

8 Béland, F., and E. Shapiro. 1994. "Ten Provinces in Search of a Long Term Care

8 Policy." In V. Marshall and B. McPherson, eds., *Aging: Canadian Perspectives*, 245–67. Peterborough, ON: Broadview Press.

8 Béland, F., and E. Shapiro. 1995. "Policy Issues in Care for the Elderly in Canada." *Canadian Journal on Aging* 14(2). Special Issue.

5 Bélanger, A., L. Martel, J.-M. Berthelot, R. Wilkins. 2002. "Gender Differences in Disability-Free Life Expectancy for Selected Risk Factors and Chronic Conditions in Canada." *Journal of Women and Aging* 14(1/2): 61–83.

2 Bengtson, V.L., E.O. Burgess, and T.M. Parrott. 1997. "Theory, Explanation, and a Third Generation of Theoretical Development in Social Gerontology." *Journals of Gerontology Series B* 52(2): S72–88.

3 Bengtson, V.L., J.J. Dowd, D.H. Smith, and A. Inkeles. 1975. "Modernization, Modernity and Perceptions of Aging: A Cross-Cultural Study." *Journal of Gerontology* 30: 688–95.

13 Bengtson, V.L., and J.A. Kuypers. 1971. "Generational Differences and the Developmental Stake." *International Journal of Aging and Human Development* 2: 249–60.

2 Bengtson, V.L., C.J. Rice, and M.L. Johnson. 1999. "Are Theories of Aging Important? Models and Explanations in Gerontology at the Turn of the Century." In V.L. Bengtson and K.W. Shaie, eds., *Handbook of Theories of Aging*. New York: Springer Publishing.

2 Bengtson, V.L., C.J. Rosenthal, and L.M. Burton. 1996. "Parodoxes of Families and Aging." In R.H. Binstock and L.K. George, eds., *Handbook of Aging and the Social Sciences*, 4th ed. San Diego: Academic Press.

2 Bengtson, V.L., and K.W. Schaie, eds. 1999. *Handbook of Theories of Aging*. New York: Springer.

3 Benoit, C.M. 2000. *Women, Work and Social Rights*. Scarborough, ON: Prentice Hall Allyn and Bacon Canada.

8 Berdes, C. 1996. "Driving the System: Long-Term Care Coordination in Manitoba, Canada." *Journal of Case Management* 5(4): 68–72.

2 Berg, B.L. 1998. *Qualitative Research Methods for the Social Sciences*. 3rd ed. Boston: Allyn and Bacon.

2 Berger, P., and Luckman, T. 1967. *The Social Construction of Reality*. Garden City, NY: Archor.

13 Berger, R.M., ed. 1996. *Gay and Grey: The Older Homosexual Man*, 2nd ed. New York: Harrington Park.

13 Berger, R.M. 1996. "What Are Older Homosexual Men Like?" In R.M. Berger, ed., *Gay and Grey: The Older Homosexual Man*, 2nd ed., 155–99. New York: Harrington Park.

8 Bergob, M. 2004. "Drug Use among Senior Canadians." Statistics Canada, http://www.statcan.ca/english/ads/11-008-XIE/drugs.html, accessed on August 4, 2004.

3 Berkner, Lutz. 1972. "The Stem Family and the Development Cycle of the Peasant Household: An Eighteenth-Century Austrian Example." *American Historical Review* 77: 398–418.

1 Berman, L., and I. Sobkowska-Ashcroft. 1986. "The Old in Language and Literature." *Language and Communication* 6: 139–45.

1 Berman, L., and I. Sobkowska-Ashcroft. 1987. *Images and Impressions of Old Age in the Great Works of Western Literature (700 B.C.–1900 A.D.)*. Lewiston, NY: Edwin Mellen Press.

11 Bess, I. 1999a. "Seniors behind the Wheel." *Canadian Social Trends* (Autumn): 2–7.

13 Bess, I. 1999b. "Widows Living Alone." *Canadian Social Trends* (Summer): 2–5.

3 Bhat, A.K., and R. Dhruvarajan. 2001. "Ageing in India: Drifting Intergenerational Relations, Challenges and Options." *Ageing and Society* 21 (Part 5): 621–40.

1 Bieman, C.S., and R.E. Bouchard. 1998. "Age-Biased Interpretation of Memory Successes and Failures in Adulthood." *Journals of Gerontology Series B* 53(2): P105–P111.

7 Bienvenue, R., and B. Havens. 1986. "Structural Inequalities, Informal Networks: A Comparison of Native and Non-Native Elderly." *Canadian Journal on Aging* 5: 241–48.

3 Biesele, M., and N. Howell. 1981. "'The Old Give You Life': Aging among Kung Hunter-Gatherers." In P.T. Amoss and S. Harrell, eds., *Other Ways of Growing Old: Anthropological Perspectives*. Stanford, CA: Stanford University Press.

3 Biggs, B., and R. Bollman. 1991. "Urbanization in Canada." *Canadian Social Trends* (Summer): 22–27.

1 Binstock, R.H. 1983. "The Aged as Scapegoats." *Gerontologist* 23(2): 136–41.

1 Binstock, R.H. 1992. "The Oldest Old and Intergenerational Equity." In R.M. Suzman, D.P. Willis, and K.G. Manton, eds., *The Oldest*

Old, 394–417. New York: Oxford University Press.

8 Binstock, R.H. 1993. "Healthcare Costs around the World: Is Aging a Fiscal 'Black Hole'?" *Generations* (Winter): 37–42.

6 Birren, J.E., and K.W. Schaie, eds. 2001. *Handbook of the Psychology of Aging*, 5th ed. San Diego: Academic Press.

6 Birren, J.E., and J.F. Schroots. 1996. "History, Concepts, and Theory in the Psychology of Aging." In J.E. Birren and K.W. Schaie, eds., *Handbook of the Psychology of Aging*, 4th ed., 3–23. San Diego: Academic Press.

8 Black, C., N.P. Roos, B. Havens, and L. MacWilliam. 1995. "Rising Use of Physician Services by the Elderly: The Contribution of Morbidity." *Canadian Journal on Aging* 14(2): 225–44.

11 Blackwell, T. 2002. "Ottawa to Test Safety Devices for Elderly Drivers." *National Post*, September 17.

12 Blair, S.N., H.W. Kohl, R.S. Paffenbarger, D.G. Clark, K.H. Cooper, and L.H. Gibbons. 1989. "Physical Fitness and All-Cause Mortality." *Journal of the American Medical Association* 262(17): 2395–401.

11 Blakeney, M. 1992. "Canadians in Subsidized Housing." *Canadian Social Trends* Winter: 20–24.

7 Blanchard-Fields, F., and R.P. Abeles. 1996. "Social Cognition and Aging." In J.E. Birren, and K.W. Schaie, eds., *Handbook of the Psychology of Aging*, 4th ed., 159–61. San Diego: Academic Press.

7 Blandford, A.A., and N.L. Chappell. 1990. "Subjective Well-Being among Native and Non-Native Elderly Persons: Do Differences Exist?" *Canadian Journal on Aging* 9: 386–99.

11 Blandford, A.A., N.L. Chappell, and S. Marshall. 1989. "Tenant Resource Coordinators: An Experiment in Supportive Housing." *Gerontologist* 29: 826–29.

13 Blaser, C.J. 1998. "The Case against Paid Family Caregivers: Ethical and Practical Issues." *Generations* 22(3): 65–69.

7 Blau, Z.S. 1973. *Old Age in a Changing Society*. New York: New Viewpoints.

8 Blomqvist, A. 1994. "Introduction: Economic Issues in Canadian Health Care." In A. Blomqvist and D.M. Brown, eds., *Limits to Care: Reforming Canada's Health System in an*

Age of Restraint, 3–50. Ottawa: C.D. Howe Institute.

14 Blouin, M. 1995. "Care-in-Dying: A Call to Action." *Catholic Health Association of Canada Review* 23(1): 23.

13 Boaz, R.F., J. Hu, and Y. Ye. 1999. "The Transfer of Resources from Middle-Aged Children to Functionally Limited Elderly Parents: Providing Time, Giving Money, Sharing Space." *Gerontologist* 39(6): 648–57.

12 Bocksnick, J.G., and B.L. Hall. 1994. "Recreation Activity Programming for the Institutionalized Older Adult." *Activities, Adaptation and Aging* 19(1): 1–25.

8 Bogaert, M. 1980. "Restrained in Canada—Free in Britain." *Health Care*(July): 22.

13 Bogard, R., and B. Spilka. 1996. "Self-Disclosure and Marital Satisfaction in Mid-Life and Late-Life Remarriages." *International Journal of Aging and Human Development* 42: 161–72.

10 Bolger, Joe. 1980. "Bill C-12 and the Debate over Public Service Pension Indexing." Unpublished master's essay. Ottawa: Carleton University.

12 Bond, J.B., Jr. 1982. "Volunteerism and Life Satisfaction among Older Adults." *Canadian Counsellor* 16: 168–72.

13 Bond, J.B. Jr., R. Cuddy, G.L. Dixon, K.A. Duncan, and D.L. Smith. 1999. "Financial Abuse of Mentally Incompetent Older Adults: A Canadian Study." *Journal of Elder Abuse and Neglect* 11(4): 23–38.

13 Bond, J.B., Jr., R.L. Penner, and P. Yellen. 1995. "Perceived Effectiveness of Legislation Concerning Abuse of the Elderly: A Survey of Professionals in Canada and the United States." *Canadian Journal on Aging* 14 (Suppl. 2): 118–35.

8 Bonifazi, W.L. 1998. "Get Me Out!" *Contemporary Long Term Care* 21(10): 54–56.

13 Boon, S.D., and M.J. Brussoni. 1998. "Popular Images of Grandparents: Examining Young Adults' Views of Their Closest Grandparents." *Personal Relationships* 5: 105–19.

11 Borden, L., and J. McGregor. 1994. "Current Realities and Challenges in Providing Services to Seniors: The Home Care Perspective." In G. Gutman and A.V. Wister, eds., *Progressive Accommodation for Seniors: Interfacing Shelter and Services*, 47–56. Vancouver: Gerontology Research Centre, Simon Fraser University.

6 Borovoy, A. 1982. "Guardianship and Civil Liberties." *Health Law in Canada* 3(3): 51–52.

6 Bosman, E. 1993. "Age-Related Differences in the Motoric Aspects of Transcription Typing Skill." *Psychology and Aging* 8(1): 87–102.

6 Botwinick, J. 1984. *Aging and Behavior*, 3rd ed. New York: Springer.

6 Bourret, S. 2000. "Poet Evokes Images of Times Past." *Hamilton Spectator*, February 15, E2.

1 Bowd, A.D. 2003. "Stereotypes of Elderly Persons in Narrative Jokes." *Research on Aging* 25(1): 22–23.

13 Bowers, B.F., and B.J. Myers. 1999. "Grandmothers Providing Care for Grand-children: Consequences of Various Levels of Caregiving." *Family Relations* 48(3): 303–11.

6 Bowles, N.L., and L.W. Poon. 1982. "An Analysis of the Effect of Aging on Memory." *Journal of Gerontology* 37(2): 212–19.

14 Boyd, K.J. 1993. "Palliative Care in the Community: Views of General Practitioners and District Nurses in East London." *Journal of Palliative Care* 9(2): 33–37.

13 Boyd, M., and D. Norris. 1999. "The Crowded Nest: Young Adults at Home." *Canadian Social Trends* (Spring): 2–5.

3 Braburn, H.H.H. 1969. *Eskimos without Igloos.* Boston: Little, Brown.

3 Bradbury, B. 1983. "The Family Economy and Work in an Industrializing City: Montreal in the 1970s." In W.P. Ward, ed., *The Social Development of Canada: Readings.* Richmond, BC: Open Learning Institute.

13 Brandl, B. 2000. "Power and Control: Understanding Domestic Abuse in Later Life." *Generations* 24: 39–45.

3 Braudel, F. 1981. *Civilization and Capitalism: 15th–18th Century.* Vol. 1: The Structure of Everyday Life. Trans. Sian Reynolds. New York: Harper and Row.

7 Braun, P., and R. Sweet. 1983–84. "Passages: Fact or Fiction?" *International Journal of Aging and Human Development* 18(3): 161–76.

8 Bravo, G., M.-F. Dubois, M. Charpentier, P. De Wals, and A. Emond. 1999. "Quality of Care in Unlicensed Homes for the Aged in the Eastern Townships of Quebec." *Canadian Medical Association Journal* 160(10): 1441–48.

12 Bravo, G., P. Gauthier, P.M. Roy, H. Payette, and P. Gaulin. 1996a. "Comparison of Group-versus a Home-Based Exercise Program in Osteopenic Women." *Journal of Aging and Physical Activity* 4(2): 51–64.

12 Bravo, G., P. Gauthier, P.M. Roy, H. Payette, and P. Gaulin. 1996b. "Impact of a 12-Month Exercise Program on the Physical and Psychological Health of Osteopenic Women." *Journal of the American Geriatrics Society* 44(7): 756–62.

7 Breytspraak, L.M. 1995. "The Development of Self in Later Life." In M. Novak, ed., *Aging and Society: A Canadian Reader*, 92–103. Toronto: Nelson Canada.

1 Brillon, Y. 1987. *Victimization and Fear of Crime among the Elderly.* Trans. D.R. Crelinsten. Toronto: Butterworths.

8 Brillon, Y. 1992. "Editorial: The 'Right' to Age in an Institution." *Canadian Journal on Aging* 12(1): 7–11.

1 Brimacombe, C.A.E., Q. Nyla, N. Nance, and L. Garrioch. 1997. "Is Age Irrelevant? Perceptions of Young and Old Adult Eyewitnesses." *Law and Human Behavior* 21(6): 619–34.

11 Brink, S. 1994. "Social Policy Models for Shelter and Services: An International Perspective." In G. Gutman and A.V. Wister, eds., *Progressive Accommodation for Seniors: Interfacing Shelter and Services,* 101–18. Vancouver: Gerontology Research Centre.

5 Brink, S. 1997. "The Twin Challenges of Information Technology and Population Aging." *Generations* 21(3): 7–10.

5 Brink, S. 1998. "Blending Research, Private and Public Sector Agendas in the Information Economy." In G.M. Gutman, ed., *Technology Innovation for an Aging Society: Blending Research, Public and Private Sectors*, 131–45. Vancouver: Gerontology Research Centre, Simon Fraser University.

5 Brink S. 2001. "Digital Divide or Digital Dividend? Ensuring Benefits to Seniors from Information Technology." In J. Jessome, C. Parks, and M. MacLellan, eds., *Seniors and Technology,* 19–32. Cat. No. 0-662-30932-4. Ottawa: Minister of Public Works and Government Services Canada.

14 British Columbia. 1996. *Health Care (Consent) and Care Facility (Admission) Act.* Revised Statutes and Consolidated Regulations of British Columbia. Victoria: Queen's Printer. http://www.qp.gov.bc.ca/statreg/stat/H/ 96181_01.htm, accessed on October 18, 2003.

13 Brody, E.M. 1981. "'Women in the Middle' and Family Help to Older People." *Gerontologist* 18: 471–80.

13 Brody, E.M. 1990. *Women in the Middle: Their Parent-Care Years.* New York: Springer.

5 Bronnum-Hansen, H., and K. Juel. 2001. "Abstention from Smoking Extends Life and Compresses Morbidity: A Population Based Study of Health Expectancy among Smokers and Never Smokers in Denmark." *Tobacco Control* 10(3): 273–78.

3 Bronowski, J. 1976. *The Ascent of Man.* London: BBC Publishing.

12 Brooks, J.D. 1994. "What We Know about Exercise and Where We Should Go from Here." Paper presented at the Midwest Sociological Association annual meeting, St. Louis, March.

4,9 Brotman, S. 1998. "The Incidence of Poverty among Seniors in Canada: Exploring the Impact of Gender, Ethnicity, and Race." *Canadian Journal on Aging* 17(2): 166–85.

13 Brotman, S., B. Ryan, and R. Cormier. 2002. "Mental Health Issues of Particular Groups: Gay and Lesbian Seniors." In *Writings in Gerontology: Mental Health and Aging*, 56–67. Cat. No. H71-2/1-18-2002E. Ottawa: Minister of Public Works and Government Services Canada.

13 Brown, L.B., S.G. Sarosy, T.C. Cook, and J.G. Quarto. 1997. *Gay Men and Aging.* New York: Garland.

9 Brown, R.L. 1995. "Security for Social Security—Raise the Age of Entitlement?" In E.M. Gee and G.M. Gutman, eds., *Rethinking Retirement*, 69–73. Vancouver: Gerontology Research Centre, Simon Fraser University.

9 Brown, R.L. 1997. "Security for Social Security: Is Privatization the Answer?" *Canadian Journal on Aging* 16(3): 499–518.

6 Browne, A., M. Blake, M. Donnelly, and D. Herbert. 2002. "On Liberty for the Old." *Canadian Journal on Aging* 21(2): 283–93.

9 Bryden, K. 1974. *Old Age Pensions and Policy-Making in Canada.* Montreal: McGill-Queen's University Press.

13 Buchignani, N., and C. Armstrong-Esther. 1999. "Informal Care and Older Native Canadians." *Ageing and Society* 19(1): 3–32.

14 Buckingham, R.W., III, S.A. Lack, G.M. Mount, L.D. MacLean, and J.T. Collins. 1976. "Living with the Dying." *Canadian Medical Association Journal* 115: 1211–15.

12 Buckwalter, J.A. 1997. "Exercise Your Independence." *Physician and Sportsmedicine* 25(9). http://www.physsportsmed.com/issues/1997/09sep/buck_pa.htm, accessed on August 28, 2004.

7 Bühler, C. 1951. "Maturation and Motivation." *Personality* 1: 184–211.

12 Burden, C., and A.J. Lee. 1992. "Older Volunteers: An Agency Perspective." *The Journal of Volunteer Administration* 11(1): 19–21.

4 Burke, M.A. 1991. "Implications of an Aging Society." *Canadian Social Trends* (Spring): 6–8.

6 Burke, M.A., J. Lindsay, I. McDowell, and G. Hill. 1997. "Dementia among Seniors." *Canadian Social Trends* (Summer): 24–27.

11 Burke, M.A., and A. Spector. 1991. "Falling through the Cracks: Women Aged 55–64 Living on Their Own." *Canadian Social Trends* (Winter): 14–17.

1 Butler, R.N. 1969. "Age-ism: Another Form of Bigotry." *Gerontologist* 9: 243–46.

6 Butler, R.N. 1974. "The Creative Life and Old Age." In E. Pfeiffer, ed., *Successful Aging.* Durham, NC: Center for the Study of Aging and Human Development, Duke University.

7 Butler, R.N. 1975. *Why Survive? Being Old in America.* New York: Harper and Row.

1 Butler, R.N. 1993. "Dispelling Ageism: The Cross-Cutting Intervention." *Generations* 17(2): 75–78.

13 Butler, R.N., and M.I. Lewis. 1976. *Sex after 60: A Guide for Men and Women for Their Later Years.* New York: Harper and Row.

6 Butler, R.N., and M.I. Lewis. 1982. *Aging and Mental Health*, 3rd ed. St. Louis, MO: Mosby.

8 Buzzell, M. 1981. "So Very Vulnerable." *Journal of Gerontological Nursing* 7: 286–87.

11 Byszewski, A. 2002. "Driving and Dementia: A toolkit to Assist Physicians in Dealing with the Issue." *Geriatrics and Aging* 5(4): 68–73.

5 Cairney, J. 2000. "Socio-Economic Status and Self-Rated Health among Older Canadians." *Canadian Journal on Aging* 19(4): 456–78.

10 Calasanti, T.M. 1988. "Participation in a Dual Economy and Adjustment to Retirement." *International Journal of Aging and Human Development* 26: 13–27.

2 Calasanti, T.M. 1996. "Incorporating Diversity: Meaning, Levels of Research, and Implications for Theory." *Gerontologist* 36: 147–56.

2   Calasanti, T.M., and K.F. Slevin. 2001. *Gender, Social Inequalities, and Aging.* Walnut Creek, CA: AltaMira Press.

4   *Calgary Herald.* 1998. "Long-Lived Problems: Canada's Aging Population Must Prepare Now for Longer Retirement." Editorial, A10.

1   Callahan, D. 1987. *Setting Limits: Medical Goals in an Aging Society.* New York: Simon and Schuster.

13   Callahan, J.J. 1986. "Guest Editor's Perspective." *Pride Institute Journal of Long-Term Home Health Care* 5: 2–3.

13   Campbell, L.D. 2002. "Men Who Care: Exploring the Male Experience of Filial Caregiving." Paper presented at the International Symposium Reconceptualising Gender and Ageing, University of Surrey, Guildford, U.K., June 25–27.

13   Campbell, L.D., I.A. Connidis, and L. Davies. 1999. "Sibling Ties in Later Life: A Social Network Analysis." *Journal of Family Issues* 20(1): 114–48.

13   Campbell, L.D., and A. Martin-Matthews. 2000a. "Caring Sons: Exploring Men's Involvement in Filial Care." *Canadian Journal on Aging* 19(1): 57–79.

13   Campbell, L.D., and A. Martin-Matthews. 2000b. "Primary and Proximate: The Importance of Coresidence and Being Primary Provider of Care for Men's Filial Care Involvement." *Journal of Family Issues* 21(8): 1006–30.

2,13   Campbell, L.D., and A. Martin-Matthews. 2003. "The Gendered Nature of Men's Filial Care." *Journals of Gerontology Series B* 58(6): S350–58.

10   Campolieti, M. 2001. "Disability Insurance and the Labour Force Participation of Older Men and Women in Canada." *Canadian Public Policy* 27(2): 179–94.

8   Canada. 1984. *Canada Health Act,* R.S.C. 1985, c. C-6. Ottawa: Queen's Printer. http://laws.justice.gc.ca/en/C-6/index.html, accessed on August 4, 2004.

3   Canada Coordinating Committee. 1999. *Canada, a Society for All Ages.* Ottawa: Canada Coordinating Committee.

11   Canada Mortgage and Housing Corporation. 1978. *Housing the Elderly.* Ottawa: Minister of Supply and Services.

11   Canada Mortgage and Housing Corporation. 1987. *Garden Suites: A New Housing Option for Elderly Canadians?* Ottawa: Minister of Supply and Services.

11   Canada Mortgage and Housing Corporation. 1992. *Housing Choices for Canadians with Disabilities.* Cat. No. NH15-74/1992E. Ottawa: Canada Mortgage and Housing Corporation.

11   Canada Mortgage and Housing Corporation. 2002a. "Housing Conditions of Women and Girls, and Female-Led Households." *Research Highlights.* Special Studies on 1996 Census Data, Socio-Economic Series, Issue 55-9. http://www.cmhc-schl.gc.ca/publications/en/rh-pr/socio/socio055-9-e.pdf, accessed on December 7, 2003.

11   Canada Mortgage and Housing Corporation. 2002b. "Housing the Boom, Bust and Echo Generations." *Research Highlights.* Special Studies on 1996 Census Data, Socio-Economic Series, Issue 77. http://www.cmhc-schl.gc.ca/publications/en/rh-pr/socio/ socio77-e.pdf, accessed on December 7, 2003.

11   Canada Mortgage and Housing Corporation. 2002c. "Seniors' Housing Conditions." *Research Highlights.* Special Studies on 1996 Census Data, Socio-Economic Series, Issue 55-8. http://www.cmhc-schl.gc.ca/publications/en/rh-pr/socio/socio055-8e.pdf, accessed on December 7, 2003.

11   Canada Mortgage and Housing Corporation. 2003a. "Alternate Tenure Arrangements." Socio-Economic Series, Issue 65. http://www.cmhc-schl.gc.ca/publications/en/rh-pr/socio/socio065.pdf, accessed on December 6, 2003.

11   Canada Mortgage and Housing Corporation. 2003b. "Home Adaptations for Seniors' Independence (HASI)." *Programs and Financial Assistance.* http://www.cmhc-schl.gc.ca/en/prfias/abhoas/readaspr_002.cfm, accessed on December 6, 2003.

11   Canada Mortgage and Housing Corporation. 2003c. "Housing Options for Elderly or Chronically Ill Shelter Users." *Research Highlights.* Socio-Economic Series 03-019. http://www.cmhc-schl.gc.ca/publications/en/rh-pr/socio/socio03-019-e.pdf, accessed on December 6, 2003.

11   Canada Mortgage and Housing Corporation. 2003d. "Improving Quality and Affordability: Flexhousing." http://www.cmhc-schl.gc.ca/en/imquaf/flho/index.cfm, accessed on December 6, 2003.

11 Canada Mortgage and Housing Corporation. 2003e. "Homeowner Residential Rehabilitation Assistance Program (Homeowner RRAP)." *Programs and Financial Assistance*. http://www.cmhc-schl.gc.ca/en/prfias/rerepr/readaspr_003.cfm, accessed on August 29, 2004.

10 Canadian Association of University Teachers. 1991. "Mandatory Retirement." *CAUT Bulletin* 38: 1–5.

8 Canadian Association on Gerontology. 1999. "Women, Older Patients Less Likely to Get Proven Treatments for Cardiovascular Diseases." News Release. May 13. E-mail communication.

2 Canadian Association on Gerontology. 2002. "Notes to Authors." *Canadian Journal on Aging* 22(1): cover page.

4 Canadian Council on Social Development. 1999. "Social Spending across the Life Course: Summary Report." http://www.ccsd.ca/pubs/hc/spend.htm, accessed on July 26, 2004.

9 Canadian Council on Social Development. 2003. *2002 Poverty Lines*. http://www.ccsd.ca/factsheets/fs_lic02.htm, accessed on August 22, 2004.

12 Canadian Executive Service Organization. 2003. "Welcome to CESO." http://www.ceso-saco.com/home.htm, accessed on November 26, 2003.

8 Canadian Home Care Association. 1998. *Portrait of Canada: An Overview of Public Home Care Programs*. Ottawa: Canadian Home Care Association.

9 Canadian Institute of Actuaries. 1993. *Canadian Retirement Income Social Security Programs*. Report of the Task Force on Social Security Funding. November. Ottawa: Canadian Institute of Actuaries.

8 Canadian Institute for Health Information. 2003. *National Health Expenditure Trends, 1975–2003*. Ottawa: Canadian Institute for Health Information.

6,14 Canadian Medical Association. 1987. *Health Care for the Elderly: Today's Challenges, Tomorrow's Options*. Ottawa: Canadian Medical Association.

14 Canadian Medical Association. 1995. "Policy Summary: Joint Statement on Resuscitative Intervention (Update 1995)." *Canadian Medical Association Journal* 153(11): 1652a–52c.

6 Canadian Study of Health and Aging Working Group. 1994. "Canadian Study of Health and Aging: Study Methods and Prevalence of Dementia." *Canadian Medical Association Journal* 150(6): 899–913.

13 Cantor, M.H., and V. Little. 1985. "Aging and Social Care." In R.H. Binstock and E. Shanas, eds., *Handbook of Aging and the Social Sciences*. New York: Van Nostrand Reinhold.

6 Cappliez, P. 1988. "Some Thoughts on the Prevalence and Etiology of Depressive Conditions in the Elderly." *Canadian Journal on Aging* 7: 431–40.

9 Carey, B., and A. Yamada. 2002. *Getting Older, Getting Poorer? A Study of the Earnings, Pensions, Assets, and Living Arrangements of Older People in Nine Countries*. Labour Market and Social Policy Occasional Paper No. 60. Paris: Organization for Economic Co-operation and Development.

8 Carrière, Y. 2000. "The Impact of Population Aging and Hospital Days: Will There Be a Problem?" In E.M. Gee and G.M. Gutman, eds., *The Overselling of Population Aging: Apocalyptic Demography, Intergenerational Challenges, and Social Policy*, 26–44. Don Mills, ON: Oxford University Press.

6 Carswell-Opzoomer, A., J. Puxty, M. Teaffe, and W. Walop. 1993. "Dementia in Long-Term Care Facilities: A Survey of the Ottawa-Carleton Region." *Canadian Journal on Aging* 12(3): 360–72.

12 Casperson, C.J., K. Powell, and G.M. Christenson. 1985. "Physical Activity, Exercise, and Physical Fitness: Definitions for Health Related Research." *Public Health Reports* 100: 126–30.

6 Cattell, R.B. 1963. "Theory of Fluid and Crystallized Intelligence: An Initial Experiment." *Journal of Educational Psychology* 54: 105–11.

6 Cavanaugh, J.C. 1983. "Comprehension and Retention of Television Programs by 20- and 60-Year Olds." *Journal of Gerontology* 38: 190–96.

6 Cavanaugh, J.C., J.A. Grady, and M. Perlmutter. 1983. "Forgetting and Use of Memory Aids in 20 to 70 Year-Olds' Everyday Life." *International Journal of Aging and Human Development* 17: 113–22.

6 Cerella, J. 1990. "Aging and Information-Processing Rate." In J.E. Birren and K.W.

Schaie, eds., *Handbook of the Psychology of Aging*, 3rd ed. San Diego: Academic Press.

6 Cerella, J., J. Rybash, W. Hoyer, and M.L. Commons, eds. 1993. *Adult Information Processing: Limits on Loss.* San Diego: Academic Press.

13 Chan, C.G., and G.H. Elder, Jr. 2000. "Matrilineal Advantage in Grandchild– Grandparent Relations." *Gerontologist* 40(2): 179–90.

7 Chan, L. 2003. "Is Spirituality Healthful?" *Wellness Options* 4(12): 26–27.

8 Chan, P., and S.R. Kenny. 2001. "National Consistency and Provincial Diversity in Delivery of Long-Term Care in Canada." *Journal of Aging and Social Policy* 13(2–3): 83–99.

8 Chappell, N.L. 1983. "Who Benefits from Adult Day Care? Changes in Functional Ability and Mental Functioning during Attendance." *Canadian Journal on Aging* 2: 9–26.

9 Chappell, N.L. 1987. "Canadian Income and Health-Care Policy: Implications for the Elderly." In V.W. Marshall, ed., *Aging in Canada,* 2nd ed. Toronto: Fitzhenry and Whiteside.

8 Chappell, N.L. 1988. "Long-Term Care in Canada." In E. Rathbone-McCuan and B. Havens, eds., *North American Elders: United States and Canadian Perspectives.* New York: Greenwood Press.

13 Chappell, N.L. 1989. "Health and Helping among the Elderly: Gender Differences." *Journal of Aging and Health* 1: 102–20.

5 Chappell, N.L. 1993a. "Technology and Aging." *Journal of Canadian Studies* 28(1): 45–58.

8 Chappell, N.L. 1993b. "The Future of Health Care in Canada." *International Social Policy* 22(4): 487–505.

8 Chappell, N.L. 1993c. "Implications of Shifting Health Care Policy for Caregiving in Canada." *Journal of Aging and Social Policy* 5(1/2): 39–55.

2 Chappell, N.L. 1995. "Gerontological Research in the '90s: Strengths, Weaknesses, and Contributions to Policy." *Canadian Journal on Aging* 14 (Suppl. 1): 23–36.

13 Chappell, N.L. 1997. *National Respite Project: Evaluation Report.* Victoria: Centre on Aging, University of Victoria.

3 Chappell, N.L. 1999a. "Director's Perspective." *Centre on Aging Bulletin* 7(2): 1–3.3. Centre on Aging, University of Victoria.

8 Chappell, N.L. 1999b. "Editorial: Canadian Association on Gerontology Policy Statement on Home Care in Canada." *Canadian Journal on Aging* 18(3): i–iii.

8 Chappell, N.L. 1999c. "Editorial: Canadian Association on Gerontology Policy Statement on Home Care in Canada." *Canadian Journal on Aging* 18(3): i–vii.

8 Chappell, N.L., and A.A. Blandford. 1987. "Adult Day Care and Medical and Hospital Claims." *Gerontologist* 7: 773–79.

12 Chappell, N.L., Health Canada, Volunteer Canada, and Manulife Financial. 1999d. *Volunteering and Healthy Aging: What We Know.* Ottawa: Volunteer Canada.

13 Chappell, N.L., and V.K. Kuehne. 1998. "Congruence among Husband and Wife Caregivers." *Journal of Aging Studies* 12(3): 239–54.

8 Chappell, N.L., M. Maclure, H. Brunt, and J. Hopkinson. 1997. "Seniors' Views of Medication Reimbursement Policies: Bridging Research and Policy at the Point of Policy Impact." *Canadian Journal on Aging/Canadian Public Policy* 16 (Suppl.): 114–31.

8 Chappell, N.L., and M.J. Penning. 1979. "The Trend Away from Institutionalization: Humanism or Economic Efficiency?" *Research on Aging* 1: 361–87.

12 Chappell, N.L., and M.J. Prince. 1997. "Reasons Why Canadian Seniors Volunteer." *Canadian Journal on Aging* 16(2): 336–53.

13 Chappell, N.L., and R.C. Reid. 2002. "Burden and Well-Being among Caregivers: Examining the Distinction." *Gerontologist* 42(6): 772–80.

13 Chappell, N.L., R.C. Reid, and E. Dow. 2001. "Respite Reconsidered: A Typology of Meanings Based on the Caregiver's Point of View." *Journal of Aging Studies* 15(2): 201–16.

13 Chappell, N.L., Alexander Segall, and Doris G. Lewis. 1990. "Gender and Helping Networks among Day Hospital and Senior Centre Participants." *Canadian Journal on Aging* 9: 220–33.

8 Chappell, N.L., L.A. Strain, and A.A. Blandford. 1986. *Aging and Health Care: A Social Perspective.* Toronto: Holt, Rinehart, and Winston of Canada.

13 Chapple, M.J., S. Kippax, and G. Smith. 1998. "'Semi-Straight Sort of Sex': Class and Gay Community Attachment Explored within a

Framework of Older Homosexually Active Men." *Journal of Homosexuality* 35(2): 65–83.

7,9 Chard, J. 1995. "Women in a Visible Minority." In Statistics Canada, *Women in Canada: A Statistical Report*, 3rd ed., 133–46. Cat. No. 89-503E. Ottawa: Minister of Supply and Services.

9 Chard, J. 2000. "Women in a Visible Minority." In C. Lindsay, ed. *Women in Canada 2000: A Gender-Based Statistical Report*. Cat. No. 89-503-XPE. Ottawa: Statistics Canada.

4 Chard, J., J. Badets., and L.H. Leo. 2000. "Immigrant Women." In Statistics Canada, *Women in Canada 2000: A Gender-Based Statistical Report*. Cat. No. 89-503-XPE. Ottawa: Minister Responsible for Statistics Canada.

8 Charles, C., and C. Schalm. 1992a. "Alberta's Resident Classification System for Long-Term Care Facilities. Part I: Conceptual and Methodological Development." *Canadian Journal on Aging* 11(3): 219–32.

8 Charles, C., and C. Schalm. 1992b. "Alberta's Resident Classification System for Long-Term Care Facilities. Part II: First-Year Results and Policy Implications." *Canadian Journal on Aging* 11(3): 233–48.

6 Charness, N. 1981. "Aging and Skilled Problem Solving." *Journal of Experimental Psychology: General* 110(1): 21–38.

6 Charness, N. 1985. "Aging and Problem-Solving Performance." In N. Charness, ed., *Aging and Human Performance*. Chichester, U.K.: John Wiley and Sons.

6 Charness, Neil. 1987. "Component Processes in Bridge Bidding and Novel Problem-Solving Tasks." *Canadian Journal of Psychology* 41(2): 223–43.

11 Charness, N.H. 1993. "Whither Technology and Aging?" *Gerontology News* (April): 2ff.

2 Charness, N. 1995. "Psychological Models of Aging: How, Who, and What? A Comment." *Canadian Journal on Aging* 14(1): 67–73.

6 Charness, N., and J.I.D. Campbell. 1988. "Acquiring Skill at Mental Calculation in Adulthood: A Task Decomposition." *Journal of Experimental Psychology: General* 117: 115–29.

4 Che-Alford, J., and K. Stevenson. 1998. "Older Canadians on the Move." *Canadian Social Trends* 48: 15–18.

11 Che-Alford, J., and B. Hamm. 1999. "Under One Roof: Three Generations Living Together." *Canadian Social Trends* (Summer): 6–9.

9 Cheal, D. 1985a. *Moral Economy: Gift Giving in an Urban Society*. Winnipeg Area Study Report No. 5. Winnipeg: Institute for Social and Economic Research, University of Manitoba.

9 Cheal, D. 1985b. "The System of Transfers to and from Households in Canada." *Western Economic Review* 4: 35–39.

4 Cheal, D. 2000. "Aging and Demographic Change." *Canadian Public Policy* 26 (Suppl. 2): S109–22.

6 Checkland, D., and M. Silberfeld. 1993. "Competence and the Three A's: Autonomy, Authenticity, and Aging." *Canadian Journal on Aging* 12(4): 453–68.

3 Chee, Y.K. 2000. "Elder Care in Korea: The Future Is Now." *Ageing International* 26(1/2): 25–37.

8 Chen, J., and F. Hou. 2002. "Unmet Needs for Health Care." *Health Reports* 13(2): 23–34.

8 Chen, J., F. Hou, C. Sanmartin, C. Hould, S. Tremblay, and J.-M. Berthelot. 2002. "Unmet Health Care Needs." *Canadian Social Trends* (Winter): 18–22.

5 Chen, J., and W.J. Millar. 2000. "Are Recent Cohorts Healthier Than Their Predecessors?" *Health Reports* 11(4): 9–24.

12 Chen, J., and W.J. Millar. 2001. "Starting and Sustaining Physical Activity." *Health Reports* 12(4): 33–43.

4 Chen, Yung-Ping. 1987. "Making Assets Out of Tomorrow's Elderly." *Gerontologist* 27: 410–16.

12 Chené, A. 1994. "Community-Based Older Learners: Being with Others." *Educational Gerontology* 20: 765–81.

12 Chené, A., and R. Sigouin. 1997. "Reciprocity and Older Learners." *Educational Gerontology* 23(3): 253–72.

13 Cherlin, A., and F.F. Furstenberg. 1985. "Styles and Strategies of Grand-Parenting." In V.L. Bengtson and J.F. Robertson, eds., *Grandparenthood*. Beverly Hills: Sage.

8 Cherniack, E., R.S. Senzel, and C.X. Pan. 2001. "Correlates of Use of Alternative Medicine by the Elderly in an Urban Population." *Journal of Alternative and Complementary Medicine* 7(3): 277–80.

5 Chernoff, R. 2002. "Health Promotion for Older Women: Benefits of Nutrition and Exercise Programs." *Topics in Geriatric Rehabilitation* 18(1): 59–67.

3   Cherry, R., and S. Magnuson-Martinson. 1981. "Modernization and the Status of the Aged in China: Decline or Equalization?" *Sociological Quarterly* 22: 253–61.

13   Chevan, A. 1996. "As Cheaply as One: Cohabitation in the Older Population." *Journal of Marriage and the Family* 58(3): 656–67.

3   Chi, I. 2001. "Commentary: Asian Perspectives on Sociological Issues for the Millennium." *Canadian Journal on Aging* 20 (Suppl. 1): 118–24.

7   Chipperfield, J.G., and B. Havens. 1992. "A Longitudinal Analysis of Perceived Respect among Elders: Changing Perceptions of Some Ethnic Groups." *Canadian Journal on Aging* 11(2): 15–30.

13   Chipperfield, J.G., and B. Havens. 2001. "Gender Differences in the Relationship between Marital Status Transitions and Life Satisfaction in Later Life." *Journals of Gerontology Series B* 56(3): P176–86.

2   Chipperfield, J.G., B. Havens, and W.D. Doig. 1997. "Method and Description of the Aging in Manitoba Project: A 20-Year Longitudinal Study." *Canadian Journal on Aging* 16(4): 606–25.

8   Church, J., and P. Barker. 1998. "Regionalization of Health Services in Canada: A Critical Perspective." *International Journal of Health Services* 28(3): 467–86.

5   Clarfield, M. 2002. "Is Old Age a Disease or Just Another of Life's Stages?" *Geriatrics and Aging* 5(1): 58–59.

12   Clark, F., A.F. Heller, C. Rafman, and J. Walker. 1997. "Peer Learning: A Popular Model for Seniors' Education." *Educational Gerontology* 23(8): 751–62.

14   Clark, G.T. 1993. *Personal Meanings of Grief and Bereavement.* Doctoral dissertation. Edmonton: University of Alberta.

1   Clark, P.G. 1993. "Moral Discourse and Public Policy in Aging: Framing Problems, Seeking Solutions, and 'Public Ethics.' " *Canadian Journal on Aging* 12(4): 485–508.

8   Clark, P.G. 1995. "The Moral Economy of Health and Aging in Canada and the United States." *Canadian–American Public Policy* 23 (November): 1–46.

8   Clark, P.G. 1999. "Moral Economy and the Social Construction of the Crisis of Aging and Health Care: Differing Canadian and U.S.

Perspectives." In M. Minkler and C.L. Estes, eds., *Critical Gerontology*, 147–67. Amityville, NY: Baywood Publishing.

7   Clark, W. 2000. "Patterns of Religious Attendance." *Canadian Social Trends* Winter: 23–26.

11,12   Clark, W. 2002. "Time Alone." *Canadian Social Trends* (Autumn): 2–6.

7   Clark, W. 2003. "Pockets of Belief: Religious Attendance Patterns in Canada. *Canadian Social Trends* (Spring): 2–5.

8   Clarke, A.E. 1997. "Arthritis Patient Education: How Economic Evaluations Can Inform Health Policy." *Canadian Journal on Aging/Canadian Public Policy* 16 (Suppl.): 162–76.

1   Clarke, L.C.H. 2002. "Beauty in Later Life: Older Women's Perceptions of Physical Attractiveness." *Canadian Journal on Aging* 21(3): 429–42.

1,5,7   Clarke, P.J., V.W. Marshall, C.D. Ryff, and C.J. Rosenthal. 2000. "Well-Being in Canadian Seniors: Findings from the Canadian Study of Health and Aging." *Canadian Journal on Aging* 19(2): 139–59.

13   Cohen, C.A., A. Colantonio, and L. Vernich. 2002. "Positive Aspects of Caregiving: Rounding out the Caregiver Experience." *International Journal of Geriatric Psychiatry* 17(2): 184–88.

6   Cohen, G.D. 1990. "Psychopathology and Mental Health in the Mature and Elderly Adult." In J.E. Birren and K.W. Schaie, eds., *Handbook of the Psychology of Aging*, 3rd ed. San Diego: Academic Press.

13   Cohen, G.D. 1999. "Marriage and Divorce in Later Life: Editorial." *American Journal of Geriatric Psychiatry* 7(3): 185–87.

3   Cohn, R. 1982. "Economic Development and Status Change of the Aged." *American Journal of Sociology* 87: 1150–61.

13   Colantonio, A., C. Cohen, and S. Corlett. 1998. "Support Needs of Elderly Caregivers of Persons with Dementia." *Canadian Journal on Aging* 17(3): 330–45.

3   Cole, T.R. 1992. *The Journey of Life.* New York: Cambridge University Press.

12   Coleman, D., and S.E. Iso-Ahola. 1993. "Leisure and Health: The Role of Social Support and Self-Determination." *Journal of Leisure Research* 25: 111–28.

3   Collings, P. 2000. "Aging and Life Course Development in an Inuit Community." *Arctic Anthropology* 37(2): 111–25.

3   Collings, P. 2001. "'If You Got Everything, It's Good Enough': Perspectives on Successful Aging in a Canadian Inuit Community. *Journal of Cross-Cultural Gerontology* 16(2): 127–55.

6   Collins, B., and A. Tellier. 1994. "Differences in Conceptual Flexibility with Age as Measured by a Modified Version of the Visual Verbal Test." *Canadian Journal on Aging* 13(3): 368–77.

3   Colson, E., and T. Scudder. 1981. "Old Age in Gwembe District, Zambia." In P.T. Amoss and S. Harrell, eds., *Other Ways of Growing Old: Anthropological Perspectives*. Stanford, CA: Stanford University Press.

8   Commission on the Future of Health Care in Canada. 2002. *Building on Values: The Future of Health Care in Canada: Final Report* (Romanow Report). Ottawa: Government of Canada. http://www.hc-sc.gc.ca/english/ pdf/care/romanow_e.pdf, accessed on July 10, 2003.

1   Commonwealth Fund. 1993. "Commonwealth Fund Survey: Over 65 in Five Nations." *Ageing International* 20(1): 43–45.

3   Condon. 1987. *Inuit Youth: Growth and Change in the Canadian Arctic.* New Brunswick, NJ: Rutgers University Press.

4,8   Conference of Deputy Ministers of Health. 1999. *Toward a Healthy Future: Second Report on the Health of Canadians*. Ottawa: Government of Canada. http:// www.hc-sc.gc.ca/hppb/phdd/report/toward/ index.html, accessed on August 4, 2004.

6   Conn, D.K. 2002. "An Overview of Common Mental Disorders among Seniors." In *Writings in Gerontology: Mental Health and Aging*, 19–31. Ottawa: National Advisory Council on Aging.

2   Connell, B.R. 1998. "A Picture Is Worth 1000 Words: Using Video-Based Technology to Understand Behavior Problems in Long Term Care Settings." In G.M. Gutman, ed., *Technology Innovation for an Aging Society: Blending Research, Public and Private Sectors*, 69–82. Vancouver: Gerontology Research Centre, Simon Fraser University.

8   Connell, F.E.A., G. Tan, I. Gupta, P. Gompertz, G.C. J. Bennett, and J.L. Herzberg. 2001. "Can Aromatherapy Promote Sleep in Elderly Hospitalized Patients?" *Geriatrics Today* 4(4): 191–95.

9   Connelly, M.P., and M. MacDonald. 1990. *Women and the Labour Force*. Cat. No. 98-125. Ottawa: Minister of Supply and Services.

10   Connidis, I. 1982. "Women and Retirement: The Effect of Multiple Careers on Retirement Adjustment." *Canadian Journal on Aging* 1: 17–27.

11   Connidis, I.A. 1983a. "Living Arrangement Choices of Older Residents: Assessing Quantitative Results with Qualitative Data." *Canadian Journal of Sociology* 8: 359–75.

7   Connidis, I.A. 1983b. "The Pros, Cons and Worries of Aging." Paper presented at the Canadian Association on Gerontology 12th Annual Scientific and Educational Meeting, Moncton.

1,13   Connidis, I.A. 2001. *Family Ties and Aging*. Thousand Oaks, CA: Sage.

13   Connidis, I.A., and L.D. Campbell. 1995. "Closeness, Confiding, and Contact among Siblings in Middle and Late Adulthood." *Journal of Family Issues* 16(6): 722–45.

13   Connidis, I.A., and J.A. McMullin. 1999. "Permanent Childlessness: Perceived Advantages and Disadvantages among Older Persons." *Canadian Journal on Aging* 18(4): 447–65.

11   Connidis, I., and J. Rempel. 1983. "The Living Arrangements of Older Residents: The Role of Gender, Marital Status, Age, and Family Size." *Canadian Journal on Aging* 2: 91–105.

13   Connidis, I.A., C.J. Rosenthal, and J.A. McMullin. 1996. "Impact of Family Composition on Providing Help to Older Parents." *Research on Aging* 18(4): 402–29.

14   Connor, S.R. 1998. *Hospice: Practice, Pitfalls, and Promise*. Washington, DC: Taylor and Fancis.

13   Cooley, M.E. 2002. "Sex over Sixty." *Expression* 15(2). Ottawa: National Advisory Council on Aging.

13   Cooney, T., and K. Dunne. 2001. "Intimate Relationships in Later Life, Current Realities, Future Prospects." *Journal of Family Issues* 22(7): 838–58.

8   Coons, D.H., and N.L. Mace. 1996. *Quality of Life in Long-Term Care*. New York: Haworth Press.

12 Corbeil, J.-P. 1995. "Sport Participation in Canada." *Canadian Social Trends* (Spring): 18–23.

6 Cornelius, S.W., and A. Caspi. 1987. "Everyday Problem Solving in Adulthood and Old Age." *Psychology and Aging* 2(2): 144–53.

7 Costello, J. 1994. "Growing Older, Growing Bolder." *The Moment* 21: 11. Jesuit Centre for Social Faith and Justice.

8 Cott, C.A., and M.T. Fox. 2001. "Health and Happiness for Elderly Institutionalized Canadians." *Canadian Journal on Aging* 20(4): 527–35.

5 Cott, C.A., and M.A.M. Gignac. 1999. "Independence and Dependence for Older Adults with Osteoarthritis or Osteoporosis." *Canadian Journal on Aging* 18(1): 1–25.

13 Cotten, S. 1999. "Marital Status and Mental Health Revisited: Examining the Importance of Risk Factors and Resources." *Family Relations* 48(3): 225–33.

13 Council against Abuse of Older Persons. 2002. "Abuse and Neglect of an Older or Vulnerable Person." Laminated handout. Sponsored by St. Joseph's Health Care, Hamilton Health Sciences, St. Peter's Hospital, Hamilton Academy of Medicine, Hamilton Academy of Dentistry, Hamilton Police Service, and McMaster Centre for Gerontological Studies, Hamilton, ON: Promark Printing.

12 Cousins, S.O. 1993. "Turn of the Century Tomboys: Does Older Women's Efficacy for Late Life Exercise Originate in Childhood?" In E. Beregi, I.A. Gergely, and K. Rajczi, eds., *Recent Advances in Aging Science, 1911–1916.* Bologna: Monduzzi Editore.

12 Cousins, S.O. 1995. "Social Support for Exercise among Elderly Women in Canada." *Health Promotion International* 10(4): 273–82.

12 Cousins, S.O. 1996. "Exercise Cognition among Elderly Women." *Journal of Applied Sport Psychology* 8: 131–45.

12 Cousins, S.O. 1997. "Elderly Tomboys? Sources of Self-Efficacy for Physical Activity in Later Life." *Journal of Aging and Physical Activity* 5(3): 229–43.

5 Cousins, S.O. 1998. *Exercise, Aging, and Health: Overcoming Barriers to an Active Old Age.* Philadelphia: Taylor and Francis.

12 Cousins, S.O. 2000. "'My Health Couldn't Take It': Older Women's Beliefs about Exercise Benefits and Risks." *Journals of Gerontology Series B* 55(5): P283–94.

12 Cousins, S.O. 2001. "Thinking Out Loud: What Older Adults Say about Triggers for Physical Activity." *Journal of Aging and Physical Activity* 9(4): 347–63.

12 Cousins, S.O., and A. Burgess. 1992. "Perspectives on Older Adults in Physical Activity and Sports." *Educational Gerontology* 18: 461–81.

5 Cousins, S.O., and D. Goodwin. 2002. "Balance Your Life! The Metaphors of Falling." *Wellspring* 13(3): 6–7.

8 Cousins, S.O., and T. Horne, eds. 1999. *Active Living among Older Adults: Health Benefits and Outcomes.* Philadelphia: Brunner/Mazel.

12 Cousins, S.O., and N. Keating. 1995. "Life Cycle Patterns of Physical Activity among Sedentary and Active Older Women." *Journal of Aging and Physical Activity* 3: 340–59.

3 Cowgill, D.O. 1972. "A Theory of Aging in Cross-Cultural Perspective." In D. Cowgill and L. Holmes, eds., *Aging and Modernization.* New York: Appleton-Century-Crofts.

3,10 Cowgill, D.O. 1974. "Aging and Modernization: A Revision of the Theory." In J.F. Gubrium, ed., *Late Life.* Springfield, IL: Charles C. Thomas.

3 Cowgill, D.O. 1986. *Aging around the World.* Belmont, CA: Wadsworth.

2,3 Cowgill, D.O., and L.D. Holmes, eds. 1972. *Aging and Modernization.* New York: Appleton-Century-Crofts.

8 Coyte, P.C. 2000. "Home Care in Canada: Passing the Buck." Paper commissioned by the Dialogue on Health Reform. http://www.utoronto.ca/hpme/dhr, accessed on August 5, 2004.

6 Craik, F.I.M. 2000. "Age-Related Changes in Human Memory." In D.C. Park and N. Schwarz, eds., *Cognitive Aging: A Primer,* 75–92. Philadelphia: Taylor and Francis.

6 Craik, F.I.M., and T.A. Salthouse, eds. 2000. *The Handbook of Aging and Cognition,* 2nd ed. Mahwah, NJ: Lawrence Erlbaum Associates.

14 Cramer, K., H. Tuokko, and D. Evans. 2001. "Extending Autonomy for Health Care Preferences in Late Life." *Aging Neuropsychology and Cognition* 8(3): 213–24.

13 Cranswick, K. 1997. "Canada's Caregivers." *Canadian Social Trends* (Winter). Cat. No. 11-008XPE. http://www.statcan.ca/english/ads/

11-008-XIE/care.pdf, accessed on August 29, 2004.

13 Cranswick, K. 1999. "Help Close at Hand: Relocating to Give or Receive Care." *Canadian Social Trends* (Winter).

13 Cranswick, K. 2003. *Caring for an Aging Society.* Cat. No. 89-582-XIE. Ottawa: Statistics Canada.

12 Creative Retirement Manitoba. 1992. *Annual Report.* Winnipeg: Creative Retirement Manitoba.

5 Crews, D.E. 1993. "Biological Aging: Book Review Essay." *Journal of Cross-Cultural Gerontology* 8: 281–90.

13 Crompton, S., and A. Kemeny. 1999. "In Sickness and in Health: The Well-Being of Married Seniors." *Canadian Social Trends* (Winter).

3,4 Cross, D.S. 1983. "The Neglected Majority: The Changing Role of Women in Nineteenth-Century Montreal." In P.W. Ward, ed., *The Social Development of Canada: Readings.* Richmond, BC: Open Learning Institute.

6 Crosson, C.W., and E.A. Robertson-Tchabo. 1983. "Age and Preference for Complexity among Manifestly Creative Women." *Human Development* 26: 149–55.

8 Crowell, S.J., K. Rockwood, P. Stolee, S.K. Buehler, B.M. James, A. Kozma, and J.M. Gray. 1996. "Use of Home Care Services among the Elderly in Eastern Canada." *Canadian Journal on Aging* 15(3): 413–26.

5 Crowther, M.R., M.W. Parker, W.A. Achenbaum, W.L. Larimore, and H.G. Koenig. 2002. "Rowe and Kahn's Model of Successful Aging Revisited: Positive Spirituality—The Forgotten Factor." *Gerontologist* 42(5): 613–20.

1 Cruikshank, M. 2003. *Learning to Be Old: Gender, Culture, and Aging.* Lanham, MD: Rowman and Littlefield.

13 Crystal, S. 1986. "Social Policy and Elder Abuse." In K.A. Pillemer and R.S. Wolf, eds., *Elder Abuse: Conflict in the Family.* Dover, MA: Auburn House.

2,7 Cumming, E., and W.E. Henry. 1961. *Growing Old: The Process of Disengagement.* New York: Basic Books.

12 Cunningham, D.A., P.A. Rechnitzer, J.H. Howard, and A.P. Donner. 1987. "Exercise Training of Men at Retirement: A Clinical Trial." *Journal of Gerontology* 42: 17–23.

12 Curtis, J.E., and B.D. McPherson. 1987. "Regional Differences in the Leisure Physical Activity of Canadians: Testing Some Alternative Interpretations." *Sociology of Sport Journal* 4: 363–75.

12 Curtis, J., W. McTeer, and P. White. 1999. "Exploring Effects of School Sport Experiences on Sport Participation in Later Life." *Sociology of Sport Journal* 16(4): 348–65.

12 Cusack, S.A., and W.J.A. Thompson. 1999. *Leadership for Older Adults: Aging with Purpose and Passion.* New York: Brunner/Mazel.

6 Cusack, S.A., W.J.A. Thompson, and M.E. Rogers. 2003. "Mental Fitness for Life: Assessing the Impact of an 8-Week Mental Fitness Program on Healthy Aging." *Educational Gerontology* 29(5): 393–403.

13 Cuthbertson, D. 2003. "Never Too Old for Love." *Sarnia Observer*, December 20, A1–2.

11 Cvitkovich, Y., and A. Wister. 2001. "Importance of Transportation and Prioritization of Environmental Needs to Sustain Well-Being among Older Adults." *Environment and Behavior* 33(6): 809–29.

12 Cyr, J., and M.M. Schnore. 1982. "Level of Education of the Future Elderly: Demographic Characteristics and Clinical Implications." *Essence* 5: 153–67.

11 Daigneault, G., P. Joly, and J-Y Frigon. 2002. "Previous Convictions or Accidents and the Risk of Subsequent Accidents of Older Drivers." *Accident Analysis and Prevention* 34(2): 257–61.

7 d'Anglure, B.S. 1994. "Recycling the 'Elders' in the Inuit Social Life." In National Advisory Council on Aging, *Aboriginal Seniors' Issues*, 59–64. Cat. No. H71-2/1-15-1994E. Ottawa: Minister of Supply and Services.

13 Dauvergne, M. 2003. "Family Violence against Seniors." *Canadian Social Trends* (Spring): 10–14.

10 David, H. 1993. "Canada's Labor Market: Older Workers Need Not Apply." *Ageing International* 20(3): 21–25.

13 Davidson, K., S. Arber, and J. Ginn. 2000. "Gendered Meanings of Care Work within Late Life Marital Relationships." *Canadian Journal on Aging* 19(4): 536–53.

13 Davies, L. 1995. "A Closer Look at Gender and Distress among the Never Married." *Women and Health* 23(2): 13–30.

9   Davies, S., and M. Denton. 2001. *The Economic Well-Being of Older Women Who Become Divorced or Separated in Mid and Later Life.* SEDAP Research Paper No. 66. Hamilton, ON: McMaster University.

9,13   Davies, S., and M. Denton. 2002. "Economic Well-Being of Older Women Who Became Divorced or Separated in Mid- or Later Life." *Canadian Journal on Aging* 21(4): 477–93.

11   Davis, C., D. Flett, L. Johnson, L. Gosselin, L. Holmes, and E. Gerrits. 2000. *Supportive Housing for Seniors.* Ottawa: Canada Mortgage and Housing Corporation.

13   Davis, I. 1996. "Grandparenting Denied." *Maturity* (March/April): 25–26.

13   Dawson, P., and C.J. Rosenthal. 1996. "Wives of Institutionalized Elderly Men: What Influences Satisfaction with Care?" *Canadian Journal on Aging* 15(2): 245–63.

12   Dawson, R. "A Personal Odyssey." *Maturity* (January/February): 26–27.

4   Deacon, J. 1992. "Enjoying the Good Life." *Maclean's,* August 24, 50.

8   Deber, R.B., S.L. Mhatre, and G.R. Baker. 1994. "A Review of Provincial Initiatives." In A. Blomqvist and D.M. Brown, eds., *Limits to Care: Reforming Canada's Health System in an Age of Restraint,* 91–124. Ottawa: C.D. Howe Institute.

8   Deber, R.B., and A.P. Williams. 1995. "Policy, Payment, and Participation: Long-Term Care Reform in Ontario." *Canadian Journal on Aging* 14(2): 294–318.

7   DeGenova, M.K. 1992. "If You Had Your Life to Live Over Again: What Would You Do Differently?" *International Journal of Aging and Human Development* 34: 135–43.

2   Del Balso, M., and A.D. Lewis. 1997. *First Steps: A Guide to Social Research.* Scarborough, ON: Nelson.

3   DeLehr, Esther Contreras. 1988. "Today's and Tomorrow's Aging in Latin America." In *Aging around the World: A Report on the President's Symposium on Aging in Tomorrow's World: An International Perspective.* Washington, DC: Gerontological Society of America.

7   Delisle, M.A. 1988. "What Does Solitude Mean to the Aged?" *Canadian Journal on Aging* 7: 358–71.

8   Dello Buono, M., O. Urciuoli, P. Marietta, W. Padoani, and D. De Leo. 2001. "Alternative Medicine in a Sample of 655 Community-Dwelling Elderly." *Journal of Psychosomatic Research* 50(3): 147–54.

6   Dennis, W. 1968. "Creative Productivity between the Ages of 20 and 80 Years." In B.L. Neugarten, ed., *Middle Age and Aging.* Chicago: University of Chicago Press.

4   Denton, F.T., C.H. Feaver, and B.G. Spencer. 1986. "Prospective Aging of the Population and Its Implications for the Labour Force and Government Expenditures." *Canadian Journal on Aging* 5: 75–98.

4   Denton, F.T., C.H. Feaver, and B.G. Spencer. 1998. "The Future Population of Canada, Its Age Distribution, and Dependency Relations." *Canadian Journal on Aging* 17(1): 83–109.

4   Denton, F.T., C.H. Feaver, and B.G. Spencer. 2000. *Projections of the Population and Labour Force to 2046.* SEDAP Research Paper No. 15. Hamilton, ON: McMaster University.

9, 10   Denton, F.T., D. Fretz, and B.G. Spencer, eds. 2000. *Independence and Economic Security in Old Age.* Vancouver: UBC Press.

8   Denton, F.T., A. Gafni, and B.G. Spencer. 2001. *Exploring the Effects of Population Change on the Costs of Physician Services.* SEDAP Research Paper No. 43. Hamilton, ON: McMaster University.

12   Denton, F.T., P.C. Pineo, and B.G. Spencer. 1988. "Participation in Adult Education by the Elderly: A Multivariate Analysis and Some Implications for the Future." *Canadian Journal on Aging* 7: 4–16.

4,8   Denton, F.T., and B.G. Spencer. 1995. "Demographic Change and the Cost of Publicly Funded Health Care." *Canadian Journal on Aging* 14(2): 174–92.

4   Denton, F.T., and B.G. Spencer. 1997. "Population Aging and the Maintenance of Social Support Systems." *Canadian Journal on Aging* 16(3): 485–98.

4   Denton, F.T., and B.G. Spencer. 1999. *Population Aging and Its Economic Costs: A Survey of the Issues and Evidence.* SEDAP Research Paper No. 1. Hamilton, ON: McMaster University.

4   Denton, F.T., and B.G. Spencer. 2000. "Population Aging and Its Economic Costs: A Survey of the Issues and Evidence". *Canadian Journal on Aging* 19 (Suppl. 1): 1–31.

4   Denton, F.T., and B.G. Spencer. 2002. "Some Demographic Consequences of Revising the Definition of 'Old Age' to Reflect Future

4 Changes in Life Table Probabilities." *Canadian Journal on Aging* 21(3): 349–56.

4 Denton, F.T., and B.G. Spencer. 2003. *Population Change and Economic Growth: The Long-Term Outlook*. SEDAP Research Paper No. 12. Hamilton, ON: McMaster University.

2,13 Denton, M. 1997. "The Linkages between Informal and Formal Care of the Elderly." *Canadian Journal on Aging* 16(1): 30–50.

4 Desjardins, B. 1993. *Population Ageing and the Elderly*. Cat. No. 91-533E. Ottawa: Minister of Industry, Science, and Technology.

12 Devereaux, M.S. 1985. *One in Every Five: A Survey of Adult Education in Canada*. Cat. No. SZ-139/1984E. Ottawa: Minister of Supply and Services.

4 Devereaux, M.S. 1987. "Aging of the Canadian Population." *Canadian Social Trends* (Winter): 37–38.

8 Devine, B.A. 1980. "Old Age Stereotyping: A Comparison of Nursing Staff Attitudes toward the Elderly." *Journal of Gerontological Nursing* 6: 25–32.

14 De Vries, B., ed. 1999. *End of Life Issues: Interdisciplinary and Multidimensional Perspectives*. New York: Springer.

13 De Vries, B., C. Jacoby, and C.G. Davis. 1996. "Ethnic Differences in Later Life Friendship." *Canadian Journal on Aging* 15(2): 226–44.

12 DeVries, H.A. 1975. "Physiology of Exercise and Aging." In D.S. Woodruff and J.E. Birren, eds., *Aging: Scientific Perspectives and Social Issues*. New York: D. Van Nostrand Co.

3 de Vries, P. 1987. "Every Old Person Is Somebody: The Image of Aging in Canadian Children's Literature." *Canadian Children's Literature* 46: 37–44.

12 Diamond, M. 1984. "A Love Affair with the Brain." *Psychology Today* (November): 62–73.

12 DiPietro, L., and J. Dziura. 2000. "Exercise: A Prescription to Delay the Effects of Aging." *The Physician and Sportsmedicine* 28(10). http://www.physsportsmed.com/issues/2000/10_00/dipietro.htm, accessed on November 25, 2003.

6 Dixon, R.A. 2000. "Concepts and Mechanisms of Gains in Cognitive Aging." In D.C. Park and N. Schwarz, eds., *Cognitive Aging: A Primer*, 23–41. Philadelphia: Taylor and Francis.

6 Dixon, R.A., and L. Bäckman. 1993. "The Concept of Compensation in Cognitive Aging: The Case of Prose Processing in Adulthood."

International Journal of Aging and Human Development 36(3): 199–217.

6,7 Dixon, R.A., and A.-L. Cohen. 2001. "The Psychology of Aging: Canadian Research in an International Context." *Canadian Journal on Aging* 20 (Suppl. 1): 125–48.

4 Dominion Bureau of Statistics. 1964. *Census of Canada (1961 Census). Bulletin* 7: 1–4. Ottawa: Queen's Printer.

1 Donahue, P.J.D. 2001. *Fraud in Ethnocultural Seniors' Communities*. SEDAP Research Paper No. 37. Hamilton, ON: SEDAP Research Program, McMaster University.

8 Donelan, K., R.J. Blendon, C. Shoen, K. Binns, R. Osborn, and K. Davis. 2000. "Elderly in Five Nations: The Importance of Universal Coverage." *Health Affairs* 19(3): 226–35.

1 Dooley, Stephen, and B. Gail Frankel. 1990. "Improving Attitudes toward Elderly People: Evaluation of an Intervention Program for Adolescents." *Canadian Journal on Aging* 9: 400–9.

14 Doutre, D., D.M. Stillwell, and I. Ajemian. 1979. "Physiotherapy in Palliative Care." *Essence* 3: 69–77.

10 Dowd, J.J. 1980. *Stratification among the Aged*. Monterey, CA: Brooks/Cole.

13 Downs, K.J.M., M. Coleman, and L. Ganong. 2000. "Divorced Families over the Life Course." In S.J. Price, P.C. McKenry, and M.J. Murphy, eds., *Families across Time: A Life Course Perspective*, 24–36. Los Angeles: Roxbury Publishing Company.

11 Doyle, V. 1994. "Choice, Control and the Right to Age in Place." In G. Gutman and A.V. Wister, eds., *Progressive Accommodation for Seniors: Interfacing Shelter and Services*, 33–44. Vancouver: Gerontology Research Centre.

4 Driedger, Leo, and N.L. Chappell. 1987. *Aging and Ethnicity: Toward an Interface*. Toronto: Butterworths.

8 Dubois, M.-F., G. Bravo, and M. Charpentier. 2001. "Which Residential Care Facilities Are Delivering Inadequate Care? A Simple Case-Finding Questionnaire." *Canadian Journal on Aging* 20(3): 339–55.

2 Dukoff, R., and T. Sunderland. 1997. "Durable Power of Attorney and Informed Consent with Alzheimer's Disease Patients: A Clinical Study." *American Journal of Psychiatry* 154(8): 1070–75.

12   Dulka, I.M., M.J. Yaffe, B. Goldin, and W.S. Rowe. 1999. "Use of Senior Volunteers in the Care of Discharged Geriatric Patients." *Journal of Sociology and Social Welfare* 26(1): 69–85.

4   Dumas, J. 1990. *Current Demographic Analysis: Report on the Demographic Situation in Canada 1988.* Statistics Canada. Cat. No. 91-209E. Ottawa: Minister of Supply and Services.

4,5   Dumas, J., and A. Bélanger. 1994. *Report on the Demographic Situation in Canada 1994.* Cat. No. 91-209E. Ottawa: Minister of Industry, Science, and Technology.

5   Dunn, P.A. 1990. *Barriers Confronting Seniors with Disabilities in Canada. Special Topics Series: The Health and Activity Limitation Survey.* Statistics Canada. Cat. No. 82-615. Ottawa: Minister of Supply and Services.

11   Dunn, P.A. 1997. "A Comparative Analysis of Barrier-Free Housing: Policies for Elderly People in the United States and Canada." In L.A. Patalan, ed., *Shelter and Service Issues for Aging Populations: International Perspectives,* 37–53. New York: Haworth Press.

13   Dunn, Prov. J. 1993. Godwin versus Bolsco. *Reports of Family Law,* Vol. 45, 3rd ed., 310–27.

5   Dunphy, C. 2003. "Going Strong." *Comfort Life.* Our Kids Publications. http://www.ourkids.net/comfortlife/uf2003_amazing_himes.shtml, accessed on July 28, 2004.

13   Dupuis, S.L. 2000. "Institution-Based Caregiving as a Container for Leisure." *Leisure Sciences* 22(4): 259–80.

7,12   Dupuis, S.L., and B.J.A. Smale. 1995. "An Examination of Relationship between Psychological Well-Being and Depression and Leisure Activity Participation among Older Adults." *Society and Leisure* 18(1): 67–92.

13   Dupuis, S.L., and B.J.A. Smale. 2000. "Bittersweet Journeys: Meanings of Leisure in the Institution-Based Caregiving Context." *Journal of Leisure Research* 32(3): 303–40.

13   Dupuis, S.L., and B.J.A. Smale. 2004. *In Their Own Voices: Dementia Caregivers Identify the Issues.* Final report prepared for the Minstry of Health and Long-Term Care and the Ontario Senior's Secretariat as part of Initiative No. 6 of Ontario's Alzheimer Strategy. Waterloo, ON: Murray Alzheimer Research and Education Program.

7   Durkheim, E. 1951. *Suicide: A Study in Sociology.* New York: Free Press.

13   Dykstra, P.A. 1995. "Loneliness among the Never and Formerly Married: The Importance of Supportive Friendships and a Desire for Independence." *Journals of Gerontology Series B* 50: S321–29.

8   Eagle, D.J., G. Guyatt, C. Patterson, and I. Turpie. 1987. "Day Hospitals' Cost and Effectiveness: A Summary." *Gerontologist* 27: 735–40.

8   Eakin, J.M. 1987. "Care of the Unwanted: Stroke Patients in a Canadian Hospital." In D. Coburn, C. D'Arcy, G. Torrance, and P. New, eds., *Health and Canadian Society: Sociological Perspectives,* 2nd ed. Toronto: Fitzhenry and Whiteside.

14   Eastaugh, A.M. 1996. "Approaches to Palliative Care by Primary Health Care Teams: A Survey." *Journal of Palliative Care* 12(4): 47–50.

2   Eastwood, R., H. Nobbs, J. Lindsay, and I. McDowell. 1992. "Canadian Study of Health and Aging." *Dementia* 3(4): 209–12.

6,8   Eaton, B., M.J. Stones, and K. Rockwood. 1986. "Poor Mental Status in Older Hospital Patients: Prevalence and Correlates." *Canadian Journal on Aging* 5: 231–39.

14   Eaton, J.W. 1964. "The Art of Aging and Dying." *Gerontologist* 4: 94–112.

5   Edwards, N., D. Lockett, F. Aminzadeh, and R.C. Nair. 2003. "Predictors of Bath Grab-Bar Use among Community-Living Older Adults." *Canadian Journal on Aging* 22(2): 217–27.

3   Eisdorfer, C. 1981. "Foreword." In P.T. Amoss and S. Harrell, eds., *Other Ways of Growing Old: Anthropological Perspectives.* Stanford, CA: Stanford University Press.

10   Ekos Research Associates. 1998. Ottawa. *Rethinking Generations: Preliminary Findings.*

2   Elder, G.H., Jr. 2000. "The Life Course." In E.F. Borgatta and R.J.V. Montgomery, eds., *The Encyclopedia of Sociology,* Vol. 3, 2nd ed., 939–91. New York: Wiley.

12   Elderhostel. 1981. *Annual Report.* Boston: Elderhostel.

12   Elderhostel. 2003. "What Is Elderhostel?" http://www.elderhostel.org/about/what_is.asp, accessed on November 26, 2003.

12   Elderhostel. 2004. "About Us." http://www.elderhostel.org/about/default.asp, accessed on August 28, 2004.

5   Elgar, F.J., G. Worrall, and J.C. Knight. 2002. "Functional Assessment of Elderly Clients of a Rural Community–Based Long-Term Care

Program: A 10-Year Cohort Study." *Canadian Journal on Aging* 21(3): 455–63.

6   Elo, A.E. 1965. "Age Changes in Master Chess Performance." *Journal of Gerontology* 20: 289–99.

6   Engelman, M. 2000. "Here's to the Belleville Ladies: Creativity in Aging." *Activities, Adaptation and Aging* 24(4): 19–26.

11   Enman, A., and M.H. Rogers. 2002. "Aging Well in Rural Places." *The Guardian* (Charlottetown), June 4, D19.

8   Epp, J. 1986. *Achieving Health for All: A Framework for Health Promotion.* Cat. No. H39-102/1986E. Ottawa: Minister of Supply and Services.

12   Ericsson, K.A. 1990. "Peak Performance and Age: An Examination of Peak Performance in Sports." In P.B. Baltes and M.M. Baltes, eds., *Successful Aging: Perspectives from the Behavioral Sciences.* Cambridge: Cambridge University Press.

7   Erikson, E.H. 1950. "Growth and Crises of the Healthy Personality." In M.J. Senn, ed., *Symposium on the Healthy Personality, Supplement II: Problems of Infancy and Childhood.* Transaction of Fourth Conference. New York: Josiah Macy, Jr., Foundation.

7   Erikson, E.H. 1959. "Identity and the Life Cycle: Selected Issues." *Psychological Issues* 1: 50–100, Appendix.

7,14 Erikson, E.H. 1963. *Childhood and Society*, 2nd ed. New York: W.W. Norton.

7   Erikson, E.H. 1982. *The Life Cycle Completed.* New York: W.W. Norton.

12   Estabrooks, P.A., and A.V. Carron. 2000. "Predicting Scheduling Self-Efficacy in Older Adult Exercisers: The Role of Task Cohesion." *Journal of Aging and Physical Activity* 8(1): 41–50.

2   Estes, C.L. 1999. "The Aging Enterprise Revisited." In M. Minkler and C.L. Estes, eds., *Critical Gerontology: Perspectives from Political and Moral Economy*, 135–46. Amityville, NY: Baywood.

11   Evans, A.T., and G.J.M. Purdie. 1985. "Private Sector Financing for Elderly Housing." In G. Gutman and N. Blackie, eds., *Innovations in Housing and Living Arrangements for Seniors.* Vancouver: Gerontology Research Centre, Simon Fraser University.

8   Evans, J.G. 1996. "Health Care for Older People: A Look across a Frontier." *Journal of*

the *American Medical Association* 275(18): 1449–50.

11   Evans, L. 1988. "Older Driver Involvement in Fatal and Severe Traffic Crashes." *Journals of Gerontology Series B* 43: S186–93.

8   Evans, R.G. 1984. *Strained Mercy: The Economics of Canadian Health Care.* Toronto: Butterworths.

8   Evans, R.G., M.L. Barer, and G.L. Stoddart. 1995. "User Fees for Health Care: Why a Bad Idea Keeps Coming Back (or, What's Health Got to Do with It?)." *Canadian Journal on Aging* 14(2): 360–90.

4,5,8 Evans, R.G., K.M. McGrail, S.G. Morgan, M.L. Barer, and C. Hertzman. 2001. "Apocalypse No: Population Aging and the Future of Health Care Systems." *Canadian Journal on Aging* 20 (Suppl. 1): 160–91.

13   Fairchild, S.K., G.E. Carrino, and M. Ramirez. 1996. "Social Workers' Perceptions of Staff Attitudes toward Resident Sexuality in a Random Sample of New York State Nursing Homes: A Pilot Study." *Journal of Gerontological Social Work* 26(1/2): 153–69.

9   Fast, J., and M. Da Pont. 1997. "Changes in Women's Work Continuity." *Canadian Social Trends* (Autumn): 2–7.

6   Featherman, D.L., J. Smith, and J.G. Peterson. 1990. "Successful Aging in a Post-Retired Society." In P.B. Baltes and M.M. Baltes, eds., *Successful Aging: Perspectives from the Behavioral Sciences*, 50–93. Cambridge: Cambridge University Press.

8   Federal/Provincial/Territorial Subcommittee on Continuing Care. 1992. *Future Directions in Continuing Care.* Cat. No. H39-260/1002E. Ottawa: Minister of Supply and Services.

8   Federal/Provincial/Territorial Working Group on Home Care. 1990. *Report on Home Care.* Cat. No. H39-186/1990E. Ottawa: Minister of Supply and Services.

8   Fedorak, S.A., and C. Griffin. 1986. "Developing a Self-Advocacy Program for Seniors: The Essential Component of Health Promotion." *Canadian Journal on Aging* 5: 269–77.

8   Feeny, D. 1994. "Technology Assessment and Health Policy in Canada." In A. Blomqvist and D.M. Brown, eds., *Limits to Care: Reforming Canada's Health System in an Age of Restraint*, 293–326. Ottawa: C.D. Howe Institute.

5   Ferrucci, L., G. Izmirlian, S.G. Léveillé, C.L. Phillips, M.C. Corti, D.B. Brock, and J.M. Guralnik. 1999. "Smoking, Physical Activity, and Active Life Expectancy." *American Journal of Epidemiology* 149(7): 645–53.

13 Field, D. 1999. "Continuity and Change in Friendships in Advanced Old Age: Findings from the Berkeley Older Generation Study." *International Journal of Aging and Human Development* 48(4): 325–46.

10 Finlayson, A. 1985. "The Lure of Early Retirement." *Maclean's,* February 4.

8   Finlayson, M., and B. Havens. 2001. "Changes over Time in Long-Term Care Use, ADL, and IADL among the Oldest-Old Participants of the Aging in Manitoba Longitudinal Study." *Canadian Journal on Aging* 20(2): 271–90.

11 Finlayson, M., and J. Kaufert. 2002. "Older Women's Community Mobility: A Qualitative Exploration." *Canadian Journal on Aging* 21(1): 75–84.

5   Finn, J. 1997. "The Promise and the Challenge." *Generations* 21(3): 5–6.

3   Fischer, D.H. 1978. *Growing Old in America*, expanded ed. New York: Oxford University Press.

8   Fisher, R.H., and M.L. Zorzitto. 1983. "Placement Problem: Diagnosis, Disease or Term of Denigration?" *Canadian Medical Association Journal* 129: 331–33.

13 Fitzpatrick, J.A., and K.S. Wampler. 2000. "Marital Relationships: A Life Course Perspective." In S.J. Price, P.C. McKenry, and M.J. Murphy, eds., *Families across Time: A Life Course Perspective*, 92–104. Los Angeles: Roxbury Publishing Company.

1   Fletcher, S. 1990. "Seniors in the Marketplace." *Canadian Business Review* (Winter): 36–39.

5   Fletcher P.C., and J.P. Hirdes. 2002. "Risk Factors for Serious Falls among Community-Based Seniors: Results from the National Population Health Survey." *Canadian Journal on Aging* 21(1): 103–16.

6   Foisy, P. 1995. "Variations in Age-Related Deficits among Episodic Memory Tasks: An Archival Study." *Canadian Journal on Aging* 14(4): 686–96.

10 Foot, D.K., and K.J. Gibson. 1993. "Population Aging in the Canadian Labour Force: Changes and Challenges." *Journal of Canadian Studies* 28(1): 59–74.

1,4,12 Foot, D.K., and D. Stoffman. 1998. *Boom, Bust, and Echo 2000: Profiting from the Demographic Shift in the New Millennium.* Toronto: Macfarlane Walter & Ross.

8   Forbes, D.A. 2001. "Canadian Community-Dwelling Young-Old and Old-Old: Determinants of Satisfaction with Health Care." *Canadian Journal on Aging* 20(1): 113–26.

8   Forbes, W.F., J.A. Jackson, and A.S. Kraus. 1987. *Institutionalization of the Elderly in Canada.* Toronto: Butterworths.

2   Foundations Project. 1980. "Foundations for Gerontological Education." *Gerontologist* 20: Part II.

5   Fox, M.T., and B.A. Gooding. 1998. "Physical Mobility and Social Integration: Their Relationship to the Well-Being of Older Canadians." *Canadian Journal on Aging* 17(4): 372–83.

11 Fox, P.L. 1995. "Environmental Modifications in the Homes of Elderly Canadians with Disabilities." *Disability and Rehabilitation: An International Multidisciplinary Journal* 17(1): 3–49.

5   Fozard, J.L. 1990. "Vision and Hearing." In J.E. Birren and K.W. Schaie, eds., *Handbook of the Psychology of Aging*, 3rd ed. San Diego: Academic Press.

6   France, A.I. 1990. "Psychology of Aging: Stability and Change in Intelligence and Personality." In K.F. Ferraro, ed., *Gerontology: Perspectives and Issues,* 87–109. New York: Springer.

7   Frankl, V. 1990. "Facing the Transitoriness of Human Existence." *Generations* 15(4): 7–10.

13 Frederick, J.A., and J.E. Fast. 1999. "Eldercare in Canada: Who Does How Much?" *Canadian Social Trends* (Autumn).

9   Freeman, A. 1994. "CPP Dips into Surplus Fund." *Globe and Mail,* April 21, B1–2.

7   French, S.E., M. Denton, A. Gafni, A. Joshi, J. Lian, P. Raina, C.J. Rosenthal, and D.J. Willison. 2000. "Independence of Older Persons: Meaning and Determinants." In F.T. Denton, D. Fretz, and B.G. Spencer, eds., *Independence and Economic Security in Old Age,* 59–84. Vancouver: UBC Press.

9   Frenken, H. 1995. "RRSPs: Unused Opportunities." *Perspectives* (Winter): 20–25.

7   Frideres, J. 1994. "The Future of Our Past: Native Elderly in Canadian Society." In

National Advisory Council on Aging, *Aboriginal Seniors' Issues*, 17–37. Cat. No. H71-2/1-15-1994E. Ottawa: Minister of Supply and Services.

4 Friedland, R.B., and L. Summer. 1999. *Demography Is Not Destiny*. Washington, DC: National Academy on an Aging Society.

13 Friend, R.A. 1996. "Older Lesbian and Gay People: A Theory of Successful Aging." In R. Berger, ed., *Gay and Grey: The Older Homosexual Man*, 2nd ed., 277–98. New York: Harrington Park.

5 Fries, James F. 1980. "Aging, Natural Death, and the Compression of Morbidity." *New England Journal of Medicine* 303: 130–36.

5 Fries, James F. 1986. "The Elimination of Premature Disease." In K. Dychtwald and J. MacLean, eds., *Wellness and Health Promotion for the Elderly*. Rockville, MD: Aspen.

5 Fries, James F. 1990. "Medical Perspectives upon Successful Aging." In Paul B. Baltes and Margaret M. Baltes, eds., *Successful Aging: Perspectives from the Behavioral Sciences*. Cambridge: Cambridge University Press.

5 Fries, J.F., and L.M. Crapo. 1981. *Vitality and Aging*. San Francisco: W.H. Freeman.

7 Fry, P.S. 2000. "Religious Involvement, Spirituality and Personal Meaning for Life: Existential Predictors of Psychological Well-Being in Community-Residing and Institutional Care Elders." *Aging and Mental Health* 4(4): 375–87.

13 Fullmer, E.M. 1995. "Challenging Biases against Families of Older Gays and Lesbians." In G.C. Smith, S.S. Tobin, E.A. Robertson-Tchabo, and P.W. Power, eds., *Strengthening Aging Families: Diversity in Practice and Policy*, 99–119. Thousand Oaks, CA: Sage.

2 Fullmer, E.M., D. Shenk, and L.J. Eastland. 1999. "Negating Identity: A Feminist Analysis of the Social Invisibility of Older Lesbians." *Journal of Women and Aging* 11(2/3): 131–48.

12 Furlong, M. 1997. "Creating Online Community for Older Adults." *Generations* 21(3): 33–35.

4 Gagan, D. 1983a. "Geographical and Social Mobility in Nineteenth-Century Ontario: A Microstudy." In P.W. Ward, ed., *The Social Development of Canada: Readings*. Richmond, BC: Open Learning Institute.

3,4 Gagan, D. 1983b. "Land, Population, and Social Change: The 'Critical Years' in Rural Canada West." In P.W. Ward, ed., *The Social Development of Canada: Readings*. Richmond, BC: Open Learning Institute.

10 Gall, T.L., and D.R. Evans. 2000. "Preretirement Expectations and the Quality of Life of Male Retirees in Later Retirement." *Canadian Journal of Behavioural Science* 32(3): 187–97.

13 Gallagher, E.M., and B. Hagen. 1996. "Outcome Evaluation of a Group Education and Support Program for Family Caregivers." *Gerontology and Geriatrics Education* 17(1): 33–50.

2 Garfinkel, H. 1967. *Studies in Ethnomethodology*. Englewood Cliffs, NJ: Prentice-Hall.

6 Gatz, M., and M.A. Smyer. 2001. "Mental Health and Aging at the Outset of the Twenty-First Century." In J.E. Birren and K.W. Schaie, eds., *Handbook of the Psychology of Aging*, 5th ed. San Diego: Academic Press.

10 Gauthier, Pierre. 1991. "Canada's Seniors." *Canadian Social Trends* (Autumn): 16–20.

12 Gauthier, P., and A. Haman. 1992. "Physical Fitness." *Canadian Social Trends* (Summer): 18–20.

6 Gauthier, S., I. McDowell, and G. Hill. 1990. "Canadian Study of Health and Aging (CaSHA)." *Psychiatry Journal of the University of Ottawa* 15(4): 227–29.

13 Gee, E.M. 1988. "The Changing Demography of Intergenerational Relations in Canada." Paper presented at the 17th Annual Scientific and Educational Meeting of the Canadian Association on Gerontology, Halifax, October.

7 Gee, E.M. 1990. "Preferred Timing of Women's Life Events: A Canadian Study." *International Journal of Aging and Human Development* 31(4): 279–94.

13 Gee, E.M. 1995a. "Families in Later Life." In R. Beaujot, E.M. Gee, F. Rajulton, and Z. Ravanera, eds., *Families over the Life Course: Current Demographic Analysis*. Statistics Canada. Ottawa: Minister of Industry.

9,10 Gee, E.M. 1995b. "Population Aging: A Contested Terrain of Social Policy." In E.M. Gee and G.M. Gutman, eds., *Rethinking Retirement*, 13–29. Vancouver: Gerontology Research Centre, Simon Fraser University.

1,4 Gee, E.M., and G.M. Gutman, eds. 2000. *The Overselling of Population Aging: Apocalyptic Demography, Intergenerational Challenges, and*

10   *Social Policy.* Don Mills, ON: Oxford University Press.

10   Gee, E.M., and M.M. Kimball. 1987. *Women and Aging.* Toronto: Butterworths.

4   Gee, E.M., K.M. Kobayashi, and S.G. Prus. 2003. *Examining the 'Healthy Immigrant Effect' in Later Life: Findings from the Canadian Community Health Survey.* SEDAP Research Paper No. 98. Hamilton, ON: SEDAP Research Program, McMaster University.

13   Gendron, C., L. Poitras, D.P. Dastoor, and G. Perodeau. 1996. "Cognitive-Behavioral Group Intervention for Spousal Caregivers: Findings and Clinical Considerations." *Clinical Gerontologist* 17(1): 3–19.

2,13   George, L.K. 1996. "Missing Links: The Case for a Social Psychology of the Life Course." *Gerontologist* 36(2): 248–55.

4   George, M.V., M.J. Norris, F. Nault, S. Loh, and S.Y. Dai. 1994. *Population Projections for Canada, Provinces and Territories 1993–2016.* Cat. No. 91-520. Ottawa: Ministry of Industry, Science and Technology.

4   Gerber, L.M. 1983. "Ethnicity Still Matters: Socio-Demographic Profiles of the Ethnic Elderly in Ontario." *Canadian Ethnic Studies* 15: 60–80.

14   Gesser, G., P.T.P. Wong, and G.T. Reker. 1986. "Death Attitudes across the Life-Span: The Development and Validation of the Death Attitude Profile (DAP)." Personal communication.

8   Gibbs, P. 1996. "How to Make Visits Count." *BC Caregiver News* 1(5): 4.

2   Gibson, D. 1996. "Broken Down by Age and Gender—'The Problem of Old Women' Redefined." *Gender and Society* 10(4): 433–48.

1   Gibson, H.B. 2000. "It Keeps Us Young." *Ageing and Society* 20 (Part 6): 773–79.

10   Gibson, K.J., W.J. Zerbe, and R.E. Franken. 1993. "The Influence of Rater and Ratee Age on Judgments of Work-Related Attributes." *Journal of Psychology* 127(3): 271–80.

7   Gibson, R.C. 1988. "Minority Aging Research: Opportunity and Challenge." *Gerontologist* 28: 559–60.

5   Gignac, M.A.M., C. Cott, and E.M. Badley. 2000. "Adaptation to Chronic Illness and Disability and Its Relationship to Perceptions of Independence and Dependence." *Journals of Gerontology Series B* 55(6): P362–72.

13   Gignac, M.A.M., E.K. Kelloway, and B.H. Gottlieb. 1996. "The Impact of Caregiving on Employment: A Mediational Model of Work–Family Conflict." *Canadian Journal on Aging* 15(4): 525–42.

6,8   Gilbart, E.E., and J.P. Hirdes. 2000. "Stress, Social Engagement, and Psychological Well-Being in Institutional Settings: Evidence Based on the Minimum Data Set 2.0." *Canadian Journal on Aging* 19 (Suppl. 2): 50–66.

3   Gillin, C.T. 1986. "Aging in the Developing World." Paper presented at the Canadian Sociology and Anthropology Annual Meeting. Winnipeg.

5   Gillis, K.J., and J.P. Hirdes. 1996. "The Quality of Life Implications of Health Practices among Older Adults: Evidence from the 1991 Canadian General Social Survey." *Canadian Journal on Aging* 15(2): 299–314.

9   Ginn, J., D. Street, and S. Arber. 2001. "Cross-National Trends in Women's Work." In J. Ginn, D. Street, and S. Arber, eds., *Women, Work, and Pensions: International Issues and Prospects,* 11–30. Buckingham, U.K.: Open University Press.

9   Ginn, J., D. Street, and S. Arber, eds. 2001. *Women, Work, and Pensions: International Issues and Prospects.* Buckingham, U.K.: Open University Press.

13   Giranda, M., J.E. Luk, and K.A. Atchison. 1999. "Social Networks of Elders without Children." *Journal of Gerontological Social Work* 31(1/2): 63–83.

5   Gitlin, L.N. 1995. "Why Older People Accept or Reject Assistive Technology." *Generations* 19(1): 41–46.

13   Gladstone, J.W. 1989. "Grandmother–Grandchild Contact: The Mediating Influence of the Middle Generation Following Marriage Breakdown and Remarriage." *Canadian Journal on Aging* 8: 355–65.

8   Gladstone, J.W. 1992. "Identifying the Living Arrangements of Elderly Married Couples in Long-Term Care Institutions." *Canadian Journal on Aging* 11: 184–96.

13   Gladstone, J.W. 1995. "The Marital Perceptions of Elderly Persons Living or Having a Spouse Living in a Long-Term Care Institution in Canada." *Gerontologist* 35(1): 52–60.

13   Gladstone, J., and E. Wexler. 2000. "Family Perspective of Family/Staff Interaction in

Long-Term Care Facilities." *Geriatric Nursing* 21(1): 16–19.

13 Gladstone, J., and E. Wexler. 2002a. "Exploring the Relationships between Families and Staff Caring for Residents in Long-Term Care Facilities: Family Members' Perspectives." *Canadian Journal on Aging* 21(1): 39–45.

13 Gladstone, J., and E. Wexler. 2002b. "The Development of Relationships between Families and Staff in Long-Term Care Facilities: Nurses' Perspectives." *Canadian Journal on Aging* 21(2): 217–28.

3 Glascock, A.P., and S.L. Feinman. 1981. "Social Asset or Social Burden: Treatment of the Aged in Non-Industrial Societies." In C.L. Fry, ed., *Dimensions: Aging, Culture, and Health.* New York: Praeger.

1 Glass, K.C. 1993. "Ethical Principles and Age-Based Rationing of Health Care." In National Advisory Council on Aging, *Ethics and Aging,* 69–83. Cat. No. H71-3/16-1993E. Ottawa: Minister of Supply and Services.

5 Glass, P.-Y. 1995. "He Didn't Know She'd Live Forever." *Winnipeg Free Press,* December 29, 1.

13 Glendenning, F. 1999. "Elder Abuse and Neglect in Residential Settings: The Need for Inclusiveness in Elder Abuse Research." *Journal of Elder Abuse and Neglect* 10(1–2): 1–11.

4 *Globe and Mail.* 1993. "Will We Still Feed Them, When They're 64?" Editorial, November 15.

8 Glor, E.D. 1991. "An Effective Evaluation of a Small-Scale Seniors Health Promotion Centre: A Case Study." *Canadian Journal on Aging* 10: 64–73.

6 Gold, D.P., D. Andres, J. Etezadi, T. Arbuckle, and A. Schwartzman. 1995. "Structural Equation Model of Intellectual Change and Continuity and Predictors of Intelligence in Older Men." *Psychology and Aging* 10(2): 294–303.

7 Gold, Y. 1980. "Ethnic and Cultural Aspects of Aging." Paper presented at the 9th Annual Scientific and Educational Meeting of the Canadian Association on Gerontology, Saskatoon.

13 Goldberg, D.L. 2003. "Grandparent–Grandchild Access: A Legal Analysis." Paper presented to Family, Children, and Youth Section, Department of Justice Canada. Minister of Justice and Attorney General of Canada.

6 Goldmeier, John. 1986. "Pets or People: Another Research Note." *Gerontologist* 26: 203–6.

13 Goodman, C. 1999a. "Intimacy and Autonomy in Long Term Marriage." *Journal of Gerontological Social Work* 32: 83–97.

10 Goodman, C. 1999b. "Retirement Patterns in Canada." *Horizons* 2(2): 16–17.

10 Goodwin, J.L., and M.Y.T. Chen. 1991. "From Pastor to Pensioner: A Study of Retired Canadian Protestant Clergy from he Continuity Perspective." *Journal of Religious Gerontology* 7(3): 69–79.

7 Gordon, S. 1976. *Lonely in America.* New York: Simon and Schuster.

14 Gorer, G. 1965. *Death, Grief, and Mourning in Contemporary Britain.* London: Cresset.

14 Gorer, G. 1967. *Death, Grief and Mourning.* New York: Anchor.

12 Gordon, S.A., T.J. Overend, and A.A. Vandervoort. 2001. "Country Line Dancing: An Aerobic Activity for Older Women?" *Journal of Aging and Physical Activity* 9(4): 364–71.

12 Gottlieb, B.H. 2002. "Older Volunteers: A Precious Resource under Pressure." *Canadian Journal on Aging* 21(1): 5–9.

13 Gottlieb, B.H., and J. Johnson. 2000. "Respite Programs for Caregivers of Persons with Dementia: A Review with Practice Implica-tions." *Aging and Mental Health* 4(2): 119–29.

13 Gottlieb, B.H., and K. Kelloway. 1993. "Eldercare and Employment." *Human Resources Management in Canada* (June): 597–604.

13 Gottlieb, B.H., E.K. Kelloway, and M. Fraboni. 1994. "Aspects of Eldercare That Place Employees at Risk." *Gerontologist* 34(6): 815–21.

7 Gould, R.L. 1978. *Transformations: Growth and Change in Adult Life.* New York: Simon and Schuster.

9 Government of Canada. 1982. *Better Pensions for Canadians (Green Paper).* Ottawa: Minister of Supply and Services.

13 Government of Canada. 1999. "Help Given to Children in the Parents' Senior Years." *Info-Age* 20 (January).

10 Gower, D. 1995. "Men Retiring Early: How Are They Doing?" *Perspectives* (Winter): 30–34.

12 Graham, D.F., I. Graham, and M.J. MacLean. 1991. "Going to the Mall: A Leisure Activity of Urban Elderly People." *Canadian Journal on Aging* 10(4): 345–58.

3 Graham, I.D., and P.M. Baker. 1989. "Status, Age, and Gender: Perceptions of Old and Young People." *Canadian Journal on Aging* 8: 255–67.

8 Graham, K., and K. Braun. 1999. "Concordance of Use of Alcohol and Other Substances among Older Adult Couples." *Addictive Behaviors* 24(6): 839–56.

13,14 Grand'Maison, J., and S. Lefebvre. 1996. *Sharing the Blessings: The Role of Seniors in Today's Society.* Trans. Jane Brierly. Sherbrooke: Mediaspaul.

12 Grant, B.C. 2002. "Physical Activity: Not a Popular Leisure Choice in Later Life." *Loisir et société/Society and Leisure* 25(2): 285–302.

1 Grant, M.J., A.S. Ross, C.M. Button, T.E. Hannah, and R. Hoskins. 2001. "Attitudes and Stereotypes about Attitudes across the Lifespan." *Social Behavior and Personality* 29(8): 749–62.

11 Grant, P.R., and B. Rice. 1983. "Transportation Problems of the Rural Elderly: A Needs Assessment." *Canadian Journal on Aging* 2: 107–24.

10 Gratton, B. 1993. "The Creation of Retirement: Families, Individuals, and the Social Security Movement." In K.W. Schaie and W.A. Achenbaum, eds., *Societal Impact on Aging: Historical Perspectives.* New York: Springer.

3 Greene, J.P., ed. 1965. *Diary of Colonel Landon Carter of Sabine Hall, 1752–1778.* 2 vols. Charlottesville, VA: University Press of Virginia.

1 Greenslade, V. 1986. "Evaluation of Postgraduate Gerontological Nursing Education." Unpublished manuscript.

3 Gregg, J. 2000. "Confronting an Aging World." *Washington Quarterly* 23(3): 213–24.

8 Gregor, F. 1997. "From Women to Women: Nurses, Informal Caregivers and the Gender Dimension of Health Care Reform in Canada." *Health and Social Care in the Community* 5(1): 30–36.

8 Griffin, R.L., and E. Vitro. 1998. "Overview of Therapeutic Touch and Its Application to Patients with Alzheimer's Disease." *American Journal of Alzheimer's Disease* 13(4): 211–16.

8 Gross, J., and C. Schwenger. 1981. *Health Care Costs for the Elderly in Ontario: 1976–2026.* Occasional Paper 11. Toronto: Ontario Economic Council.

13 Grossman, A.H. 1997. "The Virtual and Actual Identities of Older Lesbians and Gay Men." In M. Duberman, ed., *A Queer World: The Center for Lesbian and Gay Studies Reader,* 615–26. New York: New York University Press.

10 Gruber, J., and D. Wise. 1999a. "Social Security Programs and Retirement around the World." *Research in Labor Economics* 18: 1–40.

10 Gruber, J., and D. Wise. 1999b. "Social Security, Retirement Incentives, and Retirement Behavior: An International Perspective." *EBRI Issue Brief No. 209* (May): 1–22.

5 Grundy, E. 1984. "Mortality and Morbidity among the Old." *British Medical Journal* 288: 663–64.

13 Guberman, N. 1999. "Daughters-in-Law as Caregivers: How and Why Do They Come to Care?" *Journal of Women and Aging* 11(1): 85–102.

2,13 Guberman, N., and P. Maheu. 1999. "Combining Employment and Caregiving: An Intricate Juggling Act." *Canadian Journal on Aging* 18(1): 84–106.

2 Gubrium, J.F., and J.A. Holstein. 1997. *The New Language of Qualitative Methods.* New York: Oxford University Press.

3 Guemple, L. 1974. "The Dilemma of the Aging Eskimo." In C. Beattie and S. Crysdale, eds., *Sociology Canada: Readings,* 203–14. Toronto: Butterworths.

3 Guemple, L. 1977. "The Dilemma of the Aging Eskimo." In C. Beattie and S. Chrysdale, eds., *Sociology Canada: Readings,* 2nd ed. Toronto: Butterworths.

3 Guemple, L. 1980. "Growing Old in Inuit Society." In V.W. Marshall, ed., *Aging in Canada: Social Perspectives.* Toronto: Fitzhenry and Whiteside.

10 Guillemard, A.M. 1977. "The Call to Activity amongst the Old: Rehabilitation or Regimentation." In B.T. Wigdor, ed., *Canadian Gerontological Collection I.* Winnipeg: Canadian Association on Gerontology.

10 Guillemard, A.M. 1997. "Re-Writing Social Policy and Changes within the Life Course Organisation. A European Perspective." *Canadian Journal on Aging* 16(3): 441–64.

10 Guppy, N. 1989. "The Magic of 65: Issues and Evidence in the Mandatory Retirement Debate." *Canadian Journal on Aging* 8: 174–86.

11 Gutman, G.M. 1983. *The Long Term Impact of Multi-Level, Multi-Service Accommodation for Seniors.* Senior Citizen Housing Study Report No. 3. Ottawa: Canada Mortgage and Housing Corporation.

11 Gutman, G.M., ed. 1992. *Shelter and Care of Persons with Dementia.* Vancouver: Gerontology Research Centre, Simon Fraser University.

5 Gutman, G.M. 1998. "Introduction: Technology, Aging and Disability in Canada." In G.M. Gutman, ed., *Technology Innovation for an Aging Society: Blending Research, Public and Private Sectors,* 7–21. Vancouver: Gerontology Research Centre, Simon Fraser University.

5 Gutman, G.M. 1999a. *Aging, Technology, and Policy: An International Perspective.* Vancouver: Gerontology Research Centre and Programs, Simon Fraser University.

5 Gutman, G.M. 1999b. "Technology Innovation for an Aging Society: Application to Environmental Design." *Gerontology Research Centre News* 18(1): 3–5.

8 Gutman, G., C. Jackson, A.J. Stark, and B. McCashin. 1986. "Mortality Rates Five Years after Admission to a Long-Term Care Program." *Canadian Journal on Aging* 5: 9–17.

3,10 Haber, C. 1978. "Mandatory Retirement in Nineteenth-Century America: The Conceptual Basis for a New York Cycle." *Journal of Social History* 12: 77–96.

3 Haber, C. 1983. *Beyond Sixty-Five: The Dilemma of Old Age in America's Past.* Cambridge: Cambridge University Press.

3 Haber, C. 1993. "'And the Fear of the Poorhouse': Perceptions of Old Age Impoverishment in Early Twentieth-Century America." *Generations* (Spring/Summer): 46–50.

3 Haber, C., and B. Gratton. 1994. *Old Age and the Search for Security: An American Social History.* Bloomington: Indiana University Press.

8 Haber, D. 1999. *Health Promotion and Aging,* 2nd ed. New York: Springer.

13 Hagen, B., E.M. Gallagher, and S. Simpson. 1997. "Family Caregiver Education and Support Programs: Using Humanistic Approaches to Evaluate Program Effects." *Educational Gerontology* 23(2): 129–42.

13 Hagestad, G.O. 1985. "Continuity and Connectedness." In V.L. Bengtson and J.F. Robertson, eds., *Grandparenthood.* Beverly Hills: Sage.

7 Hagestad, G.O. 1990. "Social Perspectives on the Life Course." In R.H. Binstock and L.K. George, eds., *Handbook of Aging and the Social Sciences,* 3rd ed. San Diego: Academic Press.

13 Haines, V.A., and L.J. Henderson. 2002. "Targeting Social Support: A Network Assessment of the Convoy Model of Social Support." *Canadian Journal on Aging* 21(2): 243–56.

11 Haldemann, V., and A. Wister. 1992. "Environment and Aging." *Journal of Canadian Studies* 28(1): 30–44.

7 Hall, B.L. 1993. "Elderly Vietnamese Immigrants: Family and Community Connections." *Community Alternatives* 5(2): 81–96.

13 Hall, C.M. 1999. *The Special Mission of Grandparents: Hearing, Seeing, Telling.* Westport, CT: Greenwood.

7 Hall, M., and B. Havens. "Social Isolation and Social Loneliness." In *Writing in Gerontology: Mental Health and Aging,* No. 18, 33–44. Ottawa: National Advisory Council on Aging.

8 Hall, R., and P.C. Coyte. 2001. "Determinants of Home Care Utilization: Who Uses Home Care in Ontario?" *Canadian Journal on Aging* 20(2): 175–92.

11 Hallman, B.C., and A.E. Joseph. 1997. "Housing the Rural Elderly: A Place for Abbeyfield?" In L.A. Patalan, ed., *Shelter and Service Issues for Aging Populations: International Perspectives,* 83–103. New York: Haworth Press.

13 Hallman, B.C., and A.E. Joseph. 1999. "Getting There: Mapping the Gendered Geography of Caregiving to Elderly Relatives." *Canadian Journal on Aging* 18(4): 397–414.

14 Hamel, C.F., L.W. Guse, P.G. Hawranik, J.B. Bond. 2002. "Advance Directives and Community-Dwelling Older Adults." *Western Journal of Nursing Research* 24(2): 143–58.

11 Hamilton, K., and T. Brehaut. 1992. *Older Women: A Study of the Housing and Support Service Needs of Older "Single" Women.* A Report for the Canada Mortgage and

8 Housing Corporation. Charlottetown: Renaissance Communications.

8 Hamilton, N., and T. Bhatti. 1996. *Population Health Promotion: An Integrated Model of Population Health and Health Promotion.* Ottawa: Health Promotion Development Division, Health Canada.

12 Hanley, M. 1999. "Grandma's Leap of Faith (from a Plane)," *Hamilton Spectator*, July 7, A12.

13 Hamon, R.R. 1995. "Parents as Resources When Adult Children Divorce." *Journal of Divorce and Remarriage* 23(1/2): 171–83.

13 Harbison, J. 1999a. "Models of Intervention for 'Elder Abuse and Neglect': A Canadian Perspective on Ageism, Participation, and Empowerment." *Journal of Elder Abuse and Neglect* 10(3–4): 1–17.

13 Harbison, J. 1999b. "Changing Career of 'Elder Abuse and Neglect' as a Social Problem in Canada: Learning from Feminist Frameworks?" *Journal of Elder Abuse and Neglect* 11(4): 59–80.

2 Harbison, J., and M. Morrow. 1998. "Re-examining the Social Construction of 'Elder Abuse and Neglect': A Canadian Perspective." *Ageing and Society* 18: 691–711.

13 Harlton, S.V., N. Keating, and J. Fast. 1998. "Defining Eldercare for Policy and Practice: Perspectives Matter." *Family Relations* 47(3): 281–88.

11 Harper, I. 1984. *Housing Options for the Elderly in the Capital Region: Sheltered Housing and Other Alternatives.* Victoria: Capital Regional Hospital District, Hospital and Health Planning Commission.

13 Harris, P.B. 1998. "Listening to Caregiving Sons: Misunderstood Realities." *Gerontologist* 38(3): 342–52.

6 Harrison, C. 1993. "Personhood, Dementia and Integrity of Life." *Canadian Journal on Aging* 12(4): 428–40.

14 Harvard Medical School. 1968. "A Definition of Irreversible Coma: Report of the Ad Hoc Committee of the Harvard Medical School to Examine the Definition of Brain Death." *Journal of the American Medical Association* 205(5): 677–79.

12 Harvey, A.S., K. Marshall, and J.A. Frederick. 1991. *Where Does Time Go?* Cat. No. 11-612E, No. 4. Ottawa: Ministry of Industry, Science and Technology.

13 Hatch, R.G. 1995. *Aging and Cohabitation.* New York: Garland.

8 Havens, B. 1980. "Differentiation of Unmet Needs Using Analysis by Age/Sex Cohorts." In V.W. Marshall, ed., *Aging in Canada.* Toronto: Fitzhenry and Whiteside.

2,8 Havens, B. 1995a. "Long-Term Care Diversity within the Care Continuum." *Canadian Journal on Aging* 14(2): 245–62.

2 Havens, B. 1995b. "Overview of Longitudinal Research on Aging." *Canadian Journal on Aging* 14 (Suppl. 1): 119–34.

8 Havens, B. 1995c. "Canadian Long-Term Care Use: What Is the Future?" In S.R. Ingman, X. Pei, C.D. Ekstrom, H.J. Friedsam, and K.R. Bartlett, eds., *An Aging Population, an Aging Planet, and a Sustainable Future.* Denton, TX: Texas Institute for Research and Education on Aging, University of North Texas.

8,11 Havens, B., and D. Bray. 1996. "International Comparisons of Long-Term Care: Canada, with Specific Reference to Manitoba." *Canadian Journal on Aging* 15 (Suppl. 1): 31–45.

7 Havens, B., and N.L. Chappell. 1983. "Triple Jeopardy: Age, Sex and Ethnicity." *Canadian Ethnic Studies* 15: 119–32.

12 Hawkins, Terry. 1980. *Never Too Old: A Report to the Northumberland Newcastle Board of Education on the Educational Needs of Senior Adults Living in the Area Served by Its Schools.* Northumberland Newcastle, ON: Board of Education.

13 Hawranik, P. 2002. "Inhome Service Use by Caregivers and Their Elders: Does Cognitive Status Make a Difference?" *Canadian Journal on Aging* 21(2): 257–72.

4 Hayward, L.M. 2001. *Mid-Life Patterns and the Residential Mobility of Older Men.* SEDAP Research Paper No. 64. Hamilton, ON: McMaster University.

10 He, Y.H., A. Colantonio, and V.W. Marshall. 2003. "Later-Life Career Disruption and Self-Rated Health: An Analysis of General Social Survey Data." *Canadian Journal on Aging* 22(1): 45–57.

10 Health and Welfare Canada. 1979. *Retirement Age.* Ottawa: Minister of Supply and Services.

8,10 Health and Welfare Canada. 1982a. *Canadian Governmental Report on Aging.* Ottawa: Minister of Supply and Services.

14 Health and Welfare Canada. 1982b. *Palliative Care in Canada*. Ottawa: Minister of Supply and Services.

6 Health and Welfare Canada. 1984. *Alzheimer's Disease: A Family Information Handbook*. Ottawa: Minister of Supply and Services.

8 Health and Welfare Canada. 1988. *Active Health Report: The Active Health Report on Seniors*. Cat No. H-39-124/1988E. Ottawa: Minister of Supply and Services.

6 Health and Welfare Canada. 1991. *Mental Health Problems among Canada's Seniors: Demographic and Epidemiologic Considerations*. Ottawa: Supply and Services.

12 Health and Welfare Canada. 1993. *Ageing and Independence: Overview of a National Survey*. Cat. No. H88-3/13-1993E. Ottawa: Minister of Supply and Services.

6 Health and Welfare Canada and Statistics Canada. 1981. *The Health of Canadians (The Canada Health Survey)*. Cat. No. 82-538E. Ottawa: Minister of Supply and Services.

7,14 Health Canada. 1994. *Suicide in Canada: Update of the Report of the Task Force on Suicide in Canada*. Cat. No. 39-107/1995E. Ottawa: Minister of National Health and Welfare.

5 Health Canada. 1999a. *Canada's Physical Activity Guide to Healthy Active Living for Older Adults: Handbook*. Ottawa: Canada's Communications Group.

8 Health Canada. 1999b. "Canada's Seniors. No. 12: Living in Institutions." http://www.hc-sc.gc.ca/seniors-aines/pubs/factoids/1999/pdf/entire_e.pdf, accessed on July 26, 2004.

8 Health Canada. 1999c. "Canada's Seniors. No. 13: Living in Institutions—In All Provinces." http://www.hc-sc.gc.ca/seniors-aines/pubs/factoids/1999/pdf/entire_e.pdf, accessed on July 26, 2004.

4 Health Canada. 1999d. "Many Seniors in All Provinces." *Canada's Seniors, Snapshot No. 3*. http://www.hc-sc.gc.ca/seniors-aines/pubs/factoids/1999/pdf/entire_e.pdf, accessed on July 26, 2004.

1,4 Health Canada. 2001a. "Canada's Seniors. No.1: A Growing Population." http://www.hc-sc.gc.ca/seniors-aines/pubs/factoids/2001/ no01_e.htm, accessed on December 27, 2003.

4 Health Canada. 2001b. "Canada's Seniors. No. 2: Canada's Oldest Seniors." http://www.hc-sc.gc.ca/seniors-aines/pubs/factoids/2001/no02_e.htm, accessed on December 27, 2003.

10 Health Canada. 2001c. "Canada's Seniors. No. 9: Decline in Employment among Men Aged 55 to 64." http://www.hc-sc.gc.ca/seniors-aines/pubs/factoids/2001/no09_e.htm, accessed on August 11, 2004.

12 Health Canada. 2001d. "Canada's Seniors. No. 24: Travel in Canada and around the World." http://www.hc-sc.gc.ca/seniors-aines-pubs/factoids/2001/no24_e.htm, accessed on August 17, 2004.

5,9 Health Canada. 2002a. *Canada's Aging Population*. Cat. No. H39-608/2002E. Ottawa: Minister of Public Works and Government Services.

5 Health Canada. 2002b. *Dare to Age Well!: Healthy Aging, Physical Activity and Older Adults*. Cat. No. H39-612/2002-4E. Ottawa: Minister of Public Works and Government Services Canada.

5 Health Canada. 2002c. *Healthy Aging: Tobacco Use and Smoking Cessation among Seniors*. Cat. No. H39-612/2002-E. Minister of Public Works and Government Services Canada.

6 Health Canada. 2002d. *A Report on Mental Illnesses in Canada*. Ottawa: Health Canada Editorial Board.

8 Heath, Y., and R. Gifford. 2001. "Post-Occupancy Evaluation of Therapeutic Gardens in a Multi-Level Care Facility for the Aged." *Activities, Adaptation and Aging* 25(2): 21–43.

8 Hébert, R. 2003. "Yes to Home Care, But Don't Forget Older Canadians." *Canadian Journal on Aging* 22(1): 9–10.

8 Hébert, R., N. Dubuc, M. Buteau, J. Desrosiers, G. Bravo, L. Trottier, C. St-Hilaire, and C. Roy. 2001. "Resources and Costs Associated with Disabilities of Elderly People Living at Home and in Institutions." *Canadian Journal on Aging* 20(1): 1–21.

13 Hébert, R., L. Lévesque, J. Vézina, J.P. Lavoie, F. Ducharme, C. Gendron, M. Préville, L. Voyer, and M.F. Dubois. 2003. "Efficacy of a Psychoeducative Group Program for Caregivers of Demented Persons Living at Home: A Randomized Controlled Trial." *Journals of Gerontology Series B* 58(1): S58–67.

13 Heidemann, B., O. Suhomlinova, and A.M. O'Rand. 1998. "Economic Independence, Economic Status, and Empty Nest in Midlife Marital Disruption." *Journal of Marriage and the Family* 60: 219–31.

12   Heinzl, J. 1995. "What We're Buying," *Globe and Mail,* July 8, B19.

3   Hendricks, J. 1982. "The Elderly in Society: Beyond Modernization." *Social Science History* 6: 321–45.

2   Hendricks, J. 1997. "Bridging Contested Terrain: Chaos or Prelude to a Theory." *Canadian Journal on Aging* 16(2): 197–217.

5,12   Hendrix, C.C., and K.M. Sakauye. 2001. "Teaching Elderly Individuals on Computer Use." *Journal of Gerontological Nursing* 27(6): 47–53.

4   Henripin, J. 1972. *Trends and Factors of Fertility in Canada.* Ottawa: Statistics Canada (Dominion Bureau of Statistics).

3   Henripin, J. 1994. "The Financial Consequences of Population Aging." *Canadian Public Policy* 20(1): 78–94.

4   Henripin, J., and Y. Peron. 1972. "The Demographic Transition of the Province of Quebec." In D. Glass and R. Revelle, eds., *Population and Social Change.* London: Edward Arnold.

6   Hermann, N. 1991. "Confusion and Dementia in the Elderly." In National Advisory Council on Aging, *Mental Health and Aging,* 31–48. Ottawa: National Advisory Council on Aging.

6   Hertzog, C. 1996. "Research Design in Studies of Aging and Cognition." In J.E. Birren and K.W. Schaie, eds., *Handbook of the Psychology of Aging,* 4th ed., 24–37. San Diego: Academic Press.

3   Hess, B., and E. Markson. 1987. "The Dega and the Nacirema." In *Growing Old in America,* 3rd ed. New Brunswick, NJ: Transaction Publishers.

8   Hicks, V. 1999. "The Evolution of Public and Private Health Care Spending in Canada, 1960–1997." Ottawa: Canadian Institute for Health Information, Health Action Coalition, Health Canada.

13   Hightower, J., M.J. Smith, C.A. Ward-Hall, and H.C. Hightower. 1999. "Meeting the Needs of Abused Older Women? A British Columbia and Yukon Transition House Survey." *Journal of Elder Abuse and Neglect* 11(4): 39–57.

13   Hillman, J.L., and G. Stricker. 1996. "College Students' Attitudes toward Elderly Sexuality: A Two Factor Solution." *Canadian Journal on Aging* 14(4): 543–58.

13   Hilton, J.M., and D.P. Macari. 1997. "Grandparent Involvement Following Divorce: A Comparison in Single-Mother and Single-Father Families." *Journal of Divorce and Remarriage* 28(1/2): 203–24.

8   Hirdes, J.P., and K.S. Brown. 1996. "A Survival Analysis of Institutional Relocation in a Chronic Care Hospital." *Canadian Journal on Aging* 15(4): 514–24.

8   Hirdes, J.P., K.S. Brown, W.F. Forbes, D. Vigoda, and L. Crawford. 1986. "The Association between Self-Reported Income and Perceived Health Based on the Ontario Longitudinal Study of Aging." *Canadian Journal on Aging* 6: 189–204.

13   Hirdes, J.P., and L.A. Strain. 1995. "The Balance of Exchange in Instrumental Support with Network Members Outside the Household." *Journals of Gerontology Series B* 50(3): S134–42.

11   Hodge, G. 1987. "Assisted Housing for Ontario's Rural Elderly: Shortfalls in Product and Location." *Canadian Journal on Aging* 6: 141–54.

11   Hodge, G., and L. McKay. 1992. *Small Town Seniors and Their Freedom to Move.* Final report on Seniors' Independence Project No. 4687-9-88/029. Vancouver: Gerontology Research Centre, Simon Fraser University.

13   Hodgson, L.G. 1995. "Adult Grandchildren and Their Grandparents: The Enduring Bond."" In J. Hendricks, ed., *The Ties of Later Life,* 155–70. Amityville, NY: Baywood.

5   Hoenig, H., D.H. Taylor, Jr., and F.A. Sloan. 2003. "Does Assistive Technology Substitute for Personal Assistance among the Disabled Elderly?" *American Journal of Public Health* 93(2): 330–37.

5   Hogan, D.B., E.M. Ebly, and T.S. Fung. 1999. "Disease, Disability, and Age in Cognitively Intact Seniors: Results from the Canadian Study of Health and Aging." *Journals of Gerontology Series A* 54(2): M77–82.

13   Holladay, S., D. Denton, D. Harding, M. Lee, R. Lackovich, and M. Coleman. 1997. "Granddaughters' Accounts of the Influence of Parental Mediation on Relational Closeness with Maternal Grandmothers." *International Journal of Aging and Human Development* 45(1): 23–38.

13   Holladay, S., R. Lackovich, M. Lee, M. Coleman, D. Harding, and D. Denton. 1998. "(Re)constructing Relationships with Grandparents: A Turning Point Analysis of

6 Granddaughters' Relational Development and Maternal Grandmothers." *International Journal of Aging and Human Development* 46(4): 287–303.

8 Hollander, M.J. 2001. *Comparative Cost Analysis of Home Care and Residential Care Services.* http://www.homecarestudy.com/reports/summaries/ss01-es.html, accessed on July 12, 2003.

8 Hollander, M.J., and N. Chappell. 2002. *Overview of the National Evaluation of the Cost-Effectiveness of Home Care.* Victoria: Hollander Analytical Services and the Centre on Aging at the University of Victoria. http://www.homecarestudy.com/overview/index.html#cost, accessed on July 12, 2003.

7 Holmen, K., et al. 1992. "Loneliness among Elderly People Living in Stockholm: A Population Study." *Journal of Advanced Nursing* 17(1): 43–51.

3 Holmes, E.R., and L.D. Holmes. 1995. *Other Cultures, Elder Years.* 2nd ed. Thousand Oaks, CA: Sage.

6 Holt, J. 1978. *Never Too Late.* New York: Delacorte Press.

7 Holzberg, C.S. 1981. "Cultural Gerontology: Toward an Understanding of Ethnicity and Aging." *Culture* 1: 110–22.

7 Holzberg, C.S. 1982. "Ethnicity and Aging: Anthropological Perspectives on More Than Just the Minority Elderly." *Gerontologist* 22: 249–57.

2 Homans, George C. 1961. *Social Behaviour: Its Elementary Forms.* New York: Harcourt Brace Jovanovich.

12 Homebound Learning Opportunities. 1989. "1988–1989 Program Statistics and Comments about HLO." Personal communication.

2 Hooyman, N.R., C.V. Browne, R. Ray, and V. Richardson. 2002. "Feminist Gerontology and the Life Course: Policy, Research, and Teaching Issues." *Gerontology and Geriatrics Education* 22(4): 3–26.

1 Hooyman, N.R., and H.A. Kiyak. 1993. *Social Gerontology: A Multidisciplinary Perspective,* 3rd ed. Boston: Allyn and Bacon.

12 Horgas, A.L., H-U. Wilms, and M.M. Baltes. 1998. "Daily Life in Very Old Age: Everyday Activities as Expression of Successful Living." *Gerontologist* 38(5): 556–68.

6 Horn, J.L. 1978. "Human Ability Systems." In P.B. Baltes, ed., *Life-Span Development and Behavior.* Vol. 1. New York: Academic Press.

6 Horn, J.L., and R.B. Cattell. 1966. "Age Differences in Primary Mental Ability Factors." *Journal of Gerontology* 21(2): 210–20.

6 Horn, J.L., and R.B. Cattell. 1967. "Age Differences in Fluid and Crystallized Intelligence." *Acta Psychologica* 26 (2): 107–29.

11 Hough, G.S. 1981. *Tenant Receptiveness: Family and Senior Citizen Mixing in Public Housing.* Toronto: Ministry of Municipal Affairs and Housing, Policy and Program Development Secretariat.

9 House of Commons Canada. 1983. *Report of the Parliamentary Task Force on Pension Reform* (Frith Commission). Ottawa: Supply and Services Canada.

9 Hudson, D. 2003. "RRSP Contribution Limits." http://www.rrsp.org/contrlimit.htm, accessed on August 24, 2003.

2 Hudson, R.B. 1999. "The Evolution of the Welfare State: Shifting Rights and Responsibilities for the Old." In M. Minkler and C.L. Estes, eds., *Critical Gerontology: Perspectives from Political and Moral Economy*, 329–43. Amityville, NY: Baywood.

3 Hufton, O. 1975. *The Poor in Eighteenth-Century France.* Oxford: Oxford University Press.

7 Hughes, E.C., and H.M. Hughes. 1952. *Where Peoples Meet.* Glencoe, IL: Free Press.

6 Hultsch, D.F., and F. Deutsch. 1981. *Adult Development and Aging: A Life-Span Perspective.* New York: McGraw-Hill.

6 Hultsch, D.F., and R.A. Dixon. 1983. "The Role of Pre-Experimental Knowledge in Text Processing in Adulthood." *Experimental Aging Research* 9(1): 7–22.

6 Hultsch, D.F., and R.A. Dixon. 1990. "Learning and Memory in Aging." In J.E. Birren and K.W. Schaie, eds., *Handbook of the Psychology of Aging*, 3rd ed. San Diego: Academic Press.

6 Hultsch, D.F., C. Hertzog, B.J. Small, L. McDonald-Miszczak, and R.A. Dixon. 1992. "Short-Term Longitudinal Change in Cognitive Performance in Later Life." *Psychology and Aging* 7(4): 571–84.

5 Hum, D., and W. Simpson. 2002. "Disability Onset among Aging Canadians: Evidence from Panel Data." *Canadian Journal on Aging* 21(1): 117–36.

3 *Human Behavior Magazine.* 1977. "Retirement to the Porch." In S.H. Zarit, ed., *Readings in*

Aging and Death: Contemporary Perspectives.
New York: Harper and Row.

10   Human Resources Development Canada.
2001. "Income Security Programs: Evaluation
of Public and Private Financial Incentives for
Retirement." SP-AH087-05-01E. http://
www11.hrdc-drhc.gc.ca/pls/edd/ EPPFI_
221000.htm, accessed on October 19, 2003.

4,9   Human Resources Development Canada.
2003a. "Income Security Programs: Table of
Rates in Effect July–September 2003."
http://www.hrdc-drhc.gc.ca/isp/oas/
tabrates2003.pdf, accessed on August 24, 2003.

9   Human Resources Development Canada.
2003b. "The ISP Stats Book: Statistics Related
to Income Security Programs." http://
www.sdc.gc.ca/en/isp/statistics/pdf/
ispstatbook2003.pdf, accessed on August 10,
2004.

14   Humphry, D. 2000. *Supplement to Final Exit.*
Junction City, OR: Norris Lane Press.

3   Ikels, C. 1981. "The Coming of Age in Chinese
Society: Traditional Patterns and Contemporary
Hong Kong." In C.L. Fry, ed., *Dimensions:
Aging, Culture, and Health.* New York: Praeger.

5   "Impact of Smoking on Life Expectancy and
Disability." 2001. *The Daily*, June 22.
http://www.statcan.ca/english/edu/feature/
smk.htm, accessed on November 24, 2003; see
also http://www.statcan.ca/Daily/English/
010622/d010622a.htm.

13   Ingram, P. 1996. "Senior Suffers Abuse of
Trust." *Winnipeg Free Press*, January 11, A6.

14   Institute of Medicine. 1997. *Approaching
Death.* Washington, DC: National Academy
Press.

2   Inter-Council Program Directorate. 1988.
*Open Letter and Call for Proposal Submissions
for Networks of Centres of Excellence.* Ottawa:
Government of Canada.

12   Iso-Ahola, S.E. 1989. "Motivation for Leisure."
In E.L. Jackson and T. Burton, eds.,
Understanding Leisure and Recreation. State
College, PA: Venture Publishing.

12   Iso-Ahola, S.E. 1993. "Leisure Lifestyles and
Health." In D. Compton and S.E. Iso-Ahola,
eds., *Leisure and Mental Health.* Park City,
UT: Family Development Resources Inc.

13   Iwasiw, C., D. Goldenberg, N. Bol, and E.
MacMaster. 2003. "Resident and Family
Perspectives: The First Year in a Long-Term

Care Facility." *Journal of Gerontological Nursing*
29(1): 45–54.

12   Jaberg, S.J. 1996. "Internet Comes to the
Nursing Home." *Nursing Homes Long Term
Care Management* 45(1): 15–16.

8   Jackson, M.F. 1983. "Day Care for
Handicapped Elders: An Evaluation Study."
Canadian Journal of Public Health 74:
348–51.

1   Jacobs, B. 1990. "Aging and Politics." In Robert
H. Binstock and Linda K. George, eds.,
Handbook of Aging and the Social Sciences, 3rd
ed. San Diego: Academic Press.

13   Jacobs, R.J., L.A. Rasmussen, and M.M.
Hohman. 1999. "The Social Support Needs of
Older Lesbians, Gay Men, and Bisexuals."
Journal of Gay and Lesbian Social Services 9(1):
1–30.

13   Jacoby, S. 1999. "Great Sex: What's Age Got to
Do with It?" *Modern Maturity* (October): 41ff.

6   Jacquish, G.A., and R.E. Ripple. 1981.
"Cognitive Creative Abilities and Self-Esteem
across the Adult Life-Span." *Human
Development* 24: 110–19.

13   Jerrome, D. 1996. "Continuity and Change in
the Study of Family Relationships." *Ageing and
Society* 16(1): 93–104.

5   Jessome, J., C. Parks, and M. MacLellan. 2001.
"Everyday Technology and Older Adults:
Friends or Foes?" In J. Jessome, C. Parks, and
M. MacLellan, eds., *Seniors and Technology*,
15–18. Cat. No. 0-662-30932-4. Ottawa:
Minister of Public Works and Government
Services Canada.

13   Joffres, C. 2002. "Barriers to Residential
Planning: Perspectives from Selected Older
Parents Caring for Adult Offrspring with
Lifelong Disabilities." *Canadian Journal on
Aging* 21(2): 303–11.

13   Johnson, B. 1997. "Older Adults' Suggestions
for Health Care Providers Regarding
Discussions of Sex." *Geriatric Nursing* 18:
65–66.

10   Johnson, E.S., and J.B. Williamson. 1987.
"Retirement in the United States." In K.S.
Markides and C.L. Cooper, eds., *Retirement in
Industrialized Societies.* New York: Wiley.

12   Johnston, D.W. 1999. *Cyberseniors: Exploring
the Use of Communication and Information
Technologies by Older Adults.* M.A. thesis,
University of Calgary, Graduate Program in
Communication Studies.

14   Joint Statement on Terminal Illness. 1984. "A Protocol for Health Professionals Regarding Resuscitation Intervention for the Terminally Ill." *Canadian Nurse* 80(6): 24.

6   Jones, H.E., and H.S. Conrad. 1933. "The Growth and Decline of Intelligence." *Genetic Psychology Monographs* 12: 223–98.

11   Joseph, A.E., and A.M. Fuller. 1991. "Towards an Integrative Perspective on the Housing, Services and Transportation Implications of Rural Aging." *Canadian Journal on Aging* 10: 127–48.

13   Joseph, A.E., and B.C. Hallman. 1996. "Caught in the Triangle: The Influence of Home, Work, and Elder Location on Work–Family Balance." *Canadian Journal on Aging* 15(3): 393–412.

11   Joseph, A.E., and A. Martin-Matthews. 1993. "Growing Old in Aging Communities." *Journal of Canadian Studies* 28(1): 14–29.

7   Jung, C.G. 1976. "The Stages of Life." In J. Campbell, ed., *The Portable Jung.* Harmondsworth, U.K.: Penguin.

13   Jutras, S., and J.-P. Lavoie. 1995. "Living with an Impaired Elderly Person: The Informal Caregiver's Physical and Mental Health." *Journal of Aging and Health* 7(1): 46–73.

13   Kahn, R.L., and T.C. Antonucci. 1980. "Convoys over the Life Course: Attachments, Roles, and Social Support." *Life-Span Development and Behavior* 3: 253–86.

11   Kaill, R.C. 1980. "Housing Canada's Aging." *Essence* 4: 79–86.

4   Kalbach, W.E., and W.W. McVey. 1979. *The Demographic Bases of Canadian Society*, 2nd ed. Toronto: McGraw-Hill Ryerson.

14   Kalish, R.A. 1963. "An Approach to the Study of Death Attitudes." *American Behavioral Scientist* 6: 68–70.

1   Kalish, R.A. 1979. "The New Ageism and the Failure Models: A Polemic." *Gerontologist* 19: 398–402.

14   Kane, R.L., J. Wales, L. Bernstein, A. Leibowitz, and S. Kaplan. 1984. "A Randomized Controlled Trial of Hospice Care." *Lancet* 1: 890–94.

5   Kaplan, D. 1997. "Access to Technology: Unique Challenges for People with Disabilities." *Generations* 21(3): 24–27.

2   Karlawish, J. 2004. "Ethics of Research in Dementia." In S. Gauthier, P. Scheltens, and J.L. Cummings, eds., *Alzheimer's Disease and Related Disorders Annual 2004*, 123–36. London: Martin Dunitz.

14   Kastenbaum, R.J. 1999. "Foreword." In B. de Vries, ed., *End of Life Issues,* xv–xvii. New York: Springer.

14   Kastenbaum, R.J. 2001. *Death, Society, and Human Experience.* Boston: Allyn and Bacon.

3   Kastenbaum, R.J., and B. Ross. 1975. "Historical Perspectives on Care." In J.G. Howells, ed., *Modern Perspectives in the Psychiatry of Old Age.* New York: Brunner/Mazel.

6   Katz, I.R. 1999. "Expanding the Place of Geriatric Mental Health within Health Systems: Integrated Care, Prevention, and Rehabilitation." *Gerontologist* 39: 626–30.

3   Katz, M.B. 1975. *The People of Hamilton, Canada West: Family and Class in a Mid-Nineteenth-Century City.* Cambridge, MA: Harvard University Press.

3   Katz, S. 1996. *Disciplining Old Age: The Formation of Gerontological Knowledge.* Charlottesville, VA: University Press of Virginia.

1   Katz, S., and B. Marshall. 2003. "New Sex for Old: Lifestyle Consumerism and the Ethics of Aging Well." *Journal of Aging Studies* 17(1): 3–16.

1   Kaufert, P.A., and M. Lock. 1997. "Medicalization of Women's Third Age." *Journal of Psychosomatic Obstetrics and Gynaecology* 18: 81–86.

6   Kausler, D.H. 1982. *Experimental Psychology and Human Aging.* New York: Wiley.

10   Kaye, L.W., and A. Monk. 1984. "Sex Role Traditions and Retirement from Academe." *Gerontologist* 24: 420–26.

2   Kayser-Jones, J., and B.A. Koenig. 1994. "Ethical Issues." In J.F. Gubrium and A. Sankar, eds., *Qualitative Methods in Aging Research*, 15–32. Thousand Oaks, CA: Sage.

11   Keating, N.C. 1991. *Aging in Rural Canada.* Toronto: Butterworths.

3   Keating, N.C. 1996. "Legacy, Aging, and Succession in Farm Families." *Generations* 20(3): 61–64.

13   Keating, N.C., J.E. Fast, I.A. Connidis, M.J. Penning, and J. Keefe. 1997. "Bridging Policy and Research in Eldercare." *Canadian Journal on Aging/Canadian Public Policy* 16 (Suppl.): 22–41.

8   Keating, N.C., J.E. Fast, D. Dosman, and J. Eales. 2001. "Services Provided by Informal and Formal Caregivers to Seniors in Residential Continuing Care." *Canadian Journal on Aging* 20(1): 23–45.

13   Keating, N.C., J.E. Fast, J. Frederick, K. Cranswick, and C. Perrier. 1999. *Eldercare in Canada: Context, Content, and Consequences.* Cat. No. 89-570-XPE. Ottawa: Minister of Industry.

10   Keating, N.C., and B. Jeffrey. 1983. "Work Careers of Ever Married and Never Married Retired Women." *Gerontologist* 23: 416–21.

13   Keefe, J.M., and P. Fancey. 1997. "Financial Compensation or Home Help Services: Examining Differences among Program Recipients." *Canadian Journal on Aging* 16(2): 254–78.

13   Keefe, J.M., and P. Fancey. 2000. "Care Continues: Responsibility for Elderly Relatives Before and After Admission to a Long-Term Care Facility." *Family Relations* 49(3): 235–44.

13   Keefe, J.M., and P.J. Fancey. 2002. "Work and Eldercare: Reciprocity between Older Mothers and Their Employed Daughters." *Canadian Journal on Aging* 21(2): 229–41.

13   Keefe, J.M., and S. Medjuck. 1997. "The Contribution of Long-Term Economic Costs to Predicting Strain among Employed Women Caregivers." *Journal of Women and Aging* 9(3): 3–25.

13   Keefe, J.M., C. Rosenthal, and F. Béland. 2000. "Impact of Ethnicity on Helping Older Relatives." *Canadian Journal on Aging* 19: 317–42.

8   Kelk, D. 1989. "CRD Quick-Response Team Keeps Woman, 89, Mobile." *Victoria Times-Colonist,* February 4.

5   Keller, H.H., T. Ostbye, E. Bright-See, and M.K. Campbell. 1999. "Activity Limitation and Food Intake in Community-Living Seniors." *Canadian Journal on Aging* 18(1): 47–63.

11   Kelley, M.L., and M.J. MacLean. 1997. "I Want to Live Here for the Rest of My Life: The Challenge of Case Management for Rural Seniors." *Journal of Case Management* 6(4): 174–82.

14   Kelly, J.L., G. Elphick, V. Mepham, and D.W. Molloy. 1989. *Let Me Decide.* Hamilton: McMaster University Press.

12   Kelly, J.R., M.W. Steinkamp, and J.R. Kelly. 1987. "Later-Life Satisfaction: Does Leisure Contribute?" *Leisure Sciences* 9: 189–200.

8   Kelly, L.E., V.J. Knox, and W.L. Gekoski. 1998. "Women's Views of Institutional versus Community-Based Long-Term Care." *Research on Aging* 20(2): 218–45.

12   Kelly, P. 1987. "Learning Begins at Home for Shut-In Seniors." *Seniors Today,* December 30.

13   Kemp, C. 2003. "The Social and Demographic Contours of Contemporary Grandparent-hood: Mapping Patterns in Canada and the United States." *Journal of Comparative Family Studies* 34(2): 187–212.

13   Kemp, C. 2004. "'Grand' Expectations: The Experiences of Grandparents and Adult Grandchildren." *Canadian Journal of Sociology* (forthcoming).

13   Kemp, C.L., and M. Denton. 2003. "The Allocation of Responsibility for Later Life: Canadian Reflections on the Roles of Individuals, Government, Employers, and Families." *Ageing and Society* 23(6): 737–60.

1   Kenyon, G.M. 1992. "Editorial: Why Is Ageism a Serious Social Problem and What Can Be Done about It?" *Canadian Journal on Aging* 11(1): 2–5.

11   Kerr, R., and R. Normand. 1992. "Independent Living and Psychomotor Performance." *Canadian Journal on Aging* 11(1): 92–100.

3   Kertzer, D.I. 1995. "Toward a Historical Demography of Aging." In D.I. Kertzer and P. Laslett, eds., *Aging in the Past: Demography, Society, and Old Age,* 363–83. Berkeley: University of California Press.

10   Kieran, P. 2001. "Early Retirement Trends." *Perspectives on Labour and Income* 13(4): 7–13.

8   King, R.H.T. 1994. "An Update on the Future of Medicare in Canada." *Employee Benefits Journal* 19(1): 17–20.

13   King, V., and G.H. Elder, Jr. 1997. "The Legacy of Grandparenting: Childhood Experiences with Grandparents and Current Involvement with Grandchildren." *Journal of Marriage and the Family* 59(4): 848–59.

11   Kinnis, R. 1997. *"Garden Suites" Pilot Project: Case Study.* Ottawa: Canada Mortgage and Housing Corporation.

12   Kinsley, B., and F. Graves. 1983. *The Time of Our Lives.* Ottawa: Employment and Immigration Canada.

10 Klassen, T.R., and C.T. Gillin. 1999. "The Heavy Hand of the Law: The Canadian Supreme Court and Mandatory Retirement." *Canadian Journal on Aging* 18(2): 259–76.

1 Kleyman, P. 2002. "Journalism's Age-Beat Continues Steady Heartbeat Despite Ageist Media Economics." *Contemporary Gerontology* 8(4): 115–18.

5 Kline, D.W. 1994. "Optimising the Visibility of Displays for Older Observers." *Experimental Aging Research* 20(1): 11–23.

1,3 Knox, V.J., and W.L. Gekoski. 1989. "The Effect of Judgement Context on Assessments of Age Groups." *Canadian Journal on Aging* 8: 244–54.

7,13 Kobayashi, K.M. 2000. *The Nature of Support from Adult Sansei (Third Generation) Children to Older Nisei (Second Generation) Parents in Japanese Canadian Families.* SEDAP Research Paper No. 18. Hamilton, ON: McMaster University.

7 Kobayashi, K.M., A. Martin-Matthews, C. Rosenthal, and S. Matthews. 2001. *The Timing and Duration of Women's Life Course Events: A Study of Mothers with at Least Two Children.* SEDAP Research Paper No. 55. Hamilton, ON: McMaster University.

6 Koch, K. 1977. *I Never Told Anybody: Teaching Poetry Writing in a Nursing Home.* New York: Random House.

6 Koch, K. 1982. "Teaching Poetry Writing in a Nursing Home." In S.H. Zarit, ed., *Readings in Aging and Death: Contemporary Perspectives,* 2nd ed. New York: Harper and Row.

7 Koenig, H., L. George, and I. Siegler. 1988. "Religion and Well-Being in Later Life." *Gerontologist* 28(1): 18–28.

11 Kormos, W., and T.L. Horton. 1994. *Are We Spending Our Children's Inheritance?* Ottawa: National Advisory Council on Aging.

14 Koster, J., and J. Prather. 1999. "Around the World: Canada." *AARP Global Aging e-Report,* April. E-mail communication.

13 Kozak, J.F., T. Elmslie, and J. Verdon. 1995. "Epidemiological Perspectives on the Abuse and Neglect of Seniors: A Review of the National and International Research Literature." In M.J. MacLean, ed., *Abuse and Neglect of Older Canadians: Strategies for Change,* 129–41. Toronto: Thompson Educational Publishing.

7 Kozma, A., and M.J. Stones. 1978. "Some Research Issues and Findings in the Study of Psychological Well-Being in the Aged." *Canadian Psychological Review* 19: 241–49.

8 Kozyrskyi, A.L. 2003. "Romanow on Pharmaceuticals: A Strong Case for Access to Quality Medication Therapy." *Canadian Journal on Aging* 22(1): 25–28.

5 Kraus, A.S. 1987. "The Increase in the Usual Life Span in North America." *Canadian Journal on Aging* 6: 19–32.

5 Kraus, A.S. 1988. "Is a Compression of Morbidity in Late Life Occurring? Examination of Death Certificate Evidence." *Canadian Journal on Aging* 7: 58–70.

12 Kraus, H., and W. Raab. 1961. *Hypokinetic Disease.* Springfield, IL: Charles C. Thomas.

14 Krauthammer, C. 1996. "First and Last, Do No Harm." *Time,* April 15, 61.

8 Krueger, P., K. Brazil, L. Lohfeld, J. daPonte, and M. Slobodnik. 2000. *Canadian Journal of Public Health* 91(6): 445–48.

13 Kruk, E. 1995. "Grandparent–Grandchild Contact Loss: Findings from a Study of 'Grandparent Rights' Members." *Canadian Journal on Aging* 14(4): 737–54.

14 Kübler-Ross, Elisabeth. 1969. *On Death and Dying.* New York: Macmillan.

2 Kuehne, V.S. 1998. "Building Intergenerational Communities through Research and Evaluation." *Generations* 22(4): 82–87.

13 Kunemund, H., and M. Rein. 1999. "There Is More to Receiving Than Needing: Theoretical Arguments and Empirical Explorations of Crowding In and Crowding Out." *Ageing and Society* 19(1): 93–121.

7 Kuypers, J.A., and V.L. Bengtson. 1973. "Social Breakdown and Competence: A Model of Normal Aging." *Human Development* 6: 181–201.

7 Labillois, M. 1994. "Aboriginal Housing: A Personal Perspective." In National Advisory Council on Aging, *Aboriginal Seniors' Issues,* 11–15. Cat. No. H71-2/1-15-1994E. Ottawa: Minister of Supply and Services.

10 Labour Canada. 1986. *Women in the Labour Force, 1985–1986.* Cat. No. L38-30/1986. Ottawa: Minister of Supply and Services.

9 *Labour Gazette.* 1924.

6 Labouvie-Vief, G. 1985. "Intelligence and Cognition." In J.E. Birren and K.W. Schaie,

eds., *Handbook of the Psychology of Aging*, 2nd ed. New York: Van Nostrand Reinhold.

7 Lacy, W.B., and J. Hendricks. 1980. "Developmental Models of Adult Life: Myth or Reality." *International Journal of Aging and Human Development* 11: 89–110.

6 Lai, D.W.L. 2000. "Depression among the Elderly Chinese in Canada." *Canadian Journal on Aging* 19(3): 409–29.

5,12 Lalive d'Epinay, C.J., and J.F. Bickel. 2003. "Do 'Young-Old' Exercisers Feel Better Than Sedentary Persons? A Cohort Study in Switzerland." *Canadian Journal on Aging* 22(2): 155–65.

8 Lalonde, Marc. 1974. *A New Perspective on the Health of Canadians*. Ottawa: Minister of Supply and Services.

7 Lam, L. 1994. "Self-Assessment of Health Status of Aged Chinese-Canadians." *Journal of Asian and African Studies* 29(1–2): 77–90.

9 Lam, N., M.J. Prince, and J. Cutt. 1996. "Restoring the Canada Pension Plan: Simulating the Future and Stimulating the Social Policy Debate." In J.B. Burbridge et al., eds., *When We're 65: Reforming Canada's Retirement Income System*, 129–70. Toronto: C.D. Howe Institute.

7 Langlois, S., and P. Morrison. 2002. "Suicide Deaths and Attempts." *Canadian Social Trends* (Autumn): 66.

6 Langton, M. 1999. "Seniority: In Their Own Words: Doris Finta, 86." *Hamilton Spectator*, September 23.

7 Lapierre, S., J. Pronovost, M. Dubé, and I. Delisle. 1992. "Risk Factors Associated with Suicide in the Community." *Canada's Mental Health* 40(3): 8–12.

6 Laprise, R., and J. Vézina. 1998. "Diagnostic Performance of the Geriatric Depression Scale and the Beck Depression Inventory with Nursing Home Residents." *Canadian Journal on Aging* 17(4): 401–13.

12 Larkin-Lieffers, P.A. 2000. "Older Adult and Public Library Computer Technology: A Pilot Study in a Canadian Setting." *Livri* 50(4): 225–34.

12 LaRocque P., and P.D. Campagna. 1983. "Physical Activity through Rhythmic Exercise for Elderly Persons Living in a Senior Citizen Residence." *Activities, Adaptations, and Aging* 4: 77–81.

3 Laslett, P. 1976. "Societal Development and Aging." In R.H. Binstock and E. Shanas, eds., *Handbook of Aging and the Social Sciences*. New York: Van Nostrand Reinhold.

3 Laslett, P. 1995. "Necessary Knowledge: Age and Aging in the Societies of the Past." In D.I. Kertzer and P. Laslett, eds., *Aging in the Past: Demography, Society, and Old Age*, 3–77. Berkeley: University of California Press.

14 Lavigne, P.C., and L. Lévesque. 1992. "Reactions of the Institutionalized Elderly upon Learning of the Death of a Peer." *Death Studies* 16(5): 451–61.

3,4 Lavoie, Y. 1992. "Structure in Transition: Two Centuries of Demographic Change." In J. Dumas, *Report on the Demographic Situation in Canada 1992*, 101–53. Cat. No. 91-209E. Ottawa: Minister of Industry, Science, and Technology.

14 Lavoie, M., D. Blondeau, and G. Godin. 1999. "Intentions to Select a Given Level of Care When Confronted with an Ethical Issue: The Impact of a Living Will." *Journal of Applied Social Psychology* 29(4): 772–85.

4,9 Lavoie, Y., and J. Oderkirk. 1993. "Social Consequences of Demographic Change." *Canadian Social Trends* (Winter): 2–5.

14 Law Reform Commission of Canada. 1982. *Euthanasia, Aiding Suicide and Cessation of Treatment*. Working Paper 28. Ottawa: Minister of Supply and Service.

11 Lawton, M.P. 1976. "The Relative Impact of Enriched and Traditional Housing on Elderly Tenants." *Gerontologist* 16: 237–42.

11 Lawton, M.P. 1980. *Environment and Aging*. Monterey, CA: Brooks/Cole.

11 Lawton, M.P. 1982. "Environmental Research: Issues and Methods." In R. Bayne and B. Wigdor, eds., *Research Issues in Aging: Report of a Conference, 1980*. Hamilton, ON: Gerontology Research Council of Ontario.

14 Lawton, M.P. 2001. "Quality of Life and the End of Life." In J.E. Birren and K.W. Schaie, eds., *Handbook of the Psychology of Aging*, 5th ed. San Diego: Academic Press.

11 Lawton, M.P., and L. Nahemow. 1973. "Ecology and the Aging Process." In C. Eisdorfer and M.P. Lawton, eds. *The Psychology of Adult Development and Aging*. Washington, DC: American Psychological Association.

11   Lazarowich, M. 1986. "The Perspective of the User in the Ontario Granny Flat Demonstration Project." In S. Corke, G.S. Romanick, M.Lazarowich, and J. Simon, eds., *Granny Flats: A Housing Option for the Elderly*. Report No. 13. Winnipeg: Institute of Urban Studies.

5   Lazowski, D.-A., N.A. Ecclestone, A.M. Myers, D.H. Paterson, C. Tudor-Locke, C. Fitzgerald, G. Jones, N. Shima, and D.A. Cunningham. 1999. "Randomized Outcome Evaluation of Group Exercise Programs in Long-Term Care Institutions." *Journals of Gerontology Series A* 54(12): M621–28.

4   Leacy, F., ed. 1983. *Historical Statistics of Canada*. 2nd ed. Ottawa: Minister of Supply and Services.

10   LeBlanc, L.S., and J.A. McMullin. 1997. "Falling through the Cracks: Addressing the Needs of Individuals between Employment and Retirement." *Canadian Public Policy* 23(3): 289–304.

14   Lee, B.C. 1999. "Should It Be Legal for Physicians to Expedite Death. Yes: What Experience Teaches about Legalization of Assisted Dying." *Generations* 23(1): 59–60.

13   Lee, G.R., M.C. Willetts, and K. Seccombe. 1998. "Widowhood and Depression: Gender Differences." *Research on Aging* 20: 611–30.

13   Lee, J.A. 1987. "The Invisible Lives of Canada's Gray Gays." In V.W. Marshall, ed., *Aging in Canada*, 2nd ed. Toronto: Fitzhenry and Whiteside.

12   Lefrançois, R., G. Leclerc, M. Dubé, S. Hamel, and P. Gaulin. 2001. "Valued Activities of Everyday Life among the Very Old: A One-Year Trend." *Activities, Adaptation and Aging* 25(3–4): 19–34.

12   Lefrançois, R., G. Leclerc, and N. Poulin. 1998. "Predictors of Activity Involvement among Older Adults." *Activities, Adaptation and Aging* 22(4): 15–29.

6   Lehman, H.C. 1953. *Age and Achievement*. Princeton, NJ: Princeton University Press.

6   Lehman, H.C. 1968. "The Creative Production Rates of Present versus Past Generations of Scientists." In B.L. Neugarten, ed., *Middle Age and Aging*. Chicago: University of Chicago Press.

12   Lehto, X.Y., J.T. O'Leary, and G. Lee. 2001. "Mature International Travelers: An Examination of Gender and Benefits." *Journal of Hospitality and Leisure Marketing* 9(1–2): 53–72.

13   Leigh, G.K. 2000. "Cohabiting and Never-Married Families across the Life Course." In S.J. Price, P.C. McKenry, and M.J. Murphy, eds., *Families across Time: A Life Course Perspective*, 77–89. Los Angeles: Roxbury Publishing Company.

12   Lemieux, A. 1997. "Essential Learning Contents in the Curriculum for a Certificate Degree in Personalized Education for Older Adults." *Educational Gerontology* 23(2): 143–50.

7   Lemon, B.W., V.L. Bengtson, and J.A. Peterson. 1972a. "Activity Types and Life Satisfaction in a Retirement Community." *Journal of Gerontology* 27: 511–23.

7   Lemon, B.W., V.L. Bengtson, and J.A. Peterson. 1972b. "An Exploration of the Activity Theory of Aging: Activity Types and Life Satisfaction among In-Movers to a Retirement Community." In C.S. Kart and B.B. Manard, eds., *Aging in America: Readings in Social Gerontology*, 15–38. Sherman Oaks, CA: Alfred.

7   Lenaars, A.A., and D. Lester. 1992. "Comparison of Rates and Patterns of Suicide in Canada and the United States, 1960–1988." *Death Studies* 16(5): 417–30.

3   Lenski, G., and J. Lenski. 1974. *Human Societies: An Introduction to Macrosociology*, 2nd ed. New York: McGraw-Hill.

2   Lesemann, F. 2001. "Twenty Years of Canadian Social Research on Aging: An Attempted Understanding." *Canadian Journal on Aging* 20 (Suppl. 1): 58–66.

5   Lester, J.S. 1997. "Cyclops and Me: Confessions of a Former Computerphobe." *Generations* 21(3): 30–32.

13   Lévesque, L., S. Cossette, and L. Lachance. 1998. "Predictors of the Psychological Well-Being of Primary Caregivers Living with a Demented Relative: A 1-Year Follow-up Study." *Journal of Applied Gerontology* 17(2): 240–58.

6   Lévesque, L., S. Cossette., L. Potvin, and M. Benigeri. 2000. "Community Services and Caregivers of a Demented Relative: Users and Those Perceiving a Barrier to Their Use." *Canadian Journal on Aging* 19(2): 186–209.

7   Levinson, D.J. 1978. *The Seasons of a Man's Life*. New York: Knopf.

14 Levy, J.A. 1987. "A Life Course Perspective on Hospice and the Family." *Marriage and Family Review* 11: 39–64.

6 Li, S.-C., U. Lindenberger, B. Hommel, G. Aschersleben, W. Prinz, and P.B. Baltes. 2004. "Transformations in the Couplings among Intellectual Abilities and Constituent Cognitive Processes across the Life Span." *Psychological Science* 15(3): 155–63.

13 Lichtenberg, P.A. 1997. "Clinical Perspectives on Sexual Issues in Nursing Homes." *Topics in Geriatric Rehabilitation* 12(4): 1–10.

6 Light, L.L. 1990. "Interactions between Memory and Language in Old Age." In J.E. Birren and K.W. Schaie, eds., *Handbook of the Psychology of Aging*, 3rd ed. San Diego: Academic Press.

6 Light, L.L., and J.L. Capps. 1986. "Comprehension of Pronouns in Young and Older Adults." *Developmental Psychology* 2: 580–85.

2 Lincoln, Y., and E. Guba. 2000. "Paradigmatic Controversies, Contradictions, and Emerging Confluences." In N. Denzin and Y. Lincoln, eds., *Handbook of Qualitative Research*, 2nd ed., 163–87. Thousand Oaks, CA: Sage.

14 Lindemann, E. 1944. "Symptomatology and Management of Acute Grief." *American Journal of Psychiatry* 101: 141–48.

6 Lindenberger, U., and P.B. Baltes. 1997. "Intellectual Functioning in Old and Very Old Age: Cross-Sectional Results from the Berlin Aging Study." *Psychology and Aging* 12: 410–32.

4,10,12 Lindsay, C. 1997. *A Portrait of Seniors in Canada*, 2nd ed. Cat. No. 89-519-XPE. Ottawa: Statistics Canada.

1,2,4,5,6,7,8,9,10,11,12,13,14 Lindsay, C. 1999. *A Portrait of Seniors in Canada*, 3rd ed. Cat. No. 89-519-XPE. Ottawa: Statistics Canada.

9 Lindsay, C. 2000a. "Income and Earnings." In Statistics Canada, *Women in Canada 2000: A Gender-Based Statistical Report*. Cat. No. 89-503-XPE. Ottawa: Minister Responsible for Statistics Canada.

4,9 Lindsay, C. 2000b. "Senior Women." In Statistics Canada, *Women in Canada 2000: A Gender-Based Statistical Report*. Cat. No. 89-503-XPE. Ottawa: Minister Responsible for Statistics Canada.

13 Lithwick, M., M. Beaulieu, S. Gravel, and S.M. Straka. 1999. "Mistreatment of Older Adults: Perpetrator-Victim Relationships and Interventions." *Journal of Elder Abuse and Neglect* 11(4): 95–112.

5 Little, D. 2002. "Review of Smoking in the Elderly." *Geriatrics and Aging* 5(9): 9–13.

13 Litwak, E. 1985. *Helping the Elderly: The Complementary Roles of Informal Networks and Formal Systems*. New York: Guilford Press.

4 Litwak, E., and C.F. Longino, Jr. 1987. "Migration Patterns among the Elderly: A Developmental Perspective." *Gerontologist* 27: 266–72.

5 Litwin, H. 2000. "Activity, Social Network and Well-Being: An Empirical Examination." *Canadian Journal on Aging* 19(3): 343–62.

8 Liu, L., and L. Lazaruk. 1998. "Validity of the Alberta Assessment and Placement Instrument (AAPI) for Use in Admitting Long-Term Care Clients to Home Care." *Canadian Journal on Aging* 17(3): 296–310.

11 Lo, O. 1996. "Condominium Living." *Canadian Social Trends* (Summer): 27–30.

11 Lo, O., and P. Gauthier. 1995. "Housing Affordability Problems among Renters." *Canadian Social Trends* (Spring): 14–17.

13 Loehr, J., S. Verma, and R. Séguin. 1997. "Issues of Sexuality in Older Women." *Journal of Women's Health* 6(4): 451–57.

8 Loera, J.A., S.A. Black, K.S. Markidos, D.V. Espino, and J.S. Goodwin. 2001. "Use of Herbal Medicine by Older Mexican Americans." *Journals of Gerontology Series A* 56(11): M714–18.

6 Longfellow, H.W. 1928. "Morituri Salutamus." In *The Poetical Works of Longfellow*. London: Oxford University Press.

4 Longino, C.F., Jr. 1988a. "The Gray Peril Mentality and the Impact of Retirement Migration." *Journal of Applied Gerontology* 7: 448–55.

4 Longino, C.F., Jr. 1988b. "On the Nesting of Snowbirds: Canadian-Born Residents of the United States." In L.C. Mullins and R.D. Tucker, eds., *Snowbirds in the Sun Belt: Older Canadians in Florida*. Tampa: International Exchange Center on Gerontology.

4 Longino, C.F., V.W. Marshall, L.C. Mullins, and R.D. Tucker. 1991. "On the Nesting of Snowbirds: A Question about Seasonal and Permanent Migrants." *Journal of Applied Gerontology* 10(2): 157–68.

13 Loos, C., and A. Bowd. 1997. "Caregivers of Persons with Alzheimer's Disease: Some Neglected Implications of the Experience of Personal Loss and Grief." *Death Studies* 21(5): 501–14.

13 Lopata, H.Z. 1996. *Current Widowhood: Myths and Realities.* Thousand Oaks, CA: Sage.

12 Losier, G.F., P.E. Bourque, and R.J. Vallerand. 1993. "Motivational Model of Leisure Participation in the Elderly." *Journal of Psychology* 127(2): 153–70.

1 Loveland, N.C. 1994. "It's Time for Older Canadians to Pay More." *Globe and Mail,* November 22, A21.

5,8 Lovering, M.J., C.A. Cott, D.L. Wells, J. Schleifer Taylor, and L.M. Wells. 2002. "A Study of a Secure Garden in the Care of People with Alzheimer's Disease." *Canadian Journal on Aging* 21(3): 417–27.

10 Luchak, A.A., and I.R. Gellatly. 2001. "What Kind of Commitment Does a Final-Earning Pension Plan Elicit?" *Relations Industrielles/Industrial Relations* 56(2): 394–417.

5 Lustbader, W. 1997. "On Bringing Older People into the Computer Age." *Generations* 21(3): 30–31.

6 MacCourt, P., H. Tuokko, and M. Tierney. 2002. "Editorial: Canadian Association on Gerontology Policy Statement on Issues in the Delivery of Mental Health Services to Older Adults." *Canadian Journal on Aging* 21(2): 165–74.

11 MacDonald, A. 1989. *Transportation: Options for the Future.* National Advisory Council on Aging. Cat. No. H71-2/1-5-1988E. Ottawa: Minister of Supply and Services.

9 MacDonald, M. 1990. *Family Background, the Life Cycle and Inter-Household Transfers.* NSFH Working Paper 13. Madison, WI: Center for Demography and Ecology, University of Wisconsin.

13 MacDougall, B. 1998. "A Time to Grieve." *Expression* 12(1): 1–2. Ottawa: National Advisory Council on Aging.

6 Mace, N.L., and P.V. Rabins. 1981. *The Thirty-Six-Hour Day.* Baltimore: Johns Hopkins University Press.

11 Mack, R., A. Salmoni, D.G. Viverais, E. Porter, and R. Garg. 1997. "Perceived Risks to Independent Living: The Views of Older, Community-Dwelling Adults." *Gerontologist* 37(6): 729–36.

8 MacKnight, C., B.L. Beattie, H. Bergman, W.B. Dalziel, J. Feightner, B. Goldlist, D.B. Hogan, F. Molnar, and K. Rockwood. 2003. "Response to the Romanow Report: The Canadian Geriatrics Society. *Geriatrics Today* 6(1): 11–15.

8 Maclean, M.B., and J. Oderkirk. 1991. "Surgery among Elderly People." *Canadian Social Trends* (Summer): 11–13.

8 MacLean, M.J., and R. Bonar. 1983. "The Normalization Principle and the Institutionalization of the Elderly." *Canada's Mental Health* 31: 16–18.

13 MacLean, M.J., and R.M. Williams. 1995. "Introduction." In M.J. MacLean, ed., *Abuse and Neglect of Older Canadians: Strategies for Change,* xi–xxii. Toronto: Thompson Educational Publishing.

8 MacLennan, B.A. 1983. "Some Possible Implications for Adapting the Milieu in Nursing Homes." *Activities, Adaptation and Aging* 4: 33–38.

2,13 MacRae, H. 1996. "Strong and Enduring Ties: Older Women and Their Friends." *Canadian Journal on Aging* 15(3): 374–92.

13 MacRae, H. 1999. "Managing Courtesy Stigma: The Case of Alzheimer's Disease." *Sociology of Health and Illness* 21(1): 54–70.

2,13 MacRae, H. 2002. "The Identity Maintenance Work of Family Members of Persons with Alzheimer's Disease." *Canadian Journal on Aging* 21(3): 405–15.

6 Madden, D.J. 2001. "Speed and Timing of Behavioral Processes." In J.E. Birren and K.W. Schaie, eds., *Handbook of the Psychology of Aging,* 5th ed. San Diego: Academic Press.

3 Maddox, G.L. 1988. "Overview." In *Aging around the World: A Report on the President's Symposium on Aging in Tomorrow's World: An International Perspective.* Washington, DC: Gerontological Society of America.

5,12 Malcolm, M., W.C. Mann, M.R. Tomita, L.F. Fraas, K.M. Stanton, and L. Gitlin. 2001. "Computer and Internet Use in Physically Frail Elders." *Physical and Occupational Therapy in Geriatrics* 19(3): 15–32.

8 Mamdani, M., S.V. Parikh, P.C. Austin, and R.E. Upshur. 2000. "Use of Antidepressants among Elderly Subjects: Trends and Contributing Factors." *American Journal of Psychiatry* 157(3): 360–67.

11 Mancer, K. 2003. *Life Lease Housing in Canada: A Preliminary Exploration of Some*

11   *Consumer Protection Issues.* Ottawa: Canada Mortgage and Housing Corporation.

11   Mancer, K., and D. Kosmuk. 1999. *Meeting Seniors' Housing Needs: A Guide for Community Groups.* Ottawa: Canada Mortgage and Housing Corporation.

8   Manga, P. 1993. "Health Economics and the Current Health Care Cost Crisis: Contributions and Controversies." *Health and Canadian Society* 1(1): 177–203.

12   Manitoba Health. 1997. *Core Health Services in Manitoba.* Report prepared by the Northern/Rural Regionalization Task Force. Winnipeg: Manitoba Health.

8   Manitoba Health Services Commission. 1985. *Manitoba Health Services Commission Study of Persons Age 65+ Presenting at the Emergency Departments of Three Winnipeg Hospitals.* Winnipeg: Manitoba Health Services Commission.

14   Manitoba Law Reform Commission. 1990. *Discussion Paper on Advance Directives and Durable Powers of Attorney for Health Care.* Winnipeg: Manitoba Law Reform Commission.

5   Manton, K.G. 1982. "Changing Concepts of Mortality and Morbidity in the Elderly Population." *Milbank Memorial Fund Quarterly* 60: 183–244.

5   Manton, K.G. 1986. "Past and Future Life Expectancy Increases at Later Ages: Their Implications for the Linkage of Chronic Morbidity, Disability, and Mortality." *Journal of Gerontology* 41: 672–81.

7   Markides, K.S., and C.H. Mindel. 1987. *Aging and Ethnicity.* Newbury Park, CA: Sage.

8   Marmor, T.R., and K. Sullivan. 2000. "Canada's Burning! Media Myths about Universal Health Coverage." *Washington Monthly* (July/August).

14   Marshall, V.W. 1975. "Age and Awareness of Finitude in Developmental Gerontology." *Omega* 6: 113–29.

7   Marshall, V.W. 1983. "Generations, Age Groups, and Cohorts." *Canadian Journal on Aging* 2: 51–61.

2   Marshall, V.W. 1995a. "The Next Half-Century of Aging Research—and Thoughts for the Past." *Journals of Gerontology Series B* 50(3): S131–33.

10   Marshall, V.W. 1995b. "The Older Worker in Canadian Society: Is There a Future?" In E.M. Gee and G.M. Gutman, eds., *Rethinking*

10   *Retirement,* 51–68. Vancouver: Gerontology Research Centre, Simon Fraser University.

10   Marshall, V.W. 1995c. "Rethinking Retirement: Issues for the Twenty-First Century." In E.M. Gee and G.M. Gutman, eds., *Rethinking Retirement,* 31–50. Vancouver: Gerontology Research Centre, Simon Fraser University.

2   Marshall, V.W. 1996. "The State of Theory in Aging and the Social Sciences." In R. Binstock and L. George, eds., *Handbook of Aging and the Social Sciences,* 4th ed. San Diego: Academic Press.

2   Marshall, V.W. 1999. "Analyzing Social Theories of Aging." In V.L. Bengtson and K.W. Schaie, eds., *Handbook of Theories of Aging,* 434–58. New York: Springer Publishing.

1   Marshall, V.W. 2001. "Canadian Research on Older Workers." Paper presented for a symposium, "Problems of Older Workers," at the International Association on Gerontology conference, Vancouver, July.

10   Marshall, V.W., Clarke, P.J., and P.J. Ballantyne. 2001. "Instability in the Retirement Transition: Effects on Health and Well-Being in a Canadian Study." *Research on Aging* 23(4): 379–409.

10   Marshall, V.W., and J.G. Marshall. 1999. "Age and Changes in Work: Causes and Contrasts." *Ageing International* 25(2): 46–68.

1   Marshall, V.W., and B.D. McPherson. 1993. "Aging: Canadian Perspectives." *Journal of Canadian Studies* 28(1): 3–13.

13   Marshall, V.W., C.J. Rosenthal, and J. Synge. 1983. "Concerns about Parental Health." In E.W. Markson, ed., *Older Women: Issues and Prospects.* Lexington, MA: D.C. Heath.

4   Marshall, V.W., and R.D. Tucker. 1990. "Canadian Seasonal Migrants to the Sunbelt: Boon or Burden?" *Journal of Applied Gerontology* 9(4): 420–32.

5   Martel, L., and A. Bélanger. 2000. "Dependence-Free Life Expectancy in Canada." *Canadian Social Trends* (Autumn): 26–29.

5   Martel, L., A. Belanger, and J.-M. Berthelot. 2002. "Loss and Recovery of Independence among Seniors." *Health Reports* 13(4): 35–48.

4   Martin, H.W., S.K. Hoppe, V.W. Marshall, and J.F. Daciuk. 1992. "Sociodemographic and Health Characteristics of Anglophone Canadian and U.S. Snowbirds." *Journal of Aging and Health* 4(4): 500–13.

14   Martin, K., and S. Elder. 1993. "Pathways through Grief: A Model of the Process." In J.D. Morgan, ed., *Personal Care in an Impersonal World: A Multidimensional Look at Bereavement*, 73–86. Amityville, NY: Baywood.

13   Martin-Matthews, A. 1996. "Widowhood and Widowherhood." *Encyclopedia of Gerontology* 2: 621–25.

13   Martin-Matthews, A. 1999. "Widowhood: Dominant Renditions, Changing Demography, and Variable Meaning." In S.M. Neysmith, ed., *Critical Issues for Future Social Work Practice with Aging Persons*, 27–46. New York: Columbia University Press.

9   Maser, K., and J. Begin. 2003. *Canada's Retirement Income Programs: A Statistical Overview (1990–2000)*. Ottawa: Minister of Industry.

13   Masters, W., and V. Johnson. 1970. *Human Sexual Inadequacy*. Boston: Little, Brown.

7   Matsuoka, A.K. 1993. "Collecting Qualitative Data through Interviews with Ethnic Older People." *Canadian Journal on Aging* 12(2): 216–32.

13   Matthews, A.M. 1987. "Widowhood as an Expectable Life Event." In V.W. Marshall, ed., *Aging in Canada: Social Perspectives*, 2nd ed. Toronto: Fitzhenry and Whiteside.

2   Matthews, A.M., ed. 1995. "Methodological Diversity." *Canadian Journal on Aging* 14(1). Special issue.

10   Matthews, A.M., K.H. Brown, C.K. Davis, and M.A. Denton. 1982. "A Crisis Assessment Technique for the Evaluation of Life Events: Transition to Retirement as an Example." *Canadian Journal on Aging* 1: 28–39.

13   Matthews, A.M., and L.D. Campbell. 1995. "Gender Roles, Employment and Informal Care." In S. Arber and J. Ginn, eds., *Connecting Gender and Aging: A Sociological Approach*, 129–43. Buckingham, U.K.: Open University Press.

10   Matthews, A.M., and Joseph A. Tindale. 1987. "Retirement in Canada." In K.S. Markides and C.L. Cooper, eds., *Retirement in Industrialized Societies: Social, Psychological and Health Factors*. Toronto: John Wiley and Sons.

1   Matthews, A.M., J.A. Tindale, and J.E. Norris. 1985. "The Facts on Aging Quiz: A Canadian Validation and Cross-Cultural Comparison." *Canadian Journal on Aging* 3: 165–74.

3   Matthews, C., and J.V. Thompson. 1985. "The Aged in Canadian Fiction: No Longer Tragic Figures." Paper presented at the Canadian Association on Gerontology Annual Scientific and Educational Meeting, Hamilton.

13   Matthews, S.H., and J. Heidorn. 1998. "Meeting Filial Responsibilities in Brothers-Only Sibling Groups." *Journals of Gerontology Series B* 53(5): S278–86.

13   Matthias, R.E., J.E. Lubben, L.A. Atchison, and S.O. Schweitzer. 1997. "Sexual Activity and Satisfaction among Very Old Adults: Results from a Community-Dwelling Medicare Population Survey." *Gerontologist* 37(1): 6–14.

1   Maurier, W.L., and H.C. Northcott. 2000. *Aging in Ontario: Diversity in the New Millennium*. Calgary: Detselig Enterprises.

3   Maxwell, R., and J.P. Silverman. 1977. "Information and Esteem: Cultural Considerations in the Treatment of the Aged." In W.H. Watson and R.J. Maxwell, eds., *Human Aging and Dying: A Study in Socio-cultural Gerontology*. New York: St. Martin's Press.

3   Mays, H.J. 1983. "A Place to Stand: Families, Land and Permanence in Toronto Gore Township, 1820–1890." In W.P. Ward, ed., *The Social Development of Canada: Readings*. Richmond, BC: Open Learning Institute.

7   McAdams, D.P. 1990. "Unity and Purpose in Human Lives: The Emergence of Identity as a Life Story." In A.I. Rabin, R.A. Zucker, R.A. Emmons, and S. Frank, eds., *Studying Persons and Lives*, 148–200. New York: Springer.

7   McAdams, D.P. 1996. "Narrating the Self in Adulthood." In J.E. Birren et al., eds., *Aging and Biography: Exploration in Adult Development*, 131–48. New York: Springer.

13   McCandless, N.J., and F.P. Conner. 1997. "Older Women and Grief: A New Direction for Research." *Journal of Women and Aging* 9: 85–91.

10   McClelland, S. 2001. "The Costs of an Aging Population." *Maclean's*, July 9, 18.

7   McCrae, R., and P. Costa, Jr. 1990. *Personality in Adulthood*. New York: Guilford.

6   McCrae, R.R., D. Arenberg, and P.T. Costa, Jr. 1987. "Declines in Divergent Thinking with Age-Cross-Sectional, Longitudinal, and Cross-Sequential Analyses." *Psychology and Aging* 2(2): 130–37.

4   McDaniel, S. 1986. *Canada's Aging Population.* Toronto: Butterworths.

10   McDaniel, S. 1989. "Women and Aging: A Sociological Perspective." In D.J. Garner and S.O. Mercer, eds., *Women as They Age: Challenge, Opportunity, and Triumph.* Binghamton, NY: Haworth Press.

10   McDaniel, S.A. 1995. "Work, Retirement and Women in Later Life." In E.M. Gee and G.M. Gutman, eds., *Rethinking Retirement,* 75–92. Vancouver: Gerontology Research Centre, Simon Fraser University.

10   McDaniel, S.A. 1997. "Serial Employment and Skinny Government: Reforming Caring and Sharing among Generations." *Canadian Journal on Aging* 16(3): 465–84.

9,13   McDonald, L. 1997a. "The Invisible Poor: Canada's Retired Widows." *Canadian Journal on Aging* 16(3): 553–83.

10   McDonald, L. 1997b. "The Link between Social Research and Social Policy Options: Reverse Retirement as a Case in Point." *Canadian Journal on Aging/Canadian Public Policy* 16 (Suppl.): 90–113.

10   McDonald, L. 2002. *The Invisible Retirement of Women.* SEDAP Research Paper No. 69. Hamilton, ON: McMaster University.

9,10   McDonald, L., and M.Y.T. Chen. 1995. "The Youth Freeze and the Retirement Bulge: Older Workers and the Impending Labour Shortage." *Journal of Canadian Studies* 28(1): 75–101.

13   McDonald, L., and A. Collins. 2000. *Abuse and Neglect of Older Adults: A Discussion Paper.* Ottawa: Health Canada, National Clearing-house on Family Violence.

10   McDonald, L., and P. Donahue. 2000. "Poor Health and Retirement Income: The Canadian Case." *Aging and Society* 20 (Pt. 5): 493–522.

10   McDonald, L., P. Donahue, and V. Marshall. 2000. "The Economic Consequences of Unexpected Early Retirement." In F.T. Denton, D. Fretz, and B.G. Spencer, eds., *Independence and Economic Security in Old Age,* 267–92. Vancouver: UBC Press.

10,13   McDonald, L., R. Donahue, and B. Moore. 2000a. "The Poverty of Retired Widows." In F.T. Denton, D. Fretz, and B.G. Spencer, eds., *Independence and Economic Security in Old Age,* 328–45. Vancouver: UBC Press.

7,10   McDonald, L., P. Donahue, and B. Moore. 2000b. "Retirement through Unemployment: What Social Work Needs to Know." *Canadian Social Work Review* 17(1): 69–85.

9   McDonald, L., and A.L. Robb. 2003. *The Economic Legacy of Divorced and Separated Women in Old Age.* SEDAP Research Paper No. 104. Hamilton, ON: McMaster University.

10   McDonald, P.L., and R.A. Wanner. 1984. "Socioeconomic Determinants of Early Retirement in Canada." *Canadian Journal on Aging* 3: 105–16.

10   McDonald, P.L., and R.A. Wanner. 1987. "Retirement in a Dual Economy: The Canadian Case." In V.W. Marshall, ed., *Aging in Canada: Social Perspectives,* 2nd ed. Toronto: Fitzhenry and Whiteside.

1,10   McDonald, P.L., and R.A. Wanner. 1990. *Retirement in Canada.* Toronto: Butterworths.

7   McFadden, S.H. 1996. "Religion, Spirituality, and Aging." In J.E. Birren and K.W. Schaie, eds., *Handbook of the Psychology of Aging,* 4th ed., 162–77. San Diego: Academic Press.

10   McFadgen, L., and L. Zimmerman. 1995. "Women's Retirement: Shifting Ground." In E.M. Gee and G.M. Gutman, eds., *Rethinking Retirement,* 93–118. Vancouver: Gerontology Research Centre, Simon Fraser University.

13   McGarry, K., and R.F. Schoeni. 1995. *Transfer Behavior within the Family: Results from the Asset and Health Dynamics Survey.* Working Paper No. 5099. Cambridge, MA: National Bureau of Economic Research.

10   McGoldrick, A.E., and C.L. Cooper. 1988. *Early Retirement.* Gower: Brookfield, VT.

12   McGuire, F.A., F.D. Dottavio, and J.T. O'Leary. 1987. "The Relationship of Early Life Experiences to Later Life Leisure Involve-ment." *Leisure Sciences* 9: 251–57.

4   McInnis, R.M. 1977. "Childbearing and Land Availability: Some Evidence from Individual Household Data." In R. Lee, ed., *Population Patterns in the Past.* New York: Academic Press.

6   McIntyre, J.S., and F.I.M. Craik. 1987. "Age Differences in Memory for Item and Source Information." *Canadian Journal of Psychology* 41(2): 175–92.

4   McKie, C. 1993. "Population Aging: Baby Boomers into the 21st Century." *Canadian Social Trends* (Summer): 2–6.

7   McMellon, C.A., and L.G. Schiffman. 2002. "Cybersenior Empowerment: How Some Older Individuals Are Taking Control of Their

Lives." *Journal of Applied Gerontology* 21(2): 157–75.

2   McMullin, J.A. 1995. "Theorizing Age and Gender Relations." In S. Arber and J. Ginn, eds., *Connecting Gender and Ageing: A Sociological Approach*, 30–41. Buckingham, U.K.: Open University Press.

2   McMullin, J.A. 2000. "Diversity and the State of Sociological Aging Theory." *Gerontologist* 40(5): 517–30.

13   McMullin, J.A., and V.W. Marshall. 1996. "Family, Friends, Stress, and Well-Being: Does Childlessness Make a Difference?" *Canadian Journal on Aging* 15(3): 355–73.

10   McMullin, J.A., and V.W. Marshall. 1999. "Structure and Agency in the Retirement Process: A Case Study of Montreal Garment Workers." In C.D. Ryff and V.W. Marshall, eds., *The Self and Society in Aging Processes*, 305–38. New York: Springer.

1,2 McMullin, J.A., and V.W. Marshall. 2001. "Ageism, Age Relations, and Garment Industry Work in Montreal." *Gerontologist* 41(1): 111–22.

12   McPherson, B.D. 1983. *Aging as a Social Process.* Toronto: Butterworths.

2   McPherson, B.D. 2001. "Commentary: Are There Two Solitudes in Canadian Geron-tology?' *Canadian Journal on Aging* 20 (Suppl. 1): 76–81.

12   McPherson, B.D., and C. Kozlik. 1980. "Canadian Leisure Patterns: Disengagement, Continuity or Ageism." In V.W. Marshall, ed., *Aging in Canada.* Toronto: Fitzhenry and Whiteside.

12   McPherson, B.D., and C. Kozlik. 1987. "Age Patterns in Leisure Participation: The Canadian Case." In V.W. Marshall, ed., *Aging in Canada*, 2nd ed. Toronto: Fitzhenry and Whiteside.

13   McQuillan, K., and M. Belle. 2001. "Lone-Father Families in Canada, 1971–1996." *Canadian Studies in Population* 28(1): 67–88.

6   McShane, R., K. Gedling, J. Keene, C. Fairburn, R. Jacoby, and T. Hope. 1998. "Getting Lost in Dementia: A Longitudinal Study of a Behavioral Symptom." *International Psychogeriatrics* 10(3): 253–60.

3   McVey, W.W. 1987. Personal communication.

5,8 McWilliam, C.L., W.L. Diehl-Jones, J. Jutai, and S. Tadrissi. 2000. "Care Delivery Approaches and Seniors' Independence."

Canadian Journal on Aging 19 (Suppl. 1): 101–24.

2   Mead, G.H. 1934. *Mind, Self, and Society: From the Standpoint of a Social Behaviorist.* Chicago: University of Chicago Press.

13   Medjuck, S., J.M. Keefe, and P.J. Fancey. 1998. "Available But Not Accessible: An Examination of the Use of Workplace Policies for Caregivers of Elderly Kin." *Journal of Family Issues* 19(3): 274–99.

14   Meier, D.E. 1999. "Should It Be Legal for Physicians to Expedite Death? No: A Change of Heart on Assisted Suicide." *Generations* 23(1): 58–60.

14   Meier, E.E., H. Myers, and P.R. Muskin. 1999. "When a Patient Requests Help Committing Suicide." *Generations* 23(1): 61–68.

5   Melzer, D., B. McWilliams, C. Brayne, T. Johnson, and J. Bond. 2000. "Socioeconomic State and the Expectation of Disability in Old Age: Estimates for England." *Journal of Epidemiology and Community Health* 54(2): 28–92.

12   Menec, V.H. 2003. "Relation between Everyday Activities and Successful Aging: A 6-Year Longitudinal Study." *Journals of Gerontology Series B* 58(2): S74–82.

5   Menec, V.H., J.G. Chipperfield, and R.P. Perry. 1999. "Self-Perceptions of Health: A Prospective Analysis of Mortality, Control, and Health." *Journals of Gerontology Series B* 54(2): P85–93.

5   Menec, V.H., L. Lix, and J. MacWilliam. 2003. "Living Longer, Living Healthier? Trends in the Health Status of Older Manitobans." Paper presented at the 32nd Annual Scientific and Educational Meeting of the Canadian Association on Gerontology, Toronto, October 30–November 1.

13   Merrill, D.M. 1997. *Caring for Elderly Parents: Juggling Work, Family, and Caregiving in Middle and Working Class Families.* Westport, CT: Auburn House.

10   Méthot, S. 1987. "Employment Patterns of Elderly Canadians." *Canadian Social Trends* (Autumn): 7–11.

13   Metz, M.E., and M.H. Miner. 1998. "Psychosexual and Psychosocial Aspects of Male Aging and Sexual Health." *Canadian Journal of Human Sexuality* 7(3): 245–59.

8   Mhatre, S.L., and R.B. Deber. 1992. "From Equal Access to Health Care to Equitable

Access to Health: A Review of Canadian Provincial Health Commissions and Reports." *International Journal of Health Services* 22(4): 271–82.

1 Michalos, A.C., A.M. Hubley, B.D. Zumbo, and D. Hemingway. 2001. "Health and Other Aspects of the Quality of Life of Older People." *Social Indicators Research* 54(3): 239–74.

7 Miedema, B., and S. Tatemichi. 2003. "Gender, Marital Status, Social Networks, and Health: Their Impact on Loneliness in the Very Old." *Geriatrics Today* 6(2): 95–99.

13 Milan, A.M. 2000. "One Hundred Years of Families." *Canadian Social Trends* (Spring): 2–12.

13 Milan, A.M., and B. Hamm. 2003. "Across the Generations: Grandparents and Grandchildren." *Canadian Social Trends* Winter.

13 Milan, A.M., and A. Peters. 2003. "Couples Living Apart." *Canadian Social Trends* (Summer).

6 Miles, C.C., and W.R. Miles. 1932. "The Correlation of Intelligence Scores and Chronological Age from Early to Late Maturity." *American Journal of Psychology* 44: 44–78.

11 Millar, W.J. 1999. "Older Drivers: A Complex Public Health Issue." *Health Reports* 11(2): 59–71.

13 Miller, B., and J.E. Kaufman. 1996. "Beyond Gender Stereotypes: Spouse Caregivers of Persons with Dementia." *Journal of Aging Studies* 10(3): 189–204.

13 Miller, R.B., K. Hemesath, and B. Nelson. 1997. "Marriage in Middle and Later Life." In T.D. Hargrave and S.M. Hanna, eds., *The Aging Family: New Visions in Theory, Practice, and Reality.* New York: Brunner/Mazel.

13 Mills, T.L. 1999. "When Grandchildren Grow Up: Role Transition and Family Solidarity among Baby Boomer Grandchildren and Their Grandparents." *Journal of Aging Studies* 13(2): 219–39.

13 Miner, S., and P. Uhlenberg. 1997. "Intergenerational Proximity and the Social Role of Sibling Neighbors after Midlife." *Family Relations* 46(2): 145–53.

12 Minerva Senior Studies Institute. 2003. "Fall 2003 Programs and Courses." http://www.minerva.macewan.ca/minerva.pdf, accessed on November 26, 2003.

13 Minkler, M. 1999a. "Intergenerational Households Headed by Grandparents: Contexts, Realities, and Implications for Policy." *Journal of Aging Studies* 13(2): 199–218.

2 Minkler, M. 1999b. "Introduction." In M. Minkler and C.L. Estes, eds. *Critical Gerontology: Perspectives from Political and Moral Economy*, 1–13. Amityville, NY: Baywood.

2 Minkler, M., and C.L. Estes. 1999. *Critical Gerontology: Perspectives from Political and Moral Economy.* Amityville, NY: Baywood.

11 Minuk, M., and K. Davidson. 1981. *A Report on the Research Findings on the MHRC 1981 Shelter Allowance Program Review.* Winnipeg: Manitoba Housing and Renewal Corporation.

7 Mireault, M., and A.F. de Man. 1996. *Social Behavior and Personality* 24(4): 385–92.

6 Mireles, D.E., and N. Charness. 2002. "Computational Explorations of the Influence of Structured Knowledge on Age-Related Cognitive Decline." *Psychology and Aging* 17(2): 245–59.

13 Mitchell, B.A. 2003. "Would I Share a Home with an Elderly Parent? Exploring Ethnocultural Diversity and Intergenerational Support Relations during Young Adulthood." *Canadian Journal on Aging* 22(1): 69–82.

5 Mitchell, E. 1996. "Yo, Van Gogh! What's Up?" *Time,* February 26, 60.

8 Mitchell-Pedersen, L., L. Edmund, E. Fingerote, and C. Powell. 1985. "Let's Untie the Elderly." *OAHA Quarterly* (October): 10–14.

12 Mittelman, K., S. Crawford, S. Holliday, G. Gutman, and G. Bhakthan. 1989. "The Older Cyclist: Anthropometric, Physiological, and Psychosocial Changes Observed during a Trans-Canada Cycle Tour." *Canadian Journal on Aging* 8: 144–56.

7 Moberg, D.O. 1997. "Religion and Aging." In K.F. Ferraro, ed., *Gerontology: Perspectives and Issues*, 2nd ed., 193–220. New York: Springer.

7 Moberg, D.O. 2001. "The Reality and Centrality of Spirituality." In D.O. Moberg, ed., *Aging and Spirituality*, 3–20. New York: Haworth Press.

12 Mobily, K.E., R. Nilson, L.J. Ostiguy, R.D. MacNeil, and R.B. Wallace. 1995. "Seasonal

Variation in Physical Activity in Older Adults." *Topics in Geriatric Rehabilitation* 10(3): 11–22.

10   Moen, P., V. Fields, H.E. Quick, and H. Hofmeister. 2000. "A Life-Course Approach to Retirement and Social Integration." In K. Pillemer, P. Moen, E. Wethington, and N. Glasgow, eds., *Social Integration in the Second Half of Life*, 75–107. Baltimore: Johns Hopkins University Press.

7   Moen, P., K. Pillemer, E. Wethington, N. Glasgow, and G. Vesey. 2000. "Closing Thoughts and Future Directions." In K. Pillemer, P. Moen, E. Wethington, and N. Glasgow, eds., *Social Integration in the Second Half of Life*. Baltimore: Johns Hopkins University Press.

14   Molloy, D.W., G.H. Guyatt, R. Russo, R. Goeree, B.J. O'Brien, M. Bédard, W.A. Willan, J. Watson, C. Patterson, and C. Harrison. 2000. "Systematic Implementation of an Advance Directive Program in Nursing Homes: A Randomized Controlled Trial." *Journal of the American Medical Association* 283(11): 1437–44.

14   Molloy, D.W., R. Russo., D. Pedlar, and M. Bédard. 2000. "Implementation of Advance Directives among Community-Dwelling Veterans." *Gerontologist* 40(2): 213–17.

8   Montgomery, P.R., and W.M. Fallis. 2003. "South Winnipeg Integrated Geriatric Program (SWING): A Rapid Community-Response for the Frail Elderly." *Canadian Journal on Aging* 22(3): 275–81.

8   Montgomery, P.R., A.J. Kirshen, and N.P. Roos. 1988. "Long-Term Care and Impending Mortality: Influence upon Place of Death and Hospital Utilization." *Gerontologist* 28: 351–54.

3,8   Montigny, E.-A. 1997. *Foisted upon the Government? State Responsibilities, Family Obligations, and the Care of the Dependent Aged in Late Nineteenth-Century Ontario*. Montreal and Kingston: McGill-Queen's University Press.

3   Moodie, S. 1853. *Life in the Clearings versus the Bush*. New York: DeWitt and Davenport.

12   Moody, H.R. 1988. *Abundance of Life: Human Development Policies for an Aging Society*. New York: Columbia University Press.

13   Moore, A.J., and D.C. Stratton. 2002. *Resilient Widowers: Older Men Speak for Themselves*. New York: Springer.

7   Moore, E.G. 1995. "Aboriginal Women in Canada." In Statistics Canada, *Women in Canada: A Statistical Report*, 3rd ed., 147–62. Cat. No. 89-503E. Ottawa: Minister of Supply and Services.

4   Moore, E.G., and M.A. Pacey. 2003. *Geographic Dimensions of Aging in Canada 1991–2001*. SEDAP Research Paper No. 97. Hamilton, ON: SEDAP Research Program, McMaster University.

5   Moore, E.G., M.W. Rosenberg, and S.H. Fitzgibbon. 1999. "Activity Limitations and Chronic Conditions in Canada's Elderly, 1986–2011." *Disability and Rehabilitation* 21(5/6): 196–210.

4,13   Moore, E.G., M.W. Rosenberg, and D. McGuinness. 1997. *Growing Old in Canada: Demographic and Geographic Perspectives*. Toronto: ITP Nelson and Statistics Canada.

6   Morantz, A. 1990. "The Right to Decide." Today's Health (Suppl.), *Globe and Mail*, September, 39–44.

12   Morgan, W.P., and P.J. O'Connor. 1988. "Exercise and Mental Health." In R. Dishman, ed., *Exercise Adherence: Its Impact on Public Health*. Champaign, IL: Human Kinetics.

14   Mori, M. 1991. *Palliative Care of the Elderly: An Overview and Annotated Bibliography*. Vancouver: Gerontology Research Centre, Simon Fraser University.

8   Morris, J.N., I. Carpenter, K. Berg, and R.N. Jones. 2000. "Outcome Measures for Use with Home Care Clients." *Canadian Journal on Aging* 19 (Suppl. 2): 87–105.

10   Morrissette, R., and M. Drolet. 2001, "Pension Coverage and Retirement Savings." *Perspectives on Labour and Income* 13(2): 39–46.

5   Morrongiello, B.A., and B.H. Gottlieb. 2000. "Self-Care among Older Adults." *Canadian Journal on Aging* 19 (Suppl. 1): 32–57.

14   Moss, M.S., and S.Z. Moss. 1984–85. "Some Aspects of the Elderly Widow(er)'s Persistent Tie with the Deceased Spouse." *Omega* 15: 195–206.

14   Mount, R.M., A. Jones, and A. Patterson. 1974. "Death and Dying: Attitudes in a Teaching Hospital." *Urology* 4: 741.

4   Mullins, Larry C., R. Tucker, C.F. Longino, Jr., and V.W. Marshall. 1989. "An Examination of Loneliness among Elderly Canadian Seasonal Residents in Florida." *Journal of Gerontology* 44: S80–86.

14 Murray, M.E. 1981. "Palliative Care." *Canadian Nurse* 77(5): 16–17.

7 Mussell, W.J. 1994. "First Nations Elders as Resource Persons/Educators." In National Advisory Council on Aging, *Aboriginal Seniors' Issues*, 49–58. Cat. No. H71-2/1-15-1994E. Ottawa: Minister of Supply and Services.

12 Myers, A.M., and G. Gonda. 1986. "Research on Physical Activity in the Elderly: Practical Implications for Program Planning." *Canadian Journal on Aging* 5: 175–87.

12 Myers, A.M., and N. Hamilton. 1985. "Evaluation of the Canadian Red Cross Society's Fun and Fitness Program for Seniors." *Canadian Journal on Aging* 4: 201–12.

9 Myles, J. 1981. "Income Inequality and Status Maintenance." *Research on Aging* 3: 123–41.

4,9 Myles, J. 1982. "Social Implications of a Changing Age Structure." In G. Gutman, ed., *Canada's Changing Age Structure: Implications for the Future*. Vancouver: Simon Fraser University Publications.

2,9,10 Myles, J. 1984. *Old Age in the Welfare State: The Political Economy of Public Pensions*. Boston: Little, Brown.

9 Myles, J. 1988. "Social Policy in Canada." In E. Rathbone-McEwan and B. Havens, eds., *North American Elders: United States and Canadian Perspectives*. New York: Greenwood.

13 Myles, J. 1991. "Women, the Welfare State, and Care-Giving." *Canadian Journal on Aging* 10: 82–85.

1,2,9 Myles, J. 2000. "The Maturation of Canada's Retirement Income System: Income Levels, Income Inequality, and Low Income among Older Persons." *Canadian Journal on Aging* 19(3): 287–316.

3,9 Myles, J. 2002. "Editorial: Back to Bismarck? The Public Policy Implications of Living Longer." *Canadian Journal on Aging* 21(3): 325–29.

4,8,12 Myles, J., and M. Boyd. 1982. "Population Aging and the Elderly." In D. Forcese and S. Richer, eds., *Social Issues: Sociological Views of Canada*. Scarborough, ON: Prentice-Hall.

9 Myles, J., and D. Street. 1995. "Should the Economic Life Course Be Redesigned? Old Age Security in a Time of Transition." *Canadian Journal on Aging* 14(2): 335–59.

1,9 Myles, J., and L. Teichroew. 1991. "The Politics of Dualism: Pension Policy in Canada." In J. Myles and J. Quadagno, eds., *States, Labor Markets, and the Future of Old-Age Policy*, 84–104. Philadelphia: Temple University Press.

6 Naglie, G., M. Silberfeld, K. O'Rourke, B. Fried, N. Durham, C. Bombardier, and A. Detsky. 1995. "Convening Expert Panels to Identify Mental Capacity Assessment Items." *Canadian Journal on Aging* 14(4): 697–705.

4 Nagnur, D. 1986. *Longevity and Historical Life Tables, 1921–1981 (Abridged): Canada and the Provinces*. Statistics Canada. Cat. No. 89-506. Ottawa: Minister of Supply and Services.

4 Nagnur, D., and M. Nagrodski. 1988. "Cardiovascular Disease, Cancer and Life Expectancy." *Canadian Social Trends* (Winter): 25–27.

12 Nahmiash, D. 1985. "Intergenerational Relationships." Paper presented at the Canadian Association on Gerontology 14th Annual Scientific and Educational Meeting, Hamilton, ON.

6 Nahmiash, D. 1995. "Informal Caregiving: Women's Care or Work?" In E. Sawyer and M. Stephenson, eds., *Continuing the Care: The Issues and Challenges of Long-Term Care*, 247–69. Ottawa: Canadian Healthcare Association Press.

8 Nahmiash, D., and F. Lesemann. 1993. *Home Care: A Love Affair*. North York, ON: Captus Press.

8 Nahmiash, D., and M. Reis. 1992. *An Exploratory Study of Private Home Care Services in Canada*. Cat. No. H39-248/1992E. Ottawa: Minister of Supply and Services Canada.

13 Nahmiash, D., and M. Reis. 2000. "Most Successful Intervention Strategies for Abused Older Adults." *Journal of Elder Abuse and Neglect* 12(3–4): 53–70.

5,12 Namazi, K.H., and M. McClintic. 2003. "Computer Use among Elderly Persons in Long-Term Care Facilities." *Educational Gerontology* 29(6): 535–50.

3 Nason, J.D. 1981. "Respected Elder or Old Person: Aging in a Micronesian Community." In P.T. Amoss and S. Harrell, eds., *Other Ways of Growing Old: Anthropological Perspectives*. Stanford, CA: Stanford University Press.

11 National Advisory Council on Aging. 1985. *Expression* 2(4). Ottawa: National Advisory Council on Aging.

11   National Advisory Council on Aging. 1986. *Expression* 3(1). Ottawa: National Advisory Council on Aging.

8   National Advisory Council on Aging. 1989. *Understanding Seniors' Independence Report No. 1: The Barriers and Suggestions for Action.* Cat. No. H71-3/11-1-1989E. Ottawa: Minister of Supply and Services.

8   National Advisory Council on Aging. 1990a. *The NACA Position on Community Services in Health Care for Seniors.* Cat. No. H71-2/2-8-1990. Ottawa: Minister of Supply and Services.

12   National Advisory Council on Aging. 1990b. *The NACA Position on Lifelong Learning.* Cat. No. H71-2/2-10-1990. Ottawa: Minister of Supply and Services.

4   National Advisory Council on Aging. 1992a. *The NACA Position on Canada's Oldest Seniors: Maintaining the Quality of Their Lives.* Ottawa: National Advisory Council on Aging.

10   National Advisory Council on Aging. 1992b. *The NACA Position on Managing an Aging Labour Force.* Cat. No. H71-2/2-12-1991. Ottawa: Minister of Supply and Services Canada.

7   National Advisory Council on Aging. 1992c. "Spirituality and Meaning." *Expression* 8(4): 3–8. Ottawa: National Advisory Council on Aging.

6   National Advisory Council on Aging. 1993a. "Competency and Risk." *Expression* 9(2): 3–4. Ottawa: National Advisory Council on Aging.

13   National Advisory Council on Aging. 1993b. *Ethics and Aging.* Ottawa: Minister of Supply and Services.

6   National Advisory Council on Aging. 1993c. "Freedom and Responsibility: Home Alone." *Expression* 9(2): 2. Ottawa: National Advisory Council on Aging.

11   National Advisory Council on Aging. 1993d. "The Freedom to Drive a Car." *Expression* 9(2): 7. Ottawa: National Advisory Council on Aging.

1   National Advisory Council on Aging. 1993e. *The NACA Position on the Image of Aging.* Cat. No. H71-2/5-1993. Ottawa: Minister of Supply and Services.

7   National Advisory Council on Aging. 1993f. *The NACA Position on Women's Life-Course Events.* Cat. No. H71-2/2-15-1993. Ottawa: Minister of Supply and Services Canada.

6,8   National Advisory Council on Aging. 1993g. "Rights and Limits to Risk." *Expression* 9(2): 1–8. Ottawa: National Advisory Council on Aging.

7   National Advisory Council on Aging. 1994a. *Aboriginal Seniors' Issues.* Ottawa: Minister of Supply and Services.

14   National Advisory Council on Aging. 1994b. "Euthanasia and Assisted Suicide: What They Mean." *Expression* 10(1). Ottawa: National Advisory Council on Aging.

5   National Advisory Council on Aging. 1994d. "A State of Optimal Well-Being." *Expression* 10(2): 2–7. Ottawa: National Advisory Council on Aging.

8   National Advisory Council on Aging. 1995a. *The NACA Position on Community Services in Health Care for Seniors: Progress and Challenges.* Ottawa: National Advisory Council on Aging.

8   National Advisory Council on Aging. 1995b. *The NACA Position on Determining Priorities in Health Care: The Seniors' Perspective.* Ottawa: National Advisory Council on Aging.

5   National Advisory Council on Aging. 1995c. *The NACA Position on Health Care Technology and Aging.* Cat. No. H71-2/2-18-1995. Ottawa: Minister of Supply and Services Canada.

8   National Advisory Council on Aging. 1996a. "Are Seniors Heavier Users of Hospital Care?" Aging Vignette No. 29. http://www.hc-sc.gc.ca/seniors-aines/pubs/vignette/pdf/vig21-33_e.pdf, accessed on August 5, 2004.

5   National Advisory Council on Aging. 1996b. "Health Consequences of Inadequate Incomes." *Info-Age* 14 (March).

6   National Advisory Council on Aging. 1996c. "How Many People Are Affected?" Aging Vignette No. 35. http://www.hc-sc.gc.ca/seniors-aines/ pubs/vignette/pdf/vig34-50_e .pdf, accessed on August 5, 2004.

6   National Advisory Council on Aging. 1996d. "What Is the Prevalence of Alzheimer's Disease?" Aging Vignette No. 42. http://www.hc-sc.gc.ca/seniors-aines/pubs/vignette/pdf/vig34-50_e.pdf, accessed on August 5, 2004.

6   National Advisory Council on Aging. 1999a. "How Many in Institutions?" Aging Vignette No. 5. http://www.hc-sc.gc.ca/seniors-aines/ seniors/pubs/vignette/vig5_e.htm, accessed on August 5, 2004.

11   National Advisory Council on Aging. 1999b. "Senior Friendly Communities." *Expression* 13(1). Ottawa: National Advisory Council on Aging.

8   National Advisory Council on Aging. 2000a. "Choice." *Expression* 14(1): 5. Ottawa: National Advisory Council on Aging.

8   National Advisory Council on Aging. 2000b. *The NACA Position on Home Care.* No. 20. Ottawa: National Advisory Council on Aging.

10   National Advisory Council on Aging. 2000c. "The 'New' Retirement." *Expression* 13(2): 5.

8   National Advisory Council on Aging. 2000d. "SIPA Success." *Expression* 14(1): 9. Ottawa: National Advisory Council on Aging.

1   National Advisory Council on Aging. 2001a. "Seniors a Target." *Expression* 14(2). Ottawa: National Advisory Council on Aging.

5   National Advisory Council on Aging. 2001b. *Seniors and Technology.* Cat. No. 0-662-30932-4. Ottawa: Minister of Public Works and Government Services Canada.

5   National Advisory Council on Aging. 2001c. *Seniors in Canada: A Report Card.* Cat. No. H88-3/29-2001E. Minister of Public Works and Government Services Canada.

3   National Advisory Council on Aging. 2002a. "AIDS and Age." *Expression* 15(4): 7. Ottawa: National Advisory Council on Aging.

8,11   National Advisory Council on Aging. 2002b. *The NACA Position on Supportive Housing for Seniors.* No. 22. Ottawa: Minister of Public Works and Government Services Canada.

6   National Advisory Council on Aging. 2002c. *Writings in Gerontology.* No. 18. Ottawa: Minister of Public Works and Government Services.

11   National Advisory Council on Aging. 2002–03. "Let's Get Moving!" *Expression* 16(1): 1–8. Ottawa: National Advisory Council on Aging.

7   National Advisory Council on Aging. 2003a. *Interim Report Card: Seniors in Canada 2003.* Cat. No. H88-3/29-2003E. Ottawa: Minister of Public Works and Government Services.

5,7,8   National Advisory Council on Aging. 2003. *Seniors in Canada 2003: Interim Report Card.* Cat. No. H88-3/29-2003E. Minister of Public Works and Government Services Canada.

5   National Council on Disability. 1993. *Study on the Financing of Assistive Technology Devices and Services for Individuals with Disabilities.* Washington, DC.

9   National Council of Welfare. 1979. *Women and Poverty.* Ottawa: Minister of Supply and Services.

9   National Council of Welfare. 1984. *Sixty-Five and Older.* Cat. No. H68-11/1984E. Ottawa: Minister of Supply and Services.

9   National Council of Welfare. 1989a. *The 1989 Budget and Social Policy.* Cat. No. H68-22/1989E. Ottawa: Minister of Supply and Services.

9   National Council of Welfare. 1989b. *A Pension Primer.* Cat. No. H68-23/1989E. Ottawa: Minister of Supply and Services.

9   National Council of Welfare. 1990a. *Pension Reform.* Cat. No. H68-24/1990E. Ottawa: Minister of Supply and Services.

9   National Council of Welfare. 1990b. *Women and Poverty Revisited.* Cat. No. H68-25/1990E. Ottawa: Minister of Supply and Services.

9   National Council of Welfare. 1996a. *A Pension Primer.* Cat. No. H68-23/1996E. Ottawa: Minister of Supply and Services.

9   National Council of Welfare. 1996b. *Poverty Profile, 1994.* Cat. No. H67-1/4-1994E. Ottawa: Minister of Supply and Services Canada.

13   National Council of Welfare. 1996c. *Women and Poverty Revisited* 16: 134. Ottawa: Minister of Supply and Services Canada.

7,9   National Council of Welfare. 1998. *Poverty Profile, 1996.* Ottawa: National Council of Welfare.

9   National Council of Welfare. 1999. *A Pension Primer.* Cat. No. H68-49/1999E. Ottawa: Minister of Public Works and Government Services Canada.

13   National Forum on Health. 1997. "An Overview of Women's Health: Implications for Policies and Programs." In *Canada Health Action: Building on the Legacy.* Vol. 2. Ottawa: Health Canada. http://www.hc-sc.gc.ca/english/care/health_forum/publications/finvol2/womens, accessed on August 18, 2004.

9   National Health and Welfare. 1973. *Working Paper on Social Security in Canada.* 2nd ed. Ottawa: Queen's Printer.

5   National Health and Welfare. 1993. *Ageing and Independence: Overview of a National Survey.* Cat. No. H88-3/13-1993E. Ottawa: Minister of Supply and Services.

5   Needham, G. 1997. "Institutions Changing under the Force of New Information Technology." *Generations* 21(3): 11–14.

1   Nemeth, M. 1994. "Amazing Greys." *Maclean's,* January 10, 32–33.

13   Nemeth, M., and J. Howse. 1994. "Sandwich Generation." *Maclean's,* January 10, 34–35.

7   Neugarten, B.L. 1964. *Personality in Middle and Late Life.* New York: Atherton Press.

3,10 Neugarten, B.L. 1980. "Acting One's Age: New Rules for Old" (interview with Elizabeth Hall). *Psychology Today* (April).

2,7 Neugarten, B.L., R.J. Havighurst, and S. Tobin. 1968. "Personality and Patterns of Aging." In B.L. Neugarten, ed., *Middle Age and Aging.* Chicago: University of Chicago Press.

7   Neugarten, B.L., and J.W. Moore. 1968. "The Changing Age-Status System." In B.L. Neugarten, ed., *Middle Age and Aging.* Chicago: University of Chicago Press.

7   Neugarten, B.L., J.W. Moore, and J.C. Lowe. 1968. "Age Norms, Age Constraints, and Adult Socialization." In B.L. Neugarten, ed., *Middle Age and Aging.* Chicago: University of Chicago Press.

13   Neugarten, B.L., and Karol K. Weinstein. 1964. "The Changing American Grandparent." *Journal of Marriage and the Family* 26: 199–204.

2   Neuman, W.L. 2003. *Social Research Methods: Qualitative and Quantitative Approaches.* 5th ed. Boston: Allyn and Bacon.

9   Neysmith, S.M. 1984. "Poverty in Old Age: Can Pension Reform Meet the Needs of Women?" *Canadian Woman Studies* 5: 17–21.

8   Neysmith, S.M. 1993. "Developing a Home Care System to Meet the Needs of Aging Canadians and Their Families." In J. Hendricks and C.J. Rosenthal, eds., *The Remainder of Their Days: Domestic Policy and Older Families in the United States and Canada,* 145–67. New York: Garland.

2   Neysmith, S.M. 1995a. "Feminist Methodologies: A Consideration of Principles and Practice for Research in Gerontology." *Canadian Journal on Aging* 14(1): 100–18.

13   Neysmith, S.M. 1995b. "Power in Relationships of Trust: A Feminist Analysis of Elder Abuse." In M.J. MacLean, ed., *Abuse and Neglect of Older Canadians: Strategies for Change,* 43–54. Toronto: Thompson Educational Publishing.

3   Neysmith, S.M., and J. Edwardh. 1983. "Ideological Underpinnings of the World Assembly on Aging." *Canadian Journal on Aging* 2: 125–36.

1   Ng, E. 1992. "Children and Elderly People: Sharing Public Income Resources." *Canadian Social Trends* (Summer): 12–17.

7   Nichols, B., and P. Leonard, eds. 1995. *Gender, Aging, and the State.* Toronto: Black Rose Books.

11   Niewind, A.C., M. Krondl, and D. Lau. 1988. "Relative Impact of Selected Factors on Food Choices of Elderly Individuals." *Canadian Journal on Aging* 8: 32–47.

10   Nishio, H.K., and H. Lank. 1987. "Patterns of Labour Participation of Older Female Workers." In V.W. Marshall, ed., *Aging in Canada: Social Perspectives,* 2nd ed. Toronto: Fitzhenry and Whiteside.

4   Norland, J.A. 1976. *The Age–Sex Structure of Canada's Population.* Cat. No. 99-703. Ottawa: Statistics Canada.

4,5,9,11 Norland, J.A. 1994. *Profile of Canada's Seniors.* Cat. No. 96-312E. Ottawa: Statistics Canada and Prentice-Hall Canada.

4,6 Normand, J. 2000. "The Health of Women." In Statistics Canada, *Women in Canada 2000: A Gender-Based Statistical Report.* Cat. No. 89-503-XPE. Ottawa: Minister Responsible for Statistics Canada.

10   Norris, J.E. 1993. "'Why Not Think Carnegie Hall?' Working and Retiring among Older Professionals." *Canadian Journal on Aging* 12(2): 182–99.

6   Norris, J.E. 1998. "Editorial: A Psychology of Aging: Who Needs It?" *Canadian Journal on Aging* 17(4): i–xi.

1,7 Northcott, H.C. 1982. "The Best Years of Your Life." *Canadian Journal on Aging* 1: 72–78.

4   Northcott, H.C. 1988. *Changing Residence: The Geographic Mobility of Elderly Canadians.* Toronto: Butterworths.

4   Northcott, H.C. 1992. *Aging in Alberta: Rhetoric and Reality.* Calgary: Detselig Enterprises.

1   Northcott, H.C. 1994. "Public Perceptions of the Population Aging 'Crisis.'" *Canadian Public Policy* 20(1): 66–77.

3,14 Northcott, H.C., and D.M. Wilson. 2001. *Dying and Death in Canada.* Aurora, ON: Garamond Press.

7,14 Novak, M. 1985. *Successful Aging: The Myths, Realities, and Future of Aging in Canada.* Markham, ON: Penguin.

7   Novak, M. 1985–86. "Biography after the End of Metaphysics." *International Journal of Aging and Human Development* 22(3): 189–204.

6   Novak, M., N. Chappell, and C. Miles-Tapping. 1990. "Nursing Assistant Stress and the Cognitively Impaired Elderly." Paper presented at the 43rd Scientific Meeting of the Gerontological Society of America, Boston.

6   Novak, M., and C. Guest. 1985. "Social Correlates of Caregiver Burden." Paper presented at the Canadian Association on Gerontology 14th Annual Scientific and Education Meeting, Hamilton.

12   Novak, M., and A. Percival. 1993. *Adult Education: A Study of Motivations, Preferences, and Financial Support in a Winnipeg Sample.* Winnipeg Area Study Research Reports Series. Winnipeg: Winnipeg Area Study.

13   Novak, M., and L.O. Stone. 1985. "Changing Patterns of Aging." Paper presented at the Annual Meeting of the Canadian Sociology and Anthropology Association, Montreal.

13   O'Brien, C., and A. Goldberg. 2000. "Lesbians and Gay Men Inside and Outside Families." In N. Mandell and A. Duffy. eds., *Canadian Families: Diversity, Conflict, and Change,* 115–45. Toronto: Harcourt Brace.

13   O'Brien, M. 1991. "Never Married Older Women: The Life Experience." *Social Indicators Research* 24: 301–15.

12   O'Brien, S.J., and P.R. Conger. 1991. "No Time to Look Back: Approaching the Finish Line of Life's Course." *International Journal of Aging and Human Development* 33(1): 75–87.

5,12   O'Brien, S.J., and P.A. Vertinsky. 1991. "Unfit Survivors: Exercise as a Resource for Aging Women." *Gerontologist* 31: 347–57.

13   O'Connor, B.P. 1995. "Family and Friend Relationships among Older and Younger Adults: Interaction Motivation, Mood, and Quality." *International Journal of Aging and Human Development* 40(1): 9–29.

8   O'Connor, B.P., and R.J. Vallerand. 1994. "Motivation, Self-Determination, and Person–Environment Fit as Predictors of Psychological Adjustment among Nursing Home Residents." *Psychology and Aging* 9(2): 189–94.

2,13   O'Connor, D. 1999. "Living with a Memory-Impaired Spouse: (Re)cognizing the Experience." *Canadian Journal on Aging* 18(2): 211–35.

9   Oderkirk, J. 1996. "Canada and Quebec Pension Plans." *Canadian Social Trends* (Spring): 8–15.

3   Oh, K.M., and A.M. Warnes. 2001. "Care Services for Frail Older People in South Korea." *Ageing and Society* 21 (Part 6): 701–20.

11   Okraku, I.O. 1987. "Age and Attitudes toward Multigenerational Residence, 1973 to 1983." *Journal of Gerontology* 42: 280–87.

11   Ontario Advisory Council on the Physically Handicapped and Ontario Advisory Council on Senior Citizens. 1987. *The Freedom to Move Is Life Itself: A Report on Transportation in Ontario.* Toronto: Ontario Advisory Council on the Physically Handicapped and Ontario Advisory Council on Senior Citizens.

11   Ontario Advisory Council on Senior Citizens. 1978. *Through the Eyes of Others.* Toronto: Ontario Advisory Council on Senior Citizens.

11   Ontario Advisory Council on Senior Citizens. 1980–81. *Seniors Tell All.* Toronto: Ontario Advisory Council on Senior Citizens.

7   Ontario Advisory Council on Senior Citizens. 1993. *Denied Too Long.* Toronto: Ontario Advisory Council on Senior Citizens.

11   Ontario Ministry of Health and Long-Term Care. 2004. "Seniors' Care: Supportive Housing." http://www.health.gov.on.ca/english/public/program/ltc/13_housing.html, accessed on August 28, 2004.

11   Ontario Ministry of Municipal Affairs and Housing. 1983. *Towards Community Planning for an Aging Society.* Toronto: Queen's Printer for Ontario.

4   Ontario Ministry of Treasury and Economics. 1979. *Issues in Pension Policy: Demographic and Economic Aspects of Canada's Ageing Population.* Ontario Treasury Studies 16. Toronto: Ministry of Treasury and Economics, Taxation and Fiscal Policy Branch.

1   Ontario Provincial Police. 1997. *Phonebusters—A National Task Force Combating Telemarketing Fraud.*

3,10   O'Rand, A.M. 1990. "Stratification and the Life Course." In R.H. Binstock and L.K. George, eds., *Handbook of Aging and the Social Sciences,* 3rd ed. San Diego: Academic Press.

13   O'Rourke, N., and P. Cappeliez. 2002. "Perceived Control, Coping, and Expressed Burden among Spouses of Suspected Dementia Patients: Analysis of the Goodness-of-Fit Hypothesis." *Canadian Journal on Aging* 21(3): 385–92.

13   O'Rourke, N., B.E. Haverkamp, H. Tuokko, S. Hayden, and B.L. Beattie. 1996. "The Relative

Contribution of Subjective Factors to Expressed Burden among Spousal Caregivers of Suspected Dementia Patients." *Canadian Journal on Aging* 15(4): 583–96.

13 O'Rourke, N., and C.A. Wenaus. 1998. "Marital Aggrandizement as a Mediator of Burden among Spouses of Suspected Dementia Patients." *Canadian Journal on Aging* 17(4): 384–400.

7 Osgood, N.J., B.A. Brant, and A. Lipman. 1991. *Suicide among the Elderly in Long-Term Care Facilities.* New York: Greenwood Press.

5 *Ottawa Citizen.* 1999. "Designs for Living." August 14.

13 Otto, J. 2000. "The Role of Adult Protective Services in Addressing Abuse." *Generations* 24: 33–38.

12 Ouellet, P. 1986. "The Leisure Participation and Enjoyment Patterns of French and English-Speaking Members of Senior Citizens' Clubs in New Brunswick, Canada." *Canadian Journal on Aging* 5: 257–68.

4 Owram, D. 1996. *Born at the Right Time: A History of the Baby-Boom Generation.* Toronto: University of Toronto Press.

7 Pacey, M.A. 2002. *Living Alone and Living with Children: The Living Arrangements of Canadian and Chinese-Canadian Seniors.* SEDAP Research Paper No. 74. Hamilton, ON: McMaster University.

1 Page, S. 1997. "Accommodating the Elderly: Words and Actions in the Community." In L.A. Pastalan, ed., *Shelter and Service Issues for Aging Populations: International Perspectives,* 55–61. New York: Haworth Press.

9 Palameta, B. 2001. "Who Contributes to RRSPs? A Re-Examination." *Perspectives on Labour and Income* 13(3): 7–13.

1 Palmore, E.B. 1971. "Attitudes toward Aging as Shown in Humor." *Gerontologist* 11: 181–86.

1 Palmore, E.B. 1977. "Facts on Aging: A Short Quiz." *Gerontologist* 17: 315–20.

1 Palmore, E.B. 1988. *The Facts on Aging Quiz: A Handbook of Uses and Results.* New York: Springer.

1 Palmore, E.B. 1994. "When Is Humor about Aging 'Good' and When Is It 'Ageist'?" *Perspectives on Aging* 23(3): 9–10.

3 Palmore, E.B., and K. Manton. 1974. "Modernization and the Status of the Aged: International Correlations." *Journal of Gerontology* 29: 205–10.

3 Palmore, E.B., and F. Whittington. 1971. "Trends in the Relative Status of the Aged." *Social Forces* 50: 84–91.

8 Parboosingh, J.E., and D.E. Larsen. 1987. "Factors Influencing Frequency and Appropriateness of Utilization of the Emergency Room by the Elderly." *Medical Care* 25: 1139–47.

8 Parboosingh, J., S. Stachenko, and S. Inhaber. 1997. "Model of Consumer Participation: The Canadian Breast Cancer Initiative." *Canadian Journal on Aging* 16 (Suppl.): 177–86.

8 Paré, I. 2000. "Des projets-pilotes prometteurs en santé." *Le Devoir,* October 27.

10 Paris, H. 1989. *The Corporate Response to Workers with Family Responsibilities.* Report 43-89. Ottawa: Conference Board of Canada.

6 Park, D.C. 2000. "The Basic Mechanisms Accounting for Age-Related Decline in Cognitive Function." In D.C. Park and N. Schwarz, eds., *Cognitive Aging: A Primer,* 3–21. Philadelphia: Taylor and Francis.

6,10 Park, D.C., and A.H. Gutchess. 2000. "Cognitive Aging and Everyday Life." In D.C. Park and N. Schwarz, eds., *Cognitive Aging: A Primer,* 217–32. Philadelphia: Taylor and Francis.

6 Park, D.C., and N. Schwarz, eds. 2001. *Cognitive Aging: A Primer.* Philadelphia: Taylor and Francis.

4 Parliament, J.-A. 1987. "Increased Life Expectancy, 1921–1986." *Canadian Social Trends* (Summer): 15–19.

4 Parliament, J.-A. 1989. "The Decline in Cardio-Vascular Disease Mortality." *Canadian Social Trends* (Autumn): 28–29.

11 Parmelee, P.A., and M.P. Lawton. 1990. "The Design of Special Environments for the Aged." In J.E. Birren and K.W. Schaie, eds., *Handbook of the Psychology of Aging,* 3rd ed. San Diego: Academic Press.

13 Patterson, J. 1996. "Participation in Leisure Activities by Older Adults after a Stressful Life Event: The Loss of a Spouse." *International Journal of Aging and Human Development* 42: 123–42.

13 Parsons, K. 1997. "The Male Experience of Caregiving for a Family Member with Alzheimer's Disease." *Qualitative Health Research* 7(3): 391–407.

13 Parsons, J., and J.A. Tindale. 2001. "Parents Who Sue Their Adult Children for Support:

An Examination of Decisions by Canadian Court Judges." *Canadian Journal on Aging* 20(4): 451–70.

2 Parsons, T. 1937. *The Structure of Social Action*. New York: McGraw-Hill.

2 Parsons, T. 1951. *The Social System*. New York: Free Press.

8 Passini, R., C. Rainville, N. Marchand, and Y. Joanette. 1998. "Wayfinding and Dementia: Some Research Findings and a New Look at Design." *Journal of Architectural and Planning Research* 15(2): 133–51.

8 Paterson, J. 1989. "New Services Help Seniors Convalesce in Own Home." *Victoria Times Colonist*, November 28.

5 Paul, A. 1994. "AIDS Stalking the Elderly." *Winnipeg Free Press*, October 15, A17.

7,14 Peck, R.C. [1955] 1968. "Psychological Aspects of Aging." In J.E. Anderson, ed. *Proceedings of a Conference on Planning Research, Bethesda, MD, April 24–27, 1955*. Washington, DC: American Psychological Association. Excerpted in "Psychological Developments in the Second Half of Life," in B.L. Neugarten, ed., *Middle Age and Aging*. Chicago: University of Chicago Press, 1968.

13 Pederson, A. 2002. "Who Cares?" *Centres of Excellence for Women's Health Research Bulletin* 3(1): 1–3.

13 Penning, M.J. 1990. "Receipt of Assistance by Elderly People: Hierarchical Selection and Task Specificity." *Gerontologist* 30: 220–27.

13 Penning, M.J. 1998. "In the Middle: Parental Caregiving in the Context of Other Roles." *Journals of Gerontology Series B* 53(4): S188–97.

13 Penning, M.J. 2002. "Hydra Revisited: Substituting Formal for Self- and Informal In-Home Care among Older Adults with Disabilities." *Gerontologist* 42(1): 4–16.

8 Penning, M.J., and N.L. Chappell. 1982. "Mental Health Status: A Comparison of Different Socio-Cultural Environments for the Elderly." *Essence* 5: 169–82.

5 Penning, M.J., and N.L. Chappell. 1990. "Self-Care in Relation to Informal and Formal Care." *Ageing and Society* 10: 41–59.

8 Penning, M.J., and N.L. Chappell. 1993. "Age-Related Differences." In T. Stephens and D.F. Graham, eds., *Canada's Health Promotion Survey 1990: Technical Report*, 248–61. Cat.

No. H39-263/2-1990E. Ottawa: Minister of Supply and Services.

5 Penning, M.J., and L.A. Strain. 1994. "Gender Differences in Disability, Assistance, and Subjective Well-Being in Later Life." *Journals of Gerontology* 49(4): S202–8.

12 Penning, M.J., and D. Wasyliw. 1992. "Homebound Learning Opportunities: Reaching Out to Older Shut-Ins and Their Caregivers." *Gerontologist* 32: 704–7.

6 Perfect, T.J., and Z.R.R. Dasgupta. 1997. "What Underlies the Deficit in Reported Recollective Experience in Old Age?" *Memory and Cognition* 25(6): 849–58.

7 Perlman, D., A.C. Gerson, and B. Spinner. 1978. "Loneliness among Senior Citizens: An Empirical Report." *Essence* 2: 239–48.

8 Perodeau, G.M., and G.G. du Fort. 2000. "Psychotropic Drug Use and the Relation between Social Support, Life Events, and Mental Health in the Elderly." *Journal of Applied Gerontology* 19(1): 23–41.

13 Peters, A., and A.C. Liefbroer. 1997. "Beyond Marital Status: Partner History and Well-Being in Old Age." *Journal of Marriage and the Family* 59(3): 687–99.

13 Pfeiffer, E., A. Verwoerdt, and H.S. Wang. 1968. "Sexual Behavior in Aged Men and Women, I: Observations on 254 Community Volunteers." *Archives of General Psychiatry* 19: 753–58.

2 Phillipson, C. 1999. "The Social Construction of Retirement: Perspectives from Critical Theory and Political Economy." In M. Minkler and C.L. Estes, *Critical Gerontology: Perspectives from Political and Moral Economy*, 315–27. Amityville, NY: Baywood.

4 Philpot, H.J. 1871. *Guide Book to the Canadian Dominion Containing Full Information for the Emigrant, the Tourist, the Sportsman and the Small Capitalist*. London: E. Stanford.

13 Pierce, T., J.E. Lydon, and S. Yang. 2001. "Enthusiasm and Moral Commitment: What Sustains Family Caregivers of Those with Dementia." *Basic and Applied Social Psychology* 23(1): 29–41.

12 Pihlchyn, P. 1995. "Seniors Set Up Shop on Internet." *Winnipeg Free Press*, March 14, C6.

13 Pillemer, K., and D. Finkelhor. 1988. "The Prevalence of Elder Abuse: A Random Sample Survey." *Gerontologist* 28: 51–57.

13   Pittaway, E. and E. Gallagher. 1995. *A Guide to Enhancing Service for Abused Older Canadians.* Victoria: Centre on Aging, University of Victoria.

13   Pittaway, E.D., E. Gallagher, M. Stones, J. Kosberg, D. Nahmiash, E. Podnieks, L. Strain, and J. Bond. 1995. *Services for Abused Older Canadians.* Report for the Interministry Committee on Elder Abuse, Office for Seniors, Province of British Columbia. Victoria: Ministry of Health and Ministry Responsible for Seniors.

13   Pittaway, E.D., A. Westhues, and T. Peressini. 1995. "Risk Factors for Abuse and Neglect among Older Adults." *Canadian Journal on Aging* 14 (Suppl. 2): 20–44.

3   Plath, D.W. 1972. "Japan: The After Years." In D.O. Cowgill and L.D. Holmes, eds., *Aging and Modernization.* New York: Appleton-Century-Crofts.

13   Ploeg, J., L. Biehler, K. Willison, B. Hutchinson, and J. Blythe. 2001. "Perceived Support Needs of Family Caregivers and Implications for a Telephone Support Service." *Canadian Journal of Nursing Research* 33(2): 43–61.

13   Ploeg, J., L.D. Campbell, M. Denton, A. Joshi, and S. Davies. 2003. *Helping to Build and Rebuild Secure Lives and Futures: Intergenerational Financial Transfers from Parents to Adult Children and Grandchildren.* SEDAP Research Paper No. 96. Hamilton, ON: McMaster University.

1   Plouffe, L. 1991. *Consumer Fraud and Seniors.* Ottawa: National Advisory Council on Aging.

1   Podnieks, E., K. Pillemer, J.P. Nicholson, T. Shillington, and A. Frizzell. 1989. *National Survey of Abuse of the Elderly in Canada: Preliminary Findings.* Toronto: Ryerson Office of Research and Innovation.

13   Podnieks, E., K. Pillemer, J.P. Nicholson, T. Shillington, and A. Frizzel. 1990. *National Survey on Abuse of the Elderly in Canada.* Toronto: Ryerson Polytechnic Institute.

8   Poirier, D. 1992. "Power of Social Workers in the Creation and Application of Elder Protection Statutory Norms in New Brunswick and Nova Scotia." *Journal of Elder Abuse and Neglect* 4: 13–33.

8   Poirier, S., and G. Barbeau. 1999. "In-Home Medication Inventory among Elderly Receiving Home Care Services." *Journal of Geriatric Drug Therapy* 12(3): 43–54.

8   Policy, Planning, and Information Branch. 1993. *Health Expenditures in Canada: Fact Sheets.* March. Ottawa: Health Canada.

6   Poon, L.W. 1985. "Differences in Human Memory with Aging: Nature, Causes, and Clinical Implications." In J.E. Birren and K.W. Schaie, eds., *Handbook of the Psychology of Aging,* 2nd ed. New York: Van Nostrand Reinhold.

3   Prentice, A., P. Bourne, G.C. Brandt, B. Light, W. Mitchinson, and N. Black. 1996. *Canadian Women: A History.* 2nd ed. Toronto: Harcourt Brace.

3   Press, I., and M. McKool. 1972. "Social Structure and Status of the Aged: Toward Some Valid Cross-Cultural Generalizations." *Aging and Human Development* 3: 297–306.

8   Préville, M., R. Hébert, R. Boyer, and G. Bravo. 2001. "Correlates of Psychotropic Drug Use in the Elderly Compared to Adults Aged 18–64: Results from the Quebec Health Survey." *Aging and Mental Health* 5(3): 216–24.

6   Préville, M., R. Hébert, G. Bravo, and R. Boyer. 2002. "Predisposing and Facilitating Factors of Severe Psychological Distress among Frail Elderly Adults." *Canadian Journal on Aging* 21(2): 195–204.

13   Price, S.J., P.C. McKenry, and M.J. Murphy. 2000. "Families across Time: A Life Course Perspective." In S.J. Price, P.C. McKenry, and M.J. Murphy, eds., *Families across Time: A Life Course Perspective,* 2–22. Los Angeles: Roxbury Publishing Company.

12   Prince, M.J., and N.L. Chappell. 1994. *Voluntary Action by Seniors in Canada: Executive Summary.* A report published by the Centre on Aging, University of Victoria, Victoria.

8   Pringle, D. 1998. "Aging and the Health Care System: Am I in the Right Queue?" *Forum Collection Series.* Ottawa: National Advisory Council on Aging.

6   Prull, M.W., J.D.E. Gabrieli, and S.A. Bunge. 2000. "Age-Related Changes in Memory: A Cognitive Neuroscience Perspective." In F.I.M. Craik and T.A. Salthouse, eds., *The Handbook of Aging and Cognition,* 2nd ed., 91–153. Mahwah, NJ: Lawrence Erlbaum Associates.

9   Prus, S.G. 1999. *Income Inequality as a Canadian Cohort Ages: An Analysis of the Later*

9   *Life Course.* SEDAP Research Paper No. 10. Hamilton, ON: McMaster University.

9   Prus, S.G. 2000. "Income Inequality as a Canadian Cohort Ages: An Analysis of the Later Life Course." *Research on Aging* 22(3): 211–37.

9   Prus, S.G. 2002. "Changes in Income within a Cohort over the Later Life Course: Evidence for Income Status Convergence." *Canadian Journal on Aging* 21(4): 475–504.

6   Puner, M. 1979. *Vital Maturity.* New York: Universe Books.

3   Quadagno, J. 1980. "The Modernization Controversy: A Socio-Historical Analysis of Retirement in Nineteenth Century England." Paper presented at the Annual Meeting of the American Sociological Association, New York.

1   Quadagno, J. 1991. "Interest-Group Politics and the Future of U.S. Social Security." In J. Myles and J. Quadagno, eds., *States, Labor Markets, and the Future of Old-Age Policy,* 36–58. Philadelphia: Temple University Press.

2   Quadagno, J., and J. Reid. 1999. "The Political Economy Perspective in Aging." In V.L. Bengtson and K.W. Schaie, eds., *Handbook of Theories of Aging,* 344–58. New York: Springer Publishing.

8   Queen's Health Policy Research Unit. 1999. *Putting a Face on Home Care: CARP's Report on Home Care in Canada 1999.* Toronto: Canadian Association of Retired Persons.

8   Quick Response Team. n.d. *A Report on the Capital Regional District Quick Response Team.* Victoria: Quick Response Team.

10   Quinn, J.F. 1981. "The Extent and Correlates of Partial Retirement." *Gerontologist* 21: 634–43.

10   Quinn, J.F., and R.V. Burkhauser. 1990. "Work and Retirement." In R.H. Binstock and L.K. George, eds., *Handbook of Aging and the Social Sciences,* 3rd ed. San Diego: Academic Press.

7   Quirouette, C.C., and D. Pushkar. 1999. "Views of Future Aging among Middle-Aged, University Educated Women." *Canadian Journal on Aging* 18(2): 236–58.

8   Rachlis, M.M. 2000. "Modernizing Medicare for the Twenty-First Century." Victoria: British Columbia Ministry of Health and Ministry Responsible for Seniors.

1   Ragan, A.M., and A.M. Bowen. 2001. "Improving Attitudes Regarding the Elderly Population: The Effects of Information and Reinforcement for Change." *Gerontologist* 41(4): 511–15.

8   Rattenbury, C., and M.J. Stones. 1989. "A Controlled Evaluation of Reminiscence and Current Topics Discussion Groups in a Nursing Home Context." *Gerontologist* 29: 768–71.

2   Ray, R.E. 2003. "Uninvited Guest: Mother/Daughter Conflict in Feminist Gerontology." *Journal of Aging Studies* 17(1): 113–28.

6   Raz, N. 2000. "Aging of the Brain and Its Impact on Cognitive Performance: Integration of Structural and Functional Findings." In F.I.M. Craik and T.A. Salthouse, eds., *The Handbook of Aging and Cognition,* 2nd ed., 1–90. Mahwah, NJ: Lawrence Erlbaum Associates.

13 Reis, M., and D. Nahmiash. 1997. "Abuse of Seniors: Personality, Stress, and Other Indicators." *Journal of Mental Health and Aging* 3(3): 337–56.

13 Reis, M., and D. Nahmiash. 1998. "Validation of the Indicators of Abuse (IOA) Screen." *Gerontologist* 38(4): 471–80.

6   Reker, G.T. 1997. "Personal Meaning, Optimism, and Choice: Existential Predictors of Depression in Community and Institutional Elderly." *Gerontologist* 37(6): 709–16.

5   Reker, G.T. 2001–02. "Prospective Predictors of Successful Aging in Community-Residing and Institutionalized Canadian Elderly." *Ageing International* 27(1): 42–64.

7   Reker, G.T., E.J. Peacock, and P.T.P. Wong. 1987. "Meaning and Purpose in Life and Well-Being: A Life-Span Perspective." *Journal of Gerontology* 42: 44–49.

12 Rhodes, R.E., A.D. Martin, and J.E. Taunton. 2001. "Temporal Relationships of Self-Efficacy and Social Support as Predictors of Adherence in a 6-Month Strength-Training Program for Older Women." *Perceptual and Motor Skills* 93(3): 693–703.

4   Richardson, R., S. Lowenstein, and M. Weissberg. 1989. "Coping with the Suicidal Elderly: A Physician's Guide." *Geriatrics* 44(9): 43–47, 51.

2   Richardson, V.E. 1999. "Women and Retirement." *Journal of Women and Aging* 11(2/3): 49–66.

7   Riegel, K.F. 1975. "Adult Life Crises: A Dialectic Interpretation of Development." In N. Datan and L.H. Ginsberg, eds., *Life-Span Developmental Psychology: Normative Life Crisis.* New York: Academic Press.

7   Riegel, K.F. 1976. "The Dialectics of Human Development." *American Psychologist* 31: 689–700.

2   Riley, M.W. 1971. "Social Gerontology and the Age Stratification of Society." *Gerontologist* 11: 79–87.

2   Riley, M.W. 1987. "On the Significance of Age in Sociology." *American Sociological Review* 52: 1–14.

2   Riley, M.W. 1994. "Aging and Society: Past, Present and Future." *Gerontologist* 34: 436–46.

2   Riley, M.W., A. Foner, and J.W. Riley, Jr. 1999. "The Aging and Society Paradigm." In V.L. Bengtson and K.W. Schaie, eds., *Handbook of Theories of Aging,* 327–43. New York: Springer Publishing.

2   Riley, M.W., A. Foner, and J. Waring. 1988. "Sociology of Age." In N. Smelser, ed., *Handbook of Sociology.* Beverly Hills: Sage.

2,7,10   Riley, M.W., M.E. Johnson, and A. Foner, eds. 1972. *Aging and Society.* Vol. 3: A Sociology of Age Stratification. New York: Russell Sage Foundation.

7   Ritzer, G. 1992. *Contemporary Sociological Theory,* 3rd ed. New York: McGraw-Hill.

12,13   Robb, R., M. Denton, A. Gafni, A. Joshi, J. Lian, C. Rosenthal, and D. Willison. 1999. "Valuation of Unpaid Help by Seniors in Canada: An Empirical Analysis." *Canadian Journal on Aging* 18(4): 430–46.

8   Roberge, R., and R. Beauséjour. 1988. "Use of Restraints in Chronic Care Hospitals and Nursing Homes." *Canadian Journal on Aging* 8: 377–81.

5,8   Roberge, R., J.-M. Berthelot, and M. Wolfson. 1995. "Health and Socio-Economic Inequalities." *Canadian Social Trends* (Summer): 15–19.

2   Roberge, D., F. Ducharme, P. Lebel, R. Pineault, and J. Losielle. 2002. "Qualité des soins dispensés en unités de courte durée gériatriques: la perspective des aidants familiaux." *Canadian Journal on Aging* 21(3): 393–403.

13   Roberto, K.A., and J. Stroes. 1995. "Grandchildren and Grandparents: Roles, Influences, and Relationships." In J. Hendricks, ed., *The Ties of Later Life,* 141–54. Amityville, NY: Baywood.

6   Roberts, J., G. Browne, A. Gafni, M. Varieur, P. Loney, and M. de Ruijter. 2000. "Specialized Continuing Care Models for Persons with Dementia: A Systematic Review of the Research Literature." *Canadian Journal on Aging* 19(1): 106–26.

10   Robertson, A. 2000. "'I Saw the Handwriting on the Wall': Shades of Meaning in Reasons for Early Retirement." *Journal of Aging Studies* 14(1): 63–79.

5   Robine, J.M., P. Mormiche, and C. Sermet. 1998. "Examination of the Causes and Mechanisms of the Increase in Disability-Free Life Expectancy." *Journal of Aging and Health* 10(2): 171–91.

10   Robinson, P.K., S. Coberly, and C.E. Paul. 1985. "Work and Retirement." In R.H. Binstock and E. Shanas, eds., *Handbook of Aging and the Social Sciences,* 2nd ed. New York: Van Nostrand Reinhold.

1   Robinson, T.E. 1998. *Portraying Older People in Advertising.* New York: Garland.

9   Robson, W.B.P. 1996. "Ponzi's Pawns: Young Canadians and the Canada Pension Plan." In J.B. Burbridge et al., eds., *When We're 65: Reforming Canada's Retirement Income System,* 27–56. Toronto: C.D. Howe Institute.

4   Robson, W.B.P. 2001. *Will the Baby Boomers Bust the Health Budget? Demographic Change and Health Care Financing Reform.* Commentary No. 148. Toronto: C.D. Howe Institute.

10   Robson, W.B.P., and British–North American Committee. 2001. *Aging Populations and the Workforce: Challenge for Employers.* Washington, DC: British–North American Committee.

11   Rodriguez, Luis. 1997. *Canada's Response to the Housing Needs of Its Aging Population.* Ottawa: Canada Mortgage and Housing Corporation.

13   Roe, K.M., and M. Minkler. 1998. "Grandparents Raising Grandchildren: Challenges and Responses." *Generations* 22(4): 25–32.

5   Roos, N.P., and B. Havens. 1991. "Predictors of Successful Aging: A Twelve-Year Study of Manitoba Elderly." *American Journal of Public Health* 81: 63–68.

13   Rose, H., and E. Bruce. 1995. "Mutual Care but Differential Esteem: Caring between Older Couples." In S. Arber and J. Ginn, eds.,

Connecting Gender and Ageing: A Sociological Approach, 114–28. Buckingham, U.K.: Open University Press.

5   Rose, M.R. 1993. "Evolutionary Gerontology and Critical Gerontology: Let's Just Be Friends." In T.R. Cole, W.A. Achenbaum, P.L. Jakobi, and R. Kastenbaum, eds., *Voices and Visions of Aging: Toward a Critical Gerontology*, 64–75. New York: Springer.

8   Rosenberg, M.W. 2000. *The Effects of Population Ageing on the Canadian Health Care System*. SEDAP Research Paper No. 14. Hamilton, ON: McMaster University.

8   Rosenberg, M.W., and A.M. James. 2000. "Medical Services Utilization Patterns by Seniors." *Canadian Journal on Aging* 19 (Suppl.1): 125–42.

11   Rosenmayr, L., and E. Kockeis. 1963. "Propositions for a Sociological Theory of Aging and the Family." *International Social Science Journal* 15: 410–26.

7   Rosenthal, C.J. 1983. "The Anglo-Canadian Family: A Perspective on Ethnicity and Support to the Elderly." Paper presented at the 12th Annual Scientific and Educational Meeting of the Canadian Association on Gerontology, Moncton.

7   Rosenthal, C.J. 1986a. "Family Supports in Later Life: Does Ethnicity Make a Difference?" *Gerontologist* 26: 19–24.

7   Rosenthal, C.J. 1986b. *Intergenerational Solidarity in Later Life: Ethnic Contrasts in Jewish and Anglo Families*. Research Paper No. 4. Toronto: Program in Gerontology, University of Toronto.

13   Rosenthal, C.J. 1994. "Editorial: Long-Term Care Reform and 'Family' Care: A Worrisome Combination." *Canadian Journal on Aging* 13(3): 419–27.

13   Rosenthal, C.J. 1995. "The Comforter." In M. Novak, ed., *Aging and Society: A Canadian Reader*, 326–31. Scarborough, ON: Nelson Canada.

13   Rosenthal, C.J. 1997. "Changing Contexts of Family Care in Canada." *Ageing International* 24(1): 13–31.

13   Rosenthal, C.J. 2000. "Aging Families: Have Current Changes and Challenges Been 'Oversold'?" In E.M. Gee and G.M. Gutman, eds., *The Overselling of Population Aging: Apocalyptic Demography, Intergenerational*

Challenges, and Social Policy, 45–63. Don Mills, ON: Oxford University Press.

13   Rosenthal, C., and P. Dawson. 1991. "Wives of Institutionalized Husbands." *Journal of Aging and Health* 3(3): 315–34.

13   Rosenthal, C.J., V.W. Marshall, and J. Synge. 1980. "The Succession of Lineage Roles as Families Age." *Essence* 4: 179–93.

13   Rosenthal, C.J., A. Martin-Matthews, L. Hayward, and M. Denton. 1999. "Women's Multiple Roles: How Contraining Is Employment on the Provision of Parent Care?" Paper presented at the 52nd Annual Scientific Meeting of the Gerontological Society of America, San Francisco, November 19–23.

13   Rosenthal, C.J., A. Martin-Matthews, and S.H. Matthews. 1996. "Caught in the Middle? Occupancy in Multiple Roles and Help to Parents in a National Probability Sample of Canadian Adults." *Journals of Gerontology Series B* 51(6): S274–83.

1   Rosenzweig, Robert M. 1991. "Generational Conflict Brewing, GSA Members Warned." *Gerontology News* (January).

3   Rosow, I. 1965. "And Then We Were Old." *Transaction* 2: 20–26.

13   Ross, M.M., A. Carswell, and W.B. Dalziel. 2002. "Family Caregiving in Long-Term Care Facilities: Visiting and Task Performance." *Geriatrics Today* 5(4): 179–82.

14   Ross, M.M., M.J. MacLean, R. Cain, S. Sellick, and R. Fisher. 2002. "End of Life Care: The Experience of Seniors and Informal Caregivers." *Canadian Journal on Aging* 21(1): 137–46.

14   Ross, M.M., and B. McDonald. 1994. "Providing Palliative Care to Older Adults: Context and Challenges." *Journal of Palliative Care* 10(4): 5–10.

13   Ross, M.M., C.J. Rosenthal, and P. Dawson. 1994. "The Continuation of Caregiving Following the Institutionalization of Elderly Husbands." In National Advisory Council on Aging, *Marital Disruption in Later Life*, 23–32. Cat. No. H71-3/17-1994E. Ottawa: Minister of Supply and Services.

13   Ross, M.M., C.J. Rosenthal, and P.G. Dawson. 1997a. "Spousal Caregiving in the Institutional Setting: Task Performance." *Canadian Journal on Aging* 16(1): 51–69.

13   Ross, M.M., C.J. Rosenthal, and P. Dawson. 1997b. "Spousal Caregiving in the Institutional Setting: Visiting." *Journal of Clinical Nursing* 6(6): 473–83.

10   Rowe, G., and H. Nguyen. 2003. "Older Workers and the Labour Market." *Perspectives on Labour and Income* 15(1): 55–58.

5   Rowe, J.W., and R.L. Kahn. 1991. "Human Aging: Usual and Successful." In H. Cox, ed., *Aging*, 7th ed. Guilford, CT: Dushkin. Originally published in *Science* 237 (1987): 143–49.

5   Rowe, J.W., and R.L. Kahn. 1995. "Successful Aging." *Gerontologist* 37(4): 433–40.

13   Rowe, J.W., and R.L. Kahn, 1998. *Successful Aging*. New York: Dell Publishing.

13   Rubinstein, R.L. 1996. "Childless, Legacy, and Generativity." *Generations* 20(3): 58–60.

3   Rubio, M., and E. Waterson, eds. 1986. *Selected Journals of L.M. Montgomery*. Vol. 1: 1889–1910. Toronto: Oxford University Press.

13   Russell, R. 2001. "In Sickness and in Health: A Qualitative Study of Elderly Men Who Care for Wives with Dementia." *Journal of Aging Studies* 15: 351–67.

2   Russell, C. 1999. "Interviewing Vulnerable Old People: Ethical and Methodological Implications of Imagining Our Subjects." *Journal of Aging Studies* 13(4): 403–17.

7   Ruth, J., and P. Coleman. 1996. "Personality and Aging: Coping and Management of the Self in Later Life." In J.E. Birren and K.W. Schaie, eds. *Handbook of the Psychology of Aging*, 4th ed., 308–22. San Diego: Academic Press.

11   Rutman, D., and J.L. Freedman. 1988. "Anticipating Relocation: Coping Strategies and the Meaning of Home for Older People." *Canadian Journal on Aging* 7: 17–31.

5   Ryan, E.B., A.P. Anas, M. Beamer, and S. Bajorek. 2003. "Coping with Age-Related Vision Loss in Everyday Reading Activities." *Educational Gerontology* 29(1): 37–54.

1   Ryan, E.B., A.P. Anas, M.L. Hummert, and I.A. Laver. 1998. "Young and Older Adults' Views of Telephone Talk: Conversation Problems and Social Uses." *Journal of Applied Communication Research* 26(1): 83–98.

1   Ryan, E.B., and R.K.B. Heaven. 1988. "The Impact of Situational Context on Age-Based Attitudes." *Social Behaviour* 3: 105–18.

5   Ryan, J. 2001. "Technology and Older Adults: A Senior's Perspective." In J. Jessome, C. Parks, and M. MacLellan, eds., *Seniors and Technology*, 33–38. Cat. No. 0-662-30932-4. Ottawa: Minister of Public Works and Government Services Canada.

7   Ryan, M.C. 1998. "The Relationship between Loneliness, Social Support, and Decline in Cognitive Function in the Hospitalized Elderly." *Journal of Gerontological Nursing* 24(3): 19–27.

6   Rybash, J.M., W.J. Hoyer, and P.A. Roodin. 1986. *Adult Cognition and Aging: Developmental Changes in Processing, Knowing, and Thinking*. New York: Pergamon Press.

7   Ryff, C.D., C.M.L. Kwan, and B.H. Singer. 2001. "Personality and Aging: Flourishing Agendas and Future Challenges." In J.E. Birren and K.W. Schaie, eds., *Handbook of the Psychology of Aging*, 5th ed. San Diego: Academic Press.

7   Ryff, C.D., W.J. Magee, K.C. Kling, and E.H. Wing. 1999. "Forging Macro–Micro Linkages in the Study of Psychological Well-Being." In C.D. Ryff and V.W. Marshall, eds. *The Self and Society in Aging Processes*, 247–78. New York: Springer.

7   Ryff, C.D., and V.W. Marshall, eds. 1999. *The Self and Society in Aging Processes*. New York: Springer.

7   Ryff, C.D., and B. Singer. 1996. "Psychological Well-Being: Meaning, Measurement and Implications for Psychotherapy Research." *Psychotherapy and Psychosomatics* 65: 14–23.

1   Sacco, V.F., and R.M. Nakhaie. 2001. "Coping with Crime: An Examination of Elderly and Nonelderly Adaptations." *International Journal of Law and Psychiatry* 24(2/3): 305–23.

6   Sainsbury, R.S., and M. Coristine. 1986. "Affective Discrimination in Moderately to Severely Demented Patients." *Canadian Journal on Aging* 5: 99–104.

6,14 Saint-Arnaud, J. 1993. "Autonomy, Self-Determination, and the Decision-Making Process Concerning End-of-Life Treatment." In National Advisory Council on Aging, *Ethics and Aging*, 33–49. Cat. No. H71-3/16-1993E. Ottawa: Minister of Supply and Services.

6   Salthouse, T.A., and R.L. Babcock. 1991. "Decomposing Adult Age Differences in Working Memory." *Developmental Psychology* 27(5): 763–76.

6 Salthouse, T.A., and F.I.M. Craik. 2000. "Closing Comments." In F.I.M. Craik and T.A. Salthouse, eds., *The Handbook of Aging and Cognition*, 2nd ed., 689–703. Mahwah, NJ: Lawrence Erlbaum Associates.

10 Salthouse, T.A., and T.J. Maurer. 1996. "Aging, Job Performance, and Career Development." In J.E. Birren and K.W. Schaie, eds., *Handbook of the Psychology of Aging*, 4th ed., 353–64. San Diego: Academic Press.

6 Salvatori, P., M. Tremblay, J. Sandys, and D. Maraccio. 1998. "Aging with an Intellectual Disability: A Review of Canadian Literature." *Canadian Journal on Aging* 17(3): 249–71.

14 Sanders, C.M. 1980–81. "Comparison of Younger and Older Spouses in Bereavement Outcome." *Omega* 11: 217–32.

6 Sanders, R.E., M.D. Murphy, F.A. Schmitt, and K.K. Walsh. 1980. "Age Differences in Free Recall Rehearsal Strategies." *Journal of Gerontology* 35: 550–58.

13 Sands, R., and R.S. Goldberg-Glen. 2000. "Factors Associated with Stress among Grandparents Raising their Grandchildren. *Family Relations* 49(1): 97–105.

8 Sanmartin, C., C. Houle, S. Tremblay, and J.-M. Berthelot. 2002. "Changes in Unmet Health Care Needs." *Health Reports* 13(3): 15–17

8 Saskatchewan Health Services Utilization Research Commission, *Hospital and Home Care Study*. Summary Report No. 10. Saskatoon: Saskatchewan Health.

14 Saunders, C. 1984. "St. Christopher's Hospice." In E.S. Shneidman, ed., *Death: Current Perspectives*, 3rd ed. Palo Alto, CA: Mayfield.

8 Saunders, L.D., A. Alibhai, D.B. Hogan, C.J. Maxwell, H. Quan, and D. Johnson. 2001. "Trends in the Utilization of Health Services by Seniors in Alberta." *Canadian Journal on Aging* 20(4): 493–516.

4 Scarth, W. 2003. *Population Aging, Productivity, and Growth in Living Standards*. SEDAP Research Paper No. 90. Hamilton, ON: SEDAP Research Program, McMaster University.

6 Schaie, K.W. 1990a. "Intellectual Development in Adulthood." In J.E. Birren and K.W. Schaie, eds., *Handbook of the Psychology of Aging*, 3rd ed. San Diego: Academic Press.

6 Schaie, K.W. 1990b. "The Optimization of Cognitive Functioning in Old Age: Predictions Based on Cohort-Sequential and Longitudinal Data." In P.B. Baltes and M.M. Baltes, eds., *Successful Aging: Perspectives from the Behavioral Sciences*. Cambridge: Cambridge University Press.

6 Schaie, K.W. 1996. "Intellectual Development in Adulthood." In J.E. Birren and K.W. Schaie, eds., *Handbook of the Psychology of Aging*, 4th ed., 266–86. San Diego: Academic Press.

6 Schaie, K.W., and G. Labouvie-Vief. 1974. "Generational versus Ontogenetic Components of Change in Adult Cognitive Behaviour: A Fourteen-Year Cross-Sequential Study." *Developmental Psychology* 10: 305–20.

6 Scheibel, A.B. 1996. "Structural and Functional Changes in the Aging Brain." In J.E. Birren and K.W. Schaie, eds., *Handbook of the Psychology of Aging*, 4th ed., 105–28. San Diego: Academic Press.

10 Schellenberg, G. 1994. *Older Workers and Canada's Aging Labour Force*. Ottawa: One Voice—the Seniors Network (Canada) Ltd.

10 Schellenberg, G. 1995. "Summary of Address to Statistics Canada Symposium on Greying of the Workforce." *Perspectives on Labour and Income* 7(1): 33–38.

11 Schiff, M., and N. Gnaedinger. 1997. *Adapting Municipal Housing to Meet the Needs of Older Tenants with Dementia*. Ottawa: Canada Mortgage and Housing Corporation.

13 Schlesinger, B. 1996. "Sexless Years or Sex Rediscovered." *Journal of Gerontological Social Work* 26(1/2): 117–31.

5 Schneider, E.L., and J.A. Brody. 1983. "Aging, Natural Death, and the Compression of Morbidity: Another View." *New England Journal of Medicine* 309: 854–56.

5 Schneider, E.L., and J.W. Rowe, eds. 1996. *Handbook of the Biology of Aging*. 4th ed. San Diego: Academic Press.

8 Schoenborn, C.A. 1993. "Trends in Health Status and Practices: Canada and the United States." *Canadian Social Trends* (Winter): 16–21.

12 Scholz, W.D. 1993. "New Prospects at the Third Stage of Life: Older People at University." *Journal of Educational Gerontology* 8: 33–46.

13 Schone, B.S., and R.M. Weinick. 1998. "Health-Related Behaviors and the Benefits of Marriage for Elderly Persons." *Gerontologist* 38(5): 618–27.

6,11 Schooler, C. 1990. "Psychosocial Factors and Effective Cognitive Functioning in Adulthood." In J.E. Birren and K.W. Schaie, eds., *Handbook of the Psychology of Aging*, 3rd ed. San Diego: Academic Press.

6 Schroots, J.F. 1995. "Psychological Models of Aging." *Canadian Journal on Aging* 14(1): 44–66.

3,10 Schulz, J.H. 1980. *The Economics of Aging*. 2nd ed. Belmont, CA: Wadsworth.

10 Schulz, J.H. 1985. *The Economics of Aging*. 3rd ed. Belmont, CA: Wadsworth.

10 Schulz, J.H. 1991. "Epilogue: The 'Buffer Years': Market Incentives and Evolving Retirement Policies." In J. Myles and J. Quadagno, eds., *States, Labor Markets, and the Future of Old-Age Policy*, 295–308. Philadelphia: Temple University Press.

14 Schulz, R. 1978. *The Psychology of Death, Dying, and Bereavement*. Reading, MA: Addison-Wesley.

7 Schulz-Hipp, P.L. 2001. "Do Spirituality and Religiosity Increase with Age?" In D.O. Moberg, ed., *Aging and Spirituality*, 85–98. New York: Haworth Press.

13 Schwartz, P., and V. Rutter. 1998. *The Gender of Sexuality*. Thousand Oaks, CA: Pine Forge.

6 Schwartzman, A.E., D. Gold, D. Andres, T.Y. Arbuckle, and J. Chaikelson. 1987. "Stability of Intelligence: A 40-Year Follow-Up." *Canadian Journal of Psychology* 41(2): 244–56.

12 Searle, M.S., and M.J. Mahon. 1991. "Leisure Education in a Day Hospital: The Effects of Selected Social-Psychological Variables among Older Adults." *Canadian Journal of Community Mental Health* 10(2): 95–109.

12 Searle, M.S., M.J. Mahon, S.E. Iso-Ahola, and H.A. Sdrolias. 1995. "Enhancing a Sense of Independence and Psychological Well-Being among the Elderly: A Field Experiment." *Journal of Leisure Research* 27(2): 107–24.

12 Searle, M.S., M.J. Mahon, S.E. Iso-Ahola, H.A. Sdrolias, and J. van Dyck. 1998. "Examining the Long Term Effects of Leisure Education on a Sense of Independence and Psychological Well-Being among the Elderly." *Journal of Leisure Research* 30(3): 331–40.

3 Secretariat of the Economic Commission for Europe. 1992. "Aging, the Public Sector and Age Profiles." In G.J. Stolnitz, ed., *Demographic Causes and Economic Consequences of Population Aging: Europe and North America*, 383–96. New York: United Nations.

8 Segall, A. 1987. "Age Differences in Lay Conceptions of Health and Self-Care Responses to Illness." *Canadian Journal on Aging* 6: 47–65.

9,10 Senate of Canada. 1979. *Retirement without Tears: A Report of the Special Senate Committee on Retirement Age Policies* (Croll Commission). Ottawa: Minister of Supply and Services.

14 Senate of Canada. 1995. *Of Life and Death*. Report of the Special Senate Commmittee on Euthanasia and Assisted Suicide. Ottawa: Queen's Printer of Canada.

11 Senior Citizens' Provincial Council. 1981. *Regina Social Support Survey*. Regina: Senior Citizens' Provincial Council.

7 Senior Citizens' Provincial Council. 1988. *A Study of Unmet Needs of Off-Reserve Indian and Metis Elderly in Saskatchewan*. Regina: Senior Citizens' Provincial Council.

8 Seniors Advisory Council. 1999. *Seniors Involvement in the Governance of Health Services in British Columbia*. British Columbia.

6 *Seniors Today*. 1995. "National Alzheimer Registry Created." *Seniors Today*, July 1, 3.

3 Sennott-Miller, L. 1994. "Research on Aging in Latin America: Present Status and Future Directions." *Journal of Cross-Cultural Gerontology* 9: 87–97.

7 Sermat, V. 1978. "Sources of Loneliness." *Essence* 2: 271–76.

14 Sewell, D. 2003. "Giving the Gift of Peace." *Reader's Digest Canada*. http://www.readersdigest.ca/mag/2003/08/palliative.html, accessed on September 25, 2003.

13 Shanas, Ethel. 1967. "Family Help Patterns and Social Class in Three Societies." *Journal of Marriage and the Family* 29: 257–66.

13 Shanas, E. 1979. "The Family as a Social Support System in Old Age." *Gerontologist* 19: 169–74.

14 Shapiro, E. 1983. "Impending Death and the Use of Hospitals by the Elderly." *Journal of the American Geriatrics Society* 31: 348–51.

8 Shapiro, E. 1992. "Editorial: We've Come a Long Way but Are We There?" *Canadian Journal on Aging* 11(3): 206–9.

8 Shapiro, E. 1994. "Community and Long-Term Health Care in Canada." In A. Blomqvist and D.M. Brown, eds., *Limits to Care: Reforming*

Canada's Health System in an Age of Restraint, 327–62. Ottawa: C.D. Howe Institute.

8 Shapiro, E. 1995. "Long-Term Care and Population Aging." In M. Novak, ed., *Aging and Society: A Canadian Reader*, 154–60. Toronto: Nelson Canada.

8 Shapiro, E. 2003. "The Romanow Commission Report and Home Care." *Canadian Journal on Aging* 22(1): 13–17.

5,8 Shapiro, E., and B. Havens. 2000. "Bridging the Knowledge Gap: From Evidence to Policy and Practice That Fosters Seniors' Independence." *Canadian Journal on Aging* 19 (Suppl. 1): 176–90.

10 Shapiro, E., and N.P. Roos. 1982. "Retired and Employed Elderly Persons: Their Utilization of Health Care Services." *Gerontologist* 22: 187–93.

8 Shapiro, E., and N.P. Roos. 1986. "High Users of Hospital Days." *Canadian Journal on Aging* 5: 165–74.

6,8 Shapiro, E., and R.B. Tate. 1997. "The Use and Cost of Community Care Services by Elders with Unimpaired Cognitive Function, with Cognitive Impairment/No Dementia and with Dementia." *Canadian Journal on Aging* 16(4): 665–81.

8 Shapiro, E., and R.B. Tate. 1988a. "Survival Patterns of Nursing Home Admissions and Their Policy Implications." *Canadian Journal of Public Health* 79: 268–74.

8 Shapiro, E., and R. Tate. 1988b. "Who Is Really at Risk of Institutionalization?" *Gerontologist* 28: 237–45.

8 Shapiro, E., R.B. Tate, and N.P. Roos. 1987. "Do Nursing Homes Reduce Hospital Use?" *Medical Care* 25: 1–8.

2,8 Shapiro, E., R.B. Tate, RB. Wright, and J. Plohman. 2000. "Changes in the Perception of Health Care Policy and Delivery among Manitoba Elders during the Downsizing of the Hospital Sector." *Canadian Journal on Aging* 19(1): 18–34.

3 Sharp, H.S. 1981. "Old Age among the Chipewyan." In P.T. Amoss and S. Harrell, eds., *Other Ways of Growing Old: Anthropological Perspectives*. Stanford, CA: Stanford University Press.

6 Sharps, M.J., and J.L. Price Sharps. 1996. "Visual Memory Support: An Effective Mnemonic Device for Older Adults." *Gerontologist* 36(5): 706–8.

14 Shedletsky, R., and R. Fisher. 1986. "Terminal Illness: Attitudes in Both an Acute and an Extended Care Teaching Hospital." *Journal of Palliative Care* 2: 16–21.

14 Shedletsky, R., R. Fisher, and G. Nadon. 1982. "Assessment of Palliative Care for Dying Hospitalized Elderly." *Canadian Journal on Aging* 1: 11–15.

12 Shephard, R.J. 1986. "Physical Activity and Aging in a Post-Industrial Society." In B.D. McPherson, ed., *Sport and Aging: The 1984 Olympic Scientific Congress Proceedings*, Vol. 5. Champaign, IL: Human Kinetics.

12 Shephard, R.J. 1990. "Measuring Physical Activity in the Elderly: Some Implications for Nutrition." *Canadian Journal on Aging* 9: 188–203.

10 Shephard, R.J. 1995. "A Personal Perspective on Aging and Productivity, with Particular Reference to Physically Demanding Work." *Ergonomics* 38(4): 617–36.

10 Sheppard, H.L. 1991. "Early Retirement: Questions and Speculations." In J. Myles and J. Quadagno, eds., *States, Labor Markets, and the Future of Old-Age Policy*, 290–94. Philadelphia: Temple University Press.

13 Shernoff, M. 1997. *Gay Widowers: Life after Death of a Partner*. New York: Haworth Press.

6 Shidler, S. 1998. "Participation of Chronically Ill Older Adults in Their Life-Prolonging Treatment Decisions: Rights and Opportunity." *Canadian Journal on Aging* 17(1): 1–23.

5 Shields, M., and S. Shooshtari. 2001. "Determinants of Self-Perceived Health." *Health Reports* 13(1): 35–52.

14 Shneidman, E.S. 1984. "Malignancy: Dialogues with Life-Threatening Illnesses." In E.S. Shneidman, ed. *Death: Current Perspectives*, 3rd ed. Palo Alto, CA: Mayfield.

3 Shrestra, L.B. 2000. "Population Aging in Developing Countries." *Health Affairs* 19(3): 204–12.

12 Sidney, K.H., and Shephard, R.J. 1978. *Exercise and Aging: The Scientific Basis*. Hillsdale, NJ: Enslow Publishers.

13 Siegel, J.M. 1995. "Looking for Mr. Right? Older Single Women Who Become Mothers." *Journal of Family Issues* 16(2): 194–211.

4 Siegel, J.S. 1994. "Plotting the Source: Individual Aging and Population Aging in the West." *Gerontologist* 34(3).

12 Sijpkes, P., M. MacLean, and D. Brown. 1983. "Hanging around the Mall." *Recreation Canada* (February).

6 Silberfeld, M. 1992. "The Use of 'Risk' in Decision-Making." *Canadian Journal on Aging* 11(2): 124–36.

6 Silberfeld, M. 1994. "Evaluating Decisions in Mental Capacity Assessments." *International Journal of Geriatric Psychiatry* 9: 365–71.

6 Silberfeld, M., R. Grundstein Amando, D. Stephens, and R. Deber. 1996. "Family and Physicians' Views of Surrogate Decision-Making: The Roles and How to Choose." *International Psychogeriatrics* 8(4): 589–96.

11 Silver, C., and R. Van Diepen. 1995. "Housing Tenure Trends 1951–1991." *Canadian Social Trends* (Spring): 8–12.

13 Silverstein, M., and J.D. Long. 1998. "Trajectories of Grandparents' Perceived Solidarity with Adult Grandchildren: A Growth Curve Analysis over 23 Years." *Journal of Marriage and the Family* 60(4): 912–23.

3 Simmons, L.W. 1960. "Aging in Preindustrial Societies." In C. Tibbitts, ed., *Handbook of Social Gerontology: Societal Aspects of Aging.* Chicago: University of Chicago Press.

3 Simmons, L.W. 1970. *The Role of the Aged in Primitive Society.* New Haven, CT: Yale University.

13 Simons, R.L. 1983–84. "Specificity and Substitution in the Social Networks of the Elderly." *International Journal of Aging and Human Development* 18: 121–39.

6 Simonton, D.K. 1977. "Creative Productivity, Age, and Stress: A Biographical Time-Series Analysis of 10 Classical Composers." *Journal of Personality and Social Psychology* 35(11): 791–804.

6 Simonton, D.K. 1988a. "Age and Outstanding Achievement: What Do We Know after Over a Century of Research?" *Psychological Bulletin* 104: 251–67.

6 Simonton, D.K. 1988b. *Scientific Genius: A Psychology of Science.* Cambridge: Cambridge University Press.

6 Simonton, D.K. 1990. "Creativity and Wisdom in Aging." In J.E. Birren and K.W. Schaie, eds., *Handbook of the Psychology of Aging*, 3rd ed. San Diego: Academic Press.

8 Simpson, J. 1999. "Paying for Your Health." *Globe and Mail*, December 23.

7 Singer, B.H., and C.D. Ryff. 1999. "Hierarchies of Life Histories and Associated Health Risks." In N.D. Adler, B.S. McEwen, and M. Marmot, eds., *Socioeconomic Status in Industrialized Countries: Annals of the New York Academy of Sciences* 896: 96–115.

12 Singleton, J.F., W.F. Forbes, and N. Agwani. 1993. "Stability of Activity across the Lifespan." *Activities, Adaptation and Aging* 18(1): 19–27.

14 Skelton, D. 1982. "The Hospice Movement: A Human Approach to Palliative Care." *Canadian Medical Association Journal* 126: 556–58.

8 Skinner, M.W., and M.W. Rosenberg. 2002. *Health Care in Rural Communities: Exploring the Development of Informal and Voluntary Care.* SEDAP Research Paper No. 79. Hamilton, ON: McMaster University.

7,12 Smale, B.J.A., and S.L. Dupuis. 1993. "The Relationship between Leisure Activity Participation and Psychological Well-Being across the Lifespan." *Journal of Applied Recreation Research* 18(4): 281–300.

6 Smale, B., and S.L. Dupuis. 2003a. *In Their Own Voices: A Profile of Dementia Caregivers in Ontario. Stage 1: Survey Results.* Waterloo, ON: University of Waterloo.

6 Smale, B., and S.L. Dupuis. 2003b. *In Their Own Voices: A Profile of Dementia Caregivers in Ontario. Stage 2: The Focus Group.* Waterloo, ON: University of Waterloo.

6 Smith, A.D. 1996. "Memory." In J.E. Birren and K.W. Schaie, eds., *Handbook of the Psychology of Aging*, 4th ed., 236–50. San Diego: Academic Press.

11 Smith, G.C. 1998. "Change in Elderly Residential Segregation in Canadian Metropolitan Areas, 1981–91." *Canadian Journal on Aging* 17(1): 59–82.

9 Smith, R., L. Magee, A.L. Robb, and J.B. Burbidge. 2000. "The Independence and Economic Security of Older Women Living Alone." In F.T. Denton, D. Fretz, and B.G. Spencer, eds. *Independence and Economic Security in Old Age*, 293–327. Vancouver: UBC Press.

6 Smyer, M.A., S.H. Zarit, and S.H. Qualls. 1990. "Psychological Intervention with the Aging Individual." In J.E. Birren and K.W. Schaie, eds., *Handbook of the Psychology of Aging*, 3rd ed. San Diego: Academic Press.

13 Snell, J.G. 1990. "Filial Responsibility Laws in Canada: An Historical Study." *Canadian Journal on Aging* 9: 268–77.

9 Snell, J.G. 1993. "The Gendered Construction of Elderly Marriage, 1900–1950." *Canadian Journal on Aging* 12(4): 509–23.

3,9,10 Snell, J.G. 1996. *The Citizen's Wage: The State and the Elderly in Canada, 1900–1951.* Toronto: University of Toronto Press.

10 Snell, M.L., and K. Brown. 1987. "Financial Strategies of the Recently Retired." *Canadian Journal on Aging* 6: 290–303.

9 Social Development Canada. 2002. "Income Security Programs Information Card (Rate Card): Old Age Security." http://www.sdc.gc.ca/asp/gateway.asp?hr=/en/isp/statistics/octdec02.shtml&hs=ozs#topic3, accessed on August 22, 2004.

9 Social Development Canada. 2004. "Old Age Security (OAS) Payment Rates—July–September 2004." http://www.sdc.gc.ca/asp/gateway.asp?hr=/en/isp/oas/oasrates.shtml&hs=ozs, accessed on August 22, 2004.

3 Sokolovsky, J., ed. 1990. *The Cultural Context of Aging: Worldwide Perspectives.* New York: Bergin and Garvey.

1 Solicitor General of Canada. 1983. *Canadian Urban Victimization Survey. Bulletin 1: Victims of Crime.* Ottawa: Minister of Supply and Services.

6 Sparks, B., V. Temple, M. Springer, and K.P. Stoddart. 2000. "Service Provision to Older Adults with Developmental Disabilities: A Survey of Service Providers." *Canadian Journal on Aging* 19(2): 210–22.

12 Spirduso, W.W., and P.G. MacRae. 1991. "Physical Activity and Quality of Life in the Frail Elderly." In J.E. Birren, D.E. Deutchman, J. Lubben, and J. Rowe, eds., *The Concept and Measurement of the Quality of Life in the Frail Elderly.* New York: Academic Press.

14 St. John, P., and M. Man-Son-Hing. 2002. "Requests for Physician-Assisted Suicide in Older Persons: An Approach." *Geriatrics Today* 5(2): 81–83.

12 Stacey, C., A. Kozma, and M.J. Stones. 1985. "Simple Cognitive and Behavioral Changes Resulting from Improved Physical Fitness in Persons over 50 Years of Age." *Canadian Journal on Aging* 4: 67–74.

13 Stack, S., and J.R. Eshleman. 1998. "Marital Status and Happiness: A 17-Nation Study." *Journal of Marriage and the Family* 60: 527–36.

4 Statistics Canada. 1968. *1966 Census of Canada.* Vol. 1 (1–11). Ottawa: Queen's Printer.

4 Statistics Canada. 1973. *Census of Canada (1971 Census). Bulletin* 1: 2–3. Ottawa: Information Canada.

4 Statistics Canada. 1978. *Vital Statistics.* Vol. III: Births–Deaths, 1975 and 1976. Cat. No. 84-204. Ottawa: Health Division, Vital Statistics and Diseases Registry Section, Statistics Canada, Ministry of Supply and Services.

4 Statistics Canada. 1981. *Canada Year Book, 1980–81.* Ottawa: Minister of Supply and Services.

7 Statistics Canada. 1984a. *Canada's Immigrants.* Cat. No. 99-936. Ottawa: Minister of Supply and Services.

7 Statistics Canada. 1984b. *The Elderly in Canada.* Cat. No. 99-932. Ottawa: Minister of Supply and Services.

10 Statistics Canada. 1986. *The Labour Force, August 1986.* Cat. No. 71-001. Ottawa: Minister of Supply and Services.

12 Statistics Canada. 1987. *Health and Social Support, 1985: General Social Survey Analysis Series.* No. 1. Cat. No. 11-612E. Ottawa: Minister of Supply and Services.

4,5 Statistics Canada. 1989a. *Canada Year Book 1990.* Cat. No. 11-402E/1990. Ottawa: Minister of Supply and Services.

12 Statistics Canada. 1989b. *Family Expenditure in Canada, 1986.* Cat. No. 62-555. Ottawa: Minister of Supply and Services.

8 Statistics Canada. 1990a. *Canada Year Book.* Ottawa: Minister of Supply and Services.

5 Statistics Canada. 1990b. *Highlights: Disabled Persons in Canada.* Cat. No. 82-602. Ottawa: Minister of Supply and Services.

4 Statistics Canada. 1991. *Population Projections 1990–2011.* Ottawa: Statistics Canada, Demography Division.

4 Statistics Canada. 1992. "Age, Sex, and Marital Status." *1991 Census of Canada.* Cat. No. 93-310. Ottawa: Statistics Canada.

5 Statistics Canada. 1993. *Aging and Independence.* Ottawa: Statistics Canada, Household Surveys Division.

1   Statistics Canada. 1994. *Canadian Crime Statistics.* Cat. No. 85-205-XIE. Ottawa: Minister of Industry, Science, and Technology.

9   Statistics Canada. 1995. *Women in Canada: A Statistical Report.* 3rd ed. Cat. No. 89-503E. Ottawa: Minister of Industry.

9   Statistics Canada. 1996. *Canada's Retirement Income Programs: A Statistical Overview.* Cat. No. 74-507-XPB. Ottawa: Minister of Industry.

10   Statistics Canada. 1998. *Labour Force Update: Older Workers* 2(2). Ottawa: Statistics Canada, Household Surveys Division.

8   Statistics Canada. 1999a. *Canada Year Book.* Cat. No. 11-402E/1999. Ottawa: Ministry of Industry, Science, and Technology.

5   Statistics Canada. 1999b. "Health Expectancy in Canada." *Canadian Statistics.* http://www.statcan.ca/english/Pgdb/People/Health/health38.htm.

5   Statistics Canada. 2000a. "Stress and Well-Being." *Health Reports* 12(3). Cat. No. 82-003-XIE. http://www.statcan.ca/english/freepub/82-003-XIE/art2.pdf, accessed on November 23, 2003.

5   Statistics Canada. 2000b. "Taking Risks/Taking Care." *Health Reports* 12(3). Cat. No. 82-003-XIE. http://www.statcan.ca/english/freepub/82-003-XIE/art1.pdf, accessed on November 23, 2003.

4   Statistics Canada 2001a. "Bring Your Families to Canada." http://142.206.72.67/02/02a/02a_005_e.htm#t01, accessed on July 26, 2004.

13   Statistics Canada. 2001b. *Changing Conjugal Life in Canada.* Cat. No. 89-576-XIE. Ottawa: Statistics Canada.

5   Statistics Canada. 2001c. "How Healthy Are Canadians?" *Health Reports* 12(3). Cat. No. 82-003. http://www.statcan.ca/english/freepub/82-003-XIE/free.htm, accessed on July 28, 2004.

12   Statistics Canada. 2001d. "Internet Use among Older Canadians." http://www.statcan.ca:8096/bsolc/english/bsolc?catno=56F0004M2001004, accessed on September 15, 2004.

4   Statistics Canada. 2001e. "Mobility Status 1 Year Ago, 2001 Counts for the Age." *2001 Census.* http://www12.statcan.ca/english/census01/products/highlight/Mobility/Page.cfm?Lang=E&Geo=PR&View=1&Code=0&Table=1e1&StartRec=1&Sort=7&B1=Counts1&B2=4564, accessed on July 26, 2004.

10   Statistics Canada. 2001f. "Trends in Early Retirement." *The Daily*, September 19, 2001. http://www.statcan.ca/Daily/English/010919/d010919c.htm, accessed on August 10, 2004.

4   Statistics Canada. 2002a. "Median Age, Canada, 1901–2011." http://www12.statcan.ca/english/census01/Products/Analytic/companion/age/cdamedaget.cfm, accessed on September 27, 2003.

4   Statistics Canada. 2002b. "Median Age Reaches All-Time High." http://www12.statcan.ca/english/census01/Products/Analytic/companion/age/canada.cfm#median_age, accessed on July 26, 2004.

1   Statistics Canada. 2002c. "Time Line: The Events Today's Centenarians Have Witnessed in Their Lifetime." http://www12.statcan.ca/english/census01/Products/Analytic/companion/age/timelinet.cfm, accessed on September 15, 2004.

4   Statistics Canada. 2003a. "Aboriginal Peoples of Canada: A Demographic Profile." *2001 Census: Analysis Series.* Cat. No. 96F0030XIE2001007. http://www12.statcan.ca/english/census01/products/analytic/companion/abor/pdf/96F0030XIE2001007.pdf, accessed on September 28, 2003.

9   Statistics Canada. 2003b. "Average Earnings by Sex and Work Pattern." *Canadian Statistics.* http://www.statcan.ca/english/Pgdb/labor01a.htm, accessed on August 10, 2004.

6   Statistics Canada. 2003c. *Canadian Community Health Survey: Mental Health and Well-Being.* Cat. No. 82-617-XIE. Ottawa: Ministry of Industry. http://www.statcan.ca:8096/bsolc/english/bsolc?catno=82-617-X, accessed on August 2, 2004.

4,14 Statistics Canada. 2003d. "Deaths." *The Daily*, September 25, 2003. http://www.statcan.ca/Daily/English/030925/td030925.htm, accessed on July 26, 2004.

9   Statistics Canada. 2003e. "Gender Differences in Low Income." http://www.hc-sc.gc.ca/seniors-aines/pubs/factoids/2001/no15_e.htm, accessed on August 10, 2004.

10   Statistics Canada. 2003f. "General Social Survey: Social Support and Aging." *The Daily*, September 2. http://www.statcan.ca/Daily/English/030902/d030902a.htm, accessed on September 2, 2004.

13   Statistics Canada. 2003g. "Grandparents and Grandchildren." *The Daily*, December 9, 2003.

http://www.statcan.can/Daily/English/031209/
d031209b.htm, accessed on August 18, 2004.

10 Statistics Canada. 2003h. "Labour Force and
Participation Rates by Sex and Age Group."
Canadian Statistics. http://www.statcan.ca/
english/Pgdb/labor05.htm, accessed on
October 10, 2003.

5 Statistics Canada. 2003i. "Pain or Discomfort
That Affects Activities, by Age Group and Sex,
Household Population Aged 12 and Over,
Canada." *Health Indicators* 2003(1). Cat. No.
82-221-XIE.

13 Statistics Canada. 2003j. "The People: Breakup." *Canada e-Book.* Cat. No. 11-404-XIE.
Ottawa: Statistics Canada.

13 Statistics Canada. 2003k. "The People:
Common-Law." *Canada e-Book.* Cat. No. 11-
404-XIE. Ottawa: Statistics Canada.

8 Statistics Canada. 2003l. "The People:
Hospitals." *Canada e-Book.* http://142.206.72.67/
02/02b/02b_008c_e.htm, accessed on
December 19, 2003.

13 Statistics Canada. 2003m. "The People:
Marriage." *Canada e-Book.* Cat. No. 11-404-
XIE. Ottawa: Statistics Canada.

13 Statistics Canada. 2003n. "The People:
Widowhood." *Canada e-Book.* Cat. No. 11-
404-XIE. Ottawa: Statistics Canada.

4 Statistics Canada. 2003o. "Population and
Growth Components, 1851–2001 Censuses."
http://www.statcan.ca/english/Pgdb/
demo03.htm, accessed on October 22, 2003.

4 Statistics Canada. 2003p. "Population by Sex
and Age Group." CANSIMII, Table 051-0001.
http://www.statcan.ca/english/Pgdb/demo10a
.htm, accessed on September 27, 2003.

9 Statistics Canada. 2003q. "Proportion of
Labour Force and Paid Workers Covered by a
Registered Pension Plan (RPP)." *Canadian
Statistics.* http://www.statcan.ca/english/Pgdb/
labor26a.htm, accessed on August 10, 2004.

10 Statistics Canada. 2003r. "Reasons for Part-
Time Work by Sex and Age Group." *Canadian
Statistics.* http://www.statcan.ca/english/Pgdb/
labor63a.htm, accessed on October 10, 2003.

7 Statistics Canada. 2003s. "Religion and Age
Groups for Population, for Canada, Provinces,
Territories, Census Metropolitan Areas 1 and
Census Agglomerations, 2001 Census."
http://www12.statcan.ca/english/census01/
products/highlight/Religion/Page.cfm?Lang=E
&Geo=PR&View=1a&Code=01&Table=1&

StartRec=1&Sort=2&B1=Canada&B2=1,
accessed on August 22, 2004.

9 Statistics Canada. 2003t. "Retirement Savings
through RRSPs and RPPs." *Canadian Statistics.*
http://www.statcan.ca/english/Pgdb/
labor55.htm, accessed on July 9, 2003.

10 Statistics Canada. 2003u. "The Retirement
Wave." *The Daily,* February 21, 2003.
http://www.statcan.ca/Daily/English/030221/
d030221f.htm, accessed on August 10, 2004.

1 Statistics Canada. 2003v. "Satisfaction with
Life, by Age Group and Sex, Household
Population Aged 15 and Over, Canada
Excluding Territories, 2002." *Canadian
Community Health Survey: Mental Health and
Well-Being 2002,* Table 21. Cat. No. 82-617-
XIE. Ottawa: Ministry of Industry. http://
www.statcan.ca/english/freepub/
82-617-XIE/htm/51100115.htm, accessed on
September 15, 2004.

5 Statistics Canada. 2003w. "Self-Rated Health,
by Age Group and Sex, Household Population
Aged 12 and Over, Canada, 2000/01." *Health
Indicators* 2003(1). Cat. No. 82-221-XIE.
http://www.statcan.ca/english/freepub/
82-221-XIE/00503/tables/html/1115.htm,
accessed on November 22, 2003.

13 Statistics Canada. 2003x. "Social Support and
Mortality among Seniors." *The Daily,* May 23.
Health Statistics Division.

13 Statistics Canada. 2004a. "Divorces." *The
Daily,* May 4. http://www.statcan.ca/Daily/
English/040504/d040504a.htm.

9 Statistics Canada. 2004b. "Low Income."
http://www12.statcan.ca/English/census01/
products/analytic/companion/inc/
canada.cfm#4, accessed on September
15, 2004.

3 Stearns, P.N. 1967. *European Society in
Upheaval.* New York: Macmillan.

3 Stearns, P.N. 1977. *Old Age in European
Society: The Case of France.* London: Croom
Helm.

13 Stein, P. 1981. "Understanding Single
Adulthood." In P.J. Stein, ed., *Single Life:
Unmarried Adults in Social Context,* 9–21.
New York: St. Martin's.

6 Stelmach, L., C. Konnert, and K. Dobson.
2001. "Obtaining Informed Consent from
Continuing Care Residents: Issues and
Recommendations." *Canadian Journal on
Aging* 20(3): 385–406.

12   Steptoe, A., and D.S. Cox. 1988. "Acute Effects of Aerobic Exercise on Mood." *Health Psychology* 7: 329–40.

5   Stipp, D. 1999. "Hell No, We Won't Go!" *Fortune,* July 19, 102–8.

2   Stoller, E.P., and R.C. Gibson. 1997. *Worlds of Difference: Inequality in the Aging Experience.* 2nd ed. Thousand Oaks, CA: Pine Forge Press.

5   Stone, D.S. 2003. "Disability, Dependence, and Old Age: Problematic Constructions." *Canadian Journal on Aging* 22(1): 59–67.

6   Stone, L.O. 1986. "On the Demography of Dementia." In M.R. Easterwood, *Alzheimer's Disease and Other Dementias: The Magnitude and Management of the Problem.* Symposium presented at the Clarke Institute of Psychiatry, Toronto.

12,13   Stone, L.O. 1988. *Family and Friendship Ties among Canada's Seniors.* Cat. No. 89-508. Ottawa: Minister of Supply and Services.

10   Stone, L.O. 1994. "Men's Work over the Life Course." *Info-Age* 10 (March).

4   Stone, L.O., and S. Fletcher. 1980. *A Profile of Canada's Older Population.* Montreal: Institute for Research on Public Policy.

8   Stone, L.O., and S. Fletcher. 1986. *The Seniors Boom.* Cat. No. 89-515E. Ottawa: Minister of Supply and Services.

4   Stone, L.O., and H. Frenken. 1988. *Canada's Seniors.* Cat. No. 98-121. Ottawa: Minister of Supply and Services.

1,13   Stone, L.O., C.J. Rosenthal, and I.A. Connidis. 1998. *Parent–Child Exchanges of Supports and Intergenerational Equity.* Cat. No. 89-557-XPE. Ottawa: Ministry of Industry.

13   Stones, L., and M. Stones. 1996. *Sex May Be Wasted on the Young.* North York, ON: Captus.

13   Stones, M.J. 1994. *Rules and Tools: The Meaning and Measurement of Elder Abuse.* A Manual for Milestones. Newfoundland.

13   Stones, M.J., and M. Bédard. 2002. "Higher Thresholds for Elder Abuse with Age and Rural Residence." *Canadian Journal on Aging* 21(4): 577–86.

12   Stones, M.J., and D. Dawe. 1993. "Acute Exercise Facilitates Semantically Cued Memory in Nursing Home Residents." *Journal of the American Geriatrics Society* 41(5): 531–34.

8   Stones, M.J., B. Dornan, and A. Kozma. 1989. "The Prediction of Mortality in Elderly Institution Residents." *Journal of Gerontology Series B* 44(3): P72–79.

13   Stones, M.J., and D. Pittman. 1995. "Individual Differences in Attitudes about Elder Abuse: The Elder Abuse Attitude Test (EAAT)." *Canadian Journal of Aging* 14 (Suppl. 2): 61–71.

8   Strain, L.A. 1991. "Use of Health Services in Later Life: The Influence of Health Beliefs." *Journals of Gerontology Series B* 46(3): S143–50.

12   Strain, L.A. 2001. "Senior Centres: Who Participates?" *Canadian Journal on Aging* 20(4): 471–91.

13   Strain, L.A., and A.A. Blandford. 2003. "Caregiving Networks in Later Life: Does Cognitive Status Make a Difference?" *Canadian Journal on Aging* 22(3): 261–73.

7   Strain, L.A., and N.L. Chappell. 1984. "Social Support among Elderly Canadian Natives: A Comparison with Elderly Non-Natives." Paper presented at the Canadian Association on Gerontology 13th Annual Scientific and Educational Meeting, Vancouver.

12   Strain, L.A., C.C. Grabusic, M.S. Searle, and N.J. Dunn. 2002. "Continuing and Ceasing Leisure Activities in Later Life: A Longitudinal Study." *Gerontologist* 42(2): 217–23.

9   Street, D., and I. Connidis. 2001. "Creeping Selectivity in Canadian Women's Pensions." In J. Ginn, D. Street, and S. Arber, eds., *Women, Work, and Pensions: International Issues and Prospects,* 158–78. Buckingham, U.K.: Open University Press.

10   Stryckman, J. 1987. "Work Sharing and the Older Worker in a Unionized Setting." In V.W. Marshall, ed., *Aging in Canada: Social Perspectives,* 2nd ed. Toronto: Fitzhenry and Whiteside.

8   Sturdy, C., and J.A. Tindale. 1985. "The Social Organization of Health Care Provision to the Elderly in Ontario." Paper presented at the Canadian Association on Gerontology 14th Annual Scientific and Educational Meeting, Hamilton.

14   Subcommittee on Institutional Program Guidelines. 1989. *Palliative Care Services.* Health and Welfare Canada. Cat. No. H39-32/1989E. Ottawa: Minister of Supply and Services.

8   Sullivan, T., and P.M. Baranek. 2002. *First Do No Harm: Making Sense of Canadian Health Reform.* Vancouver: UBC Press.

8   Sullivan, T., and C. Mustard. 2001. "Canada: More State, More Market?" In J.B. Davis, ed., *The Social Economics of Health Care.* London: Routledge.

8   Sulman, J., and S. Wilkinson. 1989. "An Activity Group for Long-Stay Elderly Patients in an Acute Care Hospital: Program Evaluation." *Canadian Journal on Aging* 8: 34–50.

5   Sutton, D., M.A.M. Gignac, and C. Cott. 2002. "Medical and Everyday Assistive Device Use among Older Adults with Arthritis." *Canadian Journal on Aging* 21(4): 535–48.

12   Swedburg, R.B. 1993. "Educational Institutes: Models for and by Seniors." Report for Elderhostel Canada sponsored by Health and Welfare Canada and the Seniors Independence Program, Ottawa.

3   Synge, Jane. 1980. "Work and Family Support Patterns of the Aged in the Early Twentieth Century." In V.W. Marshall, ed., *Aging in Canada: Social Perspectives.* Toronto: Fitzhenry and Whiteside.

10   Szinovacz, M.E. 1982. "Introduction: Research on Women's Retirement." In M. Szinovacz, ed., *Women's Retirement.* Beverly Hills, CA: Sage.

10   Szinovacz, M.E. 1983. "Beyond the Hearth: Older Women and Retirement." In E.W. Markson, ed., *Older Women: Issues and Prospects.* Lexington, MA: D.C. Heath.

13   Talbott, M.M. 1998. "Older Widows' Attitudes towards Men and Remarriage." *Journal of Aging Studies* 12(4): 429–49.

8   Tamblym, R., and R. Perreault. 2000. "Prescription Drug Use and Seniors." *Canadian Journal on Aging* 19 (Suppl. 1): 143–75.

7   Tasse, L. 1993. "Promised Lands: The Social Role and Filiation of Elderly Algonquins of Kitigan Zibi." *International Review of Community Development* 29(69): 25–36.

6   Taub, H.A. 1979. "Comprehension and Memory of Prose Materials by Young and Old Adults." *Experimental Aging Research* 5(1): 3–13.

14   Taylor, K. 1999. "Hospice Palliative Care: A Growing Movement in B.C." *Gerontology Research Centre News* (February): 4–5.

10   Taylor, P.S. 1995. "Grandma! Grandpa! Back to Work!" *Saturday Night,* June, 18.

1   Taylor, S.C. 1995. "Primetime's Big Sleep." *Modern Maturity* (November/December): 38–43.

12   Thacker, C., and M. Novak. 1991. "Middle-Aged Re-Entry Women and Student Role Supports: Application of a Life Event Model." *Canadian Journal of Higher Education* 21: 13–36.

13   Thomas, L.E. 1982. "Sexuality and Aging: Essential Vitamin or Popcorn?" *Gerontologist* 22, 240–43.

14   Thompson, E.H. 1985–86. "Palliative and Curative Care: Nurses' Attitudes toward Dying and Death in the Hospital Setting." *Omega* 16: 233–42.

6   Tierney, M.C. 1997. "Editorial: How Safe Are Cognitively Impaired Seniors Who Live Alone?" *Canadian Journal on Aging* 16(2): 177–89.

6   Tierney, M.C., and J. Charles. 2002. "The Care and Treatment of People with Dementia and Cognitive Impairment: An Update." In *Writings in Gerontology: Mental Health and Aging,* 97–112. Ottawa: National Advisory Council on Aging.

7   Tindale, J. 1980. "Identity Maintenance Processes of Old Poor Men." In V.W. Marshall, ed., *Aging in Canada.* Toronto: Fitzhenry and Whiteside.

10   Tindale, J. 1991. *Older Workers in an Aging Work Force.* Cat. No. H71-2/1-10-1991E. Ottawa: Minister of Supply and Services.

10   Tompa, E. 1999. *Transitions to Retirement: Determinants of Age of Social Security Take Up.* SEDAP Research Paper No. 6. Hamilton, ON: McMaster University.

7   Tornstam, L. 1994. "Gero-Transcendence: A Theoretical and Empirical Exploration." In L.E. Thopmas and S.A. Eisenhandler, eds., *Aging and the Religious Dimension,* 203–25. Westport, CT: Greenwood.

4   Torrance, G.M. 1981. "Introduction: Socio-Historical Overview: The Development of the Canadian Health System." In D. Coburn, C. D'Arcy, P. New, and G. Torrance, eds., *Health and Canadian Society: Sociological Perspectives.* Toronto: Fitzhenry and Whiteside.

5   Toufexis, A. 1986. "New Rub for the Skin Game." *Time,* March 31.

10 Tournier, Paul. 1972. *Learning to Grow Old.* London: SCM Press.

13 Townsend-Batten, B. 2002. "Staying in Touch: Contact between Adults and their Parents." *Canadian Social Trends* (Spring): 9–12.

1 Townson, M. 1994. *The Social Contract and Seniors: Preparing for the 21st Century.* Ottawa: National Advisory Council on Aging.

13 Trevitt, C., and E. Gallagher, E. 1996. "Elder Abuse in Canada and Australia: Implications for Nurses." *International Journal of Nursing Studies* 33(6): 651–59.

3 Trexler, R.C. 1982. "A Widows' Asylum of the Renaissance: The Orbatello of Florence." In P.N. Stearns, ed., *Old Age in Preindustrial Society.* New York: Holmes and Meier.

11 Trickey, F., D. Maltais, C. Gosselin, Y. Robitaille. 1993. "Adapting Older Persons' Homes to Promote Independence." *Physical and Occupational Therapy in Geriatrics* 12(1): 1–14.

12 Trombo, B. 1995. *Seniors Computer Information Projects, Spring 1995, Survey Results.* Report of Creative Retirement Manitoba. Winnipeg.

8 Trottier, H., L. Martel, C. Houle, J.-M. Berthelot, and J. Legare. 2000. "Living at Home or in an Institution: What Makes the Difference for Seniors?" *Health Indicators* 11(4): 49–62.

7 Trovato, F. 1988. "Suicide in Canada: A Further Look at the Effects of Age, Period, and Cohort." *Canadian Journal of Public Health* 79: 37–44.

8 Tsang, H., L. Cheung, and D.C. Lak. 2002. "Qigong as a Psychosocial Intervention for Depressed Elderly with Chronic Physical Illnesses." *International Journal of Geriatric Psychiatry* 17(12): 1146–54.

4 Tucker, R.D., and V. Marshall. 1988. "Descriptive Overview of Older Anglophone Canadians in Florida." In L.C. Mullins and R.D. Tucker, eds., *Snowbirds in the Sun Belt: Older Canadians in Florida.* Tampa, FL: International Exchange Center on Gerontology.

4 Tucker, R.D., V.W. Marshall, C.F. Longino, Jr., and L.C. Mullins. 1988. "Older Anglophone Canadian Snowbirds in Florida: A Descriptive Profile." *Canadian Journal on Aging* 7: 218–32.

4 Tucker, R.D., L.C. Mullins, F. Béland, C.F. Longino, Jr., and V.W. Marshall. 1992. "Older Canadians in Florida: A Comparison of Anglophone and Francophone Seasonal Migrants." *Canadian Journal on Aging* 11(3): 281–97.

12 Tudor-Locke, C., A.M. Myers, C.S. Jacob, G. Jones, D. Lazowski, and N.A. Ecclestone. 2000. "Development and Formative Evaluation of the Centre for Activity and Ageing's Home Support Exercise Program for Frail Older Adults." *Journal of Aging and Physical Activity* 8(1): 59–75.

3 Turnbull, C. 1961. *The Forest People.* New York: Simon and Schuster.

12 "Two-Wheel Adventurers Brook No Complaints." 1999. *Fifty Plus, Victoria Times Colonist* advertising feature, October 5.

2 Uhlenberg, P., and S. Miner. 1996. "Life Course and Aging: A Cohort Perspective." In R.H. Binstock and L.K. George, eds., *Handbook of Aging and the Social Sciences*, 4th ed., 208–28. San Diego: Academic Press.

6 Ujfalussy, D. 1999. "Terrific Turroni Still Turning It Out." *Hamilton Spectator*, October 13.

1 Underhill, S.C., V.W. Marshall, and S. Deliencourt. 1997. *Options 45+ HRCC Survey Final Report.* Toronto: Institute for Human Development, Life Course and Aging, University of Toronto; and Ottawa: One Voice: Canadian Seniors Network.

3 United Nations. Department of Economics and Social Affairs. 1995. *World Population Prospects: The 1994 Review.* United Nations Publication, Sales No. E.95.XIII.16.

3,4 United Nations. Population Division. 2002. "World Population Ageing: 1950–2050." http://www.un.org/esa/population/publications/worldageing19502050, accessed on July 8, 2003.

11 United Senior Citizens of Ontario. 1985. *Elderly Residents in Ontario: Their Current Housing Situation and Their Interest in Various Housing Options.* Ontario: Minister for Senior Citizen Affairs.

13 Van den Hoonaard, D.K. 1997. "Identity Foreclosure: Women's Experiences of Widowhood as Expressed in Autobiographical Accounts." *Ageing and Society* 17(5): 533–51.

13 Van den Hoonaard, D.K. 1999. "No Regrets: Widows' Stories about the Last Days of Their Husbands' Lives." *Journal of Aging Studies* 13(1): 59–72.

13 Van den Hoonaard, D.K. 2001. *The Widowed Self: The Older Woman's Journey through Widowhood.* Waterloo, ON: Wilfrid Laurier University Press.

7 Vanderburgh, R.M. 1988. "The Impact of Government Support for Indian Culture on Canada's Aged Indians." In E. Rathbone-McEwan and B. Havens, eds., *North American Elders: United States and Canadian Perspectives.* New York: Greenwood.

12 Van der Veen, R. 1990. "Third Age or Inter-Age Universities?" *Journal of Educational Gerontology* 5: 96–105.

3 Vatuk, S. 1982. "Old Age in India." In P.N. Stearns, ed., *Old Age in Preindustrial Society.* New York: Holmes and Meier.

11 Veevers, Jean E. 1987. "The 'Real' Marriage Squeeze: Mate Selection, Mortality and the Mating Gradient." Paper presented at the Annual Meeting of the Pacific Sociological Association.

4 Venne, R.A. 2001. "Population Aging in Canada and Japan: Implications for Labour Force and Career Patterns." *Canadian Journal of Administrative Sciences* 18(1): 40–49.

13 Verwoerdt, A., E. Pfeiffer, and H.S. Wang. 1969. "Sexual Behavior in Senescence—Changes in Sexual Activity and Interest of Aging Men and Women." *Journal of Geriatric Psychiatry* 2: 163–80.

12 Vigoda, D., L. Crawford, and J. Hirdes. 1985. "The Continuity Theory: Empirical Support." In N.K. Blackie, Sister A. Robichaud, and S. MacDonald, eds., *Aging, Mirror of Humanity: Canadian Gerontological Collection IV.* Winnipeg: Canadian Association on Gerontology.

6 Vintners, H.V. 2001. "Aging and the Human Nervous System." In J.E. Birren and K.W. Schaie, eds., *Handbook of the Psychology of Aging,* 5th ed. San Diego: Academic Press.

2 Vinton, L. 1999. "Working with Abused Older Women from a Feminist Perspective." *Journal of Women and Aging* 11(2/3): 85–100.

12 Wagner, D.L. 1995. "Senior Center Research in America: An Overview of What We Know." In D. Shollenberger, ed., *Senior Centers in America: A Blueprint for the Future.* Washington, DC: National Council on the Aging and National Eldercare Institute on Multipurpose Senior Centers and Community Focal Points.

13 Wahl, J., and S. Purdy. 2001. *Elder Abuse: The Hidden Crime.* 7th ed. Toronto: Advocacy Centre for the Elderly.

12 Waldron, M.K., and G.A.B. Moore. 1991. *Helping Adults Learn.* Toronto: Thompson Educational Publishing.

13 Waldrop, D.P., and J.A. Weber. 2001. "From Grandparent to Caregiver: The Stress and Satisfaction of Raising Grandchildren." *Families in Society* 82(5): 361–472.

13 Walker, A. 1996. "Intergenerational Relations and the Provision of Welfare." In A. Walker, ed., *The New Generational Contract: Intergenerational Relations, Old Age and Welfare,* 10–36. London: UCL Press.

13 Walker, B.L., and P.H. Ephross. 1999. "Knowledge and Attitudes toward Sexuality of a Group of Elderly." *Journal of Gerontological Social Work* 31(1/2): 85–107.

13 Walker, B.L., N.J. Osgood, J.P. Richardson, and P.H. Ephross. 1998. "Staff and Elderly Knowledge and Attitudes toward Elderly Sexuality." *Educational Gerontology* 24: 471–89.

14 Walton, D.N., and W.H. Fleming. 1980. "Responsibility for the Discontinuation of Treatment." *Essence* 4: 57–61.

7 Wanner, R.A., and P.L. McDonald. 1986. "The Vertical Mosaic in Later Life: Ethnicity and Retirement in Canada." *Journal of Gerontology* 41: 662–71.

13 Ward-Griffin, C. 2002. "Boundaries and Connections between Formal and Informal Caregivers." *Canadian Journal on Aging* 21(2): 205–16.

13 Ward-Griffin, C., and V.W. Marshall. 2003. "Reconceptualizing the Relationship between 'Public' and 'Private' Eldercare." *Journal of Aging Studies* 17(2): 189–208.

8 Ward-Griffin, C., and J. Ploeg. 1997. "A Feminist Approach to Health Promotion for Older Women." *Canadian Journal on Aging* 16(2): 279–96.

8 Watzke, J.R., and A.V. Wister. 1993. "Staff Attitudes: Monitoring Technology in Long-Term Care." *Journal of Gerontological Nursing* 19(11): 23–29.

6 Waugh, N.C., and R.A. Barr. 1982. "Encoding Deficits in Aging." In F.I.M. Craik and S. Trehub, eds., *Aging and Cognitive Processes.* New York: Plenum Press.

2   Weber, M. 1905/1955. *The Protestant Ethic and the Spirit of Capitalism.* New York: Charles Scribner's Sons.

2   Webster, J.D. 1997. "Attachment Style and Well-Being in Elderly Adults: A Preliminary Investigation." *Canadian Journal on Aging* 16(1): 101–11.

1   Webster, J.D. 1998. "Attachment Styles, Reminiscence Functions, and Happiness in Young and Elderly Adults." *Journal of Aging Studies* 12(3): 315–30.

6   Wechsler, D. 1939. *A Measurement of Adult Intelligence.* Baltimore: Williams and Wilkins.

6   Wechsler, D. 1981. *WAIS-R Manual* (Wechsler Adult Intelligence Scale Revised). New York: Harcourt Brace Jovanovich.

8   Weeks, L.E., and K.A. Roberto. 2002. "Comparison of Adult Day Services in Atlantic Canada, Maine, and Vermont." *Canadian Journal on Aging* 21(2): 273–82.

13   Weg, R.B. 1983. "The Physiological Perspective." In R.B. Weg, ed., *Sexuality in Later Years: Roles and Behaviour.* New York: Academic Press.

7   Weiss, R.S., ed. 1973. *Loneliness: The Experience of Emotional and Social Isolation.* Cambridge, MA: MIT Press.

4   Weller, R.H., and L.F. Bouvier. 1981. *Population: Demography and Policy.* New York: St. Martin's Press.

8   Wells, D.L. 1997. "A Critical Ethnography of the Process of Discharge Decision-Making for Elderly Patients." *Canadian Journal on Aging* 16(4): 682–99.

6   White, K. 1993. "How the Mind Ages." *Psychology Today* 26(6): 38–42, 80.

8   Wiener, J.M., and L.H. Illston. 1996. "The Financing and Organization of Health Care for Older Americans." In R.H. Binstock and L.K. George, eds., *Handbook of Aging and the Social Sciences,* 427–45. San Diego: Academic Press.

8   Wilkins, K., and M.P. Beaudet. 2000. "Changes in Social Support in Relation to Seniors' Use of Home Care." *Health Reports* 11(4): 39–48.

2   Wilkins, S. 2001. "Aging, Chronic Illness and Self-Concept: A Study of Women with Osteoporosis." *Journal of Women and Aging* 13(1): 73–92.

12   Williams, A.M., and W.J. Montelpare. 1998. "Lifelong Learning in Niagara: Identifying the Educational Needs of a Retirement Community." *Educational Gerontology* 24(8): 699–717.

8   Williams, A.P., J. Barnslety, S. Leggat, R. Deber, and P. Baranek. 1999. "Long-Term Care Goes to Market: Managed Competition and Ontario's Reform of Community-Based Services." *Canadian Journal on Aging* 18(2): 125–53.

6   Willis, S.L. 1990. "Contributions of Cognitive Training Research to Understanding Late Life Potential." In M. Perlmutter, ed., *Late Life Potential,* 25–42. Washington, DC: Gerontological Society of America.

6   Willis, S.L. 1996. "Everyday Problem Solving." In J.E. Birren and K.W. Schaie, eds., *Handbook of the Psychology of Aging,* 4th ed., 287–307. San Diego: Academic Press.

1   Wisensale, S.K. 1993. "Generational Equity." In R. Kastenbaum, ed., *Encyclopedia of Adult Development,* 175–80. Phoenix, AZ: Oryx.

11   Wister, A.V. 1985. "Living Arrangement Choices among the Elderly." *Canadian Journal on Aging* 4: 127–44.

8   Wister, A.V. 1992. "Residential Attitudes and Knowledge, Use, and Future Use of Home Support." *Journal of Applied Gerontology* 11(1): 84–100.

5   Wister, A.V. 1998. "Introduction." In A.V. Wister and G.M. Gutman, eds., *Health Systems and Aging in Selected Pacific Rim Countries: Cultural Diversity and Change,* 9–17. Vancouver: Gerontology Research Centre, Simon Fraser University.

13   Wister, A.V., and P.A. Dykstra. 2000. "Formal Assistance among Dutch Older Adults: An Examination of the Gendered Nature of Marital History." *Canadian Journal on Aging* 19(4): 508–35.

11   Wister, A.V., and G. Gutman. 1997. "Housing Older Canadians: Current Patterns, Preferences and Policies." *Journal of Housing for the Elderly* 12(1/2): 19–35.

5   Wister, A.V., G. Gutman, and B. Mitchell. 1998. "The North Shore Self-Care Study." In L.W. Green, G. Gutman, P. McGowan, and A. Wister, eds., *Seniors Independence through Self-Care, Self-Help, and Mutual Aid.* Vancouver: Institute of Health Promotion Research, University of British Columbia.

7,8 Wister, A.V., and C. Moore. 1998. "First Nations Elders in Canada: Issues, Problems and Successes in Health Care Policy." In A.V.

Wister and G. Gutman, eds., *Health Systems and Aging in Selected Pacific Rim Countries: Cultural Diversity and Change,* 103–24. Vancouver: Gerontology Research Centre, Simon Fraser University.

12   Wister, A.V., and Z. Romeder. 2002. "The Chronic Illness Context and Change in Exercise Self-Care among Older Adults: A Longitudinal Analysis." *Canadian Journal on Aging* 21(4): 521–34.

13   Wolf, R.S. 1996. "Understanding Elder Abuse and Neglect." *Aging* 367: 4.

13   Wolf, R.S. 2001. "Support Groups for Older Victims of Domestic Violence." *Journal of Women and Aging* 13(4): 71–83.

13   Wolf, R.S., and K.A. Pillemer. 1989. *Helping Elderly Victims: The Reality of Elder Abuse.* New York: Columbia University Press.

7   Wong, P.T.P., and G.T. Reker. 1985. "Stress, Coping, and Well-Being in Anglo and Chinese Elderly." *Canadian Journal on Aging* 4: 29–38.

8   World Health Organization. 1984. "Health Promotion: A World Health Organization Document on the Concept and Principles." *Canadian Public Health Association Digest* 8: 101–2.

13   World Health Organization/International Network for the Prevention of Elder Abuse. 2002. *Missing Voices: Views of Older Persons on Elder Abuse.* Geneva: World Health Organization.

1,3   Wortley, J. 1998. "Aging and the Aged in 'The Greek Anthology.'" *International Journal of Aging and Human Development* 47(1): 53–68.

14   Wortman, C.B., and R.C. Silver. 1990. "Successful Mastery of Bereavement and Widowhood: A Life-Course Perspective." In P.B. Baltes and M.M. Baltes, eds., *Successful Aging.* Cambridge: Cambridge University Press.

13   Wu, Z. 1995. "Remarriage after Widowhood: A Marital History Study of Older Canadians." *Canadian Journal on Aging* 14(4): 719–36.

13   Wu, Z., and M.J. Penning. 1997. "Marital Instability after Midlife." *Journal of Family Issues* 18(5): 459–78.

5   Wylde, M.A. 1998. "How to Effectively Research and Market Technology to Older People." In G.M. Gutman, ed., *Technology Innovation for an Aging Society: Blending Research, Public and Private Sectors,* 41–50. Vancouver: Gerontology Research Centre, Simon Fraser University.

6   Zacks, R.T., L. Hasher, and K.Z.H. Li. 2000. "Human Memory." In F.I.M. Craik and T.A. Salthouse, eds., *The Handbook of Aging and Cognition,* 2nd ed., 293–357. Mahwah, NJ: Lawrence Erlbaum Associates.

11   Zamprelli, J. 1985. "Shelter Allowances for Older Adults: Programs in Search of a Policy." In G. Gutman and N. Blackie, eds., *Innovations in Housing and Living Arrangements for Seniors.* Vancouver: Gerontology Research Centre, Simon Fraser University.

5   Zimmer, Z., and N.L. Chappell. 1994. "Mobility Restriction and the Use of Devices." *Journal of Aging and Health* 6(2): 185–208.

11   Zimmer, Z., and N. Chappell, 1997. "Rural-Urban Differences in Seniors' Neighbourhood Preferences." In L.A. Patalan, ed., *Shelter and Service Issues for Aging Populations: International Perspectives,* 105–24. New York: Haworth Press.

5   Zimmer, Z., and N.L. Chappell. 1999. "Receptivity to New Technology among Older Adults." *Disability and Rehabilitation* 21(5/6): 222–30.

5,12   Zimmer, Z., T. Hickey, and M.S. Searle. 1997. "Pattern of Change in Leisure Activity Behavior among Older Adults with Arthritis." *Gerontologist* 37(3): 384–92.

5   Zimmer, Z., and A. Myers. 1997. "Receptivity to Protective Garments among the Elderly." *Journal of Aging and Health* 9(3): 355–72.

2,10   Zimmerman, L., B. Mitchell, A. Wister, and G. Gutman. 2000. "Unanticipated Consequences: A Comparison of Expected and Actual Retirement Timing among Older Women." *Journal of Women and Aging* 12(1–2): 109–28.

6   Zuckerman, H. 1977. *Scientific Elite: Studies of Nobel Laureates in the United States.* New York: Free Press.

11   Zukewich Ghalam, N. 1996. "Living with Relatives." *Canadian Social Trends* (Autumn): 20–24.

12   Zuzanek, J., and S.J. Box. 1988. "Life Course and the Daily Lives of Older Adults in Canada." In K. Altergott, ed., *Daily Life in Later Life: Comparative Perspectives.* Newbury Park, CA: Sage.

Index